Chaplain
Mike
269-449-7601

W9-ABA-128

CLEAN

A RECOVERY COMPANION

COMPLETE WITH NEW TESTAMENT, PSALMS & PROVERBS

Dr. Robert Hemfelt
and
Dr. Richard Fowler

THOMAS NELSON
Since 1798

NASHVILLE   DALLAS   MEXICO CITY   RIO DE JANEIRO   BEIJING

www.thomasnelson.com

1 2 3 4 5 6 7 8 9 10 11 12 13 14 15 16 17 18 19 20—14 13 12 11 10 09 08 07

About the Authors

Dr. Robert Hemfelt is a psychologist in private practice in Dallas, Texas; and he specializes in the treatment of relationships, addictions, and adult-children-of-abuse issues. Dr. Hemfelt has coauthored multiple best-selling books that have been translated into numerous foreign languages. (Telephone: 972-960-7505; Web site: renewcc.com)

Dr. Richard Fowler, author of eleven books, has a wide background in higher education, counseling, administration, and public speaking. He presently serves as the director of a Christian counseling clinic in Dallas, Texas. (Telephone: 972-382-4122; Email: note4pcc@aol.com)

Notes of Appreciation

The authors wish to thank Joseph B. Snider for his sensitivity in revising the manuscripts for the introductory material and the meditations and Evan Buja for his care in reviewing the content prior to publication. Joseph Snider is a writer and editor who resides in Fort Wayne, Indiana. Evan Buja is a licensed professional counselor and director of Celebrate Recovery at Fellowship Bible Church, Dallas, Texas.

The publisher is grateful to A.A. World Services, Inc., for permission to quote briefly from the following sources:

Alcoholics Anonymous Comes of Age: A Brief History of A.A. Copyright ©1957, 1985 by Alcoholics Anonymous Publishing, Inc. (now known as A.A. World Services, Inc.).

Alcoholics Anonymous, Third Edition. Copyright © 1939, 1955, 1976 by Alcoholics Anonymous World Services, Inc.

The Twelve Steps of Alcoholics Anonymous*

1. We admitted we were powerless over alcohol—that our lives had become unmanageable.
2. Came to believe that a Power greater than ourselves could restore us to sanity.
3. Made a decision to turn our will and our lives over to the care of God *as we understood Him*.
4. Made a searching and fearless moral inventory of ourselves.
5. Admitted to God, to ourselves, and to another human being the exact nature of our wrongs.
6. Were entirely ready to have God remove all these defects of character.
7. Humbly asked Him to remove our shortcomings.
8. Made a list of all persons we had harmed, and became willing to make amends to them all.
9. Made direct amends to such people wherever possible, except when to do so would injure them or others.
10. Continued to take personal inventory and when we were wrong promptly admitted it.
11. Sought through prayer and meditation to improve our conscious contact with God *as we understood Him*, praying only for knowledge of His will for us and the power to carry that out.
12. Having had a spiritual awakening as the result of these steps, we tried to carry this message to alcoholics, and to practice these principles in all our affairs.

---

*The Twelve Steps are reprinted with permission of Alcoholics Anonymous World Services, Inc. Permission to reprint and adapt the Twelve Steps does not mean that A.A. has reviewed or approved the contents of this publication, nor that A.A. agrees with the views expressed herein. A.A. is a program of recovery from alcoholism. Use of the Twelve Steps in connection with programs that are patterned after A.A. but that address other problems does not imply otherwise.

Contents

Books of the New Testament, Psalms, and Proverbs

A Word from the Publisher

What's robbing you of freedom? What's become so important it feels like a god to you? Is it sex, drugs, or alcohol? Maybe it's an eating disorder, pornography, or gambling. It could be a relationship, work, getting good grades, or any other compulsive behavior. What is it? What fills your thoughts, messes with your emotions, and compels your actions? That's what you need to come clean about. That's where you're playing with an addiction or a dependency. Whatever it is you named holds the potential to cripple your life. *Clean: A Recovery Companion* can help you take a courageous look at yourself and your addiction from God's point of view as expressed in the New Testament and the Old Testament books of Psalms and Proverbs.

Maybe you come from a pretty messed up family. A dysfunctional family can leave you with the makings of an adult addictive personality. We hope *Clean* guides you to recognize and resolve some old emotional wounds.

We've packed away in the pages of *Clean* an introduction to the Twelve Steps of recovery, called "Steps to Freedom." Don't skip these. They'll help you get handles on what each step is about and how the Twelve Steps mesh with Scripture. After each step description you'll find a listing of recovery meditations and the Bible passages they're based on. When you look up these Bible readings, you'll find them highlighted so they stand out. We've highlighted nearly five hundred recovery Bible passages. Of these, we've focused on seven for each of the Twelve Steps so we can give you eighty-four recovery meditations to cheer you on and give you hope. The seven meditations for any given step to freedom are cross-referenced, so you can go from one to the next without going back to the list at the front. If you want, you can easily read through the meditations for a step—one each day—in a week.

SPECIAL NOTE: Be aware that Step 4 (page 33) will challenge you to make a personal inventory to help you name your areas of addiction, dependency, or codependency. Don't skip over it.

An adventure awaits you. Read and meditate on the Scripture and the meditations in *Clean*. As you do, you will begin to sense the God of the Bible speaking directly to your dependency needs. Let him set you free from your hurts, habits, and hang-ups and give you a whole and healthy life to be lived in relationship with him.

Finding Encouragement

Clean: A Recovery Companion can point you a long way down your road to spiritual healing and growth, but there are a lot of other places you can find additional help. Don't be afraid to look into professional therapy, pastoral counseling, or joining a Twelve Step program. Here are some of the big national groups that help people with various issues. You could discover what's in your area by calling a large church, by checking the white pages of your telephone directory, or by talking with your local library's reference specialist.

Alcoholics Anonymous
P.O. Box 459
Grand Central Station
New York, NY 10163
(212) 870-3400

Al-Anon/Alateen Family Group Headquarters, Inc.
1600 Corporate Landing
 Parkway
Virginia Beach, VA 23454-5617
(757) 563-1600

Debtors Anonymous
General Service Office
P.O. Box 920888
Needham, MA 02492-0009
(781) 453-2745

Incest Survivors Anonymous
P.O. Box 17245
Long Beach, CA 90807-7245

Narcotics Anonymous, World Service Office
P.O. Box 9999
Van Nuys, CA 91409-9099
(818) 773-9999

National Association for Children of Alcoholics
www.nacoa.org
11426 Rockville Pike, Suite 301
Rockville, MD 20852
(301) 468-0987

Overcomers Outreach
P.O. Box 922950
Sylmar, CA 91392-2950
Phones Toll Free: 1-800-310-3001 or 1-877-9OVERCOME
(Alcoholics and Adult Children Claiming Christ's Promises and Accepting His Healing)

Adult Children of Alcoholics, World Service Organization, Inc.
P.O. Box 3216
Torrance, CA 90510 USA
(310) 534-1815 (message only)

SAMHSA's National Clearinghouse for Alcohol and Drug Information
P.O. Box 2345
Rockville, MD 20847-2345
(240) 221-4019
1-800-729-6686

Gamblers Anonymous
P.O. Box 17173
Los Angeles, CA 90017
(213) 386-8789

Emotions Anonymous International
P.O. Box 4245
St. Paul, MN 55104-0245
(651) 647-9712

Overeaters Anonymous, World Service Office
P.O. Box 44020
Rio Rancho, NM 87174-4020
(505) 891-2664

These groups aren't as widespread as the first group. If one looks like a good fit for you, check whether there is a group anywhere near you.

- Adult Children Anonymous
- Al-Atot
- Alcoholics Victorious (Christian recovery support group)
- Bulimics/Anorexics Anonymous
- Celebrate Recovery (www.celebraterecovery.com)
- Child Abusers Anonymous
- Cocaine Anonymous
- Codependents of Sex Addicts
- Parents Anonymous
- Pills Anonymous
- Sex Addicts Anonymous
- Sexaholics Anonymous
- Sex and Love Addicts Anonymous
- Shoplifters Anonymous
- Smokers Anonymous
- Spenders Anonymous
- Victims of Incest Can Emerge Survivors (VOICES)
- Workaholics Anonymous

Becoming Clean
Getting Started

You probably wouldn't have picked up *Clean* unless you or someone you love is interested in a Twelve Step recovery program. We go after recovery when we need freedom from one or more addictive agents. Addictive agents are people or things we've formed an excessive dependency on. A catalog of addictive agents would include things like these:

1) Alcohol or drugs
2) Work, achievement, and success
3) Money addictions, such as overspending, gambling, hoarding
4) Control addictions, especially if they surface in personal, sexual, family, and business relationships
5) Food addictions
6) Sexual addictions
7) Approval dependency (the need to please people)
8) Rescuing patterns toward other persons
9) Dependency on toxic relationships (relationships that are damaging and hurtful)
10) Physical illness (hypochondria)
11) Exercise and physical conditioning
12) Cosmetics, clothes, cosmetic surgery, trying to look good on the outside
13) Academic pursuits and excessive intellectualizing
14) Religiosity or religious legalism (preoccupation with the form and the rules and regulations of religion, rather than benefiting from the real spiritual message)
15) General perfectionism
16) Cleaning and avoiding contamination and other obsessive-compulsive symptoms
17) Organizing, structuring (the need always to have everything in its place)
18) Materialism

Where did you see yourself on that list? Most of us are there somewhere, to some extent. And all of us can benefit from the truths contained in Twelve Step recovery, because all of us are, to some degree, codependent. What does that mean? Codependency is trying to control how you feel about yourself by manipulating people, things, and events around you. We start this because of things that go wrong during childhood—usually things in our family. Maybe you grew up in a home where love and acceptance were scarce. Or maybe things went the other way and you were smothered by adults who never gave you enough room to mature emotionally, spiritually, and mentally. Face it. A dysfunctional family, whether it involved open abuse or being treated in a way that was less than nurturing, may be the original source of your codependent pain. In turn, the pain becomes the root of your present addiction. Beyond all that, when you feel cut off from real love in your biological family, you tend to feel alienated from a second important "family"—the spiritual family. If you're struggling with habits, hurts, and hang-ups, you may feel uncomfortable with God as your Father. You may assume other members of God's family will judge you and reject you. After all, if you didn't find real love at home, why should you expect God or his people to love and care for you?

Sound complicated? In a way, it is. However, by facing our pain we create an opportunity to find peace and gain insight into why we picked up our destructive habits in the first place. Healing has to start and keep going in several dimensions of your life:

1) **You have to heal your relationships with people—maybe with several people. You have to go back and deal with painful memories from your dysfunctional family of origin, and you have to work on your key present relationships, too.**
2) **You really need to choose a recovery family. This can be a support group, a Twelve Step group, or a church community; but you need a new, healthy chosen family to stand with you and give you strength.**

3) **You need to get in touch with God in a spiritual family. Both the church and recovery groups, such as Alcoholics Anonymous, Overeaters Anonymous, and Emotions Anonymous, all say this is crucial to the success of your recovery.**

You may not have thought about it, but another reason to come clean and beat your hurts, habits, and hang-ups is the future of your children. Maybe you haven't even thought about children yet, but you probably will someday. Psychologists say we pass on our codependent love-hunger to the next generation, just as we got it from our parents. Emotionally dysfunctional families perpetuate themselves until someone breaks the cycle in one branch of the family tree.

This is a book about finding healing solutions to this love hunger. Both the Twelve Steps and the Bible address these healing solutions to our hurts, habits, and hang-ups. Let's take a glance at the history of the Twelve Steps in order to see why they align so nicely with the teachings of the Bible.

Where the Twelve Steps Came From

Twelve Step programs started in the mid-1930s with the birth of Alcoholics Anonymous. Alcoholics Anonymous was based on the ideas of a Christian revival organization known as the Oxford Group. In 1908 a Lutheran minister named Frank Buchman attended a deeper spiritual life conference in England. He had lost his job as the director of a hospice after a dispute with his board of directors and was angry and bitter over the experience. During a session at that conference, Dr. Buchman had an intense spiritual experience in which he had a vision of the face of Jesus as he suffered on the cross. The vision made Buchman realize how his bitterness separated him from Christ and the people he wanted to help as a pastor. By the time he returned to Pennsylvania, Dr. Buchman had started thinking in terms of a cycle of surrender, restitution, and sharing as basic spiritual principles for restoring broken lives—surrender to God, restitution for past wrongs, and sharing one's story to help others.

Dr. Buchman first put his "Oxford Principles" to work as an evangelist with the YMCA in Pennsylvania. The YMCA was an aggressive movement throughout the era of World War I. Through a series of revivals Buchman developed student groups that followed his ideas at Princeton, Yale, Harvard, Williams, Smith, and Vassar. His influence reached back to England where groups arose in Oxford and other universities. Eventually, Princeton and others banned the Oxford Group from campus for being too aggressive; but the Group continued off-campus in homes. Members were encouraged to find and help people who suffered from problems similar to their own. That meant recovering alcoholics were encouraged to reach out to others who suffered from alcohol dependencies.

In November 1934, an Oxford Group member named Ebby Thatcher visited an old friend, Bill Wilson, to encourage him to break free from alcoholism. Thatcher had found sobriety through the Group and was following the principle of sharing with someone else. Wilson didn't respond, but a month later Thatcher visited him again—this time in a hospital where Wilson was being treated for alcoholism. That night Wilson listened to the Oxford Principles. Twenty years later, Bill Wilson described his conversion experience that night:

> My depression deepened unbearably and finally it seemed to me as though I were at the very bottom of the pit. I still gagged badly at the notion of a Power greater than myself, but finally, just for the moment, the last vestige of my proud obstinacy was crushed. All at once I found myself crying out, "If there is a God, let Him show Himself! I am ready to do anything, anything!"
>
> Suddenly, the room lit up with a great white light. I was caught up into an ecstasy which there are no

words to describe. It seemed to me, in the mind's eye, that I was on a mountain and that a wind not of air but of spirit was blowing. And then it burst upon me that I was a free man. Slowly the ecstasy subsided. I lay on the bed, but now for a time I was in another world, a new world of consciousness. All about me and through me there was a wonderful feeling of Presence, and I thought to myself, "So this is the God of the preachers!" A great peace stole over me and I thought, "No matter how wrong things seem to be, they are still all right. Things are all right with God and His world."

(*Alcoholics Anonymous Comes of Age: A Brief History of A.A.* , **p. 63**)

For three years, Bill Wilson pursued his recovery through the Oxford Group, which emphasized these ideas:

1) **Complete deflation (of false pride)**
2) **Dependence and guidance from a Higher Power**
3) **Moral inventory**
4) **Confession**
5) **Restitution**
6) **Continued work with other suffering persons**

Early in that three-year period, Bill made a business trip to Akron, Ohio, on which he experienced strong urges to drink. He knew he was going to fall off the wagon, so he began calling churches and asking if there was an alcoholic in that town he could talk to. The Oxford Principles told him he could only retain his recovery if he actively involved himself in helping someone else. Wilson found an alcoholic surgeon, Dr. Bob Smith. It was May 1935. Wilson shared his life story and his newfound realization that if he persisted in drinking, he would either go mad or die. They talked night after night until Dr. Bob, too, began sharing frankly with his new friend. After ten days of sobriety, Dr. Bob went on a binge that ended with the last drink he ever took. It was June 10, 1935. Many people say that's when Alcoholics Anonymous began, although it would not be known by that name for another four years.

In August 1937, Wilson broke away from the Oxford Group because many alcoholics had trouble with its aggressive evangelism. Several were Catholics prohibited by Canon Law from joining religious movements outside their church. Also, Frank Buchman started getting more politically involved; and Wilson wanted to avoid any possible fallout from that.

As Alcoholics Anonymous became its own organization, it still relied on the ideas of the Oxford Group and the Bible as its foundation. The Twelve Steps of A.A. expand the six principles of the Oxford Group. Reliance on a Higher Power stands as a cornerstone of A.A. The tradition of sharing and story-telling that was common in the house meetings of the Oxford Group lives on in every A.A. and in other recovery group meetings today. No Oxford Group member ever appeared alone to represent the group as a whole. Likewise in A.A., there is no leader, no president, no representative for the organization.

Today tens of millions of Americans suffer from dependency problems, ranging from chemical addiction to sexual compulsion. Additionally, over 100 million live in families codependently related to these addicted men and women. That's the bad news. The good news is that recovery is possible. Something like 15 million men, women, and children are actively involved in 500,000 recovery groups, such as Alcoholics Anonymous, Al-Anon, Emotions Anonymous, and Overeaters Anonymous.

Do you want to know more about each of the Twelve Steps that have helped millions battle their addictions? Read on! As you do, you'll discover, too, where to find recovery meditations and related Bible passages, highlighted throughout the Bible text.

STEP I

We admitted we were powerless
over our dependencies—that our lives
had become unmanageable.

Why would anyone want to admit powerlessness— that they were
unable to do something? We're taught to say, "I'm strong! I'm the
master of my destiny!" On top of that, when we're addicted, there's
a tape in our head that repeats, "You're a pro at this! Do it more!
You can handle it!"

Right here at the beginning you face what may be your biggest
challenge in coming clean and getting free. There's an upside-
down bit of logic that kick-starts the whole process. You can only
find strength by admitting you don't have any. You find the road to
self-control by turning a corner and admitting you're hopelessly out
of control.

You have to say you're powerless to beat your addiction. The
reason for this is tied up in the five stages of the addiction cycle
that go like this:

1) Pain

   ▼

2) Reaching out for a fix from drugs, pornography, work, food,
   sex, alcohol, or dependent relationships to make the pain go
   away

   ▼

3) Temporary pleasure or good feelings

   ▼

4) Negative consequences

   ▼

5) Shame and guilt, which result in more pain or feelings of worthlessness

Here's an example. A cocaine addict gets anxious because he's behind on a project at school (pain). He snorts a line to escape his frustrations (addictive agent) and feels the familiar rush of elation. But the happiness wears off after a while, and he still hasn't made any progress on his project. In fact, he's lost more time. He stays up late and still doesn't get done. His roommate is mad at him for having the lights on all night (multiple negative consequences). He's done this so much that it isn't really guilt he feels. He doesn't feel much of anything—just a numb sense of worthlessness and a sad knowledge he'll probably do it again tomorrow or the next day.

If you stop and think a while about this addiction cycle, you might see why the Oxford Group and Bill Wilson (see "Becoming Clean: Getting Started") felt admitting powerlessness had to be the first step to recovery. If the cocaine addict just tries harder and harder to stop doing the drug, he's missed the point. His primary problem is the pain that drives the addiction. When he fights coke with willpower, he pumps up his fearful feelings of failure. Unfortunately, he only knows one sure-fired way of relieving that pain. So the more he relies on willpower to beat his addiction, the more he feels a need for it. Step 1 calls us to do less—to yield, to surrender, to stop looking inside ourselves for a kind of strength that can't be there.

Don't be surprised if you're skeptical about this so far. Two things go on in most peoples' heads that try to keep them from taking Step 1. They are 1) fear of withdrawal and 2) denial.

First, in order to take Step 1, you have to get past the fear of stepping off the addiction treadmill. You may dread the fight and pain it will take to come clean. Doctors, for instance, used to think that withdrawal for drug addicts was mainly biochemical and physical. It is true that when heroin addicts stop taking heroin, for example, their minds and bodies literally rebel as they struggle to restore balance. However, experts now agree that the emotional and spiritual struggles of withdrawal from addiction are more intense than the physical aspects. A woman with an eating disorder, for example, goes through withdrawal when she tries to follow a normal diet. Her real fear is that she will lose control over her appearance and how others see her. The paradox of Step 1 is that the act of surrendering addictive control starts to bring you back into a state of healthy control.

Second, you have to break your pattern of denial about your addiction. Denial is a cloak of self-deception we throw over our thinking that lets us avoid an honest assessment of our dependencies. We send ourselves denial messages such as these: "I can stop any time I want to." "Things aren't that bad." "This is normal now." "I only practice my addiction because I want to." "When things get better, I'll stop my addiction." A lot of us blame someone else, saying, "You make me do what I do!" All of these messages divert our attention away from the damage our addiction is causing.

Often you have to "hit bottom" before you can break out of denial. You "hit bottom" when something so bad happens that you can't go on the way you are. "Hitting bottom" forces you to admit your powerlessness over your addictive lifestyle. You can hit bottom physically as your health breaks because of your addiction. You can hit bottom emotionally with a mental breakdown or suicide attempt. You can hit bottom spiritually when there is nothing left to live for unless God steps in.

Here are some common examples of "bottom" crises that have helped people get past denial to recovery:

1) A physical breakdown (a perfectionistic college student suffers panic attacks as graduation nears)

2) A confrontation by a family member or friend (a drug addict's family stages an intervention)

3) Vocational crisis (an alcoholic loses a job because of absenteeism)

4) A financial crisis (a compulsive gambler misses three student loan payments and starts getting calls from a collection agency)

5) A spiritual crisis (a girl living with her boyfriend can't pray and feels God hates her)

This is where you start to break the addiction cycle. You give up trying to do it yourself and yield to a Power outside yourself. In reality, you'll have to surrender again and again, as you admit your powerlessness over your primary addiction and various other parts of your life that impact it. You'll come to realize you are ultimately powerless over lots of people, places, and situations. You'll learn to let those things go. For example, when a macho driver cuts you off in rush hour traffic, instead of getting mad and trying to punish him, you need to admit that you can't change or fix what happened. In the most trivial issues we face, we must learn to flex. Don't be surprised if you find yourself switching addictions or transferring obsessions as you move through the Twelve Steps. If you do, you need to apply the first step to your new dependency, too.

If you don't know it already, addicts are control freaks. Control, or the lack of it, is central to every aspect of life. As you admit your powerlessness, you grab hold of the antidote for control addiction. For example, an alcoholic overcontrols efforts to escape stress and frustration. In the process, she undercontrols her family life, her emotional stability, and her spiritual life. By admitting she is powerless to deal with her alcoholism, she opens the door for God to teach her new ways to handle stress and frustration. Then she can invest more energy in all the things she's been undercontrolling. With her life in better balance, she's less likely to feel the need to hide in a bottle.

Admitting powerlessness is not the same thing as passively sitting by while life beats you up. You admit personal powerlessness as a step toward discovering God's will and power. In the long run, you're counting on him to make your life better than you ever imagined it could be.

STEP I

Recovery Meditations

What does the Bible say about the unmanageability of our lives? To find out, read the recovery meditations on the following passages:

Scripture	Page	Scripture	Page
Matthew 9:36	13	Psalm 38:1–9	412
Romans 7:18–20	212	Psalm 44:15–16	417
Psalm 6:2–4	385	Psalm 72:12–13	436
Psalm 31:9–10	403		

STEP I

Recovery Scriptures Highlighted in the Text

STEP 2

Came to believe that a Power greater than
ourselves could restore us to sanity.

The Step 2 phrase "came to believe" suggests a process of faith
that took some time to become effective in your life. Alcoholics
Anonymous likes to talk about three stages in this process. First, *we
came.* For an alcoholic that may mean showing up and stumbling in
the door at a meeting. Second, *we came to,* that is, you sobered up.
You have to come to your senses and see reality from a different
perspective. Only then can you experience emotional sobriety.
Third, *we came to believe.* Faith is the last stage of your process.
Then spiritual growth can kick in. In this way, Step 2 fits nicely with
the Christian teaching that you have to come to an individual,
personal knowledge of God.

Step 2 unfolds logically from Step 1. In Step 1, you admitted your
powerlessness, so you need a new source of strength to help you
get well and whole. Some people experience dramatic spiritual
conversions when they first come into contact with God. Most get
to know Him more gradually. In the same way you grow and mature
emotionally, you also grow spiritually.

It's easy to say it's time to welcome in a new Power into your life to
restore you to wellness. It's quite another thing to do it. You
probably will have some emotional and spiritual baggage to deal
with.

1) You have to identify all the addictive agents you've been using to ease the pains of daily living. You have to get ready to think about them differently. You have to get money, sex, career, food, gambling, pornography, drugs—anything and everything that's dominated your life—into proper perspective. You've got to get those things off the pedestal where you've unconsciously worshiped them in your denial.

2) You need to get ready to think about God differently, especially if religion has been mainly a set of rules or a catechism you learned as a child. You're going to need to start treating God as a person you talk to and rely on.

3) You have to learn to stop playing God yourself. Addicts are controllers. They use habits and substances to soothe themselves. Step 2 says it's time to get beyond selfishness, self-absorption, and dramatic attempts to fix things.

4) You may have to admit putting certain people, relationships, or things in God's place and commit to stop doing that.

None of this is easy to do. You may have a track record of self-destructive behaviors. Steps 1 and 2 say it's time to break with things that don't work and turn to someone who has real power. Maybe you're thinking at this point that you're mad at God. Maybe you feel he can't be trusted.

1) You may identify God with an abusive parent.

2) You may think the church is full of hypocrites, bigots, and judgmental jerks.

3) You may feel crushed by a sense that God has failed you—that he hasn't done anything to keep you out of the personal mess you're in.

4) You may be angry with God because he hasn't instantaneously healed you from your addictive illnesses when you've asked him to.

No matter what you've thought of God in the past, it's time to start over. Wipe the slate clean. Admit your own powerlessness to help yourself, and turn to a higher power who has power to restore you to sanity. You will find that recovery takes a lifetime. You don't do it alone. You need God and you need others who are fighting the same battle. You'll find meetings and recovery literature important tools for keeping in touch with others fighting the good fight. You'll find the Bible to be an important tool for keeping in touch with God. Let *Clean* guide you in finding passages and readings that will introduce you to God. The better you know him, the more confident you will be about how he wants you to succeed in life.

STEP 2

Recovery Meditations

What does the Bible have to say about God's power to make your life whole? To find out, read the recovery meditations based on the following passages:

STEP 2

Passages Highlighted in the Text

STEP 3

Made a decision to turn our will and our lives over to the care of God **as we understood Him.**

Step 3 completes what you started in Steps 1 and 2. In Step 1, you admitted your life was out of control and that you were powerless to change things through your own ability. In Step 2, you started looking to a higher Power to restore you to wholeness. You stopped relying on all the old failed ways you had turned to in the past. In Step 3, you call that higher Power God and ask him to take control of every part of your life.

Twelve Step recovery groups use the phrase "Turn it over" a lot. Recovering people learn to turn over to God's care not only the big, obvious addictions like alcoholism, but also the little frustrations of taking care of children, trying to make a broken toaster work, or coping with rush-hour traffic. Whenever you're irritated and could feel the urge to act out, you need to say time and again, "Turn it over; turn it over; turn it over."

There are a lot of things that seem contradictory in recovery. Step 3 recognizes that an addict is often proud and self-centered. At the same time, that pride and selfishness acts as a mask for a scared, insecure soul. Alcoholics Anonymous, the granddaddy of Twelve Step groups, calls an alcoholic "an egomaniac with an inferiority complex." Step 3 invites you to get out of the center of your universe and give that place back to God.

An addicted person becomes more self-centered, self-absorbed, and self-preoccupied while trying to ease the pain that drives the addiction. In a vicious cycle, this self-preoccupation drags the addict deeper into the destructive habit. Focusing on self only intensifies a person's feelings of pain, loneliness, and isolation. By its nature an addiction pulls the addict deeper into its pain cycle. To get out of that pain cycle, the addict has to do the last thing he or she wants to—focus on someone else.

Here's another apparent contradiction of recovery. Focusing on someone else doesn't mean you have to ignore or deny your needs. People in recovery find that when they focus on God, they discover themselves while they're discovering him. At the same time you discover healthy, God-directed ways to meet your emotional and physical needs, you become less needy, less selfish, less self-preoccupied. Discovering what your needs are and asking God to meet those needs will be one of the most *unselfish* things you do.

We all have needs. We all make choices about how to meet those needs. Addictions and compulsive behaviors turn out to be bogus ways of satisfying our most basic physical, emotional, and spiritual hungers. With God's help you can find real ways of satisfying them.

You may be saying, "I'd like to turn my life over to God, but how do I do that?" The key to giving control of your life to God is *willingness*. If you crack open the door a little bit, God will guide you in the process. In Revelation 3:20, Jesus says: "Here I am! I stand at the door and knock. If you hear my voice and open the door, I will come in and eat with you, and you will eat with me."

A.A. has a Third Step Prayer to help alcoholics express their new willingness to let God control their lives. Its language is old-fashioned, and its last sentence is complicated; but its ideas are terrific. Think about how you would say this prayer in your own words:

"God, I offer myself to Thee—to build with me and to do with me as Thou wilt. Relieve me of the bondage of self, that I may better do Thy will. Take away my difficulties, that victory over them may bear witness to those I would help of Thy power, Thy love, and Thy way of life. May I do Thy will always!" (*Alcoholics Anonymous*, p. 63).

STEP 3

Recovery Meditations

What does the Bible have to say about surrendering your will and life to God? To find out, read the recovery meditations based on the following passages:

STEP 3

Passages Highlighted in the Text

STEP 4

Made a searching and fearless moral
inventory of ourselves.

In the first three steps, you've identified a reliable source of power for recovery from your hurts, habits, and hang-ups. During Step 4 you will do the hard work of looking inside yourself to note the damage your addiction has done to you and also looking outside yourself to see what it's done to others. This inventory will serve as a roadmap to direct your new spiritual growth. It will identify character traits you'll want to keep and develop and those you need to change or eliminate.

You're probably wondering what in the world a "moral inventory" is. A moral inventory is a description of your addiction, its causes, and its consequences. Your inventory will have all or most of the following six parts.

First, you need to "tell your story." It helps to do some journaling, that is, write out the story of your addiction. That gives you a framework for sharing your story in recovery meetings or one-on-one conversations. Telling your story means it isn't a secret any more. You don't have to hide your addiction. There's a story in the Bible about a woman who'd ruined five marriages and was living with a man she hadn't married. When she found out that Jesus knew all about her and still accepted her, she was set free to welcome the power of God into her life (John 4). Telling your story can have that sort of liberating impact.

When you're getting your story ready, you can think through the major events of your life. Going step-by-step through your past journey helps you look honestly at your present situations. Telling your story to somebody else brings that person into your closest circle of friends where they can help you heal your life.

The second thing you want to accomplish with your inventory is to discover the roots of your addictions and compulsions. Usually that involves examining your childhood. What did you need from your childhood that you didn't get? What bad things happened inside your family? Did your family have any of these six kinds of family breakdowns that can lead to adult addiction or codependency?

1) *Active abuse.* This occurs when a parent releases anger or frustration on a child in the form of direct physical, verbal, or sexual abuse.

2) *Passive abuse.* Passive abuse takes place when a parent neglects a child's emotional needs. A son or daughter needs fifteen to twenty years of steady, consistent love from two sane, sober, relatively happy parents. A child requires time, attention, and affection. Anything, such as workaholism, that hinders a parent's ability to give these things can result in passive abuse.

3) *Emotional incest.* In some troubled families, the parents behave so immaturely that the children have to take on adult roles and take care of their parents. Imagine that seven-year-old Suzie's mom is an alcoholic. Suzie gets herself up for school, fixes her own breakfast, and urges her mom out of bed in the afternoon so daddy won't throw a fit when he gets home. Suzie is becoming a mother to her own mother. That isn't doing Suzie any good.

4) *Unfinished business.* Sometimes parents try to make up for their failures and disappointments through their children. A father who is frustrated and unsuccessful in his work may push his sons and daughters to be compulsive,

perfectionistic, and workaholics in order to make himself feel better about not getting further on his own.

5) *Negative messages about who and what the child is.* Sometimes parents say incredibly cruel, hurtful things to their children. These destroy feelings of self-worth and become part of the child's personality. Too many adults remember parents saying things such as: "You'll never amount to anything." "Can't you do anything right?" "You make me sick!" Other times parents send hurtful messages without using words. The son whose father works all the time soon realizes his dad doesn't care to be with him. The daughter whose mother makes all her decisions eventually can't make them on her own.

6) *Dead-end feelings or needs.* Members of dysfunctional families deny their feelings and bury their needs. In time, they may not feel much; or they may not know what their feelings mean. Their emotions can come out in odd ways. A young woman whose mother gripes at her regularly about her grades and her weight may learn to keep quiet and stay out of her way. Her need to assert herself may come out in shoplifting or cutting herself.

Keep in mind that looking for the roots of your hurts, habits, and hang-ups isn't looking for somebody to blame. You just need to know all you can about where your addiction or compulsive behavior came from.

Third, you have to face up to the full extent of your dependencies. When you do, two things will happen. You will learn just how bad your primary addiction is, and you may find out you have one or more secondary addictions you'd never thought about. This is where you start identifying symptoms and addictions you've ignored while you focused on the big problem. All those hours on the Internet may not be so harmless. What about that craving for chocolate? Is it over the top? You need how much caffeine? You may have nothing to deal with but your primary addiction. But there may be other issues affecting your life. (See page 11, "Becoming Clean: Getting Started," for a list of common addictions.)

Fourth, you want to think back carefully over your relationship history with the people who have been important to your life—parents, teachers, friends, boyfriends, or girlfriends. Write out a list of all the ways you have hurt each of these people through your addiction. If you name ten people, you make ten lists. You do this as a step toward getting rid of anger and shame.

When we feel insecure, we fear we will fail and look bad. So we resent the people we blame for putting us in these insecure settings. We say things to hurt them. We do things to hurt them. These are the people you make lists for. The lists involve what you said and did to hurt them. You want to understand better what drove you to hurt them. What made you afraid? What made you feel insecure? You have to know before you can deal with these things.

Fifth, you want to deal with your guilt feelings. Face it. Most addictions are fueled by shame. In order to take away the power of shame, you need to distinguish between two kinds of guilt:

1) *False shame.* A lot of addicts blame themselves for situations they have no control over. Children and teens blame themselves for their parents' divorce. The children of a once-respected businessman who embezzled money can't seem to form lasting relationships, either in marriage or friendships. Many adults go through life feeling false shame for wrong things their parents did years before.

2) *Authentic guilt.* We all do selfish things that the Bible calls sin. We all hurt people in lots of little and big ways—by things we say, things we do, and things we should do but don't. We're guilty of these things.

You need to distinguish between these two types of guilt. Don't let yourself be a victim of false shame, but accept responsibility for what you truly have done wrong. Be willing to ask forgiveness of people you've hurt.

Sixth, you must "look for the good." Step 4 isn't an exercise in beating yourself up for being worthless. Your Step 4 inventory should include both the positive and the negative things you discover about yourself. 1) What positive things came out of your childhood? 2) What worthwhile survival skills have you learned in your struggles to cope? For example, an overachieving student may turn out to be an excellent teacher with great job skills. 3) What are your skills, talents, and interests? 4) What recovery steps and positive changes are you working on currently?

NOTE: If you uncover addictions or dependencies you hadn't recognized before, you may need to return to Step 1 to start working on these.

STEP 4

Recovery Meditations

What does the Bible have to say about the personal inventorying of your life? To find out, read the recovery meditations based on the following passages:

STEP 4

Passages Highlighted in the Text

STEP 5

Admitted to God, to ourselves, and to another human being the exact nature of our wrongs.

This is one of the hardest steps in the recovery process, because you have to stop hiding your hurts, habits, and hang-ups. At the same time, this is the step where you start noticing real progress because it pulls you out of your isolation and gets you talking to somebody else. Step 5 requires a three-part sharing of everything you found out about yourself in your Step 4 inventory. You will admit what's going wrong in your life to God, to yourself, and to somebody else.

There are five kinds of "wrongs" you need to share:

1) You need to admit *all* of your addictions.

2) You need to tell the things that went wrong in your families that played a part in making you try to escape your pain.

3) You need to talk about how your parents got to be the way they are. Try to understand the families your parents grew up in and feel compassion for them.

4) You need to identify the problems in all major relationships in your life.

5) You need to admit the specific ways in which you have wronged others by practicing your addictions.

These are intensely personal and sensitive issues. Be very careful in choosing who you share all of this with. Don't just pick your best friend, unless that person is extremely mature, dependable, and able to keep secrets really well. Most people in recovery make this confession to a counselor, a pastor, or a trusted member of their support group. You may want to think in terms of an older person who is compassionate and accepting, not condemning.

You can expect four really good results from Step 5 sharing:

1) You'll sense a sharp drop in feelings of shame and guilt. Christians have always practiced confession as part of spiritual growth. No wonder it works wonders in the healing and renewal process.

2) Your Step 5 sharing gives you a chance to grieve—to tell how bad you feel about all that has happened and all that you've done wrong right up to the present. These are the things that are keeping you from living life to the fullest.

3) This confession lets you take a major step toward honesty. Nothing keeps you trapped in your addiction like the need to hide who you really are and how you really feel. In Step 5 sharing, maybe for the first time in your life, you open your deepest, darkest secrets and hurts to somebody else.

4) Remember that addictions isolate you from other people and from God. Step 5 sharing breaks down the walls you have built through your addictions and lets in the light and fresh air that comes from knowing someone else knows all about you and still likes you.

Step 5 sharing is the beginning of the end of your lonely isolation.

STEP 5

Recovery Meditations

What does the Bible have to say about confession's role in your recovery? To find out, read the recovery meditations based on the following passages:

STEP 5

Passages Highlighted in the Text

STEP 6

Were entirely ready to have God
remove all these defects of character.

Step 6 looks easier than it is. You don't have to ask God to remove any character defects. You just have to be ready to ask him. Think about that. Are you really *ready* to ask God to remove *all* of your addictions and dependencies? Maybe the sheer agony of drug abuse or the fright of waking up in the hospital because of an eating disorder forced you into recovery. You're ready to get clean from that one. But what about a sneakier dependency that you like and want to hold on to? You might be ready to ask God to take away your addiction to alcohol but be in denial about a destructive relationship with a boyfriend or girlfriend. Maybe he hasn't beaten you too badly yet. Maybe you haven't noticed you can't afford everything she wants. In fact, you may lean on that relationship even more as you get free of alcohol.

Do you see what the real struggle is in Step 6? Are you *entirely* ready to ask God to remove *all* of your defects, even the ones you'd like to cling to? This isn't easy. You have to start asking yourself what else is going on in your life that you need to get rid of. Ask God to point out things he wants you to work on. Ask wise older people—maybe the one you shared with in Step 5—to tell you if they see destructive patterns in your life that you don't see.

Look back at the relationship inventory you conducted in Step 4. If you see repeating patterns in how you handle people and problems, you may be onto something. Do you always end up the doormat in important relationships? Or do you end up using and overcontrolling people? How are you at setting boundaries? Do you frequently let people take advantage of you? Or do you regularly push people away? Do you see and respect the boundaries of others? Problems in areas like these are defects you need to give to God. Can you?

You need to be really *specific* when identifying *individual* defects of character. You also have to be specific about what changes you need to make to fix them. One cure does not fit all! The way you approach one addiction may not work at all for another. For instance, if your problem is uncontrollable anger, you're going to work on reducing anger expression. But if you're afraid of anger and never let yourself get mad, you have to learn how to feel anger in right ways and assert yourself when necessary. The treatment has to be very specifically tailored to the defect and to you.

Generally, your defects of character involve some imbalance in the way you express and experience basic human needs. For example, sexuality and ambition aren't bad unless you let them get out of hand. If you are addicted to sex or driven by ambition to the point of workaholism, those are defects you have to deal with. You wouldn't pray, "Take away my sexuality" or "Take away my ambition." Instead, you might pray, "Help me know healthy sexual feelings" or "Channel my ambition into building a successful personal and work life."

When you tell God about your defects of character, don't beat yourself up. You want to let go of these things and find God's help. He doesn't want you to punish yourself. He wants you to discover his love and acceptance. Also be prepared to find that being willing to let go of your defects takes time. You may have to do it several times before you really are ready to let go of everything. Recovery is a daily struggle to understand yourself and learn how to cooperate with God in keeping the needs of your life in balance.

STEP 6

Recovery Meditations

What does the Bible have to say about choosing to yield your character defects to God? To find out, read the recovery meditations based on the following passages:

STEP 6

Passages Highlighted in the Text

STEP 7

Humbly asked Him to remove our shortcomings.

Steps 6 and 7 go together. They combine to invite God to do what he needs to as he deals with your character defects. In Step 6, you became completely *willing* to give these flaws to God. Now, in Step 7, you *humbly ask* him to handle your shortcomings. Be careful not to confuse *humility* with *humiliation*. God isn't out to make you feel bad about yourself. He wants you to submit your will to his.

Maybe humility doesn't appeal to you very much. Actually, you need humility for three reasons:

1) *To recognize how bad your character defects really are.* Addicts are notorious for denying or playing down just how much pain they've caused other people. Therefore, when you take stock of your character defects, you need humility to face all that you've done to people around you.

2) *To admit your own inability to correct these character defects.* You cannot overcome your hurts, habits, and hang-ups on your own. You can't do it with sheer willpower. You can't think your way or talk your way out of the habit that has you in its grip.

3) *To grasp just how great God's power is for making your life new.*

When you humble yourself to ask God to change you, you're not telling yourself you're worthless or helpless. This is how you start becoming confident and self-controlled. People who hate themselves often put on a mask of false pride. They pretend they're in control and don't need God or anybody else. When you start feeling good about yourself, you don't need to pretend to be tough. You know what you can do and what you can't. You can ask for help from God or others and feel glad to get it. When you're comfortable with yourself, humility isn't so hard.

To get to the point of having life-changing humility, you have to realize a couple of things. First, being happy doesn't depend on how rich you are, how smart you are, or how good-looking you are. Second, you have to know your limits before you will put God in control of your life. You'll never overcome your character defects until God gets in the driver's seat of your life and stays there.

Step 7 is the shortest of the Twelve Steps. It has the fewest words, but it packs one of the biggest wallops of all the steps. When you embrace this step and turn over to God all your brokenness and pain, you set in motion the miracle of transformation. God will start molding you into a healthy, effective personality. A.A.'s Seventh Step Prayer asks God to take control like this:

> My Creator, I am now willing that you should have all of me, good and bad. I pray that you now remove from me every single defect of character which stands in the way of my usefulness to you and my fellows. Grant me strength, as I go out from here, to do your bidding. Amen.

> (*Alcoholics Anonymous*, p. 76)

STEP 7

Recovery Meditations

What does the Bible have to say about the importance of asking God to remove your shortcomings? To find out, read the recovery meditations based on the following passages:

STEP 7

Passages Highlighted in the Text

STEP 8

Made a list of all persons we had harmed,
and became willing to make amends to them all.

In Steps 4 and 5, you started getting rid of shame by making a moral inventory and admitting to another person the full extent of your addictive behavior. In Step 8, you go even farther to eliminate guilt. In this step, you make preparations to go to people you've wronged with your addictive behavior and try to make things right.

You might ask, "Who should I put on my list of people to make amends to?" Here are four suggestions. They overlap, so your list may be done before you get to the fourth one.

1) Include everybody you may have hurt because of your addiction.

2) Look back at everybody you included in your Step 4 relationship history. You probably owe some amends to most of them.

3) Don't overlook people younger than you, such as younger brothers and sisters or your own children, who have suffered because of your addiction and compulsive behaviors.

4) Consider whether you need to make amends to the following "family" groups:

a) All members of your family of origin, living and dead. (You may even owe amends to an abusive parent. Making amends does not mean that you pretend the abuse didn't happen or doesn't matter anymore. Making amends means you take back the hatred and nastiness you threw on the fires of that relationship.)

b) All sexual partners, your spouse, and any children.

c) People you work with or go to school with.

d) People you know in your neighborhood.

e) People you go to church with.

f) People you've mistreated because of their race, gender, sexual orientation, politics, and so on.

Steps 8 and 9 assume that it's a really bad thing to hurt people and never try to repair the damage you've done. It's bad for your relationships, and it's bad for your soul. You can't be a healthy, free person without forgiving those who hurt you and asking forgiveness from those you've hurt. Steps 8 and 9 give you a procedure for doing this.

Remember this. You need to work through your own bad feelings about people who have hurt you before you can honestly make amends with those you have hurt. If you try to make amends with somebody you hate, you're putting a Band-Aid on a cancer. That doesn't heal anything. You have to do a lot of forgiving before you can accept forgiveness with emotional integrity.

STEP 8

Recovery Meditations

What does the Bible have to say about the importance of your willingness to make amends to the people you have harmed? To find out, read the recovery meditations based on the following passages:

STEP 8

Passages Highlighted in the Text

STEP 9

Made direct amends to such people
wherever possible, except when to
do so would injure them or others.

It's easy to make a list of people you should make amends to.
Actually making amends is really hard, especially when you
struggle with the kinds of insecurities and fears that lead to
addictive or compulsive behavior. As you think about making
amends, remember these things. Genuine efforts to make up for
past wrongs can accomplish three important things. There also is a
fourth and phony way of looking at amends.

Sincere amends do these things:

1) They apologize for past harm.

2) They build bridges to new and better future relationships.

3) They get you out from under the weight of guilt and shame
   for things you've done as an addict.

Here's the fourth thing that your amends should *never* seek to do.
Don't ask for forgiveness as a way of proving you'll never make any
more mistakes. Don't promise anyone else perfection, and don't
expect it of yourself. People with addictive personalities tend to think
they have to prove they aren't worthless by becoming perfect. If you
think you have to be perfect, you'll just set yourself up for failure.

Don't miss the second half of Step 9. In some cases, there may be
a person or two you shouldn't try to make things right with
because you'll only hurt them more. An alcoholic who killed

someone driving drunk may not be able to talk with the victim's mother. A drug addict who raped a woman may not be able to make amends to the victim. Amends in these cases must be made to God. However, don't use this exception as an excuse for avoiding a confrontation you dread.

Who should you make amends to? In Step 8, you made a list of everyone you've hurt. You need to be willing to make amends to everyone on your list. However, when it comes down to going to people to heal past wounds, you have to use your head about who you actually talk to, as well as when and how you do it. Here are four main groups you can divide your Step 8 list into:

1) Those you need to talk with soon and fully, such as close family members and good friends.

2) Those you will talk with in a limited way so you don't hurt somebody else. Maybe you were addicted to drugs. When you make amends to people outside your former circle of drug users, you don't want to mention anything that identifies or could lead somebody to guess the identity of another user. You're making amends for what *you* did.

3) Those you need to wait a while to talk with. You may have hurt someone so badly that you need to give them some time before you can expect them to forgive you. Or it may be that you need to work through some anger and bitterness before you're ready to make amends to people you've hurt because they have hurt you, too.

4) Those rare individuals you shouldn't try to make amends to. For example, sex addicts can't always make amends to former partners they've mistreated. Sometimes trust has been damaged so badly in a relationship that one person simply will not have contact with the other.

The amends process of Step 9 is one-sided. You admit to the individuals you see what you have done wrong to them and ask them to forgive you. They may forgive you right then. They may forgive you later. They may refuse to forgive you. You'd rather they forgive you, but the goal of Step 9 is your confession more than their forgiveness. You're throwing out the garbage of the past so you can be free and clean.

STEP 9

Recovery Meditations

What does the Bible have to say about how to reconcile with people you have harmed? To find out, read the recovery meditations based on the following passages:

STEP 9

Passages Highlighted in the Text

STEP 10

Continued to take personal inventory
and when we were wrong promptly admitted it.

People in Twelve Step groups often call Steps 10, 11, and 12 the maintenance steps. These steps will keep you cycling through the healing process of the earlier steps. They help you "work the steps" on a day-to-day basis.

Step 10 encourages you to take a personal inventory regularly. Most recovering people need to do this every day to keep from slipping back into their addictive habits. A daily maintenance inventory has five components:

1) What are your needs? Be conscious of your needs for love, acceptance, and security. Think about whether they are being met in some reasonable fashion.

2) What are your feelings? Many addicts become emotionally numb and have to work at having normal feelings. Let yourself grieve over the mess your life is in. Watch out for deep feelings of resentment. Resentment hides anger. Anger covers up hurt. Hurt usually conceals fear. And the deepest fear is fear of rejection or abandonment.

3) What addictive means are you using to meet your needs? Are you manipulating anyone? Are you overcontrolling anyone? Are you being perfectionistic or compulsive? Are you playing the martyr or the victim in your relationships? Are you "rescuing" or enabling someone who is bad for you?

4) Are you maintaining your personal boundaries so no one takes advantage of you, and are you respecting the boundaries of your friends and family members? You need boundaries that are neither too rigid nor too fragile. Can you keep people out as you need to? Can you let people in as you need to? Do you honor the boundaries of the people in your life in the same way you want them to respect yours?

5) When someone violates your boundaries, are you able to tell them not to? Are you able to restore your boundaries quickly? When you violate someone else's boundaries, do you make amends right away?

6) Do you admit your wrongs promptly? When you do, you keep your conscience clean and free. When you don't, your conscience becomes cluttered with unresolved issues. This can make it easier for you to fall back into your old ways of trying to meet your needs.

Your daily inventory also needs to ask how your relationship with God is going. Are you still yielding your will to him? At the heart of addiction is the attempt to replace God's control with some behavior we hope will take away all the pain of life. Addicts can get very stubborn about their habits. You will need to surrender your will to God on a daily basis for the rest of your life. We will take a closer look at what that means in Step 11.

STEP 10

Recovery Meditations

What does the Bible have to say about the need for an ongoing inventory of your life? To find out, read the recovery meditations based on the following passages:

STEP 10

Passages Highlighted in the Text

STEP 11

Sought through prayer and meditation to improve our conscious contact with God **as we understood Him,** praying only for knowledge of His will for us and the power to carry that out.

When you work on Step 11, you're developing an everyday relationship with God. In the early stages of recovery, you will depend on support group meetings and recovery reading material for spiritual and emotional growth. But the longer you're in recovery, the more you'll want your own one-on-one contact with God. You'll need to connect with a church that meets your needs. You'll want to read your Bible regularly and spend daily time in prayer so you can tell God what's going on in your life and "listen" for his responses to you. Step 11 asks you to slow down, take yourself out of the driver's seat, and follow God's will for you as you discover it.

Studying the Bible helps you know God better and shows you what he wants for your life. *Clean: A Recovery Companion* guides you through a series of Bible readings and meditations geared directly to the Twelve Steps. A lot of other parts of the Bible are highlighted in *Clean* so you can find other things God has to say about recovery and spiritual growth. If you want to, you can use *Clean* quite a while in your daily time with God.

Maybe you've not prayed much in the past. Just start out simply talking to God about what concerns you and what excites you. Don't be completely problem-oriented when you pray. Tell God about good things that happen and thank him for them. If you tend to be a perfectionist, get rid of any ideas of the "right way" to pray.

Picture God as your loving heavenly Father. Even if your physical father has not been a good parent, you can imagine God as the perfect Father who wants to hear from you and respond to you.

As you get more comfortable with God, you will find yourself talking with him as with a trusted friend. He will be the one Person to whom you can pour out your daily inventories of bad feelings and temptations toward your past addictive behaviors. You will also start experiencing his answers to your prayers. He's not a heavenly vending machine that spits out everything you ask for. Much better than that, he's a loving God who gives you what's best in the long run. Trust him.

There's one more step to go. When you read about Step 12, you will discover how important it is for your recovery to share what you discover with others who need to find how to be free and clean of their hurts, habits, and hang-ups.

STEP 11

Recovery Meditations

What does the Bible have to say about the value of prayer and meditation in seeking God's will and power for your life? To find out, read the recovery meditations based on the following passages:

STEP 11

Passages Highlighted in the Text

STEP 12

Having had a spiritual awakening as the
result of these steps, we tried to carry
this message to others, and to practice
these principles in all our affairs.

When you start into recovery, you have one thing in mind—kicking
your habit. It's interesting that people in recovery find they get a
whole lot more than that. They find they've been made new from
the inside out by a God they may have thought they hated in the
past. In a way, your addiction, your pain, and the healing of your
addiction become stepping-stones to a whole new life. A.A. and
other Twelve Step groups have a tradition that people in meetings
introduce themselves by saying, "Hi, I'm _____, and I'm a
grateful recovering alcoholic." What they mean is that they're glad
that their addiction or dependency led them to where they are.

The second phrase in Step 12 reads: "we tried to carry this
message to others." Twelve Step programs all encourage members
to reach out to other addicts. Another A.A. saying goes, "You can't
keep it unless you give it away." You hang onto your healing best
when you help somebody else along the same road. That's one way
Twelve Step recovery is similar to the Christian church. Both share
good news about a better life with hurting people.

Therapists observe all the time that people who share the same
addiction feel a bond with one another. That's why A.A. works as
well as it does. Nobody can help an alcoholic like another alcoholic
who's found how to beat the bottle. You name your addiction.
Nobody can help you like someone recovering from the same

problem. As you recover, you have the ability to help someone else find freedom and cleansing.

The last line of Step 12 says to practice the Twelve Step principles "in all our affairs." The changes God makes in you will touch every part of your life, and people around you will notice the changes. Of course, they'll know you're not practicing your addiction anymore. But they'll also see you aren't as angry as before, or that you don't let them walk all over you. They'll realize you're more interested in others more than in yourself. They'll know your sex life is different, and on and on.

Healing your addictions or codependencies isn't where recovery ends. That's where it starts. You want your addiction under control and your life in balance. That can happen for you. Believe it! Believe also that God will remake every part of your life if you let him. Have you wondered why the founders of A.A. referred to God with the phrase "God as we understood Him"? They realized that many alcoholics come into recovery with bad feelings about God. Some start as agnostics. Maybe they come to think of their support group as their higher power and look to their friends for strength. Gradually, most accept a vague notion of god, that grows to a more personal god. They start praying to this god. Eventually, they come to know the one true God told about in the Bible.

As you search for the true God, tune in to the God of the Scriptures. Spend time reading *Clean* and thinking over what you read. Then you, too, can know this caring, loving, and merciful Father.

STEP 12

Recovery Meditations

What does the Bible have to say about sharing your spiritual awakening with others through message and example? To find out, read the recovery meditations based on the following passages:

STEP 12

Passages Highlighted in the Text

NEW TESTAMENT

MATTHEW

Matthew Tells About Jesus the King of the Jews

1 This is the family history of Jesus Christ. He came from the family of David, and David came from the family of Abraham.

²Abraham was the father of Isaac.
Isaac was the father of Jacob.
Jacob was the father of Judah and his brothers.
³Judah was the father of Perez and Zerah.
  (Their mother was Tamar.)
Perez was the father of Hezron.
Hezron was the father of Ram.
⁴Ram was the father of Amminadab.
Amminadab was the father of Nahshon.
Nahshon was the father of Salmon.
⁵Salmon was the father of Boaz.
  (Boaz's mother was Rahab.)
Boaz was the father of Obed.
  (Obed's mother was Ruth.)
Obed was the father of Jesse.
⁶Jesse was the father of King David.
David was the father of Solomon.
  (Solomon's mother had been Uriah's wife.)
⁷Solomon was the father of Rehoboam.
Rehoboam was the father of Abijah.
Abijah was the father of Asa.
⁸Asa was the father of Jehoshaphat.
Jehoshaphat was the father of Jehoram.
Jehoram was the ancestor of Uzziah.
⁹Uzziah was the father of Jotham.
Jotham was the father of Ahaz.
Ahaz was the father of Hezekiah.
¹⁰Hezekiah was the father of Manasseh.
Manasseh was the father of Amon.
Amon was the father of Josiah.
¹¹Josiah was the grandfather of Jehoiachin and his brothers.
  (This was at the time that the people were taken to Babylon.)
¹²After they were taken to Babylon:
Jehoiachin was the father of Shealtiel.
Shealtiel was the grandfather of Zerubbabel.
¹³Zerubbabel was the father of Abiud.
Abiud was the father of Eliakim.
Eliakim was the father of Azor.
¹⁴Azor was the father of Zadok.
Zadok was the father of Akim.
Akim was the father of Eliud.
¹⁵Eliud was the father of Eleazar.
Eleazar was the father of Matthan.
Matthan was the father of Jacob.
¹⁶Jacob was the father of Joseph.
Joseph was the husband of Mary, and Mary was the mother of Jesus.
Jesus is called the Christ.

¹⁷So there were fourteen generations from Abraham to David. And there were fourteen generations from David until the people were taken to Babylon. And there were fourteen generations from the time when the people were taken to Babylon until Christ was born.

¹⁸This is how the birth of Jesus Christ came about. His mother Mary was engaged to marry Joseph, but before they married, she learned she was pregnant by the power of the Holy Spirit. ¹⁹Because Mary's husband, Joseph, was a good man, he did not want to disgrace her in public, so he planned to divorce her secretly.

²⁰While Joseph thought about these things, an angel of the Lord came to him in a dream. The angel said, "Joseph,

descendant of David, don't be afraid to take Mary as your wife, because the baby in her is from the Holy Spirit. ²¹She will give birth to a son, and you will name him Jesus, because he will save his people from their sins."

²²All this happened to bring about what the Lord had said through the prophet: ²³"The virgin will be pregnant. She will have a son, and they will name him Immanuel," which means "God is with us."

²⁴When Joseph woke up, he did what the Lord's angel had told him to do. Joseph took Mary as his wife, ²⁵but he did not have sexual relations with her until she gave birth to the son. And Joseph named him Jesus.

2 Jesus was born in the town of Bethlehem in Judea during the time when Herod was king. When Jesus was born, some wise men from the east came to Jerusalem. ²They asked, "Where is the baby who was born to be the king of the Jews? We saw his star in the east and have come to worship him."

³When King Herod heard this, he was troubled, as were all the people in Jerusalem. ⁴Herod called a meeting of all the leading priests and teachers of the law and asked them where the Christ would be born. ⁵They answered, "In the town of Bethlehem in Judea. The prophet wrote about this in the Scriptures:

⁶'But you, Bethlehem, in the land of
        Judah,
   are not just an insignificant village
        in Judah.
A ruler will come from you
   who will be like a shepherd for my
        people Israel.' "   *Micah 5:2*

⁷Then Herod had a secret meeting with the wise men and learned from them the exact time they first saw the star. ⁸He sent the wise men to Bethlehem,

saying, "Look carefully for the child. When you find him, come tell me so I can worship him too."

⁹After the wise men heard the king, they left. The star that they had seen in the east went before them until it stopped above the place where the child was. ¹⁰When the wise men saw the star, they were filled with joy. ¹¹They came to the house where the child was and saw him with his mother, Mary, and they bowed down and worshiped him. They opened their gifts and gave him treasures of gold, frankincense, and myrrh. ¹²But God warned the wise men in a dream not to go back to Herod, so they returned to their own country by a different way.

¹³After they left, an angel of the Lord came to Joseph in a dream and said, "Get up! Take the child and his mother and escape to Egypt, because Herod is starting to look for the child so he can kill him. Stay in Egypt until I tell you to return."

¹⁴So Joseph got up and left for Egypt during the night with the child and his mother. ¹⁵And Joseph stayed in Egypt until Herod died. This happened to bring about what the Lord had said through the prophet: "I called my son out of Egypt."

¹⁶When Herod saw that the wise men had tricked him, he was furious. So he gave an order to kill all the baby boys in Bethlehem and in the surrounding area who were two years old or younger. This was in keeping with the time he learned from the wise men. ¹⁷So what God had said through the prophet Jeremiah came true:

¹⁸"A voice was heard in Ramah
      of painful crying and deep
          sadness:
   Rachel crying for her children.
      She refused to be comforted,
      because her children are dead."
                          Jeremiah 31:15

[19]After Herod died, an angel of the Lord spoke to Joseph in a dream while he was in Egypt. [20]The angel said, "Get up! Take the child and his mother and go to the land of Israel, because the people who were trying to kill the child are now dead."

[21]So Joseph took the child and his mother and went to Israel. [22]But he heard that Archelaus was now king in Judea since his father Herod had died. So Joseph was afraid to go there. After being warned in a dream, he went to the area of Galilee, [23]to a town called Nazareth, and lived there. And so what God had said through the prophets came true: "He will be called a Nazarene."

3 About that time John the Baptist began preaching in the desert area of Judea. [2]John said, "Change your hearts and lives because the kingdom of heaven is near." [3]John the Baptist is the one Isaiah the prophet was talking about when he said:

"This is a voice of one
    who calls out in the desert:
'Prepare the way for the Lord.
    Make the road straight for him.' "
                              Isaiah 40:3

[4]John's clothes were made from camel's hair, and he wore a leather belt around his waist. For food, he ate locusts and wild honey. [5]Many people came from Jerusalem and Judea and all the area around the Jordan River to hear John. [6]They confessed their sins, and he baptized them in the Jordan River.

[7]Many of the Pharisees and Sadducees came to the place where John was baptizing people. When John saw them, he said, "You are snakes! Who warned you to run away from God's coming punishment? [8]Do the things that show you really have changed your hearts and lives. [9]And don't think you can

say to yourselves, 'Abraham is our father.' I tell you that God could make children for Abraham from these rocks. [10]The ax is now ready to cut down the trees, and every tree that does not produce good fruit will be cut down and thrown into the fire.

[11]"I baptize you with water to show that your hearts and lives have changed. But there is one coming after me who is greater than I am, whose sandals I am not good enough to carry. He will baptize you with the Holy Spirit and fire. [12]He will come ready to clean the grain, separating the good grain from the chaff. He will put the good part of the grain into his barn, but he will burn the chaff with a fire that cannot be put out."

[13]At that time Jesus came from Galilee to the Jordan River and wanted John to baptize him. [14]But John tried to stop him, saying, "Why do you come to me to be baptized? I need to be baptized by you!"

[15]Jesus answered, "Let it be this way for now. We should do all things that are God's will." So John agreed to baptize Jesus.

[16]As soon as Jesus was baptized, he came up out of the water. Then heaven opened, and he saw God's Spirit coming down on him like a dove. [17]And a voice from heaven said, "This is my Son, whom I love, and I am very pleased with him."

4 Then the Spirit led Jesus into the desert to be tempted by the devil. [2]Jesus fasted for forty days and nights. After this, he was very hungry. [3]The devil came to Jesus to tempt him, saying, "If you are the Son of God, tell these rocks to become bread."

[4]Jesus answered, "It is written in the Scriptures, 'A person lives not on bread alone, but by everything God says.' "

[5]Then the devil led Jesus to the holy

STEP
6

3

city of Jerusalem and put him on a high place of the Temple. [6]The devil said, "If you are the Son of God, jump down, because it is written in the Scriptures:

'He has put his angels in charge of
      you.
   They will catch you in their
         hands
so that you will not hit your foot on a
      rock.' "   *Psalm 91:11–12*

[7]Jesus answered him, "It also says in the Scriptures, 'Do not test the Lord your God.' "

[8]Then the devil led Jesus to the top of a very high mountain and showed him all the kingdoms of the world and all their splendor. [9]The devil said, "If you will bow down and worship me, I will give you all these things."

[10]Jesus said to the devil, "Go away from me, Satan! It is written in the Scriptures, 'You must worship the Lord your God and serve only him.' "

[11]So the devil left Jesus, and angels came and took care of him.

[12]When Jesus heard that John had been put in prison, he went back to Galilee. [13]He left Nazareth and went to live in Capernaum, a town near Lake Galilee, in the area near Zebulun and Naphtali. [14]Jesus did this to bring about what the prophet Isaiah had said:

[15]"Land of Zebulun and land of Naphtali
      along the sea,
   beyond the Jordan River.
   This is Galilee where the non-
         Jewish people live.
[16]These people who live in darkness
      will see a great light.
   They live in a place covered with the
         shadows of death,
   but a light will shine on them."
                              Isaiah 9:1–2

[17]From that time Jesus began to preach, saying, "Change your hearts and lives, because the kingdom of heaven is near."

[18]As Jesus was walking by Lake Galilee, he saw two brothers, Simon (called Peter) and his brother Andrew. They were throwing a net into the lake because they were fishermen. [19]Jesus said, "Come follow me, and I will make you fish for people." [20]So Simon and Andrew immediately left their nets and followed him.

[21]As Jesus continued walking by Lake Galilee, he saw two other brothers, James and John, the sons of Zebedee. They were in a boat with their father Zebedee, mending their nets. Jesus told them to come with him. [22]Immediately they left the boat and their father, and they followed Jesus.

[23]Jesus went everywhere in Galilee, teaching in the synagogues, preaching the Good News about the kingdom of heaven, and healing all the people's diseases and sicknesses. [24]The news about Jesus spread all over Syria, and people brought all the sick to him. They were suffering from different kinds of diseases. Some were in great pain, some had demons, some were epileptics, and some were paralyzed. Jesus healed all of them. [25]Many people from Galilee, the Ten Towns, Jerusalem, Judea, and the land across the Jordan River followed him.

5 When Jesus saw the crowds, he went up on a hill and sat down. His followers came to him, [2]and he began to teach them, saying:

[3]"They are blessed who realize their
         spiritual poverty,   STEP 6
   for the kingdom of heaven
         belongs to them.
[4]They are blessed who grieve,
   for God will comfort them.
[5]They are blessed who are humble,
   for the whole earth will be theirs.

4

STEP 11

⁶They are blessed who hunger and
        thirst after justice,
    for they will be satisfied.
⁷They are blessed who show mercy to
        others,
    for God will show mercy to them.

STEP 10

⁸They are blessed whose thoughts are
        pure,
    for they will see God.

STEP 9

⁹They are blessed who work for peace,
    for they will be called God's
        children.

¹⁰They are blessed who are persecuted
        for doing good,
    for the kingdom of heaven
        belongs to them.

¹¹"People will insult you and hurt you. They will lie and say all kinds of evil things about you because you follow me. But when they do, you will be blessed. ¹²Rejoice and be glad, because you have a great reward waiting for you in heaven. People did the same evil things to the prophets who lived before you.

¹³"You are the salt of the earth. But if the salt loses its salty taste, it cannot be made salty again. It is good for nothing, except to be thrown out and walked on.

¹⁴"You are the light that gives light to the world. A city that is built on a hill cannot be hidden. ¹⁵And people don't hide a light under a bowl. They put it on a lampstand so the light shines for all the people in the house.

STEP 12

¹⁶In the same way, you should be a light for other people. Live so that they will see the good things you do and will praise your Father in heaven.

¹⁷"Don't think that I have come to destroy the law of Moses or the teaching of the prophets. I have not come to destroy them but to bring about what they said. ¹⁸I tell you the truth, nothing will disappear from the law until heaven and earth are gone. Not even the smallest letter or the smallest part of a letter will be lost un-

til everything has happened. ¹⁹Whoever refuses to obey any command and teaches other people not to obey that command will be the least important in the kingdom of heaven. But whoever obeys the commands and teaches other people to obey them will be great in the kingdom of heaven. ²⁰I tell you that if you are no more obedient than the teachers of the law and the Pharisees, you will never enter the kingdom of heaven.

²¹"You have heard that it was said to our people long ago, 'You must not murder anyone. Anyone who murders another will be judged.' ²²But I tell you, if you are angry with a brother or sister, you will be judged. If you say bad things to a brother or sister, you will be judged by the council. And if you call someone a fool, you will be in danger of the fire of hell.

STEP 9

²³"So when you offer your gift to God at the altar, and you remember that your brother or sister has something against you, ²⁴leave your gift there at the altar. Go and make peace with that person, and then come and offer your gift.

²⁵"If your enemy is taking you to court, become friends quickly, before you go to court. Otherwise, your enemy might turn you over to the judge, and the judge might give you to a guard to put you in jail. ²⁶I tell you the truth, you will not leave there until you have paid everything you owe.

STEP 4

²⁷"You have heard that it was said, 'You must not be guilty of adultery.' ²⁸But I tell you that if anyone looks at a woman and wants to sin sexually with her, in his mind he has already done that sin with the woman. ²⁹If your right eye causes you to sin, take it out and throw it away. It is better to lose one part of your body than to have your whole body thrown into hell. ³⁰If your right hand causes you to sin, cut

STEP 9

Made direct amends to such people
wherever possible, except when to
do so would injure them or others.

Matthew 5:9

Do you want peace in your life? Most people do. But peace doesn't just happen. You don't stumble across it by chance. You make it. You become a peacemaker. You don't find peace by sweeping the past under the rug. That's an escapist approach. Peacemakers face problems head-on and deal with them.

You need courage and wisdom to make peace. Fortunately, God sends his love to work through us to give us courage and wisdom. First John 3:1 says, "The Father has loved us so much that we are called children of God." So God's love will guide your peacemaking. And he wants you to succeed; John 14:27 promises that God's special peace will not "let your hearts be troubled or afraid."

When your heart is full of God's love and peace, you can forgive those who hurt you and make appropriate amends to those you hurt. You can be a peacemaker!

FOR YOUR NEXT **STEP 9** MEDITATION, TURN TO **PAGE 224.** ▶▶

it off and throw it away. It is better to lose one part of your body than for your whole body to go into hell.

³¹"It was also said, 'Anyone who divorces his wife must give her a written divorce paper.' ³²But I tell you that anyone who divorces his wife forces her to be guilty of adultery. The only reason for a man to divorce his wife is if she has sexual relations with another man. And anyone who marries that divorced woman is guilty of adultery.

³³"You have heard that it was said to our people long ago, 'Don't break your promises, but keep the promises you make to the Lord.' ³⁴But I tell you, never swear an oath. Don't swear an oath using the name of heaven, because heaven is God's throne. ³⁵Don't swear an oath using the name of the earth, because the earth belongs to God. Don't swear an oath using the name of Jerusalem, because that is the city of the great King. ³⁶Don't even swear by your own head, because you cannot make one hair on your head become white or black. ³⁷Say only yes if you mean yes, and no if you mean no. If you say more than yes or no, it is from the Evil One.

³⁸"You have heard that it was said, 'An eye for an eye, and a tooth for a tooth.' ³⁹But I tell you, don't stand up against an evil person. If someone slaps you on the right cheek, turn to him the other cheek also. ⁴⁰If someone wants to sue you in court and take your shirt, let him have your coat also. ⁴¹If someone forces you to go with him one mile, go with him two miles. ⁴²If a person asks you for something, give it to him. Don't refuse to give to someone who wants to borrow from you.

⁴³"You have heard that it was said, 'Love your neighbor and hate your enemies.' ⁴⁴But I say to you, love your enemies. Pray for those who hurt you. ⁴⁵If you do this, you will be true children of your Father in heaven. He causes the sun to rise on good people and on evil people, and he sends rain to those who do right and to those who do wrong. ⁴⁶If you love only the people who love you, you will get no reward. Even the tax collectors do that. ⁴⁷And if you are nice only to your friends, you are no better than other people. Even those who don't know God are nice to their friends. ⁴⁸So you must be perfect, just as your Father in heaven is perfect.

6 "Be careful! When you do good things, don't do them in front of people to be seen by them. If you do that, you will have no reward from your Father in heaven.

²"When you give to the poor, don't be like the hypocrites. They blow trumpets in the synagogues and on the streets so that people will see them and honor them. I tell you the truth, those hypocrites already have their full reward. ³So when you give to the poor, don't let anyone know what you are doing. ⁴Your giving should be done in secret. Your Father can see what is done in secret, and he will reward you.

⁵"When you pray, don't be like the hypocrites. They love to stand in the synagogues and on the street corners and pray so people will see them. I tell you the truth, they already have their full reward. ⁶When you pray, you should go into your room and close the door and pray to your Father who cannot be seen. Your Father can see what is done in secret, and he will reward you.

⁷"And when you pray, don't be like those people who don't know God. They continue saying things that mean nothing, thinking that God will hear them because of their many words. ⁸Don't be like

them, because your Father knows the things you need before you ask him. [9]So when you pray, you should pray like this:

'Our Father in heaven,
    may your name always be kept holy.
 [10]May your kingdom come
    and what you want be done,
       here on earth as it is in heaven.
 [11]Give us the food we need for each day.
 [12]Forgive us for our sins,
    just as we have forgiven those
       who sinned against us.
 [13]And do not cause us to be tempted,
    but save us from the Evil One.' [The
       kingdom, the power, and the
       glory are yours forever.
       Amen.]

STEP 8 [14]Yes, if you forgive others for their sins, your Father in heaven will also forgive you for your sins. [15]But if you don't forgive others, your Father in heaven will not forgive your sins.

[16]"When you fast, don't put on a sad face like the hypocrites. They make their faces look sad to show people they are fasting. I tell you the truth, those hypocrites already have their full reward. [17]So when you fast, comb your hair and wash your face. [18]Then people will not know that you are fasting, but your Father, whom you cannot see, will see you. Your Father sees what is done in secret, and he will reward you.

[19]"Don't store treasures for yourselves here on earth where moths and rust will destroy them and thieves can break in and steal them. [20]But store your treasures in heaven where they cannot be destroyed by moths or rust and where thieves cannot break in and steal them. [21]Your heart will be where your treasure is.

[22]"The eye is a light for the body. If your eyes are good, your whole body will be full of light. [23]But if your eyes are evil, your whole body will be full of darkness.

And if the only light you have is really darkness, then you have the worst darkness.

[24]"No one can serve two masters. The person will hate one master and love the other, or will follow one master and refuse to follow the other. You cannot serve both God and worldly riches.

[25]"So I tell you, don't worry about the food or drink you need to live, or about the clothes you need for your body. Life is more than food, and the body is more than clothes. [26]Look at the birds in the air. They don't plant or harvest or store food in barns, but your heavenly Father feeds them. And you know that you are worth much more than the birds. [27]You cannot add any time to your life by worrying about it.

[28]"And why do you worry about clothes? Look at how the lilies in the field grow. They don't work or make clothes for themselves. [29]But I tell you that even Solomon with his riches was not dressed as beautifully as one of these flowers. [30]God clothes the grass in the field, which is alive today but tomorrow is thrown into the fire. So you can be even more sure that God will clothe you. Don't have so little faith! **STEP 3** [31]Don't worry and say, 'What will we eat?' or 'What will we drink?' or 'What will we wear?' [32]The people who don't know God keep trying to get these things, and your Father in heaven knows you need them. [33]Seek first God's kingdom and what God wants. Then all your other needs will be met as well. [34]So don't worry about tomorrow, because tomorrow will have its own worries. Each day has enough trouble of its own.

7 "Don't judge others, or you will be judged. **STEP 8** [2]You will be judged in the same way that you judge others, and the amount you give to others will be given to you.

³"Why do you notice the little piece of dust in your friend's eye, but you don't notice the big piece of wood in your own eye? ⁴How can you say to your friend, 'Let me take that little piece of dust out of your eye'? Look at yourself! You still have that big piece of wood in your own eye. ⁵You hypocrite! First, take the wood out of your own eye. Then you will see clearly to take the dust out of your friend's eye.

⁶"Don't give holy things to dogs, and don't throw your pearls before pigs. Pigs will only trample on them, and dogs will turn to attack you.

STEP 7

⁷"Ask, and God will give to you. Search, and you will find. Knock, and the door will open for you. ⁸Yes, everyone who asks will receive. Everyone who searches will find. And everyone who knocks will have the door opened.

⁹"If your children ask for bread, which of you would give them a stone? ¹⁰Or if your children ask for a fish, would you give them a snake? ¹¹Even though you are bad, you know how to give good gifts to your children. How much more will your heavenly Father will give good things to those who ask him!

STEP 9

¹²"Do to others what you want them to do to you. This is the meaning of the law of Moses and the teaching of the prophets.

¹³"Enter through the narrow gate. The gate is wide and the road is wide that leads to hell, and many people enter through that gate. ¹⁴But the gate is small and the road is narrow that leads to true life. Only a few people find that road.

¹⁵"Be careful of false prophets. They come to you looking gentle like sheep, but they are really dangerous like wolves. ¹⁶You will know these people by what they do. Grapes don't come from thornbushes, and figs don't come from thorny weeds. ¹⁷In the same way, every good tree produces good fruit, but a bad tree produces bad fruit. ¹⁸A good tree cannot produce bad fruit, and a bad tree cannot produce good fruit. ¹⁹Every tree that does not produce good fruit is cut down and thrown into the fire. ²⁰In the same way, you will know these false prophets by what they do.

²¹"Not all those who say 'You are our Lord' will enter the kingdom of heaven. The only people who will enter the kingdom of heaven are those who do what my Father in heaven wants. ²²On the last day many people will say to me, 'Lord, Lord, we spoke for you, and through you we forced out demons and did many miracles.' ²³Then I will tell them clearly, 'Get away from me, you who do evil. I never knew you.'

STEP 6

²⁴"Everyone who hears my words and obeys them is like a wise man who built his house on rock. ²⁵It rained hard, the floods came, and the winds blew and hit that house. But it did not fall, because it was built on rock. ²⁶Everyone who hears my words and does not obey them is like a foolish man who built his house on sand. ²⁷It rained hard, the floods came, and the winds blew and hit that house, and it fell with a big crash."

²⁸When Jesus finished saying these things, the people were amazed at his teaching, ²⁹because he did not teach like their teachers of the law. He taught like a person who had authority.

8 When Jesus came down from the hill, great crowds followed him. ²Then a man with a skin disease came to Jesus. The man bowed down before him and said, "Lord, you can heal me if you will."

³Jesus reached out his hand and touched the man and said, "I will. Be healed!" And immediately the man was healed from his disease. ⁴Then Jesus said to him, "Don't tell anyone about this. But

go and show yourself to the priest and offer the gift Moses commanded for people who are made well. This will show the people what I have done."

⁵When Jesus entered the city of Capernaum, an army officer came to him, begging for help. ⁶The officer said, "Lord, my servant is at home in bed. He can't move his body and is in much pain."

⁷Jesus said to the officer, "I will go and heal him."

⁸The officer answered, "Lord, I am not worthy for you to come into my house. You only need to command it, and my servant will be healed. ⁹I, too, am a man under the authority of others, and I have soldiers under my command. I tell one soldier, 'Go,' and he goes. I tell another soldier, 'Come,' and he comes. I say to my servant, 'Do this,' and my servant does it.

¹⁰When Jesus heard this, he was amazed. He said to those who were following him, "I tell you the truth, this is the greatest faith I have found, even in Israel. ¹¹Many people will come from the east and from the west and will sit and eat with Abraham, Isaac, and Jacob in the kingdom of heaven. ¹²But those people who should be in the kingdom will be thrown outside into the darkness, where people will cry and grind their teeth with pain."

¹³Then Jesus said to the officer, "Go home. Your servant will be healed just as you believed he would." And his servant was healed that same hour.

¹⁴When Jesus went to Peter's house, he saw that Peter's mother-in-law was sick in bed with a fever. ¹⁵Jesus touched her hand, and the fever left her. Then she stood up and began to serve Jesus.

¹⁶That evening people brought to Jesus many who had demons. Jesus spoke and the demons left them, and he healed all the sick. ¹⁷He did these things to bring about what Isaiah the prophet had said:

"He took our suffering on him
    and carried our diseases."

Isaiah 53:4

¹⁸When Jesus saw the crowd around him, he told his followers to go to the other side of the lake. ¹⁹Then a teacher of the law came to Jesus and said, "Teacher, I will follow you any place you go."

²⁰Jesus said to him, "The foxes have holes to live in, and the birds have nests, but the Son of Man has no place to rest his head."

²¹Another man, one of Jesus' followers, said to him, "Lord, first let me go and bury my father."

²²But Jesus told him, "Follow me, and let the people who are dead bury their own dead."

²³Jesus got into a boat, and his followers went with him. ²⁴A great storm arose on the lake so that waves covered the boat, but Jesus was sleeping. ²⁵His followers went to him and woke him, saying, "Lord, save us! We will drown!"

²⁶Jesus answered, "Why are you afraid? You don't have enough faith." Then Jesus got up and gave a command to the wind and the waves, and it became completely calm.

²⁷The men were amazed and said, "What kind of man is this? Even the wind and the waves obey him!"

²⁸When Jesus arrived at the other side of the lake in the area of the Gadarene people, two men who had demons in them met him. These men lived in the burial caves and were so dangerous that people could not use the road by those caves. ²⁹They shouted, "What do you want with us, Son of God? Did you come here to torture us before the right time?"

³⁰Near that place there was a large herd of pigs feeding. ³¹The demons begged Jesus, "If you make us leave

these men, please send us into that herd of pigs."

[32]Jesus said to them, "Go!" So the demons left the men and went into the pigs. Then the whole herd rushed down the hill into the lake and were drowned. [33]The herdsmen ran away and went into town, where they told about all of this and what had happened to the men who had demons. [34]Then the whole town went out to see Jesus. When they saw him, they begged him to leave their area.

9 Jesus got into a boat and went back across the lake to his own town. [2]Some people brought to Jesus a man who was paralyzed and lying on a mat. When Jesus saw the faith of these people, he said to the paralyzed man, "Be encouraged, young man. Your sins are forgiven."

[3]Some of the teachers of the law said to themselves, "This man speaks as if he were God. That is blasphemy!"

[4]Knowing their thoughts, Jesus said, "Why are you thinking evil thoughts? [5]Which is easier: to say, 'Your sins are forgiven,' or to tell him, 'Stand up and walk'? [6]But I will prove to you that the Son of Man has authority on earth to forgive sins." Then Jesus said to the paralyzed man, "Stand up, take your mat, and go home." [7]And the man stood up and went home. [8]When the people saw this, they were amazed and praised God for giving power like this to human beings.

[9]When Jesus was leaving, he saw a man named Matthew sitting in the tax collector's booth. Jesus said to him, "Follow me," and he stood up and followed Jesus.

[10]As Jesus was having dinner at Matthew's house, many tax collectors and "sinners" came and ate with Jesus and his followers. [11]When the Pharisees saw this, they asked Jesus' followers, "Why does your teacher eat with tax collectors and sinners?"

[12]When Jesus heard them, he said, "It is not the healthy people who need a doctor, but the sick. [13]Go and learn what this means: 'I want kindness more than I want animal sacrifices.' I did not come to invite good people but to invite sinners."

[14]Then the followers of John came to Jesus and said, "Why do we and the Pharisees often fast for a certain time, but your followers don't?"

[15]Jesus answered, "The friends of the bridegroom are not sad while he is with them. But the time will come when the bridegroom will be taken from them, and then they will fast.

[16]"No one sews a patch of unshrunk cloth over a hole in an old coat. If he does, the patch will shrink and pull away from the coat, making the hole worse. [17]Also, people never pour new wine into old leather bags. Otherwise, the bags will break, the wine will spill, and the wine bags will be ruined. But people always pour new wine into new wine bags. Then both will continue to be good."

[18]While Jesus was saying these things, a leader of the synagogue came to him. He bowed down before Jesus and said, "My daughter has just died. But if you come and lay your hand on her, she will live again." [19]So Jesus and his followers stood up and went with the leader.

[20]Then a woman who had been bleeding for twelve years came behind Jesus and touched the edge of his coat. [21]She was thinking, "If I can just touch his clothes, I will be healed."

[22]Jesus turned and saw the woman and said, "Be encouraged, dear woman. You are made well because you believed." And the woman was healed from that moment on.

[23]Jesus continued along with the

leader and went into his house. There he saw the funeral musicians and many people crying. ²⁴Jesus said, "Go away. The girl is not dead, only asleep." But the people laughed at him. ²⁵After the crowd had been thrown out of the house, Jesus went into the girl's room and took hold of her hand, and she stood up. ²⁶The news about this spread all around the area.

²⁷When Jesus was leaving there, two blind men followed him. They cried out, "Have mercy on us, Son of David!"

²⁸After Jesus went inside, the blind men went with him. He asked the men, "Do you believe that I can make you see again?"

They answered, "Yes, Lord."

²⁹Then Jesus touched their eyes and said, "Because you believe I can make you see again, it will happen." ³⁰Then the men were able to see. But Jesus warned them strongly, saying, "Don't tell anyone about this." ³¹But the blind men left and spread the news about Jesus all around that area.

³²When the two men were leaving, some people brought another man to Jesus. This man could not talk because he had a demon in him. ³³After Jesus forced the demon to leave the man, he was able to speak. The crowd was amazed and said, "We have never seen anything like this in Israel."

³⁴But the Pharisees said, "The prince of demons is the one that gives him power to force demons out."

³⁵Jesus traveled through all the towns and villages, teaching in their synagogues, preaching the Good News about the kingdom, and healing all kinds of diseases and sicknesses. ³⁶When he saw the crowds, he felt sorry for them because they were hurting and helpless, like sheep without a shepherd. ³⁷Jesus said to his followers, "There are many people to harvest but only a few workers to help harvest them. ³⁸Pray to the Lord, who owns the harvest, that he will send more workers to gather his harvest."

10 Jesus called his twelve followers together and gave them authority to drive out evil spirits and to heal every kind of disease and sickness. ²These are the names of the twelve apostles: Simon (also called Peter) and his brother Andrew; James son of Zebedee, and his brother John; ³Philip and Bartholomew; Thomas and Matthew, the tax collector; James son of Alphaeus, and Thaddaeus; ⁴Simon the Zealot and Judas Iscariot, who turned against Jesus.

⁵Jesus sent out these twelve men with the following order: "Don't go to the non-Jewish people or to any town where the Samaritans live. ⁶But go to the people of Israel, who are like lost sheep. ⁷When you go, preach this: 'The kingdom of heaven is near.' ⁸Heal the sick, raise the dead to life again, heal those who have skin diseases, and force demons out of people. I give you these powers freely, so help other people freely. ⁹Don't carry any money with you—gold or silver or copper. ¹⁰Don't carry a bag or extra clothes or sandals or a walking stick. Workers should be given what they need.

¹¹"When you enter a city or town, find some worthy person there and stay in that home until you leave. ¹²When you enter that home, say, 'Peace be with you.' ¹³If the people there welcome you, let your peace stay there. But if they don't welcome you, take back the peace you wished for them. ¹⁴And if a home or town refuses to welcome you or listen to you, leave that place and shake its dust off your feet. ¹⁵I tell you the truth, on the Judgment Day it will be better for the towns of Sodom and Gomorrah than for the people of that town.

STEP I

STEP 1

We admitted we were powerless
over our dependencies—that our lives
had become unmanageable.

Matthew 9:36

Step 1 challenges you to admit your addictive lifestyle is chaotic and out of control. One of the odd things about every addiction is that the more you try to control yourself and others around you, the more out of control you become.

What phony ways do you use to try and make yourself feel good in a world that seems out of control? Maybe you escape into pornography. Maybe you obsess about your appearance and starve yourself or binge and purge. Maybe you pop pills, drink too much, or do dope to get along. Maybe you prefer depression or hypochondria as ways of withdrawing from the rat race. Or maybe you have to have someone in your bed to make you feel you're loved.

In all those addictive, compulsive, codependent ways we act like sheep, "hurting and helpless." Read the Gospels and you find out that Jesus is the True Shepherd. He looks at the brokenness of your heart and life and feels deep compassion for you. You don't have to pretend to be in control to impress Jesus. He invites you into Twelve Step recovery where you can admit your life is out of control without fear that he will judge you and reject you.

FOR YOUR NEXT **STEP 1** MEDITATION, TURN TO **PAGE 212.** ▶▶

¹⁶"Listen, I am sending you out like sheep among wolves. So be as clever as snakes and as innocent as doves. ¹⁷Be careful of people, because they will arrest you and take you to court and whip you in their synagogues. ¹⁸Because of me you will be taken to stand before governors and kings, and you will tell them and the non-Jewish people about me. ¹⁹When you are arrested, don't worry about what to say or how to say it. At that time you will be given the things to say. ²⁰It will not really be you speaking but the Spirit of your Father speaking through you.

²¹"Brothers will give their own brothers to be killed, and fathers will give their own children to be killed. Children will fight against their own parents and have them put to death. ²²All people will hate you because you follow me, but those people who keep their faith until the end will be saved. ²³When you are treated badly in one city, run to another city. I tell you the truth, you will not finish going through all the cities of Israel before the Son of Man comes.

²⁴"A student is not better than his teacher, and a servant is not better than his master. ²⁵A student should be satisfied to become like his teacher; a servant should be satisfied to become like his master. If the head of the family is called Beelzebul, then the other members of the family will be called worse names!

²⁶"So don't be afraid of those people, because everything that is hidden will be shown. Everything that is secret will be made known. ²⁷I tell you these things in the dark, but I want you to tell them in the light. What you hear whispered in your ear you should shout from the housetops. ²⁸Don't be afraid of people, who can kill the body but cannot kill the soul. The only one you should fear is the one who can destroy the soul and the body in hell. ²⁹Two sparrows cost only a penny, but not even one of them can die without your Father's knowing it. ³⁰God even knows how many hairs are on your head. ³¹So don't be afraid. You are worth much more than many sparrows.

³²"All those who stand before others and say they believe in me, I will say before my Father in heaven that they belong to me. ³³But all who stand before others and say they do not believe in me, I will say before my Father in heaven that they do not belong to me.

³⁴"Don't think that I came to bring peace to the earth. I did not come to bring peace, but a sword. ³⁵I have come so that

'a son will be against his father,
     a daughter will be against her
          mother,
a daughter-in-law will be against her
          mother-in-law.
³⁶   A person's enemies will be
          members of his own family.'

Micah 7:6

³⁷"Those who love their father or mother more than they love me are not worthy to be my followers. Those who love their son or daughter more than they love me are not worthy to be my followers. ³⁸Whoever is not willing to carry the cross and follow me is not worthy of me. ³⁹Those who try to hold on to their lives will give up true life. Those who give up their lives for me will hold on to true life. ⁴⁰Whoever accepts you also accepts me, and whoever accepts me also accepts the One who sent me. ⁴¹Whoever meets a prophet and accepts him will receive the reward of a prophet. And whoever accepts a good person because that person is good will receive the reward of a good person. ⁴²Those who give one of these little ones a cup of cold water because they

STEP 3

I 4

are my followers will truly get their reward."

11 After Jesus finished telling these things to his twelve followers, he left there and went to the towns in Galilee to teach and preach.

²John the Baptist was in prison, but he heard about what the Christ was doing. So John sent some of his followers to Jesus. ³They asked him, "Are you the One who is to come, or should we wait for someone else?"

⁴Jesus answered them, "Go tell John what you hear and see: ⁵The blind can see, the crippled can walk, and people with skin diseases are healed. The deaf can hear, the dead are raised to life, and the Good News is preached to the poor. ⁶Those who do not stumble in their faith because of me are blessed."

⁷As John's followers were leaving, Jesus began talking to the people about John. Jesus said, "What did you go out into the desert to see? A reed blown by the wind? ⁸What did you go out to see? A man dressed in fine clothes? No, those who wear fine clothes live in kings' palaces. ⁹So why did you go out? To see a prophet? Yes, and I tell you, John is more than a prophet. ¹⁰This was written about him:

'I will send my messenger ahead of you,
who will prepare the way for you.'

Malachi 3:1

¹¹I tell you the truth, John the Baptist is greater than any other person ever born, but even the least important person in the kingdom of heaven is greater than John. ¹²Since the time John the Baptist came until now, the kingdom of heaven has been going forward in strength, and people have been trying to take it by force. ¹³All the prophets and the law of Moses told about what would happen until the time John came. ¹⁴And if you will believe what they said, you will believe that John is Elijah, whom they said would come. ¹⁵Let those with ears use them and listen!

¹⁶"What can I say about the people of this time? What are they like? They are like children sitting in the marketplace, who call out to each other,

¹⁷'We played music for you, but you did not dance;
we sang a sad song, but you did not cry.'

¹⁸John came and did not eat or drink like other people. So people say, 'He has a demon.' ¹⁹The Son of Man came, eating and drinking, and people say, 'Look at him! He eats too much and drinks too much wine, and he is a friend of tax collectors and sinners.' But wisdom is proved to be right by what she does."

²⁰Then Jesus criticized the cities where he did most of his miracles, because the people did not change their lives and stop sinning. ²¹He said, "How terrible for you, Korazin! How terrible for you, Bethsaida! If the same miracles I did in you had happened in Tyre and Sidon, those people would have changed their lives a long time ago. They would have worn rough cloth and put ashes on themselves to show they had changed. ²²But I tell you, on the Judgment Day it will be better for Tyre and Sidon than for you. ²³And you, Capernaum, will you be lifted up to heaven? No, you will be thrown down to the depths. If the miracles I did in you had happened in Sodom, its people would have stopped sinning, and it would still be a city today. ²⁴But I tell you, on the Judgment Day it will be better for Sodom than for you."

²⁵At that time Jesus said, "I praise you, Father, Lord of heaven and earth, because you have hidden these things from

the people who are wise and smart. But you have shown them to those who are like little children. ²⁶Yes, Father, this is what you really wanted.

²⁷"My Father has given me all things. No one knows the Son, except the Father. And no one knows the Father, except the Son and those whom the Son chooses to tell.

STEP 3

²⁸"Come to me, all of you who are tired and have heavy loads, and I will give you rest. ²⁹Accept my teachings and learn from me, because I am gentle and humble in spirit, and you will find rest for your lives. ³⁰The burden that I ask you to accept is easy; the load I give you to carry is light."

12 At that time Jesus was walking through some fields of grain on a Sabbath day. His followers were hungry, so they began to pick the grain and eat it. ²When the Pharisees saw this, they said to Jesus, "Look! Your followers are doing what is unlawful to do on the Sabbath day."

³Jesus answered, "Have you not read what David did when he and the people with him were hungry? ⁴He went into God's house, and he and those with him ate the holy bread, which was lawful only for priests to eat. ⁵And have you not read in the law of Moses that on every Sabbath day the priests in the Temple break this law about the Sabbath day? But the priests are not wrong for doing that. ⁶I tell you that there is something here that is greater than the Temple. ⁷The Scripture says, 'I want kindness more than I want animal sacrifices.' You don't really know what those words mean. If you understood them, you would not judge those who have done nothing wrong.

⁸"So the Son of Man is Lord of the Sabbath day."

⁹Jesus left there and went into their synagogue, ¹⁰where there was a man with a crippled hand. They were looking for a reason to accuse Jesus, so they asked him, "Is it right to heal on the Sabbath day?"

¹¹Jesus answered, "If any of you has a sheep, and it falls into a ditch on the Sabbath day, you will help it out of the ditch. ¹²Surely a human being is more important than a sheep. So it is lawful to do good things on the Sabbath day."

¹³Then Jesus said to the man with the crippled hand, "Hold out your hand." The man held out his hand, and it became well again, like the other hand. ¹⁴But the Pharisees left and made plans to kill Jesus.

¹⁵Jesus knew what the Pharisees were doing, so he left that place. Many people followed him, and he healed all who were sick. ¹⁶But Jesus warned the people not to tell who he was. ¹⁷He did these things to bring about what Isaiah the prophet had said:

STEP 2

¹⁸"Here is my servant whom I have
        chosen.
    I love him, and I am pleased with
        him.
I will put my Spirit upon him,
    and he will tell of my justice to all
        people.
¹⁹He will not argue or cry out;
    no one will hear his voice in the
        streets.
²⁰He will not break a crushed blade of
        grass
    or put out even a weak flame
until he makes justice win the victory.
²¹   In him will the non-Jewish people
        find hope."   *Isaiah 42:1–4*

²²Then some people brought to Jesus a man who was blind and could not talk, because he had a demon. Jesus healed the man so that he could talk and see. ²³All the people were amazed and said, "Perhaps this man is the Son of David!"

STEP 3

Made a decision to turn our will and our lives over to the care of God **as we understood Him.**

Matthew 11:28-30

Maybe you have felt crushed under a load of guilt, shame, bitterness, fear, and discouragement ever since childhood. Are you tired of trying to stand—let alone walk—under such a heavy load? Let God's healing love act like an ointment on your heart wounds. Let him heal your hurts and give rest to your weary soul.

Does it strike you odd that Jesus talked about rest and carrying a burden (or yoke) in the same sentence? Farmers of his day trained young farm animals by teaming them with an experienced one. A young ox that knew nothing about plowing a straight furrow did it easily when yoked with a veteran. Jesus promises to do life with you. He'll get in the harness with you and show you how to succeed at things you don't have the experience or wisdom to handle by yourself. Being a follower of Jesus is a light load to carry compared to the crushing weight of your addiction with its guilt and shame. Drop that burden at Jesus' feet and don't pick it up again.

FOR YOUR NEXT **STEP 3** MEDITATION, TURN TO **PAGE 26.** ▶▶

STEP 2

Came to believe that a Power greater than
ourselves could restore us to sanity.

Matthew 12:18–21

Jesus quoted a part of Isaiah that tells about the servant of the
Lord. In fact, Jesus fulfilled those prophecies by being a special
servant to the weakest and neediest people of his day and of every
era since.

Jesus was more than a good man and a great teacher. He came to
earth as God in the flesh. His actions and life show us what God's
character is like. He demonstrated that God has great tenderness
toward people struggling with life. He is careful not to break a
crushed blade of grass. He will not put out a weak flame struggling
to stay lit.

Jesus showed this compassion over and over through his earthly
life. Nobody expected him to reject them or have no time for them.
At the same time, this gentle man exercised great and awesome
power to help the helpless. He raised the dead, drove out demons,
and controlled the very forces of nature.

Guess what. The power that raised Jesus from the dead is the same
power he uses to raise you from the living death of your addiction
and create in you a healthy, clean life.

FOR YOUR NEXT **STEP 2** MEDITATION, TURN TO **PAGE 64.** ▶▶

[24] When the Pharisees heard this, they said, "Jesus uses the power of Beelzebul, the ruler of demons, to force demons out of people."

[25] Jesus knew what the Pharisees were thinking, so he said to them, "Every kingdom that is divided against itself will be destroyed. And any city or family that is divided against itself will not continue. [26] And if Satan forces out himself, then Satan is divided against himself, and his kingdom will not continue. [27] You say that I use the power of Beelzebul to force out demons. If that is true, then what power do your people use to force out demons? So they will be your judges. [28] But if I use the power of God's Spirit to force out demons, then the kingdom of God has come to you.

[29] "If anyone wants to enter a strong person's house and steal his things, he must first tie up the strong person. Then he can steal the things from the house.

[30] "Whoever is not with me is against me. Whoever does not work with me is working against me. [31] So I tell you, people can be forgiven for every sin and everything they say against God. But whoever speaks against the Holy Spirit will not be forgiven. [32] Anyone who speaks against the Son of Man can be forgiven, but anyone who speaks against the Holy Spirit will not be forgiven, now or in the future.

[33] "If you want good fruit, you must make the tree good. If your tree is not good, it will have bad fruit. A tree is known by the kind of fruit it produces. [34] You snakes! You are evil people, so how can you say anything good? The mouth speaks the things that are in the heart.

STEP 9 [35] Good people have good things in their hearts, and so they say good things. But evil people have evil in their hearts, so they say evil things. [36] And I tell you that on the Judgment Day people will be responsible for every careless thing they have said. [37] The words you have said will be used to judge you. Some of your words will prove you right, but some of your words will prove you guilty."

[38] Then some of the Pharisees and teachers of the law answered Jesus, saying, "Teacher, we want to see you work a miracle as a sign."

[39] Jesus answered, "Evil and sinful people are the ones who want to see a miracle for a sign. But no sign will be given to them, except the sign of the prophet Jonah. [40] Jonah was in the stomach of the big fish for three days and three nights. In the same way, the Son of Man will be in the grave three days and three nights. [41] On the Judgment Day the people from Nineveh will stand up with you people who live now, and they will show that you are guilty. When Jonah preached to them, they were sorry and changed their lives. And I tell you that someone greater than Jonah is here. [42] On the Judgment Day, the Queen of the South will stand up with you people who live today. She will show that you are guilty, because she came from far away to listen to Solomon's wise teaching. And I tell you that someone greater than Solomon is here.

[43] "When an evil spirit comes out of a person, it travels through dry places, looking for a place to rest, but it doesn't find it. [44] So the spirit says, 'I will go back to the house I left.' When the spirit comes back, it finds the house still empty, swept clean, and made neat. [45] Then the evil spirit goes out and brings seven other spirits even more evil than it is, and they go in and live there. So the person has even more trouble than before. It is the same way with the evil people who live today."

[46] While Jesus was talking to the people,

his mother and brothers stood outside, trying to find a way to talk to him. ⁴⁷Someone told Jesus, "Your mother and brothers are standing outside, and they want to talk to you."

⁴⁸He answered, "Who is my mother? Who are my brothers?" ⁴⁹Then he pointed to his followers and said, "Here are my mother and my brothers. ⁵⁰My true brother and sister and mother are those who do what my Father in heaven wants."

13 That same day Jesus went out of the house and sat by the lake. ²Large crowds gathered around him, so he got into a boat and sat down, while the people stood on the shore. ³Then Jesus used stories to teach them many things. He said: "A farmer went out to plant his seed. ⁴While he was planting, some seed fell by the road, and the birds came and ate it all up. ⁵Some seed fell on rocky ground, where there wasn't much dirt. That seed grew very fast, because the ground was not deep. ⁶But when the sun rose, the plants dried up, because they did not have deep roots. ⁷Some other seed fell among thorny weeds, which grew and choked the good plants. ⁸Some other seed fell on good ground where it grew and produced a crop. Some plants made a hundred times more, some made sixty times more, and some made thirty times more. ⁹Let those with ears use them and listen."

¹⁰The followers came to Jesus and asked, "Why do you use stories to teach the people?"

¹¹Jesus answered, "You have been chosen to know the secrets about the kingdom of heaven, but others cannot know these secrets. ¹²Those who have understanding will be given more, and they will have all they need. But those who do not have understanding, even what they have will be taken away from them. ¹³This is

why I use stories to teach the people: They see, but they don't really see. They hear, but they don't really hear or understand. ¹⁴So they show that the things Isaiah said about them are true:

'You will listen and listen, but you will
    not understand.
You will look and look, but you will
    not learn.
¹⁵For the minds of these people have
    become stubborn.
They do not hear with their ears,
    and they have closed their eyes.
Otherwise they might really
    understand
what they see with their eyes
    and hear with their ears.
They might really understand in their
    minds
and come back to me and be
    healed.'   *Isaiah 6:9–10*

¹⁶But you are blessed, because you see with your eyes and hear with your ears. ¹⁷I tell you the truth, many prophets and good people wanted to see the things that you now see, but they did not see them. And they wanted to hear the things that you now hear, but they did not hear them.

¹⁸"So listen to the meaning of that story about the farmer. ¹⁹What is the seed that fell by the road? That seed is like the person who hears the message about the kingdom but does not understand it. The Evil One comes and takes away what was planted in that person's heart. ²⁰And what is the seed that fell on rocky ground? That seed is like the person who hears the teaching and quickly accepts it with joy. ²¹But he does not let the teaching go deep into his life, so he keeps it only a short time. When trouble or persecution comes because of the teaching he accepted, he quickly gives up. ²²And what is the seed that fell among the thorny weeds? That seed is like the person who hears the

teaching but lets worries about this life and the temptation of wealth stop that teaching from growing. So the teaching does not produce fruit in that person's life. ²³But what is the seed that fell on the good ground? That seed is like the person who hears the teaching and understands it. That person grows and produces fruit, sometimes a hundred times more, sometimes sixty times more, and sometimes thirty times more."

²⁴Then Jesus told them another story: "The kingdom of heaven is like a man who planted good seed in his field. ²⁵That night, when everyone was asleep, his enemy came and planted weeds among the wheat and then left. ²⁶Later, the wheat sprouted and the heads of grain grew, but the weeds also grew. ²⁷Then the man's servants came to him and said, 'You planted good seed in your field. Where did the weeds come from?' ²⁸The man answered, 'An enemy planted weeds.' The servants asked, 'Do you want us to pull up the weeds?' ²⁹The man answered, 'No, because when you pull up the weeds, you might also pull up the wheat. ³⁰Let the weeds and the wheat grow together until the harvest time. At harvest time I will tell the workers, "First gather the weeds and tie them together to be burned. Then gather the wheat and bring it to my barn." ' "

³¹Then Jesus told another story: "The kingdom of heaven is like a mustard seed that a man planted in his field. ³²That seed is the smallest of all seeds, but when it grows, it is one of the largest garden plants. It becomes big enough for the wild birds to come and build nests in its branches."

³³Then Jesus told another story: "The kingdom of heaven is like yeast that a woman took and hid in a large tub of flour until it made all the dough rise."

³⁴Jesus used stories to tell all these things to the people; he always used stories to teach them. ³⁵This is as the prophet said:

"I will speak using stories;
    I will tell things that have been
        secret since the world was
        made."   *Psalm 78:2*

³⁶Then Jesus left the crowd and went into the house. His followers came to him and said, "Explain to us the meaning of the story about the weeds in the field."

³⁷Jesus answered, "The man who planted the good seed in the field is the Son of Man. ³⁸The field is the world, and the good seed are all of God's children who belong to the kingdom. The weeds are those people who belong to the Evil One. ³⁹And the enemy who planted the bad seed is the devil. The harvest time is the end of the age, and the workers who gather are God's angels.

⁴⁰"Just as the weeds are pulled up and burned in the fire, so it will be at the end of the age. ⁴¹The Son of Man will send out his angels, and they will gather out of his kingdom all who cause sin and all who do evil. ⁴²The angels will throw them into the blazing furnace, where the people will cry and grind their teeth with pain. ⁴³Then the good people will shine like the sun in the kingdom of their Father. Let those with ears use them and listen.

⁴⁴"The kingdom of heaven is like a treasure hidden in a field. One day a man found the treasure, and then he hid it in the field again. He was so happy that he went and sold everything he owned to buy that field.

⁴⁵"Also, the kingdom of heaven is like a man looking for fine pearls. ⁴⁶When he found a very valuable pearl, he went and sold everything he had and bought it.

⁴⁷"Also, the kingdom of heaven is like a net that was put into the lake and caught

many different kinds of fish. [48]When it was full, the fishermen pulled the net to the shore. They sat down and put all the good fish in baskets and threw away the bad fish. [49]It will be this way at the end of the age. The angels will come and separate the evil people from the good people. [50]The angels will throw the evil people into the blazing furnace, where people will cry and grind their teeth with pain."

[51]Jesus asked his followers, "Do you understand all these things?"

They answered, "Yes, we understand."

[52]Then Jesus said to them, "So every teacher of the law who has been taught about the kingdom of heaven is like the owner of a house. He brings out both new things and old things he has saved."

[53]When Jesus finished teaching with these stories, he left there. [54]He went to his hometown and taught the people in the synagogue, and they were amazed. They said, "Where did this man get this wisdom and this power to do miracles? [55]He is just the son of a carpenter. His mother is Mary, and his brothers are James, Joseph, Simon, and Judas. [56]And all his sisters are here with us. Where then does this man get all these things?" [57]So the people were upset with Jesus.

But Jesus said to them, "A prophet is honored everywhere except in his hometown and in his own home."

[58]So he did not do many miracles there because they had no faith.

14

At that time Herod, the ruler of Galilee, heard the reports about Jesus. [2]So he said to his servants, "Jesus is John the Baptist, who has risen from the dead. That is why he can work these miracles."

[3]Sometime before this, Herod had arrested John, tied him up, and put him into prison. Herod did this because of Herodias, who had been the wife of Philip, Herod's brother. [4]John had been telling Herod, "It is not lawful for you to be married to Herodias." [5]Herod wanted to kill John, but he was afraid of the people, because they believed John was a prophet.

[6]On Herod's birthday, the daughter of Herodias danced for Herod and his guests, and she pleased him. [7]So he promised with an oath to give her anything she wanted. [8]Herodias told her daughter what to ask for, so she said to Herod, "Give me the head of John the Baptist here on a platter." [9]Although King Herod was very sad, he had made a promise, and his dinner guests had heard him. So Herod ordered that what she asked for be done. [10]He sent soldiers to the prison to cut off John's head. [11]And they brought it on a platter and gave it to the girl, and she took it to her mother. [12]John's followers came and got his body and buried it. Then they went and told Jesus.

[13]When Jesus heard what had happened to John, he left in a boat and went to a lonely place by himself. But the crowds heard about it and followed him on foot from the towns. [14]When he arrived, he saw a great crowd waiting. He felt sorry for them and healed those who were sick.

[15]When it was evening, his followers came to him and said, "No one lives in this place, and it is already late. Send the people away so they can go to the towns and buy food for themselves."

[16]But Jesus answered, "They don't need to go away. You give them something to eat."

[17]They said to him, "But we have only five loaves of bread and two fish."

[18]Jesus said, "Bring the bread and the fish to me." [19]Then he told the people to

sit down on the grass. He took the five loaves and the two fish and, looking to heaven, he thanked God for the food. Jesus divided the bread and gave it to his followers, who gave it to the people. ²⁰All the people ate and were satisfied. Then the followers filled twelve baskets with the leftover pieces of food. ²¹There were about five thousand men there who ate, not counting women and children.

²²Immediately Jesus told his followers to get into the boat and go ahead of him across the lake. He stayed there to send the people home. ²³After he had sent them away, he went by himself up into the hills to pray. It was late, and Jesus was there alone. ²⁴By this time, the boat was already far away from land. It was being hit by waves, because the wind was blowing against it.

²⁵Between three and six o'clock in the morning, Jesus came to them, walking on the water. ²⁶When his followers saw him walking on the water, they were afraid. They said, "It's a ghost!" and cried out in fear.

²⁷But Jesus quickly spoke to them, "Have courage! It is I. Do not be afraid."

²⁸Peter said, "Lord, if it is really you, then command me to come to you on the water."

²⁹Jesus said, "Come."

And Peter left the boat and walked on the water to Jesus. ³⁰But when Peter saw the wind and the waves, he became afraid and began to sink. He shouted, "Lord, save me!"

³¹Immediately Jesus reached out his hand and caught Peter. Jesus said, "Your faith is small. Why did you doubt?"

³²After they got into the boat, the wind became calm. ³³Then those who were in the boat worshiped Jesus and said, "Truly you are the Son of God!"

³⁴When they had crossed the lake, they came to shore at Gennesaret. ³⁵When the people there recognized Jesus, they told people all around there that Jesus had come, and they brought all their sick to him. ³⁶They begged Jesus to let them touch just the edge of his coat, and all who touched it were healed.

15 Then some Pharisees and teachers of the law came to Jesus from Jerusalem. They asked him, ²"Why don't your followers obey the unwritten laws which have been handed down to us? They don't wash their hands before they eat."

³Jesus answered, "And why do you refuse to obey God's command so that you can follow your own teachings? ⁴God said, 'Honor your father and your mother,' and 'Anyone who says cruel things to his father or mother must be put to death.' ⁵But you say a person can tell his father or mother, 'I have something I could use to help you, but I have given it to God already.' ⁶You teach that person not to honor his father or his mother. You rejected what God said for the sake of your own rules. ⁷You are hypocrites! Isaiah was right when he said about you:

⁸'These people show honor to me with
      words,
   but their hearts are far from me.
⁹Their worship of me is worthless.
   The things they teach are nothing
      but human rules.' "

Isaiah 29:13

¹⁰After Jesus called the crowd to him, he said, "Listen and understand what I am saying. ¹¹It is not what people put into their mouths that makes them unclean. It is what comes out of their mouths that makes them unclean."

¹²Then his followers came to him and asked, "Do you know that the Pharisees are angry because of what you said?"

¹³Jesus answered, "Every plant that my

Father in heaven has not planted himself will be pulled up by the roots. [14]Stay away from the Pharisees; they are blind leaders. And if a blind person leads a blind person, both will fall into a ditch."

[15]Peter said, "Explain the example to us."

[16]Jesus said, "Do you still not understand? [17]Surely you know that all the food that enters the mouth goes into the stomach and then goes out of the body. [18]But what people say with their mouths comes from the way they think; these are the things that make people unclean. [19]Out of the mind come evil thoughts, murder, adultery, sexual sins, stealing, lying, and speaking evil of others. [20]These things make people unclean; eating with unwashed hands does not make them unclean."

[21]Jesus left that place and went to the area of Tyre and Sidon. [22]A Canaanite woman from that area came to Jesus and cried out, "Lord, Son of David, have mercy on me! My daughter has a demon, and she is suffering very much."

[23]But Jesus did not answer the woman. So his followers came to Jesus and begged him, "Tell the woman to go away. She is following us and shouting."

[24]Jesus answered, "God sent me only to the lost sheep, the people of Israel."

[25]Then the woman came to Jesus again and bowed before him and said, "Lord, help me!"

[26]Jesus answered, "It is not right to take the children's bread and give it to the dogs."

[27]The woman said, "Yes, Lord, but even the dogs eat the crumbs that fall from their masters' table."

[28]Then Jesus answered, "Woman, you have great faith! I will do what you asked." And at that moment the woman's daughter was healed.

[29]After leaving there, Jesus went along the shore of Lake Galilee. He went up on a hill and sat there.

[30]Great crowds came to Jesus, bringing with them the lame, the blind, the crippled, those who could not speak, and many others. They put them at Jesus' feet, and he healed them. [31]The crowd was amazed when they saw that people who could not speak before were now able to speak. The crippled were made strong. The lame could walk, and the blind could see. And they praised the God of Israel for this.

[32]Jesus called his followers to him and said, "I feel sorry for these people, because they have already been with me three days, and they have nothing to eat. I don't want to send them away hungry. They might faint while going home."

[33]His followers asked him, "How can we get enough bread to feed all these people? We are far away from any town."

[34]Jesus asked, "How many loaves of bread do you have?"

They answered, "Seven, and a few small fish."

[35]Jesus told the people to sit on the ground. [36]He took the seven loaves of bread and the fish and gave thanks to God. Then he divided the food and gave it to his followers, and they gave it to the people. [37]All the people ate and were satisfied. Then his followers filled seven baskets with the leftover pieces of food. [38]There were about four thousand men there who ate, besides women and children. [39]After sending the people home, Jesus got into the boat and went to the area of Magadan.

16 The Pharisees and Sadducees came to Jesus, wanting to trick him. So they asked him to show them a miracle from God.

[2]Jesus answered, "At sunset you

say we will have good weather, because the sky is red. ³And in the morning you say that it will be a rainy day, because the sky is dark and red. You see these signs in the sky and know what they mean. In the same way, you see the things that I am doing now, but you don't know their meaning. ⁴Evil and sinful people ask for a miracle as a sign, but they will not be given any sign, except the sign of Jonah." Then Jesus left them and went away.

⁵Jesus' followers went across the lake, but they had forgotten to bring bread. ⁶Jesus said to them, "Be careful! Beware of the yeast of the Pharisees and the Sadducees."

⁷His followers discussed the meaning of this, saying, "He said this because we forgot to bring bread."

⁸Knowing what they were talking about, Jesus asked them, "Why are you talking about not having bread? Your faith is small. ⁹Do you still not understand? Remember the five loaves of bread that fed the five thousand? And remember that you filled many baskets with the leftovers? ¹⁰Or the seven loaves of bread that fed the four thousand and the many baskets you filled then also? ¹¹I was not talking to you about bread. Why don't you understand that? I am telling you to beware of the yeast of the Pharisees and the Sadducees." ¹²Then the followers understood that Jesus was not telling them to beware of the yeast used in bread but to beware of the teaching of the Pharisees and the Sadducees.

¹³When Jesus came to the area of Caesarea Philippi, he asked his followers, "Who do people say the Son of Man is?"

¹⁴They answered, "Some say you are John the Baptist. Others say you are Elijah, and still others say you are Jeremiah or one of the prophets."

¹⁵Then Jesus asked them, "And who do you say I am?"

¹⁶Simon Peter answered, "You are the Christ, the Son of the living God."

¹⁷Jesus answered, "You are blessed, Simon son of Jonah, because no person taught you that. My Father in heaven showed you who I am. ¹⁸So I tell you, you are Peter. On this rock I will build my church, and the power of death will not be able to defeat it. ¹⁹I will give you the keys of the kingdom of heaven; the things you don't allow on earth will be the things that God does not allow, and the things you allow on earth will be the things that God allows." ²⁰Then Jesus warned his followers not to tell anyone he was the Christ.

²¹From that time on Jesus began telling his followers that he must go to Jerusalem, where the Jewish elders, the leading priests, and the teachers of the law would make him suffer many things. He told them he must be killed and then be raised from the dead on the third day.

²²Peter took Jesus aside and told him not to talk like that. He said, "God save you from those things, Lord! Those things will never happen to you!"

²³Then Jesus said to Peter, "Go away from me, Satan! You are not helping me! You don't care about the things of God, but only about the things people think are important."

²⁴Then Jesus said to his followers, "If people want to follow me, they must give up the things they want. They must be willing even to give up their lives to follow me. ²⁵Those who want to save their lives will give up true life, and those who give up their lives for me will have true life. ²⁶It is worthless to have the whole world if they lose their souls. They could never pay enough to buy back their souls. ²⁷The Son of Man will come again with his Father's glory and with his angels. At that

STEP 3

STEP 3

Made a decision to turn our will and our lives
over to the care of God **as we understood Him.**

Matthew 16:21–26

Coming clean from an addiction depends on a process that
involves several important paradoxes—things that at first glance
appear contradictory or illogical. The central paradox of recovery is
that you have to give up in order to win. Jesus said it this way:
"Those who want to save their lives will give up true life, and those
who give up their lives for me will have true life" (verse 25).

Face it. It's never easy to stop doing things your way and start
doing them God's way. That means you have to put him in charge.
Sometimes what God wants doesn't appeal to you. That's always
been true. Peter was one of Jesus' most trusted friends, and even
he didn't always like what Jesus was up to. When Jesus started
talking about going to Jerusalem to die on the cross, Peter opposed
the idea. Jesus got angry with Peter and told him he didn't "care
about the things of God, but only about the things people think are
important" (verse 23).

Those were harsh words on Jesus' part, but they remind us that
spiritual growth depends on giving your life to God no matter what
he asks of you. Those who have fought their addiction and won
with God's help say, "Half measures availed us nothing. We stood at
the turning point. We asked His protection and care with complete
abandon" (*Alcoholics Anonymous*, p. 59).

FOR YOUR NEXT **STEP 3** MEDITATION, TURN TO **PAGE 270.** ▶▶

time, he will reward them for what they have done. ²⁸I tell you the truth, some people standing here will see the Son of Man coming with his kingdom before they die."

17 Six days later, Jesus took Peter, James, and John, the brother of James, up on a high mountain by themselves. ²While they watched, Jesus' appearance was changed; his face became bright like the sun, and his clothes became white as light. ³Then Moses and Elijah appeared to them, talking with Jesus.

⁴Peter said to Jesus, "Lord, it is good that we are here. If you want, I will put up three tents here—one for you, one for Moses, and one for Elijah."

⁵While Peter was talking, a bright cloud covered them. A voice came from the cloud and said, "This is my Son, whom I love, and I am very pleased with him. Listen to him!"

⁶When his followers heard the voice, they were so frightened they fell to the ground. ⁷But Jesus went to them and touched them and said, "Stand up. Don't be afraid." ⁸When they looked up, they saw Jesus was now alone.

⁹As they were coming down the mountain, Jesus commanded them not to tell anyone about what they had seen until the Son of Man had risen from the dead.

¹⁰Then his followers asked him, "Why do the teachers of the law say that Elijah must come first?"

¹¹Jesus answered, "They are right to say that Elijah is coming and that he will make everything the way it should be. ¹²But I tell you that Elijah has already come, and they did not recognize him. They did to him whatever they wanted to do. It will be the same with the Son of Man; those same people will make the Son of Man suffer." ¹³Then the followers understood that Jesus was talking about John the Baptist.

¹⁴When Jesus and his followers came back to the crowd, a man came to Jesus and bowed before him. ¹⁵The man said, "Lord, have mercy on my son. He has epilepsy and is suffering very much, because he often falls into the fire or into the water. ¹⁶I brought him to your followers, but they could not cure him."

¹⁷Jesus answered, "You people have no faith, and your lives are all wrong. How long must I put up with you? How long must I continue to be patient with you? Bring the boy here." ¹⁸Jesus commanded the demon inside the boy. Then the demon came out, and the boy was healed from that time on.

¹⁹The followers came to Jesus when he was alone and asked, "Why couldn't we force the demon out?"

²⁰Jesus answered, "Because your faith is too small. I tell you the truth, if your faith is as big as a mustard seed, you can say to this mountain, 'Move from here to there,' and it will move. All things will be possible for you. [²¹That kind of spirit comes out only if you use prayer and fasting.]"

²²While Jesus' followers were gathering in Galilee, he said to them, "The Son of Man will be handed over to people, ²³and they will kill him. But on the third day he will be raised from the dead." And the followers were filled with sadness.

²⁴When Jesus and his followers came to Capernaum, the men who collected the Temple tax came to Peter. They asked, "Does your teacher pay the Temple tax?"

²⁵Peter answered, "Yes, Jesus pays the tax."

Peter went into the house, but before he could speak, Jesus said to him, "What do you think? The kings of the earth collect different kinds of taxes. But who pays the taxes—the king's children or others?"

[26]Peter answered, "Other people pay the taxes."

Jesus said to Peter, "Then the children of the king don't have to pay taxes. [27]But we don't want to upset these tax collectors. So go to the lake and fish. After you catch the first fish, open its mouth and you will find a coin. Take that coin and give it to the tax collectors for you and me."

18 At that time the followers came to Jesus and asked, "Who is greatest in the kingdom of heaven?"

[2]Jesus called a little child to him and stood the child before his followers. [3]Then he said, "I tell you the truth, you must change and become like little children. Otherwise, you will never enter the kingdom of heaven. [4]The greatest person in the kingdom of heaven is the one who makes himself humble like this child.

[5]"Whoever accepts a child in my name accepts me. [6]If one of these little children believes in me, and someone causes that child to sin, it would be better for that person to have a large stone tied around the neck and be drowned in the sea. [7]How terrible for the people of the world because of the things that cause them to sin. Such things will happen, but how terrible for the one who causes them to happen! [8]If your hand or your foot causes you to sin, cut it off and throw it away. It is better for you to lose part of your body and live forever than to have two hands and two feet and be thrown into the fire that burns forever. [9]If your eye causes you to sin, take it out and throw it away. It is better for you to have only one eye and live forever than to have two eyes and be thrown into the fire of hell.

[10]"Be careful. Don't think these little children are worth nothing. I tell you that they have angels in heaven who are always with my Father in heaven. [[11]The Son of Man came to save lost people.]

[12]"If a man has a hundred sheep but one of the sheep gets lost, he will leave the other ninety-nine on the hill and go to look for the lost sheep. [13]I tell you the truth, if he finds it he is happier about that one sheep than about the ninety-nine that were never lost. [14]In the same way, your Father in heaven does not want any of these little children to be lost.

[15]"If your fellow believer sins against you, go and tell him in private what he did wrong. If he listens to you, you have helped that person to be your brother or sister again. [16]But if he refuses to listen, go to him again and take one or two other people with you. 'Every case may be proved by two or three witnesses.' [17]If he refuses to listen to them, tell the church. If he refuses to listen to the church, then treat him like a person who does not believe in God or like a tax collector.

[18]"I tell you the truth, the things you don't allow on earth will be the things God does not allow. And the things you allow on earth will be the things that God allows.

[19]"Also, I tell you that if two of you on earth agree about something and pray for it, it will be done for you by my Father in heaven. [20]This is true because if two or three people come together in my name, I am there with them."

[21]Then Peter came to Jesus and asked, "Lord, when my fellow believer sins against me, how many times must I forgive him? Should I forgive him as many as seven times?"

[22]Jesus answered, "I tell you, you must forgive him more than seven times. You must forgive him even if he wrongs you seventy times seven.

STEP 7

Humbly asked Him to remove our shortcomings.

Matthew 18:4

Children are supposed to be innocent and unspoiled because adults protect them from the uglier realities of life. They need protection because their emotions aren't meant to deal with brutality and terror. Innocent children respond to their world with honesty, spontaneity, and delight. Unfortunately, their openness also leaves children vulnerable to abuse. Worst of all, the most damaging abuse children suffer comes from family members and other trusted caregivers.

So, when Jesus tells you to become like a little child in order to enter the kingdom of heaven, if you were abused as a child, that sounds like a scary idea. You may be trying hard to forget the memories of your childhood and may hate the idea of childlike faith. Didn't that kind of trust leave you scarred and addicted to the very habits you're trying to get away from?

God can be a trustworthy heavenly Father to you, even if your earthly parents weren't trustworthy. In the same way, you can be a trusting child to God, even though you couldn't trust your earthly family. It takes incredible courage for adult children of abuse to take the first step of trusting God.

But you can do it. Tell God just how hard it is for you to trust him. Tell him why it's hard. Ask for his help in becoming a trusting child so you can do what he asks you to with confidence that all will be well because your Father is good and kind and watching out for you.

FOR YOUR NEXT **STEP 7** MEDITATION, TURN TO **PAGE 165.** ▶▶

²³"The kingdom of heaven is like a king who decided to collect the money his servants owed him. ²⁴When the king began to collect his money, a servant who owed him several million dollars was brought to him. ²⁵But the servant did not have enough money to pay his master, the king. So the master ordered that everything the servant owned should be sold, even the servant's wife and children. Then the money would be used to pay the king what the servant owed.

²⁶"But the servant fell on his knees and begged, 'Be patient with me, and I will pay you everything I owe.' ²⁷The master felt sorry for his servant and told him he did not have to pay it back. Then he let the servant go free.

²⁸"Later, that same servant found another servant who owed him a few dollars. The servant grabbed him around the neck and said, 'Pay me the money you owe me!'

²⁹"The other servant fell on his knees and begged him, 'Be patient with me, and I will pay you everything I owe.'

³⁰"But the first servant refused to be patient. He threw the other servant into prison until he could pay everything he owed. ³¹When the other servants saw what had happened, they were very sorry. So they went and told their master all that had happened.

³²"Then the master called his servant in and said, 'You evil servant! Because you begged me to forget what you owed, I told you that you did not have to pay anything. ³³You should have showed mercy to that other servant, just as I showed mercy to you.' ³⁴The master was very angry and put the servant in prison to be punished until he could pay everything he owed.

³⁵"This king did what my heavenly Father will do to you if you do not forgive your brother or sister from your heart."

19 After Jesus said all these things, he left Galilee and went into the area of Judea on the other side of the Jordan River. ²Large crowds followed him, and he healed them there.

³Some Pharisees came to Jesus and tried to trick him. They asked, "Is it right for a man to divorce his wife for any reason he chooses?"

⁴Jesus answered, "Surely you have read in the Scriptures: When God made the world, 'he made them male and female.' ⁵And God said, 'So a man will leave his father and mother and be united with his wife, and the two will become one body.' ⁶So there are not two, but one. God has joined the two together, so no one should separate them."

⁷The Pharisees asked, "Why then did Moses give a command for a man to divorce his wife by giving her divorce papers?"

⁸Jesus answered, "Moses allowed you to divorce your wives because you refused to accept God's teaching, but divorce was not allowed in the beginning. ⁹I tell you that anyone who divorces his wife and marries another woman is guilty of adultery. The only reason for a man to divorce his wife is if his wife has sexual relations with another man."

¹⁰The followers said to him, "If that is the only reason a man can divorce his wife, it is better not to marry."

¹¹Jesus answered, "Not everyone can accept this teaching, but God has made some able to accept it. ¹²There are different reasons why some men cannot marry. Some men were born without the ability to become fathers. Others were made that way later in life by other people. And some men have given up marriage because of the kingdom of heaven. But the person who can marry should accept this teaching about marriage."

STEP 8

Made a list of all persons we had harmed,
and became willing to make amends to them all.

Matthew 18:21–35

In Step 8, you learn to accept your responsibility for the part you played in problem situations and broken relationships.

Jesus told Peter a story about a servant who received forgiveness for a huge debt he owed his master. Then he refused to forgive a tiny debt another servant owed him. Jesus used this story to teach a negative lesson—don't be like that servant. Whether you need to receive forgiveness or to grant forgiveness, you should do it. That's the essence of Step 8.

Think about it this way. God, in his mercy, forgave you and saved you, even when you were in the depths of your addiction. Now you must be willing "from your heart" (verse 35) to forgive and be reconciled to the people who hurt you in the past.

You also need to make amends for wrongs you have done. As you do, the underlying attitude must still be "from your heart." When God sees that your heart is willing to obey him, regardless of the outcome, he will bless you beyond what you "can ask or imagine" (Ephesians 3:20).

FOR YOUR NEXT **STEP 8** MEDITATION, TURN TO **PAGE 90.** ▶▶

¹³Then the people brought their little children to Jesus so he could put his hands on them and pray for them. His followers told them to stop, ¹⁴but Jesus said, "Let the little children come to me. Don't stop them, because the kingdom of heaven belongs to people who are like these children." ¹⁵After Jesus put his hands on the children, he left there.

¹⁶A man came to Jesus and asked, "Teacher, what good thing must I do to have life forever?"

¹⁷Jesus answered, "Why do you ask me about what is good? Only God is good. But if you want to have life forever, obey the commands."

¹⁸The man asked, "Which commands?"

Jesus answered, " 'You must not murder anyone; you must not be guilty of adultery; you must not steal; you must not tell lies about your neighbor; ¹⁹honor your father and mother; and love your neighbor as you love yourself.' "

²⁰The young man said, "I have obeyed all these things. What else do I need to do?"

²¹Jesus answered, "If you want to be perfect, then go and sell your possessions and give the money to the poor. If you do this, you will have treasure in heaven. Then come and follow me."

²²But when the young man heard this, he left sorrowfully, because he was rich.

²³Then Jesus said to his followers, "I tell you the truth, it will be hard for a rich person to enter the kingdom of heaven. ²⁴Yes, I tell you that it is easier for a camel to go through the eye of a needle than for a rich person to enter the kingdom of God."

²⁵When Jesus' followers heard this, they were very surprised and asked, "Then who can be saved?"

²⁶Jesus looked at them and said, "For people this is impossible, but for God all things are possible."

²⁷Peter said to Jesus, "Look, we have left everything and followed you. So what will we have?"

²⁸Jesus said to them, "I tell you the truth, when the age to come has arrived, the Son of Man will sit on his great throne. All of you who followed me will also sit on twelve thrones, judging the twelve tribes of Israel. ²⁹And all those who have left houses, brothers, sisters, father, mother, children, or farms to follow me will get much more than they left, and they will have life forever. ³⁰Many who are first now will be last in the future. And many who are last now will be first in the future.

20 "The kingdom of heaven is like a person who owned some land. One morning, he went out very early to hire some people to work in his vineyard. ²The man agreed to pay the workers one coin for working that day. Then he sent them into the vineyard to work. ³About nine o'clock the man went to the marketplace and saw some other people standing there, doing nothing. ⁴So he said to them, 'If you go and work in my vineyard, I will pay you what your work is worth.' ⁵So they went to work in the vineyard. The man went out again about twelve o'clock and three o'clock and did the same thing. ⁶About five o'clock the man went to the marketplace again and saw others standing there. He asked them, 'Why did you stand here all day doing nothing?' ⁷They answered, 'No one gave us a job.' The man said to them, 'Then you can go and work in my vineyard.'

⁸"At the end of the day, the owner of the vineyard said to the boss of all the workers, 'Call the workers and pay them.

32

Start with the last people I hired and end with those I hired first.'

⁹"When the workers who were hired at five o'clock came to get their pay, each received one coin. ¹⁰When the workers who were hired first came to get their pay, they thought they would be paid more than the others. But each one of them also received one coin. ¹¹When they got their coin, they complained to the man who owned the land. ¹²They said, 'Those people were hired last and worked only one hour. But you paid them the same as you paid us who worked hard all day in the hot sun.' ¹³But the man who owned the vineyard said to one of those workers, 'Friend, I am being fair to you. You agreed to work for one coin. ¹⁴So take your pay and go. I want to give the man who was hired last the same pay that I gave you. ¹⁵I can do what I want with my own money. Are you jealous because I am good to those people?'

¹⁶"So those who are last now will someday be first, and those who are first now will someday be last."

¹⁷While Jesus was going to Jerusalem, he took his twelve followers aside privately and said to them, ¹⁸"Look, we are going to Jerusalem. The Son of Man will be turned over to the leading priests and the teachers of the law, and they will say that he must die. ¹⁹They will give the Son of Man to the non-Jewish people to laugh at him and beat him with whips and crucify him. But on the third day, he will be raised to life again."

²⁰Then the wife of Zebedee came to Jesus with her sons. She bowed before him and asked him to do something for her.

²¹Jesus asked, "What do you want?"

She said, "Promise that one of my sons will sit at your right side and the other will sit at your left side in your kingdom."

²²But Jesus said, "You don't understand what you are asking. Can you drink the cup that I am about to drink?"

The sons answered, "Yes, we can."

²³Jesus said to them, "You will drink from my cup. But I cannot choose who will sit at my right or my left; those places belong to those for whom my Father has prepared them."

²⁴When the other ten followers heard this, they were angry with the two brothers.

²⁵Jesus called all the followers together and said, "You know that the rulers of the non-Jewish people love to show their power over the people. And their important leaders love to use all their authority. ²⁶But it should not be that way among you. Whoever wants to become great among you must serve the rest of you like a servant. ²⁷Whoever wants to become first among you must serve the rest of you like a slave. ²⁸In the same way, the Son of Man did not come to be served. He came to serve others and to give his life as a ransom for many people."

²⁹When Jesus and his followers were leaving Jericho, a great many people followed him. ³⁰Two blind men sitting by the road heard that Jesus was going by, so they shouted, "Lord, Son of David, have mercy on us!"

³¹The people warned the blind men to be quiet, but they shouted even more, "Lord, Son of David, have mercy on us!"

³²Jesus stopped and said to the blind men, "What do you want me to do for you?"

³³They answered, "Lord, we want to see."

³⁴Jesus felt sorry for the blind men and touched their eyes, and at once they could see. Then they followed Jesus.

STEP 2

21 As Jesus and his followers were coming closer to Jerusalem, they stopped at Bethphage at the hill called the Mount of Olives. From there Jesus sent two of his followers ²and said to them, "Go to the town you can see there. When you enter it, you will quickly find a donkey tied there with its colt. Untie them and bring them to me. ³If anyone asks you why you are taking the donkeys, say that the Master needs them, and he will send them at once."

⁴This was to bring about what the prophet had said:

⁵"Tell the people of Jerusalem,
  'Your king is coming to you.
He is gentle and riding on a donkey,
  on the colt of a donkey.' "

Isaiah 62:11; Zechariah 9:9

⁶The followers went and did what Jesus told them to do. ⁷They brought the donkey and the colt to Jesus and laid their coats on them, and Jesus sat on them. ⁸Many people spread their coats on the road. Others cut branches from the trees and spread them on the road. ⁹The people were walking ahead of Jesus and behind him, shouting,

"Praise to the Son of David!
God bless the One who comes in the
    name of the Lord!

Psalm 118:26

Praise to God in heaven!"

¹⁰When Jesus entered Jerusalem, all the city was filled with excitement. The people asked, "Who is this man?"

¹¹The crowd said, "This man is Jesus, the prophet from the town of Nazareth in Galilee."

¹²Jesus went into the Temple and threw out all the people who were buying and selling there. He turned over the tables of those who were exchanging different kinds of money, and he upset the benches of those who were selling doves.

¹³Jesus said to all the people there, "It is written in the Scriptures, 'My Temple will be called a house for prayer.' But you are changing it into a 'hideout for robbers.' "

¹⁴The blind and crippled people came to Jesus in the Temple, and he healed them. ¹⁵The leading priests and the teachers of the law saw that Jesus was doing wonderful things and that the children were praising him in the Temple, saying, "Praise to the Son of David." All these things made the priests and the teachers of the law very angry.

¹⁶They asked Jesus, "Do you hear the things these children are saying?"

Jesus answered, "Yes. Haven't you read in the Scriptures, 'You have taught children and babies to sing praises'?"

¹⁷Then Jesus left and went out of the city to Bethany, where he spent the night.

¹⁸Early the next morning, as Jesus was going back to the city, he became hungry. ¹⁹Seeing a fig tree beside the road, Jesus went to it, but there were no figs on the tree, only leaves. So Jesus said to the tree, "You will never again have fruit." The tree immediately dried up.

²⁰When his followers saw this, they were amazed. They asked, "How did the fig tree dry up so quickly?"

²¹Jesus answered, "I tell you the truth, if you have faith and do not doubt, you will be able to do what I did to this tree and even more. You will be able to say to this mountain, 'Go, fall into the sea.' And if you have faith, it will happen. ²²If you believe, you will get anything you ask for in prayer."

STEP 7

²³Jesus went to the Temple, and while he was teaching there, the leading priests and the elders of the people came to him. They said, "What authority do you have to do these things? Who gave you this authority?"

²⁴Jesus answered, "I also will ask you a question. If you answer me, then I will tell you what authority I have to do these things. ²⁵Tell me: When John baptized people, did that come from God or just from other people?"

They argued about Jesus' question, saying, "If we answer, 'John's baptism was from God,' Jesus will say, 'Then why didn't you believe him?' ²⁶But if we say, 'It was from people,' we are afraid of what the crowd will do because they all believe that John was a prophet."

²⁷So they answered Jesus, "We don't know."

Jesus said to them, "Then I won't tell you what authority I have to do these things.

²⁸"Tell me what you think about this: A man had two sons. He went to the first son and said, 'Son, go and work today in my vineyard.' ²⁹The son answered, 'I will not go.' But later the son changed his mind and went. ³⁰Then the father went to the other son and said, 'Son, go and work today in my vineyard.' The son answered, 'Yes, sir, I will go and work,' but he did not go. ³¹Which of the two sons obeyed his father?"

The priests and leaders answered, "The first son."

Jesus said to them, "I tell you the truth, the tax collectors and the prostitutes will enter the kingdom of God before you do. ³²John came to show you the right way to live. You did not believe him, but the tax collectors and prostitutes believed him. Even after seeing this, you still refused to change your ways and believe him.

³³"Listen to this story: There was a man who owned a vineyard. He put a wall around it and dug a hole for a winepress and built a tower. Then he leased the land to some farmers and left for a trip. ³⁴When it was time for the grapes to be picked, he sent his servants to the farmers to get his share of the grapes. ³⁵But the farmers grabbed the servants, beat one, killed another, and then killed a third servant with stones. ³⁶So the man sent some other servants to the farmers, even more than he sent the first time. But the farmers did the same thing to the servants that they had done before. ³⁷So the man decided to send his son to the farmers. He said, 'They will respect my son.' ³⁸But when the farmers saw the son, they said to each other, 'This son will inherit the vineyard. If we kill him, it will be ours!' ³⁹Then the farmers grabbed the son, threw him out of the vineyard, and killed him. ⁴⁰So what will the owner of the vineyard do to these farmers when he comes?"

⁴¹The priests and leaders said, "He will surely kill those evil men. Then he will lease the vineyard to some other farmers who will give him his share of the crop at harvest time."

⁴²Jesus said to them, "Surely you have read this in the Scriptures:

'The stone that the builders rejected
    became the cornerstone.
The Lord did this,
    and it is wonderful to us.'

Psalm 118:22–23

⁴³"So I tell you that the kingdom of God will be taken away from you and given to people who do the things God wants in his kingdom. ⁴⁴The person who falls on this stone will be broken, and on whomever that stone falls, that person will be crushed."

⁴⁵When the leading priests and the Pharisees heard these stories, they knew Jesus was talking about them. ⁴⁶They wanted to arrest him, but they were afraid of the people, because the people believed that Jesus was a prophet.

22 Jesus again used stories to teach them. He said, ²"The kingdom of heaven is like a king who prepared a wedding feast for his son. ³The king invited some people to the feast. When the feast was ready, the king sent his servants to tell the people, but they refused to come.

⁴"Then the king sent other servants, saying, 'Tell those who have been invited that my feast is ready. I have killed my best bulls and calves for the dinner, and everything is ready. Come to the wedding feast.'

⁵"But the people refused to listen to the servants and left to do other things. One went to work in his field, and another went to his business. ⁶Some of the other people grabbed the servants, beat them, and killed them. ⁷The king was furious and sent his army to kill the murderers and burn their city.

⁸"After that, the king said to his servants, 'The wedding feast is ready. I invited those people, but they were not worthy to come. ⁹So go to the street corners and invite everyone you find to come to my feast.' ¹⁰So the servants went into the streets and gathered all the people they could find, both good and bad. And the wedding hall was filled with guests.

¹¹"When the king came in to see the guests, he saw a man who was not dressed for a wedding. ¹²The king said, 'Friend, how were you allowed to come in here? You are not dressed for a wedding.' But the man said nothing. ¹³So the king told some servants, 'Tie this man's hands and feet. Throw him out into the darkness, where people will cry and grind their teeth with pain.'

¹⁴"Yes, many are invited, but only a few are chosen."

¹⁵Then the Pharisees left that place and made plans to trap Jesus in saying something wrong. ¹⁶They sent some of their own followers and some people from the group called Herodians. They said, "Teacher, we know that you are an honest man and that you teach the truth about God's way. You are not afraid of what other people think about you, because you pay no attention to who they are. ¹⁷So tell us what you think. Is it right to pay taxes to Caesar or not?"

¹⁸But knowing that these leaders were trying to trick him, Jesus said, "You hypocrites! Why are you trying to trap me? ¹⁹Show me a coin used for paying the tax." So the men showed him a coin. ²⁰Then Jesus asked, "Whose image and name are on the coin?"

²¹The men answered, "Caesar's."

Then Jesus said to them, "Give to Caesar the things that are Caesar's, and give to God the things that are God's."

²²When the men heard what Jesus said, they were amazed and left him and went away.

²³That same day some Sadducees came to Jesus and asked him a question. (Sadducees believed that people would not rise from the dead.) ²⁴They said, "Teacher, Moses said if a married man dies without having children, his brother must marry the widow and have children for him. ²⁵Once there were seven brothers among us. The first one married and died. Since he had no children, his brother married the widow. ²⁶Then the second brother also died. The same thing happened to the third brother and all the other brothers. ²⁷Finally, the woman died. ²⁸Since all seven men had married her, when people rise from the dead, whose wife will she be?"

²⁹Jesus answered, "You don't understand, because you don't know what the Scriptures say, and you don't know about the power of God. ³⁰When people rise from the dead, they will not marry, nor will they be given to someone to marry.

They will be like the angels in heaven. [31]Surely you have read what God said to you about rising from the dead. [32]God said, 'I am the God of Abraham, the God of Isaac, and the God of Jacob.' God is the God of the living, not the dead."

[33]When the people heard this, they were amazed at Jesus' teaching.

[34]When the Pharisees learned that the Sadducees could not argue with Jesus' answers to them, the Pharisees met together. [35]One Pharisee, who was an expert on the law of Moses, asked Jesus this question to test him: [36]"Teacher, which command in the law is the most important?"

[37]Jesus answered, " 'Love the Lord your God with all your heart, all your soul, and all your mind.' [38]This is the first and most important command. [39]And the second command is like the first: 'Love your neighbor as you love yourself.' [40]All the law and the writings of the prophets depend on these two commands."

[41]While the Pharisees were together, Jesus asked them, [42]"What do you think about the Christ? Whose son is he?"

They answered, "The Christ is the Son of David."

[43]Then Jesus said to them, "Then why did David call him 'Lord'? David, speaking by the power of the Holy Spirit, said,

[44]'The Lord said to my Lord,

"Sit by me at my right side,

until I put your enemies under your control." ' *Psalm 110:1*

[45]David calls the Christ 'Lord,' so how can the Christ be his son?"

[46]None of the Pharisees could answer Jesus' question, and after that day no one was brave enough to ask him any more questions.

23 Then Jesus said to the crowds and to his followers, [2]"The teachers of

the law and the Pharisees have the authority to tell you what the law of Moses says. [3]So you should obey and follow whatever they tell you, but their lives are not good examples for you to follow. They tell you to do things, but they themselves don't do them. [4]They make strict rules and try to force people to obey them, but they are unwilling to help those who struggle under the weight of their rules.

[5]"They do good things so that other people will see them. They enlarge the little boxes holding Scriptures that they wear, and they make their special prayer clothes very long. [6]Those Pharisees and teachers of the law love to have the most important seats at feasts and in the synagogues. [7]They love people to greet them with respect in the marketplaces, and they love to have people call them 'Teacher.'

[8]"But you must not be called 'Teacher,' because you have only one Teacher, and you are all brothers and sisters together. [9]And don't call any person on earth 'Father,' because you have one Father, who is in heaven. [10]And you should not be called 'Master,' because you have only one Master, the Christ. [11]Whoever is your servant is the greatest among you. [12]Whoever makes himself great will be made humble. Whoever makes himself humble will be made great.

[13]"How terrible for you, teachers of the law and Pharisees! You are hypocrites! You close the door for people to enter the kingdom of heaven. You yourselves don't enter, and you stop others who are trying to enter. [[14]How terrible for you, teachers of the law and Pharisees. You are hypocrites. You take away widows' houses, and you say long prayers so that people will notice you. So you will have a worse punishment.]

[15]"How terrible for you, teachers of the

law and Pharisees! You are hypocrites! You travel across land and sea to find one person who will change to your ways. When you find that person, you make him more fit for hell than you are.

[16]"How terrible for you! You guide the people, but you are blind. You say, 'If people swear by the Temple when they make a promise, that means nothing. But if they swear by the gold that is in the Temple, they must keep that promise.' [17]You are blind fools! Which is greater: the gold or the Temple that makes that gold holy? [18]And you say, 'If people swear by the altar when they make a promise, that means nothing. But if they swear by the gift on the altar, they must keep that promise.' [19]You are blind! Which is greater: the gift or the altar that makes the gift holy? [20]The person who swears by the altar is really using the altar and also everything on the altar. [21]And the person who swears by the Temple is really using the Temple and also everything in the Temple. [22]The person who swears by heaven is also using God's throne and the One who sits on that throne.

[23]"How terrible for you, teachers of the law and Pharisees! You are hypocrites! You give to God one-tenth of everything you earn—even your mint, dill, and cumin. But you don't obey the really important teachings of the law—justice, mercy, and being loyal. These are the things you should do, as well as those other things. [24]You guide the people, but you are blind! You are like a person who picks a fly out of a drink and then swallows a camel!

[25]"How terrible for you, teachers of the law and Pharisees! You are hypocrites! You wash the outside of your cups and dishes, but inside they are full of things you got by cheating others and by pleasing only yourselves. [26]Pharisees, you are blind! First make the inside of the cup clean, and then the outside of the cup can be truly clean.

[27]"How terrible for you, teachers of the law and Pharisees! You are hypocrites! You are like tombs that are painted white. Outside, those tombs look fine, but inside, they are full of the bones of dead people and all kinds of unclean things. [28]It is the same with you. People look at you and think you are good, but on the inside you are full of hypocrisy and evil.

[29]"How terrible for you, teachers of the law and Pharisees! You are hypocrites! You build tombs for the prophets, and you show honor to the graves of those who lived good lives. [30]You say, 'If we had lived during the time of our ancestors, we would not have helped them kill the prophets.' [31]But you give proof that you are descendants of those who murdered the prophets. [32]And you will complete the sin that your ancestors started.

[33]"You are snakes! A family of poisonous snakes! How are you going to escape God's judgment? [34]So I tell you this: I am sending to you prophets and wise men and teachers. Some of them you will kill and crucify. Some of them you will beat in your synagogues and chase from town to town. [35]So you will be guilty for the death of all the good people who have been killed on earth—from the murder of that good man Abel to the murder of Zechariah son of Berakiah, whom you murdered between the Temple and the altar. [36]I tell you the truth, all of these things will happen to you people who are living now.

[37]"Jerusalem, Jerusalem! You kill the prophets and stone to death those who are sent to you. Many times I wanted to gather your people as a hen gathers her chicks under her wings, but you did not let me. [38]Now your house will be left

STEP 4

Made a searching and fearless moral
inventory of ourselves.

Matthew 23:23-28

Research into addictive behavior indicates that all addictions and compulsions are shame-based. Some people feel intense shame because of early childhood events they saw or experienced. Others experience shame because of their habits. In either case, the shame has to go before lasting recovery can occur. The Bible says cleansing has to start on the inside with your heart and work its way out into your actions. Twelve Step recovery offers the tool of a "searching and fearless moral inventory" as a way of going about this inner cleansing.

If you want your inventory to work, you have to deal with both false and real shame. You may carry false guilt by feeling responsible for childhood sexual abuse or your parents' drug use. Or you may experience real feelings of guilt about hurting family and friends through your own addictive behaviors.

Step 4 gives you a special opportunity to open the dark recesses of your life to the cleansing light of God's Spirit.

FOR YOUR NEXT **STEP 4** MEDITATION, TURN TO **PAGE 102.** ▶▶

completely empty. ³⁹I tell you, you will not see me again until that time when you will say, 'God bless the One who comes in the name of the Lord.' "

24 As Jesus left the Temple and was walking away, his followers came up to show him the Temple's buildings. ²Jesus asked, "Do you see all these buildings? I tell you the truth, not one stone will be left on another. Every stone will be thrown down to the ground."

³Later, as Jesus was sitting on the Mount of Olives, his followers came to be alone with him. They said, "Tell us, when will these things happen? And what will be the sign that it is time for you to come again and for this age to end?"

⁴Jesus answered, "Be careful that no one fools you. ⁵Many will come in my name, saying, 'I am the Christ,' and they will fool many people. ⁶You will hear about wars and stories of wars that are coming, but don't be afraid. These things must happen before the end comes. ⁷Nations will fight against other nations; kingdoms will fight against other kingdoms. There will be times when there is no food for people to eat, and there will be earthquakes in different places. ⁸These things are like the first pains when something new is about to be born.

⁹"Then people will arrest you, hand you over to be hurt, and kill you. They will hate you because you believe in me. ¹⁰At that time, many will lose their faith, and they will turn against each other and hate each other. ¹¹Many false prophets will come and cause many people to believe lies. ¹²There will be more and more evil in the world, so most people will stop showing their love for each other. ¹³But those people who keep their faith until the end will be saved. ¹⁴The Good News about God's kingdom will be preached in all the world, to every nation. Then the end will come.

¹⁵"Daniel the prophet spoke about 'a blasphemous object that brings destruction.' You will see this standing in the holy place." (You who read this should understand what it means.) ¹⁶"At that time, the people in Judea should run away to the mountains. ¹⁷If people are on the roofs of their houses, they must not go down to get anything out of their houses. ¹⁸If people are in the fields, they must not go back to get their coats. ¹⁹At that time, how terrible it will be for women who are pregnant or have nursing babies! ²⁰Pray that it will not be winter or a Sabbath day when these things happen and you have to run away, ²¹because at that time there will be much trouble. There will be more trouble than there has ever been since the beginning of the world until now, and nothing as bad will ever happen again. ²²God has decided to make that terrible time short. Otherwise, no one would go on living. But God will make that time short to help the people he has chosen. ²³At that time, someone might say to you, 'Look, there is the Christ!' Or another person might say, 'There he is!' But don't believe them. ²⁴False Christs and false prophets will come and perform great wonders and miracles. They will try to fool even the people God has chosen, if that is possible. ²⁵Now I have warned you about this before it happens.

²⁶"If people tell you, 'The Christ is in the desert,' don't go there. If they say, 'The Christ is in the inner room,' don't believe it. ²⁷When the Son of Man comes, he will be seen by everyone, like lightning flashing from the east to the west. ²⁸Wherever the dead body is, there the vultures will gather.

²⁹"Soon after the trouble of those days,
    'the sun will grow dark,
        and the moon will not give its light.

The stars will fall from the sky.
And the powers of the heavens
will be shaken.'

Isaiah 13:10; 34:4

[30]"At that time, the sign of the Son of Man will appear in the sky. Then all the peoples of the world will cry. They will see the Son of Man coming on clouds in the sky with great power and glory. [31]He will use a loud trumpet to send his angels all around the earth, and they will gather his chosen people from every part of the world.

[32]"Learn a lesson from the fig tree: When its branches become green and soft and new leaves appear, you know summer is near. [33]In the same way, when you see all these things happening, you will know that the time is near, ready to come. [34]I tell you the truth, all these things will happen while the people of this time are still living. [35]Earth and sky will be destroyed, but the words I have said will never be destroyed.

[36]"No one knows when that day or time will be, not the angels in heaven, not even the Son. Only the Father knows. [37]When the Son of Man comes, it will be like what happened during Noah's time. [38]In those days before the flood, people were eating and drinking, marrying and giving their children to be married, until the day Noah entered the boat. [39]They knew nothing about what was happening until the flood came and destroyed them. It will be the same when the Son of Man comes. [40]Two men will be in the field. One will be taken, and the other will be left. [41]Two women will be grinding grain with a mill. One will be taken, and the other will be left.

[42]"So always be ready, because you don't know the day your Lord will come. [43]Remember this: If the owner of the house knew what time of night a thief was coming, the owner would watch and not let the thief break in. [44]So you also must be ready, because the Son of Man will come at a time you don't expect him.

[45]"Who is the wise and loyal servant that the master trusts to give the other servants their food at the right time? [46]When the master comes and finds the servant doing his work, the servant will be blessed. [47]I tell you the truth, the master will choose that servant to take care of everything he owns. [48]But suppose that evil servant thinks to himself, 'My master will not come back soon,' [49]and he begins to beat the other servants and eat and get drunk with others like him? [50]The master will come when that servant is not ready and is not expecting him. [51]Then the master will cut him in pieces and send him away to be with the hypocrites, where people will cry and grind their teeth with pain.

25 "At that time the kingdom of heaven will be like ten bridesmaids who took their lamps and went to wait for the bridegroom. [2]Five of them were foolish and five were wise. [3]The five foolish bridesmaids took their lamps, but they did not take more oil for the lamps to burn. [4]The wise bridesmaids took their lamps and more oil in jars. [5]Because the bridegroom was late, they became sleepy and went to sleep.

[6]"At midnight someone cried out, 'The bridegroom is coming! Come and meet him!' [7]Then all the bridesmaids woke up and got their lamps ready. [8]But the foolish ones said to the wise, 'Give us some of your oil, because our lamps are going out.' [9]The wise bridesmaids answered, 'No, the oil we have might not be enough for all of us. Go to the people who sell oil and buy some for yourselves.'

[10]"So while the five foolish bridesmaids went to buy oil, the bridegroom came. The bridesmaids who were ready

went in with the bridegroom to the wedding feast. Then the door was closed and locked.

¹¹"Later the others came back and said, 'Sir, sir, open the door to let us in.' ¹²But the bridegroom answered, 'I tell you the truth, I don't want to know you.'

¹³"So always be ready, because you don't know the day or the hour the Son of Man will come.

¹⁴"The kingdom of heaven is like a man who was going to another place for a visit. Before he left, he called for his servants and told them to take care of his things while he was gone. ¹⁵He gave one servant five bags of gold, another servant two bags of gold, and a third servant one bag of gold, to each one as much as he could handle. Then he left. ¹⁶The servant who got five bags went quickly to invest the money and earned five more bags. ¹⁷In the same way, the servant who had two bags invested them and earned two more. ¹⁸But the servant who got one bag went out and dug a hole in the ground and hid the master's money.

¹⁹"After a long time the master came home and asked the servants what they did with his money. ²⁰The servant who was given five bags of gold brought five more bags to the master and said, 'Master, you trusted me to care for five bags of gold, so I used your five bags to earn five more.' ²¹The master answered, 'You did well. You are a good and loyal servant. Because you were loyal with small things, I will let you care for much greater things. Come and share my joy with me.'

²²"Then the servant who had been given two bags of gold came to the master and said, 'Master, you gave me two bags of gold to care for, so I used your two bags to earn two more.' ²³The master answered, 'You did well. You are a good and loyal servant. Because you were loyal

with small things, I will let you care for much greater things. Come and share my joy with me.'

²⁴"Then the servant who had been given one bag of gold came to the master and said, 'Master, I knew that you were a hard man. You harvest things you did not plant. You gather crops where you did not sow any seed. ²⁵So I was afraid and went and hid your money in the ground. Here is your bag of gold.' ²⁶The master answered, 'You are a wicked and lazy servant! You say you knew that I harvest things I did not plant and that I gather crops where I did not sow any seed. ²⁷So you should have put my gold in the bank. Then, when I came home, I would have received my gold back with interest.'

²⁸"So the master told his other servants, 'Take the bag of gold from that servant and give it to the servant who has ten bags of gold. ²⁹Those who have much will get more, and they will have much more than they need. But those who do not have much will have everything taken away from them.' ³⁰Then the master said, 'Throw that useless servant outside, into the darkness where people will cry and grind their teeth with pain.'

³¹"The Son of Man will come again in his great glory, with all his angels. He will be King and sit on his great throne. ³²All the nations of the world will be gathered before him, and he will separate them into two groups as a shepherd separates the sheep from the goats. ³³The Son of Man will put the sheep on his right and the goats on his left.

³⁴"Then the King will say to the people on his right, 'Come, my Father has given you his blessing. Receive the kingdom God has prepared for you since the world was made. ³⁵I was hungry, and you gave me food. I was thirsty, and you gave me something to drink. I was alone and away

from home, and you invited me into your house. ³⁶I was without clothes, and you gave me something to wear. I was sick, and you cared for me. I was in prison, and you visited me.'

³⁷"Then the good people will answer, 'Lord, when did we see you hungry and give you food, or thirsty and give you something to drink? ³⁸When did we see you alone and away from home and invite you into our house? When did we see you without clothes and give you something to wear? ³⁹When did we see you sick or in prison and care for you?'

⁴⁰"Then the King will answer, 'I tell you the truth, anything you did for even the least of my people here, you also did for me.'

⁴¹"Then the King will say to those on his left, 'Go away from me. You will be punished. Go into the fire that burns forever that was prepared for the devil and his angels. ⁴²I was hungry, and you gave me nothing to eat. I was thirsty, and you gave me nothing to drink. ⁴³I was alone and away from home, and you did not invite me into your house. I was without clothes, and you gave me nothing to wear. I was sick and in prison, and you did not care for me.'

⁴⁴"Then those people will answer, 'Lord, when did we see you hungry or thirsty or alone and away from home or without clothes or sick or in prison? When did we see these things and not help you?'

⁴⁵"Then the King will answer, 'I tell you the truth, anything you refused to do for even the least of my people here, you refused to do for me.'

⁴⁶"These people will go off to be punished forever, but the good people will go to live forever."

26 After Jesus finished saying all these things, he told his followers,

²"You know that the day after tomorrow is the day of the Passover Feast. On that day the Son of Man will be given to his enemies to be crucified."

³Then the leading priests and the elders had a meeting at the palace of the high priest, named Caiaphas. ⁴At the meeting, they planned to set a trap to arrest Jesus and kill him. ⁵But they said, "We must not do it during the feast, because the people might cause a riot."

⁶Jesus was in Bethany at the house of Simon, who had a skin disease. ⁷While Jesus was there, a woman approached him with an alabaster jar filled with expensive perfume. She poured this perfume on Jesus' head while he was eating.

⁸His followers were upset when they saw the woman do this. They asked, "Why waste that perfume? ⁹It could have been sold for a great deal of money and the money given to the poor."

¹⁰Knowing what had happened, Jesus said, "Why are you troubling this woman? She did an excellent thing for me. ¹¹You will always have the poor with you, but you will not always have me. ¹²This woman poured perfume on my body to prepare me for burial. ¹³I tell you the truth, wherever the Good News is preached in all the world, what this woman has done will be told, and people will remember her."

¹⁴Then one of the twelve apostles, Judas Iscariot, went to talk to the leading priests. ¹⁵He said, "What will you pay me for giving Jesus to you?" And they gave him thirty silver coins. ¹⁶After that, Judas watched for the best time to turn Jesus in.

¹⁷On the first day of the Feast of Unleavened Bread, the followers came to Jesus. They said, "Where do you want us to prepare for you to eat the Passover meal?"

¹⁸Jesus answered, "Go into the city to a

certain man and tell him, 'The Teacher says: "The chosen time is near. I will have the Passover with my followers at your house." ' " [19]The followers did what Jesus told them to do, and they prepared the Passover meal.

[20]In the evening Jesus was sitting at the table with his twelve followers. [21]As they were eating, Jesus said, "I tell you the truth, one of you will turn against me."

[22]This made the followers very sad. Each one began to say to Jesus, "Surely, Lord, I am not the one who will turn against you, am I?"

[23]Jesus answered, "The man who has dipped his hand with me into the bowl is the one who will turn against me. [24]The Son of Man will die, just as the Scriptures say. But how terrible it will be for the person who hands the Son of Man over to be killed. It would be better for him if he had never been born."

[25]Then Judas, who would give Jesus to his enemies, said to Jesus, "Teacher, surely I am not the one, am I?"

Jesus answered, "Yes, it is you."

[26]While they were eating, Jesus took some bread and thanked God for it and broke it. Then he gave it to his followers and said, "Take this bread and eat it; this is my body."

[27]Then Jesus took a cup and thanked God for it and gave it to the followers. He said, "Every one of you drink this. [28]This is my blood which is the new agreement that God makes with his people. This blood is poured out for many to forgive their sins. [29]I tell you this: I will not drink of this fruit of the vine again until that day when I drink it new with you in my Father's kingdom."

[30]After singing a hymn, they went out to the Mount of Olives.

[31]Jesus told his followers, "Tonight you will all stumble in your faith on ac-count of me, because it is written in the Scriptures:

'I will kill the shepherd,
　　and the sheep will scatter.'
Zechariah 13:7

[32]But after I rise from the dead, I will go ahead of you into Galilee."

[33]Peter said, "Everyone else may stumble in their faith because of you, but I will not."

[34]Jesus said, "I tell you the truth, tonight before the rooster crows you will say three times that you don't know me."

[35]But Peter said, "I will never say that I don't know you! I will even die with you!" And all the other followers said the same thing.

[36]Then Jesus went with his followers to a place called Gethsemane. He said to them, "Sit here while I go over there and pray." [37]He took Peter and the two sons of Zebedee with him, and he began to be very sad and troubled. [38]He said to them, "My heart is full of sorrow, to the point of death. Stay here and watch with me."

[39]After walking a little farther away from them, Jesus fell to the ground and prayed, "My Father, if it is possible, do not give me this cup of suffering. But do what you want, not what I want." [40]Then Jesus went back to his followers and found them asleep. He said to Peter, "You men could not stay awake with me for one hour? [41]Stay awake and pray for strength against temptation. The spirit wants to do what is right, but the body is weak."

[42]Then Jesus went away a second time and prayed, "My Father, if it is not possible for this painful thing to be taken from me, and if I must do it, I pray that what you want will be done."

[43]Then he went back to his followers, and again he found them asleep, because their eyes were heavy. [44]So Jesus left

them and went away and prayed a third time, saying the same thing.

⁴⁵Then Jesus went back to his followers and said, "Are you still sleeping and resting? The time has come for the Son of Man to be handed over to sinful people. ⁴⁶Get up, we must go. Look, here comes the man who has turned against me."

⁴⁷While Jesus was still speaking, Judas, one of the twelve apostles, came up. With him were many people carrying swords and clubs who had been sent from the leading priests and the Jewish elders of the people. ⁴⁸Judas had planned to give them a signal, saying, "The man I kiss is Jesus. Arrest him." ⁴⁹At once Judas went to Jesus and said, "Greetings, Teacher!" and kissed him.

⁵⁰Jesus answered, "Friend, do what you came to do."

Then the people came and grabbed Jesus and arrested him. ⁵¹When that happened, one of Jesus' followers reached for his sword and pulled it out. He struck the servant of the high priest and cut off his ear.

⁵²Jesus said to the man, "Put your sword back in its place. All who use swords will be killed with swords. ⁵³Surely you know I could ask my Father, and he would give me more than twelve armies of angels. ⁵⁴But it must happen this way to bring about what the Scriptures say."

⁵⁵Then Jesus said to the crowd, "You came to get me with swords and clubs as if I were a criminal. Every day I sat in the Temple teaching, and you did not arrest me there. ⁵⁶But all these things have happened so that it will come about as the prophets wrote." Then all of Jesus' followers left him and ran away.

⁵⁷Those people who arrested Jesus led him to the house of Caiaphas, the high priest, where the teachers of the law and the elders were gathered. ⁵⁸Peter followed far behind to the courtyard of the high priest's house, and he sat down with the guards to see what would happen to Jesus.

⁵⁹The leading priests and the whole Jewish council tried to find something false against Jesus so they could kill him. ⁶⁰Many people came and told lies about him, but the council could find no real reason to kill him. Then two people came and said, ⁶¹"This man said, 'I can destroy the Temple of God and build it again in three days.'"

⁶²Then the high priest stood up and said to Jesus, "Aren't you going to answer? Don't you have something to say about their charges against you?" ⁶³But Jesus said nothing.

Again the high priest said to Jesus, "I command you by the power of the living God: Tell us if you are the Christ, the Son of God."

⁶⁴Jesus answered, "Those are your words. But I tell you, in the future you will see the Son of Man sitting at the right hand of God, the Powerful One, and coming on clouds in the sky."

⁶⁵When the high priest heard this, he tore his clothes and said, "This man has said things that are against God! We don't need any more witnesses; you all heard him say these things against God. ⁶⁶What do you think?"

The people answered, "He should die."

⁶⁷Then the people there spat in Jesus' face and beat him with their fists. Others slapped him. ⁶⁸They said, "Prove to us that you are a prophet, you Christ! Tell us who hit you!"

⁶⁹At that time, as Peter was sitting in the courtyard, a servant girl came to him and said, "You also were with Jesus of Galilee."

⁷⁰But Peter said to all the people there

that he was never with Jesus. He said, "I don't know what you are talking about."

STEP 10

[71]When he left the courtyard and was at the gate, another girl saw him. She said to the people there, "This man was with Jesus of Nazareth."

[72]Again, Peter said he was never with him, saying, "I swear I don't know this man Jesus!"

[73]A short time later, some people standing there went to Peter and said, "Surely you are one of those who followed Jesus. The way you talk shows it."

[74]Then Peter began to place a curse on himself and swear, "I don't know the man." At once, a rooster crowed. [75]And Peter remembered what Jesus had told him: "Before the rooster crows, you will say three times that you don't know me." Then Peter went outside and cried painfully.

27 Early the next morning, all the leading priests and elders of the people decided that Jesus should die. [2]They tied him, led him away, and turned him over to Pilate, the governor.

[3]Judas, the one who had given Jesus to his enemies, saw that they had decided to kill Jesus. Then he was very sorry for what he had done. So he took the thirty silver coins back to the priests and the leaders, [4]saying, "I sinned; I handed over to you an innocent man."

The leaders answered, "What is that to us? That's your problem, not ours."

[5]So Judas threw the money into the Temple. Then he went off and hanged himself.

[6]The leading priests picked up the silver coins in the Temple and said, "Our law does not allow us to keep this money with the Temple money, because it has paid for a man's death." [7]So they decided to use the coins to buy Potter's Field as a place to bury strangers who died in Jeru-

salem. [8]That is why that field is still called the Field of Blood. [9]So what Jeremiah the prophet had said came true: "They took thirty silver coins. That is how little the Israelites thought he was worth. [10]They used those thirty silver coins to buy the potter's field, as the Lord commanded me."

[11]Jesus stood before Pilate the governor, and Pilate asked him, "Are you the king of the Jews?"

Jesus answered, "Those are your words."

[12]When the leading priests and the elders accused Jesus, he said nothing.

[13]So Pilate said to Jesus, "Don't you hear them accusing you of all these things?"

[14]But Jesus said nothing in answer to Pilate, and Pilate was very surprised at this.

[15]Every year at the time of Passover the governor would free one prisoner whom the people chose. [16]At that time there was a man in prison, named Barabbas, who was known to be very bad. [17]When the people gathered at Pilate's house, Pilate said, "Whom do you want me to set free: Barabbas or Jesus who is called the Christ?" [18]Pilate knew that they turned Jesus in to him because they were jealous.

[19]While Pilate was sitting there on the judge's seat, his wife sent this message to him: "Don't do anything to that man, because he is innocent. Today I had a dream about him, and it troubled me very much."

[20]But the leading priests and elders convinced the crowd to ask for Barabbas to be freed and for Jesus to be killed. [21]Pilate said, "I have Barabbas and Jesus. Which do you want me to set free for you?"

The people answered, "Barabbas."

²²Pilate asked, "So what should I do with Jesus, the one called the Christ?"

They all answered, "Crucify him!"

²³Pilate asked, "Why? What wrong has he done?"

But they shouted louder, "Crucify him!"

²⁴When Pilate saw that he could do nothing about this and that a riot was starting, he took some water and washed his hands in front of the crowd. Then he said, "I am not guilty of this man's death. You are the ones who are causing it!"

²⁵All the people answered, "We and our children will be responsible for his death."

²⁶Then he set Barabbas free. But Jesus was beaten with whips and handed over to the soldiers to be crucified.

²⁷The governor's soldiers took Jesus into the governor's palace, and they all gathered around him. ²⁸They took off his clothes and put a red robe on him. ²⁹Using thorny branches, they made a crown, put it on his head, and put a stick in his right hand. Then the soldiers bowed before Jesus and made fun of him, saying, "Hail, King of the Jews!" ³⁰They spat on Jesus. Then they took his stick and began to beat him on the head. ³¹After they finished, the soldiers took off the robe and put his own clothes on him again. Then they led him away to be crucified.

³²As the soldiers were going out of the city with Jesus, they forced a man from Cyrene, named Simon, to carry the cross for Jesus. ³³They all came to the place called Golgotha, which means the Place of the Skull. ³⁴The soldiers gave Jesus wine mixed with gall to drink. He tasted the wine but refused to drink it. ³⁵When the soldiers had crucified him, they threw lots to decide who would get his clothes. ³⁶The soldiers sat there and continued watching him. ³⁷They put a sign above Jesus' head with a charge against him. It said: THIS IS JESUS, THE KING OF THE JEWS. ³⁸Two robbers were crucified beside Jesus, one on the right and the other on the left. ³⁹People walked by and insulted Jesus and shook their heads, ⁴⁰saying, "You said you could destroy the Temple and build it again in three days. So save yourself! Come down from that cross if you are really the Son of God!"

⁴¹The leading priests, the teachers of the law, and the Jewish elders were also making fun of Jesus. ⁴²They said, "He saved others, but he can't save himself! He says he is the king of Israel! If he is the king, let him come down now from the cross. Then we will believe in him. ⁴³He trusts in God, so let God save him now, if God really wants him. He himself said, 'I am the Son of God.' " ⁴⁴And in the same way, the robbers who were being crucified beside Jesus also insulted him.

⁴⁵At noon the whole country became dark, and the darkness lasted for three hours. ⁴⁶About three o'clock Jesus cried out in a loud voice, "Eli, Eli, lama sabachthani?" This means, "My God, my God, why have you abandoned me?"

⁴⁷Some of the people standing there who heard this said, "He is calling Elijah."

⁴⁸Quickly one of them ran and got a sponge and filled it with vinegar and tied it to a stick and gave it to Jesus to drink. ⁴⁹But the others said, "Don't bother him. We want to see if Elijah will come to save him."

⁵⁰But Jesus cried out again in a loud voice and died.

⁵¹Then the curtain in the Temple was torn into two pieces, from the top to the bottom. Also, the earth shook and rocks broke apart. ⁵²The graves opened, and many of God's people who had died were raised from the dead. ⁵³They came

out of the graves after Jesus was raised from the dead and went into the holy city, where they appeared to many people.

⁵⁴When the army officer and the soldiers guarding Jesus saw this earthquake and everything else that happened, they were very frightened and said, "He really was the Son of God!"

⁵⁵Many women who had followed Jesus from Galilee to help him were standing at a distance from the cross, watching. ⁵⁶Mary Magdalene, and Mary the mother of James and Joseph, and the mother of James and John were there.

⁵⁷That evening a rich man named Joseph, a follower of Jesus from the town of Arimathea, came to Jerusalem. ⁵⁸Joseph went to Pilate and asked to have Jesus' body. So Pilate gave orders for the soldiers to give it to Joseph. ⁵⁹Then Joseph took the body and wrapped it in a clean linen cloth. ⁶⁰He put Jesus' body in a new tomb that he had cut out of a wall of rock, and he rolled a very large stone to block the entrance of the tomb. Then Joseph went away. ⁶¹Mary Magdalene and the other woman named Mary were sitting near the tomb.

⁶²The next day, the day after Preparation Day, the leading priests and the Pharisees went to Pilate. ⁶³They said, "Sir, we remember that while that liar was still alive he said, 'After three days I will rise from the dead.' ⁶⁴So give the order for the tomb to be guarded closely till the third day. Otherwise, his followers might come and steal the body and tell people that he has risen from the dead. That lie would be even worse than the first one."

⁶⁵Pilate said, "Take some soldiers and go guard the tomb the best way you know." ⁶⁶So they all went to the tomb and made it safe from thieves by sealing the stone in the entrance and putting soldiers there to guard it.

28 The day after the Sabbath day was the first day of the week. At dawn on the first day, Mary Magdalene and another woman named Mary went to look at the tomb.

²At that time there was a strong earthquake. An angel of the Lord came down from heaven, went to the tomb, and rolled the stone away from the entrance. Then he sat on the stone. ³He was shining as bright as lightning, and his clothes were white as snow. ⁴The soldiers guarding the tomb shook with fear because of the angel, and they became like dead men.

⁵The angel said to the women, "Don't be afraid. I know that you are looking for Jesus, who has been crucified. ⁶He is not here. He has risen from the dead as he said he would. Come and see the place where his body was. ⁷And go quickly and tell his followers, 'Jesus has risen from the dead. He is going into Galilee ahead of you, and you will see him there.' " Then the angel said, "Now I have told you."

⁸The women left the tomb quickly. They were afraid, but they were also very happy. They ran to tell Jesus' followers what had happened. ⁹Suddenly, Jesus met them and said, "Greetings." The women came up to him, took hold of his feet, and worshiped him. ¹⁰Then Jesus said to them, "Don't be afraid. Go and tell my followers to go on to Galilee, and they will see me there."

¹¹While the women went to tell Jesus' followers, some of the soldiers who had been guarding the tomb went into the city to tell the leading priests everything that had happened. ¹²Then the priests met with the elders and made a plan. They paid the soldiers a large amount of money ¹³and said to them, "Tell the people that Jesus' followers came during the night and stole the body while you were

asleep. [14]If the governor hears about this, we will satisfy him and save you from trouble." [15]So the soldiers kept the money and did as they were told. And that story is still spread among the people even today.

[16]The eleven followers went to Galilee to the mountain where Jesus had told them to go. [17]On the mountain they saw Jesus and worshiped him, but some of them did not believe it was really Jesus. [18]Then Jesus came to them and said, "All power in heaven and on earth is given to me. [19]So go and make followers of all people in the world. Baptize them in the name of the Father and the Son and the Holy Spirit. [20]Teach them to obey everything that I have taught you, and I will be with you always, even until the end of this age."

MARK

Mark Tells About Jesus the Suffering Messiah

---

1 This is the beginning of the Good News about Jesus Christ, the Son of God, [2]as the prophet Isaiah wrote:

"I will send my messenger ahead of
    you,
who will prepare your way."

Malachi 3:1

[3]"This is a voice of one
    who calls out in the desert:
'Prepare the way for the Lord.
    Make the road straight for him.' "

Isaiah 40:3

[4]John was baptizing people in the desert and preaching a baptism of changed hearts and lives for the forgiveness of sins. [5]All the people from Judea and Jerusalem were going out to him. They confessed their sins and were baptized by him in the Jordan River. [6]John wore clothes made from camel's hair, had a leather belt around his waist, and ate locusts and wild honey. [7]This is what John preached to the people: "There is one coming after me who is greater than I; I am not good enough even to kneel down and untie his sandals. [8]I baptize you with water, but he will baptize you with the Holy Spirit."

[9]At that time Jesus came from the town of Nazareth in Galilee and was baptized by John in the Jordan River. [10]Immediately, as Jesus was coming up out of the water, he saw heaven open. The Holy Spirit came down on him like a dove, [11]and a voice came from heaven: "You are my Son, whom I love, and I am very pleased with you."

[12]Then the Spirit sent Jesus into the desert. [13]He was in the desert forty days and was tempted by Satan. He was with the wild animals, and the angels came and took care of him.

[14]After John was put in prison, Jesus went into Galilee, preaching the Good News from God. [15]He said, "The right time has come. The kingdom of God is near. Change your hearts and lives and believe the Good News!"

[16]When Jesus was walking by Lake Galilee, he saw Simon and his brother Andrew throwing a net into the lake because they were fishermen. [17]Jesus said to them, "Come follow me, and I will make you fish for people." [18]So Simon and Andrew immediately left their nets and followed him.

[19]Going a little farther, Jesus saw two more brothers, James and John, the sons of Zebedee. They were in a boat, mending their nets. [20]Jesus immediately called them, and they left their father in the boat with the hired workers and followed Jesus.

[21]Jesus and his followers went to Capernaum. On the Sabbath day he went to the synagogue and began to teach. [22]The people were amazed at his teaching, because he taught like a person who had authority, not like their teachers of the law. [23]Just then, a man was there in the synagogue who had an evil spirit in him. He shouted, [24]"Jesus of Nazareth! What do you want with us? Did you come to destroy us? I know who you are—God's Holy One!"

[25]Jesus commanded the evil spirit, "Be quiet! Come out of the man!" [26]The evil spirit shook the man violently, gave a loud cry, and then came out of him.

[27]The people were so amazed they asked each other, "What is happening here? This man is teaching something new, and with authority. He even gives

commands to evil spirits, and they obey him." [28]And the news about Jesus spread quickly everywhere in the area of Galilee.

[29]As soon as Jesus and his followers left the synagogue, they went with James and John to the home of Simon and Andrew. [30]Simon's mother-in-law was sick in bed with a fever, and the people told Jesus about her. [31]So Jesus went to her bed, took her hand, and helped her up. The fever left her, and she began serving them.

[32]That evening, after the sun went down, the people brought to Jesus all who were sick and had demons in them. [33]The whole town gathered at the door. [34]Jesus healed many who had different kinds of sicknesses, and he forced many demons to leave people. But he would not allow the demons to speak, because they knew who he was.

[35]Early the next morning, while it was still dark, Jesus woke and left the house. He went to a lonely place, where he prayed. [36]Simon and his friends went to look for Jesus. [37]When they found him, they said, "Everyone is looking for you!"

[38]Jesus answered, "We should go to other towns around here so I can preach there too. That is the reason I came." [39]So he went everywhere in Galilee, preaching in the synagogues and forcing out demons.

[40]A man with a skin disease came to Jesus. He fell to his knees and begged Jesus, "You can heal me if you will."

[41]Jesus felt sorry for the man, so he reached out his hand and touched him and said, "I will. Be healed!" [42]Immediately the disease left the man, and he was healed.

[43]Jesus told the man to go away at once, but he warned him strongly, [44]"Don't tell anyone about this. But go and show yourself to the priest. And offer the gift Moses commanded for people who are made well. This will show the people what I have done." [45]The man left there, but he began to tell everyone that Jesus had healed him, and so he spread the news about Jesus. As a result, Jesus could not enter a town if people saw him. He stayed in places where nobody lived, but people came to him from everywhere.

2 A few days later, when Jesus came back to Capernaum, the news spread that he was at home. [2]Many people gathered together so that there was no room in the house, not even outside the door. And Jesus was teaching them God's message. [3]Four people came, carrying a paralyzed man. [4]Since they could not get to Jesus because of the crowd, they dug a hole in the roof right above where he was speaking. When they got through, they lowered the mat with the paralyzed man on it. [5]When Jesus saw the faith of these people, he said to the paralyzed man, "Young man, your sins are forgiven."

[6]Some of the teachers of the law were sitting there, thinking to themselves, [7]"Why does this man say things like that? He is speaking as if he were God. Only God can forgive sins."

[8]Jesus knew immediately what these teachers of the law were thinking. So he said to them, "Why are you thinking these things? [9]Which is easier: to tell this paralyzed man, 'Your sins are forgiven,' or to tell him, 'Stand up. Take your mat and walk'? [10]But I will prove to you that the Son of Man has authority on earth to forgive sins." So Jesus said to the paralyzed man, [11]"I tell you, stand up, take your mat, and go home." [12]Immediately the paralyzed man stood up, took his mat, and

walked out while everyone was watching him.

The people were amazed and praised God. They said, "We have never seen anything like this!"

¹³Jesus went to the lake again. The whole crowd followed him there, and he taught them. ¹⁴While he was walking along, he saw a man named Levi son of Alphaeus, sitting in the tax collector's booth. Jesus said to him, "Follow me," and he stood up and followed Jesus.

¹⁵Later, as Jesus was having dinner at Levi's house, many tax collectors and "sinners" were eating there with Jesus and his followers. Many people like this followed Jesus. ¹⁶When the teachers of the law who were Pharisees saw Jesus eating with the tax collectors and "sinners," they asked his followers, "Why does he eat with tax collectors and sinners?"

¹⁷Jesus heard this and said to them, "It is not the healthy people who need a doctor, but the sick. I did not come to invite good people but to invite sinners."

¹⁸Now the followers of John and the Pharisees often fasted for a certain time. Some people came to Jesus and said, "Why do John's followers and the followers of the Pharisees often fast, but your followers don't?"

¹⁹Jesus answered, "The friends of the bridegroom do not fast while the bridegroom is still with them. As long as the bridegroom is with them, they cannot fast. ²⁰But the time will come when the bridegroom will be taken from them, and then they will fast.

²¹"No one sews a patch of unshrunk cloth over a hole in an old coat. Otherwise, the patch will shrink and pull away—the new patch will pull away from the old coat. Then the hole will be worse.

²²Also, no one ever pours new wine into old leather bags. Otherwise, the new wine will break the bags, and the wine will be ruined along with the bags. But new wine should be put into new leather bags."

²³One Sabbath day, as Jesus was walking through some fields of grain, his followers began to pick some grain to eat. ²⁴The Pharisees said to Jesus, "Why are your followers doing what is not lawful on the Sabbath day?"

²⁵Jesus answered, "Have you never read what David did when he and those with him were hungry and needed food? ²⁶During the time of Abiathar the high priest, David went into God's house and ate the holy bread, which is lawful only for priests to eat. And David also gave some of the bread to those who were with him."

²⁷Then Jesus said to the Pharisees, "The Sabbath day was made to help people; they were not made to be ruled by the Sabbath day. ²⁸So then, the Son of Man is Lord even of the Sabbath day."

3 Another time when Jesus went into a synagogue, a man with a crippled hand was there. ²Some people watched Jesus closely to see if he would heal the man on the Sabbath day so they could accuse him.

³Jesus said to the man with the crippled hand, "Stand up here in the middle of everyone."

⁴Then Jesus asked the people, "Which is lawful on the Sabbath day: to do good or to do evil, to save a life or to kill?" But they said nothing to answer him.

⁵Jesus was angry as he looked at the people, and he felt very sad because they were stubborn. Then he said to the man, "Hold out your hand." The man held out his hand and it was healed. ⁶Then the Pharisees left and began making plans

with the Herodians about a way to kill Jesus.

[7]Jesus left with his followers for the lake, and a large crowd from Galilee followed him. [8]Also many people came from Judea, from Jerusalem, from Idumea, from the lands across the Jordan River, and from the area of Tyre and Sidon. When they heard what Jesus was doing, many people came to him. [9]When Jesus saw the crowds, he told his followers to get a boat ready for him to keep people from crowding against him. [10]He had healed many people, so all the sick were pushing toward him to touch him. [11]When evil spirits saw Jesus, they fell down before him and shouted, "You are the Son of God!" [12]But Jesus strongly warned them not to tell who he was.

[13]Then Jesus went up on a mountain and called to him those he wanted, and they came to him. [14]Jesus chose twelve and called them apostles. He wanted them to be with him, and he wanted to send them out to preach [15]and to have the authority to force demons out of people. [16]These are the twelve men he chose: Simon (Jesus named him Peter), [17]James and John, the sons of Zebedee (Jesus named them Boanerges, which means "Sons of Thunder"), [18]Andrew, Philip, Bartholomew, Matthew, Thomas, James the son of Alphaeus, Thaddaeus, Simon the Zealot, [19]and Judas Iscariot, who later turned against Jesus.

[20]Then Jesus went home, but again a crowd gathered. There were so many people that Jesus and his followers could not eat. [21]When his family heard this, they went to get him because they thought he was out of his mind. [22]But the teachers of the law from Jerusalem were saying, "Beelzebul is living inside him! He uses power from the ruler of demons to force demons out of people."

[23]So Jesus called the people together and taught them with stories. He said, "Satan will not force himself out of people. [24]A kingdom that is divided cannot continue, [25]and a family that is divided cannot continue. [26]And if Satan is against himself and fights against his own people, he cannot continue; that is the end of Satan. [27]No one can enter a strong person's house and steal his things unless he first ties up the strong person. Then he can steal things from the house. [28]I tell you the truth, all sins that people do and all the things people say against God can be forgiven. [29]But anyone who speaks against the Holy Spirit will never be forgiven; he is guilty of a sin that continues forever."

[30]Jesus said this because the teachers of the law said that he had an evil spirit inside him.

[31]Then Jesus' mother and brothers arrived. Standing outside, they sent someone in to tell him to come out. [32]Many people were sitting around Jesus, and they said to him, "Your mother and brothers are waiting for you outside."

[33]Jesus asked, "Who are my mother and my brothers?" [34]Then he looked at those sitting around him and said, "Here are my mother and my brothers! [35]My true brother and sister and mother are those who do what God wants."

4 Again Jesus began teaching by the lake. A great crowd gathered around him, so he sat down in a boat near the shore. All the people stayed on the shore close to the water. [2]Jesus taught them many things, using stories. He said, [3]"Listen! A farmer went out to plant his seed. [4]While he was planting, some seed fell by the road, and the birds came and ate it up. [5]Some seed fell on rocky ground where there wasn't much

dirt. That seed grew very fast, because the ground was not deep. [6]But when the sun rose, the plants dried up because they did not have deep roots. [7]Some other seed fell among thorny weeds, which grew and choked the good plants. So those plants did not produce a crop. [8]Some other seed fell on good ground and began to grow. It got taller and produced a crop. Some plants made thirty times more, some made sixty times more, and some made a hundred times more."

[9]Then Jesus said, "Let those with ears use them and listen!"

[10]Later, when Jesus was alone, the twelve apostles and others around him asked him about the stories.

[11]Jesus said, "You can know the secret about the kingdom of God. But to other people I tell everything by using stories [12]so that:

'They will look and look, but they will
        not learn.
    They will listen and listen, but they
        will not understand.
If they did learn and understand,
    they would come back to me and
        be forgiven.' "   *Isaiah 6:9–10*

[13]Then Jesus said to his followers, "Don't you understand this story? If you don't, how will you understand any story? [14]The farmer is like a person who plants God's message in people. [15]Sometimes the teaching falls on the road. This is like the people who hear the teaching of God, but Satan quickly comes and takes away the teaching that was planted in them. [16]Others are like the seed planted on rocky ground. They hear the teaching and quickly accept it with joy. [17]But since they don't allow the teaching to go deep into their lives, they keep it only a short time. When trouble or persecution comes because of the teaching they accepted,

they quickly give up. [18]Others are like the seed planted among the thorny weeds. They hear the teaching, [19]but the worries of this life, the temptation of wealth, and many other evil desires keep the teaching from growing and producing fruit in their lives. [20]Others are like the seed planted in the good ground. They hear the teaching and accept it. Then they grow and produce fruit—sometimes thirty times more, sometimes sixty times more, and sometimes a hundred times more."

[21]Then Jesus said to them, "Do you hide a lamp under a bowl or under a bed? No! You put the lamp on a lampstand. [22]Everything that is hidden will be made clear and every secret thing will be made known. [23]Let those with ears use them and listen!

[24]"Think carefully about what you hear. The way you give to others is the way God will give to you, but God will give you even more. [25]Those who have understanding will be given more. But those who do not have understanding, even what they have will be taken away from them."

[26]Then Jesus said, "The kingdom of God is like someone who plants seed in the ground. [27]Night and day, whether the person is asleep or awake, the seed still grows, but the person does not know how it grows. [28]By itself the earth produces grain. First the plant grows, then the head, and then all the grain in the head. [29]When the grain is ready, the farmer cuts it, because this is the harvest time."

[30]Then Jesus said, "How can I show you what the kingdom of God is like? What story can I use to explain it? [31]The kingdom of God is like a mustard seed, the smallest seed you plant in the ground. [32]But when planted, this seed

grows and becomes the largest of all garden plants. It produces large branches, and the wild birds can make nests in its shade."

³³Jesus used many stories like these to teach the crowd God's message—as much as they could understand. ³⁴He always used stories to teach them. But when he and his followers were alone, Jesus explained everything to them.

STEP 1

³⁵That evening, Jesus said to his followers, "Let's go across the lake." ³⁶Leaving the crowd behind, they took him in the boat just as he was. There were also other boats with them. ³⁷A very strong wind came up on the lake. The waves came over the sides and into the boat so that it was already full of water. ³⁸Jesus was at the back of the boat, sleeping with his head on a cushion. His followers woke him and said, "Teacher, don't you care that we are drowning!"

³⁹Jesus stood up and commanded the wind and said to the waves, "Quiet! Be still!" Then the wind stopped, and it became completely calm.

⁴⁰Jesus said to his followers, "Why are you afraid? Do you still have no faith?"

⁴¹The followers were very afraid and asked each other, "Who is this? Even the wind and the waves obey him!"

5 Jesus and his followers went to the other side of the lake to the area of the Gerasene people. ²When Jesus got out of the boat, instantly a man with an evil spirit came to him from the burial caves. ³This man lived in the caves, and no one could tie him up, not even with a chain. ⁴Many times people had used chains to tie the man's hands and feet, but he always broke them off. No one was strong enough to control him. ⁵Day and night he would wander around the burial caves and on the hills, screaming and cutting himself with stones. ⁶While Jesus was still

far away, the man saw him, ran to him, and fell down before him.

⁷The man shouted in a loud voice, "What do you want with me, Jesus, Son of the Most High God? I command you in God's name not to torture me!" ⁸He said this because Jesus was saying to him, "You evil spirit, come out of the man."

⁹Then Jesus asked him, "What is your name?"

He answered, "My name is Legion, because we are many spirits." ¹⁰He begged Jesus again and again not to send them out of that area.

¹¹A large herd of pigs was feeding on a hill near there. ¹²The demons begged Jesus, "Send us into the pigs; let us go into them." ¹³So Jesus allowed them to do this. The evil spirits left the man and went into the pigs. Then the herd of pigs—about two thousand of them—rushed down the hill into the lake and were drowned.

¹⁴The herdsmen ran away and went to the town and to the countryside, telling everyone about this. So people went out to see what had happened. ¹⁵They came to Jesus and saw the man who used to have the many evil spirits, sitting, clothed, and in his right mind. And they were frightened. ¹⁶The people who saw this told the others what had happened to the man who had the demons living in him, and they told about the pigs. ¹⁷Then the people began to beg Jesus to leave their area.

¹⁸As Jesus was getting back into the boat, the man who was freed from the demons begged to go with him.

STEP 12

¹⁹But Jesus would not let him. He said, "Go home to your family and tell them how much the Lord has done for you and how he has had mercy on you." ²⁰So the man left and began to tell the people in

STEP 12

Having had a spiritual awakening as the
result of these steps, we tried to carry
this message to others, and to practice
these principles in all our affairs.

Mark 5:18–20

After the demon-possessed man had been healed by Jesus, he
wanted to stay with Jesus as one of his followers. After all, if he
stayed with Jesus, he'd always be near the source of his healing.
However, Jesus sent the man back to his family and community so
he could tell everybody how he had been made well.

Recovery groups like to say, "You have to give it away to keep it."
Step 12 is one of the maintenance steps of your recovery. One of
the ways you keep your recovery on track is by sharing with other
addicts how you got to the place where you are in your healing.

How do you share the message? First, tell the story of your
recovery through your new lifestyle, free of the destructive
behaviors of your past. Second, share your life story and recovery
experiences in support groups and one-on-one conversations.
Finally, be willing to confront other addicts trapped in denial about
their own dependencies. Sometimes that's the only way you can
carry out Jesus' instruction to tell others what great things God has
done for you.

FOR YOUR NEXT **STEP 12** MEDITATION, TURN TO **PAGE 237.** ▶▶

the Ten Towns about what Jesus had done for him. And everyone was amazed.

²¹When Jesus went in the boat back to the other side of the lake, a large crowd gathered around him there. ²²A leader of the synagogue, named Jairus, came there, saw Jesus, and fell at his feet. ²³He begged Jesus, saying again and again, "My daughter is dying. Please come and put your hands on her so she will be healed and will live." ²⁴So Jesus went with him.

A large crowd followed Jesus and pushed very close around him. ²⁵Among them was a woman who had been bleeding for twelve years. ²⁶She had suffered very much from many doctors and had spent all the money she had, but instead of improving, she was getting worse. ²⁷When the woman heard about Jesus, she came up behind him in the crowd and touched his coat. ²⁸She thought, "If I can just touch his clothes, I will be healed." ²⁹Instantly her bleeding stopped, and she felt in her body that she was healed from her disease.

³⁰At once Jesus felt power go out from him. So he turned around in the crowd and asked, "Who touched my clothes?"

³¹His followers said, "Look at how many people are pushing against you! And you ask, 'Who touched me?' "

³²But Jesus continued looking around to see who had touched him. ³³The woman, knowing that she was healed, came and fell at Jesus' feet. Shaking with fear, she told him the whole truth. ³⁴Jesus said to her, "Dear woman, you are made well because you believed. Go in peace; be healed of your disease."

³⁵While Jesus was still speaking, some people came from the house of the synagogue leader. They said, "Your daughter is dead. There is no need to bother the teacher anymore."

³⁶But Jesus paid no attention to what they said. He told the synagogue leader, "Don't be afraid; just believe."

³⁷Jesus let only Peter, James, and John the brother of James go with him. ³⁸When they came to the house of the synagogue leader, Jesus found many people there making lots of noise and crying loudly. ³⁹Jesus entered the house and said to them, "Why are you crying and making so much noise? The child is not dead, only asleep." ⁴⁰But they laughed at him. So, after throwing them out of the house, Jesus took the child's father and mother and his three followers into the room where the child was. ⁴¹Taking hold of the girl's hand, he said to her, "Talitha, koum!" (This means, "Young girl, I tell you to stand up!") ⁴²At once the girl stood right up and began walking. (She was twelve years old.) Everyone was completely amazed. ⁴³Jesus gave them strict orders not to tell people about this. Then he told them to give the girl something to eat.

6 Jesus left there and went to his hometown, and his followers went with him. ²On the Sabbath day he taught in the synagogue. Many people heard him and were amazed, saying, "Where did this man get these teachings? What is this wisdom that has been given to him? And where did he get the power to do miracles? ³He is just the carpenter, the son of Mary and the brother of James, Joseph, Judas, and Simon. And his sisters are here with us." So the people were upset with Jesus.

⁴Jesus said to them, "A prophet is honored everywhere except in his hometown and with his own people and in his own home." ⁵So Jesus was not able to work any miracles there except to heal a few sick people by putting his hands on them. ⁶He was amazed at how many people had no faith.

STEP 2

Then Jesus went to other villages in that area and taught. [7]He called his twelve followers together and got ready to send them out two by two and gave them authority over evil spirits. [8]This is what Jesus commanded them: "Take nothing for your trip except a walking stick. Take no bread, no bag, and no money in your pockets. [9]Wear sandals, but take only the clothes you are wearing. [10]When you enter a house, stay there until you leave that town. [11]If the people in a certain place refuse to welcome you or listen to you, leave that place. Shake its dust off your feet as a warning to them."

[12]So the followers went out and preached that people should change their hearts and lives. [13]They forced many demons out and put olive oil on many sick people and healed them.

[14]King Herod heard about Jesus, because he was now well known. Some people said, "He is John the Baptist, who has risen from the dead. That is why he can work these miracles."

[15]Others said, "He is Elijah."

Other people said, "Jesus is a prophet, like the prophets who lived long ago."

[16]When Herod heard this, he said, "I killed John by cutting off his head. Now he has risen from the dead!"

[17]Herod himself had ordered his soldiers to arrest John and put him in prison in order to please his wife, Herodias. She had been the wife of Philip, Herod's brother, but then Herod had married her. [18]John had been telling Herod, "It is not lawful for you to be married to your brother's wife." [19]So Herodias hated John and wanted to kill him. But she couldn't, [20]because Herod was afraid of John and protected him. He knew John was a good and holy man. Also, though John's preaching always bothered him, he enjoyed listening to John.

[21]Then the perfect time came for Herodias to cause John's death. On Herod's birthday, he gave a dinner party for the most important government leaders, the commanders of his army, and the most important people in Galilee. [22]When the daughter of Herodias came in and danced, she pleased Herod and the people eating with him.

So King Herod said to the girl, "Ask me for anything you want, and I will give it to you." [23]He promised her, "Anything you ask for I will give to you—up to half of my kingdom."

[24]The girl went to her mother and asked, "What should I ask for?"

Her mother answered, "Ask for the head of John the Baptist."

[25]At once the girl went back to the king and said to him, "I want the head of John the Baptist right now on a platter."

[26]Although the king was very sad, he had made a promise, and his dinner guests had heard it. So he did not want to refuse what she asked. [27]Immediately the king sent a soldier to bring John's head. The soldier went and cut off John's head in the prison [28]and brought it back on a platter. He gave it to the girl, and the girl gave it to her mother. [29]When John's followers heard this, they came and got John's body and put it in a tomb.

[30]The apostles gathered around Jesus and told him about all the things they had done and taught. [31]Crowds of people were coming and going so that Jesus and his followers did not even have time to eat. He said to them, "Come away by yourselves, and we will go to a lonely place to get some rest."

[32]So they went in a boat by themselves to a lonely place. [33]But many people saw them leave and recognized them. So from all the towns they ran to the place where Jesus was going, and they got

there before him. ³⁴When he arrived, he saw a great crowd waiting. He felt sorry for them, because they were like sheep without a shepherd. So he began to teach them many things.

³⁵When it was late in the day, his followers came to him and said, "No one lives in this place, and it is already very late. ³⁶Send the people away so they can go to the countryside and towns around here to buy themselves something to eat."

³⁷But Jesus answered, "You give them something to eat."

They said to him, "We would all have to work a month to earn enough money to buy that much bread!"

³⁸Jesus asked them, "How many loaves of bread do you have? Go and see."

When they found out, they said, "Five loaves and two fish."

³⁹Then Jesus told his followers to have the people sit in groups on the green grass. ⁴⁰So they sat in groups of fifty or a hundred. ⁴¹Jesus took the five loaves and two fish and, looking up to heaven, he thanked God for the food. He divided the bread and gave it to his followers for them to give it to the people. Then he divided the two fish among them all. ⁴²All the people ate and were satisfied. ⁴³The followers filled twelve baskets with the leftover pieces of bread and fish. ⁴⁴There were five thousand men who ate.

⁴⁵Immediately Jesus told his followers to get into the boat and go ahead of him to Bethsaida across the lake. He stayed there to send the people home. ⁴⁶After sending them away, he went into the hills to pray.

⁴⁷That night, the boat was in the middle of the lake, and Jesus was alone on the land. ⁴⁸He saw his followers struggling hard to row the boat, because the wind was blowing against them. Between three

and six o'clock in the morning, Jesus came to them, walking on the water, and he wanted to walk past the boat. ⁴⁹But when they saw him walking on the water, they thought he was a ghost and cried out. ⁵⁰They all saw him and were afraid. But quickly Jesus spoke to them and said, "Have courage! It is I. Do not be afraid." ⁵¹Then he got into the boat with them, and the wind became calm. The followers were greatly amazed. ⁵²They did not understand about the miracle of the five loaves, because their minds were closed.

⁵³When they had crossed the lake, they came to shore at Gennesaret and tied the boat there. ⁵⁴When they got out of the boat, people immediately recognized Jesus. ⁵⁵They ran everywhere in that area and began to bring sick people on mats wherever they heard he was. ⁵⁶And everywhere he went—into towns, cities, or countryside—the people brought the sick to the marketplaces. They begged him to let them touch just the edge of his coat, and all who touched it were healed.

7 When some Pharisees and some teachers of the law came from Jerusalem, they gathered around Jesus. ²They saw that some of Jesus' followers ate food with hands that were not clean, that is, they hadn't washed them. ³(The Pharisees and all the Jews never eat before washing their hands in the way required by their unwritten laws. ⁴And when they buy something in the market, they never eat it until they wash themselves in a special way. They also follow many other unwritten laws, such as the washing of cups, pitchers, and pots.)

⁵The Pharisees and the teachers of the law said to Jesus, "Why don't your followers obey the unwritten laws which have been handed down to us? Why do your followers eat their food with hands that are not clean?"

⁶Jesus answered, "Isaiah was right when he spoke about you hypocrites. He wrote,

'These people show honor to me with words,
but their hearts are far from me.
⁷Their worship of me is worthless.
The things they teach are nothing but human rules.'

Isaiah 29:13

⁸You have stopped following the commands of God, and you follow only human teachings."

⁹Then Jesus said to them, "You cleverly ignore the commands of God so you can follow your own teachings. ¹⁰Moses said, 'Honor your father and your mother,' and 'Anyone who says cruel things to his father or mother must be put to death.' ¹¹But you say a person can tell his father or mother, 'I have something I could use to help you, but it is Corban—a gift to God.' ¹²You no longer let that person use that money for his father or his mother. ¹³By your own rules, which you teach people, you are rejecting what God said. And you do many things like that."

¹⁴After Jesus called the crowd to him again, he said, "Every person should listen to me and understand what I am saying. ¹⁵There is nothing people put into their bodies that makes them unclean. People are made unclean by the things that come out of them. [¹⁶Let those with ears use them and listen.]"

¹⁷When Jesus left the people and went into the house, his followers asked him about this story. ¹⁸Jesus said, "Do you still not understand? Surely you know that nothing that enters someone from the outside can make that person unclean. ¹⁹It does not go into the mind, but into the stomach. Then it goes out of the body." (When Jesus said this, he meant that no longer was any food unclean for people to eat.)

²⁰And Jesus said, "The things that come out of people are the things that make them unclean. ²¹All these evil things begin inside people, in the mind: evil thoughts, sexual sins, stealing, murder, adultery, ²²greed, evil actions, lying, doing sinful things, jealousy, speaking evil of others, pride, and foolish living. ²³All these evil things come from inside and make people unclean."

²⁴Jesus left that place and went to the area around Tyre. When he went into a house, he did not want anyone to know he was there, but he could not stay hidden. ²⁵A woman whose daughter had an evil spirit in her heard that he was there. So she quickly came to Jesus and fell at his feet. ²⁶She was Greek, born in Phoenicia, in Syria. She begged Jesus to force the demon out of her daughter.

²⁷Jesus told the woman, "It is not right to take the children's bread and give it to the dogs. First let the children eat all they want."

²⁸But she answered, "Yes, Lord, but even the dogs under the table can eat the children's crumbs."

²⁹Then Jesus said, "Because of your answer, you may go. The demon has left your daughter."

³⁰The woman went home and found her daughter lying in bed; the demon was gone.

³¹Then Jesus left the area around Tyre and went through Sidon to Lake Galilee, to the area of the Ten Towns. ³²While he was there, some people brought a man to him who was deaf and could not talk plainly. The people begged Jesus to put his hand on the man to heal him.

³³Jesus led the man away from the crowd, by himself. He put his fingers in the man's ears and then spit and touched

the man's tongue. ³⁴Looking up to heaven, he sighed and said to the man, "Ephphatha!" (This means, "Be opened.") ³⁵Instantly the man was able to hear and to use his tongue so that he spoke clearly.

³⁶Jesus commanded the people not to tell anyone about what happened. But the more he commanded them, the more they told about it. ³⁷They were completely amazed and said, "Jesus does everything well. He makes the deaf hear! And those who can't talk he makes able to speak."

8 Another time there was a great crowd with Jesus that had nothing to eat. So Jesus called his followers and said, ²"I feel sorry for these people, because they have already been with me for three days, and they have nothing to eat. ³If I send them home hungry, they will faint on the way. Some of them live a long way from here."

⁴Jesus' followers answered, "How can we get enough bread to feed all these people? We are far away from any town."

⁵Jesus asked, "How many loaves of bread do you have?"

They answered, "Seven."

⁶Jesus told the people to sit on the ground. Then he took the seven loaves, gave thanks to God, and divided the bread. He gave the pieces to his followers to give to the people, and they did so. ⁷The followers also had a few small fish. After Jesus gave thanks for the fish, he told his followers to give them to the people also. ⁸All the people ate and were satisfied. Then his followers filled seven baskets with the leftover pieces of food. ⁹There were about four thousand people who ate. After they had eaten, Jesus sent them home. ¹⁰Then right away he got into a boat with his followers and went to the area of Dalmanutha.

¹¹The Pharisees came to Jesus and began to ask him questions. Hoping to trap him, they asked Jesus for a miracle from God. ¹²Jesus sighed deeply and said, "Why do you people ask for a miracle as a sign? I tell you the truth, no sign will be given to you." ¹³Then Jesus left the Pharisees and went in the boat to the other side of the lake.

¹⁴His followers had only one loaf of bread with them in the boat; they had forgotten to bring more. ¹⁵Jesus warned them, "Be careful! Beware of the yeast of the Pharisees and the yeast of Herod."

¹⁶His followers discussed the meaning of this, saying, "He said this because we have no bread."

¹⁷Knowing what they were talking about, Jesus asked them, "Why are you talking about not having bread? Do you still not see or understand? Are your minds closed? ¹⁸You have eyes, but you don't really see. You have ears, but you don't really listen. Remember when ¹⁹I divided five loaves of bread for the five thousand? How many baskets did you fill with leftover pieces of food?"

They answered, "Twelve."

²⁰"And when I divided seven loaves of bread for the four thousand, how many baskets did you fill with leftover pieces of food?"

They answered, "Seven."

²¹Then Jesus said to them, "Don't you understand yet?"

²²Jesus and his followers came to Bethsaida. There some people brought a blind man to Jesus and begged him to touch the man. ²³So Jesus took the blind man's hand and led him out of the village. Then he spit on the man's eyes and put his hands on the man and asked, "Can you see now?"

²⁴The man looked up and said, "Yes, I see people, but they look like trees walking around."

²⁵Again Jesus put his hands on the man's eyes. Then the man opened his

eyes wide and they were healed, and he was able to see everything clearly. 26Jesus told him to go home, saying, "Don't go into the town."

27Jesus and his followers went to the towns around Caesarea Philippi. While they were traveling, Jesus asked them, "Who do people say I am?"

28They answered, "Some say you are John the Baptist. Others say you are Elijah, and others say you are one of the prophets."

29Then Jesus asked, "But who do you say I am?"

Peter answered, "You are the Christ."

30Jesus warned his followers not to tell anyone who he was.

31Then Jesus began to teach them that the Son of Man must suffer many things and that he would be rejected by the Jewish elders, the leading priests, and the teachers of the law. He told them that the Son of Man must be killed and then rise from the dead after three days. 32Jesus told them plainly what would happen. Then Peter took Jesus aside and began to tell him not to talk like that. 33But Jesus turned and looked at his followers. Then he told Peter not to talk that way. He said, "Go away from me, Satan! You don't care about the things of God, but only about things people think are important."

34Then Jesus called the crowd to him, along with his followers. He said, "If people want to follow me, they must give up the things they want. They must be willing even to give up their lives to follow me. 35Those who want to save their lives will give up true life. But those who give up their lives for me and for the Good News will have true life. 36It is worthless to have the whole world if they lose their souls. 37They could never pay enough to buy back their souls. 38The people who

live now are living in a sinful and evil time. If people are ashamed of me and my teaching, the Son of Man will be ashamed of them when he comes with his Father's glory and with the holy angels."

9 Then Jesus said to the people, "I tell you the truth, some people standing here will see the kingdom of God come with power before they die."

2Six days later, Jesus took Peter, James, and John up on a high mountain by themselves. While they watched, Jesus' appearance was changed. 3His clothes became shining white, whiter than any person could make them. 4Then Elijah and Moses appeared to them, talking with Jesus.

5Peter said to Jesus, "Teacher, it is good that we are here. Let us make three tents—one for you, one for Moses, and one for Elijah." 6Peter did not know what to say, because he and the others were so frightened.

7Then a cloud came and covered them, and a voice came from the cloud, saying, "This is my Son, whom I love. Listen to him!"

8Suddenly Peter, James, and John looked around, but they saw only Jesus there alone with them.

9As they were coming down the mountain, Jesus commanded them not to tell anyone about what they had seen until the Son of Man had risen from the dead. 10So the followers obeyed Jesus, but they discussed what he meant about rising from the dead.

11Then they asked Jesus, "Why do the teachers of the law say that Elijah must come first?"

12Jesus answered, "They are right to say that Elijah must come first and make everything the way it should be. But why does the Scripture say that the Son of

Man will suffer much and that people will treat him as if he were nothing? [13]I tell you that Elijah has already come. And people did to him whatever they wanted to do, just as the Scriptures said it would happen."

[14]When Jesus, Peter, James, and John came back to the other followers, they saw a great crowd around them and the teachers of the law arguing with them. [15]But as soon as the crowd saw Jesus, the people were surprised and ran to welcome him.

[16]Jesus asked, "What are you arguing about?"

[17]A man answered, "Teacher, I brought my son to you. He has an evil spirit in him that stops him from talking. [18]When the spirit attacks him, it throws him on the ground. Then my son foams at the mouth, grinds his teeth, and becomes very stiff. I asked your followers to force the evil spirit out, but they couldn't."

[19]Jesus answered, "You people have no faith. How long must I stay with you? How long must I put up with you? Bring the boy to me."

[20]So the followers brought him to Jesus. As soon as the evil spirit saw Jesus, it made the boy lose control of himself, and he fell down and rolled on the ground, foaming at the mouth.

[21]Jesus asked the boy's father, "How long has this been happening?"

The father answered, "Since he was very young. [22]The spirit often throws him into a fire or into water to kill him. If you can do anything for him, please have pity on us and help us."

STEP 2
[23]Jesus said to the father, "You said, 'If you can!' All things are possible for the one who believes."

[24]Immediately the father cried out, "I do believe! Help me to believe more!"

[25]When Jesus saw that a crowd was quickly gathering, he ordered the evil spirit, saying, "You spirit that makes people unable to hear or speak, I command you to come out of this boy and never enter him again!"

[26]The evil spirit screamed and caused the boy to fall on the ground again. Then the spirit came out. The boy looked as if he were dead, and many people said, "He is dead!" [27]But Jesus took hold of the boy's hand and helped him to stand up.

[28]When Jesus went into the house, his followers began asking him privately, "Why couldn't we force that evil spirit out?"

[29]Jesus answered, "That kind of spirit can only be forced out by prayer."

[30]Then Jesus and his followers left that place and went through Galilee. He didn't want anyone to know where he was, [31]because he was teaching his followers. He said to them, "The Son of Man will be handed over to people, and they will kill him. After three days, he will rise from the dead." [32]But the followers did not understand what Jesus meant, and they were afraid to ask him.

[33]Jesus and his followers went to Capernaum. When they went into a house there, he asked them, "What were you arguing about on the road?" [34]But the followers did not answer, because their argument on the road was about which one of them was the greatest.

[35]Jesus sat down and called the twelve apostles to him. He said, "Whoever wants to be the most important must be last of all and servant of all."

[36]Then Jesus took a small child and had him stand among them. Taking the child in his arms, he said, [37]"Whoever accepts a child like this in my name accepts me. And whoever accepts me accepts the One who sent me."

[38]Then John said, "Teacher, we saw

STEP 2

Came to believe that a Power greater than
ourselves could restore us to sanity.

Mark 9:23–24

Once you've been held captive by addictive behaviors for any
length of time, it's hard to believe you will ever be free of them.
You need to hear and believe the words of Luke 1:37 deep in your
heart: "God can do anything!"

A frightened and doubting father discovered the truth of these
words when he brought his demon-possessed son to Jesus for
healing. His hope was nearly gone, but he begged, "If you can do
anything for him, please have pity on us and help us" (Mark 9:22).

Jesus didn't criticize this father for his lack of impressive faith.
Instead, he appealed to the faith the man did have. Only faith can
call on God to do what is humanly impossible. The father's
response probably echoes the cry of your heart, "I do believe! Help
me to believe more!" He declared his faith, even as he admitted his
weakness.

If you truly want to believe in God's great power to deliver you, he
will help you. He will help you get rid of doubt and break your
addictions through growing, active trust in him.

FOR YOUR NEXT **STEP 2** MEDITATION, TURN TO **PAGE 106**. ▶▶

someone using your name to force demons out of a person. We told him to stop, because he does not belong to our group."

³⁹But Jesus said, "Don't stop him, because anyone who uses my name to do powerful things will not easily say evil things about me. ⁴⁰Whoever is not against us is with us. ⁴¹I tell you the truth, whoever gives you a drink of water because you belong to the Christ will truly get his reward.

⁴²"If one of these little children believes in me, and someone causes that child to sin, it would be better for that person to have a large stone tied around his neck and be drowned in the sea. ⁴³If your hand causes you to sin, cut it off. It is better for you to lose part of your body and live forever than to have two hands and go to hell, where the fire never goes out. [⁴⁴In hell the worm does not die; the fire is never put out.] ⁴⁵If your foot causes you to sin, cut it off. It is better for you to lose part of your body and to live forever than to have two feet and be thrown into hell. [⁴⁶In hell the worm does not die; the fire is never put out.] ⁴⁷If your eye causes you to sin, take it out. It is better for you to enter the kingdom of God with only one eye than to have two eyes and be thrown into hell. ⁴⁸In hell the worm does not die; the fire is never put out. ⁴⁹Every person will be salted with fire.

⁵⁰"Salt is good, but if the salt loses its salty taste, you cannot make it salty again. So, be full of salt, and have peace with each other."

10 Then Jesus left that place and went into the area of Judea and across the Jordan River. Again, crowds came to him, and he taught them as he usually did.

²Some Pharisees came to Jesus and tried to trick him. They asked, "Is it right for a man to divorce his wife?"

³Jesus answered, "What did Moses command you to do?"

⁴They said, "Moses allowed a man to write out divorce papers and send her away."

⁵Jesus said, "Moses wrote that command for you because you were stubborn. ⁶But when God made the world, 'he made them male and female.' ⁷'So a man will leave his father and mother and be united with his wife, ⁸and the two will become one body.' So there are not two, but one. ⁹God has joined the two together, so no one should separate them."

¹⁰Later, in the house, his followers asked Jesus again about the question of divorce. ¹¹He answered, "Anyone who divorces his wife and marries another woman is guilty of adultery against her. ¹²And the woman who divorces her husband and marries another man is also guilty of adultery."

¹³Some people brought their little children to Jesus so he could touch them, but his followers told them to stop. ¹⁴When Jesus saw this, he was upset and said to them, "Let the little children come to me. Don't stop them, because the kingdom of God belongs to people who are like these children. ¹⁵I tell you the truth, you must accept the kingdom of God as if you were a little child, or you will never enter it." ¹⁶Then Jesus took the children in his arms, put his hands on them, and blessed them.

¹⁷As Jesus started to leave, a man ran to him and fell on his knees before Jesus. The man asked, "Good teacher, what must I do to have life forever?"

¹⁸Jesus answered, "Why do you call me good? Only God is good. ¹⁹You know the commands: 'You must not murder

anyone. You must not be guilty of adultery. You must not steal. You must not tell lies about your neighbor. You must not cheat. Honor your father and mother.' "

²⁰The man said, "Teacher, I have obeyed all these things since I was a boy."

²¹Jesus, looking at the man, loved him and said, "There is one more thing you need to do. Go and sell everything you have, and give the money to the poor, and you will have treasure in heaven. Then come and follow me."

²²He was very sad to hear Jesus say this, and he left sorrowfully, because he was rich.

²³Then Jesus looked at his followers and said, "How hard it will be for the rich to enter the kingdom of God!"

²⁴The followers were amazed at what Jesus said. But he said again, "My children, it is very hard to enter the kingdom of God! ²⁵It is easier for a camel to go through the eye of a needle than for a rich person to enter the kingdom of God."

²⁶The followers were even more surprised and said to each other, "Then who can be saved?"

²⁷Jesus looked at them and said, "For people this is impossible, but for God all things are possible."

²⁸Peter said to Jesus, "Look, we have left everything and followed you."

²⁹Jesus said, "I tell you the truth, all those who have left houses, brothers, sisters, mother, father, children, or farms for me and for the Good News ³⁰will get more than they left. Here in this world they will have a hundred times more homes, brothers, sisters, mothers, children, and fields. And with those things, they will also suffer for their belief. But in this age they will have life forever. ³¹Many who are first now will be last in the future. And many who are last now will be first in the future."

³²As Jesus and the people with him were on the road to Jerusalem, he was leading the way. His followers were amazed, but others in the crowd who followed were afraid. Again Jesus took the twelve apostles aside and began to tell them what was about to happen in Jerusalem. ³³He said, "Look, we are going to Jerusalem. The Son of Man will be turned over to the leading priests and the teachers of the law. They will say that he must die, and they will turn him over to the non-Jewish people, ³⁴who will laugh at him and spit on him. They will beat him with whips and crucify him. But on the third day, he will rise to life again."

³⁵Then James and John, sons of Zebedee, came to Jesus and said, "Teacher, we want to ask you to do something for us."

³⁶Jesus asked, "What do you want me to do for you?"

³⁷They answered, "Let one of us sit at your right side and one of us sit at your left side in your glory in your kingdom."

³⁸Jesus said, "You don't understand what you are asking. Can you drink the cup that I must drink? And can you be baptized with the same kind of baptism that I must go through?"

³⁹They answered, "Yes, we can."

Jesus said to them, "You will drink the same cup that I will drink, and you will be baptized with the same baptism that I must go through. ⁴⁰But I cannot choose who will sit at my right or my left; those places belong to those for whom they have been prepared."

⁴¹When the other ten followers heard this, they began to be angry with James and John.

⁴²Jesus called them together and said, "The other nations have rulers. You know that those rulers love to show their power over the people, and their important lead-

ers love to use all their authority. [43]But it should not be that way among you. Whoever wants to become great among you must serve the rest of you like a servant. [44]Whoever wants to become the first among you must serve all of you like a slave. [45]In the same way, the Son of Man did not come to be served. He came to serve others and to give his life as a ransom for many people."

[46]Then they came to the town of Jericho. As Jesus was leaving there with his followers and a great many people, a blind beggar named Bartimaeus son of Timaeus was sitting by the road. [47]When he heard that Jesus from Nazareth was walking by, he began to shout, "Jesus, Son of David, have mercy on me!"

[48]Many people warned the blind man to be quiet, but he shouted even more, "Son of David, have mercy on me!"

[49]Jesus stopped and said, "Tell the man to come here."

So they called the blind man, saying, "Cheer up! Get to your feet. Jesus is calling you." [50]The blind man jumped up, left his coat there, and went to Jesus.

[51]Jesus asked him, "What do you want me to do for you?"

The blind man answered, "Teacher, I want to see."

[52]Jesus said, "Go, you are healed because you believed." At once the man could see, and he followed Jesus on the road.

11 As Jesus and his followers were coming closer to Jerusalem, they came to the towns of Bethphage and Bethany near the Mount of Olives. From there Jesus sent two of his followers [2]and said to them, "Go to the town you can see there. When you enter it, you will quickly find a colt tied, which no one has ever ridden. Untie it and bring it here to me. [3]If anyone asks you why you are doing this,

tell him its Master needs the colt, and he will send it at once."

[4]The followers went into the town, found a colt tied in the street near the door of a house, and untied it. [5]Some people were standing there and asked, "What are you doing? Why are you untying that colt?" [6]The followers answered the way Jesus told them to answer, and the people let them take the colt.

[7]They brought the colt to Jesus and put their coats on it, and Jesus sat on it. [8]Many people spread their coats on the road. Others cut branches in the fields and spread them on the road. [9]The people were walking ahead of Jesus and behind him, shouting,

"Praise God!

God bless the One who comes in the name of the Lord!

Psalm 118:26

[10]God bless the kingdom of our father David!

That kingdom is coming!

Praise to God in heaven!"

[11]Jesus entered Jerusalem and went into the Temple. After he had looked at everything, since it was already late, he went out to Bethany with the twelve apostles.

[12]The next day as Jesus was leaving Bethany, he became hungry. [13]Seeing a fig tree in leaf from far away, he went to see if it had any figs on it. But he found no figs, only leaves, because it was not the right season for figs. [14]So Jesus said to the tree, "May no one ever eat fruit from you again." And Jesus' followers heard him say this.

[15]When Jesus returned to Jerusalem, he went into the Temple and began to throw out those who were buying and selling there. He turned over the tables of those who were exchanging different kinds of money, and he upset the

benches of those who were selling doves. [16]Jesus refused to allow anyone to carry goods through the Temple courts. [17]Then he taught the people, saying, "It is written in the Scriptures, 'My Temple will be called a house for prayer for people from all nations.' But you are changing God's house into a 'hideout for robbers.' "

[18]The leading priests and the teachers of the law heard all this and began trying to find a way to kill Jesus. They were afraid of him, because all the people were amazed at his teaching. [19]That evening, Jesus and his followers left the city.

[20]The next morning as Jesus was passing by with his followers, they saw the fig tree dry and dead, even to the roots. [21]Peter remembered the tree and said to Jesus, "Teacher, look! The fig tree you cursed is dry and dead!"

[22]Jesus answered, "Have faith in God. [23]I tell you the truth, you can say to this mountain, 'Go, fall into the sea.' And if you have no doubts in your mind and believe that what you say will happen, God will do it for you. [24]So I tell you to believe that you have received the things you ask for in prayer, and God will give them to you. [25]When you are praying, if you are angry with someone, forgive him so that your Father in heaven will also forgive your sins. [26]But if you don't forgive other people, then your Father in heaven will not forgive your sins.]"

[27]Jesus and his followers went again to Jerusalem. As Jesus was walking in the Temple, the leading priests, the teachers of the law, and the elders came to him. [28]They said to him, "What authority do you have to do these things? Who gave you this authority?"

[29]Jesus answered, "I will ask you one question. If you answer me, I will tell you

what authority I have to do these things. [30]Tell me: When John baptized people, was that authority from God or just from other people?"

[31]They argued about Jesus' question, saying, "If we answer, 'John's baptism was from God,' Jesus will say, 'Then why didn't you believe him?' [32]But if we say, 'It was from other people,' the crowd will be against us." (These leaders were afraid of the people, because all the people believed that John was a prophet.)

[33]So they answered Jesus, "We don't know."

Jesus said to them, "Then I won't tell you what authority I have to do these things."

12 Jesus began to use stories to teach the people. He said, "A man planted a vineyard. He put a wall around it and dug a hole for a winepress and built a tower. Then he leased the land to some farmers and left for a trip. [2]When it was time for the grapes to be picked, he sent a servant to the farmers to get his share of the grapes. [3]But the farmers grabbed the servant and beat him and sent him away empty-handed. [4]Then the man sent another servant. They hit him on the head and showed no respect for him. [5]So the man sent another servant, whom they killed. The man sent many other servants; the farmers beat some of them and killed others.

[6]"The man had one person left to send, his son whom he loved. He sent him last of all, saying, 'They will respect my son.'

[7]"But the farmers said to each other, 'This son will inherit the vineyard. If we kill him, it will be ours.' [8]So they took the son, killed him, and threw him out of the vineyard.

[9]"So what will the owner of the vineyard do? He will come and kill those

STEP 8

farmers and will give the vineyard to other farmers. [10]Surely you have read this Scripture:

'The stone that the builders rejected
    became the cornerstone.
[11]The Lord did this,
    and it is wonderful to us.' "

Psalm 118:22–23

[12]The Jewish leaders knew that the story was about them. So they wanted to find a way to arrest Jesus, but they were afraid of the people. So the leaders left him and went away.

[13]Later, the Jewish leaders sent some Pharisees and Herodians to Jesus to trap him in saying something wrong. [14]They came to him and said, "Teacher, we know that you are an honest man. You are not afraid of what other people think about you, because you pay no attention to who they are. And you teach the truth about God's way. Tell us: Is it right to pay taxes to Caesar or not? [15]Should we pay them, or not?"

But knowing what these men were really trying to do, Jesus said to them, "Why are you trying to trap me? Bring me a coin to look at." [16]They gave Jesus a coin, and he asked, "Whose image and name are on the coin?"

They answered, "Caesar's."

[17]Then Jesus said to them, "Give to Caesar the things that are Caesar's, and give to God the things that are God's." The men were amazed at what Jesus said.

[18]Then some Sadducees came to Jesus and asked him a question. (Sadducees believed that people would not rise from the dead.) [19]They said, "Teacher, Moses wrote that if a man's brother dies, leaving a wife but no children, then that man must marry the widow and have children for his brother. [20]Once there were seven brothers. The first brother married and died, leaving no children. [21]So the second brother married the widow, but he also died and had no children. The same thing happened with the third brother. [22]All seven brothers married her and died, and none of the brothers had any children. Finally the woman died too. [23]Since all seven brothers had married her, when people rise from the dead, whose wife will she be?"

[24]Jesus answered, "Why don't you understand? Don't you know what the Scriptures say, and don't you know about the power of God? [25]When people rise from the dead, they will not marry, nor will they be given to someone to marry. They will be like the angels in heaven. [26]Surely you have read what God said about people rising from the dead. In the book in which Moses wrote about the burning bush, it says that God told Moses, 'I am the God of Abraham, the God of Isaac, and the God of Jacob.' [27]God is the God of the living, not the dead. You Sadducees are wrong!"

[28]One of the teachers of the law came and heard Jesus arguing with the Sadducees. Seeing that Jesus gave good answers to their questions, he asked Jesus, "Which of the commands is most important?"

[29]Jesus answered, "The most important command is this: 'Listen, people of Israel! The Lord our God is the only Lord. [30]Love the Lord your God with all your heart, all your soul, all your mind, and all your strength.' [31]The second command is this: 'Love your neighbor as you love yourself.' There are no commands more important than these."

[32]The man answered, "That was a good answer, Teacher. You were right when you said God is the only Lord and there is no other God besides him. [33]One must love God with all his heart, all his

mind, and all his strength. And one must love his neighbor as he loves himself. These commands are more important than all the animals and sacrifices we offer to God."

³⁴When Jesus saw that the man answered him wisely, Jesus said to him, "You are close to the kingdom of God." And after that, no one was brave enough to ask Jesus any more questions.

³⁵As Jesus was teaching in the Temple, he asked, "Why do the teachers of the law say that the Christ is the son of David? ³⁶David himself, speaking by the Holy Spirit, said:

'The Lord said to my Lord,
   "Sit by me at my right side,
      until I put your enemies under your
         control." '   Psalm 110:1
³⁷David himself calls the Christ 'Lord,' so how can the Christ be his son?" The large crowd listened to Jesus with pleasure.

³⁸Jesus continued teaching and said, "Beware of the teachers of the law. They like to walk around wearing fancy clothes, and they love for people to greet them with respect in the marketplaces. ³⁹They love to have the most important seats in the synagogues and at feasts. ⁴⁰But they cheat widows and steal their houses and then try to make themselves look good by saying long prayers. They will receive a greater punishment."

⁴¹Jesus sat near the Temple money box and watched the people put in their money. Many rich people gave large sums of money. ⁴²Then a poor widow came and put in two small copper coins, which were only worth a few cents.

⁴³Calling his followers to him, Jesus said, "I tell you the truth, this poor widow gave more than all those rich people. ⁴⁴They gave only what they did not need. This woman is very poor, but she gave all she had; she gave all she had to live on."

13 As Jesus was leaving the Temple, one of his followers said to him, "Look, Teacher! How beautiful the buildings are! How big the stones are!"

²Jesus said, "Do you see all these great buildings? Not one stone will be left on another. Every stone will be thrown down to the ground."

³Later, as Jesus was sitting on the Mount of Olives, opposite the Temple, he was alone with Peter, James, John, and Andrew. They asked Jesus, ⁴"Tell us, when will these things happen? And what will be the sign that they are going to happen?"

⁵Jesus began to answer them, "Be careful that no one fools you. ⁶Many people will come in my name, saying, 'I am the One,' and they will fool many people. ⁷When you hear about wars and stories of wars that are coming, don't be afraid. These things must happen before the end comes. ⁸Nations will fight against other nations, and kingdoms against other kingdoms. There will be earthquakes in different places, and there will be times when there is no food for people to eat. These things are like the first pains when something new is about to be born.

⁹"You must be careful. People will arrest you and take you to court and beat you in their synagogues. You will be forced to stand before kings and governors, to tell them about me. This will happen to you because you follow me. ¹⁰But before these things happen, the Good News must be told to all people. ¹¹When you are arrested and judged, don't worry ahead of time about what you should say. Say whatever is given you to say at that time, because it will not really be you speaking; it will be the Holy Spirit.

¹²"Brothers will give their own brothers to be killed, and fathers will give their own children to be killed. Children will

fight against their own parents and cause them to be put to death. [13]All people will hate you because you follow me, but those people who keep their faith until the end will be saved.

[14]"You will see 'a blasphemous object that brings destruction' standing where it should not be." (You who read this should understand what it means.) "At that time, the people in Judea should run away to the mountains. [15]If people are on the roofs of their houses, they must not go down or go inside to get anything out of their houses. [16]If people are in the fields, they must not go back to get their coats. [17]At that time, how terrible it will be for women who are pregnant or have nursing babies! [18]Pray that these things will not happen in winter, [19]because those days will be full of trouble. There will be more trouble than there has ever been since the beginning, when God made the world, until now, and nothing as bad will ever happen again. [20]God has decided to make that terrible time short. Otherwise, no one would go on living. But God will make that time short to help the people he has chosen. [21]At that time, someone might say to you, 'Look, there is the Christ!' Or another person might say, 'There he is!' But don't believe them. [22]False Christs and false prophets will come and perform great wonders and miracles. They will try to fool even the people God has chosen, if that is possible. [23]So be careful. I have warned you about all this before it happens.

[24]"During the days after this trouble comes,

'the sun will grow dark,

and the moon will not give its light.
[25]The stars will fall from the sky.

And the powers of the heavens
will be shaken.'

Isaiah 13:10; 34:4

[26]"Then people will see the Son of Man coming in clouds with great power and glory. [27]Then he will send his angels all around the earth to gather his chosen people from every part of the earth and from every part of heaven.

[28]"Learn a lesson from the fig tree: When its branches become green and soft and new leaves appear, you know summer is near. [29]In the same way, when you see these things happening, you will know that the time is near, ready to come. [30]I tell you the truth, all these things will happen while the people of this time are still living. [31]Earth and sky will be destroyed, but the words I have said will never be destroyed.

[32]"No one knows when that day or time will be, not the angels in heaven, not even the Son. Only the Father knows. [33]Be careful! Always be ready, because you don't know when that time will be. [34]It is like a man who goes on a trip. He leaves his house and lets his servants take care of it, giving each one a special job to do. The man tells the servant guarding the door always to be watchful. [35]So always be ready, because you don't know when the owner of the house will come back. It might be in the evening, or at midnight, or in the morning while it is still dark, or when the sun rises. [36]Always be ready. Otherwise he might come back suddenly and find you sleeping. [37]I tell you this, and I say this to everyone: 'Be ready!' "

14 It was now only two days before the Passover and the Feast of Unleavened Bread. The leading priests and teachers of the law were trying to find a trick to arrest Jesus and kill him. [2]But they said, "We must not do it during the feast, because the people might cause a riot."

[3]Jesus was in Bethany at the house of Simon, who had a skin disease. While Jesus was eating there, a woman

approached him with an alabaster jar filled with very expensive perfume, made of pure nard. She opened the jar and poured the perfume on Jesus' head.

⁴Some who were there became upset and said to each other, "Why waste that perfume? ⁵It was worth a full year's work. It could have been sold and the money given to the poor." And they got very angry with the woman.

⁶Jesus said, "Leave her alone. Why are you troubling her? She did an excellent thing for me. ⁷You will always have the poor with you, and you can help them anytime you want. But you will not always have me. ⁸This woman did the only thing she could do for me; she poured perfume on my body to prepare me for burial. ⁹I tell you the truth, wherever the Good News is preached in all the world, what this woman has done will be told, and people will remember her."

¹⁰One of the twelve apostles, Judas Iscariot, went to talk to the leading priests to offer to hand Jesus over to them. ¹¹These priests were pleased about this and promised to pay Judas money. So he watched for the best time to turn Jesus in.

¹²It was now the first day of the Feast of Unleavened Bread when the Passover lamb was sacrificed. Jesus' followers said to him, "Where do you want us to go and prepare for you to eat the Passover meal?"

¹³Jesus sent two of his followers and said to them, "Go into the city and a man carrying a jar of water will meet you. Follow him. ¹⁴When he goes into a house, tell the owner of the house, 'The Teacher says: "Where is my guest room in which I can eat the Passover meal with my followers?" ' ¹⁵The owner will show you a large room upstairs that is furnished and ready. Prepare the food for us there."

¹⁶So the followers left and went into the city. Everything happened as Jesus had said, so they prepared the Passover meal.

¹⁷In the evening, Jesus went to that house with the twelve. ¹⁸While they were all eating, Jesus said, "I tell you the truth, one of you will turn against me—one of you eating with me now."

¹⁹The followers were very sad to hear this. Each one began to say to Jesus, "I am not the one, am I?"

²⁰Jesus answered, "It is one of the twelve—the one who dips his bread into the bowl with me. ²¹The Son of Man will die, just as the Scriptures say. But how terrible it will be for the person who hands the Son of Man over to be killed. It would be better for him if he had never been born."

²²While they were eating, Jesus took some bread and thanked God for it and broke it. Then he gave it to his followers and said, "Take it; this is my body."

²³Then Jesus took a cup and thanked God for it and gave it to the followers, and they all drank from the cup.

²⁴Then Jesus said, "This is my blood which is the new agreement that God makes with his people. This blood is poured out for many. ²⁵I tell you the truth, I will not drink of this fruit of the vine again until that day when I drink it new in the kingdom of God."

²⁶After singing a hymn, they went out to the Mount of Olives.

²⁷Then Jesus told the followers, "You will all stumble in your faith, because it is written in the Scriptures:

'I will kill the shepherd,
     and the sheep will scatter.'
                                    Zechariah 13:7

²⁸But after I rise from the dead, I will go ahead of you into Galilee."

²⁹Peter said, "Everyone else may stumble in their faith, but I will not."

30Jesus answered, "I tell you the truth, tonight before the rooster crows twice you will say three times you don't know me."

31But Peter insisted, "I will never say that I don't know you! I will even die with you!" And all the other followers said the same thing.

32Jesus and his followers went to a place called Gethsemane. He said to them, "Sit here while I pray." 33Jesus took Peter, James, and John with him, and he began to be very sad and troubled. 34He said to them, "My heart is full of sorrow, to the point of death. Stay here and watch."

35After walking a little farther away from them, Jesus fell to the ground and prayed that, if possible, he would not have this time of suffering. 36He prayed, "Abba, Father! You can do all things. Take away this cup of suffering. But do what you want, not what I want."

37Then Jesus went back to his followers and found them asleep. He said to Peter, "Simon, are you sleeping? Couldn't you stay awake with me for one hour?

STEP 10 38Stay awake and pray for strength against temptation. The spirit wants to do what is right, but the body is weak."

39Again Jesus went away and prayed the same thing. 40Then he went back to his followers, and again he found them asleep, because their eyes were very heavy. And they did not know what to say to him.

41After Jesus prayed a third time, he went back to his followers and said to them, "Are you still sleeping and resting? That's enough. The time has come for the Son of Man to be handed over to sinful people. 42Get up, we must go. Look, here comes the man who has turned against me."

43At once, while Jesus was still speaking, Judas, one of the twelve apostles, came up. With him were many people carrying swords and clubs who had been sent from the leading priests, the teachers of the law, and the Jewish elders.

44Judas had planned a signal for them, saying, "The man I kiss is Jesus. Arrest him and guard him while you lead him away." 45So Judas went straight to Jesus and said, "Teacher!" and kissed him. 46Then the people grabbed Jesus and arrested him. 47One of his followers standing nearby pulled out his sword and struck the servant of the high priest and cut off his ear.

48Then Jesus said, "You came to get me with swords and clubs as if I were a criminal. 49Every day I was with you teaching in the Temple, and you did not arrest me there. But all these things have happened to make the Scriptures come true." 50Then all of Jesus' followers left him and ran away.

51A young man, wearing only a linen cloth, was following Jesus, and the people also grabbed him. 52But the cloth he was wearing came off, and he ran away naked.

53The people who arrested Jesus led him to the house of the high priest, where all the leading priests, the elders, and the teachers of the law were gathered. 54Peter followed far behind and entered the courtyard of the high priest's house. There he sat with the guards, warming himself by the fire.

55The leading priests and the whole Jewish council tried to find something that Jesus had done wrong so they could kill him. But the council could find no proof of anything. 56Many people came and told false things about him, but all said different things—none of them agreed.

STEP 10

Continued to take personal inventory
and when we were wrong promptly admitted it.

Mark 14:38

You never get to where your old way of life stops pulling on your weaknesses and selfish desires. Every now and then you'll want to go back to your addictions. In this story in Mark 14, Jesus called Peter by his old name, Simon (verse 37). It's as though Jesus wanted Peter to see just how close he was to falling back into his old way of living. Soon after, Peter denied knowing Jesus.

When Jesus told his followers to "stay awake" (verse 38), he was warning them to be on the lookout for spiritual dangers around them. When he told them to pray, he meant they needed to rely on God rather than on themselves to face the dangers around them. Jesus knew that his followers wanted to please him in their hearts. But he also knew their human weaknesses and how easily they could give in to them. We're the same way. You need to "stay awake" so your old habits don't catch you by surprise. You need to pray often for wisdom and strength to stay clean—one day at a time.

FOR YOUR NEXT **STEP 10** MEDITATION, TURN TO **PAGE 220.** ▶▶

[57]Then some people stood up and lied about Jesus, saying, [58]"We heard this man say, 'I will destroy this Temple that people made. And three days later, I will build another Temple not made by people.' " [59]But even the things these people said did not agree.

[60]Then the high priest stood before them and asked Jesus, "Aren't you going to answer? Don't you have something to say about their charges against you?" [61]But Jesus said nothing; he did not answer.

The high priest asked Jesus another question: "Are you the Christ, the Son of the blessed God?"

[62]Jesus answered, "I am. And in the future you will see the Son of Man sitting at the right hand of God, the Powerful One, and coming on clouds in the sky."

[63]When the high priest heard this, he tore his clothes and said, "We don't need any more witnesses! [64]You all heard him say these things against God. What do you think?"

They all said that Jesus was guilty and should die. [65]Some of the people there began to spit at Jesus. They blindfolded him and beat him with their fists and said, "Prove you are a prophet!" Then the guards led Jesus away and beat him.

[66]While Peter was in the courtyard, a servant girl of the high priest came there. [67]She saw Peter warming himself at the fire and looked closely at him.

Then she said, "You also were with Jesus, that man from Nazareth."

[68]But Peter said that he was never with Jesus. He said, "I don't know or understand what you are talking about." Then Peter left and went toward the entrance of the courtyard. And the rooster crowed.

[69]The servant girl saw Peter there, and again she said to the people who were standing nearby, "This man is one of those who followed Jesus." [70]Again Peter said that it was not true.

A short time later, some people were standing near Peter saying, "Surely you are one of those who followed Jesus, because you are from Galilee, too."

[71]Then Peter began to place a curse on himself and swear, "I don't know this man you're talking about!"

[72]At once, the rooster crowed the second time. Then Peter remembered what Jesus had told him: "Before the rooster crows twice, you will say three times that you don't know me." Then Peter lost control of himself and began to cry.

15 Very early in the morning, the leading priests, the elders, the teachers of the law, and all the Jewish council decided what to do with Jesus. They tied him, led him away, and turned him over to Pilate, the governor.

[2]Pilate asked Jesus, "Are you the king of the Jews?"

Jesus answered, "Those are your words."

[3]The leading priests accused Jesus of many things. [4]So Pilate asked Jesus another question, "You can see that they are accusing you of many things. Aren't you going to answer?"

[5]But Jesus still said nothing, so Pilate was very surprised.

[6]Every year at the time of the Passover the governor would free one prisoner whom the people chose. [7]At that time, there was a man named Barabbas in prison who was a rebel and had committed murder during a riot. [8]The crowd came to Pilate and began to ask him to free a prisoner as he always did.

[9]So Pilate asked them, "Do you want me to free the king of the Jews?" [10]Pilate knew that the leading priests had turned Jesus in to him because they were jealous.

[11]But the leading priests had persuaded the people to ask Pilate to free Barabbas, not Jesus.

[12]Then Pilate asked the crowd again, "So what should I do with this man you call the king of the Jews?"

[13]They shouted, "Crucify him!"

[14]Pilate asked, "Why? What wrong has he done?"

But they shouted even louder, "Crucify him!"

[15]Pilate wanted to please the crowd, so he freed Barabbas for them. After having Jesus beaten with whips, he handed Jesus over to the soldiers to be crucified.

[16]The soldiers took Jesus into the governor's palace (called the Praetorium) and called all the other soldiers together. [17]They put a purple robe on Jesus and used thorny branches to make a crown for his head. [18]They began to call out to him, "Hail, King of the Jews!" [19]The soldiers beat Jesus on the head many times with a stick. They spit on him and made fun of him by bowing on their knees and worshiping him. [20]After they finished, the soldiers took off the purple robe and put his own clothes on him again. Then they led him out of the palace to be crucified.

[21]A man named Simon from Cyrene, the father of Alexander and Rufus, was coming from the fields to the city. The soldiers forced Simon to carry the cross for Jesus. [22]They led Jesus to the place called Golgotha, which means the Place of the Skull. [23]The soldiers tried to give Jesus wine mixed with myrrh to drink, but he refused. [24]The soldiers crucified Jesus and divided his clothes among themselves, throwing lots to decide what each soldier would get.

[25]It was nine o'clock in the morning when they crucified Jesus. [26]There was a sign with this charge against Jesus written on it: THE KING OF THE JEWS. [27]They also put two robbers on crosses beside Jesus, one on the right, and the other on the left. [[28]And the Scripture came true that says, "They put him with criminals."] [29]People walked by and insulted Jesus and shook their heads, saying, "You said you could destroy the Temple and build it again in three days. [30]So save yourself! Come down from that cross!"

[31]The leading priests and the teachers of the law were also making fun of Jesus. They said to each other, "He saved other people, but he can't save himself. [32]If he is really the Christ, the king of Israel, let him come down now from the cross. When we see this, we will believe in him." The robbers who were being crucified beside Jesus also insulted him.

[33]At noon the whole country became dark, and the darkness lasted for three hours. [34]At three o'clock Jesus cried in a loud voice, "Eloi, Eloi, lama sabachthani." This means, "My God, my God, why have you abandoned me?"

[35]When some of the people standing there heard this, they said, "Listen! He is calling Elijah."

[36]Someone there ran and got a sponge, filled it with vinegar, tied it to a stick, and gave it to Jesus to drink. He said, "We want to see if Elijah will come to take him down from the cross."

[37]Then Jesus cried in a loud voice and died.

[38]The curtain in the Temple was torn into two pieces, from the top to the bottom. [39]When the army officer who was standing in front of the cross saw what happened when Jesus died, he said, "This man really was the Son of God!"

[40]Some women were standing at a distance from the cross, watching; among them were Mary Magdalene, Salome, and Mary the mother of James and Joseph. (James was her youngest son.)

⁴¹These women had followed Jesus in Galilee and helped him. Many other women were also there who had come with Jesus to Jerusalem.

⁴²This was Preparation Day. (That means the day before the Sabbath day.) That evening, ⁴³Joseph from Arimathea was brave enough to go to Pilate and ask for Jesus' body. Joseph, an important member of the Jewish council, was one of the people who was waiting for the kingdom of God to come. ⁴⁴Pilate was amazed that Jesus would have already died, so he called the army officer who had guarded Jesus and asked him if Jesus had already died. ⁴⁵The officer told Pilate that he was dead, so Pilate told Joseph he could have the body. ⁴⁶Joseph bought some linen cloth, took the body down from the cross, and wrapped it in the linen. He put the body in a tomb that was cut out of a wall of rock. Then he rolled a very large stone to block the entrance of the tomb. ⁴⁷And Mary Magdalene and Mary the mother of Joseph saw the place where Jesus was laid.

16 The day after the Sabbath day, Mary Magdalene, Mary the mother of James, and Salome bought some sweet-smelling spices to put on Jesus' body. ²Very early on that day, the first day of the week, soon after sunrise, the women were on their way to the tomb. ³They said to each other, "Who will roll away for us the stone that covers the entrance of the tomb?"

⁴Then the women looked and saw that the stone had already been rolled away, even though it was very large. ⁵The women entered the tomb and saw a young man wearing a white robe and sitting on the right side, and they were afraid.

⁶But the man said, "Don't be afraid. You are looking for Jesus from Nazareth, who has been crucified. He has risen from the dead; he is not here. Look, here is the place they laid him. ⁷Now go and tell his followers and Peter, 'Jesus is going into Galilee ahead of you, and you will see him there as he told you before.' "

⁸The women were confused and shaking with fear, so they left the tomb and ran away. They did not tell anyone about what happened, because they were afraid.

Verses 9–20 are not included in some of the earliest surviving Greek copies of Mark.

[⁹After Jesus rose from the dead early on the first day of the week, he showed himself first to Mary Magdalene. One time in the past, he had forced seven demons out of her. ¹⁰After Mary saw Jesus, she went and told his followers, who were very sad and were crying. ¹¹But Mary told them that Jesus was alive. She said that she had seen him, but the followers did not believe her.

¹²Later, Jesus showed himself to two of his followers while they were walking in the country, but he did not look the same as before. ¹³These followers went back to the others and told them what had happened, but again, the followers did not believe them.

¹⁴Later Jesus showed himself to the eleven apostles while they were eating, and he criticized them because they had no faith. They were stubborn and refused to believe those who had seen him after he had risen from the dead.

¹⁵Jesus said to his followers, "Go everywhere in the world, and tell the Good News to everyone. ¹⁶Anyone who believes and is baptized will be saved, but anyone who does not believe will be punished. ¹⁷And those who believe will be able to do these things as proof: They will use my

name to force out demons. They will speak in new languages. [18]They will pick up snakes and drink poison without being hurt. They will touch the sick, and the sick will be healed."

[19]After the Lord Jesus said these things to his followers, he was carried up into heaven, and he sat at the right side of God. [20]The followers went everywhere in the world and told the Good News to people, and the Lord helped them. The Lord proved that the Good News they told was true by giving them power to work miracles.]

LUKE

Luke Tells About Jesus the Savior for All People

1 Many have tried to report on the things that happened among us. ²They have written the same things that we learned from others—the people who saw those things from the beginning and served God by telling people his message. ³Since I myself have studied everything carefully from the beginning, most excellent Theophilus, it seemed good for me to write it out for you. I arranged it in order, ⁴to help you know that what you have been taught is true.

⁵During the time Herod ruled Judea, there was a priest named Zechariah who belonged to Abijah's group. Zechariah's wife, Elizabeth, came from the family of Aaron. ⁶Zechariah and Elizabeth truly did what God said was good. They did everything the Lord commanded and were without fault in keeping his law. ⁷But they had no children, because Elizabeth could not have a baby, and both of them were very old.

⁸One day Zechariah was serving as a priest before God, because his group was on duty. ⁹According to the custom of the priests, he was chosen by lot to go into the Temple of the Lord and burn incense. ¹⁰There were a great many people outside praying at the time the incense was offered. ¹¹Then an angel of the Lord appeared to Zechariah, standing on the right side of the incense table. ¹²When he saw the angel, Zechariah was startled and frightened. ¹³But the angel said to him, "Zechariah, don't be afraid. God has heard your prayer. Your wife, Elizabeth, will give birth to a son, and you will name him John. ¹⁴He will bring you joy and gladness, and many people will be happy because of his birth. ¹⁵John will be a great

man for the Lord. He will never drink wine or beer, and even from birth, he will be filled with the Holy Spirit. ¹⁶He will help many people of Israel return to the Lord their God. ¹⁷He will go before the Lord in spirit and power like Elijah. He will make peace between parents and their children and will bring those who are not obeying God back to the right way of thinking, to make a people ready for the coming of the Lord."

¹⁸Zechariah said to the angel, "How can I know that what you say is true? I am an old man, and my wife is old, too."

¹⁹The angel answered him, "I am Gabriel. I stand before God, who sent me to talk to you and to tell you this good news. ²⁰Now, listen! You will not be able to speak until the day these things happen, because you did not believe what I told you. But they will really happen."

²¹Outside, the people were still waiting for Zechariah and were surprised that he was staying so long in the Temple. ²²When Zechariah came outside, he could not speak to them, and they knew he had seen a vision in the Temple. He could only make signs to them and remained unable to speak. ²³When his time of service at the Temple was finished, he went home.

²⁴Later, Zechariah's wife, Elizabeth, became pregnant and did not go out of her house for five months. Elizabeth said, ²⁵"Look what the Lord has done for me! My people were ashamed of me, but now the Lord has taken away that shame."

²⁶During Elizabeth's sixth month of pregnancy, God sent the angel Gabriel to Nazareth, a town in Galilee, ²⁷to a virgin. She was engaged to marry a man named

Joseph from the family of David. Her name was Mary. ²⁸The angel came to her and said, "Greetings! The Lord has blessed you and is with you."

²⁹But Mary was very startled by what the angel said and wondered what this greeting might mean.

³⁰The angel said to her, "Don't be afraid, Mary; God has shown you his grace. ³¹Listen! You will become pregnant and give birth to a son, and you will name him Jesus. ³²He will be great and will be called the Son of the Most High. The Lord God will give him the throne of King David, his ancestor. ³³He will rule over the people of Jacob forever, and his kingdom will never end."

³⁴Mary said to the angel, "How will this happen since I am a virgin?"

³⁵The angel said to Mary, "The Holy Spirit will come upon you, and the power of the Most High will cover you. For this reason the baby will be holy and will be called the Son of God. ³⁶Now Elizabeth, your relative, is also pregnant with a son though she is very old. Everyone thought she could not have a baby, but she has been pregnant for six months. ³⁷God can do anything!"

³⁸Mary said, "I am the servant of the Lord. Let this happen to me as you say!" Then the angel went away.

³⁹Mary got up and went quickly to a town in the hills of Judea. ⁴⁰She came to Zechariah's house and greeted Elizabeth. ⁴¹When Elizabeth heard Mary's greeting, the unborn baby inside her jumped, and Elizabeth was filled with the Holy Spirit. ⁴²She cried out in a loud voice, "God has blessed you more than any other woman, and he has blessed the baby to which you will give birth. ⁴³Why has this good thing happened to me, that the mother of my Lord comes to me? ⁴⁴When I heard your voice, the baby inside

me jumped with joy. ⁴⁵You are blessed because you believed that what the Lord said to you would really happen."

⁴⁶Then Mary said,

"My soul praises the Lord;
⁴⁷   my heart rejoices in God my
          Savior,
⁴⁸because he has shown his concern
          for his humble servant girl.
   From now on, all people will say that I
          am blessed,
⁴⁹   because the Powerful One has
          done great things for me.
   His name is holy.
⁵⁰God will show his mercy forever and
          ever
       to those who worship and serve
          him.
⁵¹He has done mighty deeds by his
          power.
       He has scattered the people who
          are proud
       and think great things about
          themselves.
⁵²He has brought down rulers from
          their thrones
       and raised up the humble.
⁵³He has filled the hungry with good
          things
       and sent the rich away with
          nothing.
⁵⁴He has helped his servant, the people
          of Israel,
       remembering to show them mercy
⁵⁵as he promised to our ancestors,
       to Abraham and to his children
          forever."

⁵⁶Mary stayed with Elizabeth for about three months and then returned home.

⁵⁷When it was time for Elizabeth to give birth, she had a boy. ⁵⁸Her neighbors and relatives heard how good the Lord was to her, and they rejoiced with her.

⁵⁹When the baby was eight days old, they came to circumcise him. They

wanted to name him Zechariah because this was his father's name, ⁶⁰but his mother said, "No! He will be named John."

⁶¹The people said to Elizabeth, "But no one in your family has this name." ⁶²Then they made signs to his father to find out what he would like to name him.

⁶³Zechariah asked for a writing tablet and wrote, "His name is John," and everyone was surprised. ⁶⁴Immediately Zechariah could talk again, and he began praising God. ⁶⁵All their neighbors became alarmed, and in all the mountains of Judea people continued talking about all these things. ⁶⁶The people who heard about them wondered, saying, "What will this child be?" because the Lord was with him.

⁶⁷Then Zechariah, John's father, was filled with the Holy Spirit and prophesied:

⁶⁸"Let us praise the Lord, the God of Israel,

because he has come to help his people and has given them freedom.
⁶⁹He has given us a powerful Savior
from the family of God's servant David.
⁷⁰He said that he would do this
through his holy prophets who lived long ago:
⁷¹He promised he would save us from our enemies
and from the power of all those who hate us.
⁷²He said he would give mercy to our ancestors
and that he would remember his holy promise.
⁷³God promised Abraham, our father,
⁷⁴   that he would save us from the power of our enemies
so we could serve him without fear,

⁷⁵being holy and good before God as long as we live.

⁷⁶"Now you, child, will be called a prophet of the Most High God.
You will go before the Lord to prepare his way.
⁷⁷You will make his people know that they will be saved
by having their sins forgiven.
⁷⁸With the loving mercy of our God,
a new day from heaven will dawn upon us.
⁷⁹It will shine on those who live in darkness,
in the shadow of death.
It will guide us into the path of peace."

⁸⁰And so the child grew up and became strong in spirit. John lived in the desert until the time when he came out to preach to Israel.

2 At that time, Augustus Caesar sent an order that all people in the countries under Roman rule must list their names in a register. ²This was the first registration; it was taken while Quirinius was governor of Syria. ³And all went to their own towns to be registered.

⁴So Joseph left Nazareth, a town in Galilee, and went to the town of Bethlehem in Judea, known as the town of David. Joseph went there because he was from the family of David. ⁵Joseph registered with Mary, to whom he was engaged and who was now pregnant. ⁶While they were in Bethlehem, the time came for Mary to have the baby, ⁷and she gave birth to her first son. Because there were no rooms left in the inn, she wrapped the baby with pieces of cloth and laid him in a feeding trough.

⁸That night, some shepherds were in the fields nearby watching their sheep.

[9]Then an angel of the Lord stood before them. The glory of the Lord was shining around them, and they became very frightened. [10]The angel said to them, "Do not be afraid. I am bringing you good news that will be a great joy to all the people. [11]Today your Savior was born in the town of David. He is Christ, the Lord. [12]This is how you will know him: You will find a baby wrapped in pieces of cloth and lying in a feeding box."

[13]Then a very large group of angels from heaven joined the first angel, praising God and saying:

[14]"Give glory to God in heaven,
    and on earth let there be peace
        among the people who
            please God."

[15]When the angels left them and went back to heaven, the shepherds said to each other, "Let's go to Bethlehem. Let's see this thing that has happened which the Lord has told us about."

[16]So the shepherds went quickly and found Mary and Joseph and the baby, who was lying in a feeding trough. [17]When they had seen him, they told what the angels had said about this child. [18]Everyone was amazed at what the shepherds said to them. [19]But Mary treasured these things and continued to think about them. [20]Then the shepherds went back to their sheep, praising God and thanking him for everything they had seen and heard. It had been just as the angel had told them.

[21]When the baby was eight days old, he was circumcised and was named Jesus, the name given by the angel before the baby began to grow inside Mary.

[22]When the time came for Mary and Joseph to do what the law of Moses taught about being made pure, they took Jesus to Jerusalem to present him to the Lord. [23](It is written in the law of the Lord: "Every firstborn male shall be given to the Lord.") [24]Mary and Joseph also went to offer a sacrifice, as the law of the Lord says: "You must sacrifice two doves or two young pigeons."

[25]In Jerusalem lived a man named Simeon who was a good man and godly. He was waiting for the time when God would take away Israel's sorrow, and the Holy Spirit was in him. [26]Simeon had been told by the Holy Spirit that he would not die before he saw the Christ promised by the Lord. [27]The Spirit led Simeon to the Temple. When Mary and Joseph brought the baby Jesus to the Temple to do what the law said they must do, [28]Simeon took the baby in his arms and thanked God:

[29]"Now, Lord, you can let me, your
            servant,
    die in peace as you said.
[30]With my own eyes I have seen your
            salvation,
[31]   which you prepared before all
            people.
[32]It is a light for the non-Jewish people
            to see
    and an honor for your people, the
            Israelites."

[33]Jesus' father and mother were amazed at what Simeon had said about him. [34]Then Simeon blessed them and said to Mary, "God has chosen this child to cause the fall and rise of many in Israel. He will be a sign from God that many people will not accept [35]so that the thoughts of many will be made known. And the things that will happen will make your heart sad, too."

[36]There was a prophetess, Anna, from the family of Phanuel in the tribe of Asher. Anna was very old. She had once been married for seven years. [37]Then her husband died, and she was a widow for eighty-four years. Anna never left the

Temple but worshiped God, going without food and praying day and night. [38]Standing there at that time, she thanked God and spoke about Jesus to all who were waiting for God to free Jerusalem.

[39]When Joseph and Mary had done everything the law of the Lord commanded, they went home to Nazareth, their own town in Galilee. [40]The little child grew and became strong. He was filled with wisdom, and God's goodness was upon him.

[41]Every year Jesus' parents went to Jerusalem for the Passover Feast. [42]When he was twelve years old, they went to the feast as they always did. [43]After the feast days were over, they started home. The boy Jesus stayed behind in Jerusalem, but his parents did not know it. [44]Thinking that Jesus was with them in the group, they traveled for a whole day. Then they began to look for him among their family and friends. [45]When they did not find him, they went back to Jerusalem to look for him there. [46]After three days they found Jesus sitting in the Temple with the teachers, listening to them and asking them questions. [47]All who heard him were amazed at his understanding and answers. [48]When Jesus' parents saw him, they were astonished. His mother said to him, "Son, why did you do this to us? Your father and I were very worried about you and have been looking for you."

[49]Jesus said to them, "Why were you looking for me? Didn't you know that I must be in my Father's house?" [50]But they did not understand the meaning of what he said.

[51]Jesus went with them to Nazareth and was obedient to them. But his mother kept in her mind all that had happened. [52]Jesus became wiser and grew physically. People liked him, and he pleased God.

3 It was the fifteenth year of the rule of Tiberius Caesar. These men were under Caesar: Pontius Pilate, the ruler of Judea; Herod, the ruler of Galilee; Philip, Herod's brother, the ruler of Iturea and Traconitis; and Lysanias, the ruler of Abilene. [2]Annas and Caiaphas were the high priests. At this time, the word of God came to John son of Zechariah in the desert. [3]He went all over the area around the Jordan River preaching a baptism of changed hearts and lives for the forgiveness of sins. [4]As it is written in the book of Isaiah the prophet:

"This is a voice of one
    who calls out in the desert:
'Prepare the way for the Lord.
    Make the road straight for him.
[5]Every valley should be filled in,
    and every mountain and hill
        should be made flat.
Roads with turns should be made
        straight,
    and rough roads should be made
        smooth.
[6]And all people will know about the
        salvation of God!' "

Isaiah 40:3–5

[7]To the crowds of people who came to be baptized by John, he said, "You are all snakes! Who warned you to run away from God's coming punishment? [8]Do the things that show you really have changed your hearts and lives. Don't begin to say to yourselves, 'Abraham is our father.' I tell you that God could make children for Abraham from these rocks. [9]The ax is now ready to cut down the trees, and every tree that does not produce good fruit will be cut down and thrown into the fire."

[10]The people asked John, "Then what should we do?"

[11]John answered, "If you have two shirts, share with the person who does

not have one. If you have food, share that also."

[12]Even tax collectors came to John to be baptized. They said to him, "Teacher, what should we do?"

[13]John said to them, "Don't take more taxes from people than you have been ordered to take."

[14]The soldiers asked John, "What about us? What should we do?"

John said to them, "Don't force people to give you money, and don't lie about them. Be satisfied with the pay you get."

[15]Since the people were hoping for the Christ to come, they wondered if John might be the one.

[16]John answered everyone, "I baptize you with water, but there is one coming who is greater than I am. I am not good enough to untie his sandals. He will baptize you with the Holy Spirit and fire. [17]He will come ready to clean the grain, separating the good grain from the chaff. He will put the good part of the grain into his barn, but he will burn the chaff with a fire that cannot be put out." [18]And John continued to preach the Good News, saying many other things to encourage the people.

[19]But John spoke against Herod, the governor, because of his sin with Herodias, the wife of Herod's brother, and because of the many other evil things Herod did. [20]So Herod did something even worse: He put John in prison.

[21]When all the people were being baptized by John, Jesus also was baptized. While Jesus was praying, heaven opened [22]and the Holy Spirit came down on him in the form of a dove. Then a voice came from heaven, saying, "You are my Son, whom I love, and I am very pleased with you."

[23]When Jesus began his ministry, he was about thirty years old. People thought that Jesus was Joseph's son.

Joseph was the son of Heli.
[24]Heli was the son of Matthat.
Matthat was the son of Levi.
Levi was the son of Melki.
Melki was the son of Jannai.
Jannai was the son of Joseph.
[25]Joseph was the son of Mattathias.
Mattathias was the son of Amos.
Amos was the son of Nahum.
Nahum was the son of Esli.
Esli was the son of Naggai.
[26]Naggai was the son of Maath.
Maath was the son of Mattathias.
Mattathias was the son of Semein.
Semein was the son of Josech.
Josech was the son of Joda.
[27]Joda was the son of Joanan.
Joanan was the son of Rhesa.
Rhesa was the son of Zerubbabel.
Zerubbabel was the grandson of Shealtiel.
Shealtiel was the son of Neri.
[28]Neri was the son of Melki.
Melki was the son of Addi.
Addi was the son of Cosam.
Cosam was the son of Elmadam.
Elmadam was the son of Er.
[29]Er was the son of Joshua.
Joshua was the son of Eliezer.
Eliezer was the son of Jorim.
Jorim was the son of Matthat.
Matthat was the son of Levi.
[30]Levi was the son of Simeon.
Simeon was the son of Judah.
Judah was the son of Joseph.
Joseph was the son of Jonam.
Jonam was the son of Eliakim.
[31]Eliakim was the son of Melea.
Melea was the son of Menna.
Menna was the son of Mattatha.
Mattatha was the son of Nathan.
Nathan was the son of David.
[32]David was the son of Jesse.

Jesse was the son of Obed.

Obed was the son of Boaz.

Boaz was the son of Salmon.

Salmon was the son of Nahshon.

[33]Nahshon was the son of Amminadab.

Amminadab was the son of Admin.

Admin was the son of Arni.

Arni was the son of Hezron.

Hezron was the son of Perez.

Perez was the son of Judah.

[34]Judah was the son of Jacob.

Jacob was the son of Isaac.

Isaac was the son of Abraham.

Abraham was the son of Terah.

Terah was the son of Nahor.

[35]Nahor was the son of Serug.

Serug was the son of Reu.

Reu was the son of Peleg.

Peleg was the son of Eber.

Eber was the son of Shelah.

[36]Shelah was the son of Cainan.

Cainan was the son of Arphaxad.

Arphaxad was the son of Shem.

Shem was the son of Noah.

Noah was the son of Lamech.

[37]Lamech was the son of Methuselah.

Methuselah was the son of Enoch.

Enoch was the son of Jared.

Jared was the son of Mahalalel.

Mahalalel was the son of Kenan.

[38]Kenan was the son of Enosh.

Enosh was the son of Seth.

Seth was the son of Adam.

Adam was the son of God.

4 Jesus, filled with the Holy Spirit, returned from the Jordan River. The Spirit led Jesus into the desert [2]where the devil tempted Jesus for forty days. Jesus ate nothing during that time, and when those days were ended, he was very hungry.

[3]The devil said to Jesus, "If you are the Son of God, tell this rock to become bread."

[4]Jesus answered, "It is written in the Scriptures: 'A person does not live on bread alone.' "

[5]Then the devil took Jesus and showed him all the kingdoms of the world in an instant. [6]The devil said to Jesus, "I will give you all these kingdoms and all their power and glory. It has all been given to me, and I can give it to anyone I wish. [7]If you worship me, then it will all be yours."

[8]Jesus answered, "It is written in the Scriptures: 'You must worship the Lord your God and serve only him.' "

[9]Then the devil led Jesus to Jerusalem and put him on a high place of the Temple. He said to Jesus, "If you are the Son of God, jump down. [10]It is written in the Scriptures:

'He has put his angels in charge of you

to watch over you.'   *Psalm 91:11*
[11]It is also written:

'They will catch you in their hands

so that you will not hit your foot on a rock.' "   *Psalm 91:12*

[12]Jesus answered, "But it also says in the Scriptures: 'Do not test the Lord your God.' "

[13]After the devil had tempted Jesus in every way, he left him to wait until a better time.

[14]Jesus returned to Galilee in the power of the Holy Spirit, and stories about him spread all through the area. [15]He began to teach in their synagogues, and everyone praised him.

[16]Jesus traveled to Nazareth, where he had grown up. On the Sabbath day he went to the synagogue, as he always did, and stood up to read. [17]The book of Isaiah the prophet was given to him. He opened the book and found the place where this is written:

[18]"The Lord has put his Spirit in me,

because he appointed me to tell

the Good News to the poor.

He has sent me to tell the captives
>   they are free
> and to tell the blind that they can
>   see again.   *Isaiah 61:1*
> God sent me to free those who
>   have been treated unfairly
>   *Isaiah 58:6*

¹⁹ and to announce the time when
>   the Lord will show his
>   kindness."   *Isaiah 61:2*

²⁰Jesus closed the book, gave it back to the assistant, and sat down. Everyone in the synagogue was watching Jesus closely. ²¹He began to say to them, "While you heard these words just now, they were coming true!"

²²All the people spoke well of Jesus and were amazed at the words of grace he spoke. They asked, "Isn't this Joseph's son?"

²³Jesus said to them, "I know that you will tell me the old saying: 'Doctor, heal yourself.' You want to say, 'We heard about the things you did in Capernaum. Do those things here in your own town!' " ²⁴Then Jesus said, "I tell you the truth, a prophet is not accepted in his hometown. ²⁵But I tell you the truth, there were many widows in Israel during the time of Elijah. It did not rain in Israel for three and one-half years, and there was no food anywhere in the whole country. ²⁶But Elijah was sent to none of those widows, only to a widow in Zarephath, a town in Sidon. ²⁷And there were many with skin diseases living in Israel during the time of the prophet Elisha. But none of them were healed, only Naaman, who was from the country of Syria."

²⁸When all the people in the synagogue heard these things, they became very angry. ²⁹They got up, forced Jesus out of town, and took him to the edge of the cliff on which the town was built. They planned to throw him off the edge,

³⁰but Jesus walked through the crowd and went on his way.

³¹Jesus went to Capernaum, a city in Galilee, and on the Sabbath day, he taught the people. ³²They were amazed at his teaching, because he spoke with authority. ³³In the synagogue a man who had within him an evil spirit shouted in a loud voice, ³⁴"Jesus of Nazareth! What do you want with us? Did you come to destroy us? I know who you are—God's Holy One!"

³⁵Jesus commanded the evil spirit, "Be quiet! Come out of the man!" The evil spirit threw the man down to the ground before all the people and then left the man without hurting him.

³⁶The people were amazed and said to each other, "What does this mean? With authority and power he commands evil spirits, and they come out." ³⁷And so the news about Jesus spread to every place in the whole area.

³⁸Jesus left the synagogue and went to the home of Simon. Simon's mother-in-law was sick with a high fever, and they asked Jesus to help her. ³⁹He came to her side and commanded the fever to leave. It left her, and immediately she got up and began serving them.

⁴⁰When the sun went down, the people brought those who were sick to Jesus. Putting his hands on each sick person, he healed every one of them. ⁴¹Demons came out of many people, shouting, "You are the Son of God." But Jesus commanded the demons and would not allow them to speak, because they knew Jesus was the Christ.

⁴²At daybreak, Jesus went to a lonely place, but the people looked for him. When they found him, they tried to keep him from leaving. ⁴³But Jesus said to them, "I must preach about God's kingdom to other towns, too. This is why I was sent."

⁴⁴Then he kept on preaching in the synagogues of Judea.

5 One day while Jesus was standing beside Lake Galilee, many people were pressing all around him to hear the word of God. ²Jesus saw two boats at the shore of the lake. The fishermen had left them and were washing their nets. ³Jesus got into one of the boats, the one that belonged to Simon, and asked him to push off a little from the land. Then Jesus sat down and continued to teach the people from the boat.

⁴When Jesus had finished speaking, he said to Simon, "Take the boat into deep water, and put your nets in the water to catch some fish."

⁵Simon answered, "Master, we worked hard all night trying to catch fish, and we caught nothing. But you say to put the nets in the water, so I will." ⁶When the fishermen did as Jesus told them, they caught so many fish that the nets began to break. ⁷They called to their partners in the other boat to come and help them. They came and filled both boats so full that they were almost sinking.

⁸When Simon Peter saw what had happened, he bowed down before Jesus and said, "Go away from me, Lord. I am a sinful man!" ⁹He and the other fishermen were amazed at the many fish they caught, as were ¹⁰James and John, the sons of Zebedee, Simon's partners.

Jesus said to Simon, "Don't be afraid. From now on you will fish for people." ¹¹When the men brought their boats to the shore, they left everything and followed Jesus.

¹²When Jesus was in one of the towns, there was a man covered with a skin disease. When he saw Jesus, he bowed before him and begged him, "Lord, you can heal me if you will."

¹³Jesus reached out his hand and touched the man and said, "I will. Be healed!" Immediately the disease disappeared. ¹⁴Then Jesus said, "Don't tell anyone about this, but go and show yourself to the priest and offer a gift for your healing, as Moses commanded. This will show the people what I have done."

¹⁵But the news about Jesus spread even more. Many people came to hear Jesus and to be healed of their sicknesses, ¹⁶but Jesus often slipped away to be alone so he could pray.

¹⁷One day as Jesus was teaching the people, the Pharisees and teachers of the law from every town in Galilee and Judea and from Jerusalem were there. The Lord was giving Jesus the power to heal people. ¹⁸Just then, some men were carrying on a mat a man who was paralyzed. They tried to bring him in and put him down before Jesus. ¹⁹But because there were so many people there, they could not find a way in. So they went up on the roof and lowered the man on his mat through the ceiling into the middle of the crowd right before Jesus. ²⁰Seeing their faith, Jesus said, "Friend, your sins are forgiven."

²¹The Jewish teachers of the law and the Pharisees thought to themselves, "Who is this man who is speaking as if he were God? Only God can forgive sins."

²²But Jesus knew what they were thinking and said, "Why are you thinking these things? ²³Which is easier: to say, 'Your sins are forgiven,' or to say, 'Stand up and walk'? ²⁴But I will prove to you that the Son of Man has authority on earth to forgive sins." So Jesus said to the paralyzed man, "I tell you, stand up, take your mat, and go home."

²⁵At once the man stood up before them, picked up his mat, and went home, praising God. ²⁶All the people were fully amazed and began to praise God. They

were filled with much respect and said, "Today we have seen amazing things!"

²⁷After this, Jesus went out and saw a tax collector named Levi sitting in the tax collector's booth. Jesus said to him, "Follow me!" ²⁸So Levi got up, left everything, and followed him.

²⁹Then Levi gave a big dinner for Jesus at his house. Many tax collectors and other people were eating there, too. ³⁰But the Pharisees and the men who taught the law for the Pharisees began to complain to Jesus' followers, "Why do you eat and drink with tax collectors and sinners?"

STEP 5 ³¹Jesus answered them, "It is not the healthy people who need a doctor, but the sick. ³²I have not come to invite good people but sinners to change their hearts and lives."

³³They said to Jesus, "John's followers often fast for a certain time and pray, just as the Pharisees do. But your followers eat and drink all the time."

³⁴Jesus said to them, "You cannot make the friends of the bridegroom fast while he is still with them. ³⁵But the time will come when the bridegroom will be taken away from them, and then they will fast."

³⁶Jesus told them this story: "No one takes cloth off a new coat to cover a hole in an old coat. Otherwise, he ruins the new coat, and the cloth from the new coat will not be the same as the old cloth. ³⁷Also, no one ever pours new wine into old leather bags. Otherwise, the new wine will break the bags, the wine will spill out, and the leather bags will be ruined. ³⁸New wine must be put into new leather bags. ³⁹No one after drinking old wine wants new wine, because he says, 'The old wine is better.' "

6 One Sabbath day Jesus was walking through some fields of grain. His followers picked the heads of grain, rubbed them in their hands, and ate them. ²Some Pharisees said, "Why do you do what is not lawful on the Sabbath day?"

³Jesus answered, "Have you not read what David did when he and those with him were hungry? ⁴He went into God's house and took and ate the holy bread, which is lawful only for priests to eat. And he gave some to the people who were with him." ⁵Then Jesus said to the Pharisees, "The Son of Man is Lord of the Sabbath day."

⁶On another Sabbath day Jesus went into the synagogue and was teaching, and a man with a crippled right hand was there. ⁷The teachers of the law and the Pharisees were watching closely to see if Jesus would heal on the Sabbath day so they could accuse him. ⁸But he knew what they were thinking, and he said to the man with the crippled hand, "Stand up here in the middle of everyone." The man got up and stood there. ⁹Then Jesus said to them, "I ask you, which is lawful on the Sabbath day: to do good or to do evil, to save a life or to destroy it?" ¹⁰Jesus looked around at all of them and said to the man, "Hold out your hand." The man held out his hand, and it was healed.

¹¹But the Pharisees and the teachers of the law were very angry and discussed with each other what they could do to Jesus.

¹²At that time Jesus went off to a mountain to pray, and he spent the night praying to God. ¹³The next morning, Jesus called his followers to him and chose twelve of them, whom he named apostles: ¹⁴Simon (Jesus named him Peter), his brother Andrew, James, John, Philip, Bartholomew, ¹⁵Matthew, Thomas, James son of Alphaeus, Simon (called the Zealot), ¹⁶Judas son of James, and Judas Iscariot, who later turned Jesus over to his enemies.

¹⁷Jesus and the apostles came down from the mountain, and he stood on level ground. A large group of his followers was there, as well as many people from all around Judea, Jerusalem, and the seacoast cities of Tyre and Sidon. ¹⁸They all came to hear Jesus teach and to be healed of their sicknesses, and he healed those who were troubled by evil spirits. ¹⁹All the people were trying to touch Jesus, because power was coming from him and healing them all.

STEP 11

²⁰Jesus looked at his followers and said,
"You people who are poor are blessed,
because the kingdom of God belongs to you.
²¹You people who are now hungry are blessed,
because you will be satisfied.
You people who are now crying are blessed,
because you will laugh with joy.
²²"People will hate you, shut you out, insult you, and say you are evil because you follow the Son of Man. But when they do, you will be blessed. ²³Be full of joy at that time, because you have a great reward in heaven. Their ancestors did the same things to the prophets.
²⁴"But how terrible it will be for you who are rich,
because you have had your easy life.
²⁵How terrible it will be for you who are full now,
because you will be hungry.
How terrible it will be for you who are laughing now,
because you will be sad and cry.
²⁶"How terrible when everyone says only good things about you, because their ancestors said the same things about the false prophets.

STEP 9

²⁷"But I say to you who are listening, love your enemies. Do good to those who hate you, ²⁸bless those who curse you, pray for those who are cruel to you. ²⁹If anyone slaps you on one cheek, offer him the other cheek, too. If someone takes your coat, do not stop him from taking your shirt. ³⁰Give to everyone who asks you, and when someone takes something that is yours, don't ask for it back. ³¹Do to others what you would want them to do to you. ³²If you love only the people who love you, what praise should you get? Even sinners love the people who love them. ³³If you do good only to those who do good to you, what praise should you get? Even sinners do that! ³⁴If you lend things to people, always hoping to get something back, what praise should you get? Even sinners lend to other sinners so that they can get back the same amount! ³⁵But love your enemies, do good to them, and lend to them without hoping to get anything back. Then you will have a great reward, and you will be children of the Most High God, because he is kind even to people who are ungrateful and full of sin. ³⁶Show mercy, just as your Father shows mercy.

STEP 8

³⁷"Don't judge others, and you will not be judged. Don't accuse others of being guilty, and you will not be accused of being guilty. Forgive, and you will be forgiven. ³⁸Give, and you will receive. You will be given much. Pressed down, shaken together, and running over, it will spill into your lap. The way you give to others is the way God will give to you."

³⁹Jesus told them this story: "Can a blind person lead another blind person? No! Both of them will fall into a ditch. ⁴⁰A student is not better than the teacher, but the student who has been fully trained will be like the teacher.

STEP 10

⁴¹"Why do you notice the little piece of dust in your friend's eye, but you don't

STEP 8

Made a list of all persons we had harmed,
and became willing to make amends to them all.

Luke 6:37–38

Did you know God takes great pleasure in meeting you "more than halfway" when you turn toward him? That's a great motivator to keep working on your recovery. For example, God says he will reward a tiny seed of faith with great miracles. So, when you start making amends to others, and let go of the anger and bitterness aimed at them or yourself, God will reward your efforts. When you ask the Lord to help you stop judging and condemning people who hurt you in the past, you will soon feel a change taking place inside you. That's God's Holy Spirit healing your heart.

Forgive those who have wronged you. Make amends to those you have wronged. You'll feel the promise of verse 38 coming true in your life. Giving and receiving forgiveness will jump-start rapid spiritual and emotional growth.

FOR YOUR NEXT **STEP 8** MEDITATION, TURN TO **PAGE 115.** ▶▶

notice the big piece of wood in your own eye? ⁴²How can you say to your friend, 'Friend, let me take that little piece of dust out of your eye' when you cannot see that big piece of wood in your own eye! You hypocrite! First, take the wood out of your own eye. Then you will see clearly to take the dust out of your friend's eye.

⁴³"A good tree does not produce bad fruit, nor does a bad tree produce good fruit. ⁴⁴Each tree is known by its own fruit. People don't gather figs from thornbushes, and they don't get grapes from bushes. ⁴⁵Good people bring good things out of the good they stored in their hearts. But evil people bring evil things out of the evil they stored in their hearts. People speak the things that are in their hearts.

STEP 11

⁴⁶"Why do you call me, 'Lord, Lord,' but do not do what I say? ⁴⁷I will show you what everyone is like who comes to me and hears my words and obeys. ⁴⁸That person is like a man building a house who dug deep and laid the foundation on rock. When the floods came, the water tried to wash the house away, but it could not shake it, because the house was built well. ⁴⁹But the one who hears my words and does not obey is like a man who built his house on the ground without a foundation. When the floods came, the house quickly fell and was completely destroyed."

7 When Jesus finished saying all these things to the people, he went to Capernaum. ²There was an army officer who had a servant who was very important to him. The servant was so sick he was nearly dead. ³When the officer heard about Jesus, he sent some Jewish elders to him to ask Jesus to come and heal his servant. ⁴The men went to Jesus and begged him, saying, "This officer is wor-

thy of your help. ⁵He loves our people, and he built us a synagogue."

⁶So Jesus went with the men. He was getting near the officer's house when the officer sent friends to say, "Lord, don't trouble yourself, because I am not worthy to have you come into my house. ⁷That is why I did not come to you myself. But you only need to command it, and my servant will be healed. ⁸I, too, am a man under the authority of others, and I have soldiers under my command. I tell one soldier, 'Go,' and he goes. I tell another soldier, 'Come,' and he comes. I say to my servant, 'Do this,' and my servant does it."

⁹When Jesus heard this, he was amazed. Turning to the crowd that was following him, he said, "I tell you, this is the greatest faith I have found anywhere, even in Israel."

¹⁰Those who had been sent to Jesus went back to the house where they found the servant in good health.

¹¹Soon afterwards Jesus went to a town called Nain, and his followers and a large crowd traveled with him. ¹²When he came near the town gate, he saw a funeral. A mother, who was a widow, had lost her only son. A large crowd from the town was with the mother while her son was being carried out. ¹³When the Lord saw her, he felt very sorry for her and said, "Don't cry." ¹⁴He went up and touched the coffin, and the people who were carrying it stopped. Jesus said, "Young man, I tell you, get up!" ¹⁵And the son sat up and began to talk. Then Jesus gave him back to his mother.

¹⁶All the people were amazed and began praising God, saying, "A great prophet has come to us! God has come to help his people."

¹⁷This news about Jesus spread through all Judea and into all the places around there.

¹⁸John's followers told him about all these things. He called for two of his followers ¹⁹and sent them to the Lord to ask, "Are you the One who is to come, or should we wait for someone else?"

²⁰When the men came to Jesus, they said, "John the Baptist sent us to you with this question: 'Are you the One who is to come, or should we wait for someone else?' "

²¹At that time, Jesus healed many people of their sicknesses, diseases, and evil spirits, and he gave sight to many blind people. ²²Then Jesus answered John's followers, "Go tell John what you saw and heard here. The blind can see, the crippled can walk, and people with skin diseases are healed. The deaf can hear, the dead are raised to life, and the Good News is preached to the poor. ²³Those who do not stumble in their faith because of me are blessed!"

²⁴When John's followers left, Jesus began talking to the people about John: "What did you go out into the desert to see? A reed blown by the wind? ²⁵What did you go out to see? A man dressed in fine clothes? No, people who have fine clothes and much wealth live in kings' palaces. ²⁶But what did you go out to see? A prophet? Yes, and I tell you, John is more than a prophet. ²⁷This was written about him:

'I will send my messenger ahead of
    you,
who will prepare the way for you.'
                                    Malachi 3:1
²⁸I tell you, John is greater than any other person ever born, but even the least important person in the kingdom of God is greater than John."

²⁹(When the people, including the tax collectors, heard this, they all agreed that God's teaching was good, because they had been baptized by John. ³⁰But the Pharisees and experts on the law refused to accept God's plan for themselves; they did not let John baptize them.)

³¹Then Jesus said, "What shall I say about the people of this time? What are they like? ³²They are like children sitting in the marketplace, calling to one another and saying,

'We played music for you, but you did
    not dance;
we sang a sad song, but you did
    not cry.'
³³John the Baptist came and did not eat bread or drink wine, and you say, 'He has a demon in him.' ³⁴The Son of Man came eating and drinking, and you say, 'Look at him! He eats too much and drinks too much wine, and he is a friend of tax collectors and sinners!' ³⁵But wisdom is proved to be right by what it does."

³⁶One of the Pharisees asked Jesus to eat with him, so Jesus went into the Pharisee's house and sat at the table. ³⁷A sinful woman in the town learned that Jesus was eating at the Pharisee's house. So she brought an alabaster jar of perfume ³⁸and stood behind Jesus at his feet, crying. She began to wash his feet with her tears, and she dried them with her hair, kissing them many times and rubbing them with the perfume. ³⁹When the Pharisee who asked Jesus to come to his house saw this, he thought to himself, "If Jesus were a prophet, he would know that the woman touching him is a sinner!"

⁴⁰Jesus said to the Pharisee, "Simon, I have something to say to you."

Simon said, "Teacher, tell me."

⁴¹Jesus said, "Two people owed money to the same banker. One owed five hundred coins and the other owed fifty. ⁴²They had no money to pay what they owed, but the banker told both of them they did not have to pay him. Which person will love the banker more?"

⁴³Simon, the Pharisee, answered, "I think it would be the one who owed him the most money."

Jesus said to Simon, "You are right." ⁴⁴Then Jesus turned toward the woman and said to Simon, "Do you see this woman? When I came into your house, you gave me no water for my feet, but she washed my feet with her tears and dried them with her hair. ⁴⁵You gave me no kiss of greeting, but she has been kissing my feet since I came in. ⁴⁶You did not put oil on my head, but she poured perfume on my feet. ⁴⁷I tell you that her many sins are forgiven, so she showed great love. But the person who is forgiven only a little will love only a little."

⁴⁸Then Jesus said to her, "Your sins are forgiven."

⁴⁹The people sitting at the table began to say among themselves, "Who is this who even forgives sins?"

⁵⁰Jesus said to the woman, "Because you believed, you are saved from your sins. Go in peace."

8 After this, while Jesus was traveling through some cities and small towns, he preached and told the Good News about God's kingdom. The twelve apostles were with him, ²and also some women who had been healed of sicknesses and evil spirits: Mary, called Magdalene, from whom seven demons had gone out; ³Joanna, the wife of Cuza (the manager of Herod's house); Susanna; and many others. These women used their own money to help Jesus and his apostles.

⁴When a great crowd was gathered, and people were coming to Jesus from every town, he told them this story:

⁵"A farmer went out to plant his seed. While he was planting, some seed fell by the road. People walked on the seed, and the birds ate it up. ⁶Some seed fell on rock, and when it began to grow, it died because it had no water. ⁷Some seed fell among thorny weeds, but the weeds grew up with it and choked the good plants. ⁸And some seed fell on good ground and grew and made a hundred times more."

As Jesus finished the story, he called out, "Let those with ears use them and listen!"

⁹Jesus' followers asked him what this story meant.

¹⁰Jesus said, "You have been chosen to know the secrets about the kingdom of God. But I use stories to speak to other people so that:

'They will look, but they may not see.
    They will listen, but they may not
        understand.'   *Isaiah 6:9*

¹¹"This is what the story means: The seed is God's message. ¹²The seed that fell beside the road is like the people who hear God's teaching, but the devil comes and takes it away from them so they cannot believe it and be saved. ¹³The seed that fell on rock is like those who hear God's teaching and accept it gladly, but they don't allow the teaching to go deep into their lives. They believe for a while, but when trouble comes, they give up. ¹⁴The seed that fell among the thorny weeds is like those who hear God's teaching, but they let the worries, riches, and pleasures of this life keep them from growing and producing good fruit. ¹⁵And the seed that fell on the good ground is like those who hear God's teaching with good, honest hearts and obey it and patiently produce good fruit.

¹⁶"No one after lighting a lamp covers it with a bowl or hides it under a bed. Instead, the person puts it on a lampstand so those who come in will see the light. ¹⁷Everything that is hidden will become clear, and every secret thing will be

made known. [18]So be careful how you listen. Those who have understanding will be given more. But those who do not have understanding, even what they think they have will be taken away from them."

[19]Jesus' mother and brothers came to see him, but there was such a crowd they could not get to him. [20]Someone said to Jesus, "Your mother and your brothers are standing outside, wanting to see you."

[21]Jesus answered them, "My mother and my brothers are those who listen to God's teaching and obey it!"

[22]One day Jesus and his followers got into a boat, and he said to them, "Let's go across the lake." And so they started across. [23]While they were sailing, Jesus fell asleep. A very strong wind blew up on the lake, causing the boat to fill with water, and they were in danger.

[24]The followers went to Jesus and woke him, saying, "Master! Master! We will drown!"

Jesus got up and gave a command to the wind and the waves. They stopped, and it became calm. [25]Jesus said to his followers, "Where is your faith?"

The followers were afraid and amazed and said to each other, "Who is this that commands even the wind and the water, and they obey him?"

[26]Jesus and his followers sailed across the lake from Galilee to the area of the Gerasene people. [27]When Jesus got out on the land, a man from the town who had demons inside him came to Jesus. For a long time he had worn no clothes and had lived in the burial caves, not in a house. [28]When he saw Jesus, he cried out and fell down before him. He said with a loud voice, "What do you want with me, Jesus, Son of the Most High God? I beg you, don't torture me!" [29]He said this because Jesus was commanding the evil spirit to come out of the man. Many times it had taken hold of him. Though he had been kept under guard and chained hand and foot, he had broken his chains and had been forced by the demon out into a lonely place.

[30]Jesus asked him, "What is your name?"

He answered, "Legion," because many demons were in him. [31]The demons begged Jesus not to send them into eternal darkness. [32]A large herd of pigs was feeding on a hill, and the demons begged Jesus to allow them to go into the pigs. So Jesus allowed them to do this. [33]When the demons came out of the man, they went into the pigs, and the herd ran down the hill into the lake and was drowned.

[34]When the herdsmen saw what had happened, they ran away and told about this in the town and the countryside. [35]And people went to see what had happened. When they came to Jesus, they found the man sitting at Jesus' feet, clothed and in his right mind, because the demons were gone. But the people were frightened. [36]The people who saw this happen told the others how Jesus had made the man well. [37]All the people of the Gerasene country asked Jesus to leave, because they were all very afraid. So Jesus got into the boat and went back to Galilee.

[38]The man whom Jesus had healed begged to go with him, but Jesus sent him away, saying, [39]"Go back home and tell people how much God has done for you." So the man went all over town telling how much Jesus had done for him.

[40]When Jesus got back to Galilee, a crowd welcomed him, because everyone was waiting for him. [41]A man named Jairus, a leader of the synagogue, came to Jesus and fell at his feet, begging him to

come to his house. ⁴²Jairus' only daughter, about twelve years old, was dying.

While Jesus was on his way to Jairus' house, the people were crowding all around him. ⁴³A woman was in the crowd who had been bleeding for twelve years, but no one was able to heal her. ⁴⁴She came up behind Jesus and touched the edge of his coat, and instantly her bleeding stopped. ⁴⁵Then Jesus said, "Who touched me?"

When all the people said they had not touched him, Peter said, "Master, the people are all around you and are pushing against you."

⁴⁶But Jesus said, "Someone did touch me, because I felt power go out from me." ⁴⁷When the woman saw she could not hide, she came forward, shaking, and fell down before Jesus. While all the people listened, she told why she had touched him and how she had been instantly healed. ⁴⁸Jesus said to her, "Dear woman, you are made well because you believed. Go in peace."

⁴⁹While Jesus was still speaking, someone came from the house of the synagogue leader and said to him, "Your daughter is dead. Don't bother the teacher anymore."

⁵⁰When Jesus heard this, he said to Jairus, "Don't be afraid. Just believe, and your daughter will be well."

⁵¹When Jesus went to the house, he let only Peter, John, James, and the girl's father and mother go inside with him. ⁵²All the people were crying and feeling sad because the girl was dead, but Jesus said, "Stop crying. She is not dead, only asleep."

⁵³The people laughed at Jesus because they knew the girl was dead. ⁵⁴But Jesus took hold of her hand and called to her, "My child, stand up!" ⁵⁵Her spirit came back into her, and she stood up at once.

Then Jesus ordered that she be given something to eat. ⁵⁶The girl's parents were amazed, but Jesus told them not to tell anyone what had happened.

9 Jesus called the twelve apostles together and gave them power and authority over all demons and the ability to heal sicknesses. ²He sent the apostles out to tell about God's kingdom and to heal the sick. ³He said to them, "Take nothing for your trip, neither a walking stick, bag, bread, money, or extra clothes. ⁴When you enter a house, stay there until it is time to leave. ⁵If people do not welcome you, shake the dust off of your feet as you leave the town, as a warning to them."

⁶So the apostles went out and traveled through all the towns, preaching the Good News and healing people everywhere.

⁷Herod, the governor, heard about all the things that were happening and was confused, because some people said, "John the Baptist has risen from the dead." ⁸Others said, "Elijah has come to us." And still others said, "One of the prophets who lived long ago has risen from the dead." ⁹Herod said, "I cut off John's head, so who is this man I hear such things about?" And Herod kept trying to see Jesus.

¹⁰When the apostles returned, they told Jesus everything they had done. Then Jesus took them with him to a town called Bethsaida where they could be alone together. ¹¹But the people learned where Jesus went and followed him. He welcomed them and talked with them about God's kingdom and healed those who needed to be healed.

¹²Late in the afternoon, the twelve apostles came to Jesus and said, "Send the people away. They need to go to the towns and countryside around here and

find places to sleep and something to eat, because no one lives in this place."

¹³But Jesus said to them, "You give them something to eat."

They said, "We have only five loaves of bread and two fish, unless we go buy food for all these people." ¹⁴(There were about five thousand men there.)

Jesus said to his followers, "Tell the people to sit in groups of about fifty people."

¹⁵So the followers did this, and all the people sat down. ¹⁶Then Jesus took the five loaves of bread and two fish, and looking up to heaven, he thanked God for the food. Then he divided the food and gave it to the followers to give to the people. ¹⁷They all ate and were satisfied, and what was left over was gathered up, filling twelve baskets.

¹⁸One time when Jesus was praying alone, his followers were with him, and he asked them, "Who do the people say I am?"

¹⁹They answered, "Some say you are John the Baptist. Others say you are Elijah. And others say you are one of the prophets from long ago who has come back to life."

²⁰Then Jesus asked, "But who do you say I am?"

Peter answered, "You are the Christ from God."

²¹Jesus warned them not to tell anyone, saying, ²²"The Son of Man must suffer many things. He will be rejected by the Jewish elders, the leading priests, and the teachers of the law. He will be killed and after three days will be raised from the dead."

²³Jesus said to all of them, "If people want to follow me, they must give up the things they want. They must be willing to give up their lives daily to follow me. ²⁴Those who want to save their lives will give up true life. But those who give up their lives for me will have true life. ²⁵It is worthless to have the whole world if they themselves are destroyed or lost. ²⁶If people are ashamed of me and my teaching, then the Son of Man will be ashamed of them when he comes in his glory and with the glory of the Father and the holy angels. ²⁷I tell you the truth, some people standing here will see the kingdom of God before they die."

²⁸About eight days after Jesus said these things, he took Peter, John, and James and went up on a mountain to pray. ²⁹While Jesus was praying, the appearance of his face changed, and his clothes became shining white. ³⁰Then two men, Moses and Elijah, were talking with Jesus. ³¹They appeared in heavenly glory, talking about his departure which he would soon bring about in Jerusalem. ³²Peter and the others were very sleepy, but when they awoke fully, they saw the glory of Jesus and the two men standing with him. ³³When Moses and Elijah were about to leave, Peter said to Jesus, "Master, it is good that we are here. Let us make three tents—one for you, one for Moses, and one for Elijah." (Peter did not know what he was talking about.)

³⁴While he was saying these things, a cloud came and covered them, and they became afraid as the cloud covered them. ³⁵A voice came from the cloud, saying, "This is my Son, whom I have chosen. Listen to him!"

³⁶When the voice finished speaking, only Jesus was there. Peter, John, and James said nothing and told no one at that time what they had seen.

³⁷The next day, when they came down from the mountain, a large crowd met Jesus. ³⁸A man in the crowd shouted to him, "Teacher, please come and look at my son, because he is my only child. ³⁹An evil

spirit seizes my son, and suddenly he screams. It causes him to lose control of himself and foam at the mouth. The evil spirit keeps on hurting him and almost never leaves him. ⁴⁰I begged your followers to force the evil spirit out, but they could not do it."

⁴¹Jesus answered, "You people have no faith, and your lives are all wrong. How long must I stay with you and put up with you? Bring your son here."

⁴²While the boy was coming, the demon threw him on the ground and made him lose control of himself. But Jesus gave a strong command to the evil spirit and healed the boy and gave him back to his father. ⁴³All the people were amazed at the great power of God.

While everyone was wondering about all that Jesus did, he said to his followers, ⁴⁴"Don't forget what I tell you now: The Son of Man will be handed over to people." ⁴⁵But the followers did not understand what this meant; the meaning was hidden from them so they could not understand. But they were afraid to ask Jesus about it.

⁴⁶Jesus' followers began to have an argument about which one of them was the greatest. ⁴⁷Jesus knew what they were thinking, so he took a little child and stood the child beside him. ⁴⁸Then Jesus said, "Whoever accepts this little child in my name accepts me. And whoever accepts the One who sent me, because whoever is least among you all is really the greatest."

⁴⁹John answered, "Master, we saw someone using your name to force demons out of people. We told him to stop, because he does not belong to our group."

⁵⁰But Jesus said to him, "Don't stop him, because whoever is not against you is for you."

⁵¹When the time was coming near for Jesus to depart, he was determined to go to Jerusalem. ⁵²He sent some messengers ahead of him, who went into a town in Samaria to make everything ready for him. ⁵³But the people there would not welcome him, because he was set on going to Jerusalem. ⁵⁴When James and John, followers of Jesus, saw this, they said, "Lord, do you want us to call fire down from heaven and destroy those people?"

⁵⁵But Jesus turned and scolded them. [And Jesus said, "You don't know what kind of spirit you belong to. ⁵⁶The Son of Man did not come to destroy the souls of people but to save them."] Then they went to another town.

⁵⁷As they were going along the road, someone said to Jesus, "I will follow you any place you go."

⁵⁸Jesus said to them, "The foxes have holes to live in, and the birds have nests, but the Son of Man has no place to rest his head."

⁵⁹Jesus said to another man, "Follow me!"

But he said, "Lord, first let me go and bury my father."

⁶⁰But Jesus said to him, "Let the people who are dead bury their own dead. You must go and tell about the kingdom of God."

⁶¹Another man said, "I will follow you, Lord, but first let me go and say goodbye to my family."

⁶²Jesus said, "Anyone who begins to plow a field but keeps looking back is of no use in the kingdom of God."

10 After this, the Lord chose seventy-two others and sent them out in pairs ahead of him into every town and place where he planned to go. ²He said to them, "There are a great many people to harvest, but there are only a

STEP 2

STEP 3

few workers. So pray to God, who owns the harvest, that he will send more workers to help gather his harvest. ³Go now, but listen! I am sending you out like sheep among wolves. ⁴Don't carry a purse, a bag, or sandals, and don't waste time talking with people on the road. ⁵Before you go into a house, say, 'Peace be with this house.' ⁶If peace-loving people live there, your blessing of peace will stay with them, but if not, then your blessing will come back to you. ⁷Stay in the same house, eating and drinking what the people there give you. A worker should be given his pay. Don't move from house to house. ⁸If you go into a town and the people welcome you, eat what they give you. ⁹Heal the sick who live there, and tell them, 'The kingdom of God is near you.' ¹⁰But if you go into a town, and the people don't welcome you, then go into the streets and say, ¹¹'Even the dirt from your town that sticks to our feet we wipe off against you. But remember that the kingdom of God is near.' ¹²I tell you, on the Judgment Day it will be better for the people of Sodom than for the people of that town.

¹³"How terrible for you, Korazin! How terrible for you, Bethsaida! If the miracles I did in you had happened in Tyre and Sidon, those people would have changed their lives long ago. They would have worn rough cloth and put ashes on themselves to show they had changed. ¹⁴But on the Judgment Day it will be better for Tyre and Sidon than for you. ¹⁵And you, Capernaum, will you be lifted up to heaven? No! You will be thrown down to the depths!

¹⁶"Whoever listens to you listens to me, and whoever refuses to accept you refuses to accept me. And whoever refuses to accept me refuses to accept the One who sent me."

¹⁷When the seventy-two came back, they were very happy and said, "Lord, even the demons obeyed us when we used your name!"

¹⁸Jesus said, "I saw Satan fall like lightning from heaven. ¹⁹Listen, I have given you power to walk on snakes and scorpions, power that is greater than the enemy has. So nothing will hurt you. ²⁰But you should not be happy because the spirits obey you but because your names are written in heaven."

²¹Then Jesus rejoiced in the Holy Spirit and said, "I praise you, Father, Lord of heaven and earth, because you have hidden these things from the people who are wise and smart. But you have shown them to those who are like little children. Yes, Father, this is what you really wanted.

²²"My Father has given me all things. No one knows who the Son is, except the Father. And no one knows who the Father is, except the Son and those whom the Son chooses to tell."

²³Then Jesus turned to his followers and said privately, "You are blessed to see what you now see. ²⁴I tell you, many prophets and kings wanted to see what you now see, but they did not, and they wanted to hear what you now hear, but they did not."

²⁵Then an expert on the law stood up to test Jesus, saying, "Teacher, what must I do to get life forever?"

²⁶Jesus said, "What is written in the law? What do you read there?"

²⁷The man answered, "Love the Lord your God with all your heart, all your soul, all your strength, and all your mind." Also, "Love your neighbor as you love yourself."

²⁸Jesus said to him, "Your answer is right. Do this and you will live."

²⁹But the man, wanting to show the

STEP 8

importance of his question, said to Jesus, "And who is my neighbor?"

³⁰Jesus answered, "As a man was going down from Jerusalem to Jericho, some robbers attacked him. They tore off his clothes, beat him, and left him lying there, almost dead. ³¹It happened that a priest was going down that road. When he saw the man, he walked by on the other side. ³²Next, a Levite came there, and after he went over and looked at the man, he walked by on the other side of the road. ³³Then a Samaritan traveling down the road came to where the hurt man was. When he saw the man, he felt very sorry for him. ³⁴The Samaritan went to him, poured olive oil and wine on his wounds, and bandaged them. Then he put the hurt man on his own donkey and took him to an inn where he cared for him. ³⁵The next day, the Samaritan brought out two coins, gave them to the innkeeper, and said, 'Take care of this man. If you spend more money on him, I will pay it back to you when I come again.' "

³⁶Then Jesus said, "Which one of these three men do you think was a neighbor to the man who was attacked by the robbers?"

³⁷The expert on the law answered, "The one who showed him mercy."

Jesus said to him, "Then go and do what he did."

³⁸While Jesus and his followers were traveling, Jesus went into a town. A woman named Martha let Jesus stay at her house. ³⁹Martha had a sister named Mary, who was sitting at Jesus' feet and listening to him teach. ⁴⁰But Martha was busy with all the work to be done. She went in and said, "Lord, don't you care that my sister has left me alone to do all the work? Tell her to help me."

⁴¹But the Lord answered her, "Martha, Martha, you are worried and upset about many things. ⁴²Only one thing is important. Mary has chosen the better thing, and it will never be taken away from her."

11 One time Jesus was praying in a certain place. When he finished, one of his followers said to him, "Lord, teach us to pray as John taught his followers."

²Jesus said to them, "When you pray, say: [STEP 3]

'Father, may your name always be kept holy.
May your kingdom come.
³Give us the food we need for each day.
⁴Forgive us for our sins,
    because we forgive everyone who has done wrong to us.
And do not cause us to be tempted.' "

⁵Then Jesus said to them, "Suppose [STEP 2] one of you went to your friend's house at midnight and said to him, 'Friend, loan me three loaves of bread. ⁶A friend of mine has come into town to visit me, but I have nothing for him to eat.' ⁷Your friend inside the house answers, 'Don't bother me! The door is already locked, and my children and I are in bed. I cannot get up and give you anything.' ⁸I tell you, if friendship is not enough to make him get up to give you the bread, your boldness will make him get up and give you whatever you need. ⁹So I tell you, ask, and God will give to you. Search, and you will find. Knock, and the door will open for you. ¹⁰Yes, everyone who asks will receive. The one who searches will find. And everyone who knocks will have the door opened. ¹¹If your children ask for a fish, which of you would give them a snake instead? ¹²Or, if your children ask for an egg, would you give them a scorpion? ¹³Even though you are bad, you know how to give good

things to your children. How much more your heavenly Father will give the Holy Spirit to those who ask him!"

¹⁴One time Jesus was sending out a demon who could not talk. When the demon came out, the man who had been unable to speak, then spoke. The people were amazed. ¹⁵But some of them said, "Jesus uses the power of Beelzebul, the ruler of demons, to force demons out of people."

¹⁶Other people, wanting to test Jesus, asked him to give them a sign from heaven. ¹⁷But knowing their thoughts, he said to them, "Every kingdom that is divided against itself will be destroyed. And a family that is divided against itself will not continue. ¹⁸So if Satan is divided against himself, his kingdom will not continue. You say that I use the power of Beelzebul to force out demons. ¹⁹But if I use the power of Beelzebul to force out demons, what power do your people use to force demons out? So they will be your judges. ²⁰But if I use the power of God to force out demons, then the kingdom of God has come to you.

²¹"When a strong person with many weapons guards his own house, his possessions are safe. ²²But when someone stronger comes and defeats him, the stronger one will take away the weapons the first man trusted and will give away the possessions.

²³"Anyone who is not with me is against me, and anyone who does not work with me is working against me.

²⁴"When an evil spirit comes out of a person, it travels through dry places, looking for a place to rest. But when it finds no place, it says, 'I will go back to the house I left.' ²⁵And when it comes back, it finds that house swept clean and made neat. ²⁶Then the evil spirit goes out and brings seven other spirits more evil than it is, and they go in and live there. So

the person has even more trouble than before."

²⁷As Jesus was saying these things, a woman in the crowd called out to Jesus, "Blessed is the mother who gave birth to you and nursed you."

²⁸But Jesus said, "No, blessed are those who hear the teaching of God and obey it."

²⁹As the crowd grew larger, Jesus said, "The people who live today are evil. They want to see a miracle for a sign, but no sign will be given them, except the sign of Jonah. ³⁰As Jonah was a sign for those people who lived in Nineveh, the Son of Man will be a sign for the people of this time. ³¹On the Judgment Day the Queen of the South will stand up with the people who live now. She will show they are guilty, because she came from far away to listen to Solomon's wise teaching. And I tell you that someone greater than Solomon is here. ³²On the Judgment Day the people of Nineveh will stand up with the people who live now, and they will show that you are guilty. When Jonah preached to them, they were sorry and changed their lives. And I tell you that someone greater than Jonah is here.

³³"No one lights a lamp and puts it in a secret place or under a bowl, but on a lampstand so the people who come in can see. ³⁴Your eye is a light for the body. When your eyes are good, your whole body will be full of light. But when your eyes are evil, your whole body will be full of darkness. ³⁵So be careful not to let the light in you become darkness. ³⁶If your whole body is full of light, and none of it is dark, then you will shine bright, as when a lamp shines on you."

³⁷After Jesus had finished speaking, a Pharisee asked Jesus to eat with him. So Jesus went in and sat at the table. ³⁸But

STEP
4

the Pharisee was surprised when he saw that Jesus did not wash his hands before the meal. ³⁹The Lord said to him, "You Pharisees clean the outside of the cup and the dish, but inside you are full of greed and evil. ⁴⁰You foolish people! The same one who made what is outside also made what is inside. ⁴¹So give what is in your dishes to the poor, and then you will be fully clean. ⁴²How terrible for you Pharisees! You give God one-tenth of even your mint, your rue, and every other plant in your garden. But you fail to be fair to others and to love God. These are the things you should do while continuing to do those other things. ⁴³How terrible for you Pharisees, because you love to have the most important seats in the synagogues, and you love to be greeted with respect in the marketplaces. ⁴⁴How terrible for you, because you are like hidden graves, which people walk on without knowing."

⁴⁵One of the experts on the law said to Jesus, "Teacher, when you say these things, you are insulting us, too."

⁴⁶Jesus answered, "How terrible for you, you experts on the law! You make strict rules that are very hard for people to obey, but you yourselves don't even try to follow those rules. ⁴⁷How terrible for you, because you build tombs for the prophets whom your ancestors killed! ⁴⁸And now you show that you approve of what your ancestors did. They killed the prophets, and you build tombs for them! ⁴⁹This is why in his wisdom God said, 'I will send prophets and apostles to them. They will kill some, and they will treat others cruelly.' ⁵⁰So you who live now will be punished for the deaths of all the prophets who were killed since the beginning of the world— ⁵¹from the killing of Abel to the killing of Zechariah, who died between the altar and the Temple.

Yes, I tell you that you who are alive now will be punished for them all.

⁵²"How terrible for you, you experts on the law. You have taken away the key to learning about God. You yourselves would not learn, and you stopped others from learning, too."

⁵³When Jesus left, the teachers of the law and the Pharisees began to give him trouble, asking him questions about many things, ⁵⁴trying to catch him saying something wrong.

12 So many thousands of people had gathered that they were stepping on each other. Jesus spoke first to his followers, saying, "Beware of the yeast of the Pharisees, because they are hypocrites. ²Everything that is hidden will be shown, and everything that is secret will be made known. ³What you have said in the dark will be heard in the light, and what you have whispered in an inner room will be shouted from the housetops.

⁴"I tell you, my friends, don't be afraid of people who can kill the body but after that can do nothing more to hurt you. ⁵I will show you the one to fear. Fear the one who has the power to kill you and also to throw you into hell. Yes, this is the one you should fear.

⁶"Five sparrows are sold for only two pennies, and God does not forget any of them. ⁷But God even knows how many hairs you have on your head. Don't be afraid. You are worth much more than many sparrows.

⁸"I tell you, all those who stand before others and say they believe in me, I, the Son of Man, will say before the angels of God that they belong to me. ⁹But all who stand before others and say they do not believe in me, I will say before the angels of God that they do not belong to me.

¹⁰"Anyone who speaks against the Son

STEP 4

STEP 4

Made a searching and fearless moral
inventory of ourselves.

Luke 12:1–6

When you read the life of Jesus, it's clear he hated hypocrisy—
pretending to be something you're not. Step 4 is a hypocrisy-
buster. In it, you evaluate your life thoroughly and fearlessly accept
the truth about your past. As you go through this inventory process,
keep these truths in mind:

1) God already knows everything about you (verses 2–3). You
   don't need to hide.

2) You have to name your fears to move beyond them. If you
   don't, you stay tied up in emotional knots and can't deal with
   the most important issue in life—your relationship with God
   (verses 4–5).

3) God cares about you more than you can imagine (verses
   6–7). While you do your inventory, think about his care for
   you. Let his love and forgiveness wash over you.

So far in the Steps, you have put your trust in God. He is present
with you, helping you uncover your real self. Don't be afraid, and
don't pretend. The real you is the person God loves.

FOR YOUR NEXT **STEP 4** MEDITATION, TURN TO **PAGE 222.** ▶▶

of Man can be forgiven, but anyone who speaks against the Holy Spirit will not be forgiven.

¹¹"When you are brought into the synagogues before the leaders and other powerful people, don't worry about how to defend yourself or what to say. ¹²At that time the Holy Spirit will teach you what you must say."

¹³Someone in the crowd said to Jesus, "Teacher, tell my brother to divide with me the property our father left us."

¹⁴But Jesus said to him, "Who said I should judge or decide between you?"

STEP 4

¹⁵Then Jesus said to them, "Be careful and guard against all kinds of greed. Life is not measured by how much one owns."

¹⁶Then Jesus told this story: "There was a rich man who had some land, which grew a good crop. ¹⁷He thought to himself, 'What will I do? I have no place to keep all my crops.' ¹⁸Then he said, 'This is what I will do: I will tear down my barns and build bigger ones, and there I will store all my grain and other goods. ¹⁹Then I can say to myself, "I have enough good things stored to last for many years. Rest, eat, drink, and enjoy life!"'

²⁰"But God said to him, 'Foolish man! Tonight your life will be taken from you. So who will get those things you have prepared for yourself?'

²¹"This is how it will be for those who store up things for themselves and are not rich toward God."

²²Jesus said to his followers, "So I tell you, don't worry about the food you need to live, or about the clothes you need for your body. ²³Life is more than food, and the body is more than clothes. ²⁴Look at the birds. They don't plant or harvest, they don't have storerooms or barns, but God feeds them. And you are worth much more than birds. ²⁵You cannot add

any time to your life by worrying about it. ²⁶If you cannot do even the little things, then why worry about the big things? ²⁷Consider how the lilies grow; they don't work or make clothes for themselves. But I tell you that even Solomon with his riches was not dressed as beautifully as one of these flowers. ²⁸God clothes the grass in the field, which is alive today but tomorrow is thrown into the fire. So how much more will God clothe you? Don't have so little faith! ²⁹Don't always think about what you will eat or what you will drink, and don't keep worrying. ³⁰All the people in the world are trying to get these things, and your Father knows you need them. ³¹But seek God's kingdom, and all your other needs will be met as well.

STEP 11

³²"Don't fear, little flock, because your Father wants to give you the kingdom. ³³Sell your possessions and give to the poor. Get for yourselves purses that will not wear out, the treasure in heaven that never runs out, where thieves can't steal and moths can't destroy. ³⁴Your heart will be where your treasure is.

³⁵"Be dressed, ready for service, and have your lamps shining. ³⁶Be like servants who are waiting for their master to come home from a wedding party. When he comes and knocks, the servants immediately open the door for him. ³⁷They will be blessed when their master comes home, because he sees that they were watching for him. I tell you the truth, the master will dress himself to serve and tell the servants to sit at the table, and he will serve them. ³⁸Those servants will be blessed when he comes in and finds them still waiting, even if it is midnight or later.

STEP 12

³⁹"Remember this: If the owner of the house knew what time a thief was coming, he would not allow the thief to enter

his house. 40So you also must be ready, because the Son of Man will come at a time when you don't expect him!"

41Peter said, "Lord, did you tell this story to us or to all people?"

42The Lord said, "Who is the wise and trusted servant that the master trusts to give the other servants their food at the right time? 43When the master comes and finds the servant doing his work, the servant will be blessed. 44I tell you the truth, the master will choose that servant to take care of everything he owns. 45But suppose the servant thinks to himself, 'My master will not come back soon,' and he begins to beat the other servants, men and women, and to eat and drink and get drunk. 46The master will come when that servant is not ready and is not expecting him. Then the master will cut him in pieces and send him away to be with the others who don't obey.

47"The servant who knows what his master wants but is not ready, or who does not do what the master wants, will be beaten with many blows! 48But the servant who does not know what his master wants and does things that should be punished will be beaten with few blows. From everyone who has been given much, much will be demanded. And from the one trusted with much, much more will be expected.

49"I came to set fire to the world, and I wish it were already burning! 50I have a baptism to suffer through, and I feel very troubled until it is over. 51Do you think I came to give peace to the earth? No, I tell you, I came to divide it. 52From now on, a family with five people will be divided, three against two, and two against three. 53They will be divided: father against son and son against father, mother against daughter and daughter against mother, mother-in-law against daughter-in-law and daughter-in-law against mother-in-law."

54Then Jesus said to the people, "When you see clouds coming up in the west, you say, 'It's going to rain,' and it happens. 55When you feel the wind begin to blow from the south, you say, 'It will be a hot day,' and it happens. 56Hypocrites! You know how to understand the appearance of the earth and sky. Why don't you understand what is happening now?

57"Why can't you decide for yourselves what is right? 58If your enemy is taking you to court, try hard to settle it on the way. If you don't, your enemy might take you to the judge, and the judge might turn you over to the officer, and the officer might throw you into jail. 59I tell you, you will not get out of there until you have paid everything you owe."

13 At that time some people were there who told Jesus that Pilate had killed some people from Galilee while they were worshiping. He mixed their blood with the blood of the animals they were sacrificing to God. 2Jesus answered, "Do you think this happened to them because they were more sinful than all others from Galilee? 3No, I tell you. But unless you change your hearts and lives, you will be destroyed as they were! 4What about those eighteen people who died when the tower of Siloam fell on them? Do you think they were more sinful than all the others who live in Jerusalem? 5No, I tell you. But unless you change your hearts and lives, you will all be destroyed too!"

6Jesus told this story: "A man had a fig tree planted in his vineyard. He came looking for some fruit on the tree, but he found none. 7So the man said to his gardener, 'I have been looking for fruit on this tree for three years, but I never find any. Cut it down. Why should it waste the ground?' ⁸But the servant answered, 'Master, let the tree have one more year to produce fruit. Let me dig up the dirt around it and put on some fertilizer. ⁹If the tree produces fruit next year, good. But if not, you can cut it down.' "

STEP 2

¹⁰Jesus was teaching in one of the synagogues on the Sabbath day. ¹¹A woman was there who, for eighteen years, had an evil spirit in her that made her crippled. Her back was always bent; she could not stand up straight. ¹²When Jesus saw her, he called her over and said, "Woman, you are free from your sickness." ¹³Jesus put his hands on her, and immediately she was able to stand up straight and began praising God.

¹⁴The synagogue leader was angry because Jesus healed on the Sabbath day. He said to the people, "There are six days when one has to work. So come to be healed on one of those days, and not on the Sabbath day."

¹⁵The Lord answered, "You hypocrites! Doesn't each of you untie your work animals and lead them to drink water every day—even on the Sabbath day? ¹⁶This woman that I healed, a daughter of Abraham, has been held by Satan for eighteen years. Surely it is not wrong for her to be freed from her sickness on a Sabbath day!" ¹⁷When Jesus said this, all of those who were criticizing him were ashamed, but the entire crowd rejoiced at all the wonderful things Jesus was doing.

¹⁸Then Jesus said, "What is God's kingdom like? What can I compare it with? ¹⁹It is like a mustard seed that a man plants in his garden. The seed grows and becomes a tree, and the wild birds build nests in its branches."

²⁰Jesus said again, "What can I compare God's kingdom with? ²¹It is like yeast that a woman took and hid in a large tub of flour until it made all the dough rise."

²²Jesus was teaching in every town and village as he traveled toward Jerusalem. ²³Someone said to Jesus, "Lord, will only a few people be saved?"

Jesus said, ²⁴"Try hard to enter through the narrow door, because many people will try to enter there, but they will not be able. ²⁵When the owner of the house gets up and closes the door, you can stand outside and knock on the door and say, 'Sir, open the door for us.' But he will answer, 'I don't know you or where you come from.' ²⁶Then you will say, 'We ate and drank with you, and you taught in the streets of our town.' ²⁷But he will say to you, 'I don't know you or where you come from. Go away from me, all you who do evil!' ²⁸You will cry and grind your teeth with pain when you see Abraham, Isaac, Jacob, and all the prophets in God's kingdom, but you yourselves thrown outside. ²⁹People will come from the east, west, north, and south and will sit down at the table in the kingdom of God. ³⁰There are those who are last now who will be first in the future. And there are those who are first now who will be last in the future."

³¹At that time some Pharisees came to Jesus and said, "Go away from here! Herod wants to kill you!"

³²Jesus said to them, "Go tell that fox Herod, 'Today and tomorrow I am forcing demons out and healing people. Then, on the third day, I will reach my goal.' ³³Yet I must be on my way today and tomorrow and the next day. Surely it cannot be right for a prophet to be killed anywhere except in Jerusalem.

³⁴"Jerusalem, Jerusalem! You kill the prophets and stone to death those who are sent to you. Many times I wanted to gather your people as a hen gathers her chicks under her wings, but you would not let me. ³⁵Now your house is left

STEP 2

Came to believe that a Power greater than
ourselves could restore us to sanity.

Luke 13:10–13

This story of healing is one of many in the New Testament. It's a
short story with few details. The important feature is that Jesus
touched the woman. God's healing came through the touch of
Jesus. That's what you want in your recovery. You want the touch of
Jesus to take away your anxiety, your depression, and your
addiction.

The whole recovery movement builds on the stories of men and
women delivered from addictive cravings for alcohol, drugs, sex,
and other things. Some are dramatic stories of instantaneous
deliverance from longstanding compulsions. Most are heroic tales
of one-day-at-a-time perseverance to freedom. However the
stories go, all of them involve hanging on to God's help. He got
them all through to the other side.

Your healing is a precious thing. But in the final analysis, it's a
stepping-stone to something still more precious—your life-giving
relationship with God.

FOR YOUR NEXT **STEP 2** MEDITATION, TURN TO **PAGE 137**. ▶▶

completely empty. I tell you, you will not see me until that time when you will say, 'God bless the One who comes in the name of the Lord.'"

14 On a Sabbath day, when Jesus went to eat at the home of a leading Pharisee, the people were watching Jesus very closely. ²And in front of him was a man with dropsy. ³Jesus said to the Pharisees and experts on the law, "Is it right or wrong to heal on the Sabbath day?" ⁴But they would not answer his question. So Jesus took the man, healed him, and sent him away. ⁵Jesus said to the Pharisees and teachers of the law, "If your child or ox falls into a well on the Sabbath day, will you not pull him out quickly?" ⁶And they could not answer him.

⁷When Jesus noticed that some of the guests were choosing the best places to sit, he told this story: ⁸"When someone invites you to a wedding feast, don't take the most important seat, because someone more important than you may have been invited. ⁹The host, who invited both of you, will come to you and say, 'Give this person your seat.' Then you will be embarrassed and will have to move to the last place. ¹⁰So when you are invited, go sit in a seat that is not important. When the host comes to you, he may say, 'Friend, move up here to a more important place.' Then all the other guests will respect you. ¹¹All who make themselves great will be made humble, but those who make themselves humble will be made great."

¹²Then Jesus said to the man who had invited him, "When you give a lunch or a dinner, don't invite only your friends, your family, your other relatives, and your rich neighbors. At another time they will invite you to eat with them, and you will be repaid. ¹³Instead, when you give a feast, invite the poor, the crippled, the lame, and the blind. ¹⁴Then you will be blessed, because they have nothing and cannot pay you back. But you will be repaid when the good people rise from the dead."

¹⁵One of those at the table with Jesus heard these things and said to him, "Blessed are the people who will share in the meal in God's kingdom."

¹⁶Jesus said to him, "A man gave a big banquet and invited many people. ¹⁷When it was time to eat, the man sent his servant to tell the guests, 'Come. Everything is ready.'

¹⁸"But all the guests made excuses. The first one said, 'I have just bought a field, and I must go look at it. Please excuse me.' ¹⁹Another said, 'I have just bought five pairs of oxen; I must go and try them. Please excuse me.' ²⁰A third person said, 'I just got married; I can't come.' ²¹So the servant returned and told his master what had happened. Then the master became angry and said, 'Go at once into the streets and alleys of the town, and bring in the poor, the crippled, the blind, and the lame.' ²²Later the servant said to him, 'Master, I did what you commanded, but we still have room.' ²³The master said to the servant, 'Go out to the roads and country lanes, and urge the people there to come so my house will be full. ²⁴I tell you, none of those whom I invited first will eat with me.'"

²⁵Large crowds were traveling with Jesus, and he turned and said to them, ²⁶"If anyone comes to me but loves his father, mother, wife, children, brothers, or sisters—or even life—more than me, he cannot be my follower. ²⁷Whoever is not willing to carry his cross and follow me cannot be my follower. ²⁸If you want to build a tower, you first sit down and decide how much it will cost, to see if you have enough money to finish the job. ²⁹If you don't, you might lay the foundation,

STEP 10

but you would not be able to finish. Then all who would see it would make fun of you, [30]saying, 'This person began to build but was not able to finish.'

[31]"If a king is going to fight another king, first he will sit down and plan. He will decide if he and his ten thousand soldiers can defeat the other king who has twenty thousand soldiers. [32]If he can't, then while the other king is still far away, he will send some people to speak to him and ask for peace. [33]In the same way, you must give up everything you have to be my follower.

[34]"Salt is good, but if it loses its salty taste, you cannot make it salty again. [35]It is no good for the soil or for manure; it is thrown away.

"Let those with ears use them and listen."

15 The tax collectors and sinners all came to listen to Jesus. [2]But the Pharisees and the teachers of the law began to complain: "Look, this man welcomes sinners and even eats with them."

[3]Then Jesus told them this story:

STEP 5

[4]"Suppose one of you has a hundred sheep but loses one of them. Then he will leave the other ninety-nine sheep in the open field and go out and look for the lost sheep until he finds it. [5]And when he finds it, he happily puts it on his shoulders [6]and goes home. He calls to his friends and neighbors and says, 'Be happy with me because I found my lost sheep.' [7]In the same way, I tell you there is more joy in heaven over one sinner who changes his heart and life, than over ninety-nine good people who don't need to change.

[8]"Suppose a woman has ten silver coins, but loses one. She will light a lamp, sweep the house, and look carefully for the coin until she finds it. [9]And when she finds it, she will call her friends and neighbors and say, 'Be happy with me

because I have found the coin that I lost.' [10]In the same way, there is joy in the presence of the angels of God when one sinner changes his heart and life."

[11]Then Jesus said, "A man had two sons. [12]The younger son said to his father, 'Give me my share of the property.' So the father divided the property between his two sons. [13]Then the younger son gathered up all that was his and traveled far away to another country. There he wasted his money in foolish living. [14]After he had spent everything, a time came when there was no food anywhere in the country, and the son was poor and hungry. [15]So he got a job with one of the citizens there who sent the son into the fields to feed pigs. [16]The son was so hungry that he wanted to eat the pods the pigs were eating, but no one gave him anything. [17]When he realized what he was doing, he thought, 'All of my father's servants have plenty of food. But I am here, almost dying with hunger. [18]I will leave and return to my father and say to him, "Father, I have sinned against God and against you. [19]I am no longer worthy to be called your son, but let me be like one of your servants." ' [20]So the son left and went to his father.

STEP 5

"While the son was still a long way off, his father saw him and felt sorry for his son. So the father ran to him and hugged and kissed him. [21]The son said, 'Father, I have sinned against God and against you. I am no longer worthy to be called your son.' [22]But the father said to his servants, 'Hurry! Bring the best clothes and put them on him. Also, put a ring on his finger and sandals on his feet. [23]And get our fat calf and kill it so we can have a feast and celebrate. [24]My son was dead, but now he is alive again! He was lost, but now he is found!' So they began to celebrate.

STEP 5

Admitted to God, to ourselves, and to another human being the exact nature of our wrongs.

Luke 15:17-20

The prodigal son couldn't restore his relationship with his father until he came to realize how he had mistreated his father and decided it was time to go home and say so. Step 5 tells you that you need to do something like that, too.

You—like everyone else—are a lot like the prodigal son in Jesus' story. He wanted some excitement. In trying to get it, he wasted the resources of his life. But that's not all. In a short time, he burned through what it had taken his father years to build up. He headed home with so much shame in his heart that he could hardly stand it. But he did go home. And he did face reality. From the depths of his heart, he said, "Father, I have sinned against God and against you. I am no longer worthy to be called your son" (verses 18-19).

The father's response to his son mirrors God's response to you when you authentically confess all that you've done wrong. The prodigal son expected his father to agree with him and read him the riot act. Instead, his father ran to meet him and wrapped him in forgiveness and love. Isn't that what you want? Can you believe that God greets your confession with the same eagerness and warmth?

When you come clean with him, you find you've come home. There's a strong dose of "hitting bottom" in this story. Confession involves admitting how broken your life really is. But that's the turning point that gets your life headed home to your heavenly Father's loving embrace.

FOR YOUR NEXT **STEP 5** MEDITATION, TURN TO **PAGE 189.** ▶▶

²⁵"The older son was in the field, and as he came closer to the house, he heard the sound of music and dancing. ²⁶So he called to one of the servants and asked what all this meant. ²⁷The servant said, 'Your brother has come back, and your father killed the fat calf, because your brother came home safely.' ²⁸The older son was angry and would not go in to the feast. So his father went out and begged him to come in. ²⁹But the older son said to his father, 'I have served you like a slave for many years and have always obeyed your commands. But you never gave me even a young goat to have at a feast with my friends. ³⁰But your other son, who wasted all your money on prostitutes, comes home, and you kill the fat calf for him!' ³¹The father said to him, 'Son, you are always with me, and all that I have is yours. ³²We had to celebrate and be happy because your brother was dead, but now he is alive. He was lost, but now he is found.' "

16 Jesus also said to his followers, "Once there was a rich man who had a manager to take care of his business. This manager was accused of cheating him. ²So he called the manager in and said to him, 'What is this I hear about you? Give me a report of what you have done with my money, because you can't be my manager any longer.' ³The manager thought to himself, 'What will I do since my master is taking my job away from me? I am not strong enough to dig ditches, and I am ashamed to beg. ⁴I know what I'll do so that when I lose my job people will welcome me into their homes.'

⁵"So the manager called in everyone who owed the master any money. He asked the first one, 'How much do you owe?' ⁶He answered, 'Eight hundred gallons of olive oil.' The manager said to him,

'Take your bill, sit down quickly, and write four hundred gallons.' ⁷Then the manager asked another one, 'How much do you owe?' He answered, 'One thousand bushels of wheat.' Then the manager said to him, 'Take your bill and write eight hundred bushels.' ⁸So, the master praised the dishonest manager for being clever. Yes, worldly people are more clever with their own kind than spiritual people are.

⁹"I tell you, make friends for yourselves using worldly riches so that when those riches are gone, you will be welcomed in those homes that continue forever. ¹⁰Whoever can be trusted with a little can also be trusted with a lot, and whoever is dishonest with a little is dishonest with a lot. ¹¹If you cannot be trusted with worldly riches, then who will trust you with true riches? ¹²And if you cannot be trusted with things that belong to someone else, who will give you things of your own?

¹³"No servant can serve two masters. The servant will hate one master and love the other, or will follow one master and refuse to follow the other. You cannot serve both God and worldly riches."

¹⁴The Pharisees, who loved money, were listening to all these things and made fun of Jesus. ¹⁵He said to them, "You make yourselves look good in front of people, but God knows what is really in your hearts. What is important to people is hateful in God's sight.

STEP 4

¹⁶"The law of Moses and the writings of the prophets were preached until John came. Since then the Good News about the kingdom of God is being told, and everyone tries to enter it by force. ¹⁷It would be easier for heaven and earth to pass away than for the smallest part of a letter in the law to be changed.

¹⁸"If a man divorces his wife and marries another woman, he is guilty of adul-

tery, and the man who marries a divorced woman is also guilty of adultery."

¹⁹Jesus said, "There was a rich man who always dressed in the finest clothes and lived in luxury every day. ²⁰And a very poor man named Lazarus, whose body was covered with sores, was laid at the rich man's gate. ²¹He wanted to eat only the small pieces of food that fell from the rich man's table. And the dogs would come and lick his sores. ²²Later, Lazarus died, and the angels carried him to the arms of Abraham. The rich man died, too, and was buried. ²³In the place of the dead, he was in much pain. The rich man saw Abraham far away with Lazarus at his side. ²⁴He called, 'Father Abraham, have mercy on me! Send Lazarus to dip his finger in water and cool my tongue, because I am suffering in this fire!' ²⁵But Abraham said, 'Child, remember when you were alive you had the good things in life, but bad things happened to Lazarus. Now he is comforted here, and you are suffering. ²⁶Besides, there is a big pit between you and us, so no one can cross over to you, and no one can leave there and come here.' ²⁷The rich man said, 'Father, then please send Lazarus to my father's house. ²⁸I have five brothers, and Lazarus could warn them so that they will not come to this place of pain.' ²⁹But Abraham said, 'They have the law of Moses and the writings of the prophets; let them learn from them.' ³⁰The rich man said, 'No, father Abraham! If someone goes to them from the dead, they would believe and change their hearts and lives.' ³¹But Abraham said to him, 'If they will not listen to Moses and the prophets, they will not listen to someone who comes back from the dead.' "

17 Jesus said to his followers, "Things that cause people to sin will happen, but how terrible for the person who causes them to happen! ²It would be better for you to be thrown into the sea with a large stone around your neck than to cause one of these little ones to sin. ³So be careful!

"If another follower sins, warn him, and if he is sorry and stops sinning, forgive him. ⁴If he sins against you seven times in one day and says that he is sorry each time, forgive him."

⁵The apostles said to the Lord, "Give us more faith!"

⁶The Lord said, "If your faith were the size of a mustard seed, you could say to this mulberry tree, 'Dig yourself up and plant yourself in the sea,' and it would obey you.

⁷"Suppose one of you has a servant who has been plowing the ground or caring for the sheep. When the servant comes in from working in the field, would you say, 'Come in and sit down to eat'? ⁸No, you would say to him, 'Prepare something for me to eat. Then get yourself ready and serve me. After I finish eating and drinking, you can eat.' ⁹The servant does not get any special thanks for doing what his master commanded. ¹⁰It is the same with you. When you have done everything you are told to do, you should say, 'We are unworthy servants; we have only done the work we should do.' "

¹¹While Jesus was on his way to Jerusalem, he was going through the area between Samaria and Galilee. ¹²As he came into a small town, ten men who had a skin disease met him there. They did not come close to Jesus ¹³but called to him, "Jesus! Master! Have mercy on us!"

¹⁴When Jesus saw the men, he said, "Go and show yourselves to the priests."

As the ten men were going, they were healed. ¹⁵When one of them saw that he was healed, he went back to Jesus,

STEP 4

STEP 11

praising God in a loud voice. ¹⁶Then he bowed down at Jesus' feet and thanked him. (And this man was a Samaritan.) ¹⁷Jesus said, "Weren't ten men healed? Where are the other nine? ¹⁸Is this Samaritan the only one who came back to thank God?" ¹⁹Then Jesus said to him, "Stand up and go on your way. You were healed because you believed."

²⁰Some of the Pharisees asked Jesus, "When will the kingdom of God come?"

Jesus answered, "God's kingdom is coming, but not in a way that you will be able to see with your eyes. ²¹People will not say, 'Look, here it is!' or, 'There it is!' because God's kingdom is within you."

²²Then Jesus said to his followers, "The time will come when you will want very much to see one of the days of the Son of Man. But you will not see it. ²³People will say to you, 'Look, there he is!' or, 'Look, here he is!' Stay where you are; don't go away and search.

²⁴"When the Son of Man comes again, he will shine like lightning, which flashes across the sky and lights it up from one side to the other. ²⁵But first he must suffer many things and be rejected by the people of this time. ²⁶When the Son of Man comes again, it will be as it was when Noah lived. ²⁷People were eating, drinking, marrying, and giving their children to be married until the day Noah entered the boat. Then the flood came and killed them all. ²⁸It will be the same as during the time of Lot. People were eating, drinking, buying, selling, planting, and building. ²⁹But the day Lot left Sodom, fire and sulfur rained down from the sky and killed them all. ³⁰This is how it will be when the Son of Man comes again.

³¹"On that day, a person who is on the roof and whose belongings are in the house should not go inside to get them. A person who is in the field should not go back home. ³²Remember Lot's wife. ³³Those who try to keep their lives will lose them. But those who give up their lives will save them. ³⁴I tell you, on that night two people will be sleeping in one bed; one will be taken and the other will be left. ³⁵There will be two women grinding grain together; one will be taken, and the other will be left. [³⁶Two people will be in the field. One will be taken, and the other will be left.]"

³⁷The followers asked Jesus, "Where will this be, Lord?"

Jesus answered, "Where there is a dead body, there the vultures will gather."

18 Then Jesus used this story to teach his followers that they should always pray and never lose hope. ²"In a certain town there was a judge who did not respect God or care about people. ³In that same town there was a widow who kept coming to this judge, saying, 'Give me my rights against my enemy.' ⁴For a while the judge refused to help her. But afterwards, he thought to himself, 'Even though I don't respect God or care about people, ⁵I will see that she gets her rights. Otherwise she will continue to bother me until I am worn out.' "

⁶The Lord said, "Listen to what the unfair judge said. ⁷God will always give what is right to his people who cry to him night and day, and he will not be slow to answer them. ⁸I tell you, God will help his people quickly. But when the Son of Man comes again, will he find those on earth who believe in him?"

⁹Jesus told this story to some people who thought they were very good and looked down on everyone else: ¹⁰"A Pharisee and a tax collector both went to the Temple to pray. ¹¹The Pharisee stood alone and prayed, 'God, I thank you that I

STEP
7

am not like other people who steal, cheat, or take part in adultery, or even like this tax collector. [12]I fast twice a week, and I give one-tenth of everything I get!'

[13]"The tax collector, standing at a distance, would not even look up to heaven. But he beat on his chest because he was so sad. He said, 'God, have mercy on me, a sinner.' [14]I tell you, when this man went home, he was right with God, but the Pharisee was not. All who make themselves great will be made humble, but all who make themselves humble will be made great."

[15]Some people brought even their babies to Jesus so he could touch them. When the followers saw this, they told them to stop. [16]But Jesus called for the children, saying, "Let the little children come to me. Don't stop them, because the kingdom of God belongs to people who are like these children. [17]I tell you the truth, you must accept the kingdom of God as if you were a child, or you will never enter it."

[18]A certain leader asked Jesus, "Good Teacher, what must I do to have life forever?"

[19]Jesus said to him, "Why do you call me good? Only God is good. [20]You know the commands: 'You must not be guilty of adultery. You must not murder anyone. You must not steal. You must not tell lies about your neighbor. Honor your father and mother.' "

[21]But the leader said, "I have obeyed all these commands since I was a boy."

[22]When Jesus heard this, he said to him, "There is still one more thing you need to do. Sell everything you have and give it to the poor, and you will have treasure in heaven. Then come and follow me." [23]But when the man heard this, he became very sad, because he was very rich.

[24]Jesus looked at him and said, "It is very hard for rich people to enter the kingdom of God. [25]It is easier for a camel to go through the eye of a needle than for a rich person to enter the kingdom of God."

[26]When the people heard this, they asked, "Then who can be saved?"

[27]Jesus answered, "The things impossible for people are possible for God."

[28]Peter said, "Look, we have left everything and followed you."

[29]Jesus said, "I tell you the truth, all those who have left houses, wives, brothers, parents, or children for the kingdom of God [30]will get much more in this life. And in the age that is coming, they will have life forever."

[31]Then Jesus took the twelve apostles aside and said to them, "We are going to Jerusalem. Everything the prophets wrote about the Son of Man will happen. [32]He will be turned over to those who are evil. They will laugh at him, insult him, spit on him, [33]beat him with whips, and kill him. But on the third day, he will rise to life again." [34]The apostles did not understand this; the meaning was hidden from them, and they did not realize what was said.

[35]As Jesus came near the city of Jericho, a blind man was sitting beside the road, begging. [36]When he heard the people coming down the road, he asked, "What is happening?"

[37]They told him, "Jesus, from Nazareth, is going by."

[38]The blind man cried out, "Jesus, Son of David, have mercy on me!"

[39]The people leading the group warned the blind man to be quiet. But the blind man shouted even more, "Son of David, have mercy on me!"

[40]Jesus stopped and ordered the blind man to be brought to him. When he came

STEP 2

113

near, Jesus asked him, ⁴¹"What do you want me to do for you?"

He said, "Lord, I want to see."

⁴²Jesus said to him, "Then see. You are healed because you believed."

⁴³At once the man was able to see, and he followed Jesus, thanking God. All the people who saw this praised God.

19 Jesus was going through the city of Jericho. ²A man was there named Zacchaeus, who was a very important tax collector, and he was wealthy. ³He wanted to see who Jesus was, but he was not able because he was too short to see above the crowd. ⁴He ran ahead to a place where Jesus would come, and he climbed a sycamore tree so he could see him. ⁵When Jesus came to that place, he looked up and said to him, "Zacchaeus, hurry and come down! I must stay at your house today."

⁶Zacchaeus came down quickly and welcomed him gladly. ⁷All the people saw this and began to complain, "Jesus is staying with a sinner!"

⁸But Zacchaeus stood and said to the Lord, "I will give half of my possessions to the poor. And if I have cheated anyone, I will pay back four times more."

⁹Jesus said to him, "Salvation has come to this house today, because this man also belongs to the family of Abraham. ¹⁰The Son of Man came to find lost people and save them."

¹¹As the people were listening to this, Jesus told them a story because he was near Jerusalem and they thought God's kingdom would appear immediately. ¹²He said: "A very important man went to a country far away to be made a king and then to return home. ¹³So he called ten of his servants and gave a coin to each servant. He said, 'Do business with this money until I get back.' ¹⁴But the people in the kingdom hated the man. So they

sent a group to follow him and say, 'We don't want this man to be our king.'

¹⁵"But the man became king. When he returned home, he said, 'Call those servants who have my money so I can know how much they earned with it.'

¹⁶"The first servant came and said, 'Sir, I earned ten coins with the one you gave me.' ¹⁷The king said to the servant, 'Excellent! You are a good servant. Since I can trust you with small things, I will let you rule over ten of my cities.'

¹⁸"The second servant said, 'Sir, I earned five coins with your one.' ¹⁹The king said to this servant, 'You can rule over five cities.'

²⁰"Then another servant came in and said to the king, 'Sir, here is your coin which I wrapped in a piece of cloth and hid. ²¹I was afraid of you, because you are a hard man. You even take money that you didn't earn and gather food that you didn't plant.' ²²Then the king said to the servant, 'I will condemn you by your own words, you evil servant. You knew that I am a hard man, taking money that I didn't earn and gathering food that I didn't plant. ²³Why then didn't you put my money in the bank? Then when I came back, my money would have earned some interest.'

²⁴"The king said to the men who were standing by, 'Take the coin away from this servant and give it to the servant who earned ten coins.' ²⁵They said, 'But sir, that servant already has ten coins.' ²⁶The king said, 'Those who have will be given more, but those who do not have anything will have everything taken away from them. ²⁷Now where are my enemies who didn't want me to be king? Bring them here and kill them before me.'"

²⁸After Jesus said this, he went on toward Jerusalem. ²⁹As Jesus came near

STEP 8

STEP 8

Made a list of all persons we had harmed,
and became willing to make amends to them all.

Luke 19:8

Step 8 expresses the idea that you can only become whole and new when you admit how much you have hurt others through your addictive behavior and when you try to repair the emotional damage you've caused.

The Gospel of Luke tells the story of Zacchaeus, a crooked tax collector who met Jesus and promptly paid back with interest all the people he had cheated through the years. He becomes a pattern to copy. You need to think through your lifetime of relationships and make amends to those persons you have hurt either by actively mistreating them or passively ignoring them.

You need to go to those you've hurt, tell them humbly what you've done wrong, and ask for forgiveness. That starts a healing process for them and for you. If you've been hurt by others, especially in childhood, find counseling from a pastor or professional therapist so these hurts don't get in the way of your recovery. It's hard to overestimate the effects of childhood emotional, spiritual, and physical abuse.

FOR YOUR NEXT **STEP 8** MEDITATION, TURN TO **PAGE 150.** ▶▶

Bethphage and Bethany, towns near the hill called the Mount of Olives, he sent out two of his followers. ³⁰He said, "Go to the town you can see there. When you enter it, you will find a colt tied there, which no one has ever ridden. Untie it and bring it here to me. ³¹If anyone asks you why you are untying it, say that the Master needs it."

³²The two followers went into town and found the colt just as Jesus had told them. ³³As they were untying it, its owners came out and asked the followers, "Why are you untying our colt?"

³⁴The followers answered, "The Master needs it." ³⁵So they brought it to Jesus, threw their coats on the colt's back, and put Jesus on it. ³⁶As Jesus rode toward Jerusalem, others spread their coats on the road before him.

³⁷As he was coming close to Jerusalem, on the way down the Mount of Olives, the whole crowd of followers began joyfully shouting praise to God for all the miracles they had seen. ³⁸They said,

"God bless the king who comes in the name of the Lord!"

Psalm 118:26

There is peace in heaven and glory to God!"

³⁹Some of the Pharisees in the crowd said to Jesus, "Teacher, tell your followers not to say these things."

⁴⁰But Jesus answered, "I tell you, if my followers don't say these things, then the stones would cry out."

⁴¹As Jesus came near Jerusalem, he saw the city and cried for it, ⁴²saying, "I wish you knew today what would bring you peace. But now it is hidden from you. ⁴³The time is coming when your enemies will build a wall around you and will hold you in on all sides. ⁴⁴They will destroy you and all your people, and not one stone will be left on another. All this will happen be-

cause you did not recognize the time when God came to save you."

⁴⁵Jesus went into the Temple and began to throw out the people who were selling things there. ⁴⁶He said, "It is written in the Scriptures, 'My Temple will be a house for prayer.' But you have changed it into a 'hideout for robbers'!"

⁴⁷Jesus taught in the Temple every day. The leading priests, the experts on the law, and some of the leaders of the people wanted to kill Jesus. ⁴⁸But they did not know how they could do it, because all the people were listening closely to him.

20 One day Jesus was in the Temple, teaching the people and telling them the Good News. The leading priests, teachers of the law, and elders came up to talk with him, ²saying, "Tell us what authority you have to do these things? Who gave you this authority?"

³Jesus answered, "I will also ask you a question. Tell me: ⁴When John baptized people, was that authority from God or just from other people?"

⁵They argued about this, saying, "If we answer, 'John's baptism was from God,' Jesus will say, 'Then why did you not believe him?' ⁶But if we say, 'It was from other people,' all the people will stone us to death, because they believe John was a prophet." ⁷So they answered that they didn't know where it came from.

⁸Jesus said to them, "Then I won't tell you what authority I have to do these things."

⁹Then Jesus told the people this story: "A man planted a vineyard and leased it to some farmers. Then he went away for a long time. ¹⁰When it was time for the grapes to be picked, he sent a servant to the farmers to get some of the grapes. But they beat the servant and sent him away empty-handed. ¹¹Then he sent another servant. They beat this servant

also, and showed no respect for him, and sent him away empty-handed. [12]So the man sent a third servant. The farmers wounded him and threw him out. [13]The owner of the vineyard said, 'What will I do now? I will send my son whom I love. Maybe they will respect him.' [14]But when the farmers saw the son, they said to each other, 'This son will inherit the vineyard. If we kill him, it will be ours.' [15]So the farmers threw the son out of the vineyard and killed him.

"What will the owner of this vineyard do to them? [16]He will come and kill those farmers and will give the vineyard to other farmers."

When the people heard this story, they said, "Let this never happen!"

[17]But Jesus looked at them and said, "Then what does this verse mean:

'The stone that the builders rejected became the cornerstone'?

Psalm 118:22

[18]Everyone who falls on that stone will be broken, and the person on whom it falls, that person will be crushed!"

[19]The teachers of the law and the leading priests wanted to arrest Jesus at once, because they knew the story was about them. But they were afraid of what the people would do.

[20]So they watched Jesus and sent some spies who acted as if they were sincere. They wanted to trap Jesus in saying something wrong so they could hand him over to the authority and power of the governor. [21]So the spies asked Jesus, "Teacher, we know that what you say and teach is true. You pay no attention to who people are, and you always teach the truth about God's way. [22]Tell us, is it right for us to pay taxes to Caesar or not?"

[23]But Jesus, knowing they were trying to trick him, said, [24]"Show me a coin. Whose image and name are on it?"

They said, "Caesar's."

[25]Jesus said to them, "Then give to Caesar the things that are Caesar's, and give to God the things that are God's."

[26]So they were not able to trap Jesus in anything he said in the presence of the people. And being amazed at his answer, they became silent.

[27]Some Sadducees, who believed people would not rise from the dead, came to Jesus. [28]They asked, "Teacher, Moses wrote that if a man's brother dies and leaves a wife but no children, then that man must marry the widow and have children for his brother. [29]Once there were seven brothers. The first brother married and died, but had no children. [30]Then the second brother married the widow, and he died. [31]And the third brother married the widow, and he died. The same thing happened with all seven brothers; they died and had no children. [32]Finally, the woman died also. [33]Since all seven brothers had married her, whose wife will she be when people rise from the dead?"

[34]Jesus said to them, "On earth, people marry and are given to someone to marry. [35]But those who will be worthy to be raised from the dead and live again will not marry, nor will they be given to someone to marry. [36]In that life they are like angels and cannot die. They are children of God, because they have been raised from the dead. [37]Even Moses clearly showed that the dead are raised to life. When he wrote about the burning bush, he said that the Lord is 'the God of Abraham, the God of Isaac, and the God of Jacob.' [38]God is the God of the living, not the dead, because all people are alive to him."

[39]Some of the teachers of the law said, "Teacher, your answer was good." [40]No

one was brave enough to ask him another question.

⁴¹Then Jesus said, "Why do people say that the Christ is the Son of David? ⁴²In the book of Psalms, David himself says:

'The Lord said to my Lord,
　"Sit by me at my right side,
⁴³　　until I put your enemies under your
　　　　control." ' 　　　　*Psalm 110:1*
⁴⁴David calls the Christ 'Lord,' so how can the Christ be his son?"

⁴⁵While all the people were listening, Jesus said to his followers, ⁴⁶"Beware of the teachers of the law. They like to walk around wearing fancy clothes, and they love for people to greet them with respect in the marketplaces. They love to have the most important seats in the synagogues and at feasts. ⁴⁷But they cheat widows and steal their houses and then try to make themselves look good by saying long prayers. They will receive a greater punishment."

21 As Jesus looked up, he saw some rich people putting their gifts into the Temple money box. ²Then he saw a poor widow putting two small copper coins into the box. ³He said, "I tell you the truth, this poor widow gave more than all those rich people. ⁴They gave only what they did not need. This woman is very poor, but she gave all she had to live on."

⁵Some people were talking about the Temple and how it was decorated with beautiful stones and gifts offered to God.

But Jesus said, ⁶"As for these things you are looking at, the time will come when not one stone will be left on another. Every stone will be thrown down."

⁷They asked Jesus, "Teacher, when will these things happen? What will be the sign that they are about to take place?"

⁸Jesus said, "Be careful so you are not fooled. Many people will come in my name, saying, 'I am the One' and, 'The time has come!' But don't follow them. ⁹When you hear about wars and riots, don't be afraid, because these things must happen first, but the end will come later."

¹⁰Then he said to them, "Nations will fight against other nations, and kingdoms against other kingdoms. ¹¹In various places there will be great earthquakes, sicknesses, and a lack of food. Fearful events and great signs will come from heaven.

¹²"But before all these things happen, people will arrest you and treat you cruelly. They will judge you in their synagogues and put you in jail and force you to stand before kings and governors, because you follow me. ¹³But this will give you an opportunity to tell about me. ¹⁴Make up your minds not to worry ahead of time about what you will say. ¹⁵I will give you the wisdom to say things that none of your enemies will be able to stand against or prove wrong. ¹⁶Even your parents, brothers, relatives, and friends will turn against you, and they will kill some of you. ¹⁷All people will hate you because you follow me. ¹⁸But none of these things can really harm you. ¹⁹By continuing to have faith you will save your lives.

²⁰"When you see armies all around Jerusalem, you will know it will soon be destroyed. ²¹At that time, the people in Judea should run away to the mountains. The people in Jerusalem must get out, and those who are near the city should not go in. ²²These are the days of punishment to bring about all that is written in the Scriptures. ²³How terrible it will be for women who are pregnant or have nursing babies! Great trouble will come upon this land, and God will be angry with these people. ²⁴They will be killed by the sword and taken as prisoners to all nations. Jerusa-

lem will be crushed by non-Jewish people until their time is over.

²⁵"There will be signs in the sun, moon, and stars. On earth, nations will be afraid and confused because of the roar and fury of the sea. ²⁶People will be so afraid they will faint, wondering what is happening to the world, because the powers of the heavens will be shaken. ²⁷Then people will see the Son of Man coming in a cloud with power and great glory. ²⁸When these things begin to happen, look up and hold your heads high, because the time when God will free you is near!"

²⁹Then Jesus told this story: "Look at the fig tree and all the other trees. ³⁰When their leaves appear, you know that summer is near. ³¹In the same way, when you see these things happening, you will know that God's kingdom is near.

³²"I tell you the truth, all these things will happen while the people of this time are still living. ³³Earth and sky will be destroyed, but the words I have spoken will never be destroyed.

³⁴"Be careful not to spend your time feasting, drinking, or worrying about worldly things. If you do, that day might come on you suddenly, ³⁵like a trap on all people on earth. ³⁶So be ready all the time. Pray that you will be strong enough to escape all these things that will happen and that you will be able to stand before the Son of Man."

³⁷During the day, Jesus taught the people in the Temple, and at night he went out of the city and stayed on the Mount of Olives. ³⁸Every morning all the people got up early to go to the Temple to listen to him.

22 It was almost time for the Feast of Unleavened Bread, called the Passover Feast. ²The leading priests and teachers of the law were trying to find a way to kill Jesus, because they were afraid of the people.

³Satan entered Judas Iscariot, one of Jesus' twelve apostles. ⁴Judas went to the leading priests and some of the soldiers who guarded the Temple and talked to them about a way to hand Jesus over to them. ⁵They were pleased and agreed to give Judas money. ⁶He agreed and watched for the best time to hand Jesus over to them when he was away from the crowd.

⁷The Day of Unleavened Bread came when the Passover lambs had to be sacrificed. ⁸Jesus said to Peter and John, "Go and prepare the Passover meal for us to eat."

⁹They asked, "Where do you want us to prepare it?" ¹⁰Jesus said to them, "After you go into the city, a man carrying a jar of water will meet you. Follow him into the house that he enters, ¹¹and tell the owner of the house, 'The Teacher says: "Where is the guest room in which I may eat the Passover meal with my followers?" ' ¹²Then he will show you a large, furnished room upstairs. Prepare the Passover meal there."

¹³So Peter and John left and found everything as Jesus had said. And they prepared the Passover meal.

¹⁴When the time came, Jesus and the apostles were sitting at the table. ¹⁵He said to them, "I wanted very much to eat this Passover meal with you before I suffer. ¹⁶I will not eat another Passover meal until it is given its true meaning in the kingdom of God."

¹⁷Then Jesus took a cup, gave thanks, and said, "Take this cup and share it among yourselves. ¹⁸I will not drink again from the fruit of the vine until God's kingdom comes."

¹⁹Then Jesus took some bread, gave thanks, broke it, and gave it to the

apostles, saying, "This is my body, which I am giving for you. Do this to remember me." ²⁰In the same way, after supper, Jesus took the cup and said, "This cup is the new agreement that God makes with his people. This new agreement begins with my blood which is poured out for you.

²¹"But one of you will turn against me, and his hand is with mine on the table. ²²What God has planned for the Son of Man will happen, but how terrible it will be for that one who turns against the Son of Man."

²³Then the apostles asked each other which one of them would do that.

²⁴The apostles also began to argue about which one of them was the most important. ²⁵But Jesus said to them, "The kings of the non-Jewish people rule over them, and those who have authority over others like to be called 'friends of the people.' ²⁶But you must not be like that. Instead, the greatest among you should be like the youngest, and the leader should be like the servant. ²⁷Who is more important: the one sitting at the table or the one serving? You think the one at the table is more important, but I am like a servant among you.

²⁸"You have stayed with me through my struggles. ²⁹Just as my Father has given me a kingdom, I also give you a kingdom ³⁰so you may eat and drink at my table in my kingdom. And you will sit on thrones, judging the twelve tribes of Israel.

³¹"Simon, Simon, Satan has asked to test all of you as a farmer sifts his wheat. ³²I have prayed that you will not lose your faith! Help your brothers be stronger when you come back to me."

³³But Peter said to Jesus, "Lord, I am ready to go with you to prison and even to die with you!"

³⁴But Jesus said, "Peter, before the rooster crows this day, you will say three times that you don't know me."

³⁵Then Jesus said to the apostles, "When I sent you out without a purse, a bag, or sandals, did you need anything?"

They said, "No."

³⁶He said to them, "But now if you have a purse or a bag, carry that with you. If you don't have a sword, sell your coat and buy one. ³⁷The Scripture says, 'He was treated like a criminal,' and I tell you this scripture must have its full meaning. It was written about me, and it is happening now."

³⁸His followers said, "Look, Lord, here are two swords."

He said to them, "That is enough."

³⁹Jesus left the city and went to the Mount of Olives, as he often did, and his followers went with him. ⁴⁰When he reached the place, he said to them, "Pray for strength against temptation."

⁴¹Then Jesus went about a stone's throw away from them. He kneeled down and prayed, ⁴²"Father, if you are willing, take away this cup of suffering. But do what you want, not what I want." ⁴³Then an angel from heaven appeared to him to strengthen him. ⁴⁴Being full of pain, Jesus prayed even harder. His sweat was like drops of blood falling to the ground. ⁴⁵When he finished praying, he went to his followers and found them asleep because of their sadness. ⁴⁶Jesus said to them, "Why are you sleeping? Get up and pray for strength against temptation."

⁴⁷While Jesus was speaking, a crowd came up, and Judas, one of the twelve apostles, was leading them. He came close to Jesus so he could kiss him.

⁴⁸But Jesus said to him, "Judas, are you using the kiss to give the Son of Man to his enemies?"

⁴⁹When those who were standing around him saw what was happening,

STEP 11

they said, "Lord, should we strike them with our swords?" ⁵⁰And one of them struck the servant of the high priest and cut off his right ear.

⁵¹Jesus said, "Stop! No more of this." Then he touched the servant's ear and healed him.

⁵²Those who came to arrest Jesus were the leading priests, the soldiers who guarded the Temple, and the elders. Jesus said to them, "You came out here with swords and clubs as though I were a criminal. ⁵³I was with you every day in the Temple, and you didn't arrest me there. But this is your time—the time when darkness rules."

⁵⁴They arrested Jesus, and led him away, and brought him into the house of the high priest. Peter followed far behind them. ⁵⁵After the soldiers started a fire in the middle of the courtyard and sat together, Peter sat with them. ⁵⁶A servant girl saw Peter sitting there in the firelight, and looking closely at him, she said, "This man was also with him."

⁵⁷But Peter said this was not true; he said, "Woman, I don't know him."

⁵⁸A short time later, another person saw Peter and said, "You are also one of them."

But Peter said, "Man, I am not!"

⁵⁹About an hour later, another man insisted, "Certainly this man was with him, because he is from Galilee, too."

⁶⁰But Peter said, "Man, I don't know what you are talking about!"

At once, while Peter was still speaking, a rooster crowed. ⁶¹Then the Lord turned and looked straight at Peter. And Peter remembered what the Lord had said: "Before the rooster crows this day, you will say three times that you don't know me." ⁶²Then Peter went outside and cried painfully.

⁶³The men who were guarding Jesus began making fun of him and beating him.

⁶⁴They blindfolded him and said, "Prove that you are a prophet, and tell us who hit you." ⁶⁵They said many cruel things to Jesus.

⁶⁶When day came, the council of the elders of the people, both the leading priests and the teachers of the law, came together and led Jesus to their highest court. ⁶⁷They said, "If you are the Christ, tell us."

Jesus said to them, "If I tell you, you will not believe me. ⁶⁸And if I ask you, you will not answer. ⁶⁹But from now on, the Son of Man will sit at the right hand of the powerful God."

⁷⁰They all said, "Then are you the Son of God?"

Jesus said to them, "You say that I am."

⁷¹They said, "Why do we need witnesses now? We ourselves heard him say this."

23 Then the whole group stood up and led Jesus to Pilate. ²They began to accuse Jesus, saying, "We caught this man telling things that mislead our people. He says that we should not pay taxes to Caesar, and he calls himself the Christ, a king."

³Pilate asked Jesus, "Are you the king of the Jews?"

Jesus answered, "Those are your words."

⁴Pilate said to the leading priests and the people, "I find nothing against this man."

⁵They were insisting, saying, "But Jesus makes trouble with the people, teaching all around Judea. He began in Galilee, and now he is here."

⁶Pilate heard this and asked if Jesus was from Galilee. ⁷Since Jesus was under Herod's authority, Pilate sent Jesus to Herod, who was in Jerusalem at that time.

8When Herod saw Jesus, he was very glad, because he had heard about Jesus and had wanted to meet him for a long time. He was hoping to see Jesus work a miracle. 9Herod asked Jesus many questions, but Jesus said nothing. 10The leading priests and teachers of the law were standing there, strongly accusing Jesus. 11After Herod and his soldiers had made fun of Jesus, they dressed him in a kingly robe and sent him back to Pilate. 12In the past, Pilate and Herod had always been enemies, but on that day they became friends.

13Pilate called the people together with the leading priests and the rulers. 14He said to them, "You brought this man to me, saying he makes trouble among the people. But I have questioned him before you all, and I have not found him guilty of what you say. 15Also, Herod found nothing wrong with him; he sent him back to us. Look, he has done nothing for which he should die. 16So, after I punish him, I will let him go free." [17Every year at the Passover Feast, Pilate had to release one prisoner to the people.]

18But the people shouted together, "Take this man away! Let Barabbas go free!" 19(Barabbas was a man who was in prison for his part in a riot in the city and for murder.)

20Pilate wanted to let Jesus go free and told this to the crowd. 21But they shouted again, "Crucify him! Crucify him!"

22A third time Pilate said to them, "Why? What wrong has he done? I can find no reason to kill him. So I will have him punished and set him free."

23But they continued to shout, demanding that Jesus be crucified. Their yelling became so loud that 24Pilate decided to give them what they wanted. 25He set free the man who was in jail for rioting and murder, and he handed Jesus over to them to do with him as they wished.

26As they led Jesus away, Simon, a man from Cyrene, was coming in from the fields. They forced him to carry Jesus' cross and to walk behind him.

27A large crowd of people was following Jesus, including some women who were sad and crying for him. 28But Jesus turned and said to them, "Women of Jerusalem, don't cry for me. Cry for yourselves and for your children. 29The time is coming when people will say, 'Blessed are the women who cannot have children and who have no babies to nurse.' 30Then people will say to the mountains, 'Fall on us!' And they will say to the hills, 'Cover us!' 31If they act like this now when life is good, what will happen when bad times come?"

32There were also two criminals led out with Jesus to be put to death. 33When they came to a place called the Skull, the soldiers crucified Jesus and the criminals—one on his right and the other on his left. 34Jesus said, "Father, forgive them, because they don't know what they are doing."

The soldiers threw lots to decide who would get his clothes. 35The people stood there watching. And the leaders made fun of Jesus, saying, "He saved others. Let him save himself if he is God's Chosen One, the Christ."

36The soldiers also made fun of him, coming to Jesus and offering him some vinegar. 37They said, "If you are the king of the Jews, save yourself!" 38At the top of the cross these words were written: THIS IS THE KING OF THE JEWS.

39One of the criminals on a cross began to shout insults at Jesus: "Aren't you the Christ? Then save yourself and us."

40But the other criminal stopped him and said, "You should fear God! You are getting the same punishment he is. [41]We are punished justly, getting what we deserve for what we did. But this man has done nothing wrong." [42]Then he said, "Jesus, remember me when you come into your kingdom."

[43]Jesus said to him, "I tell you the truth, today you will be with me in paradise."

[44]It was about noon, and the whole land became dark until three o'clock in the afternoon, [45]because the sun did not shine. The curtain in the Temple was torn in two. [46]Jesus cried out in a loud voice, "Father, I give you my life." After Jesus said this, he died.

[47]When the army officer there saw what happened, he praised God, saying, "Surely this was a good man!"

[48]When all the people who had gathered there to watch saw what happened, they returned home, beating their chests because they were so sad. [49]But those who were close friends of Jesus, including the women who had followed him from Galilee, stood at a distance and watched.

[50]There was a good and religious man named Joseph who was a member of the council. [51]But he had not agreed to the other leaders' plans and actions against Jesus. He was from the town of Arimathea and was waiting for the kingdom of God to come. [52]Joseph went to Pilate to ask for the body of Jesus. [53]He took the body down from the cross, wrapped it in cloth, and put it in a tomb that was cut out of a wall of rock. This tomb had never been used before. [54]This was late on Preparation Day, and when the sun went down, the Sabbath day would begin.

[55]The women who had come from Galilee with Jesus followed Joseph and saw the tomb and how Jesus' body was laid. [56]Then the women left to prepare spices and perfumes.

On the Sabbath day they rested, as the law of Moses commanded.

24

Very early on the first day of the week, at dawn, the women came to the tomb, bringing the spices they had prepared. [2]They found the stone rolled away from the entrance of the tomb, [3]but when they went in, they did not find the body of the Lord Jesus. [4]While they were wondering about this, two men in shining clothes suddenly stood beside them. [5]The women were very afraid and bowed their heads to the ground. The men said to them, "Why are you looking for a living person in this place for the dead? [6]He is not here; he has risen from the dead. Do you remember what he told you in Galilee? [7]He said the Son of Man must be handed over to sinful people, be crucified, and rise from the dead on the third day." [8]Then the women remembered what Jesus had said.

[9]The women left the tomb and told all these things to the eleven apostles and the other followers. [10]It was Mary Magdalene, Joanna, Mary the mother of James, and some other women who told the apostles everything that had happened at the tomb. [11]But they did not believe the women, because it sounded like nonsense. [12]But Peter got up and ran to the tomb. Bending down and looking in, he saw only the cloth that Jesus' body had been wrapped in. Peter went away to his home, wondering about what had happened.

[13]That same day two of Jesus' followers were going to a town named Emmaus, about seven miles from Jerusalem. [14]They were talking about everything that had happened. [15]While they were talking and discussing, Jesus

himself came near and began walking with them, ¹⁶but they were kept from recognizing him. ¹⁷Then he said, "What are these things you are talking about while you walk?"

The two followers stopped, looking very sad. ¹⁸The one named Cleopas answered, "Are you the only visitor in Jerusalem who does not know what just happened there?"

¹⁹Jesus said to them, "What are you talking about?"

They said, "About Jesus of Nazareth. He was a prophet who said and did many powerful things before God and all the people. ²⁰Our leaders and the leading priests handed him over to be sentenced to death, and they crucified him. ²¹But we were hoping that he would free Israel. Besides this, it is now the third day since this happened. ²²And today some women among us amazed us. Early this morning they went to the tomb, ²³but they did not find his body there. They came and told us that they had seen a vision of angels who said that Jesus was alive! ²⁴So some of our group went to the tomb, too. They found it just as the women said, but they did not see Jesus."

²⁵Then Jesus said to them, "You are foolish and slow to believe everything the prophets said. ²⁶They said that the Christ must suffer these things before he enters his glory." ²⁷Then starting with what Moses and all the prophets had said about him, Jesus began to explain everything that had been written about himself in the Scriptures.

²⁸They came near the town of Emmaus, and Jesus acted as if he were going farther. ²⁹But they begged him, "Stay with us, because it is late; it is almost night." So he went in to stay with them. ³⁰When Jesus was at the table with

them, he took some bread, gave thanks, divided it, and gave it to them. ³¹And then, they were allowed to recognize Jesus. But when they saw who he was, he disappeared. ³²They said to each other, "It felt like a fire burning in us when Jesus talked to us on the road and explained the Scriptures to us."

³³So the two followers got up at once and went back to Jerusalem. There they found the eleven apostles and others gathered. ³⁴They were saying, "The Lord really has risen from the dead! He showed himself to Simon."

³⁵Then the two followers told what had happened on the road and how they recognized Jesus when he divided the bread.

³⁶While the two followers were telling this, Jesus himself stood right in the middle of them and said, "Peace be with you."

³⁷They were fearful and terrified and thought they were seeing a ghost. ³⁸But Jesus said, "Why are you troubled? Why do you doubt what you see? ³⁹Look at my hands and my feet. It is I myself! Touch me and see, because a ghost does not have a living body as you see I have."

⁴⁰After Jesus said this, he showed them his hands and feet. ⁴¹While they still could not believe it because they were amazed and happy, Jesus said to them, "Do you have any food here?" ⁴²They gave him a piece of broiled fish. ⁴³While the followers watched, Jesus took the fish and ate it.

⁴⁴He said to them, "Remember when I was with you before? I said that everything written about me must happen—everything in the law of Moses, the books of the prophets, and the Psalms."

⁴⁵Then Jesus opened their minds so

they could understand the Scriptures.

STEP 3

46He said to them, "It is written that the Christ would suffer and rise from the dead on the third day 47and that a change of hearts and lives and forgiveness of sins would be preached in his name to all nations, starting at Jerusalem. 48You are witnesses of these things. 49I will send you what my Father has promised, but you must stay in Jerusa-lem until you have received that power from heaven."

50Jesus led his followers as far as Bethany, and he raised his hands and blessed them. 51While he was blessing them, he was separated from them and carried into heaven. 52They worshiped him and returned to Jerusalem very happy. 53They stayed in the Temple all the time, praising God.

JOHN

John Tells About Jesus the Son Who Reveals the Father

1 In the beginning there was the Word. The Word was with God, and the Word was God. [2]He was with God in the beginning. [3]All things were made by him, and nothing was made without him. [4]In him there was life, and that life was the light of all people. [5]The Light shines in the darkness, and the darkness has not overpowered it.

[6]There was a man named John who was sent by God. [7]He came to tell people the truth about the Light so that through him all people could hear about the Light and believe. [8]John was not the Light, but he came to tell people the truth about the Light. [9]The true Light that gives light to all was coming into the world!

[10]The Word was in the world, and the world was made by him, but the world did not know him. [11]He came to the world that was his own, but his own people did not accept him. [12]But to all who did accept him and believe in him he gave the right to become children of God. [13]They did not become his children in any human way—by any human parents or human desire. They were born of God.

[14]The Word became a human and lived among us. We saw his glory—the glory that belongs to the only Son of the Father—and he was full of grace and truth. [15]John tells the truth about him and cries out, saying, "This is the One I told you about: 'The One who comes after me is greater than I am, because he was living before me.'"

[16]Because he was full of grace and truth, from him we all received one gift after another. [17]The law was given through Moses, but grace and truth came through Jesus Christ. [18]No one has ever seen God. But God the only Son is very close to the Father, and he has shown us what God is like.

[19]Here is the truth John told when the leaders in Jerusalem sent priests and Levites to ask him, "Who are you?"

[20]John spoke freely and did not refuse to answer. He said, "I am not the Christ."

[21]So they asked him, "Then who are you? Are you Elijah?"

He answered, "No, I am not."

"Are you the Prophet?" they asked.

He answered, "No."

[22]Then they said, "Who are you? Give us an answer to tell those who sent us. What do you say about yourself?"

[23]John told them in the words of the prophet Isaiah:

"I am the voice of one
    calling out in the desert:
'Make the road straight for the Lord.'"

Isaiah 40:3

[24]Some Pharisees who had been sent asked John: [25]"If you are not the Christ or Elijah or the Prophet, why do you baptize people?"

[26]John answered, "I baptize with water, but there is one here with you that you don't know about. [27]He is the One who comes after me. I am not good enough to untie the strings of his sandals."

[28]This all happened at Bethany on the other side of the Jordan River, where John was baptizing people.

[29]The next day John saw Jesus coming toward him. John said, "Look, the Lamb of God, who takes away the sin of the world! [30]This is the One I was talking about when I said, 'A man will come after me, but he is greater than I am, because he was living before me.' [31]Even I did not

know who he was, although I came baptizing with water so that the people of Israel would know who he is."

³²⁻³³Then John said, "I saw the Spirit come down from heaven in the form of a dove and rest on him. Until then I did not know who the Christ was. But the God who sent me to baptize with water told me, 'You will see the Spirit come down and rest on a man; he is the One who will baptize with the Holy Spirit.' ³⁴I have seen this happen, and I tell you the truth: This man is the Son of God."

³⁵The next day John was there again with two of his followers. ³⁶When he saw Jesus walking by, he said, "Look, the Lamb of God!"

³⁷The two followers heard John say this, so they followed Jesus. ³⁸When Jesus turned and saw them following him, he asked, "What are you looking for?"

They said, "Rabbi, where are you staying?" ("Rabbi" means "Teacher.")

³⁹He answered, "Come and see." So the two men went with Jesus and saw where he was staying and stayed there with him that day. It was about four o'clock in the afternoon.

⁴⁰One of the two men who followed Jesus after they heard John speak about him was Andrew, Simon Peter's brother. ⁴¹The first thing Andrew did was to find his brother Simon and say to him, "We have found the Messiah." ("Messiah" means "Christ.")

⁴²Then Andrew took Simon to Jesus. Jesus looked at him and said, "You are Simon son of John. You will be called Cephas." ("Cephas" means "Peter.")

⁴³The next day Jesus decided to go to Galilee. He found Philip and said to him, "Follow me."

⁴⁴Philip was from the town of Bethsaida, where Andrew and Peter lived. ⁴⁵Philip found Nathanael and told him,

"We have found the man that Moses wrote about in the law, and the prophets also wrote about him. He is Jesus, the son of Joseph, from Nazareth."

⁴⁶But Nathanael said to Philip, "Can anything good come from Nazareth?"

Philip answered, "Come and see."

⁴⁷As Jesus saw Nathanael coming toward him, he said, "Here is truly an Israelite. There is nothing false in him."

⁴⁸Nathanael asked, "How do you know me?"

Jesus answered, "I saw you when you were under the fig tree, before Philip told you about me."

⁴⁹Then Nathanael said to Jesus, "Teacher, you are the Son of God; you are the King of Israel."

⁵⁰Jesus said to Nathanael, "Do you believe simply because I told you I saw you under the fig tree? You will see greater things than that." ⁵¹And Jesus said to them, "I tell you the truth, you will all see heaven open and 'angels of God going up and coming down' on the Son of Man."

2 Two days later there was a wedding in the town of Cana in Galilee. Jesus' mother was there, ²and Jesus and his followers were also invited to the wedding. ³When all the wine was gone, Jesus' mother said to him, "They have no more wine."

⁴Jesus answered, "Dear woman, why come to me? My time has not yet come."

⁵His mother said to the servants, "Do whatever he tells you to do."

⁶In that place there were six stone water jars that the Jews used in their washing ceremony. Each jar held about twenty or thirty gallons.

⁷Jesus said to the servants, "Fill the jars with water." So they filled the jars to the top.

⁸Then he said to them, "Now take

some out and give it to the master of the feast."

So they took the water to the master. [9]When he tasted it, the water had become wine. He did not know where the wine came from, but the servants who had brought the water knew. The master of the wedding called the bridegroom [10]and said to him, "People always serve the best wine first. Later, after the guests have been drinking awhile, they serve the cheaper wine. But you have saved the best wine till now."

[11]So in Cana of Galilee Jesus did his first miracle. There he showed his glory, and his followers believed in him.

[12]After this, Jesus went to the town of Capernaum with his mother, brothers, and followers. They stayed there for just a few days. [13]When it was almost time for the Jewish Passover Feast, Jesus went to Jerusalem. [14]In the Temple he found people selling cattle, sheep, and doves. He saw others sitting at tables, exchanging different kinds of money. [15]Jesus made a whip out of cords and forced all of them, both the sheep and cattle, to leave the Temple. He turned over the tables and scattered the money of those who were exchanging it. [16]Then he said to those who were selling pigeons, "Take these things out of here! Don't make my Father's house a place for buying and selling!"

[17]When this happened, the followers remembered what was written in the Scriptures: "My strong love for your Temple completely controls me."

[18]Some of his people said to Jesus, "Show us a miracle to prove you have the right to do these things."

[19]Jesus answered them, "Destroy this temple, and I will build it again in three days."

[20]They answered, "It took forty-six years to build this Temple! Do you really believe you can build it again in three days?"

[21](But the temple Jesus meant was his own body. [22]After Jesus was raised from the dead, his followers remembered that Jesus had said this. Then they believed the Scripture and the words Jesus had said.)

[23]When Jesus was in Jerusalem for the Passover Feast, many people believed in him because they saw the miracles he did. [24]But Jesus did not believe in them because he knew them all. [25]He did not need anyone to tell him about people, because he knew what was in people's minds.

3 There was a man named Nicodemus who was one of the Pharisees and an important Jewish leader. [2]One night Nicodemus came to Jesus and said, "Teacher, we know you are a teacher sent from God, because no one can do the miracles you do unless God is with him."

[3]Jesus answered, "I tell you the truth, unless you are born again, you cannot be in God's kingdom."

[4]Nicodemus said, "But if a person is already old, how can he be born again? He cannot enter his mother's womb again. So how can a person be born a second time?"

[5]But Jesus answered, "I tell you the truth, unless you are born from water and the Spirit, you cannot enter God's kingdom. [6]Human life comes from human parents, but spiritual life comes from the Spirit. [7]Don't be surprised when I tell you, 'You must all be born again.' [8]The wind blows where it wants to and you hear the sound of it, but you don't know where the wind comes from or where it is going. It is the same with every person who is born from the Spirit."

[9]Nicodemus asked, "How can this happen?"

¹⁰Jesus said, "You are an important teacher in Israel, and you don't understand these things? ¹¹I tell you the truth, we talk about what we know, and we tell about what we have seen, but you don't accept what we tell you. ¹²I have told you about things here on earth, and you do not believe me. So you will not believe me if I tell you about things of heaven. ¹³The only one who has ever gone up to heaven is the One who came down from heaven—the Son of Man.

STEP 2

¹⁴"Just as Moses lifted up the snake in the desert, the Son of Man must also be lifted up. ¹⁵So that everyone who believes can have eternal life in him.

¹⁶"God loved the world so much that he gave his one and only Son so that whoever believes in him may not be lost, but have eternal life. ¹⁷God did not send his Son into the world to judge the world guilty, but to save the world through him. ¹⁸People who believe in God's Son are not judged guilty. Those who do not believe have already been judged guilty, because they have not believed in God's one and only Son. ¹⁹They are judged by this fact: The Light has come into the world, but they did not want light. They wanted darkness, because they were doing evil things. ²⁰All who do evil hate the light and will not come to the light, because it will show all the evil things they do. ²¹But those who follow the true way come to the light, and it shows that the things they do were done through God."

²²After this, Jesus and his followers went into the area of Judea, where he stayed with his followers and baptized people. ²³John was also baptizing in Aenon, near Salim, because there was plenty of water there. People were going there to be baptized. ²⁴(This was before John was put into prison.)

²⁵Some of John's followers had an ar-gument with a Jew about religious washing. ²⁶So they came to John and said, "Teacher, remember the man who was with you on the other side of the Jordan River, the one you spoke about so much? He is baptizing, and everyone is going to him."

²⁷John answered, "A man can get only what God gives him. ²⁸You yourselves heard me say, 'I am not the Christ, but I am the one sent to prepare the way for him.' ²⁹The bride belongs only to the bridegroom. But the friend who helps the bridegroom stands by and listens to him. He is thrilled that he gets to hear the bridegroom's voice. In the same way, I am really happy. ³⁰He must become greater, and I must become less important.

STEP 11

³¹"The One who comes from above is greater than all. The one who is from the earth belongs to the earth and talks about things on the earth. But the One who comes from heaven is greater than all. ³²He tells what he has seen and heard, but no one accepts what he says. ³³Whoever accepts what he says has proven that God is true. ³⁴The One whom God sent speaks the words of God, because God gives him the Spirit fully. ³⁵The Father loves the Son and has given him power over everything. ³⁶Those who believe in the Son have eternal life, but those who do not obey the Son will never have life. God's anger stays on them."

4 The Pharisees heard that Jesus was making and baptizing more followers than John, ²although Jesus himself did not baptize people, but his followers did. ³Jesus knew that the Pharisees had heard about him, so he left Judea and went back to Galilee. ⁴But on the way he had to go through the country of Samaria.

⁵In Samaria Jesus came to the town called Sychar, which is near the field Jacob gave to his son Joseph. ⁶Jacob's well was

there. Jesus was tired from his long trip, so he sat down beside the well. It was about twelve o'clock noon. ⁷When a Samaritan woman came to the well to get some water, Jesus said to her, "Please give me a drink." ⁸(This happened while Jesus' followers were in town buying some food.)

⁹The woman said, "I am surprised that you ask me for a drink, since you are a Jewish man and I am a Samaritan woman." (Jewish people are not friends with Samaritans.)

¹⁰Jesus said, "If you only knew the free gift of God and who it is that is asking you for water, you would have asked him, and he would have given you living water."

¹¹The woman said, "Sir, where will you get this living water? The well is very deep, and you have nothing to get water with. ¹²Are you greater than Jacob, our father, who gave us this well and drank from it himself along with his sons and flocks?"

STEP 11

¹³Jesus answered, "Everyone who drinks this water will be thirsty again, ¹⁴but whoever drinks the water I give will never be thirsty. The water I give will become a spring of water gushing up inside that person, giving eternal life."

¹⁵The woman said to him, "Sir, give me this water so I will never be thirsty again and will not have to come back here to get more water."

¹⁶Jesus told her, "Go get your husband and come back here."

¹⁷The woman answered, "I have no husband."

Jesus said to her, "You are right to say you have no husband. ¹⁸Really you have had five husbands, and the man you live with now is not your husband. You told the truth."

¹⁹The woman said, "Sir, I can see that you are a prophet. ²⁰Our ancestors worshiped on this mountain, but you say that Jerusalem is the place where people must worship."

²¹Jesus said, "Believe me, woman. The time is coming when neither in Jerusalem nor on this mountain will you actually worship the Father. ²²You Samaritans worship something you don't understand. We understand what we worship, because salvation comes from the Jews. ²³The time is coming when the true worshipers will worship the Father in spirit and truth, and that time is here already. You see, the Father too is actively seeking such people to worship him. ²⁴God is spirit, and those who worship him must worship in spirit and truth."

²⁵The woman said, "I know that the Messiah is coming." (Messiah is the One called Christ.) "When the Messiah comes, he will explain everything to us."

²⁶Then Jesus said, "I am he—I, the one talking to you."

²⁷Just then his followers came back from town and were surprised to see him talking with a woman. But none of them asked, "What do you want?" or "Why are you talking with her?"

²⁸Then the woman left her water jar and went back to town. She said to the people, ²⁹"Come and see a man who told me everything I ever did. Do you think he might be the Christ?" ³⁰So the people left the town and went to see Jesus.

³¹Meanwhile, his followers were begging him, "Teacher, eat something."

³²But Jesus answered, "I have food to eat that you know nothing about."

³³So the followers asked themselves, "Did somebody already bring him food?"

STEP 12

³⁴Jesus said, "My food is to do what the One who sent me wants me to do and to finish his work. ³⁵You have a saying, 'Four more months till harvest.' But I tell you, open your eyes and look at the fields ready for harvest now. ³⁶Already, the one

STEP 11

Sought through prayer and meditation to improve
our conscious contact with God **as we understood
Him,** praying only for knowledge of His will
for us and the power to carry that out.

J o h n   4 : 1 3 – 1 4

For everybody struggling with an addiction or obsession, life can be
a thirsty experience. You thirst for love, security, self-worth, and
peace. You have found yourself trying to satisfy that thirst with
manipulation, control, substance abuse, food, pornography, and
lots of other things that never truly satisfy. But finally you have
come to know Jesus who can satisfy the deepest thirst of your
heart. You have put your trust in him. Like the woman at the well,
you look to him for that promised spring of water gushing up inside
you, giving you eternal life.

Did you know you can sense the joy and peace of eternal life right
now? You do that by letting God's Word act like water for your heart
(Isaiah 55:10–11; Ephesians 5:26). You know that you have to have
water to stay alive. Thirst lets you know when you need it. So you
need a thirst for what the Bible can do for you. It cleanses your
heart and satisfies your spirit's need for connection to God. The
Bible helps you know God and his will for you. You build a
friendship with him, and you become stronger and stronger inside
as you believe in and live out truth.

FOR YOUR NEXT **STEP 11** MEDITATION, TURN TO **PAGE 214.** ▶▶

who harvests is being paid and is gathering crops for eternal life. So the one who plants and the one who harvests celebrate at the same time. ³⁷Here the saying is true, 'One person plants, and another harvests.' ³⁸I sent you to harvest a crop that you did not work on. Others did the work, and you get to finish up their work."

³⁹Many of the Samaritans in that town believed in Jesus because of what the woman said: "He told me everything I ever did." ⁴⁰When the Samaritans came to Jesus, they begged him to stay with them, so he stayed there two more days. ⁴¹And many more believed because of the things he said.

⁴²They said to the woman, "First we believed in Jesus because of what you said, but now we believe because we heard him ourselves. We know that this man really is the Savior of the world."

⁴³Two days later, Jesus left and went to Galilee. ⁴⁴(Jesus had said before that a prophet is not respected in his own country.) ⁴⁵When Jesus arrived in Galilee, the people there welcomed him. They had seen all the things he did at the Passover Feast in Jerusalem, because they had been there, too.

⁴⁶Jesus went again to visit Cana in Galilee where he had changed the water into wine. One of the king's important officers lived in the city of Capernaum, and his son was sick. ⁴⁷When he heard that Jesus had come from Judea to Galilee, he went to Jesus and begged him to come to Capernaum and heal his son, because his son was almost dead. ⁴⁸Jesus said to him, "You people must see signs and miracles before you will believe in me."

⁴⁹The officer said, "Sir, come before my child dies."

⁵⁰Jesus answered, "Go. Your son will live."

The man believed what Jesus told him and went home. ⁵¹On the way the man's servants came and met him and told him, "Your son is alive."

⁵²The man asked, "What time did my son begin to get well?"

They answered, "Yesterday at one o'clock the fever left him."

⁵³The father knew that one o'clock was the exact time that Jesus had said, "Your son will live." So the man and all the people who lived in his house believed in Jesus.

⁵⁴That was the second miracle Jesus did after coming from Judea to Galilee.

5 Later Jesus went to Jerusalem for a special feast. ²In Jerusalem there is a pool with five covered porches, which is called Bethesda in the Hebrew language. This pool is near the Sheep Gate. ³Many sick people were lying on the porches beside the pool. Some were blind, some were crippled, and some were paralyzed [, and they waited for the water to move. ⁴Sometimes an angel of the Lord came down to the pool and stirred up the water. After the angel did this, the first person to go into the pool was healed from any sickness he had]. ⁵A man was lying there who had been sick for thirty-eight years. ⁶When Jesus saw the man and knew that he had been sick for such a long time, Jesus asked him, "Do you want to be well?"

⁷The sick man answered, "Sir, there is no one to help me get into the pool when the water starts moving. While I am coming to the water, someone else always gets in before me."

⁸Then Jesus said, "Stand up. Pick up your mat and walk." ⁹And immediately the man was well; he picked up his mat and began to walk.

The day this happened was a Sabbath day. ¹⁰So the Jews said to the man who had been healed, "Today is the Sabbath. It is against our law for you to carry your mat on the Sabbath day."

[11]But he answered, "The man who made me well told me, 'Pick up your mat and walk.' "

[12]Then they asked him, "Who is the man who told you to pick up your mat and walk?"

[13]But the man who had been healed did not know who it was, because there were many people in that place, and Jesus had left.

[14]Later, Jesus found the man at the Temple and said to him, "See, you are well now. Stop sinning so that something worse does not happen to you."

[15]Then the man left and told his people that Jesus was the one who had made him well.

[16]Because Jesus was doing this on the Sabbath day, some evil people began to persecute him. [17]But Jesus said to them, "My Father never stops working, and so I keep working, too."

[18]This made them try still harder to kill him. They said, "First Jesus was breaking the law about the Sabbath day. Now he says that God is his own Father, making himself equal with God!"

[19]But Jesus said, "I tell you the truth, the Son can do nothing alone. The Son does only what he sees the Father doing, because the Son does whatever the Father does. [20]The Father loves the Son and shows the Son all the things he himself does. But the Father will show the Son even greater things than this so that you can all be amazed. [21]Just as the Father raises the dead and gives them life, so also the Son gives life to those he wants to. [22]In fact, the Father judges no one, but he has given the Son power to do all the judging [23]so that all people will honor the Son as much as they honor the Father.

Anyone who does not honor the Son does not honor the Father who sent him.

[24]"I tell you the truth, whoever hears what I say and believes in the One who sent me has eternal life. That person will not be judged guilty but has already left death and entered life. [25]I tell you the truth, the time is coming and is already here when the dead will hear the voice of the Son of God, and those who hear will have life. [26]Life comes from the Father himself, and he has allowed the Son to have life in himself as well. [27]And the Father has given the Son the approval to judge, because he is the Son of Man. [28]Don't be surprised at this: A time is coming when all who are dead and in their graves will hear his voice. [29]Then they will come out of their graves. Those who did good will rise and have life forever, but those who did evil will rise to be judged guilty.

[30]"I can do nothing alone. I judge only the way I am told, so my judgment is fair. I don't try to please myself, but I try to please the One who sent me.

[31]"If only I tell people about myself, what I say is not true. [32]But there is another who tells about me, and I know that the things he says about me are true.

[33]"You have sent people to John, and he has told you the truth. [34]It is not that I need what humans say; I tell you this so you can be saved. [35]John was like a burning and shining lamp, and you were happy to enjoy his light for a while.

[36]"But I have a proof about myself that is greater than that of John. The things I do, which are the things my Father gave me to do, prove that the Father sent me. [37]And the Father himself who sent me has given proof about me. You have never heard his voice or seen what he looks like. [38]His teaching does not live in you, because you don't believe in the One the

STEP
3

Father sent. ³⁹You carefully study the Scriptures because you think they give you eternal life. They do in fact tell about me, ⁴⁰but you refuse to come to me to have that life.

⁴¹"I don't need praise from people. ⁴²But I know you—I know that you don't have God's love in you. ⁴³I have come from my Father and speak for him, but you don't accept me. But when another person comes, speaking only for himself, you will accept him. ⁴⁴You try to get praise from each other, but you do not try to get the praise that comes from the only God. So how can you believe? ⁴⁵Don't think that I will stand before the Father and say you are wrong. The one who says you are wrong is Moses, the one you hoped would save you. ⁴⁶If you really believed Moses, you would believe me, because Moses wrote about me. ⁴⁷But if you don't believe what Moses wrote, how can you believe what I say?"

6 After this, Jesus went across Lake Galilee (or, Lake Tiberias). ²Many people followed him because they saw the miracles he did to heal the sick. ³Jesus went up on a hill and sat down there with his followers. ⁴It was almost the time for the Jewish Passover Feast.

⁵When Jesus looked up and saw a large crowd coming toward him, he said to Philip, "Where can we buy enough bread for all these people to eat?" ⁶(Jesus asked Philip this question to test him, because Jesus already knew what he planned to do.)

⁷Philip answered, "Someone would have to work almost a year to buy enough bread for each person to have only a little piece."

⁸Another one of his followers, Andrew, Simon Peter's brother, said, ⁹"Here is a boy with five loaves of barley bread and two little fish, but that is not enough for so many people."

¹⁰Jesus said, "Tell the people to sit down." There was plenty of grass there, and about five thousand men sat down there. ¹¹Then Jesus took the loaves of bread, thanked God for them, and gave them to the people who were sitting there. He did the same with the fish, giving as much as the people wanted.

¹²When they had all had enough to eat, Jesus said to his followers, "Gather the leftover pieces of fish and bread so that nothing is wasted." ¹³So they gathered up the pieces and filled twelve baskets with the pieces left from the five barley loaves.

¹⁴When the people saw this miracle that Jesus did, they said, "He must truly be the Prophet who is coming into the world."

¹⁵Jesus knew that the people planned to come and take him by force and make him their king, so he left and went into the hills alone.

¹⁶That evening Jesus' followers went down to Lake Galilee. ¹⁷It was dark now, and Jesus had not yet come to them. The followers got into a boat and started across the lake to Capernaum. ¹⁸By now a strong wind was blowing, and the waves on the lake were getting bigger. ¹⁹When they had rowed the boat about three or four miles, they saw Jesus walking on the water, coming toward the boat. The followers were afraid, ²⁰but Jesus said to them, "It is I. Do not be afraid." ²¹Then they were glad to take him into the boat. At once the boat came to land at the place where they wanted to go.

²²The next day the people who had stayed on the other side of the lake knew that Jesus had not gone in the boat with his followers but that they had left without him. And they knew that only one boat had been there. ²³But then some boats came from Tiberias and landed

near the place where the people had eaten the bread after the Lord had given thanks. [24]When the people saw that Jesus and his followers were not there now, they got into boats and went to Capernaum to find Jesus.

[25]When the people found Jesus on the other side of the lake, they asked him, "Teacher, when did you come here?"

[26]Jesus answered, "I tell you the truth, you aren't looking for me because you saw me do miracles. You are looking for me because you ate the bread and were satisfied. [27]Don't work for the food that spoils. Work for the food that stays good always and gives eternal life. The Son of Man will give you this food, because on him God the Father has put his power."

STEP 2
[28]The people asked Jesus, "What are the things God wants us to do?"

[29]Jesus answered, "The work God wants you to do is this: Believe the One he sent."

[30]So the people asked, "What miracle will you do? If we see a miracle, we will believe you. What will you do? [31]Our ancestors ate the manna in the desert. This is written in the Scriptures: 'He gave them bread from heaven to eat.' "

[32]Jesus said, "I tell you the truth, it was not Moses who gave you bread from heaven; it is my Father who is giving you the true bread from heaven. [33]God's bread is the One who comes down from heaven and gives life to the world."

[34]The people said, "Sir, give us this bread always."

STEP 3
[35]Then Jesus said, "I am the bread that gives life. Whoever comes to me will never be hungry, and whoever believes in me will never be thirsty. [36]But as I told you before, you have seen me and still don't believe. [37]The Father gives me the people who are mine. Every one of them will come to me, and I will always accept

them. [38]I came down from heaven to do what God wants me to do, not what I want to do. [39]Here is what the One who sent me wants me to do: I must not lose even one whom God gave me, but I must raise them all on the last day. [40]Those who see the Son and believe in him have eternal life, and I will raise them on the last day. This is what my Father wants."

[41]Some people began to complain about Jesus because he said, "I am the bread that comes down from heaven." [42]They said, "This is Jesus, the son of Joseph. We know his father and mother. How can he say, 'I came down from heaven'?"

[43]But Jesus answered, "Stop complaining to each other. [44]The Father is the One who sent me. No one can come to me unless the Father draws him to me, and I will raise that person up on the last day. [45]It is written in the prophets, 'They will all be taught by God.' Everyone who listens to the Father and learns from him comes to me. [46]No one has seen the Father except the One who is from God; only he has seen the Father. [47]I tell you the truth, whoever believes has eternal life. [48]I am the bread that gives life. [49]Your ancestors ate the manna in the desert, but still they died. [50]Here is the bread that comes down from heaven. Anyone who eats this bread will never die. [51]I am the living bread that came down from heaven. Anyone who eats this bread will live forever. This bread is my flesh, which I will give up so that the world may have life."

[52]Then the evil people began to argue among themselves, saying, "How can this man give us his flesh to eat?"

[53]Jesus said, "I tell you the truth, you must eat the flesh of the Son of Man and drink his blood. Otherwise, you won't have real life in you. [54]Those who eat my flesh and drink my blood have eternal

life, and I will raise them up on the last day. ⁵⁵My flesh is true food, and my blood is true drink. ⁵⁶Those who eat my flesh and drink my blood live in me, and I live in them. ⁵⁷The living Father sent me, and I live because of the Father. So whoever eats me will live because of me. ⁵⁸I am not like the bread your ancestors ate. They ate that bread and still died. I am the bread that came down from heaven, and whoever eats this bread will live forever." ⁵⁹Jesus said all these things while he was teaching in the synagogue in Capernaum.

⁶⁰When the followers of Jesus heard this, many of them said, "This teaching is hard. Who can accept it?"

⁶¹Knowing that his followers were complaining about this, Jesus said, "Does this teaching bother you? ⁶²Then will it also bother you to see the Son of Man going back to the place where he came from? ⁶³It is the Spirit that gives life. The flesh doesn't give life. The words I told you are spirit, and they give life. ⁶⁴But some of you don't believe." (Jesus knew from the beginning who did not believe and who would turn against him.) ⁶⁵Jesus said, "That is the reason I said, 'If the Father does not bring a person to me, that one cannot come.' "

⁶⁶After Jesus said this, many of his followers left him and stopped following him.

⁶⁷Jesus asked the twelve followers, "Do you want to leave, too?"

⁶⁸Simon Peter answered him, "Lord, who would we go to? You have the words that give eternal life. ⁶⁹We believe and know that you are the Holy One from God."

⁷⁰Then Jesus answered, "I chose all twelve of you, but one of you is a devil." ⁷¹Jesus was talking about Judas, the son of Simon Iscariot. Judas was one of the twelve, but later he was going to turn against Jesus.

7 After this, Jesus traveled around Galilee. He did not want to travel in Judea, because some evil people there wanted to kill him. ²It was time for the Feast of Shelters. ³So Jesus' brothers said to him, "You should leave here and go to Judea so your followers there can see the miracles you do. ⁴Anyone who wants to be well known does not hide what he does. If you are doing these things, show yourself to the world." ⁵(Even Jesus' brothers did not believe in him.)

⁶Jesus said to his brothers, "The right time for me has not yet come, but any time is right for you. ⁷The world cannot hate you, but it hates me, because I tell it the evil things it does. ⁸So you go to the feast. I will not go yet to this feast, because the right time for me has not yet come." ⁹After saying this, Jesus stayed in Galilee.

¹⁰But after Jesus' brothers had gone to the feast, Jesus went also. But he did not let people see him. ¹¹At the feast some people were looking for him and saying, "Where is that man?"

¹²Within the large crowd there, many people were whispering to each other about Jesus. Some said, "He is a good man."

Others said, "No, he fools the people." ¹³But no one was brave enough to talk about Jesus openly, because they were afraid of the elders.

¹⁴When the feast was about half over, Jesus went to the Temple and began to teach. ¹⁵The people were amazed and said, "This man has never studied in school. How did he learn so much?"

¹⁶Jesus answered, "The things I teach are not my own, but they come from him who sent me. ¹⁷If people choose to do what God wants, they will know that my

STEP 2

Came to believe that a Power greater than
ourselves could restore us to sanity.

John 6:63

Addicts try to use things to create a temporary good feeling to mask the gnawing pain or numbing emptiness inside. The Bible warns against using things outside you to satisfy your deepest spiritual and emotional needs. Living in response to physical urges is what the Bible calls "the flesh." When you try to satisfy your deepest inner hungers with things like drugs, food, money, and sex, you're exhibiting the symptoms of addiction's special form of insanity.

Step 2 promises you renewed sanity when you turn away from unhealthy dependence on "the flesh" and hook up with life from God's Spirit. This transformation is so radical and huge that you have to compare it to rebirth.

A.A. describes your rebirth and your infilling of the Holy Spirit this way in the book *Alcoholics Anonymous:* "As we felt new power flow in, as we enjoyed peace of mind, as we discovered we could face life successfully, as we became conscious of His presence, we began to lose our fear of today, tomorrow or the hereafter. We were reborn" (p. 63).

FOR YOUR NEXT **STEP 2** MEDITATION, TURN TO **PAGE 148.** ▶▶

teaching comes from God and not from me. [18]Those who teach their own ideas are trying to get honor for themselves. But those who try to bring honor to the one who sent them speak the truth, and there is nothing false in them. [19]Moses gave you the law, but none of you obeys that law. Why are you trying to kill me?"

[20]The people answered, "A demon has come into you. We are not trying to kill you."

[21]Jesus said to them, "I did one miracle, and you are all amazed. [22]Moses gave you the law about circumcision. (But really Moses did not give you circumcision; it came from our ancestors.) And yet you circumcise a baby boy on a Sabbath day. [23]If a baby boy can be circumcised on a Sabbath day to obey the law of Moses, why are you angry at me for healing a person's whole body on the Sabbath day? [24]Stop judging by the way things look, but judge by what is really right."

[25]Then some of the people who lived in Jerusalem said, "This is the man they are trying to kill. [26]But he is teaching where everyone can see and hear him, and no one is trying to stop him. Maybe the leaders have decided he really is the Christ. [27]But we know where this man is from. Yet when the real Christ comes, no one will know where he comes from."

[28]Jesus, teaching in the Temple, cried out, "Yes, you know me, and you know where I am from. But I have not come by my own authority. I was sent by the One who is true, whom you don't know. [29]But I know him, because I am from him, and he sent me."

[30]When Jesus said this, they tried to seize him. But no one was able to touch him, because it was not yet the right time. [31]But many of the people believed in Jesus. They said, "When the Christ comes,

will he do more miracles than this man has done?"

[32]The Pharisees heard the crowd whispering these things about Jesus. So the leading priests and the Pharisees sent some Temple guards to arrest him. [33]Jesus said, "I will be with you a little while longer. Then I will go back to the One who sent me. [34]You will look for me, but you will not find me. And you cannot come where I am."

[35]Some people said to each other, "Where will this man go so we cannot find him? Will he go to the Greek cities where our people live and teach the Greek people there? [36]What did he mean when he said, 'You will look for me, but you will not find me,' and 'You cannot come where I am'?"

[37]On the last and most important day of the feast Jesus stood up and said in a loud voice, "Let anyone who is thirsty come to me and drink. [38]If anyone believes in me, rivers of living water will flow out from that person's heart, as the Scripture says." [39]Jesus was talking about the Holy Spirit. The Spirit had not yet been given, because Jesus had not yet been raised to glory. But later, those who believed in Jesus would receive the Spirit.

STEP 2

[40]When the people heard Jesus' words, some of them said, "This man really is the Prophet."

[41]Others said, "He is the Christ."

Still others said, "The Christ will not come from Galilee. [42]The Scripture says that the Christ will come from David's family and from Bethlehem, the town where David lived." [43]So the people did not agree with each other about Jesus. [44]Some of them wanted to arrest him, but no one was able to touch him.

[45]The Temple guards went back to the leading priests and the Pharisees, who asked, "Why didn't you bring Jesus?"

⁴⁶The guards answered, "The words he says are greater than the words of any other person who has ever spoken!"

⁴⁷The Pharisees answered, "So Jesus has fooled you also! ⁴⁸Have any of the leaders or the Pharisees believed in him? No! ⁴⁹But these people, who know nothing about the law, are under God's curse."

⁵⁰Nicodemus, who had gone to see Jesus before, was in that group. He said, ⁵¹"Our law does not judge a person without hearing him and knowing what he has done."

⁵²They answered, "Are you from Galilee, too? Study the Scriptures, and you will learn that no prophet comes from Galilee."

Some of the earliest surviving Greek copies do not contain 7:53—8:11.

[⁵³And everyone left and went home.

STEP 3

8 Jesus went to the Mount of Olives. ²But early in the morning he went back to the Temple, and all the people came to him, and he sat and taught them. ³The teachers of the law and the Pharisees brought a woman who had been caught in adultery. They forced her to stand before the people. ⁴They said to Jesus, "Teacher, this woman was caught having sexual relations with a man who is not her husband. ⁵The law of Moses commands that we stone to death every woman who does this. What do you say we should do?" ⁶They were asking this to trick Jesus so that they could have some charge against him.

But Jesus bent over and started writing on the ground with his finger. ⁷When they continued to ask Jesus their question, he raised up and said, "Anyone here who has never sinned can throw the first stone at her." ⁸Then Jesus bent over again and wrote on the ground.

⁹Those who heard Jesus began to leave one by one, first the older men and then the others. Jesus was left there alone with the woman standing before him. ¹⁰Jesus raised up again and asked her, "Woman, where are they? Has no one judged you guilty?"

¹¹She answered, "No one, sir."

Then Jesus said, "I also don't judge you guilty. You may go now, but don't sin anymore."]

STEP 2

¹²Later, Jesus talked to the people again, saying, "I am the light of the world. The person who follows me will never live in darkness but will have the light that gives life."

¹³The Pharisees said to Jesus, "When you talk about yourself, you are the only one to say these things are true. We cannot accept what you say."

¹⁴Jesus answered, "Yes, I am saying these things about myself, but they are true. I know where I came from and where I am going. But you don't know where I came from or where I am going. ¹⁵You judge by human standards. I am not judging anyone. ¹⁶But when I do judge, I judge truthfully, because I am not alone. The Father who sent me is with me. ¹⁷Your own law says that when two witnesses say the same thing, you must accept what they say. ¹⁸I am one of the witnesses who speaks about myself, and the Father who sent me is the other witness."

¹⁹They asked, "Where is your father?"

Jesus answered, "You don't know me or my Father. If you knew me, you would know my Father, too." ²⁰Jesus said these things while he was teaching in the Temple, near where the money is kept. But no one arrested him, because the right time for him had not yet come.

²¹Again, Jesus said to the people, "I will leave you, and you will look for me, but you will die in your sins. You cannot come where I am going."

²²So the Jews asked, "Will he kill himself? Is that why he said, 'You cannot come where I am going'?"

²³Jesus said, "You people are from here below, but I am from above. You belong to this world, but I don't belong to this world. ²⁴So I told you that you would die in your sins. Yes, you will die in your sins if you don't believe that I am he."

²⁵They asked, "Then who are you?"

Jesus answered, "I am what I have told you from the beginning. ²⁶I have many things to say and decide about you. But I tell people only the things I have heard from the One who sent me, and he speaks the truth."

²⁷The people did not understand that he was talking to them about the Father. ²⁸So Jesus said to them, "When you lift up the Son of Man, you will know that I am he. You will know that these things I do are not by my own authority but that I say only what the Father has taught me. ²⁹The One who sent me is with me. I always do what is pleasing to him, so he has not left me alone." ³⁰While Jesus was saying these things, many people believed in him.

STEP 11

³¹So Jesus said to the Jews who believed in him, "If you continue to obey my teaching, you are truly my followers. ³²Then you will know the truth, and the truth will make you free."

³³They answered, "We are Abraham's children, and we have never been anyone's slaves. So why do you say we will be free?"

³⁴Jesus answered, "I tell you the truth, everyone who lives in sin is a slave to sin.

³⁵A slave does not stay with a family forever, but a son belongs to the family forever. ³⁶So if the Son makes you free, you will be truly free. ³⁷I know you are Abraham's children, but you want to kill me because you don't accept my teaching. ³⁸I am telling you what my Father has shown me, but you do what your father has told you."

³⁹They answered, "Our father is Abraham."

Jesus said, "If you were really Abraham's children, you would do the things Abraham did. ⁴⁰I am a man who has told you the truth which I heard from God, but you are trying to kill me. Abraham did nothing like that. ⁴¹So you are doing the things your own father did."

But they said, "We are not like children who never knew who their father was. God is our Father; he is the only Father we have."

⁴²Jesus said to them, "If God were really your Father, you would love me, because I came from God and now I am here. I did not come by my own authority; God sent me. ⁴³You don't understand what I say, because you cannot accept my teaching. ⁴⁴You belong to your father the devil, and you want to do what he wants. He was a murderer from the beginning and was against the truth, because there is no truth in him. When he tells a lie, he shows what he is really like, because he is a liar and the father of lies. ⁴⁵But because I speak the truth, you don't believe me. ⁴⁶Can any of you prove that I am guilty of sin? If I am telling the truth, why don't you believe me? ⁴⁷The person who belongs to God accepts what God says. But you don't accept what God says, because you don't belong to God."

⁴⁸They answered, "We say you are a Samaritan and have a demon in you. Are we not right?"

⁴⁹Jesus answered, "I have no demon in me. I give honor to my Father, but you dishonor me. ⁵⁰I am not trying to get honor for myself. There is One who wants this honor for me, and he is the judge. ⁵¹I tell you the truth, whoever obeys my teaching will never die."

⁵²They said to Jesus, "Now we know that you have a demon in you! Even Abraham and the prophets died. But you say, 'Whoever obeys my teaching will never die.' ⁵³Do you think you are greater than our father Abraham, who died? And the prophets died, too. Who do you think you are?"

⁵⁴Jesus answered, "If I give honor to myself, that honor is worth nothing. The One who gives me honor is my Father, and you say he is your God. ⁵⁵You don't really know him, but I know him. If I said I did not know him, I would be a liar like you. But I do know him, and I obey what he says. ⁵⁶Your father Abraham was very happy that he would see my day. He saw that day and was glad."

⁵⁷They said to him, "You have never seen Abraham! You are not even fifty years old."

⁵⁸Jesus answered, "I tell you the truth, before Abraham was even born, I am!" ⁵⁹When Jesus said this, the people picked up stones to throw at him. But Jesus hid himself, and then he left the Temple.

9 As Jesus was walking along, he saw a man who had been born blind. ²His followers asked him, "Teacher, whose sin caused this man to be born blind—his own sin or his parents' sin?"

³Jesus answered, "It is not this man's sin or his parents' sin that made him blind. This man was born blind so that God's power could be shown in him. ⁴While it is daytime, we must continue doing the work of the One who sent me. Night is coming, when no one can work.

⁵While I am in the world, I am the light of the world."

⁶After Jesus said this, he spit on the ground and made some mud with it and put the mud on the man's eyes. ⁷Then he told the man, "Go and wash in the Pool of Siloam." (Siloam means Sent.) So the man went, washed, and came back seeing.

⁸The neighbors and some people who had earlier seen this man begging said, "Isn't this the same man who used to sit and beg?"

⁹Some said, "He is the one," but others said, "No, he only looks like him."

The man himself said, "I am the man."

¹⁰They asked, "How did you get your sight?"

¹¹He answered, "The man named Jesus made some mud and put it on my eyes. Then he told me to go to Siloam and wash. So I went and washed, and then I could see."

¹²They asked him, "Where is this man?"

"I don't know," he answered.

¹³Then the people took to the Pharisees the man who had been blind. ¹⁴The day Jesus had made mud and healed his eyes was a Sabbath day. ¹⁵So now the Pharisees asked the man, "How did you get your sight?"

He answered, "He put mud on my eyes, I washed, and now I see."

¹⁶So some of the Pharisees were saying, "This man does not keep the Sabbath day, so he is not from God."

But others said, "A man who is a sinner can't do miracles like these." So they could not agree with each other.

¹⁷They asked the man again, "What do you say about him since it was your eyes he opened?"

The man answered, "He is a prophet."

¹⁸These leaders did not believe that he

had been blind and could now see again. So they sent for the man's parents [19]and asked them, "Is this your son who you say was born blind? Then how does he now see?"

[20]His parents answered, "We know that this is our son and that he was born blind. [21]But we don't know how he can now see. We don't know who opened his eyes. Ask him. He is old enough to speak for himself." [22]His parents said this because they were afraid of the elders, who had already decided that anyone who said Jesus was the Christ would be avoided. [23]That is why his parents said, "He is old enough. Ask him."

[24]So for the second time, they called the man who had been blind. They said, "You should give God the glory by telling the truth. We know that this man is a sinner."

[25]He answered, "I don't know if he is a sinner. One thing I do know: I was blind, and now I see."

[26]They asked, "What did he do to you? How did he make you see again?"

[27]He answered, "I already told you, and you didn't listen. Why do you want to hear it again? Do you want to become his followers, too?"

[28]Then they insulted him and said, "You are his follower, but we are followers of Moses. [29]We know that God spoke to Moses, but we don't even know where this man comes from."

[30]The man answered, "This is a very strange thing. You don't know where he comes from, and yet he opened my eyes. [31]We all know that God does not listen to sinners, but he listens to anyone who worships and obeys him. [32]Nobody has ever heard of anyone giving sight to a man born blind. [33]If this man were not from God, he could do nothing."

[34]They answered, "You were born full of sin! Are you trying to teach us?" And they threw him out.

[35]When Jesus heard that they had thrown him out, Jesus found him and said, "Do you believe in the Son of Man?"

[36]He asked, "Who is the Son of Man, sir, so that I can believe in him?"

[37]Jesus said to him, "You have seen him. The Son of Man is the one talking with you."

[38]He said, "Lord, I believe!" Then the man worshiped Jesus.

[39]Jesus said, "I came into this world so that the world could be judged. I came so that the blind would see and so that those who see will become blind."

[40]Some of the Pharisees who were nearby heard Jesus say this and asked, "Are you saying we are blind, too?"

[41]Jesus said, "If you were blind, you would not be guilty of sin. But since you keep saying you see, your guilt remains."

10 Jesus said, "I tell you the truth, the person who does not enter the sheepfold by the door, but climbs in some other way, is a thief and a robber. [2]The one who enters by the door is the shepherd of the sheep. [3]The one who guards the door opens it for him. And the sheep listen to the voice of the shepherd. He calls his own sheep by name and leads them out. [4]When he brings all his sheep out, he goes ahead of them, and they follow him because they know his voice. [5]But they will never follow a stranger. They will run away from him because they don't know his voice." [6]Jesus told the people this story, but they did not understand what it meant.

[7]So Jesus said again, "I tell you the truth, I am the door for the sheep. [8]All the people who came before me were thieves and robbers. The sheep did not listen to them. [9]I am the door, and the person who enters through me will be

STEP 2

saved and will be able to come in and go out and find pasture. ¹⁰A thief comes to steal and kill and destroy, but I came to give life—life in all its fullness.

¹¹"I am the good shepherd. The good shepherd gives his life for the sheep. ¹²The worker who is paid to keep the sheep is different from the shepherd who owns them. When the worker sees a wolf coming, he runs away and leaves the sheep alone. Then the wolf attacks the sheep and scatters them. ¹³The man runs away because he is only a paid worker and does not really care about the sheep.

¹⁴"I am the good shepherd. I know my sheep, and my sheep know me, ¹⁵just as the Father knows me, and I know the Father. I give my life for the sheep. ¹⁶I have other sheep that are not in this flock, and I must bring them also. They will listen to my voice, and there will be one flock and one shepherd. ¹⁷The Father loves me because I give my life so that I can take it back again. ¹⁸No one takes it away from me; I give my own life freely. I have the right to give my life, and I have the right to take it back. This is what my Father commanded me to do."

¹⁹Again the leaders did not agree with each other because of these words of Jesus. ²⁰Many of them said, "A demon has come into him and made him crazy. Why listen to him?"

²¹But others said, "A man who is crazy with a demon does not say things like this. Can a demon open the eyes of the blind?"

²²The time came for the Feast of Dedication at Jerusalem. It was winter, ²³and Jesus was walking in the Temple in Solomon's Porch. ²⁴Some people gathered around him and said, "How long will you make us wonder about you? If you are the Christ, tell us plainly."

²⁵Jesus answered, "I told you already, but you did not believe. The miracles I do in my Father's name show who I am. ²⁶But you don't believe, because you are not my sheep. ²⁷My sheep listen to my voice; I know them, and they follow me. ²⁸I give them eternal life, and they will never die, and no one can steal them out of my hand. ²⁹My Father gave my sheep to me. He is greater than all, and no person can steal my sheep out of my Father's hand. ³⁰The Father and I are one."

³¹Again some of the people picked up stones to kill Jesus. ³²But he said to them, "I have done many good works from the Father. Which of these good works are you killing me for?"

³³They answered, "We are not killing you because of any good work you did, but because you speak against God. You are only a human, but you say you are the same as God!"

³⁴Jesus answered, "It is written in your law that God said, 'I said, you are gods.' ³⁵This Scripture called those people gods who received God's message, and Scripture is always true. ³⁶So why do you say that I speak against God because I said, 'I am God's Son'? I am the one God chose and sent into the world. ³⁷If I don't do what my Father does, then don't believe me. ³⁸But if I do what my Father does, even though you don't believe in me, believe what I do. Then you will know and understand that the Father is in me and I am in the Father."

³⁹They tried to take Jesus again, but he escaped from them.

⁴⁰Then he went back across the Jordan River to the place where John had first baptized. Jesus stayed there, ⁴¹and many people came to him and said, "John never did a miracle, but everything John said about this man is true." ⁴²And in that place many believed in Jesus.

11 A man named Lazarus was sick. He lived in the town of Bethany, where Mary and her sister Martha lived. [2]Mary was the woman who later put perfume on the Lord and wiped his feet with her hair. Mary's brother was Lazarus, the man who was now sick. [3]So Mary and Martha sent someone to tell Jesus, "Lord, the one you love is sick."

[4]When Jesus heard this, he said, "This sickness will not end in death. It is for the glory of God, to bring glory to the Son of God." [5]Jesus loved Martha and her sister and Lazarus. [6]But when he heard that Lazarus was sick, he stayed where he was for two more days. [7]Then Jesus said to his followers, "Let's go back to Judea."

[8]The followers said, "But Teacher, some people there tried to stone you to death only a short time ago. Now you want to go back there?"

[9]Jesus answered, "Are there not twelve hours in the day? If anyone walks in the daylight, he will not stumble, because he can see by this world's light. [10]But if anyone walks at night, he stumbles because there is no light to help him see."

[11]After Jesus said this, he added, "Our friend Lazarus has fallen asleep, but I am going there to wake him."

[12]The followers said, "But, Lord, if he is only asleep, he will be all right."

[13]Jesus meant that Lazarus was dead, but his followers thought he meant Lazarus was really sleeping. [14]So then Jesus said plainly, "Lazarus is dead. [15]And I am glad for your sakes I was not there so that you may believe. But let's go to him now."

[16]Then Thomas (the one called Didymus) said to the other followers, "Let us also go so that we can die with him."

[17]When Jesus arrived, he learned that Lazarus had already been dead and in the tomb for four days. [18]Bethany was about two miles from Jerusalem. [19]Many of the Jews had come there to comfort Martha and Mary about their brother.

[20]When Martha heard that Jesus was coming, she went out to meet him, but Mary stayed home. [21]Martha said to Jesus, "Lord, if you had been here, my brother would not have died. [22]But I know that even now God will give you anything you ask."

[23]Jesus said, "Your brother will rise and live again."

[24]Martha answered, "I know that he will rise and live again in the resurrection on the last day."

[25]Jesus said to her, "I am the resurrection and the life. Those who believe in me will have life even if they die. [26]And everyone who lives and believes in me will never die. Martha, do you believe this?"

STEP
2

[27]Martha answered, "Yes, Lord. I believe that you are the Christ, the Son of God, the One coming to the world."

[28]After Martha said this, she went back and talked to her sister Mary alone. Martha said, "The Teacher is here and he is asking for you." [29]When Mary heard this, she got up quickly and went to Jesus. [30]Jesus had not yet come into the town but was still at the place where Martha had met him. [31]The Jews were with Mary in the house, comforting her. When they saw her stand and leave quickly, they followed her, thinking she was going to the tomb to cry there.

[32]But Mary went to the place where Jesus was. When she saw him, she fell at his feet and said, "Lord, if you had been here, my brother would not have died."

[33]When Jesus saw Mary crying and the Jews who came with her also crying, he was upset and was deeply troubled. [34]He asked, "Where did you bury him?"

"Come and see, Lord," they said.

[35]Jesus cried.

³⁶So the Jews said, "See how much he loved him."

³⁷But some of them said, "If Jesus opened the eyes of the blind man, why couldn't he keep Lazarus from dying?"

³⁸Again feeling very upset, Jesus came to the tomb. It was a cave with a large stone covering the entrance. ³⁹Jesus said, "Move the stone away."

Martha, the sister of the dead man, said, "But, Lord, it has been four days since he died. There will be a bad smell."

⁴⁰Then Jesus said to her, "Didn't I tell you that if you believed you would see the glory of God?"

⁴¹So they moved the stone away from the entrance. Then Jesus looked up and said, "Father, I thank you that you heard me. ⁴²I know that you always hear me, but I said these things because of the people here around me. I want them to believe that you sent me." ⁴³After Jesus said this, he cried out in a loud voice, "Lazarus, come out!" ⁴⁴The dead man came out, his hands and feet wrapped with pieces of cloth, and a cloth around his face.

Jesus said to them, "Take the cloth off of him and let him go."

⁴⁵Many of the people, who had come to visit Mary and saw what Jesus did, believed in him. ⁴⁶But some of them went to the Pharisees and told them what Jesus had done. ⁴⁷Then the leading priests and Pharisees called a meeting of the council. They asked, "What should we do? This man is doing many miracles. ⁴⁸If we let him continue doing these things, everyone will believe in him. Then the Romans will come and take away our Temple and our nation."

⁴⁹One of the men there was Caiaphas, the high priest that year. He said, "You people know nothing! ⁵⁰You don't realize that it is better for one man to die for the people than for the whole nation to be destroyed."

⁵¹Caiaphas did not think of this himself. As high priest that year, he was really prophesying that Jesus would die for their nation ⁵²and for God's scattered children to bring them all together and make them one.

⁵³That day they started planning to kill Jesus. ⁵⁴So Jesus no longer traveled openly among the people. He left there and went to a place near the desert, to a town called Ephraim and stayed there with his followers.

⁵⁵It was almost time for the Passover Feast. Many from the country went up to Jerusalem before the Passover to do the special things to make themselves pure. ⁵⁶The people looked for Jesus and stood in the Temple asking each other, "Is he coming to the Feast? What do you think?" ⁵⁷But the leading priests and the Pharisees had given orders that if anyone knew where Jesus was, he must tell them. Then they could arrest him.

12 Six days before the Passover Feast, Jesus went to Bethany, where Lazarus lived. (Lazarus is the man Jesus raised from the dead.) ²There they had a dinner for Jesus. Martha served the food, and Lazarus was one of the people eating with Jesus. ³Mary brought in a pint of very expensive perfume made from pure nard. She poured the perfume on Jesus' feet, and then she wiped his feet with her hair. And the sweet smell from the perfume filled the whole house.

⁴Judas Iscariot, one of Jesus' followers who would later turn against him, was there. Judas said, ⁵"This perfume was worth an entire year's wages. Why wasn't it sold and the money given to the poor?" ⁶But Judas did not really care about the poor; he said this because he was a thief. He was the one who kept the money box, and he often stole from it.

⁷Jesus answered, "Leave her alone. It

was right for her to save this perfume for today, the day for me to be prepared for burial. [8]You will always have the poor with you, but you will not always have me."

[9]A large crowd of people heard that Jesus was in Bethany. So they went there to see not only Jesus but Lazarus, whom Jesus raised from the dead. [10]So the leading priests made plans to kill Lazarus, too. [11]Because of Lazarus many of the Jews were leaving them and believing in Jesus.

[12]The next day a great crowd who had come to Jerusalem for the Passover Feast heard that Jesus was coming there. [13]So they took branches of palm trees and went out to meet Jesus, shouting,

"Praise God!
God bless the One who comes in the
    name of the Lord!
God bless the King of Israel!"

Psalm 118:25–26

[14]Jesus found a colt and sat on it. This was as the Scripture says,

[15]"Don't be afraid, people of Jerusalem!
Your king is coming,
sitting on the colt of a donkey."

Zechariah 9:9

[16]The followers of Jesus did not understand this at first. But after Jesus was raised to glory, they remembered that this had been written about him and that they had done these things to him.

[17]There had been many people with Jesus when he raised Lazarus from the dead and told him to come out of the tomb. Now they were telling others about what Jesus did. [18]Many people went out to meet Jesus, because they had heard about this miracle. [19]So the Pharisees said to each other, "You can see that nothing is going right for us. Look! The whole world is following him."

[20]There were some Greek people, too, who came to Jerusalem to worship at the Passover Feast. [21]They went to Philip, who was from Bethsaida in Galilee, and said, "Sir, we would like to see Jesus." [22]Philip told Andrew, and then Andrew and Philip told Jesus.

[23]Jesus said to them, "The time has come for the Son of Man to receive his glory. [24]I tell you the truth, a grain of wheat must fall to the ground and die to make many seeds. But if it never dies, it remains only a single seed. [25]Those who love their lives will lose them, but those who hate their lives in this world will keep true life forever. [26]Whoever serves me must follow me. Then my servant will be with me everywhere I am. My Father will honor anyone who serves me.

[27]"Now I am very troubled. Should I say, 'Father, save me from this time'? No, I came to this time so I could suffer. [28]Father, bring glory to your name!"

Then a voice came from heaven, "I have brought glory to it, and I will do it again."

[29]The crowd standing there, who heard the voice, said it was thunder.

But others said, "An angel has spoken to him."

[30]Jesus said, "That voice was for your sake, not mine. [31]Now is the time for the world to be judged; now the ruler of this world will be thrown down. [32]If I am lifted up from the earth, I will draw all people toward me." [33]Jesus said this to show how he would die.

[34]The crowd said, "We have heard from the law that the Christ will live forever. So why do you say, 'The Son of Man must be lifted up'? Who is this 'Son of Man'?"

[35]Then Jesus said, "The light will be with you for a little longer, so walk while you have the light. Then the darkness will not catch you. If you walk in the darkness, you will not know where you are going. [36]Believe in the light while you still have it

STEP
3

so that you will become children of light." When Jesus had said this, he left and hid himself from them.

[37]Though Jesus had done many miracles in front of the people, they still did not believe in him. [38]This was to bring about what Isaiah the prophet had said:

"Lord, who believed what we told
        them?
Who saw the Lord's power in
        this?"   *Isaiah 53:1*

[39]This is why the people could not believe: Isaiah also had said,

[40]"He has blinded their eyes,
        and he has closed their minds.
Otherwise they would see with their
        eyes
        and understand in their minds
        and come back to me and be
        healed."   *Isaiah 6:10*

[41]Isaiah said this because he saw Jesus' glory and spoke about him.

[42]But many believed in Jesus, even many of the leaders. But because of the Pharisees, they did not say they believed in him for fear they would be put out of the synagogue. [43]They loved praise from people more than praise from God.

[44]Then Jesus cried out, "Whoever believes in me is really believing in the One who sent me. [45]Whoever sees me sees the One who sent me. [46]I have come as light into the world so that whoever believes in me would not stay in darkness.

[47]"Anyone who hears my words and does not obey them, I do not judge, because I did not come to judge the world, but to save the world. [48]There is a judge for those who refuse to believe in me and do not accept my words. The word I have taught will be their judge on the last day. [49]The things I taught were not from myself. The Father who sent me told me what to say and what to teach. [50]And I know that eternal life comes from what

the Father commands. So whatever I say is what the Father told me to say."

13 It was almost time for the Passover Feast. Jesus knew that it was time for him to leave this world and go back to the Father. He had always loved those who were his own in the world, and he loved them all the way to the end.

[2]Jesus and his followers were at the evening meal. The devil had already persuaded Judas Iscariot, the son of Simon, to turn against Jesus. [3]Jesus knew that the Father had given him power over everything and that he had come from God and was going back to God. [4]So during the meal Jesus stood up and took off his outer clothing. Taking a towel, he wrapped it around his waist. [5]Then he poured water into a bowl and began to wash the followers' feet, drying them with the towel that was wrapped around him.

[6]Jesus came to Simon Peter, who said to him, "Lord, are you going to wash my feet?"

[7]Jesus answered, "You don't understand now what I am doing, but you will understand later."

[8]Peter said, "No, you will never wash my feet."

Jesus answered, "If I don't wash your feet, you are not one of my people."

[9]Simon Peter answered, "Lord, then wash not only my feet, but wash my hands and my head, too!"

[10]Jesus said, "After a person has had a bath, his whole body is clean. He needs only to wash his feet. And you men are clean, but not all of you." [11]Jesus knew who would turn against him, and that is why he said, "Not all of you are clean."

[12]When he had finished washing their feet, he put on his clothes and sat down again. He asked, "Do you understand what I have just done for you? [13]You call

STEP 2

Came to believe that a Power greater than
ourselves could restore us to sanity.

John 12:46

If you had been hidden away in a cave from the time you were a
small child, you would have grown up without knowing what bright
sunlight was. You'd have never seen yourself in revealing light.
You'd have been a child of the dark, and sunlight would have been
foreign to you. If someone had told you about it, you wouldn't have
been able to grasp the idea.

In some ways, that's what growing up with abuse and family pain is
like. You don't know love and acceptance, and you can't really
imagine what they are like. You grow up medicating your pain with
addictive behaviors, and you can't even see that what you're doing
is a bad idea. There's no "light" to show you what's wrong with
what you're doing.

When you come to the light of God's power and love, you don't
have to keep living in the dark. You can step into the light of his
love, see yourself exactly as you are—warts and all—and accept
what you see. There's power in the light of God's love to make you
new and whole. You can walk in that light for eternity.

FOR YOUR NEXT **STEP 2** MEDITATION, TURN TO **PAGE 392.** ▶▶

me 'Teacher' and 'Lord,' and you are right, because that is what I am. [14]If I, your Lord and Teacher, have washed your feet, you also should wash each other's feet. [15]I did this as an example so that you should do as I have done for you. [16]I tell you the truth, a servant is not greater than his master. A messenger is not greater than the one who sent him. [17]If you know these things, you will be blessed if you do them.

[18]"I am not talking about all of you. I know those I have chosen. But this is to bring about what the Scripture said: 'The man who ate at my table has turned against me.' [19]I am telling you this now before it happens so that when it happens, you will believe that I am he. [20]I tell you the truth, whoever accepts anyone I send also accepts me. And whoever accepts me also accepts the One who sent me."

[21]After Jesus said this, he was very troubled. He said openly, "I tell you the truth, one of you will turn against me."

[22]The followers all looked at each other, because they did not know whom Jesus was talking about. [23]One of the followers sitting next to Jesus was the follower Jesus loved. [24]Simon Peter motioned to him to ask Jesus whom he was talking about.

[25]That follower leaned closer to Jesus and asked, "Lord, who is it?"

[26]Jesus answered, "I will dip this bread into the dish. The man I give it to is the man who will turn against me." So Jesus took a piece of bread, dipped it, and gave it to Judas Iscariot, the son of Simon. [27]As soon as Judas took the bread, Satan entered him. Jesus said to him, "The thing that you will do—do it quickly." [28]No one at the table understood why Jesus said this to Judas. [29]Since he was the one who kept the money box, some of the followers thought Jesus was telling him to buy what was needed for the feast or to give something to the poor.

[30]Judas took the bread Jesus gave him and immediately went out. It was night.

[31]When Judas was gone, Jesus said, "Now the Son of Man receives his glory, and God receives glory through him. [32]If God receives glory through him, then God will give glory to the Son through himself. And God will give him glory quickly."

[33]Jesus said, "My children, I will be with you only a little longer. You will look for me, and what I told the Jews, I tell you now: Where I am going you cannot come.

[34]"I give you a new command: Love each other. You must love each other as I have loved you. [35]All people will know that you are my followers if you love each other."

STEP 8

[36]Simon Peter asked Jesus, "Lord, where are you going?"

Jesus answered, "Where I am going you cannot follow now, but you will follow later."

[37]Peter asked, "Lord, why can't I follow you now? I am ready to die for you!"

[38]Jesus answered, "Are you ready to die for me? I tell you the truth, before the rooster crows, you will say three times that you don't know me."

14 Jesus said, "Don't let your hearts be troubled. Trust in God, and trust in me. [2]There are many rooms in my Father's house; I would not tell you this if it were not true. I am going there to prepare a place for you. [3]After I go and prepare a place for you, I will come back and take you to be with me so that you may be where I am. [4]You know the way to the place where I am going."

[5]Thomas said to Jesus, "Lord, we don't know where you are going. So how can we know the way?"

STEP 8

Made a list of all persons we had harmed,
and became willing to make amends to them all.

John 13:34–35

How can you love anyone as Jesus commands?

You can't as long as you have no love. You can't give away what you don't have. If your inventory of past relationships shows you that you didn't get any love or that love was mixed up with pain and abuse, you have a problem. You need to grieve that you didn't learn love in a normal way, and you need to commit to becoming part of a loving group, such as a church, where you can make up for your past. If your inventory of present relationships shows that you are using people or controlling them, you need to make amends in two ways. First, you need to admit what you're doing and apologize to those you're hurting. Second, you have to create healthy relationship boundaries for yourself and let those boundaries be a form of "living amends" that keep you from repeating past mistakes.

John's Gospel reminds you that you should have a reputation for loving people. The source of your love will be God's love, not your family background. The more familiar you become with God's unconditional love, the more loving you will become.

FOR YOUR NEXT **STEP 8** MEDITATION, TURN TO **PAGE 241.** ▶▶

STEP 2

⁶Jesus answered, "I am the way, and the truth, and the life. The only way to the Father is through me. ⁷If you really knew me, you would know my Father, too. But now you do know him, and you have seen him."

⁸Philip said to him, "Lord, show us the Father. That is all we need."

⁹Jesus answered, "I have been with you a long time now. Do you still not know me, Philip? Whoever has seen me has seen the Father. So why do you say, 'Show us the Father'? ¹⁰Don't you believe that I am in the Father and the Father is in me? The words I say to you don't come from me, but the Father lives in me and does his own work. ¹¹Believe me when I say that I am in the Father and the Father is in me. Or believe because of the miracles I have done.

STEP 11

¹²I tell you the truth, whoever believes in me will do the same things that I do. Those who believe will do even greater things than these, because I am going to the Father. ¹³And if you ask for anything in my name, I will do it for you so that the Father's glory will be shown through the Son. ¹⁴If you ask me for anything in my name, I will do it.

¹⁵"If you love me, you will obey my commands. ¹⁶I will ask the Father, and he will give you another Helper to be with you forever— ¹⁷the Spirit of truth. The world cannot accept him, because it does not see him or know him. But you know him, because he lives with you and he will be in you.

¹⁸"I will not leave you all alone like orphans; I will come back to you. ¹⁹In a little while the world will not see me anymore, but you will see me. Because I live, you will live, too. ²⁰On that day you will know that I am in my Father, and that you are in me and I am in you. ²¹Those who know my commands and obey them are the ones who love me, and my Father will love those who love me. I will love them and will show myself to them."

²²Then Judas (not Judas Iscariot) said, "But, Lord, why do you plan to show yourself to us and not to the rest of the world?"

²³Jesus answered, "If people love me, they will obey my teaching. My Father will love them, and we will come to them and make our home with them. ²⁴Those who do not love me do not obey my teaching. This teaching that you hear is not really mine; it is from my Father, who sent me.

²⁵"I have told you all these things while I am with you. ²⁶But the Helper will teach you everything and will cause you to remember all that I told you. This Helper is the Holy Spirit whom the Father will send in my name.

²⁷"I leave you peace; my peace I give you. I do not give it to you as the world does. So don't let your hearts be troubled or afraid. ²⁸You heard me say to you, 'I am going, but I am coming back to you.' If you loved me, you should be happy that I am going back to the Father, because he is greater than I am. ²⁹I have told you this now, before it happens, so that when it happens, you will believe. ³⁰I will not talk with you much longer, because the ruler of this world is coming. He has no power over me, ³¹but the world must know that I love the Father, so I do exactly what the Father told me to do.

"Come now, let us go.

15 "I am the true vine; my Father is the gardener. ²He cuts off every branch of mine that does not produce fruit. And he trims and cleans every branch that produces fruit so that it will produce even more fruit. ³You are already clean because of the words I have spoken to you. ⁴Remain in me, and I will remain in you. A branch cannot produce fruit alone but must remain in the vine. In the same way,

STEP 11

you cannot produce fruit alone but must remain in me.

⁵"I am the vine, and you are the branches. If any remain in me and I remain in them, they produce much fruit. But without me they can do nothing. ⁶If any do not remain in me, they are like a branch that is thrown away and then dies. People pick up dead branches, throw them into the fire, and burn them. ⁷If you remain in me and follow my teachings, you can ask anything you want, and it will be given to you. ⁸You should produce much fruit and show that you are my followers, which brings glory to my Father. ⁹I loved you as the Father loved me. Now remain in my love. ¹⁰I have obeyed my Father's commands, and I remain in his love. In the same way, if you obey my commands, you will remain in my love. ¹¹I have told you these things so that you can have the same joy I have and so that your joy will be the fullest possible joy.

¹²"This is my command: Love each other as I have loved you. ¹³The greatest love a person can show is to die for his friends. ¹⁴You are my friends if you do what I command you. ¹⁵I no longer call you servants, because a servant does not know what his master is doing. But I call you friends, because I have made known to you everything I heard from my Father. ¹⁶You did not choose me; I chose you. And I gave you this work: to go and produce fruit, fruit that will last. Then the Father will give you anything you ask for in my name. ¹⁷This is my command: Love each other.

¹⁸"If the world hates you, remember that it hated me first. ¹⁹If you belonged to the world, it would love you as it loves its own. But I have chosen you out of the world, so you don't belong to it. That is why the world hates you. ²⁰Remember

what I told you: A servant is not greater than his master. If people did wrong to me, they will do wrong to you, too. And if they obeyed my teaching, they will obey yours, too. ²¹They will do all this to you on account of me, because they do not know the One who sent me. ²²If I had not come and spoken to them, they would not be guilty of sin, but now they have no excuse for their sin. ²³Whoever hates me also hates my Father. ²⁴I did works among them that no one else has ever done. If I had not done these works, they would not be guilty of sin. But now they have seen what I have done, and yet they have hated both me and my Father. ²⁵But this happened so that what is written in their law would be true: 'They hated me for no reason.'

²⁶"I will send you the Helper from the Father; he is the Spirit of truth who comes from the Father. When he comes, he will tell about me, ²⁷and you also must tell people about me, because you have been with me from the beginning.

16"I have told you these things to keep you from giving up. ²People will put you out of their synagogues. Yes, the time is coming when those who kill you will think they are offering service to God. ³They will do this because they have not known the Father and they have not known me. ⁴I have told you these things now so that when the time comes you will remember that I warned you.

"I did not tell you these things at the beginning, because I was with you then. ⁵Now I am going back to the One who sent me. But none of you asks me, 'Where are you going?' ⁶Your hearts are filled with sadness because I have told you these things. ⁷But I tell you the truth, it is better for you that I go away. When I go away, I will send the Helper to you. If I do not go away, the Helper will not come. ⁸When the Helper comes, he will prove to the people of the world the truth about sin, about being right with God, and about judgment. ⁹He will prove to them that sin is not believing in me. ¹⁰He will prove to them that being right with God comes from my going to the Father and not being seen anymore. ¹¹And the Helper will prove to them that judgment happened when the ruler of this world was judged.

¹²"I have many more things to say to you, but they are too much for you now. ¹³But when the Spirit of truth comes, he will lead you into all truth. He will not speak his own words, but he will speak only what he hears, and he will tell you what is to come. ¹⁴The Spirit of truth will bring glory to me, because he will take what I have to say and tell it to you. ¹⁵All that the Father has is mine. That is why I said that the Spirit will take what I have to say and tell it to you.

¹⁶"After a little while you will not see me, and then after a little while you will see me again."

¹⁷Some of the followers said to each other, "What does Jesus mean when he says, 'After a little while you will not see me, and then after a little while you will see me again'? And what does he mean when he says, 'Because I am going to the Father'?" ¹⁸They also asked, "What does he mean by 'a little while'? We don't understand what he is saying."

¹⁹Jesus saw that the followers wanted to ask him about this, so he said to them, "Are you asking each other what I meant when I said, 'After a little while you will not see me, and then after a little while you will see me again'? ²⁰I tell you the truth, you will cry and be sad, but the world will be happy. You will be sad, but your sadness will become joy. ²¹When a woman gives birth to a baby, she has pain, because her time has come. But

when her baby is born, she forgets the pain, because she is so happy that a child has been born into the world. ²²It is the same with you. Now you are sad, but I will see you again and you will be happy, and no one will take away your joy. ²³In that day you will not ask me for anything. I tell you the truth, my Father will give you anything you ask for in my name. ²⁴Until now you have not asked for anything in my name. Ask and you will receive, so that your joy will be the fullest possible joy.

²⁵"I have told you these things indirectly in stories. But the time will come when I will not use stories like that to tell you things; I will speak to you in plain words about the Father. ²⁶In that day you will ask the Father for things in my name. I mean, I will not need to ask the Father for you. ²⁷The Father himself loves you. He loves you because you loved me and believed that I came from God. ²⁸I came from the Father into the world. Now I am leaving the world and going back to the Father."

²⁹Then the followers of Jesus said, "You are speaking clearly to us now and are not using stories that are hard to understand. ³⁰We can see now that you know all things. You can answer a person's question even before it is asked. This makes us believe you came from God."

³¹Jesus answered, "So now you believe? ³²Listen to me; a time is coming when you will be scattered, each to your own home. That time is now here. You will leave me alone, but I am never really alone, because the Father is with me.

³³"I told you these things so that you can have peace in me. In this world you will have trouble, but be brave! I have defeated the world."

17 After Jesus said these things, he looked toward heaven and prayed,

STEP 11

STEP 12

"Father, the time has come. Give glory to your Son so that the Son can give glory to you. ²You gave the Son power over all people so that the Son could give eternal life to all those you gave him. ³And this is eternal life: that people know you, the only true God, and that they know Jesus Christ, the One you sent. ⁴Having finished the work you gave me to do, I brought you glory on earth. ⁵And now, Father, give me glory with you; give me the glory I had with you before the world was made.

⁶"I showed what you are like to those you gave me from the world. They belonged to you, and you gave them to me, and they have obeyed your teaching. ⁷Now they know that everything you gave me comes from you. ⁸I gave them the teachings you gave me, and they accepted them. They knew that I truly came from you, and they believed that you sent me. ⁹I am praying for them. I am not praying for people in the world but for those you gave me, because they are yours. ¹⁰All I have is yours, and all you have is mine. And my glory is shown through them. ¹¹I am coming to you; I will not stay in the world any longer. But they are still in the world. Holy Father, keep them safe by the power of your name, the name you gave me, so that they will be one, just as you and I are one. ¹²While I was with them, I kept them safe by the power of your name, the name you gave me. I protected them, and only one of them, the one worthy of destruction, was lost so that the Scripture would come true.

¹³"I am coming to you now. But I pray these things while I am still in the world so that these followers can have all of my joy in them. ¹⁴I have given them your teaching. And the world has hated them, because they don't belong to the world, just as I don't belong to the world.

¹⁵I am not asking you to take them out of the world but to keep them safe from the Evil One. ¹⁶They don't belong to the world, just as I don't belong to the world. ¹⁷Make them ready for your service through your truth; your teaching is truth. ¹⁸I have sent them into the world, just as you sent me into the world. ¹⁹For their sake, I am making myself ready to serve so that they can be ready for their service of the truth.

²⁰"I pray for these followers, but I am also praying for all those who will believe in me because of their teaching. ²¹Father, I pray that they can be one. As you are in me and I am in you, I pray that they can also be one in us. Then the world will believe that you sent me. ²²I have given these people the glory that you gave me so that they can be one, just as you and I are one. ²³I will be in them and you will be in me so that they will be completely one. Then the world will know that you sent me and that you loved them just as much as you loved me.

²⁴"Father, I want these people that you gave me to be with me where I am. I want them to see my glory, which you gave me because you loved me before the world was made. ²⁵Father, you are the One who is good. The world does not know you, but I know you, and these people know you sent me. ²⁶I showed them what you are like, and I will show them again. Then they will have the same love that you have for me, and I will live in them."

18 When Jesus finished praying, he went with his followers across the Kidron Valley. On the other side there was a garden, and Jesus and his followers went into it.

²Judas knew where this place was, because Jesus met there often with his followers. Judas was the one who turned against Jesus. ³So Judas came there with a group of soldiers and some guards from

the leading priests and the Pharisees. They were carrying torches, lanterns, and weapons.

⁴Knowing everything that would happen to him, Jesus went out and asked, "Who is it you are looking for?"

⁵They answered, "Jesus from Nazareth."

"I am he," Jesus said. (Judas, the one who turned against Jesus, was standing there with them.) ⁶When Jesus said, "I am he," they moved back and fell to the ground.

⁷Jesus asked them again, "Who is it you are looking for?"

They said, "Jesus of Nazareth."

⁸"I told you that I am he," Jesus said. "So if you are looking for me, let the others go." ⁹This happened so that the words Jesus said before would come true: "I have not lost any of the ones you gave me."

¹⁰Simon Peter, who had a sword, pulled it out and struck the servant of the high priest, cutting off his right ear. (The servant's name was Malchus.) ¹¹Jesus said to Peter, "Put your sword back. Shouldn't I drink the cup the Father gave me?"

¹²Then the soldiers with their commander and the guards arrested Jesus. They tied him ¹³and led him first to Annas, the father-in-law of Caiaphas, the high priest that year. ¹⁴Caiaphas was the one who told the Jews that it would be better if one man died for all the people.

¹⁵Simon Peter and another one of Jesus' followers went along after Jesus. This follower knew the high priest, so he went with Jesus into the high priest's courtyard. ¹⁶But Peter waited outside near the door. The follower who knew the high priest came back outside, spoke to the girl at the door, and brought Peter inside. ¹⁷The girl at the door said to Peter, "Aren't you also one of that man's followers?"

Peter answered, "No, I am not!"

¹⁸It was cold, so the servants and guards had built a fire and were standing around it, warming themselves. Peter also was standing with them, warming himself.

¹⁹The high priest asked Jesus questions about his followers and his teaching. ²⁰Jesus answered, "I have spoken openly to everyone. I have always taught in synagogues and in the Temple, where all the Jews come together. I never said anything in secret. ²¹So why do you question me? Ask the people who heard my teaching. They know what I said."

²²When Jesus said this, one of the guards standing there hit him. The guard said, "Is that the way you answer the high priest?"

²³Jesus answered him, "If I said something wrong, then show what it was. But if what I said is true, why do you hit me?"

²⁴Then Annas sent Jesus, who was still tied, to Caiaphas the high priest.

²⁵As Simon Peter was standing and warming himself, they said to him, "Aren't you one of that man's followers?"

Peter said it was not true; he said, "No, I am not."

²⁶One of the servants of the high priest was there. This servant was a relative of the man whose ear Peter had cut off. The servant said, "Didn't I see you with him in the garden?"

²⁷Again Peter said it wasn't true. At once a rooster crowed.

²⁸Early in the morning they led Jesus from Caiaphas's house to the Roman governor's palace. They would not go inside the palace, because they did not want to make themselves unclean; they wanted to eat the Passover meal. ²⁹So Pilate went outside to them and asked, "What charges do you bring against this man?"

³⁰They answered, "If he were not a criminal, we wouldn't have brought him to you."

³¹Pilate said to them, "Take him yourselves and judge him by your own law."

"But we are not allowed to put anyone to death," the Jews answered. ³²(This happened so that what Jesus said about how he would die would come true.)

³³Then Pilate went back inside the palace and called Jesus to him and asked, "Are you the king of the Jews?"

³⁴Jesus said, "Is that your own question, or did others tell you about me?"

³⁵Pilate answered, "I am not one of you. It was your own people and their leading priests who handed you over to me. What have you done wrong?"

³⁶Jesus answered, "My kingdom does not belong to this world. If it belonged to this world, my servants would have fought to keep me from being given over to the Jewish leaders. But my kingdom is from another place."

³⁷Pilate said, "So you are a king!"

Jesus answered, "You are the one saying I am a king. This is why I was born and came into the world: to tell people the truth. And everyone who belongs to the truth listens to me."

³⁸Pilate said, "What is truth?" After he said this, he went out to the crowd again and said to them, "I find nothing against this man. ³⁹But it is your custom that I free one prisoner to you at Passover time. Do you want me to free the 'king of the Jews'?"

⁴⁰They shouted back, "No, not him! Let Barabbas go free!" (Barabbas was a robber.)

19 Then Pilate ordered that Jesus be taken away and whipped. ²The soldiers made a crown from some thorny branches and put it on Jesus' head and put a purple robe around him. ³Then they came to him many times and said, "Hail, King of the Jews!" and hit him in the face.

⁴Again Pilate came out and said to them, "Look, I am bringing Jesus out to you. I want you to know that I find nothing against him." ⁵So Jesus came out, wearing the crown of thorns and the purple robe. Pilate said to them, "Here is the man!"

⁶When the leading priests and the guards saw Jesus, they shouted, "Crucify him! Crucify him!"

But Pilate answered, "Crucify him yourselves, because I find nothing against him."

⁷The leaders answered, "We have a law that says he should die, because he said he is the Son of God."

⁸When Pilate heard this, he was even more afraid. ⁹He went back inside the palace and asked Jesus, "Where do you come from?" But Jesus did not answer him. ¹⁰Pilate said, "You refuse to speak to me? Don't you know I have power to set you free and power to have you crucified?"

¹¹Jesus answered, "The only power you have over me is the power given to you by God. The man who turned me in to you is guilty of a greater sin."

¹²After this, Pilate tried to let Jesus go. But some in the crowd cried out, "Anyone who makes himself king is against Caesar. If you let this man go, you are no friend of Caesar."

¹³When Pilate heard what they were saying, he brought Jesus out and sat down on the judge's seat at the place called The Stone Pavement. (In the Hebrew language the name is Gabbatha.) ¹⁴It was about noon on Preparation Day of Passover week. Pilate said to the crowd, "Here is your king!"

¹⁵They shouted, "Take him away! Take him away! Crucify him!"

Pilate asked them, "Do you want me to crucify your king?"

The leading priests answered, "The only king we have is Caesar."

[16]So Pilate handed Jesus over to them to be crucified.

The soldiers took charge of Jesus. [17]Carrying his own cross, Jesus went out to a place called The Place of the Skull, which in the Hebrew language is called Golgotha. [18]There they crucified Jesus. They also crucified two other men, one on each side, with Jesus in the middle. [19]Pilate wrote a sign and put it on the cross. It read: JESUS OF NAZARETH, THE KING OF THE JEWS. [20]The sign was written in Hebrew, in Latin, and in Greek. Many of the people read the sign, because the place where Jesus was crucified was near the city. [21]The leading priests said to Pilate, "Don't write, 'The King of the Jews.' But write, 'This man said, "I am the King of the Jews." ' "

[22]Pilate answered, "What I have written, I have written."

[23]After the soldiers crucified Jesus, they took his clothes and divided them into four parts, with each soldier getting one part. They also took his long shirt, which was all one piece of cloth, woven from top to bottom. [24]So the soldiers said to each other, "We should not tear this into parts. Let's throw lots to see who will get it." This happened so that this Scripture would come true:

"They divided my clothes among
      them,
   and they threw lots for my
      clothing."   *Psalm 22:18*

So the soldiers did this.

[25]Standing near his cross were Jesus' mother, his mother's sister, Mary the wife of Clopas, and Mary Magdalene. [26]When Jesus saw his mother and the follower he loved standing nearby, he said to his mother, "Dear woman, here is your son." [27]Then he said to the follower, "Here is your mother." From that time on, the follower took her to live in his home.

[28]After this, Jesus knew that everything had been done. So that the Scripture would come true, he said, "I am thirsty." [29]There was a jar full of vinegar there, so the soldiers soaked a sponge in it, put the sponge on a branch of a hyssop plant, and lifted it to Jesus' mouth. [30]When Jesus tasted the vinegar, he said, "It is finished." Then he bowed his head and died.

[31]This day was Preparation Day, and the next day was a special Sabbath day. Since the religious leaders did not want the bodies to stay on the cross on the Sabbath day, they asked Pilate to order that the legs of the men be broken and the bodies be taken away. [32]So the soldiers came and broke the legs of the first man on the cross beside Jesus. Then they broke the legs of the man on the other cross beside Jesus. [33]But when the soldiers came to Jesus and saw that he was already dead, they did not break his legs. [34]But one of the soldiers stuck his spear into Jesus' side, and at once blood and water came out. [35](The one who saw this happen is the one who told us this, and whatever he says is true. And he knows that he tells the truth, and he tells it so that you might believe.) [36]These things happened to make the Scripture come true: "Not one of his bones will be broken." [37]And another Scripture says, "They will look at the one they stabbed."

[38]Later, Joseph from Arimathea asked Pilate if he could take the body of Jesus. (Joseph was a secret follower of Jesus, because he was afraid of some of the leaders.) Pilate gave his permission, so Joseph came and took Jesus' body away. [39]Nicodemus, who earlier had come to

Jesus at night, went with Joseph. He brought about seventy-five pounds of myrrh and aloes. ⁴⁰These two men took Jesus' body and wrapped it with the spices in pieces of linen cloth, which is how they bury the dead. ⁴¹In the place where Jesus was crucified, there was a garden. In the garden was a new tomb that had never been used before. ⁴²The men laid Jesus in that tomb because it was nearby, and they were preparing to start their Sabbath day.

20 Early on the first day of the week, Mary Magdalene went to the tomb while it was still dark. When she saw that the large stone had been moved away from the tomb, ²she ran to Simon Peter and the follower whom Jesus loved. Mary said, "They have taken the Lord out of the tomb, and we don't know where they have put him."

³So Peter and the other follower started for the tomb. ⁴They were both running, but the other follower ran faster than Peter and reached the tomb first. ⁵He bent down and looked in and saw the strips of linen cloth lying there, but he did not go in. ⁶Then following him, Simon Peter arrived and went into the tomb and saw the strips of linen lying there. ⁷He also saw the cloth that had been around Jesus' head, which was folded up and laid in a different place from the strips of linen. ⁸Then the other follower, who had reached the tomb first, also went in. He saw and believed. ⁹(They did not yet understand from the Scriptures that Jesus must rise from the dead.)

¹⁰Then the followers went back home. ¹¹But Mary stood outside the tomb, crying. As she was crying, she bent down and looked inside the tomb. ¹²She saw two angels dressed in white, sitting where Jesus' body had been, one at the head and one at the feet.

¹³They asked her, "Woman, why are you crying?"

She answered, "They have taken away my Lord, and I don't know where they have put him." ¹⁴When Mary said this, she turned around and saw Jesus standing there, but she did not know it was Jesus.

¹⁵Jesus asked her, "Woman, why are you crying? Whom are you looking for?"

Thinking he was the gardener, she said to him, "Did you take him away, sir? Tell me where you put him, and I will get him."

¹⁶Jesus said to her, "Mary."

Mary turned toward Jesus and said in the Hebrew language, "Rabboni." (This means "Teacher.")

¹⁷Jesus said to her, "Don't hold on to me, because I have not yet gone up to the Father. But go to my brothers and tell them, 'I am going back to my Father and your Father, to my God and your God.' "

¹⁸Mary Magdalene went and said to the followers, "I saw the Lord!" And she told them what Jesus had said to her.

¹⁹When it was evening on the first day of the week, Jesus' followers were together. The doors were locked, because they were afraid of the elders. Then Jesus came and stood right in the middle of them and said, "Peace be with you." ²⁰After he said this, he showed them his hands and his side. His followers were thrilled when they saw the Lord.

²¹Then Jesus said again, "Peace be with you. As the Father sent me, I now send you." ²²After he said this, he breathed on them and said, "Receive the Holy Spirit. ²³If you forgive anyone his sins, they are forgiven. If you don't forgive them, they are not forgiven."

²⁴Thomas (called Didymus), who was one of the twelve, was not with them

when Jesus came. ²⁵The other followers kept telling Thomas, "We saw the Lord."

But Thomas said, "I will not believe it until I see the nail marks in his hands and put my finger where the nails were and put my hand into his side."

²⁶A week later the followers were in the house again, and Thomas was with them. The doors were locked, but Jesus came in and stood right in the middle of them. He said, "Peace be with you." ²⁷Then he said to Thomas, "Put your finger here, and look at my hands. Put your hand here in my side. Stop being an unbeliever and believe."

²⁸Thomas said to him, "My Lord and my God!"

²⁹Then Jesus told him, "You believe because you see me. Those who believe without seeing me will be truly blessed."

³⁰Jesus did many other miracles in the presence of his followers that are not written in this book. ³¹But these are written so that you may believe that Jesus is the Christ, the Son of God. Then, by believing, you may have life through his name.

21 Later, Jesus showed himself to his followers again—this time at Lake Galilee. This is how he showed himself: ²Some of the followers were together: Simon Peter, Thomas (called Didymus), Nathanael from Cana in Galilee, the two sons of Zebedee, and two other followers. ³Simon Peter said, "I am going out to fish."

The others said, "We will go with you." So they went out and got into the boat. They fished that night but caught nothing.

⁴Early the next morning Jesus stood on the shore, but the followers did not know it was Jesus. ⁵Then he said to them, "Friends, did you catch any fish?"

They answered, "No."

⁶He said, "Throw your net on the right side of the boat, and you will find some." So they did, and they caught so many fish they could not pull the net back into the boat.

⁷The follower whom Jesus loved said to Peter, "It is the Lord!" When Peter heard him say this, he wrapped his coat around himself. (Peter had taken his clothes off.) Then he jumped into the water. ⁸The other followers went to shore in the boat, dragging the net full of fish. They were not very far from shore, only about a hundred yards. ⁹When the followers stepped out of the boat and onto the shore, they saw a fire of hot coals. There were fish on the fire, and there was bread.

¹⁰Then Jesus said, "Bring some of the fish you just caught."

¹¹Simon Peter went into the boat and pulled the net to the shore. It was full of big fish, one hundred fifty-three in all, but even though there were so many, the net did not tear. ¹²Jesus said to them, "Come and eat." None of the followers dared ask him, "Who are you?" because they knew it was the Lord. ¹³Jesus came and took the bread and gave it to them, along with the fish.

¹⁴This was now the third time Jesus showed himself to his followers after he was raised from the dead.

¹⁵When they finished eating, Jesus said to Simon Peter, "Simon son of John, do you love me more than these?"

He answered, "Yes, Lord, you know that I love you."

Jesus said, "Feed my lambs."

¹⁶Again Jesus said, "Simon son of John, do you love me?"

He answered, "Yes, Lord, you know that I love you."

Jesus said, "Take care of my sheep."

¹⁷A third time he said, "Simon son of John, do you love me?"

Peter was hurt because Jesus asked him the third time, "Do you love me?" Peter said, "Lord, you know everything; you know that I love you!"

He said to him, "Feed my sheep. ¹⁸I tell you the truth, when you were younger, you tied your own belt and went where you wanted. But when you are old, you will put out your hands and someone else will tie you and take you where you don't want to go." ¹⁹(Jesus said this to show how Peter would die to give glory to God.) Then Jesus said to Peter, "Follow me!"

²⁰Peter turned and saw that the follower Jesus loved was walking behind them. (This was the follower who had leaned against Jesus at the supper and had said, "Lord, who will turn against you?") ²¹When Peter saw him behind them, he asked Jesus, "Lord, what about him?"

²²Jesus answered, "If I want him to live until I come back, that is not your business. You follow me."

²³So a story spread among the followers that this one would not die. But Jesus did not say he would not die. He only said, "If I want him to live until I come back, that is not your business."

²⁴That follower is the one who is telling these things and who has now written them down. We know that what he says is true.

²⁵There are many other things Jesus did. If every one of them were written down, I suppose the whole world would not be big enough for all the books that would be written.

ACTS

The Good News of Jesus Spreads

---

1 To Theophilus.
The first book I wrote was about everything Jesus began to do and teach [2]until the day he was taken up into heaven. Before this, with the help of the Holy Spirit, Jesus told the apostles he had chosen what they should do. [3]After his death, he showed himself to them and proved in many ways that he was alive. The apostles saw Jesus during the forty days after he was raised from the dead, and he spoke to them about the kingdom of God. [4]Once when he was eating with them, he told them not to leave Jerusalem. He said, "Wait here to receive the promise from the Father which I told you about. [5]John baptized people with water, but in a few days you will be baptized with the Holy Spirit."

[6]When the apostles were all together, they asked Jesus, "Lord, are you now going to give the kingdom back to Israel?"

[7]Jesus said to them, "The Father is the only One who has the authority to decide dates and times. These things are not for you to know. [8]But when the Holy Spirit comes to you, you will receive power. You will be my witnesses—in Jerusalem, in all of Judea, in Samaria, and in every part of the world."

[9]After he said this, as they were watching, he was lifted up, and a cloud hid him from their sight. [10]As he was going, they were looking into the sky. Suddenly, two men wearing white clothes stood beside them. [11]They said, "Men of Galilee, why are you standing here looking into the sky? Jesus, whom you saw taken up from you into heaven, will come back in the same way you saw him go."

[12]Then they went back to Jerusalem from the Mount of Olives. (This mountain is about half a mile from Jerusalem.) [13]When they entered the city, they went to the upstairs room where they were staying. Peter, John, James, Andrew, Philip, Thomas, Bartholomew, Matthew, James son of Alphaeus, Simon (known as the Zealot), and Judas son of James were there. [14]They all continued praying together with some women, including Mary the mother of Jesus, and Jesus' brothers.

[15]During this time there was a meeting of the believers (about one hundred twenty of them). Peter stood up and said, [16-17]"Brothers and sisters, in the Scriptures the Holy Spirit said through David something that must happen involving Judas. He was one of our own group and served together with us. He led those who arrested Jesus." [18](Judas bought a field with the money he got for his evil act. But he fell to his death, his body burst open, and all his intestines poured out. [19]Everyone in Jerusalem learned about this so they named this place Akeldama. In their language Akeldama means "Field of Blood.")
[20]"In the Book of Psalms," Peter said, "this is written:

'May his place be empty;
leave no one to live in it.'
Psalm 69:25

And it is also written:

'Let another man replace him as
leader.'   *Psalm 109:8*

[21-22]"So now a man must become a witness with us of Jesus' being raised from the dead. He must be one of the men who were part of our group during all the time the Lord Jesus was among us—from the time John was baptizing people until

the day Jesus was taken up from us to heaven."

²³They put the names of two men before the group. One was Joseph Barsabbas, who was also called Justus. The other was Matthias. ²⁴⁻²⁵The apostles prayed, "Lord, you know the thoughts of everyone. Show us which one of these two you have chosen to do this work. Show us who should be an apostle in place of Judas, who turned away and went where he belongs." ²⁶Then they used lots to choose between them, and the lots showed that Matthias was the one. So he became an apostle with the other eleven.

2 When the day of Pentecost came, they were all together in one place. ²Suddenly a noise like a strong, blowing wind came from heaven and filled the whole house where they were sitting. ³They saw something like flames of fire that were separated and stood over each person there. ⁴They were all filled with the Holy Spirit, and they began to speak different languages by the power the Holy Spirit was giving them.

⁵There were some religious Jews staying in Jerusalem who were from every country in the world. ⁶When they heard this noise, a crowd came together. They were all surprised, because each one heard them speaking in his own language. ⁷They were completely amazed at this. They said, "Look! Aren't all these people that we hear speaking from Galilee? ⁸Then how is it possible that we each hear them in our own languages? We are from different places: ⁹Parthia, Media, Elam, Mesopotamia, Judea, Cappadocia, Pontus, Asia, ¹⁰Phrygia, Pamphylia, Egypt, the areas of Libya near Cyrene, Rome ¹¹(both Jews and those who had become Jews), Crete, and Arabia. But we hear them telling in our own lan-

guages about the great things God has done!" ¹²They were all amazed and confused, asking each other, "What does this mean?"

¹³But others were making fun of them, saying, "They have had too much wine."

¹⁴But Peter stood up with the eleven apostles, and in a loud voice he spoke to the crowd: "My fellow Jews, and all of you who are in Jerusalem, listen to me. Pay attention to what I have to say. ¹⁵These people are not drunk, as you think; it is only nine o'clock in the morning! ¹⁶But Joel the prophet wrote about what is happening here today:

¹⁷'God says: In the last days
     I will pour out my Spirit on all kinds
          of people.
     Your sons and daughters will
          prophesy.
     Your young men will see visions,
          and your old men will dream
          dreams.
¹⁸At that time I will pour out my Spirit
     also on my male slaves and female
          slaves,
     and they will prophesy.
¹⁹I will show miracles
     in the sky and on the earth:
     blood, fire, and thick smoke.
²⁰The sun will become dark,
     the moon red as blood,
     before the overwhelming and
          glorious day of the Lord will
          come.
²¹Then anyone who calls on the Lord
     will be saved.'   *Joel 2:28–32*   **STEP 3**

²²"People of Israel, listen to these words: Jesus from Nazareth was a very special man. God clearly showed this to you by the miracles, wonders, and signs he did through Jesus. You all know this, because it happened right here among you. ²³Jesus was given to you, and with the help of those who don't know the law,

you put him to death by nailing him to a cross. But this was God's plan which he had made long ago; he knew all this would happen. 24God raised Jesus from the dead and set him free from the pain of death, because death could not hold him. 25For David said this about him:

'I keep the Lord before me always.
Because he is close by my side,
I will not be hurt.
26So I am glad, and I rejoice.
Even my body has hope,
27because you will not leave me in the grave.
You will not let your Holy One rot.
28You will teach me how to live a holy life.
Being with you will fill me with joy.'
Psalm 16:8–11

29"Brothers and sisters, I can tell you truly that David, our ancestor, died and was buried. His grave is still here with us today. 30He was a prophet and knew God had promised him that he would make a person from David's family a king just as he was. 31Knowing this before it happened, David talked about the Christ rising from the dead. He said:

'He was not left in the grave.
His body did not rot.'

32So Jesus is the One whom God raised from the dead. And we are all witnesses to this. 33Jesus was lifted up to heaven and is now at God's right side. The Father has given the Holy Spirit to Jesus as he promised. So Jesus has poured out that Spirit, and this is what you now see and hear. 34David was not the one who was lifted up to heaven, but he said:

'The Lord said to my Lord,
"Sit by me at my right side,
35   until I put your enemies under your control." '   *Psalm 110:1*

36"So, all the people of Israel should know this truly: God has made Jesus—the man you nailed to the cross—both Lord and Christ."

37When the people heard this, they felt guilty and asked Peter and the other apostles, "What shall we do?"

38Peter said to them, "Change your hearts and lives and be baptized, each one of you, in the name of Jesus Christ for the forgiveness of your sins. And you will receive the gift of the Holy Spirit. 39This promise is for you, for your children, and for all who are far away. It is for everyone the Lord our God calls to himself."

40Peter warned them with many other words. He begged them, "Save yourselves from the evil of today's people!" 41Then those people who accepted what Peter said were baptized. About three thousand people were added to the number of believers that day. 42They spent their time learning the apostles' teaching, sharing, breaking bread, and praying together.

43The apostles were doing many miracles and signs, and everyone felt great respect for God. 44All the believers were together and shared everything. 45They would sell their land and the things they owned and then divide the money and give it to anyone who needed it. 46The believers met together in the Temple every day. They ate together in their homes, happy to share their food with joyful hearts. 47They praised God and were liked by all the people. Every day the Lord added those who were being saved to the group of believers.

3 One day Peter and John went to the Temple at three o'clock, the time set each day for the afternoon prayer service. 2There, at the Temple gate called Beautiful Gate, was a man who had been crippled all his life. Every day he was carried to this gate to beg for money from the people going into the Temple. 3The man

saw Peter and John going into the Temple and asked them for money. ⁴Peter and John looked straight at him and said, "Look at us!" ⁵The man looked at them, thinking they were going to give him some money. ⁶But Peter said, "I don't have any silver or gold, but I do have something else I can give you. By the power of Jesus Christ from Nazareth, stand up and walk!" ⁷Then Peter took the man's right hand and lifted him up. Immediately the man's feet and ankles became strong. ⁸He jumped up, stood on his feet, and began to walk. He went into the Temple with them, walking and jumping and praising God. ⁹⁻¹⁰All the people recognized him as the crippled man who always sat by the Beautiful Gate begging for money. Now they saw this same man walking and praising God, and they were amazed. They wondered how this could happen.

¹¹While the man was holding on to Peter and John, all the people were amazed and ran to them at Solomon's Porch. ¹²When Peter saw this, he said to them, "People of Israel, why are you surprised? You are looking at us as if it were our own power or goodness that made this man walk. ¹³The God of Abraham, Isaac, and Jacob, the God of our ancestors, gave glory to Jesus, his servant. But you handed him over to be killed. Pilate decided to let him go free, but you told Pilate you did not want Jesus. ¹⁴You did not want the One who is holy and good but asked Pilate to give you a murderer instead. ¹⁵And so you killed the One who gives life, but God raised him from the dead. We are witnesses to this. ¹⁶It was faith in Jesus that made this crippled man well. You can see this man, and you know him. He was made completely well because of trust in Jesus, and you all saw it happen!

STEP 2

¹⁷"Brothers and sisters, I know you did those things to Jesus because neither you nor your leaders understood what you were doing. ¹⁸God said through the prophets that his Christ would suffer and die. And now God has made these things come true in this way. ¹⁹So you must change your hearts and lives! Come back to God, and he will forgive your sins. Then the Lord will send the time of rest. ²⁰And he will send Jesus, the One he chose to be the Christ. ²¹But Jesus must stay in heaven until the time comes when all things will be made right again. God told about this time long ago when he spoke through his holy prophets. ²²Moses said, 'The Lord your God will give you a prophet like me, who is one of your own people. You must listen to everything he tells you. ²³Anyone who does not listen to that prophet will die, cut off from God's people.' ²⁴Samuel, and all the other prophets who spoke for God after Samuel, told about this time now. ²⁵You are descendants of the prophets. You have received the agreement God made with your ancestors. He said to your father Abraham, 'Through your descendants all the nations on the earth will be blessed.' ²⁶God has raised up his servant Jesus and sent him to you first to bless you by turning each of you away from doing evil."

STEP 7

4 While Peter and John were speaking to the people, priests, the captain of the soldiers that guarded the Temple, and Sadducees came up to them. ²They were upset because the two apostles were teaching the people and were preaching that people will rise from the dead through the power of Jesus. ³The older leaders grabbed Peter and John and put them in jail. Since it was already night, they kept them in jail until the next day. ⁴But many of those who had heard Peter and John preach believed the

STEP 7

Humbly asked Him to remove our shortcomings.

Acts 3:19

Step 7 depends on God's incredible power to rebuild your character and work a miracle of transformation in you.

The book *Alcoholics Anonymous* (p. 76) offers this prayer for seventh step transformation: "My Creator, I am now willing that you should have all of me, good and bad. I pray that you now remove from me every single defect of character which stands in the way of my usefulness to you and my fellows. Grant me strength, as I go out from here, to do your bidding. Amen."

What does this kind of transformation involve? You admit and yield every character flaw to God's transforming touch. You give him every relationship to guide. You let him take over every addictive and compulsive habit pattern so he can whip you into shape. In other words, you ask him to be the God of every bit of your life.

Approach repentance with a sincere heart, and you will come away from it with a refreshed spirit—a small taste of "the time of rest" the Lord will one day give you forever.

FOR YOUR NEXT **STEP 7** MEDITATION, TURN TO **PAGE 324.** ▶▶

things they said. There were now about five thousand in the group of believers.

⁵The next day the rulers, the elders, and the teachers of the law met in Jerusalem. ⁶Annas the high priest, Caiaphas, John, and Alexander were there, as well as everyone from the high priest's family. ⁷They made Peter and John stand before them and then asked them, "By what power or authority did you do this?"

⁸Then Peter, filled with the Holy Spirit, said to them, "Rulers of the people and you elders, ⁹are you questioning us about a good thing that was done to a crippled man? Are you asking us who made him well? ¹⁰We want all of you and all the people to know that this man was made well by the power of Jesus Christ from Nazareth. You crucified him, but God raised him from the dead. This man was crippled, but he is now well and able to stand here before you because of the power of Jesus. ¹¹Jesus is

'the stone that you builders rejected,
　which has become the cornerstone.'　　*Psalm 118:22*

STEP 2 ¹²Jesus is the only One who can save people. No one else in the world is able to save us."

¹³The leaders saw that Peter and John were not afraid to speak, and they understood that these men had no special training or education. So they were amazed. Then they realized that Peter and John had been with Jesus. ¹⁴Because they saw the healed man standing there beside the two apostles, they could say nothing against them. ¹⁵After the leaders ordered them to leave the meeting, they began to talk to each other. ¹⁶They said, "What shall we do with these men? Everyone in Jerusalem knows they have done a great miracle, and we cannot say it is not true. ¹⁷But to keep it from spreading among the people, we must warn them not to talk to people anymore using that name."

¹⁸So they called Peter and John in again and told them not to speak or to teach at all in the name of Jesus. ¹⁹But Peter and John answered them, "You decide what God would want. Should we obey you or God? ²⁰We cannot keep quiet. We must speak about what we have seen and heard." ²¹The leaders warned the apostles again and let them go free. They could not find a way to punish them, because all the people were praising God for what had been done. ²²The man who received the miracle of healing was more than forty years old.

²³After Peter and John left the meeting of leaders, they went to their own group and told them everything the leading priests and the elders had said to them. ²⁴When the believers heard this, they prayed to God together, "Lord, you are the One who made the sky, the earth, the sea, and everything in them. ²⁵By the Holy Spirit, through our father David your servant, you said:

'Why are the nations so angry?
　Why are the people making useless plans?
²⁶The kings of the earth prepare to fight,
　and their leaders make plans together
against the Lord
　and his Christ.'　　*Psalm 2:1–2*

²⁷These things really happened when Herod, Pontius Pilate, and some Jews and non-Jews all came together against Jesus here in Jerusalem. Jesus is your holy servant, the One you made to be the Christ. ²⁸These people made your plan happen because of your power and your will. ²⁹And now, Lord, listen to their threats. Lord, help us, your servants, to speak

your word without fear. ³⁰Show us your power to heal. Give proofs and make miracles happen by the power of Jesus, your holy servant."

³¹After they had prayed, the place where they were meeting was shaken. They were all filled with the Holy Spirit, and they spoke God's word without fear.

³²The group of believers were united in their hearts and spirit. All those in the group acted as though their private property belonged to everyone in the group. In fact, they shared everything. ³³With great power the apostles were telling people that the Lord Jesus was truly raised from the dead. And God blessed all the believers very much. ³⁴There were no needy people among them. From time to time those who owned fields or houses sold them, brought the money, ³⁵and gave it to the apostles. Then the money was given to anyone who needed it.

³⁶One of the believers was named Joseph, a Levite born in Cyprus. The apostles called him Barnabas (which means "one who encourages"). ³⁷Joseph owned a field, sold it, brought the money, and gave it to the apostles.

5 But a man named Ananias and his wife Sapphira sold some land. ²He kept back part of the money for himself; his wife knew about this and agreed to it. But he brought the rest of the money and gave it to the apostles. ³Peter said, "Ananias, why did you let Satan rule your thoughts to lie to the Holy Spirit and to keep for yourself part of the money you received for the land? ⁴Before you sold the land, it belonged to you. And even after you sold it, you could have used the money any way you wanted. Why did you think of doing this? You lied to God, not to us!" ⁵⁻⁶When Ananias heard this, he fell down and died. Some young men came in, wrapped up his body, carried it out,

and buried it. And everyone who heard about this was filled with fear.

⁷About three hours later his wife came in, but she did not know what had happened. ⁸Peter said to her, "Tell me, was the money you got for your field this much?"

Sapphira answered, "Yes, that was the price."

⁹Peter said to her, "Why did you and your husband agree to test the Spirit of the Lord? Look! The men who buried your husband are at the door, and they will carry you out." ¹⁰At that moment Sapphira fell down by his feet and died. When the young men came in and saw that she was dead, they carried her out and buried her beside her husband. ¹¹The whole church and all the others who heard about these things were filled with fear.

¹²The apostles did many signs and miracles among the people. And they would all meet together on Solomon's Porch. ¹³None of the others dared to join them, but all the people respected them. ¹⁴More and more men and women believed in the Lord and were added to the group of believers. ¹⁵The people placed their sick on beds and mats in the streets, hoping that when Peter passed by at least his shadow might fall on them. ¹⁶Crowds came from all the towns around Jerusalem, bringing their sick and those who were bothered by evil spirits, and all of them were healed.

¹⁷The high priest and all his friends (a group called the Sadducees) became very jealous. ¹⁸They took the apostles and put them in jail. ¹⁹But during the night, an angel of the Lord opened the doors of the jail and led the apostles outside. The angel said, ²⁰"Go stand in the Temple and tell the people everything about this new life." ²¹When the apostles heard this, they

obeyed and went into the Temple early in the morning and continued teaching.

When the high priest and his friends arrived, they called a meeting of the leaders and all the important elders. They sent some men to the jail to bring the apostles to them. ²²But, upon arriving, the officers could not find the apostles. So they went back and reported to the leaders. ²³They said, "The jail was closed and locked, and the guards were standing at the doors. But when we opened the doors, the jail was empty!" ²⁴Hearing this, the captain of the Temple guards and the leading priests were confused and wondered what was happening.

²⁵Then someone came and told them, "Listen! The men you put in jail are standing in the Temple teaching the people." ²⁶Then the captain and his men went out and brought the apostles back. But the soldiers did not use force, because they were afraid the people would stone them to death.

²⁷The soldiers brought the apostles to the meeting and made them stand before the leaders. The high priest questioned them, ²⁸saying, "We gave you strict orders not to continue teaching in that name. But look, you have filled Jerusalem with your teaching and are trying to make us responsible for this man's death."

²⁹Peter and the other apostles answered, "We must obey God, not human authority! ³⁰You killed Jesus by hanging him on a cross. But God, the God of our ancestors, raised Jesus up from the dead! ³¹Jesus is the One whom God raised to be on his right side, as Leader and Savior. Through him, all people could change their hearts and lives and have their sins forgiven. ³²We saw all these things happen. The Holy Spirit, whom God has given to all who obey him, also proves these things are true."

³³When the leaders heard this, they became angry and wanted to kill them. ³⁴But a Pharisee named Gamaliel stood up in the meeting. He was a teacher of the law, and all the people respected him. He ordered the apostles to leave the meeting for a little while. ³⁵Then he said, "People of Israel, be careful what you are planning to do to these men. ³⁶Remember when Theudas appeared? He said he was a great man, and about four hundred men joined him. But he was killed, and all his followers were scattered; they were able to do nothing. ³⁷Later, a man named Judas came from Galilee at the time of the registration. He also led a group of followers and was killed, and all his followers were scattered. ³⁸And so now I tell you: Stay away from these men, and leave them alone. If their plan comes from human authority, it will fail. ³⁹But if it is from God, you will not be able to stop them. You might even be fighting against God himself!"

The leaders agreed with what Gamaliel said. ⁴⁰They called the apostles in, beat them, and told them not to speak in the name of Jesus again. Then they let them go free. ⁴¹The apostles left the meeting full of joy because they were given the honor of suffering disgrace for Jesus. ⁴²Every day in the Temple and in people's homes they continued teaching the people and telling the Good News— that Jesus is the Christ.

6 The number of followers was growing. But during this same time, the Greek-speaking followers had an argument with the other followers. The Greek-speaking widows were not getting their share of the food that was given out every day. ²The twelve apostles called the whole group of followers together and said, "It is not right for us to stop our work of teaching God's word in order to serve

tables. ³So, brothers and sisters, choose seven of your own men who are good, full of the Spirit and full of wisdom. We will put them in charge of this work. ⁴Then we can continue to pray and to teach the word of God."

⁵The whole group liked the idea, so they chose these seven men: Stephen (a man with great faith and full of the Holy Spirit), Philip, Procorus, Nicanor, Timon, Parmenas, and Nicolas (a man from Antioch who had become a follower of the Jewish religion). ⁶Then they put these men before the apostles, who prayed and laid their hands on them.

⁷The word of God was continuing to spread. The group of followers in Jerusalem increased, and a great number of the Jewish priests believed and obeyed.

⁸Stephen was richly blessed by God who gave him the power to do great miracles and signs among the people. ⁹But some people were against him. They belonged to the synagogue of Free Men (as it was called), which included people from Cyrene, Alexandria, Cilicia, and Asia. They all came and argued with Stephen.

¹⁰But the Spirit was helping him to speak with wisdom, and his words were so strong that they could not argue with him. ¹¹So they secretly urged some men to say, "We heard Stephen speak against Moses and against God."

¹²This upset the people, the elders, and the teachers of the law. They came and grabbed Stephen and brought him to a meeting of the leaders. ¹³They brought in some people to tell lies about Stephen, saying, "This man is always speaking against this holy place and the law of Moses. ¹⁴We heard him say that Jesus from Nazareth will destroy this place and that Jesus will change the customs Moses gave us." ¹⁵All the people in the meeting were watching Stephen closely and saw that his face looked like the face of an angel.

7 The high priest said to Stephen, "Are these things true?"

²Stephen answered, "Brothers and fathers, listen to me. Our glorious God appeared to Abraham, our ancestor, in Mesopotamia before he lived in Haran. ³God said to Abraham, 'Leave your country and your relatives, and go to the land I will show you.' ⁴So Abraham left the country of Chaldea and went to live in Haran. After Abraham's father died, God sent him to this place where you now live. ⁵God did not give Abraham any of this land, not even a foot of it. But God promised that he would give this land to him and his descendants, even before Abraham had a child. ⁶This is what God said to him: 'Your descendants will be strangers in a land they don't own. The people there will make them slaves and will mistreat them for four hundred years. ⁷But I will punish the nation where they are slaves. Then your descendants will leave that land and will worship me in this place.' ⁸God made an agreement with Abraham, the sign of which was circumcision. And so when Abraham had his son Isaac, Abraham circumcised him when he was eight days old. Isaac also circumcised his son Jacob, and Jacob did the same for his sons, the twelve ancestors of our people.

⁹"Jacob's sons became jealous of Joseph and sold him to be a slave in Egypt. But God was with him ¹⁰and saved him from all his troubles. The king of Egypt liked Joseph and respected him because of the wisdom God gave him. The king made him governor of Egypt and put him in charge of all the people in his palace.

¹¹"Then all the land of Egypt and Canaan became so dry that nothing

would grow, and the people suffered very much. Jacob's sons, our ancestors, could not find anything to eat. [12]But when Jacob heard there was grain in Egypt, he sent his sons there. This was their first trip to Egypt. [13]When they went there a second time, Joseph told his brothers who he was, and the king learned about Joseph's family. [14]Then Joseph sent messengers to invite Jacob, his father, to come to Egypt along with all his relatives (seventy-five persons altogether). [15]So Jacob went down to Egypt, where he and his sons died. [16]Later their bodies were moved to Shechem and put in a grave there. (It was the same grave Abraham had bought for a sum of money from the sons of Hamor in Shechem.)

[17]"The promise God made to Abraham was soon to come true, and the number of people in Egypt grew large. [18]Then a new king, who did not know who Joseph was, began to rule Egypt. [19]This king tricked our people and was cruel to our ancestors, forcing them to leave their babies outside to die. [20]At this time Moses was born, and he was very beautiful. For three months Moses was cared for in his father's house. [21]When they put Moses outside, the king's daughter adopted him and raised him as if he were her own son. [22]The Egyptians taught Moses everything they knew, and he was a powerful man in what he said and did.

[23]"When Moses was about forty years old, he thought it would be good to visit his own people, the people of Israel. [24]Moses saw an Egyptian mistreating one of his people, so he defended the Israelite and punished the Egyptian by killing him. [25]Moses thought his own people would understand that God was using him to save them, but they did not. [26]The next day when Moses saw two men of Israel fighting, he tried to make peace between them. He said, 'Men, you are brothers. Why are you hurting each other?' [27]The man who was hurting the other pushed Moses away and said, 'Who made you our ruler and judge? [28]Are you going to kill me as you killed the Egyptian yesterday?' [29]When Moses heard him say this, he left Egypt and went to live in the land of Midian where he was a stranger. While Moses lived in Midian, he had two sons.

[30]"Forty years later an angel appeared to Moses in the flames of a burning bush as he was in the desert near Mount Sinai. [31]When Moses saw this, he was amazed and went near to look closer. Moses heard the Lord's voice say, [32]'I am the God of your ancestors, the God of Abraham, Isaac, and Jacob.' Moses began to shake with fear and was afraid to look. [33]The Lord said to him, 'Take off your sandals, because you are standing on holy ground. [34]I have seen the troubles my people have suffered in Egypt. I have heard their cries and have come down to save them. And now, Moses, I am sending you back to Egypt.'

[35]"This Moses was the same man the two men of Israel rejected, saying, 'Who made you a ruler and judge?' Moses is the same man God sent to be a ruler and savior, with the help of the angel that Moses saw in the burning bush. [36]So Moses led the people out of Egypt. He worked miracles and signs in Egypt, at the Red Sea, and then in the desert for forty years. [37]This is the same Moses that said to the people of Israel, 'God will give you a prophet like me, who is one of your own people.' [38]This is the Moses who was with the gathering of the Israelites in the desert. He was with the angel that spoke to him at Mount Sinai, and he was with our ancestors. He received commands from God that give life, and he gave those commands to us.

[39]"But our ancestors did not want to obey Moses. They rejected him and wanted to go back to Egypt. [40]They said to Aaron, 'Make us gods who will lead us. Moses led us out of Egypt, but we don't know what has happened to him.' [41]So the people made an idol that looked like a calf. Then they brought sacrifices to it and were proud of what they had made with their own hands. [42]But God turned against them and did not try to stop them from worshiping the sun, moon, and stars. This is what is written in the book of the prophets: God says,

'People of Israel, you did not bring me
        sacrifices and offerings
   while you traveled in the desert
        for forty years.
[43]You have carried with you
   the tent to worship Molech
   and the idols of the star god
        Rephan that you made to
        worship.

So I will send you away beyond
        Babylon.'   *Amos 5:25–27*

[44]"The Holy Tent where God spoke to our ancestors was with them in the desert. God told Moses how to make this Tent, and he made it like the plan God showed him. [45]Later, Joshua led our ancestors to capture the lands of the other nations. Our people went in, and God forced the other people out. When our people went into this new land, they took with them this same Tent they had received from their ancestors. They kept it until the time of David, [46]who pleased God and asked God to let him build a house for him, the God of Jacob. [47]But Solomon was the one who built the Temple.

[48]"But the Most High does not live in houses that people build with their hands. As the prophet says:

[49]'Heaven is my throne,

and the earth is my footstool.
So do you think you can build a house
        for me? says the Lord.
   Do I need a place to rest?
[50]Remember, my hand made all these
        things!' "   *Isaiah 66:1–2*

[51]Stephen continued speaking: "You stubborn people! You have not given your hearts to God, nor will you listen to him! You are always against what the Holy Spirit is trying to tell you, just as your ancestors were. [52]Your ancestors tried to hurt every prophet who ever lived. Those prophets said long ago that the One who is good would come, but your ancestors killed them. And now you have turned against and killed the One who is good. [53]You received the law of Moses, which God gave you through his angels, but you haven't obeyed it."

[54]When the leaders heard this, they became furious. They were so mad they were grinding their teeth at Stephen. [55]But Stephen was full of the Holy Spirit. He looked up to heaven and saw the glory of God and Jesus standing at God's right side. [56]He said, "Look! I see heaven open and the Son of Man standing at God's right side."

[57]Then they shouted loudly and covered their ears and all ran at Stephen. [58]They took him out of the city and began to throw stones at him to kill him. And those who told lies against Stephen left their coats with a young man named Saul. [59]While they were throwing stones, Stephen prayed, "Lord Jesus, receive my spirit." [60]He fell on his knees and cried in a loud voice, "Lord, do not hold this sin against them." After Stephen said this, he died.

8 Saul agreed that the killing of Stephen was good.

On that day the church of Jerusalem began to be persecuted, and all the believers, except the apostles, were scattered throughout Judea and Samaria.

²And some religious people buried Stephen and cried loudly for him. ³Saul was also trying to destroy the church, going from house to house, dragging out men and women and putting them in jail. ⁴And wherever they were scattered, they told people the Good News.

⁵Philip went to the city of Samaria and preached about the Christ. ⁶When the people there heard Philip and saw the miracles he was doing, they all listened carefully to what he said. ⁷Many of these people had evil spirits in them, but Philip made the evil spirits leave. The spirits made a loud noise when they came out. Philip also healed many weak and crippled people there. ⁸So the people in that city were very happy.

⁹But there was a man named Simon in that city. Before Philip came there, Simon had practiced magic and amazed all the people of Samaria. He bragged and called himself a great man. ¹⁰All the people—the least important and the most important—paid attention to Simon, saying, "This man has the power of God, called 'the Great Power'!" ¹¹Simon had amazed them with his magic so long that the people became his followers. ¹²But when Philip told them the Good News about the kingdom of God and the power of Jesus Christ, men and women believed Philip and were baptized. ¹³Simon himself believed, and after he was baptized, he stayed very close to Philip. When he saw the miracles and the powerful things Philip did, Simon was amazed.

¹⁴When the apostles who were still in Jerusalem heard that the people of Samaria had accepted the word of God, they sent Peter and John to them. ¹⁵When Peter and John arrived, they prayed that the Samaritan believers might receive the Holy Spirit. ¹⁶These people had been baptized in the name of the Lord Jesus, but the Holy Spirit had not yet come upon any of them. ¹⁷Then, when the two apostles began laying their hands on the people, they received the Holy Spirit.

¹⁸Simon saw that the Spirit was given to people when the apostles laid their hands on them. So he offered the apostles money, ¹⁹saying, "Give me also this power so that anyone on whom I lay my hands will receive the Holy Spirit."

²⁰Peter said to him, "You and your money should both be destroyed, because you thought you could buy God's gift with money. ²¹You cannot share with us in this work since your heart is not right before God. ²²Change your heart! Turn away from this evil thing you have done, and pray to the Lord. Maybe he will forgive you for thinking this. ²³I see that you are full of bitter jealousy and ruled by sin."

²⁴Simon answered, "Both of you pray for me to the Lord so the things you have said will not happen to me."

²⁵After Peter and John told the people what they had seen Jesus do and after they had spoken the message of the Lord, they went back to Jerusalem. On the way, they went through many Samaritan towns and preached the Good News to the people.

²⁶An angel of the Lord said to Philip, "Get ready and go south to the road that leads down to Gaza from Jerusalem—the desert road." ²⁷So Philip got ready and went. On the road he saw a man from Ethiopia, a eunuch. He was an important officer in the service of Candace, the queen of the Ethiopians; he was responsible for taking care of all her money. He had gone to Jerusalem to worship. ²⁸Now, as he was on his way home, he was sitting in his chariot reading from the Book of

Isaiah, the prophet. ²⁹The Spirit said to Philip, "Go to that chariot and stay near it."

³⁰So when Philip ran toward the chariot, he heard the man reading from Isaiah the prophet. Philip asked, "Do you understand what you are reading?"

³¹He answered, "How can I understand unless someone explains it to me?" Then he invited Philip to climb in and sit with him. ³²The portion of Scripture he was reading was this:

"He was like a sheep being led to be
    killed.
He was quiet, as a lamb is quiet
        while its wool is being cut;
he never opened his mouth.
³³   He was shamed and was treated
        unfairly.
He died without children to continue
        his family.
His life on earth has ended."

Isaiah 53:7–8

³⁴The officer said to Philip, "Please tell me, who is the prophet talking about—himself or someone else?" ³⁵Philip began to speak, and starting with this same Scripture, he told the man the Good News about Jesus.

³⁶While they were traveling down the road, they came to some water. The officer said, "Look, here is water. What is stopping me from being baptized?" [³⁷Philip answered, "If you believe with all your heart, you can." The officer said, "I believe that Jesus Christ is the Son of God."] ³⁸Then the officer commanded the chariot to stop. Both Philip and the officer went down into the water, and Philip baptized him. ³⁹When they came up out of the water, the Spirit of the Lord took Philip away; the officer never saw him again. And the officer continued on his way home, full of joy. ⁴⁰But Philip appeared in a city called Azotus and preached the Good News in all the towns on the way from Azotus to Caesarea.

9In Jerusalem Saul was still threatening the followers of the Lord by saying he would kill them. So he went to the high priest ²and asked him to write letters to the synagogues in the city of Damascus. Then if Saul found any followers of Christ's Way, men or women, he would arrest them and bring them back to Jerusalem.

³So Saul headed toward Damascus. As he came near the city, a bright light from heaven suddenly flashed around him. ⁴Saul fell to the ground and heard a voice saying to him, "Saul, Saul! Why are you persecuting me?"

⁵Saul said, "Who are you, Lord?"

The voice answered, "I am Jesus, whom you are persecuting. ⁶Get up now and go into the city. Someone there will tell you what you must do."

⁷The people traveling with Saul stood there but said nothing. They heard the voice, but they saw no one. ⁸Saul got up from the ground and opened his eyes, but he could not see. So those with Saul took his hand and led him into Damascus. ⁹For three days Saul could not see and did not eat or drink.

¹⁰There was a follower of Jesus in Damascus named Ananias. The Lord spoke to Ananias in a vision, "Ananias!"

Ananias answered, "Here I am, Lord."

¹¹The Lord said to him, "Get up and go to Straight Street. Find the house of Judas, and ask for a man named Saul from the city of Tarsus. He is there now, praying. ¹²Saul has seen a vision in which a man named Ananias comes to him and lays his hands on him. Then he is able to see again."

¹³But Ananias answered, "Lord, many people have told me about this man and the terrible things he did to your holy

people in Jerusalem. ¹⁴Now he has come here to Damascus, and the leading priests have given him the power to arrest everyone who worships you."

¹⁵But the Lord said to Ananias, "Go! I have chosen Saul for an important work. He must tell about me to those who are not Jews, to kings, and to the people of Israel. ¹⁶I will show him how much he must suffer for my name."

¹⁷So Ananias went to the house of Judas. He laid his hands on Saul and said, "Brother Saul, the Lord Jesus sent me. He is the one you saw on the road on your way here. He sent me so that you can see again and be filled with the Holy Spirit." ¹⁸Immediately, something that looked like fish scales fell from Saul's eyes, and he was able to see again! Then Saul got up and was baptized. ¹⁹After he ate some food, his strength returned.

Saul stayed with the followers of Jesus in Damascus for a few days. ²⁰Soon he began to preach about Jesus in the synagogues, saying, "Jesus is the Son of God."

²¹All the people who heard him were amazed. They said, "This is the man who was in Jerusalem trying to destroy those who trust in this name! He came here to arrest the followers of Jesus and take them back to the leading priests."

²²But Saul grew more powerful. His proofs that Jesus is the Christ were so strong that his own people in Damascus could not argue with him.

²³After many days, they made plans to kill Saul. ²⁴They were watching the city gates day and night, but Saul learned about their plan. ²⁵One night some followers of Saul helped him leave the city by lowering him in a basket through an opening in the city wall.

²⁶When Saul went to Jerusalem, he tried to join the group of followers, but they were all afraid of him. They did not believe he was really a follower. ²⁷But Barnabas accepted Saul and took him to the apostles. Barnabas explained to them that Saul had seen the Lord on the road and the Lord had spoken to Saul. Then he told them how boldly Saul had preached in the name of Jesus in Damascus.

²⁸And so Saul stayed with the followers, going everywhere in Jerusalem, preaching boldly in the name of the Lord. ²⁹He would often talk and argue with the Jewish people who spoke Greek, but they were trying to kill him. ³⁰When the followers learned about this, they took Saul to Caesarea and from there sent him to Tarsus.

³¹The church everywhere in Judea, Galilee, and Samaria had a time of peace and became stronger. Respecting the Lord by the way they lived, and being encouraged by the Holy Spirit, the group of believers continued to grow.

³²As Peter was traveling through all the area, he visited God's people who lived in Lydda. ³³There he met a man named Aeneas, who was paralyzed and had not been able to leave his bed for the past eight years. ³⁴Peter said to him, "Aeneas, Jesus Christ heals you. Stand up and make your bed." Aeneas stood up immediately. ³⁵All the people living in Lydda and on the Plain of Sharon saw him and turned to the Lord.

³⁶In the city of Joppa there was a follower named Tabitha (whose Greek name was Dorcas). She was always doing good deeds and kind acts. ³⁷While Peter was in Lydda, Tabitha became sick and died. Her body was washed and put in a room upstairs. ³⁸Since Lydda is near Joppa and the followers in Joppa heard that Peter was in Lydda, they sent two messengers to Peter. They begged him, "Hurry, please come to us!" ³⁹So Peter got ready and went with them. When he arrived,

they took him to the upstairs room where all the widows stood around Peter, crying. They showed him the shirts and coats Tabitha had made when she was still alive. ⁴⁰Peter sent everyone out of the room and kneeled and prayed. Then he turned to the body and said, "Tabitha, stand up." She opened her eyes, and when she saw Peter, she sat up. ⁴¹He gave her his hand and helped her up. Then he called the saints and the widows into the room and showed them that Tabitha was alive. ⁴²People everywhere in Joppa learned about this, and many believed in the Lord. ⁴³Peter stayed in Joppa for many days with a man named Simon who was a tanner.

10 At Caesarea there was a man named Cornelius, an officer in the Italian group of the Roman army. ²Cornelius was a religious man. He and all the other people who lived in his house worshiped the true God. He gave much of his money to the poor and prayed to God often. ³One afternoon about three o'clock, Cornelius clearly saw a vision. An angel of God came to him and said, "Cornelius!"

⁴Cornelius stared at the angel. He became afraid and said, "What do you want, Lord?"

The angel said, "God has heard your prayers. He has seen that you give to the poor, and he remembers you. ⁵Send some men now to Joppa to bring back a man named Simon who is also called Peter. ⁶He is staying with a man, also named Simon, who is a tanner and has a house beside the sea." ⁷When the angel who spoke to Cornelius left, Cornelius called two of his servants and a soldier, a religious man who worked for him. ⁸Cornelius explained everything to them and sent them to Joppa.

⁹About noon the next day as they came near Joppa, Peter was going up to the roof to pray. ¹⁰He was hungry and wanted to eat, but while the food was being prepared, he had a vision. ¹¹He saw heaven opened and something coming down that looked like a big sheet being lowered to earth by its four corners. ¹²In it were all kinds of animals, reptiles, and birds. ¹³Then a voice said to Peter, "Get up, Peter; kill and eat."

¹⁴But Peter said, "No, Lord! I have never eaten food that is unholy or unclean."

¹⁵But the voice said to him again, "God has made these things clean, so don't call them 'unholy'!" ¹⁶This happened three times, and at once the sheet was taken back to heaven.

¹⁷While Peter was wondering what this vision meant, the men Cornelius had found Simon's house and were standing at the gate. ¹⁸They asked, "Is Simon Peter staying here?"

¹⁹While Peter was still thinking about the vision, the Spirit said to him, "Listen, three men are looking for you. ²⁰Get up and go downstairs. Go with them without doubting, because I have sent them to you."

²¹So Peter went down to the men and said, "I am the one you are looking for. Why did you come here?"

²²They said, "A holy angel spoke to Cornelius, an army officer and a good man; he worships God. All the people respect him. The angel told Cornelius to ask you to come to his house so that he can hear what you have to say." ²³So Peter asked the men to come in and spend the night.

The next day Peter got ready and went with them, and some of the followers from Joppa joined him. ²⁴On the following day they came to Caesarea. Cornelius was waiting for them and had called together his relatives and close friends.

[25]When Peter entered, Cornelius met him, fell at his feet, and worshiped him. [26]But Peter helped him up, saying, "Stand up. I too am only a human." [27]As he talked with Cornelius, Peter went inside where he saw many people gathered. [28]He said, "You people understand that it is against our law for Jewish people to associate with or visit anyone who is not Jewish. But God has shown me that I should not call any person 'unholy' or 'unclean.' [29]That is why I did not argue when I was asked to come here. Now, please tell me why you sent for me."

[30]Cornelius said, "Four days ago, I was praying in my house at this same time—three o'clock in the afternoon. Suddenly, there was a man standing before me wearing shining clothes. [31]He said, 'Cornelius, God has heard your prayer and has seen that you give to the poor and remembers you. [32]So send some men to Joppa and ask Simon Peter to come. Peter is staying in the house of a man, also named Simon, who is a tanner and has a house beside the sea.' [33]So I sent for you immediately, and it was very good of you to come. Now we are all here before God to hear everything the Lord has commanded you to tell us."

[34]Peter began to speak: "I really understand now that to God every person is the same. [35]In every country God accepts anyone who worships him and does what is right. [36]You know the message that God has sent to the people of Israel is the Good News that peace has come through Jesus Christ. Jesus is the Lord of all people! [37]You know what has happened all over Judea, beginning in Galilee after John preached to the people about baptism. [38]You know about Jesus from Nazareth, that God gave him the Holy Spirit and power. You know how Jesus went everywhere doing good and healing those who were ruled by the devil, because God was with him. [39]We saw what Jesus did in Judea and in Jerusalem, but the Jews in Jerusalem killed him by hanging him on a cross. [40]Yet, on the third day, God raised Jesus to life and caused him to be seen, [41]not by all the people, but only by the witnesses God had already chosen. And we are those witnesses who ate and drank with him after he was raised from the dead. [42]He told us to preach to the people and to tell them that he is the one whom God chose to be the judge of the living and the dead. [43]All the prophets say it is true that all who believe in Jesus will be forgiven of their sins through Jesus' name."

[44]While Peter was still saying this, the Holy Spirit came down on all those who were listening. [45]The Jewish believers who came with Peter were amazed that the gift of the Holy Spirit had been given even to the nations. [46]These believers heard them speaking in different languages and praising God. Then Peter said, [47]"Can anyone keep these people from being baptized with water? They have received the Holy Spirit just as we did!" [48]So Peter ordered that they be baptized in the name of Jesus Christ. Then they asked Peter to stay with them for a few days.

11 The apostles and the believers in Judea heard that some who were not Jewish had accepted God's teaching too. [2]But when Peter came to Jerusalem, some people argued with him. [3]They said, "You went into the homes of people who are not circumcised and ate with them!"

[4]So Peter explained the whole story to them. [5]He said, "I was in the city of Joppa, and while I was praying, I had a vision. I saw something that looked like a big sheet being lowered from heaven by its four corners. It came very close to me. [6]I

looked inside it and saw animals, wild beasts, reptiles, and birds. ⁷I heard a voice say to me, 'Get up, Peter. Kill and eat.' ⁸But I said, 'No, Lord! I have never eaten anything that is unholy or unclean.' ⁹But the voice from heaven spoke again, 'God has made these things clean, so don't call them unholy.' ¹⁰This happened three times. Then the whole thing was taken back to heaven. ¹¹Right then three men who were sent to me from Caesarea came to the house where I was staying. ¹²The Spirit told me to go with them without doubting. These six believers here also went with me, and we entered the house of Cornelius. ¹³He told us about the angel he saw standing in his house. The angel said to him, 'Send some men to Joppa and invite Simon Peter to come. ¹⁴By the words he will say to you, you and all your family will be saved.' ¹⁵When I began my speech, the Holy Spirit came on them just as he came on us at the beginning. ¹⁶Then I remembered the words of the Lord. He said, 'John baptized with water, but you will be baptized with the Holy Spirit.' ¹⁷Since God gave them the same gift he gave us who believed in the Lord Jesus Christ, how could I stop the work of God?"

¹⁸When the believers heard this, they stopped arguing. They praised God and said, "So God is allowing even other nations to turn to him and live."

¹⁹Many of the believers were scattered when they were persecuted after Stephen was killed. Some of them went as far as Phoenicia, Cyprus, and Antioch telling the message to others, but only to Jews. ²⁰Some of these believers were people from Cyprus and Cyrene. When they came to Antioch, they spoke also to Greeks, telling them the Good News about the Lord Jesus. ²¹The Lord was helping the believers, and a large group of people believed and turned to the Lord.

²²The church in Jerusalem heard about all of this, so they sent Barnabas to Antioch. ²³⁻²⁴Barnabas was a good man, full of the Holy Spirit and full of faith. When he reached Antioch and saw how God had blessed the people, he was glad. He encouraged all the believers in Antioch always to obey the Lord with all their hearts, and many people became followers of the Lord.

²⁵Then Barnabas went to the city of Tarsus to look for Saul, ²⁶and when he found Saul, he brought him to Antioch. For a whole year Saul and Barnabas met with the church and taught many people there. In Antioch the followers were called Christians for the first time.

²⁷About that time some prophets came from Jerusalem to Antioch. ²⁸One of them, named Agabus, stood up and spoke with the help of the Holy Spirit. He said, "A very hard time is coming to the whole world. There will be no food to eat." (This happened when Claudius ruled.) ²⁹The followers all decided to help the believers who lived in Judea, as much as each one could. ³⁰They gathered the money and gave it to Barnabas and Saul, who brought it to the elders in Judea.

12 During that same time King Herod began to mistreat some who belonged to the church. ²He ordered James, the brother of John, to be killed by the sword. ³Herod saw that some of the people liked this, so he decided to arrest Peter, too. (This happened during the time of the Feast of Unleavened Bread.) ⁴After Herod arrested Peter, he put him in jail and handed him over to be guarded by sixteen soldiers. Herod planned to bring Peter before the people for trial after the Passover Feast. ⁵So Peter was kept in jail, but the church prayed earnestly to God for him.

⁶The night before Herod was to bring

him to trial, Peter was sleeping between two soldiers, bound with two chains. Other soldiers were guarding the door of the jail. ⁷Suddenly, an angel of the Lord stood there, and a light shined in the cell. The angel struck Peter on the side and woke him up. "Hurry! Get up!" the angel said. And the chains fell off Peter's hands. ⁸Then the angel told him, "Get dressed and put on your sandals." And Peter did. Then the angel said, "Put on your coat and follow me." ⁹So Peter followed him out, but he did not know if what the angel was doing was real; he thought he might be seeing a vision. ¹⁰They went past the first and second guards and came to the iron gate that separated them from the city. The gate opened by itself for them, and they went through it. When they had walked down one street, the angel suddenly left him.

¹¹Then Peter realized what had happened. He thought, "Now I know that the Lord really sent his angel to me. He rescued me from Herod and from all the things the people thought would happen."

¹²When he considered this, he went to the home of Mary, the mother of John Mark. Many people were gathered there, praying. ¹³Peter knocked on the outside door, and a servant girl named Rhoda came to answer it. ¹⁴When she recognized Peter's voice, she was so happy she forgot to open the door. Instead, she ran inside and told the group, "Peter is at the door!"

¹⁵They said to her, "You are crazy!" But she kept on saying it was true, so they said, "It must be Peter's angel."

¹⁶Peter continued to knock, and when they opened the door, they saw him and were amazed. ¹⁷Peter made a sign with his hand to tell them to be quiet. He explained how the Lord led him out of the jail, and he said, "Tell James and the other believers what happened." Then he left to go to another place.

¹⁸The next day the soldiers were very upset and wondered what had happened to Peter. ¹⁹Herod looked everywhere for him but could not find him. So he questioned the guards and ordered that they be killed.

Later Herod moved from Judea and went to the city of Caesarea, where he stayed. ²⁰Herod was very angry with the people of Tyre and Sidon, but the people of those cities all came in a group to him. After convincing Blastus, the king's personal servant, to be on their side, they asked Herod for peace, because their country got its food from his country.

²¹On a chosen day Herod put on his royal robes, sat on his throne, and made a speech to the people. ²²They shouted, "This is the voice of a god, not a human!" ²³Because Herod did not give the glory to God, an angel of the Lord immediately caused him to become sick, and he was eaten by worms and died.

²⁴God's message continued to spread and reach people.

²⁵After Barnabas and Saul finished their task in Jerusalem, they returned to Antioch, taking John Mark with them.

13 In the church at Antioch there were these prophets and teachers: Barnabas, Simeon (also called Niger), Lucius (from the city of Cyrene), Manaen (who had grown up with Herod, the ruler), and Saul. ²They were all worshiping the Lord and fasting for a certain time. During this time the Holy Spirit said to them, "Set apart for me Barnabas and Saul to do a special work for which I have chosen them."

³So after they fasted and prayed, they laid their hands on Barnabas and Saul and sent them out.

⁴Barnabas and Saul, sent out by the Holy Spirit, went to the city of Seleucia. From there they sailed to the island of Cyprus. ⁵When they came to Salamis, they preached the Good News of God in the synagogues. John Mark was with them to help.

⁶They went across the whole island to Paphos where they met a magician named Bar-Jesus. He was a false prophet ⁷who always stayed close to Sergius Paulus, the governor and a smart man. He asked Barnabas and Saul to come to him, because he wanted to hear the message of God. ⁸But Elymas, the magician, was against them. (Elymas is the name for Bar-Jesus in the Greek language.) He tried to stop the governor from believing in Jesus. ⁹But Saul, who was also called Paul, was filled with the Holy Spirit. He looked straight at Elymas ¹⁰and said, "You son of the devil! You are an enemy of everything that is right! You are full of evil tricks and lies, always trying to change the Lord's truths into lies. ¹¹Now the Lord will touch you, and you will be blind. For a time you will not be able to see anything—not even the light from the sun."

Then everything became dark for Elymas, and he walked around, trying to find someone to lead him by the hand. ¹²When the governor saw this, he believed because he was amazed at the teaching about the Lord.

¹³Paul and those with him sailed from Paphos and came to Perga, in Pamphylia. There John Mark left them to return to Jerusalem. ¹⁴They continued their trip from Perga and went to Antioch, a city in Pisidia. On the Sabbath day they went into the synagogue and sat down. ¹⁵After the law of Moses and the writings of the prophets were read, the leaders of the synagogue sent a message to Paul and Barnabas: "Brothers, if you have any message that will encourage the people, please speak."

¹⁶Paul stood up, raised his hand, and said, "You Israelites and you who worship God, please listen! ¹⁷The God of the Israelites chose our ancestors. He made the people great during the time they lived in Egypt, and he brought them out of that country with great power. ¹⁸And he was patient with them for forty years in the desert. ¹⁹God destroyed seven nations in the land of Canaan and gave the land to his people. ²⁰All this happened in about four hundred fifty years.

"After this, God gave them judges until the time of Samuel the prophet. ²¹Then the people asked for a king, so God gave them Saul son of Kish. Saul was from the tribe of Benjamin and was king for forty years. ²²After God took him away, God made David their king. God said about him: 'I have found in David son of Jesse the kind of man I want. He will do all I want him to do.' ²³So God has brought Jesus, one of David's descendants, to Israel to be its Savior, as he promised. ²⁴Before Jesus came, John preached to all the people of Israel about a baptism of changed hearts and lives. ²⁵When he was finishing his work, he said, 'Who do you think I am? I am not the Christ. He is coming later, and I am not worthy to untie his sandals.'

²⁶"Brothers, sons of the family of Abraham, and others who worship God, listen! The news about this salvation has been sent to us. ²⁷Those who live in Jerusalem and their leaders did not realize that Jesus was the Savior. They did not understand the words that the prophets wrote, which are read every Sabbath day. But they made them come true when they said Jesus was guilty. ²⁸They could not find any real reason for Jesus to be put to death, but they asked Pilate to have him

killed. 29When they had done to him all that the Scriptures had said, they took him down from the cross and laid him in a tomb. 30But God raised him up from the dead! 31After this, for many days, those who had gone with Jesus from Galilee to Jerusalem saw him. They are now his witnesses to the people. 32We tell you the Good News about the promise God made to our ancestors. 33God has made this promise come true for us, his children, by raising Jesus from the dead. We read about this also in Psalm 2:

'You are my Son.
    Today I have become your Father.'
                                        Psalm 2:7

34God raised Jesus from the dead, and he will never go back to the grave and become dust. So God said:

'I will give you the holy and sure
    blessings
    that I promised to David.' *Isaiah 55:3*

35But in another place God says:

'You will not let your Holy One rot.'
                                        Psalm 16:10

36David did God's will during his lifetime. Then he died and was buried beside his ancestors, and his body did rot in the grave. 37But the One God raised from the dead did not rot in the grave. 38-39Brothers, understand what we are telling you: You can have forgiveness of your sins through Jesus. The law of Moses could not free you from your sins. But through Jesus everyone who believes is free from all sins. 40Be careful! Don't let what the prophets said happen to you:

41"Listen, you people who doubt!
    You can wonder, and then die.
I will do something in your lifetime
    that you won't believe even when
        you are told about it!' "
                                        Habakkuk 1:5

42While Paul and Barnabas were leaving the synagogue, the people asked them to tell them more about these things on the next Sabbath. 43When the meeting was over, many people with those who had changed to worship God followed Paul and Barnabas from that place. Paul and Barnabas were persuading them to continue trusting in God's grace.

44On the next Sabbath day, almost everyone in the city came to hear the word of the Lord. 45Seeing the crowd, the Jewish people became very jealous and said insulting things and argued against what Paul said. 46But Paul and Barnabas spoke very boldly, saying, "We must speak the message of God to you first. But you refuse to listen. You are judging yourselves not worthy of having eternal life! So we will now go to the people of other nations. 47This is what the Lord told us to do, saying:

'I have made you a light for the
    nations;
    you will show people all over the
        world the way to be saved.' "
                                        Isaiah 49:6

48When those who were not Jewish heard Paul say this, they were happy and gave honor to the message of the Lord. And the people who were chosen to have life forever believed the message.

49So the message of the Lord was spreading through the whole country. 50But the Jewish people stirred up some of the important religious women and the leaders of the city. They started trouble against Paul and Barnabas and forced them out of their area. 51So Paul and Barnabas shook the dust off their feet and went to Iconium. 52But the followers were filled with joy and the Holy Spirit.

14 In Iconium, Paul and Barnabas went as usual to the synagogue. They spoke so well that a great many

Jews and Greeks believed. ²But some people who did not believe excited the others and turned them against the believers. ³Paul and Barnabas stayed in Iconium a long time and spoke bravely for the Lord. He showed that their message about his grace was true by giving them the power to work miracles and signs. ⁴But the city was divided. Some of the people agreed with the Jews, and others believed the apostles.

⁵Some who were not Jews, some Jews, and some of their rulers wanted to mistreat Paul and Barnabas and to stone them to death. ⁶When Paul and Barnabas learned about this, they ran away to Lystra and Derbe, cities in Lycaonia, and to the areas around those cities. ⁷They announced the Good News there, too.

⁸In Lystra there sat a man who had been born crippled; he had never walked. ⁹As this man was listening to Paul speak, Paul looked straight at him and saw that he believed God could heal him. ¹⁰So he cried out, "Stand up on your feet!" The man jumped up and began walking around. ¹¹When the crowds saw what Paul did, they shouted in the Lycaonian language, "The gods have become like humans and have come down to us!" ¹²Then the people began to call Barnabas "Zeus" and Paul "Hermes," because he was the main speaker. ¹³The priest in the temple of Zeus, which was near the city, brought some bulls and flowers to the city gates. He and the people wanted to offer a sacrifice to Paul and Barnabas. ¹⁴But when the apostles, Barnabas and Paul, heard about it, they tore their clothes. They ran in among the people, shouting, ¹⁵"Friends, why are you doing these things? We are only human beings like you. We are bringing you the Good News and are telling you to turn away from these worthless things and turn to

the living God. He is the One who made the sky, the earth, the sea, and everything in them. ¹⁶In the past, God let all the nations do what they wanted. ¹⁷Yet he proved he is real by showing kindness, by giving you rain from heaven and crops at the right times, by giving you food and filling your hearts with joy." ¹⁸Even with these words, they were barely able to keep the crowd from offering sacrifices to them.

¹⁹Then some evil people came from Antioch and Iconium and persuaded the people to turn against Paul. So they threw stones at him and dragged him out of town, thinking they had killed him. ²⁰But the followers gathered around him, and he got up and went back into the town. The next day he and Barnabas left and went to the city of Derbe.

²¹Paul and Barnabas told the Good News in Derbe, and many became followers. Paul and Barnabas returned to Lystra, Iconium, and Antioch, ²²making the followers of Jesus stronger and helping them stay in the faith. They said, "We must suffer many things to enter God's kingdom." ²³They chose elders for each church, by praying and fasting for a certain time. These elders had trusted the Lord, so Paul and Barnabas put them in the Lord's care.

²⁴Then they went through Pisidia and came to Pamphylia. ²⁵When they had preached the message in Perga, they went down to Attalia. ²⁶And from there they sailed away to Antioch where the believers had put them into God's care and had sent them out to do this work. Now they had finished.

²⁷When they arrived in Antioch, Paul and Barnabas gathered the church together. They told the church all about what God had done with them and how God had made it possible for those who

were not Jewish to believe. ²⁸And they stayed there a long time with the followers.

15 Then some people came to Antioch from Judea and began teaching the non-Jewish believers: "You cannot be saved if you are not circumcised as Moses taught us." ²Paul and Barnabas were against this teaching and argued with them about it. So the church decided to send Paul, Barnabas, and some others to Jerusalem where they could talk more about this with the apostles and elders.

³The church helped them leave on the trip, and they went through the countries of Phoenicia and Samaria, telling all about how the other nations had turned to God. This made all the believers very happy. ⁴When they arrived in Jerusalem, they were welcomed by the apostles, the elders, and the church. Paul, Barnabas, and the others told about everything God had done with them. ⁵But some of the believers who belonged to the Pharisee group came forward and said, "The non-Jewish believers must be circumcised. They must be told to obey the law of Moses."

⁶The apostles and the elders gathered to consider this problem. ⁷After a long debate, Peter stood up and said to them, "Brothers, you know that in the early days God chose me from among you to preach the Good News to the nations. They heard the Good News from me, and they believed. ⁸God, who knows the thoughts of everyone, accepted them. He showed this to us by giving them the Holy Spirit, just as he did to us. ⁹To God, those people are not different from us. When they believed, he made their hearts pure. ¹⁰So now why are you testing God by putting a heavy load around the necks of the non-Jewish believers? It is a load that nei-

ther we nor our ancestors were able to carry. ¹¹But we believe that we and they too will be saved by the grace of the Lord Jesus."

¹²Then the whole group became quiet. They listened to Paul and Barnabas tell about all the miracles and signs that God did through them among the people. ¹³After they finished speaking, James said, "Brothers, listen to me. ¹⁴Simon has told us how God showed his love for those people. For the first time he is accepting from among them a people to be his own. ¹⁵The words of the prophets agree with this too:

¹⁶'After these things I will return.
        The kingdom of David is like a
            fallen tent.
    But I will rebuild its ruins,
        and I will set it up.
¹⁷Then those people who are left alive
        may ask the Lord for help,
    and the other nations that belong
        to me,
says the Lord,
    who will make it happen.
¹⁸And these things have been known
        for a long time.' *Amos 9:11–12*

¹⁹"So I think we should not bother the other people who are turning to God. ²⁰Instead, we should write a letter to them telling them these things: Stay away from food that has been offered to idols (which makes it unclean), any kind of sexual sin, eating animals that have been strangled, and blood. ²¹They should do these things, because for a long time in every city the law of Moses has been taught. And it is still read in the synagogue every Sabbath day."

²²The apostles, the elders, and the whole church decided to send some of their men with Paul and Barnabas to Antioch. They chose Judas Barsabbas and Silas, who were respected by the believ-

ers. ²³They sent the following letter with them:

> From the apostles and elders, your brothers.
>
> To all the non-Jewish believers in Antioch, Syria, and Cilicia:
> Greetings!
> ²⁴We have heard that some of our group have come to you and said things that trouble and upset you. But we did not tell them to do this. ²⁵We have all agreed to choose some messengers and send them to you with our dear friends Barnabas and Paul— ²⁶people who have given their lives to serve our Lord Jesus Christ. ²⁷So we are sending Judas and Silas, who will tell you the same things. ²⁸It has pleased the Holy Spirit that you should not have a heavy load to carry, and we agree. You need to do only these things: ²⁹Stay away from any food that has been offered to idols, eating any animals that have been strangled, and blood, and any kind of sexual sin. If you stay away from these things, you will do well.
> Good-bye.

³⁰So they left Jerusalem and went to Antioch where they gathered the church and gave them the letter. ³¹When they read it, they were very happy because of the encouraging message. ³²Judas and Silas, who were also prophets, said many things to encourage the believers and make them stronger. ³³After some time Judas and Silas were sent off in peace by the believers, and they went back to those who had sent them [, ³⁴but Silas decided to remain there].

³⁵But Paul and Barnabas stayed in Antioch and, along with many others, preached the Good News and taught the people the message of the Lord.

³⁶After some time, Paul said to Barnabas, "We should go back to all those towns where we preached the message of the Lord. Let's visit the believers and see how they are doing."

³⁷Barnabas wanted to take John Mark with them, ³⁸but he had left them at Pamphylia; he did not continue with them in the work. So Paul did not think it was a good idea to take him. ³⁹Paul and Barnabas had such a serious argument about this that they separated and went different ways. Barnabas took Mark and sailed to Cyprus, ⁴⁰but Paul chose Silas and left. The believers in Antioch put Paul into the Lord's care, ⁴¹and he went through Syria and Cilicia, giving strength to the churches.

16 Paul came to Derbe and Lystra, where a follower named Timothy lived. Timothy's mother was Jewish and a believer, but his father was a Greek. ²The believers in Lystra and Iconium respected Timothy and said good things about him. ³Paul wanted Timothy to travel with him, but all the people living in that area knew that Timothy's father was Greek. So Paul circumcised Timothy to please his mother's people. ⁴Paul and those with him traveled from town to town and gave the decisions made by the apostles and elders in Jerusalem for the people to obey. ⁵So the churches became stronger in the faith and grew larger every day.

⁶Paul and those with him went through the areas of Phrygia and Galatia since the Holy Spirit did not let them preach the Good News in Asia. ⁷When they came near the country of Mysia, they tried to go into Bithynia, but the Spirit of Jesus did not let them. ⁸So they passed by Mysia and went to Troas. ⁹That

night Paul saw in a vision a man from Macedonia. The man stood and begged, "Come over to Macedonia and help us." [10]After Paul had seen the vision, we immediately prepared to leave for Macedonia, understanding that God had called us to tell the Good News to those people.

[11]We left Troas and sailed straight to the island of Samothrace. The next day we sailed to Neapolis. [12]Then we went by land to Philippi, a Roman colony and the leading city in that part of Macedonia. We stayed there for several days.

[13]On the Sabbath day we went outside the city gate to the river where we thought we would find a special place for prayer. Some women had gathered there, so we sat down and talked with them. [14]One of the listeners was a woman named Lydia from the city of Thyatira whose job was selling purple cloth. She worshiped God, and he opened her mind to pay attention to what Paul was saying. [15]She and all the people in her house were baptized. Then she invited us to her home, saying, "If you think I am truly a believer in the Lord, then come stay in my house." And she persuaded us to stay with her.

[16]Once, while we were going to the place for prayer, a servant girl met us. She had a special spirit in her, and she earned a lot of money for her owners by telling fortunes. [17]This girl followed Paul and us, shouting, "These men are servants of the Most High God. They are telling you how you can be saved."

[18]She kept this up for many days. This bothered Paul, so he turned and said to the spirit, "By the power of Jesus Christ, I command you to come out of her!" Immediately, the spirit came out.

[19]When the owners of the servant girl saw this, they knew that now they could not use her to make money. So they grabbed Paul and Silas and dragged them before the city rulers in the marketplace. [20]They brought Paul and Silas to the Roman rulers and said, "These men are Jews and are making trouble in our city. [21]They are teaching things that are not right for us as Romans to do."

[22]The crowd joined the attack against them. The Roman officers tore the clothes of Paul and Silas and had them beaten with rods. [23]Then Paul and Silas were thrown into jail, and the jailer was ordered to guard them carefully. [24]When he heard this order, he put them far inside the jail and pinned their feet down between large blocks of wood.

[25]About midnight Paul and Silas were praying and singing songs to God as the other prisoners listened. [26]Suddenly, there was a strong earthquake that shook the foundation of the jail. Then all the doors of the jail broke open, and all the prisoners were freed from their chains. [27]The jailer woke up and saw that the jail doors were open. Thinking that the prisoners had already escaped, he got his sword and was about to kill himself. [28]But Paul shouted, "Don't hurt yourself! We are all here."

[29]The jailer told someone to bring a light. Then he ran inside and, shaking with fear, fell down before Paul and Silas. [30]He brought them outside and said, "Men, what must I do to be saved?"

[31]They said to him, "Believe in the Lord Jesus and you will be saved—you and all the people in your house." [32]So Paul and Silas told the message of the Lord to the jailer and all the people in his house. [33]At that hour of the night the jailer took Paul and Silas and washed their wounds. Then he and all his people were baptized immediately. [34]After this the jailer took Paul and Silas home and gave them food. He

STEP 2

and his family were very happy because they now believed in God.

³⁵The next morning, the Roman officers sent the police to tell the jailer, "Let these men go free."

³⁶The jailer said to Paul, "The officers have sent an order to let you go free. You can leave now. Go in peace."

³⁷But Paul said to the police, "They beat us in public without a trial, even though we are Roman citizens. And they threw us in jail. Now they want to make us go away quietly. No! Let them come themselves and bring us out."

³⁸The police told the Roman officers what Paul said. When the officers heard that Paul and Silas were Roman citizens, they were afraid. ³⁹So they came and told Paul and Silas they were sorry and took them out of jail and asked them to leave the city. ⁴⁰So when they came out of the jail, they went to Lydia's house where they saw some of the believers and encouraged them. Then they left.

17 Paul and Silas traveled through Amphipolis and Apollonia and came to Thessalonica where there was a synagogue. ²Paul went into the synagogue as he always did, and on each Sabbath day for three weeks, he talked with his fellow Jews about the Scriptures. ³He explained and proved that the Christ must die and then rise from the dead. He said, "This Jesus I am telling you about is the Christ." ⁴Some of them were convinced and joined Paul and Silas, along with many of the Greeks who worshiped God and many of the important women.

⁵But some others became jealous. So they got some evil men from the marketplace, formed a mob, and started a riot. They ran to Jason's house, looking for Paul and Silas, wanting to bring them out to the people. ⁶But when they did not find them, they dragged Jason and some

other believers to the leaders of the city. The people were yelling, "These people have made trouble everywhere in the world, and now they have come here too! ⁷Jason is keeping them in his house. All of them do things against the laws of Caesar, saying there is another king, called Jesus."

⁸When the people and the leaders of the city heard these things, they became very upset. ⁹They made Jason and the others put up a sum of money. Then they let the believers go free.

¹⁰That same night the believers sent Paul and Silas to Berea where they went to the synagogue. ¹¹These people were more willing to listen than the people in Thessalonica. The Bereans were eager to hear what Paul and Silas said and studied the Scriptures every day to find out if these things were true. ¹²So, many of them believed, as well as many important Greek women and men. ¹³But the people in Thessalonica learned that Paul was preaching the word of God in Berea, too. So they came there, upsetting the people and making trouble. ¹⁴The believers quickly sent Paul away to the coast, but Silas and Timothy stayed in Berea. ¹⁵The people leading Paul went with him to Athens. Then they carried a message from Paul back to Silas and Timothy for them to come to him as soon as they could.

¹⁶While Paul was waiting for Silas and Timothy in Athens, he was troubled because he saw that the city was full of idols. ¹⁷In the synagogue, he talked with the Jews and the Greeks who worshiped God. He also talked every day with people in the marketplace.

¹⁸Some of the Epicurean and Stoic philosophers argued with him, saying, "This man doesn't know what he is talking about. What is he trying to say?"

Others said, "He seems to be telling us about some other gods," because Paul was telling them about Jesus and his rising from the dead. ¹⁹They got Paul and took him to a meeting of the Areopagus, where they said, "Please explain to us this new idea you have been teaching. ²⁰The things you are saying are new to us, and we want to know what this teaching means." ²¹(All the people of Athens and those from other countries who lived there always used their time to talk about the newest ideas.)

²²Then Paul stood before the meeting of the Areopagus and said, "People of Athens, I can see you are very religious in all things. ²³As I was going through your city, I saw the objects you worship. I found an altar that had these words written on it: TO A GOD WHO IS NOT KNOWN. You worship a god that you don't know, and this is the God I am telling you about! ²⁴The God who made the whole world and everything in it is the Lord of the land and the sky. He does not live in temples built by human hands. ²⁵This God is the One who gives life, breath, and everything else to people. He does not need any help from them; he has everything he needs. ²⁶God began by making one person, and from him came all the different people who live everywhere in the world. God decided exactly when and where they must live. ²⁷God wanted them to look for him and perhaps search all around for him and find him, though he is not far from any of us: ²⁸'By his power we live and move and exist.' Some of your own poets have said: 'For we are his children.' ²⁹Since we are God's children, you must not think that God is like something that people imagine or make from gold, silver, or rock. ³⁰In the past, people did not understand God, and he ignored this. But now, God tells all people in the world to change their hearts and lives. ³¹God has set a day that he will judge all the world with fairness, by the man he chose long ago. And God has proved this to everyone by raising that man from the dead!"

³²When the people heard about Jesus being raised from the dead, some of them laughed. But others said, "We will hear more about this from you later." ³³So Paul went away from them. ³⁴But some of the people believed Paul and joined him. Among those who believed was Dionysius, a member of the Areopagus, a woman named Damaris, and some others.

18 Later Paul left Athens and went to Corinth. ²Here he met a Jew named Aquila who had been born in the country of Pontus. But Aquila and his wife, Priscilla, had recently moved to Corinth from Italy, because Claudius commanded that all Jews must leave Rome. Paul went to visit Aquila and Priscilla. ³Because they were tentmakers, just as he was, he stayed with them and worked with them. ⁴Every Sabbath day he talked with the Jews and Greeks in the synagogue, trying to persuade them to believe in Jesus.

⁵Silas and Timothy came from Macedonia and joined Paul in Corinth. After this, Paul spent all his time telling people the Good News, showing them that Jesus is the Christ. ⁶But they would not accept Paul's teaching and said some evil things. So he shook off the dust from his clothes and said to them, "If you are not saved, it will be your own fault! I have done all I can do! After this, I will go to other nations." ⁷Paul left the synagogue and moved into the home of Titius Justus, next to the synagogue. This man worshiped God. ⁸Crispus was the leader of that synagogue, and he and all the people living in his house believed in the Lord.

Many others in Corinth also listened to Paul and believed and were baptized.

⁹During the night, the Lord told Paul in a vision: "Don't be afraid. Continue talking to people and don't be quiet. ¹⁰I am with you, and no one will hurt you because many of my people are in this city." ¹¹Paul stayed there for a year and a half, teaching God's word to the people.

¹²When Gallio was the governor of the country of Southern Greece, some people came together against Paul and took him to the court. ¹³They said, "This man is teaching people to worship God in a way that is against our law."

¹⁴Paul was about to say something, but Gallio spoke, saying, "I would listen to you if you were complaining about a crime or some wrong. ¹⁵But the things you are saying are only questions about words and names—arguments about your own law. So you must solve this problem yourselves. I don't want to be a judge of these things." ¹⁶And Gallio made them leave the court.

¹⁷Then they all grabbed Sosthenes, the leader of the synagogue, and beat him there before the court. But this did not bother Gallio.

¹⁸Paul stayed with the believers for many more days. Then he left and sailed for Syria, with Priscilla and Aquila. At Cenchrea Paul cut off his hair, because he had made a promise to God. ¹⁹Then they went to Ephesus, where Paul left Priscilla and Aquila. While Paul was there, he went into the synagogue and talked with the people. ²⁰When they asked him to stay with them longer, he refused. ²¹But as he left, he said, "I will come back to you again if God wants me to." And so he sailed away from Ephesus.

²²When Paul landed at Caesarea, he went and gave greetings to the church in Jerusalem. After that, Paul went to Anti-

och. ²³He stayed there for a while and then left and went through the regions of Galatia and Phrygia. He traveled from town to town in these regions, giving strength to all the followers.

²⁴A Jew named Apollos came to Ephesus. He was born in the city of Alexandria and was a good speaker who knew the Scriptures well. ²⁵He had been taught about the way of the Lord and was always very excited when he spoke and taught the truth about Jesus. But the only baptism Apollos knew about was the baptism that John taught. ²⁶Apollos began to speak very boldly in the synagogue, and when Priscilla and Aquila heard him, they took him to their home and helped him better understand the way of God. ²⁷Now Apollos wanted to go to the country of Southern Greece. So the believers helped him and wrote a letter to the followers there, asking them to accept him. These followers had believed in Jesus because of God's grace, and when Apollos arrived, he helped them very much. ²⁸He argued very strongly with the Jews before all the people, clearly proving with the Scriptures that Jesus is the Christ.

19

While Apollos was in Corinth, Paul was visiting some places on the way to Ephesus. There he found some followers ²and asked them, "Did you receive the Holy Spirit when you believed?"

They said, "We have never even heard of a Holy Spirit."

³So he asked, "What kind of baptism did you have?"

They said, "It was the baptism that John taught."

⁴Paul said, "John's baptism was a baptism of changed hearts and lives. He told people to believe in the one who would come after him, and that one is Jesus."

⁵When they heard this, they were baptized in the name of the Lord Jesus. ⁶Then Paul laid his hands on them, and the Holy Spirit came upon them. They began speaking different languages and prophesying. ⁷There were about twelve people in this group.

⁸Paul went into the synagogue and spoke out boldly for three months. He talked with the people and persuaded them to accept the things he said about the kingdom of God. ⁹But some of them became stubborn. They refused to believe and said evil things about the Way of Jesus before all the people. So Paul left them, and taking the followers with him, he went to the school of a man named Tyrannus. There Paul talked with people every day ¹⁰for two years. Because of his work, every Jew and Greek in Asia heard the word of the Lord.

¹¹God used Paul to do some very special miracles. ¹²Some people took handkerchiefs and clothes that Paul had used and put them on the sick. When they did this, the sick were healed and evil spirits left them.

¹³But some people also were traveling around and making evil spirits go out of people. They tried to use the name of the Lord Jesus to force the evil spirits out. They would say, "By the same Jesus that Paul talks about, I order you to come out!" ¹⁴Seven sons of Sceva, a leading priest, were doing this.

¹⁵But one time an evil spirit said to them, "I know Jesus, and I know about Paul, but who are you?"

¹⁶Then the man who had the evil spirit jumped on them. Because he was so much stronger than all of them, they ran away from the house naked and hurt. ¹⁷All the people in Ephesus—Jews and Greeks—learned about this and were filled with fear and gave great honor to the Lord Jesus. ¹⁸Many of the believers began to confess openly and tell all the evil things they had done. ¹⁹Some of them who had used magic brought their magic books and burned them before everyone. Those books were worth about fifty thousand silver coins.

²⁰So in a powerful way the word of the Lord kept spreading and growing.

²¹After these things, Paul decided to go to Jerusalem, planning to go through the countries of Macedonia and Southern Greece and then on to Jerusalem. He said, "After I have been to Jerusalem, I must also visit Rome." ²²Paul sent Timothy and Erastus, two of his helpers, ahead to Macedonia, but he himself stayed in Asia for a while.

²³And during that time, there was some serious trouble in Ephesus about the Way of Jesus. ²⁴A man named Demetrius, who worked with silver, made little silver models that looked like the temple of the goddess Artemis. Those who did this work made much money. ²⁵Demetrius had a meeting with them and some others who did the same kind of work. He told them, "Men, you know that we make a lot of money from our business. ²⁶But look at what this man Paul is doing. He has convinced and turned away many people in Ephesus and in almost all of Asia! He says the gods made by human hands are not real. ²⁷There is a danger that our business will lose its good name, but there is also another danger: People will begin to think that the temple of the great goddess Artemis is not important. Her greatness will be destroyed, and Artemis is the goddess that everyone in Asia and the whole world worships."

²⁸When the others heard this, they became very angry and shouted, "Artemis, the goddess of Ephesus, is great!" ²⁹The whole city became confused. The people

STEP 5

STEP 5

Admitted to God, to ourselves, and to another
human being the exact nature of our wrongs.

Acts 19:18

Have you noticed that children learn to lie almost immediately after
learning to talk? A soon as they can string together a few words,
these little bundles of energy and joy start covering up what
they've done to avoid consequences. On top of that, some kids are
born risk-takers. They have extra motivation to fib about what
they've been up to. Moms and dads find themselves constantly
disciplining their little daredevils to keep them alive. Often it seems
as though it would be easier to wink at their little lies than to do the
hard work of discipline. But the fact is that when little liars (just like
big ones) admit the truth, they feel relieved.

This principle held true for first-century Christians at Ephesus; and
it does for you in the twenty-first century, too. When you get honest
with God and tell him everything you've been doing without
excuses and blame-shifting, you will be amazed at how clean and
free the Holy Spirit can make you feel. You may think it's easier to
stay in denial and rationalize your habit, but in the long run the
relief and cleansing are worth however much struggle it takes to
come clean with God.

FOR YOUR NEXT **STEP 5** MEDITATION, TURN TO **PAGE 255.** ▶▶

grabbed Gaius and Aristarchus, who were from Macedonia and were traveling with Paul, and ran to the theater. ³⁰Paul wanted to go in and talk to the crowd, but the followers did not let him. ³¹Also, some leaders of Asia who were friends of Paul sent him a message, begging him not to go into the theater. ³²Some people were shouting one thing, and some were shouting another. The meeting was completely confused; most of them did not know why they had come together. ³³They put a man named Alexander in front of the people, and some of them told him what to do. Alexander waved his hand so he could explain things to the people. ³⁴But when they saw that Alexander was a Jew, they all shouted the same thing for two hours: "Great is Artemis of Ephesus!"

³⁵Then the city clerk made the crowd be quiet. He said, "People of Ephesus, everyone knows that Ephesus is the city that keeps the temple of the great goddess Artemis and her holy stone that fell from heaven. ³⁶Since no one can say this is not true, you should be quiet. Stop and think before you do anything. ³⁷You brought these men here, but they have not said anything evil against our goddess or stolen anything from her temple. ³⁸If Demetrius and those who work with him have a charge against anyone they should go to the courts and judges where they can argue with each other. ³⁹If there is something else you want to talk about, it can be decided at the regular town meeting of the people. ⁴⁰I say this because some people might see this trouble today and say that we are rioting. We could not explain this, because there is no real reason for this meeting." ⁴¹After the city clerk said these things, he told the people to go home.

20 When the trouble stopped, Paul sent for the followers to come to him. After he encouraged them and then told them good-bye, he left and went to the country of Macedonia. ²He said many things to strengthen the followers in the different places on his way through Macedonia. Then he went to Greece, ³where he stayed for three months. He was ready to sail for Syria, but some evil people were planning something against him. So Paul decided to go back through Macedonia to Syria. ⁴The men who went with him were Sopater son of Pyrrhus, from the city of Berea; Aristarchus and Secundus, from the city of Thessalonica; Gaius, from Derbe; Timothy; and Tychicus and Trophimus, two men from Asia. ⁵These men went on ahead and waited for us at Troas. ⁶We sailed from Philippi after the Feast of Unleavened Bread. Five days later we met them in Troas, where we stayed for seven days.

⁷On the first day of the week, we all met together to break bread, and Paul spoke to the group. Because he was planning to leave the next day, he kept on talking until midnight. ⁸We were all together in a room upstairs, and there were many lamps in the room. ⁹A young man named Eutychus was sitting in the window. As Paul continued talking, Eutychus was falling into a deep sleep. Finally, he went sound asleep and fell to the ground from the third floor. When they picked him up, he was dead. ¹⁰Paul went down to Eutychus, knelt down, and put his arms around him. He said, "Don't worry. He is alive now." ¹¹Then Paul went upstairs again, broke bread, and ate. He spoke to them a long time, until it was early morning, and then he left. ¹²They took the young man home alive and were greatly comforted.

¹³We went on ahead of Paul and sailed for the city of Assos, where he wanted to join us on the ship. Paul planned it this

way because he wanted to go to Assos by land. [14]When he met us there, we took him aboard and went to Mitylene. [15]We sailed from Mitylene and the next day came to a place near Kios. The following day we sailed to Samos, and the next day we reached Miletus. [16]Paul had already decided not to stop at Ephesus, because he did not want to stay too long in Asia. He was hurrying to be in Jerusalem on the day of Pentecost, if that were possible.

[17]Now from Miletus Paul sent to Ephesus and called for the elders of the church. [18]When they came to him, he said, "You know about my life from the first day I came to Asia. You know the way I lived all the time I was with you. [19]The evil people made plans against me, which troubled me very much. But you know I always served the Lord unselfishly, and I often cried. [20]You know I preached to you and did not hold back anything that would help you. You know that I taught you in public and in your homes. [21]I warned both Jews and Greeks to change their lives and turn to God and believe in our Lord Jesus. [22]But now I must obey the Holy Spirit and go to Jerusalem. I don't know what will happen to me there. [23]I know only that in every city the Holy Spirit tells me that troubles and even jail wait for me. [24]I don't care about my own life. The most important thing is that I complete my mission, the work that the Lord Jesus gave me—to tell people the Good News about God's grace.

[25]"And now, I know that none of you among whom I was preaching the kingdom of God will ever see me again. [26]So today I tell you that if any of you should be lost, I am not responsible, [27]because I have told you everything God wants you to know. [28]Be careful for yourselves and for all the people the Holy Spirit has given to you to oversee. You must be like shep-

herds to the church of God, which he bought with the death of his own son. [29]I know that after I leave, some people will come like wild wolves and try to destroy the flock. [30]Also, some from your own group will rise up and twist the truth and will lead away followers after them. [31]So be careful! Always remember that for three years, day and night, I never stopped warning each of you, and I often cried over you.

[32]"Now I am putting you in the care of God and the message about his grace. It is able to give you strength, and it will give you the blessings God has for all his holy people. [33]When I was with you, I never wanted anyone's money or fine clothes. [34]You know I always worked to take care of my own needs and the needs of those who were with me. [35]I showed you in all things that you should work as I did and help the weak. I taught you to remember the words Jesus said: 'It is more blessed to give than to receive.' "

[36]When Paul had said this, he knelt down with all of them and prayed. [37-38]And they all cried because Paul had said they would never see him again. They put their arms around him and kissed him. Then they went with him to the ship.

21 After we all said good-bye to them, we sailed straight to the island of Cos. The next day we reached Rhodes, and from there we went to Patara. [2]There we found a ship going to Phoenicia, so we went aboard and sailed away. [3]We sailed near the island of Cyprus, seeing it to the north, but we sailed on to Syria. We stopped at Tyre because the ship needed to unload its cargo there. [4]We found some followers in Tyre and stayed with them for seven days. Through the Holy Spirit they warned Paul not to go to Jerusalem. [5]When we finished our visit, we left and continued our trip. All the followers, even

STEP
11

the women and children, came outside the city with us. After we all knelt on the beach and prayed, ⁶we said good-bye and got on the ship, and the followers went back home.

⁷We continued our trip from Tyre and arrived at Ptolemais, where we greeted the believers and stayed with them for a day. ⁸The next day we left Ptolemais and went to the city of Caesarea. There we went into the home of Philip the preacher, one of the seven helpers, and stayed with him. ⁹He had four unmarried daughters who had the gift of prophesying. ¹⁰After we had been there for some time, a prophet named Agabus arrived from Judea. ¹¹He came to us and borrowed Paul's belt and used it to tie his own hands and feet. He said, "The Holy Spirit says, 'This is how evil people in Jerusalem will tie up the man who wears this belt. Then they will give him to the older leaders.'"

¹²When we all heard this, we and the people there begged Paul not to go to Jerusalem. ¹³But he said, "Why are you crying and making me so sad? I am not only ready to be tied up in Jerusalem, I am ready to die for the Lord Jesus!"

¹⁴We could not persuade him to stay away from Jerusalem. So we stopped begging him and said, "We pray that what the Lord wants will be done."

¹⁵After this, we got ready and started on our way to Jerusalem. ¹⁶Some of the followers from Caesarea went with us and took us to the home of Mnason, where we would stay. He was from Cyprus and was one of the first followers.

¹⁷In Jerusalem the believers were glad to see us. ¹⁸The next day Paul went with us to visit James, and all the elders were there. ¹⁹Paul greeted them and told them everything God had done among the other nations through him. ²⁰When they heard this, they praised God. Then they said to Paul, "Brother, you can see that many thousands of our people have become believers. And they think it is very important to obey the law of Moses. ²¹They have heard about your teaching, that you tell our people who live among the nations to leave the law of Moses. They have heard that you tell them not to circumcise their children and not to obey customs. ²²What should we do? They will learn that you have come. ²³So we will tell you what to do: Four of our men have made a promise to God. ²⁴Take these men with you and share in their cleansing ceremony. Pay their expenses so they can shave their heads. Then it will prove to everyone that what they have heard about you is not true and that you follow the law of Moses in your own life. ²⁵We have already sent a letter to the non-Jewish believers. The letter said: 'Do not eat food that has been offered to idols, or blood, or animals that have been strangled. Do not take part in sexual sin.'"

²⁶The next day Paul took the four men and shared in the cleansing ceremony with them. Then he went to the Temple and announced the time when the days of the cleansing ceremony would be finished. On the last day an offering would be given for each of the men.

²⁷When the seven days were almost over, some of his people from Asia saw Paul at the Temple. They caused all the people to be upset and grabbed Paul. ²⁸They shouted, "People of Israel, help us! This is the man who goes everywhere teaching against the law of Moses, against our people, and against this Temple. Now he has brought some Greeks into the Temple and has made this holy place unclean!" ²⁹(They said this because they had seen Trophimus, a man from Ephesus, with Paul in Jerusalem. They

thought that Paul had brought him into the Temple.)

³⁰All the people in Jerusalem became upset. Together they ran, took Paul, and dragged him out of the Temple. The Temple doors were closed immediately. ³¹While they were trying to kill Paul, the commander of the Roman army in Jerusalem learned that there was trouble in the whole city. ³²Immediately he took some officers and soldiers and ran to the place where the crowd was gathered. When the people saw them, they stopped beating Paul. ³³The commander went to Paul and arrested him. He told his soldiers to tie Paul with two chains. Then he asked who he was and what he had done wrong. ³⁴Some in the crowd were yelling one thing, and some were yelling another. Because of all this confusion and shouting, the commander could not learn what had happened. So he ordered the soldiers to take Paul to the army building. ³⁵When Paul came to the steps, the soldiers had to carry him because the people were ready to hurt him. ³⁶The whole mob was following them, shouting, "Kill him!"

³⁷As the soldiers were about to take Paul into the army building, he spoke to the commander, "May I say something to you?"

The commander said, "Do you speak Greek? ³⁸I thought you were the Egyptian who started some trouble against the government not long ago and led four thousand killers out to the desert."

³⁹Paul said, "No, I am a Jew from Tarsus in the country of Cilicia. I am a citizen of that important city. Please, let me speak to the people."

⁴⁰The commander gave permission, so Paul stood on the steps and waved his hand to quiet the people. When there was silence, he spoke to them in the Hebrew language.

22Paul said, "Brothers and fathers, listen to my defense to you." ²When they heard him speaking the Hebrew language, they became very quiet. Paul said, ³"I am a Jew, born in Tarsus in the country of Cilicia, but I grew up in this city. I was a student of Gamaliel, who carefully taught me everything about the law of our ancestors. I was very serious about serving God, just as are all of you here today. ⁴I persecuted the people who followed the Way of Jesus, and some of them were even killed. I arrested men and women and put them in jail. ⁵The high priest and the whole council of elders can tell you this is true. They gave me letters to the brothers in Damascus. So I was going there to arrest these people and bring them back to Jerusalem to be punished.

⁶"About noon when I came near Damascus, a bright light from heaven suddenly flashed all around me. ⁷I fell to the ground and heard a voice saying, 'Saul, Saul, why are you persecuting me?' ⁸I asked, 'Who are you, Lord?' The voice said, 'I am Jesus from Nazareth whom you are persecuting.' ⁹Those who were with me did not understand the voice, but they saw the light. ¹⁰I said, 'What shall I do, Lord?' The Lord answered, 'Get up and go to Damascus. There you will be told about all the things I have planned for you to do.' ¹¹I could not see, because the bright light had made me blind. So my companions led me into Damascus.

¹²"There a man named Ananias came to me. He was a religious man; he obeyed the law of Moses, and all the Jews who lived there respected him. ¹³He stood by me and said, 'Brother Saul, see again!' Immediately I was able to see him. ¹⁴He said, 'The God of our ancestors chose you long ago to know his plan, to see the Righteous One, and to hear words from

him. ¹⁵You will be his witness to all people, telling them about what you have seen and heard. ¹⁶Now, why wait any longer? Get up, be baptized, and wash your sins away, trusting in him to save you.'

¹⁷"Later, when I returned to Jerusalem, I was praying in the Temple, and I saw a vision. ¹⁸I saw the Lord saying to me, 'Hurry! Leave Jerusalem now! The people here will not accept the truth about me.' ¹⁹But I said, 'Lord, they know that in every synagogue I put the believers in jail and beat them. ²⁰They also know I was there when Stephen, your witness, was killed. I stood there agreeing and holding the coats of those who were killing him!' ²¹But the Lord said to me, 'Leave now. I will send you far away to the other nations.' "

²²The crowd listened to Paul until he said this. Then they began shouting, "Get rid of him! He doesn't deserve to live!" ²³They shouted, threw off their coats, and threw dust into the air.

²⁴Then the commander ordered the soldiers to take Paul into the army building and beat him. He wanted to make Paul tell why the people were shouting against him like this. ²⁵But as the soldiers were tying him up, preparing to beat him, Paul said to an officer nearby, "Do you have the right to beat a Roman citizen who has not been proven guilty?"

²⁶When the officer heard this, he went to the commander and reported it. The officer said, "Do you know what you are doing? This man is a Roman citizen."

²⁷The commander came to Paul and said, "Tell me, are you really a Roman citizen?"

He answered, "Yes."

²⁸The commander said, "I paid a lot of money to become a Roman citizen."

But Paul said, "I was born a citizen."

²⁹The men who were preparing to question Paul moved away from him im-

mediately. The commander was frightened because he had already tied Paul, and Paul was a Roman citizen.

³⁰The next day the commander decided to learn why the Jews were accusing Paul. So he ordered the leading priests and the council to meet. The commander took Paul's chains off. Then he brought Paul out and stood him before their meeting.

23 Paul looked at the council and said, "Brothers, I have lived my life without guilt feelings before God up to this day." ²Ananias, the high priest, heard this and told the men who were standing near Paul to hit him on the mouth. ³Paul said to Ananias, "God will hit you, too! You are like a wall that has been painted white. You sit there and judge me, using the law of Moses, but you are telling them to hit me, and that is against the law."

⁴The men standing near Paul said to him, "You cannot insult God's high priest like that!"

⁵Paul said, "Brothers, I did not know this man was the high priest. It is written in the Scriptures, 'You must not curse a leader of your people.' "

⁶Some of the men in the meeting were Sadducees, and others were Pharisees. Knowing this, Paul shouted to them, "My brothers, I am a Pharisee, and my father was a Pharisee. I am on trial here because I believe that people will rise from the dead."

⁷When Paul said this, there was an argument between the Pharisees and the Sadducees, and the group was divided. ⁸(The Sadducees do not believe in angels or spirits or that people will rise from the dead. But the Pharisees believe in them all.) ⁹So there was a great uproar. Some of the teachers of the law, who were Pharisees, stood up and argued, "We find

nothing wrong with this man. Maybe an angel or a spirit did speak to him."

¹⁰The argument was beginning to turn into such a fight that the commander was afraid some evil people would tear Paul to pieces. So he told the soldiers to go down and take Paul away and put him in the army building.

¹¹The next night the Lord came and stood by Paul. He said, "Be brave! You have told people in Jerusalem about me. You must do the same in Rome."

¹²In the morning some evil people made a plan to kill Paul, and they took an oath not to eat or drink anything until they had killed him. ¹³There were more than forty men who made this plan. ¹⁴They went to the leading priests and the elders and said, "We have taken an oath not to eat or drink until we have killed Paul. ¹⁵So this is what we want you to do: Send a message to the commander to bring Paul out to you as though you want to ask him more questions. We will be waiting to kill him while he is on the way here."

¹⁶But Paul's nephew heard about this plan and went to the army building and told Paul. ¹⁷Then Paul called one of the officers and said, "Take this young man to the commander. He has a message for him."

¹⁸So the officer brought Paul's nephew to the commander and said, "The prisoner, Paul, asked me to bring this young man to you. He wants to tell you something."

¹⁹The commander took the young man's hand and led him to a place where they could be alone. He asked, "What do you want to tell me?"

²⁰The young man said, "The Jews have decided to ask you to bring Paul down to their council meeting tomorrow. They want you to think they are going to ask him more questions. ²¹But don't believe them! More than forty men are hiding and waiting to kill Paul. They have all taken an oath not to eat or drink until they have killed him. Now they are waiting for you to agree."

²²The commander sent the young man away, ordering him, "Don't tell anyone that you have told me about their plan."

²³Then the commander called two officers and said, "I need some men to go to Caesarea. Get two hundred soldiers, seventy horsemen, and two hundred men with spears ready to leave at nine o'clock tonight. ²⁴Get some horses for Paul to ride so he can be taken to Governor Felix safely." ²⁵And he wrote a letter that said:

²⁶From Claudius Lysias.

To the Most Excellent Governor Felix:

Greetings.

²⁷Some of the Jews had taken this man and planned to kill him. But I learned that he is a Roman citizen, so I went with my soldiers and saved him. ²⁸I wanted to know why they were accusing him, so I brought him before their council meeting. ²⁹I learned that these people said Paul did some things that were wrong by their own laws, but no charge was worthy of jail or death. ³⁰When I was told that some of them were planning to kill Paul, I sent him to you at once. I also told them to tell you what they have against him.

³¹So the soldiers did what they were told and took Paul and brought him to the city of Antipatris that night. ³²The next day the horsemen went with Paul to Caesarea, but the other soldiers went back to the army building in Jerusalem. ³³When the horsemen came to Caesarea and

gave the letter to the governor, they turned Paul over to him. ³⁴The governor read the letter and asked Paul, "What area are you from?" When he learned that Paul was from Cilicia, ³⁵he said, "I will hear your case when those who are against you come here, too." Then the governor gave orders for Paul to be kept under guard in Herod's palace.

24 Five days later Ananias, the high priest, went to the city of Caesarea with some of the elders and a lawyer named Tertullus. They had come to make charges against Paul before the governor. ²Paul was called into the meeting, and Tertullus began to accuse him, saying, "Most Excellent Felix! Our people enjoy much peace because of you, and many wrong things in our country are being made right through your wise help. ³We accept these things always and in every place, and we are thankful for them. ⁴But not wanting to take any more of your time, I beg you to be kind and listen to our few words. ⁵We have found this man to be a troublemaker, stirring up his people everywhere in the world. He is a leader of the Nazarene group. ⁶Also, he was trying to make the Temple unclean, but we stopped him. [And we wanted to judge him by our own law. ⁷But the officer Lysias came and used much force to take him from us. ⁸And Lysias commanded those who wanted to accuse Paul to come to you.] By asking him questions yourself, you can decide if all these things are true." ⁹The others agreed and said that all of this was true.

¹⁰When the governor made a sign for Paul to speak, Paul said, "Governor Felix, I know you have been a judge over this nation for a long time. So I am happy to defend myself before you. ¹¹You can learn for yourself that I went to worship in Jerusalem only twelve days ago. ¹²Those who

are accusing me did not find me arguing with anyone in the Temple or stirring up the people in the synagogues or in the city. ¹³They cannot prove the things they are saying against me now. ¹⁴But I will tell you this: I worship the God of our ancestors as a follower of the Way of Jesus. The others say that the Way of Jesus is not the right way. But I believe everything that is taught in the law of Moses and that is written in the books of the Prophets. ¹⁵I have the same hope in God that they have—the hope that all people, good and bad, will surely be raised from the dead. ¹⁶This is why I always try to do what I believe is right before God and people.

¹⁷"After being away from Jerusalem for several years, I went back to bring money to my people and to offer sacrifices. ¹⁸I was doing this when they found me in the Temple. I had finished the cleansing ceremony and had not made any trouble; no people were gathering around me. ¹⁹But there were some people from Asia who should be here, standing before you. If I have really done anything wrong, they are the ones who should accuse me. ²⁰Or ask these people here if they found any wrong in me when I stood before the council in Jerusalem. ²¹But I did shout one thing when I stood before them: 'You are judging me today because I believe that people will rise from the dead!' "

²²Felix already understood much about the Way of Jesus. He stopped the trial and said, "When commander Lysias comes here, I will decide your case." ²³Felix told the officer to keep Paul guarded but to give him some freedom and to let his friends bring what he needed.

²⁴After some days Felix came with his wife, Drusilla, who was Jewish, and asked for Paul to be brought to him. He listened to Paul talk about believing in Christ Jesus. ²⁵But Felix became afraid when Paul

spoke about living right, self-control, and the time when God will judge the world. He said, "Go away now. When I have more time, I will call for you." ²⁶At the same time Felix hoped that Paul would give him some money, so he often sent for Paul and talked with him.

²⁷But after two years, Felix was replaced by Porcius Festus as governor. But Felix had left Paul in prison to please the Jews.

25 Three days after Festus became governor, he went from Caesarea to Jerusalem. ²There the leading priests and the important leaders made charges against Paul before Festus. ³They asked Festus to do them a favor. They wanted him to send Paul back to Jerusalem, because they had a plan to kill him on the way. ⁴But Festus answered that Paul would be kept in Caesarea and that he himself was returning there soon. ⁵He said, "Some of your leaders should go with me. They can accuse the man there in Caesarea, if he has really done something wrong."

⁶Festus stayed in Jerusalem another eight or ten days and then went back to Caesarea. The next day he told the soldiers to bring Paul before him. Festus was seated on the judge's seat ⁷when Paul came into the room. The people who had come from Jerusalem stood around him, making serious charges against him, which they could not prove. ⁸This is what Paul said to defend himself: "I have done nothing wrong against the law, against the Temple, or against Caesar."

⁹But Festus wanted to please the people. So he asked Paul, "Do you want to go to Jerusalem for me to judge you there on these charges?"

¹⁰Paul said, "I am standing at Caesar's judgment seat now, where I should be judged. I have done nothing wrong to them; you know this is true. ¹¹If I have done something wrong and the law says I must die, I do not ask to be saved from death. But if these charges are not true, then no one can give me to them. I want Caesar to hear my case!"

¹²Festus talked about this with his advisers. Then he said, "You have asked to see Caesar, so you will go to Caesar!"

¹³A few days later King Agrippa and Bernice came to Caesarea to visit Festus. ¹⁴They stayed there for some time, and Festus told the king about Paul's case. Festus said, "There is a man that Felix left in prison. ¹⁵When I went to Jerusalem, the leading priests and the elders there made charges against him, asking me to sentence him to death. ¹⁶But I answered, 'When a man is accused of a crime, Romans do not hand him over until he has been allowed to face his accusers and defend himself against their charges.' ¹⁷So when these people came here to Caesarea for the trial, I did not waste time. The next day I sat on the judge's seat and commanded that the man be brought in. ¹⁸They stood up and accused him, but not of any serious crime as I thought they would. ¹⁹The things they said were about their own religion and about a man named Jesus who died. But Paul said that he is still alive. ²⁰Not knowing how to find out about these questions, I asked Paul, 'Do you want to go to Jerusalem and be judged there?' ²¹But he asked to be kept in Caesarea. He wants a decision from the emperor. So I ordered that he be held until I could send him to Caesar."

²²Agrippa said to Festus, "I would also like to hear this man myself."

Festus said, "Tomorrow you will hear him."

²³The next day Agrippa and Bernice appeared with great show, acting like

very important people. They went into the judgment room with the army leaders and the important men of Caesarea. Then Festus ordered the soldiers to bring Paul in. ²⁴Festus said, "King Agrippa and all who are gathered here with us, you see this man. All the people, here and in Jerusalem, have complained to me about him, shouting that he should not live any longer. ²⁵When I judged him, I found no reason to order his death. But since he asked to be judged by Caesar, I decided to send him. ²⁶But I have nothing definite to write the emperor about him. So I have brought him before all of you—especially you, King Agrippa. I hope you can question him and give me something to write. ²⁷I think it is foolish to send a prisoner to Caesar without telling what charges are against him."

26 Agrippa said to Paul, "You may now speak to defend yourself."

Then Paul raised his hand and began to speak. ²He said, "King Agrippa, I am very blessed to stand before you and will answer all the charges the evil people make against me. ³You know so much about all the customs and the things they argue about, so please listen to me patiently.

⁴"All my people know about my whole life, how I lived from the beginning in my own country and later in Jerusalem. ⁵They have known me for a long time. If they want to, they can tell you that I was a good Pharisee. And the Pharisees obey the laws of my tradition more carefully than any other group. ⁶Now I am on trial because I hope for the promise that God made to our ancestors. ⁷This is the promise that the twelve tribes of our people hope to receive as they serve God day and night. My king, they have accused me because I hope for this same promise! ⁸Why do any of you people think it is im-

possible for God to raise people from the dead?

⁹"I, too, thought I ought to do many things against Jesus from Nazareth. ¹⁰And that is what I did in Jerusalem. The leading priests gave me the power to put many of God's people in jail, and when they were being killed, I agreed it was a good thing. ¹¹In every synagogue, I often punished them and tried to make them speak against Jesus. I was so angry against them I even went to other cities to find them and punish them.

¹²"One time the leading priests gave me permission and the power to go to Damascus. ¹³On the way there, at noon, I saw a light from heaven. It was brighter than the sun and flashed all around me and those who were traveling with me. ¹⁴We all fell to the ground. Then I heard a voice speaking to me in the Hebrew language, saying, 'Saul, Saul, why are you persecuting me? You are only hurting yourself by fighting me.' ¹⁵I said, 'Who are you, Lord?' The Lord said, 'I am Jesus, the one you are persecuting. ¹⁶Stand up! I have chosen you to be my servant and my witness—you will tell people the things that you have seen and the things that I will show you. This is why I have come to you today. ¹⁷I will keep you safe from your own people and also from the others. I am sending you to them ¹⁸to open their eyes so that they may turn away from darkness to the light, away from the power of Satan and to God. Then their sins can be forgiven, and they can have a place with those people who have been made holy by believing in me.'

¹⁹"King Agrippa, after I had this vision from heaven, I obeyed it. ²⁰I began telling people that they should change their hearts and lives and turn to God and do things to show they really had changed. I

told this first to those in Damascus, then in Jerusalem, and in every part of Judea, and also to the other people. [21]This is why the Jews took me and were trying to kill me in the Temple. [22]But God has helped me, and so I stand here today, telling all people, small and great, what I have seen. But I am saying only what Moses and the prophets said would happen— [23]that the Christ would die, and as the first to rise from the dead, he would bring light to all people."

[24]While Paul was saying these things to defend himself, Festus said loudly, "Paul, you are out of your mind! Too much study has driven you crazy!"

[25]Paul said, "Most excellent Festus, I am not crazy. My words are true and sensible. [26]King Agrippa knows about these things, and I can speak freely to him. I know he has heard about all of these things, because they did not happen off in a corner. [27]King Agrippa, do you believe what the prophets wrote? I know you believe."

[28]King Agrippa said to Paul, "Do you think you can persuade me to become a Christian in such a short time?"

[29]Paul said, "Whether it is a short or a long time, I pray to God that not only you but every person listening to me today would be saved and be like me—except for these chains I have."

[30]Then King Agrippa, Governor Festus, Bernice, and all the people sitting with them stood up [31]and left the room. Talking to each other, they said, "There is no reason why this man should die or be put in jail." [32]And Agrippa said to Festus, "We could let this man go free, but he has asked Caesar to hear his case."

27 It was decided that we would sail for Italy. An officer named Julius, who served in the emperor's army, guarded Paul and some other prisoners.

[2]We got on a ship that was from the city of Adramyttium and was about to sail to different ports in Asia. Aristarchus, a man from the city of Thessalonica in Macedonia, went with us. [3]The next day we came to Sidon. Julius was very good to Paul and gave him freedom to go visit his friends, who took care of his needs. [4]We left Sidon and sailed close to the island of Cyprus, because the wind was blowing against us. [5]We went across the sea by Cilicia and Pamphylia and landed at the city of Myra, in Lycia. [6]There the officer found a ship from Alexandria that was going to Italy, so he put us on it.

[7]We sailed slowly for many days. We had a hard time reaching Cnidus because the wind was blowing against us, and we could not go any farther. So we sailed by the south side of the island of Crete near Salmone. [8]Sailing past it was hard. Then we came to a place called Fair Havens, near the city of Lasea.

[9]We had lost much time, and it was now dangerous to sail, because it was already after the Day of Cleansing. So Paul warned them, [10]"Men, I can see there will be a lot of trouble on this trip. The ship, the cargo, and even our lives may be lost." [11]But the captain and the owner of the ship did not agree with Paul, and the officer believed what the captain and owner of the ship said. [12]Since that harbor was not a good place for the ship to stay for the winter, most of the men decided that the ship should leave. They hoped we could go to Phoenix and stay there for the winter. Phoenix, a city on the island of Crete, had a harbor which faced southwest and northwest.

[13]When a good wind began to blow from the south, the men on the ship thought, "This is the wind we wanted, and now we have it." So they pulled up the anchor, and we sailed very close to

the island of Crete. ¹⁴But then a very strong wind named the "northeaster" came from the island. ¹⁵The ship was caught in it and could not sail against it. So we stopped trying and let the wind carry us. ¹⁶When we went below a small island named Cauda, we were barely able to bring in the lifeboat. ¹⁷After the men took the lifeboat in, they tied ropes around the ship to hold it together. The men were afraid that the ship would hit the sandbanks of Syrtis, so they lowered the sail and let the wind carry the ship. ¹⁸The next day the storm was blowing us so hard that the men threw out some of the cargo. ¹⁹A day later with their own hands they threw out the ship's equipment. ²⁰When we could not see the sun or the stars for many days, and the storm was very bad, we lost all hope of being saved.

²¹After the men had gone without food for a long time, Paul stood up before them and said, "Men, you should have listened to me. You should not have sailed from Crete. Then you would not have all this trouble and loss. ²²But now I tell you to cheer up because none of you will die. Only the ship will be lost. ²³Last night an angel came to me from the God I belong to and worship. ²⁴The angel said, 'Paul, do not be afraid. You must stand before Caesar. And God has promised you that he will save the lives of everyone sailing with you.' ²⁵So men, have courage. I trust in God that everything will happen as his angel told me. ²⁶But we will crash on an island."

²⁷On the fourteenth night we were still being carried around in the Adriatic Sea. About midnight the sailors thought we were close to land, ²⁸so they lowered a rope with a weight on the end of it into the water. They found that the water was one hundred twenty feet deep. They

went a little farther and lowered the rope again. It was ninety feet deep. ²⁹The sailors were afraid that we would hit the rocks, so they threw four anchors into the water and prayed for daylight to come. ³⁰Some of the sailors wanted to leave the ship, and they lowered the lifeboat, pretending they were throwing more anchors from the front of the ship. ³¹But Paul told the officer and the other soldiers, "If these men do not stay in the ship, your lives cannot be saved." ³²So the soldiers cut the ropes and let the lifeboat fall into the water.

³³Just before dawn Paul began persuading all the people to eat something. He said, "For the past fourteen days you have been waiting and watching and not eating. ³⁴Now I beg you to eat something. You need it to stay alive. None of you will lose even one hair off your heads." ³⁵After he said this, Paul took some bread and thanked God for it before all of them. He broke off a piece and began eating. ³⁶They all felt better and started eating, too. ³⁷There were two hundred seventy-six people on the ship. ³⁸When they had eaten all they wanted, they began making the ship lighter by throwing the grain into the sea.

³⁹When daylight came, the sailors saw land. They did not know what land it was, but they saw a bay with a beach and wanted to sail the ship to the beach if they could. ⁴⁰So they cut the ropes to the anchors and left the anchors in the sea. At the same time, they untied the ropes that were holding the rudders. Then they raised the front sail into the wind and sailed toward the beach. ⁴¹But the ship hit a sandbank. The front of the ship stuck there and could not move, but the back of the ship began to break up from the big waves.

⁴²The soldiers decided to kill the pris-

oners so none of them could swim away and escape. ⁴³But Julius, the officer, wanted to let Paul live and did not allow the soldiers to kill the prisoners. Instead he ordered everyone who could swim to jump into the water first and swim to land. ⁴⁴The rest were to follow using wooden boards or pieces of the ship. And this is how all the people made it safely to land.

28 When we were safe on land, we learned that the island was called Malta. ²The people who lived there were very good to us. Because it was raining and very cold, they made a fire and welcomed all of us. ³Paul gathered a pile of sticks and was putting them on the fire when a poisonous snake came out because of the heat and bit him on the hand. ⁴The people living on the island saw the snake hanging from Paul's hand and said to each other, "This man must be a murderer! He did not die in the sea, but Justice does not want him to live." ⁵But Paul shook the snake off into the fire and was not hurt. ⁶The people thought that Paul would swell up or fall down dead. They waited and watched him for a long time, but nothing bad happened to him. So they changed their minds and said, "He is a god!"

⁷There were some fields around there owned by Publius, an important man on the island. He welcomed us into his home and was very good to us for three days. ⁸Publius' father was sick with a fever and dysentery. Paul went to him, prayed, and put his hands on the man and healed him. ⁹After this, all the other sick people on the island came to Paul, and he healed them, too. ¹⁰⁻¹¹The people on the island gave us many honors. When we were ready to leave, three months later, they gave us the things we needed.

We got on a ship from Alexandria that had stayed on the island during the winter. On the front of the ship was the sign of the twin gods. ¹²We stopped at Syracuse for three days. ¹³From there we sailed to Rhegium. The next day a wind began to blow from the south, and a day later we came to Puteoli. ¹⁴We found some believers there who asked us to stay with them for a week. Finally, we came to Rome. ¹⁵The believers in Rome heard that we were there and came out as far as the Market of Appius and the Three Inns to meet us. When Paul saw them, he was encouraged and thanked God.

¹⁶When we arrived at Rome, Paul was allowed to live alone, with the soldier who guarded him.

¹⁷Three days later Paul sent for the leaders there. When they came together, he said, "Brothers, I have done nothing against our people or the customs of our ancestors. But I was arrested in Jerusalem and given to the Romans. ¹⁸After they asked me many questions, they could find no reason why I should be killed. They wanted to let me go free, ¹⁹but the evil people there argued against that. So I had to ask to come to Rome to have my trial before Caesar. But I have no charge to bring against my own people. ²⁰That is why I wanted to see you and talk with you. I am bound with this chain because I believe in the hope of Israel."

²¹They answered Paul, "We have received no letters from Judea about you. None of our Jewish brothers who have come from there brought news or told us anything bad about you. ²²But we want to hear your ideas, because we know that people everywhere are speaking against this religious group."

²³Paul and the people chose a day for a meeting and on that day many more of the Jews met with Paul at the place he was staying. He spoke to them all day

long. Using the law of Moses and the prophets' writings, he explained the kingdom of God, and he tried to persuade them to believe these things about Jesus. ²⁴Some believed what Paul said, but others did not. ²⁵So they argued and began leaving after Paul said one more thing to them: "The Holy Spirit spoke the truth to your ancestors through Isaiah the prophet, saying,

²⁶'Go to this people and say:
   You will listen and listen, but you will
      not understand.
   You will look and look, but you will
      not learn,
²⁷because these people have become
      stubborn.
   They don't hear with their ears,
   and they have closed their eyes.
   Otherwise, they might really
      understand
   what they see with their eyes
   and hear with their ears.
They might really understand in their
      minds
   and come back to me and be
      healed.'   *Isaiah 6:9–10*

²⁸"I want you to know that God has also sent his salvation to all nations, and they will listen!" [²⁹After Paul said this, the Jews left. They were arguing very much with each other.]

³⁰Paul stayed two full years in his own rented house and welcomed all people who came to visit him. ³¹He boldly preached about the kingdom of God and taught about the Lord Jesus Christ, and no one stopped him.

ROMANS

God's Plan to Save Us

1 From Paul, a servant of Christ Jesus. God called me to be an apostle and chose me to tell the Good News.

²God promised this Good News long ago through his prophets, as it is written in the Holy Scriptures. ³⁻⁴The Good News is about God's Son, Jesus Christ our Lord. As a man, he was born from the family of David. But through the Spirit of holiness he was declared to be God's Son with great power by rising from the dead. ⁵Through Christ, God gave me the special work of an apostle, which was to lead people of all nations to believe and obey. I do this work for him. ⁶And you who are in Rome are also called to belong to Jesus Christ.

⁷To all of you in Rome whom God loves and has called to be his holy people:

Grace and peace to you from God our Father and the Lord Jesus Christ.

⁸First I want to say that I thank my God through Jesus Christ for all of you, because people everywhere in the world are talking about your faith. ⁹God, whom I serve with my whole heart by telling the Good News about his Son, knows that I always mention you ¹⁰every time I pray. I pray that I will be allowed to come to you, and this will happen if God wants it. ¹¹I want very much to see you, to give you some spiritual gift to make you strong. ¹²I mean that I want us to help each other with the faith we have. Your faith will help me, and my faith will help you. ¹³Brothers and sisters, I want you to know that I planned many times to come to you, but this has not been possible. I wanted to come so that I could help you grow spiritually as I have helped the other non-Jewish people.

¹⁴I have a duty to all people—Greeks and those who are not Greeks, the wise and the foolish. ¹⁵That is why I want so much to preach the Good News to you in Rome.

¹⁶I am not ashamed of the Good News, because it is the power God uses to save everyone who believes—to save the Jews first, and then to save non-Jews. ¹⁷The Good News shows how God makes people right with himself—that it begins and ends with faith. As the Scripture says, "But those who are right with God will live by faith."

¹⁸God's anger is shown from heaven against all the evil and wrong things people do. By their own evil lives they hide the truth. ¹⁹God shows his anger because some knowledge of him has been made clear to them. Yes, God has shown himself to them. ²⁰There are things about him that people cannot see—his eternal power and all the things that make him God. But since the beginning of the world those things have been easy to understand by what God has made. So people have no excuse for the bad things they do. ²¹They knew God, but they did not give glory to God or thank him. Their thinking became useless. Their foolish minds were filled with darkness. ²²They said they were wise, but they became fools. ²³They traded the glory of God who lives forever for the worship of idols made to look like earthly people, birds, animals, and snakes.

²⁴Because they did these things, God left them and let them go their sinful way, wanting only to do evil. As a result, they became full of sexual sin, using their bodies wrongly with each other. ²⁵They traded the truth of God for a lie. They

worshiped and served what had been created instead of the God who created those things, who should be praised forever. Amen.

²⁶Because people did those things, God left them and let them do the shameful things they wanted to do. Women stopped having natural sex and started having sex with other women. ²⁷In the same way, men stopped having natural sex and began wanting each other. Men did shameful things with other men, and in their bodies they received the punishment for those wrongs.

²⁸People did not think it was important to have a true knowledge of God. So God left them and allowed them to have their own worthless thinking and to do things they should not do. ²⁹They are filled with every kind of sin, evil, selfishness, and hatred. They are full of jealousy, murder, fighting, lying, and thinking the worst about each other. They gossip ³⁰and say evil things about each other. They hate God. They are rude and conceited and brag about themselves. They invent ways of doing evil. They do not obey their parents. ³¹They are foolish, they do not keep their promises, and they show no kindness or mercy to others. ³²They know God's law says that those who live like this should die. But they themselves not only continue to do these evil things, they applaud others who do them.

STEP 8

2 If you think you can judge others, you are wrong. When you judge them, you are really judging yourself guilty, because you do the same things they do. ²God judges those who do wrong things, and we know that his judging is right. ³You judge those who do wrong, but you do wrong yourselves. Do you think you will be able to escape the judgment of God? ⁴He has been very kind and patient, waiting for you to change, but you think noth-

ing of his kindness. Perhaps you do not understand that God is kind to you so you will change your hearts and lives. ⁵But you are stubborn and refuse to change, so you are making your own punishment even greater on the day he shows his anger. On that day everyone will see God's right judgments. ⁶God will reward or punish every person for what that person has done. ⁷Some people, by always continuing to do good, live for God's glory, for honor, and for life that has no end. God will give them life forever. ⁸But other people are selfish. They refuse to follow truth and, instead, follow evil. God will give them his punishment and anger. ⁹He will give trouble and suffering to everyone who does evil—to the Jews first and also to those who are not Jews. ¹⁰But he will give glory, honor, and peace to everyone who does good—to the Jews first and also to those who are not Jews. ¹¹For God judges all people in the same way.

¹²People who do not have the law and who are sinners will be lost, although they do not have the law. And, in the same way, those who have the law and are sinners will be judged by the law. ¹³Hearing the law does not make people right with God. It is those who obey the law who will be right with him. ¹⁴(Those who are not Jews do not have the law, but when they freely do what the law commands, they are the law for themselves. This is true even though they do not have the law. ¹⁵They show that in their hearts they know what is right and wrong, just as the law commands. And they show this by their consciences. Sometimes their thoughts tell them they did wrong, and sometimes their thoughts tell them they did right.) ¹⁶All these things will happen on the day when God, through Christ Jesus, will judge people's secret thoughts. The Good News that I preach says this.

¹⁷What about you? You call yourself a Jew. You trust in the law of Moses and brag that you are close to God. ¹⁸You know what he wants you to do and what is important, because you have learned the law. ¹⁹You think you are a guide for the blind and a light for those who are in darkness. ²⁰You think you can show foolish people what is right and teach those who know nothing. You have the law; so you think you know everything and have all truth. ²¹You teach others, so why don't you teach yourself? You tell others not to steal, but you steal. ²²You say that others must not take part in adultery, but you are guilty of that sin. You hate idols, but you steal from temples. ²³You brag about having God's law, but you bring shame to God by breaking his law, ²⁴just as the Scriptures say: "Those who are not Jews speak against God's name because of you."

²⁵If you follow the law, your circumcision has meaning. But if you break the law, it is as if you were never circumcised. ²⁶People who are not Jews are not circumcised, but if they do what the law says, it is as if they were circumcised. ²⁷You Jews have the written law and circumcision, but you break the law. So those who are not circumcised in their bodies, but still obey the law, will show that you are guilty. ²⁸They can do this because a person is not a true Jew if he is only a Jew in his physical body; true circumcision is not only on the outside of the body. ²⁹A person is a Jew only if he is a Jew inside; true circumcision is done in the heart by the Spirit, not by the written law. Such a person gets praise from God rather than from people.

3 So, do Jews have anything that other people do not have? Is there anything special about being circumcised? ²Yes, of course, there is in every way. The most important thing is this: God trusted the Jews with his teachings. ³If some Jews were not faithful to him, will that stop God from doing what he promised? ⁴No! God will continue to be true even when every person is false. As the Scriptures say:

"So you will be shown to be right
    when you speak,
and you will win your case."
Psalm 51:4

⁵When we do wrong, that shows more clearly that God is right. So can we say that God is wrong to punish us? (I am talking as people might talk.) ⁶No! If God could not punish us, he could not judge the world.

⁷A person might say, "When I lie, it really gives him glory, because my lie shows God's truth. So why am I judged a sinner?" ⁸It would be the same to say, "We should do evil so that good will come." Some people find fault with us and say we teach this, but they are wrong and deserve the punishment they will receive.

⁹So are we Jews better than others? No! We have already said that Jews and those who are not Jews are all guilty of sin. ¹⁰As the Scriptures say:

"There is no one who always does
    what is right,
    not even one.
¹¹There is no one who understands.
    There is no one who looks to God
      for help.
¹²All have turned away.
    Together, everyone has become
      useless.
There is no one who does anything
    good;
    there is not even one." *Psalm 14:1–3*
¹³"Their throats are like open graves;
    they use their tongues for telling
      lies." *Psalm 5:9*
"Their words are like snake poison."
Psalm 140:3

¹⁴ "Their mouths are full of cursing
          and hate."   *Psalm 10:7*
¹⁵"They are always ready to kill people.
¹⁶   Everywhere they go they cause
          ruin and misery.
¹⁷They don't know how to live in
          peace."   *Isaiah 59:7–8*
¹⁸   "They have no fear of God."
                              Psalm 36:1

¹⁹We know that the law's commands are for those who have the law. This stops all excuses and brings the whole world under God's judgment, ²⁰because no one can be made right with God by following the law. The law only shows us our sin.

STEP 3 ²¹But God has a way to make people right with him without the law, and he has now shown us that way which the law and the prophets told us about. ²²God makes people right with himself through their faith in Jesus Christ. This is true for all who believe in Christ, because all people are the same: ²³Everyone has sinned and fallen short of God's glorious standard, ²⁴and all need to be made right with God by his grace, which is a free gift. They need to be made free from sin through Jesus Christ. ²⁵God sent him to die in our place to take away our sins. We receive forgiveness through faith in the blood of Jesus' death. This showed that God always does what is right and fair, as in the past when he was patient and did not punish people for their sins. ²⁶And God gave Jesus to show today that he does what is right. God did this so he could judge rightly and so he could make right any person who has faith in Jesus.

²⁷So do we have a reason to brag about ourselves? No! And why not? It is the way of faith that stops all bragging, not the way of trying to obey the law. ²⁸A person is made right with God through faith, not through obeying the law. ²⁹Is God only the God of the Jews? Is he not also the God of those who are not Jews? ³⁰Of course he is, because there is only one God. He will make Jews right with him by their faith, and he will also make those who are not Jews right with him through their faith. ³¹So do we destroy the law by following the way of faith? No! Faith causes us to be what the law truly wants.

4 So what can we say that Abraham, the father of our people, learned about faith? ²If Abraham was made right by the things he did, he had a reason to brag. But this is not God's view, ³because the Scripture says, "Abraham believed God, and God accepted Abraham's faith, and that faith made him right with God."

⁴When people work, their pay is not given as a gift, but as something earned. ⁵But people cannot do any work that will make them right with God. So they must trust in him, who makes even evil people right in his sight. Then God accepts their faith, and that makes them right with him. ⁶David said the same thing. He said that people are truly blessed when God, without paying attention to their deeds, makes people right with himself.

⁷"Blessed are they
          whose sins are forgiven,
          whose wrongs are pardoned.
⁸Blessed is the person
          whom the Lord does not consider
               guilty."   *Psalm 32:1–2*

⁹Is this blessing only for those who are circumcised or also for those who are not circumcised? We have already said that God accepted Abraham's faith and that faith made him right with God. ¹⁰So how did this happen? Did God accept Abraham before or after he was circumcised? It was before his circumcision. ¹¹Abraham was circumcised to show that he was right with God through faith before he

was circumcised. So Abraham is the father of all those who believe but are not circumcised; he is the father of all believers who are accepted as being right with God. ¹²And Abraham is also the father of those who have been circumcised and who live following the faith that our father Abraham had before he was circumcised.

¹³Abraham and his descendants received the promise that they would get the whole world. He did not receive that promise through the law, but through being right with God by his faith. ¹⁴If people could receive what God promised by following the law, then faith is worthless. And God's promise to Abraham is worthless, ¹⁵because the law can only bring God's anger. But if there is no law, there is nothing to disobey.

¹⁶So people receive God's promise by having faith. This happens so the promise can be a free gift. Then all of Abraham's children can have that promise. It is not only for those who live under the law of Moses but for anyone who lives with faith like that of Abraham, who is the father of us all. ¹⁷As it is written in the Scriptures: "I am making you a father of many nations." This is true before God, the God Abraham believed, the God who gives life to the dead and who creates something out of nothing.

¹⁸There was no hope that Abraham would have children. But Abraham believed God and continued hoping, and so he became the father of many nations. As God told him, "Your descendants also will be too many to count." ¹⁹Abraham was almost a hundred years old, much past the age for having children, and Sarah could not have children. Abraham thought about all this, but his faith in God did not become weak. ²⁰He never doubted that God would keep his prom-

ise, and he never stopped believing. He grew stronger in his faith and gave praise to God. ²¹Abraham felt sure that God was able to do what he had promised. ²²So, "God accepted Abraham's faith, and that faith made him right with God." ²³Those words ("God accepted Abraham's faith") were written not only for Abraham ²⁴but also for us. God will accept us also because we believe in the One who raised Jesus our Lord from the dead. ²⁵Jesus was given to die for our sins, and he was raised from the dead to make us right with God.

5 Since we have been made right with God by our faith, we have peace with God. This happened through our Lord Jesus Christ, ²who through our faith has brought us into that blessing of God's grace that we now enjoy. And we are happy because of the hope we have of sharing God's glory. ³We also have joy with our troubles, because we know that these troubles produce patience. ⁴And patience produces character, and character produces hope. ⁵And this hope will never disappoint us, because God has poured out his love to fill our hearts. He gave us his love through the Holy Spirit, whom God has given to us.

⁶When we were unable to help ourselves, at the right time, Christ died for us, although we were living against God. ⁷Very few people will die to save the life of someone else. Although perhaps for a good person someone might possibly die. ⁸But God shows his great love for us in this way: Christ died for us while we were still sinners.

⁹So through Christ we will surely be saved from God's anger, because we have been made right with God by the blood of Christ's death. ¹⁰While we were God's enemies, he made us his friends through the death of his Son. Surely, now

STEP 3

STEP 11

STEP 3

STEP 3

that we are his friends, he will save us through his Son's life. ¹¹And not only that, but now we are also very happy in God through our Lord Jesus Christ. Through him we are now God's friends again.

¹²Sin came into the world because of what one man did, and with sin came death. This is why everyone must die—because everyone sinned. ¹³Sin was in the world before the law of Moses, but sin is not counted against us as breaking a command when there is no law. ¹⁴But from the time of Adam to the time of Moses, everyone had to die, even those who had not sinned by breaking a command, as Adam had.

Adam was like the One who was coming in the future. ¹⁵But God's free gift is not like Adam's sin. Many people died because of the sin of that one man. But the grace from God was much greater; many people received God's gift of life by the grace of the one man, Jesus Christ. ¹⁶After Adam sinned once, he was judged guilty. But the gift of God is different. God's free gift came after many sins, and it makes people right with God. ¹⁷One man sinned, and so death ruled all people because of that one man. But now those people who accept God's full grace and the great gift of being made right with him will surely have true life and rule through the one man, Jesus Christ.

¹⁸So as one sin of Adam brought the punishment of death to all people, one good act that Christ did makes all people right with God. And that brings true life for all. ¹⁹One man disobeyed God, and many became sinners. In the same way, one man obeyed God, and many will be made right. ²⁰The law came to make sin worse. But when sin grew worse, God's grace increased. ²¹Sin once used death to rule us, but God gave people more of his grace so that grace could rule by making

people right with him. And this brings life forever through Jesus Christ our Lord.

6 So do you think we should continue sinning so that God will give us even more grace? ²No! We died to our old sinful lives, so how can we continue living in sin? ³Did you forget that all of us became part of Christ when we were baptized? We shared his death in our baptism. ⁴When we were baptized, we were buried with Christ and shared his death. So, just as Christ was raised from the dead by the wonderful power of the Father, we also can live a new life.

STEP 5

⁵Christ died, and we have been joined with him by dying too. So we will also be joined with him by rising from the dead as he did. ⁶We know that our old life died with Christ on the cross so that our sinful selves would have no power over us and we would not be slaves to sin. ⁷Anyone who has died is made free from sin's control.

⁸If we died with Christ, we know we will also live with him. ⁹Christ was raised from the dead, and we know that he cannot die again. Death has no power over him now. ¹⁰Yes, when Christ died, he died to defeat the power of sin one time—enough for all time. He now has a new life, and his new life is with God. ¹¹In the same way, you should see yourselves as being dead to the power of sin and alive with God through Christ Jesus.

STEP 6

¹²So, do not let sin control your life here on earth so that you do what your sinful self wants to do. ¹³Do not offer the parts of your body to serve sin, as things to be used in doing evil. Instead, offer yourselves to God as people who have died and now live. Offer the parts of your body to God to be used in doing good. ¹⁴Sin will not be your master, because you are not under law but under God's grace.

¹⁵So what should we do? Should we sin because we are under grace and not

STEP 6

Were entirely ready to have God
remove all these defects of character.

Romans 6:11–12

Recovering from your hurts, habits, and hang-ups is like going through a whole series of deaths and rebirths. You die time and again to the old way of escaping into your addiction. Over and over God's Spirit will give birth to new ways of living that focus on loving God and caring more about others than about yourself.

As you work through Step 6, you ask God to remove defects of character. At times, getting rid of old ways of acting out and thinking about yourself feels like dying. God may ask you to stop clinging in a needy, pathetic way to a harmful relationship. That can feel like death. God may ask you to die to your obsession with money or control. You may have to die to dependency on mood-altering chemicals or food. If you don't, you can never satisfy your deepest spiritual needs. You have to be alive to do that.

The Holy Spirit can only recreate the life of Jesus in you to the extent that you die to your old selfish, destructive ways. You need to ask God's help in this hard process of dying in order to live, for "half measures availed us nothing" (*Alcoholics Anonymous*, p. 59).

FOR YOUR NEXT **STEP 6** MEDITATION, TURN TO **PAGE 273**. ▶▶

under law? No! ¹⁶Surely you know that when you give yourselves like slaves to obey someone, then you are really slaves of that person. The person you obey is your master. You can follow sin, which brings spiritual death, or you can obey God, which makes you right with him. ¹⁷In the past you were slaves to sin—sin controlled you. But thank God, you fully obeyed the things that you were taught. ¹⁸You were made free from sin, and now you are slaves to goodness. ¹⁹I use this example because this is hard for you to understand. In the past you offered the parts of your body to be slaves to sin and evil; you lived only for evil. In the same way now you must give yourselves to slaves of goodness. Then you will live only for God.

²⁰In the past you were slaves to sin, and goodness did not control you. ²¹You did evil things, and now you are ashamed of them. Those things only bring death. ²²But now you are free from sin and have become slaves of God. This brings you a life that is only for God, and this gives you life forever. ²³The payment for sin is death. But God gives us the free gift of life forever in Christ Jesus our Lord.

7 Brothers and sisters, all of you understand the law of Moses. So surely you know that the law rules over people only while they are alive. ²For example, a woman must stay married to her husband as long as he is alive. But if her husband dies, she is free from the law of marriage. ³But if she marries another man while her husband is still alive, the law says she is guilty of adultery. But if her husband dies, she is free from the law of marriage. Then if she marries another man, she is not guilty of adultery.

⁴In the same way, my brothers and sisters, your old selves died, and you became free from the law through the body of Christ. This happened so that you might belong to someone else—the One who was raised from the dead—and so that we might be used in service to God. ⁵In the past, we were ruled by our sinful selves. The law made us want to do sinful things that controlled our bodies, so the things we did were bringing us death. ⁶In the past, the law held us like prisoners, but our old selves died, and we were made free from the law. So now we serve God in a new way with the Spirit, and not in the old way with written rules.

⁷You might think I am saying that sin and the law are the same thing. That is not true. But the law was the only way I could learn what sin meant. I would never have known what it means to want to take something belonging to someone else if the law had not said, "You must not want to take your neighbor's things." ⁸And sin found a way to use that command and cause me to want all kinds of things I should not want. But without the law, sin has no power. ⁹I was alive before I knew the law. But when the law's command came to me, then sin began to live, ¹⁰and I died. The command was meant to bring life, but for me it brought death. ¹¹Sin found a way to fool me by using the command to make me die.

¹²So the law is holy, and the command is holy and right and good. ¹³Does this mean that something that is good brought death to me? No! Sin used something that is good to bring death to me. This happened so that I could see what sin is really like; the command was used to show that sin is very evil.

¹⁴We know that the law is spiritual, but I am not spiritual since sin rules me as if I were its slave. ¹⁵I do not understand the things I do. I do not do what I want to do, and I do the things I hate. ¹⁶And if I do not want to do the hated things I do, that

means I agree that the law is good. [17]But I am not really the one who is doing these hated things; it is sin living in me that does them. [18]Yes, I know that nothing good lives in me—I mean nothing good lives in the part of me that is earthly and sinful. I want to do the things that are good, but I do not do them. [19]I do not do the good things I want to do, but I do the bad things I do not want to do. [20]So if I do things I do not want to do, then I am not the one doing them. It is sin living in me that does these things.

[21]So I have learned this rule: When I want to do good, evil is there with me. [22]In my mind, I am happy with God's law. [23]But I see another law working in my body, which makes war against the law that my mind accepts. That other law working in my body is the law of sin, and it makes me its prisoner. [24]What a miserable man I am! Who will save me from this body that brings me death? [25]I thank God for saving me through Jesus Christ our Lord!

So in my mind I am a slave to God's law, but in my sinful self I am a slave to the law of sin.

8 So now, those who are in Christ Jesus are not judged guilty. [2]Through Christ Jesus the law of the Spirit that brings life made you free from the law that brings sin and death. [3]The law was without power, because the law was made weak by our sinful selves. But God did what the law could not do. He sent his own Son to earth with the same human life that others use for sin. By sending his Son to be an offering for sin, God used a human life to destroy sin. [4]He did this so that we could be the kind of people the law correctly wants us to be. Now we do not live following our sinful selves, but we live following the Spirit.

[5]Those who live following their sinful selves think only about things that their sinful selves want. But those who live following the Spirit are thinking about the things the Spirit wants them to do. [6]If people's thinking is controlled by the sinful self, there is death. But if their thinking is controlled by the Spirit, there is life and peace. [7]When people's thinking is controlled by the sinful self, they are against God, because they refuse to obey God's law and really are not even able to obey God's law. [8]Those people who are ruled by their sinful selves cannot please God.

[9]But you are not ruled by your sinful selves. You are ruled by the Spirit, if that Spirit of God really lives in you. But the person who does not have the Spirit of Christ does not belong to Christ. [10]Your body will always be dead because of sin. But if Christ is in you, then the Spirit gives you life, because Christ made you right with God. [11]God raised Jesus from the dead, and if God's Spirit is living in you, he will also give life to your bodies that die. God is the One who raised Christ from the dead, and he will give life through his Spirit that lives in you.

[12]So, my brothers and sisters, we must not be ruled by our sinful selves or live the way our sinful selves want. [13]If you use your lives to do the wrong things your sinful selves want, you will die spiritually. But if you use the Spirit's help to stop doing the wrong things you do with your body, you will have true life.

[14]The true children of God are those who let God's Spirit lead them. [15]The Spirit we received does not make us slaves again to fear; it makes us children of God. With that Spirit we cry out, "Father." [16]And the Spirit himself joins with our spirits to say we are God's children. [17]If we are God's children, we will receive blessings from God together with Christ. But we must suffer as Christ suffered so that we will have glory as Christ has glory.

STEP 1

We admitted we were powerless
over our dependencies—that our lives
had become unmanageable.

Romans 7:18-20

Here are two of the worst symptoms of a true addiction. First, you feel your identity is getting swallowed up in your habit. Second, you go against your conscience over and over and can't stop yourself. The apostle Paul had this sort of thing in mind when he told the Roman Christians, "If I do things I do not want to do, then I am not the one doing them. It is sin living in me that does those things" (verse 20).

Paul wasn't saying he wasn't responsible for the bad things he did. He was observing that sinful habits can take over and cripple your willpower. Sometimes it helps addicts to ask, "Is the dog wagging the tail, or is the tail wagging the dog?" When the tail takes over, the dog's in trouble. Let's say you're a workaholic who wants a nice home and a happy family, so you set out to make enough money so you can live the way you want to. But somewhere along the way, you get so involved in work that there's no time or energy left for a home or a family. And you can't stop. Your fears and perfectionism won't let you. The tail is wagging the dog. It's whipping the poor pooch all over the room.

You hit bottom when you have to say "I do the bad things I do not want to do" (verse 19) and you feel helpless and hopeless ever to climb out of that dark pit. That gut-wrenching insight forces you in the cold light of day to admit your powerlessness. God can use that insight to launch your recovery.

FOR YOUR NEXT **STEP 1** MEDITATION, TURN TO **PAGE 385.** ▶▶

¹⁸The sufferings we have now are nothing compared to the great glory that will be shown to us. ¹⁹Everything God made is waiting with excitement for God to show his children's glory completely. ²⁰Everything God made was changed to become useless, not by its own wish but because God wanted it and because all along there was this hope: ²¹that everything God made would be set free from ruin to have the freedom and glory that belong to God's children.

²²We know that everything God made has been waiting until now in pain, like a woman ready to give birth. ²³Not only the world, but we also have been waiting with pain inside us. We have the Spirit as the first part of God's promise. So we are waiting for God to finish making us his own children, which means our bodies will be made free. ²⁴We were saved, and we have this hope. If we see what we are waiting for, that is not really hope. People do not hope for something they already have. ²⁵But we are hoping for something we do not have yet, and we are waiting for it patiently.

²⁶Also, the Spirit helps us with our weakness. We do not know how to pray as we should. But the Spirit himself speaks to God for us, even begs God for us with deep feelings that words cannot explain. ²⁷God can see what is in people's hearts. And he knows what is in the mind of the Spirit, because the Spirit speaks to God for his people in the way God wants. ²⁸We know that in everything God works for the good of those who love him. They are the people he called, because that was his plan. ²⁹God knew them before he made the world, and he chose them to be like his Son so that Jesus would be the firstborn of many brothers and sisters. ³⁰God planned for them to be like his Son; and those he planned to

be like his Son, he also called; and those he called, he also made right with him; and those he made right, he also glorified.

³¹So what should we say about this? If God is for us, no one can defeat us. ³²He did not spare his own Son but gave him for us all. So with Jesus, God will surely give us all things. ³³Who can accuse the people God has chosen? No one, because God is the One who makes them right. ³⁴Who can say God's people are guilty? No one, because Christ Jesus died, but he was also raised from the dead, and now he is on God's right side, appealing to God for us. ³⁵Can anything separate us from the love Christ has for us? Can troubles or problems or sufferings or hunger or nakedness or danger or violent death? ³⁶As it is written in the Scriptures:

"For you we are in danger of death all the time.

People think we are worth no more than sheep to be killed."   Psalm 44:22

³⁷But in all these things we are completely victorious through God who showed his love for us. ³⁸Yes, I am sure that neither death, nor life, nor angels, nor ruling spirits, nothing now, nothing in the future, no powers, ³⁹nothing above us, nothing below us, nor anything else in the whole world will ever be able to separate us from the love of God that is in Christ Jesus our Lord.

9 I am in Christ, and I am telling you the truth; I do not lie. My conscience is ruled by the Holy Spirit, and it tells me I am not lying. ²I have great sorrow and always feel much sadness. ³I wish I could help my Jewish brothers and sisters, my people. I would even wish that I were cursed and cut off from Christ if that would help them. ⁴They are the people of Israel, God's chosen children. They have

STEP 11

Sought through prayer and meditation to improve
our conscious contact with God **as we understood
Him,** praying only for knowledge of His will
for us and the power to carry that out.

Romans 8:26–28

Step 11 depends on two really important ideas. First, your
emotional recovery from addiction depends on your spiritual
strength. And second, your spiritual strength depends on the
quality of your regular communication with God. You talk to God by
praying. Maybe prayer seems mysterious to you. Maybe you think
only really holy people can talk to God and expect him to pay any
attention to them.

Romans 8:26–27 should give you the confidence to talk freely and
openly to God about everything that concerns you. Sure, there's
mystery here—what with talk about the Holy Spirit praying along
with you to make sure your prayers are effective. But isn't that
great news? Your prayers are supercharged and reach God with
more power than you can imagine. In a sense, your prayers reach
God with all the selfish bits filtered out. God sees what's in your
heart and sifts the good from the bad, and the Holy Spirit prays for
us "in the way God wants" (verse 27). You'll learn to do that more
and more on your own—"asking God that you will know fully what
he wants" (Colossians 1:9).

FOR YOUR NEXT **STEP 11** MEDITATION, TURN TO **PAGE 262.** ▶▶

seen the glory of God, and they have the agreements that God made between himself and his people. God gave them the law of Moses and the right way of worship and his promises. ⁵They are the descendants of our great ancestors, and they are the earthly family into which Christ was born, who is God over all. Praise him forever! Amen.

⁶It is not that God failed to keep his promise to them. But only some of the people of Israel are truly God's people, ⁷and only some of Abraham's descendants are true children of Abraham. But God said to Abraham: "The descendants I promised you will be from Isaac." ⁸This means that not all of Abraham's descendants are God's true children. Abraham's true children are those who become God's children because of the promise God made to Abraham. ⁹God's promise to Abraham was this: "At the right time I will return, and Sarah will have a son." ¹⁰And that is not all. Rebekah's sons had the same father, our father Isaac. ¹¹⁻¹²But before the two boys were born, God told Rebekah, "The older will serve the younger." This was before the boys had done anything good or bad. God said this so that the one chosen would be chosen because of God's own plan. He was chosen because he was the one God wanted to call, not because of anything he did. ¹³As the Scripture says, "I loved Jacob, but I hated Esau."

¹⁴So what should we say about this? Is God unfair? In no way. ¹⁵God said to Moses, "I will show kindness to anyone to whom I want to show kindness, and I will show mercy to anyone to whom I want to show mercy." ¹⁶So God will choose the one to whom he decides to show mercy; his choice does not depend on what people want or try to do. ¹⁷The Scripture says to the king of Egypt: "I made you king for this reason: to show my power in you so that my name will be talked about in all the earth." ¹⁸So God shows mercy where he wants to show mercy, and he makes stubborn the people he wants to make stubborn.

¹⁹So one of you will ask me: "Then why does God blame us for our sins? Who can fight his will?" ²⁰You are only human, and human beings have no right to question God. An object should not ask the person who made it, "Why did you make me like this?" ²¹The potter can make anything he wants to make. He can use the same clay to make one thing for special use and another thing for daily use.

²²It is the same way with God. He wanted to show his anger and to let people see his power. But he patiently stayed with those people he was angry with—people who were made ready to be destroyed. ²³He waited with patience so that he could make known his rich glory to the people who receive his mercy. He has prepared these people to have his glory, ²⁴and we are those people whom God called. He called us not from the Jews only but also from those who are not Jews. ²⁵As the Scripture says in Hosea:

"I will say, 'You are my people'
    to those I had called 'not my
        people.'
And I will show my love
    to those people I did not love."

Hosea 2:1, 23

²⁶"They were called,
    'You are not my people,'
but later they will be called
    'children of the living God.'"

Hosea 1:10

²⁷And Isaiah cries out about Israel:
"The people of Israel are many,
    like the grains of sand by the sea.
But only a few of them will be
        saved,

28   because the Lord will quickly and
            completely punish the
            people on the earth."
                                    Isaiah 10:22–23

29It is as Isaiah said:
"The Lord All-Powerful
    allowed a few of our descendants
        to live.
Otherwise we would have been
            completely destroyed
    like the cities of Sodom and
        Gomorrah."   *Isaiah 1:9*

30So what does all this mean? Those who are not Jews were not trying to make themselves right with God, but they were made right with God because of their faith. 31The people of Israel tried to follow a law to make themselves right with God. But they did not succeed, 32because they tried to make themselves right by the things they did instead of trusting in God to make them right. They stumbled over the stone that causes people to stumble. 33As it is written in the Scripture:

"I will put in Jerusalem a stone that
            causes people to stumble,
    a rock that makes them fall.
Anyone who trusts in him will never
        be disappointed."
                                    Isaiah 8:14; 28:16

10 Brothers and sisters, the thing I want most is for all the Jews to be saved. That is my prayer to God. 2I can say this about them: They really try to follow God, but they do not know the right way. 3Because they did not know the way that God makes people right with him, they tried to make themselves right in their own way. So they did not accept God's way of making people right. 4Christ ended the law so that everyone who believes in him may be right with God.

5Moses writes about being made right by following the law. He says, "A person who obeys these things will live because of them." 6But this is what the Scripture says about being made right through faith: "Don't say to yourself, 'Who will go up into heaven?' " (That means, "Who will go up to heaven and bring Christ down to earth?") 7"And do not say, 'Who will go down into the world below?' " (That means, "Who will go down and bring Christ up from the dead?") 8This is what the Scripture says: "The word is near you; it is in your mouth and in your heart." That is the teaching of faith that we are telling. 9If you declare with your mouth, "Jesus is Lord," and if you believe in your heart that God raised Jesus from the dead, you will be saved. 10We believe with our hearts, and so we are made right with God. And we declare with our mouths that we believe, and so we are saved. 11As the Scripture says, "Anyone who trusts in him will never be disappointed." 12That Scripture says "anyone" because there is no difference between those who are Jews and those who are not. The same Lord is the Lord of all and gives many blessings to all who trust in him, 13as the Scripture says, "Anyone who calls on the Lord will be saved."

14But before people can ask the Lord for help, they must believe in him; and before they can believe in him, they must hear about him; and for them to hear about the Lord, someone must tell them; 15and before someone can go and tell them, that person must be sent. It is written, "How beautiful is the person who comes to bring good news." 16But not all the Jews accepted the good news. Isaiah said, "Lord, who believed what we told them?" 17So faith comes from hearing the Good News, and people hear the Good News when someone tells them about Christ.

18But I ask: Didn't people hear the

STEP
3

STEP
12

Good News? Yes, they heard—as the Scripture says:

> "Their message went out through all
> the world;
> their words go everywhere on
> earth."   *Psalm 19:4*

¹⁹Again I ask: Didn't the people of Israel understand? Yes, they did understand. First, Moses says:

> "I will use those who are not a nation
> to make you jealous.
> I will use a nation that does not
> understand to make you
> angry."   *Deuteronomy 32:21*

²⁰Then Isaiah is bold enough to say:

> "I was found by those who were not
> asking me for help.
> I made myself known to people
> who were not looking for
> me."   *Isaiah 65:1*

²¹But about Israel God says,

> "All day long I stood ready to accept
> people who disobey and are
> stubborn."   *Isaiah 65:2*

11 So I ask: Did God throw out his people? No! I myself am an Israelite from the family of Abraham, from the tribe of Benjamin. ²God chose the Israelites to be his people before they were born, and he has not thrown his people out. Surely you know what the Scripture says about Elijah, how he prayed to God against the people of Israel. ³"Lord," he said, "they have killed your prophets, and they have destroyed your altars. I am the only prophet left, and now they are trying to kill me, too." ⁴But what answer did God give Elijah? He said, "But I have left seven thousand people in Israel who have never bowed down before Baal." ⁵It is the same now. There are a few people that God has chosen by his grace. ⁶And if he chose them by grace, it is not for the things they have done. If they could be made God's people by what

they did, God's gift of grace would not really be a gift.

⁷So this is what has happened: Although the Israelites tried to be right with God, they did not succeed, but the ones God chose did become right with him. The others were made stubborn and refused to listen to God. ⁸As it is written in the Scriptures:

> "God gave the people a dull mind so
> they could not understand."
>   *Isaiah 29:10*
>
> "He closed their eyes so they could
> not see
> and their ears so they could not
> hear.
> This continues until today."
>   *Deuteronomy 29:4*

⁹And David says:

> "Let their own feasts trap them and
> cause their ruin;
> let their feasts cause them to
> stumble and be paid back.
> ¹⁰Let their eyes be closed so they
> cannot see
> and their backs be forever weak
> from troubles."
>   *Psalm 69:22–23*

¹¹So I ask: When the Jews fell, did that fall destroy them? No! But their failure brought salvation to those who are not Jews, in order to make the Jews jealous. ¹²The Jews' failure brought rich blessings for the world, and the Jews' loss brought rich blessings for the non-Jewish people. So surely the world will receive much richer blessings when enough Jews become the kind of people God wants.

¹³Now I am speaking to you who are not Jews. I am an apostle to those who are not Jews, and since I have that work, I will make the most of it. ¹⁴I hope I can make my own people jealous and, in that way, help some of them to be saved. ¹⁵When God turned away from the Jews,

he became friends with other people in the world. So when God accepts the Jews, surely that will bring them life after death.

¹⁶If the first piece of bread is offered to God, then the whole loaf is made holy. If the roots of a tree are holy, then the tree's branches are holy too.

¹⁷It is as if some of the branches from an olive tree have been broken off. You non-Jewish people are like the branch of a wild olive tree that has been joined to that first tree. You now share the strength and life of the first tree, the Jews. ¹⁸So do not brag about those branches that were broken off. If you brag, remember that you do not support the root, but the root supports you. ¹⁹You will say, "Branches were broken off so that I could be joined to their tree." ²⁰That is true. But those branches were broken off because they did not believe, and you continue to be part of the tree only because you believe. Do not be proud, but be afraid. ²¹If God did not let the natural branches of that tree stay, then he will not let you stay if you don't believe.

²²So you see that God is kind and also very strict. He punishes those who stop following him. But God is kind to you, if you continue following in his kindness. If you do not, you will be cut off from the tree. ²³And if the Jews will believe in God again, he will accept them back. God is able to put them back where they were. ²⁴It is not natural for a wild branch to be part of a good tree. And you who are not Jews are like a branch cut from a wild olive tree and joined to a good olive tree. But since those Jews are like a branch that grew from the good tree, surely they can be joined to their own tree again.

²⁵I want you to understand this secret, brothers and sisters, so you will understand that you do not know everything: Part of Israel has been made stubborn, but that will change when many who are not Jews have come to God. ²⁶And that is how all Israel will be saved. It is written in the Scriptures:

"The Savior will come from Jerusalem;
    he will take away all evil from the
        family of Jacob.
²⁷And I will make this agreement with
        those people
    when I take away their sins."
                              Isaiah 59:20–21; 27:9

²⁸The Jews refuse to accept the Good News, so they are God's enemies. This has happened to help you who are not Jews. But the Jews are still God's chosen people, and he loves them very much because of the promises he made to their ancestors. ²⁹God never changes his mind about the people he calls and the things he gives them. ³⁰At one time you refused to obey God. But now you have received mercy, because those people refused to obey. ³¹And now the Jews refuse to obey, because God showed mercy to you. But this happened so that they also can receive mercy from him. ³²God has given all people over to their stubborn ways so that he can show mercy to all.

³³Yes, God's riches are very great, and his wisdom and knowledge have no end! No one can explain the things God decides or understand his ways. ³⁴As the Scripture says,

"Who has known the mind of the
        Lord,
    or who has been able to give him
        advice?"   *Isaiah 40:13*
³⁵"No one has ever given God anything
        that he must pay back."   *Job 41:11*
³⁶Yes, God made all things, and everything continues through him and for him. To him be the glory forever! Amen.

12 So brothers and sisters, since God has shown us great mercy, I beg you to offer your lives as a living sacrifice to him. Your offering must be only for God and pleasing to him, which is the spiritual way for you to worship. ²Do not be shaped by this world; instead be changed within by a new way of thinking. Then you will be able to decide what God wants for you; you will know what is good and pleasing to him and what is perfect. ³Because God has given me a special gift, I have something to say to everyone among you. Do not think you are better than you are. You must decide what you really are by the amount of faith God has given you. ⁴Each one of us has a body with many parts, and these parts all have different uses. ⁵In the same way, we are many, but in Christ we are all one body. Each one is a part of that body, and each part belongs to all the other parts. ⁶We all have different gifts, each of which came because of the grace God gave us. The person who has the gift of prophecy should use that gift in agreement with the faith. ⁷Anyone who has the gift of serving should serve. Anyone who has the gift of teaching should teach. ⁸Whoever has the gift of encouraging others should encourage. Whoever has the gift of giving to others should give freely. Anyone who has the gift of being a leader should try hard when he leads. Whoever has the gift of showing mercy to others should do so with joy.

⁹Your love must be real. Hate what is evil, and hold on to what is good. ¹⁰Love each other like brothers and sisters. Give each other more honor than you want for yourselves. ¹¹Do not be lazy but work hard, serving the Lord with all your heart. ¹²Be joyful because you have hope. Be patient when trouble comes, and pray at all times. ¹³Share with God's people who need help. Bring strangers in need into your homes.

¹⁴Wish good for those who harm you; wish them well and do not curse them. ¹⁵Be happy with those who are happy, and be sad with those who are sad. ¹⁶Live in peace with each other. Do not be proud, but make friends with those who seem unimportant. Do not think how smart you are.

¹⁷If someone does wrong to you, do not pay him back by doing wrong to him. Try to do what everyone thinks is right. ¹⁸Do your best to live in peace with everyone. ¹⁹My friends, do not try to punish others when they wrong you, but wait for God to punish them with his anger. It is written: "I will punish those who do wrong; I will repay them," says the Lord. ²⁰But you should do this:

"If your enemy is hungry, feed him;
    if he is thirsty, give him a drink.
Doing this will be like pouring burning
        coals on his head."
                        Proverbs 25:21–22

²¹Do not let evil defeat you, but defeat evil by doing good.

13 All of you must yield to the government rulers. No one rules unless God has given him the power to rule, and no one rules now without that power from God. ²So those who are against the government are really against what God has commanded. And they will bring punishment on themselves. ³Those who do right do not have to fear the rulers; only those who do wrong fear them. Do you want to be unafraid of the rulers? Then do what is right, and they will praise you. ⁴The ruler is God's servant to help you. But if you do wrong, then be afraid. He has the power to punish; he is God's servant to punish those who do wrong. ⁵So you must yield to the government, not only because you might be punished, but because you know it is right.

⁶This is also why you pay taxes. Rulers

STEP 10

Continued to take personal inventory
and when we were wrong promptly admitted it.

Romans 12:3

Sooner or later you will find yourself wondering if all you've accomplished in recovery has been because of your own willpower. The apostle Paul's advice in this verse can keep you from getting a big head.

That doesn't mean you should beat yourself up over every little slip-up. Humility doesn't mean you hate yourself. Paul says that "you must decide what you really are," which simply means to think clearly and fairly about yourself. Step 10 can help you be objective. Honesty that includes hope for the future is important to your spiritual and emotional well-being.

Making daily and weekly inventories of your life helps you "decide what you really are." Are you knowing success in breaking old dependencies? Praise God and keep right on asking for his help. Have you failed to handle a problem? Quickly admit it and ask God to help you make it right. Your personal inventory shows you who you are and helps you find the direction God wants for your life.

FOR YOUR NEXT **STEP 10** MEDITATION, TURN TO **PAGE 291.** ▶▶

are working for God and give their time to their work. ⁷Pay everyone, then, what you owe. If you owe any kind of tax, pay it. Show respect and honor to them all.

STEP 8

⁸Do not owe people anything, except always owe love to each other, because the person who loves others has obeyed all the law. ⁹The law says, "You must not be guilty of adultery. You must not murder anyone. You must not steal. You must not want to take your neighbor's things." All these commands and all others are really only one rule: "Love your neighbor as you love yourself." ¹⁰Love never hurts a neighbor, so loving is obeying all the law.

STEP 4

¹¹Do this because we live in an important time. It is now time for you to wake up from your sleep, because our salvation is nearer now than when we first believed. ¹²The "night" is almost finished, and the "day" is almost here. So we should stop doing things that belong to darkness and take up the weapons used for fighting in the light. ¹³Let us live in a right way, like people who belong to the day. We should not have wild parties or get drunk. There should be no sexual sins of any kind, no fighting or jealousy. ¹⁴But clothe yourselves with the Lord Jesus Christ and forget about satisfying your sinful self.

14 Accept into your group someone who is weak in faith, and do not argue about opinions. ²One person believes it is right to eat all kinds of food. But another, who is weak, believes it is right to eat only vegetables. ³The one who knows that it is right to eat any kind of food must not reject the one who eats only vegetables. And the person who eats only vegetables must not think that the one who eats all foods is wrong, because God has accepted that person. ⁴You cannot judge another person's servant. The

master decides if the servant is doing well or not. And the Lord's servant will do well because the Lord helps him do well.

⁵Some think that one day is more important than another, and others think that every day is the same. Let all be sure in their own mind. ⁶Those who think one day is more important than other days are doing that for the Lord. And those who eat all kinds of food are doing that for the Lord, and they give thanks to God. Others who refuse to eat some foods do that for the Lord, and they give thanks to God. ⁷We do not live or die for ourselves.

STEP 8

⁸If we live, we are living for the Lord, and if we die, we are dying for the Lord. So living or dying, we belong to the Lord.

⁹The reason Christ died and rose from the dead to live again was so he would be Lord over both the dead and the living. ¹⁰So why do you judge your brothers or sisters in Christ? And why do you think you are better than they are? We will all stand before God to be judged, ¹¹because it is written in the Scriptures:

" 'As surely as I live,' says the Lord,
'Everyone will bow before me;
everyone will say that I am God.' "
                                                    Isaiah 45:23

STEP 5

¹²So each of us will have to answer to God.

¹³For that reason we should stop judging each other. We must make up our minds not to do anything that will make another Christian sin. ¹⁴I am in the Lord Jesus, and I know that there is no food that is wrong to eat. But if a person believes something is wrong, that thing is wrong for him. ¹⁵If you hurt your brother's or sister's faith because of something you eat, you are not really following the way of love. Do not destroy someone's faith by eating food he thinks is wrong, because Christ died for him. ¹⁶Do not allow what you think is good to become what others say is evil. ¹⁷In the kingdom of God,

STEP 4

Made a searching and fearless moral
inventory of ourselves.

Romans 13:11–14

Both Romans 13:11 and Step 4 contain wake-up calls. People struggling with addictions, compulsive behaviors, and codependent relationships need wake-up calls. It's like they are a little groggy, not quite aware of why they do what they do and feel what they feel. There were probably times when you felt like a sleepwalker, doing this and that because your habit told you to, even while it felt dreamy and unreal. God calls you to wake up and stop living like that. The night of dead emotions is over; the day of your recovery has dawned.

However, you can't throw off the "things that belong to darkness" (verse 12) until you're completely sure of what they are. Your inventory helps you nail down the identity of your things of darkness. Basically, the apostle Paul asks you to face reality. Don't deny or excuse. Don't get hot with anger or chilled by fear. Consciously choose to let the light of God's steady, loving gaze look at you.

Once you've stripped off your old way of handling life's problems, Paul tells you in verse 14 to "clothe yourselves with the Lord Jesus Christ." You do this by relying on his strength, lining up your thoughts with his Word, and choosing to do what he wants you to.

FOR YOUR NEXT **STEP 4** MEDITATION, TURN TO **PAGE 231.** ▶▶

eating and drinking are not important. The important things are living right with God, peace, and joy in the Holy Spirit. [18]Anyone who serves Christ by living this way is pleasing God and will be accepted by other people.

STEP 9

[19]So let us try to do what makes peace and helps one another. [20]Do not let the eating of food destroy the work of God. All foods are all right to eat, but it is wrong to eat food that causes someone else to sin. [21]It is better not to eat meat or drink wine or do anything that will cause your brother or sister to sin.

STEP 5

[22]Your beliefs about these things should be kept secret between you and God. People are happy if they can do what they think is right without feeling guilty. [23]But those who eat something without being sure it is right are wrong because they did not believe it was right. Anything that is done without believing it is right is a sin.

15We who are strong in faith should help the weak with their weaknesses, and not please only ourselves.

STEP 9

[2]Let each of us please our neighbors for their good, to help them be stronger in faith. [3]Even Christ did not live to please himself. It was as the Scriptures said: "When people insult you, it hurts me." [4]Everything that was written in the past was written to teach us. The Scriptures give us patience and encouragement so that we can have hope. [5]May the patience and encouragement that come from God allow you to live in harmony with each other the way Christ Jesus wants. [6]Then you will all be joined together, and you will give glory to God the Father of our Lord Jesus Christ. [7]Christ accepted you, so you should accept each other, which will bring glory to God. [8]I tell you that Christ became a servant of the Jews to show that God's promises to the Jewish ancestors are true. [9]And he also did this so that those who are not Jews could give glory to God for the mercy he gives to them. It is written in the Scriptures:

> "So I will praise you among the non-Jewish people.
> I will sing praises to your name."
> *Psalm 18:49*

[10]The Scripture also says,

> "Be happy, you who are not Jews, together with his people."
> *Deuteronomy 32:43*

[11]Again the Scripture says,

> "All you who are not Jews, praise the Lord.
> All you people, sing praises to him."
> *Psalm 117:1*

[12]And Isaiah says,

> "A new king will come from the family of Jesse.
> He will come to rule over the non-Jewish people,
> and they will have hope because of him."
> *Isaiah 11:10*

[13]I pray that the God who gives hope will fill you with much joy and peace while you trust in him. Then your hope will overflow by the power of the Holy Spirit.

[14]My brothers and sisters, I am sure that you are full of goodness. I know that you have all the knowledge you need and that you are able to teach each other. [15]But I have written to you very openly about some things I wanted you to remember. I did this because God gave me this special gift: [16]to be a minister of Christ Jesus to those who are not Jews. I served God by teaching his Good News, so that the non-Jewish people could be an offering that God would accept—an offering made holy by the Holy Spirit.

[17]So I am proud of what I have done for God in Christ Jesus. [18]I will not talk about anything except what Christ has done

STEP 9

Made direct amends to such people
wherever possible, except when to
do so would injure them or others.

Romans 15:2

Steps 8 and 9 give you the tools to repair old relationships and build healthy new ones. Everything you do—whether good or bad—impacts the people in your life. Your past addictive behaviors hurt people. Romans 15:2 challenges you to reject selfish motives and live in a way that encourages and helps your family and friends.

Your most important relationship is the one you're working on every day with God. That's the foundation of your recovery. However, your recovery has to include all of your relationships with the important people of your life. When you're angry and wanting to get even with people around you, you can't be at peace with yourself or God. It's when you're agitated and frustrated that you're most vulnerable to slipping back into the well-worn rut of your addictive pattern.

Building and maintaining good relationships is hard. It isn't all giving, and it certainly isn't all taking. The "giving" part involves helping people and paying attention to them. The "taking" part involves receiving love and friendship. Step 9 is a "giving" step. It emphasizes the giving of amends to those you've hurt as a corrective balance against any selfish taking in your old relationship style.

FOR YOUR NEXT **STEP 9** MEDITATION, TURN TO **PAGE 277.** ▶▶

through me in leading those who are not Jews to obey God. They have obeyed God because of what I have said and done, [19]because of the power of miracles and the great things they saw, and because of the power of the Holy Spirit. I preached the Good News from Jerusalem all the way around to Illyricum, and so I have finished that part of my work. [20]I always want to preach the Good News in places where people have never heard of Christ, because I do not want to build on the work someone else has already started. [21]But it is written in the Scriptures:

"Those who were not told about him
will see,
and those who have not heard
about him will understand."

Isaiah 52:15

[22]This is the reason I was stopped many times from coming to you. [23]Now I have finished my work here. Since for many years I have wanted to come to you, [24]I hope to visit you on my way to Spain. After I enjoy being with you for a while, I hope you can help me on my trip. [25]Now I am going to Jerusalem to help God's people. [26]The believers in Macedonia and Southern Greece were happy to give their money to help the poor among God's people at Jerusalem. [27]They were happy to do this, and really they owe it to them. These who are not Jews have shared in the Jews' spiritual blessings, so they should use their material possessions to help the Jews. [28]After I am sure the poor in Jerusalem get the money that has been given for them, I will leave for Spain and stop and visit you. [29]I know that when I come to you I will bring Christ's full blessing.

[30]Brothers and sisters, I beg you to help me in my work by praying to God for me. Do this because of our Lord Jesus and the love that the Holy Spirit gives us.

[31]Pray that I will be saved from the nonbelievers in Judea and that this help I bring to Jerusalem will please God's people there. [32]Then, if God wants me to, I will come to you with joy, and together you and I will have a time of rest. [33]The God who gives peace be with you all. Amen.

16 I recommend to you our sister Phoebe, who is a helper in the church in Cenchrea. [2]I ask you to accept her in the Lord in the way God's people should. Help her with anything she needs, because she has helped me and many other people also.

[3]Give my greetings to Priscilla and Aquila, who work together with me in Christ Jesus [4]and who risked their own lives to save my life. I am thankful to them, and all the non-Jewish churches are thankful as well. [5]Also, greet for me the church that meets at their house.

Greetings to my dear friend Epenetus, who was the first person in Asia to follow Christ. [6]Greetings to Mary, who worked very hard for you. [7]Greetings to Andronicus and Junia, my relatives, who were in prison with me. They are very important apostles. They were believers in Christ before I was. [8]Greetings to Ampliatus, my dear friend in the Lord. [9]Greetings to Urbanus, a worker together with me for Christ. And greetings to my dear friend Stachys. [10]Greetings to Apelles, who was tested and proved that he truly loves Christ. Greetings to all those who are in the family of Aristobulus. [11]Greetings to Herodion, my fellow citizen. Greetings to all those in the family of Narcissus who belong to the Lord. [12]Greetings to Tryphena and Tryphosa, women who work very hard for the Lord. Greetings to my dear friend Persis, who also has worked very hard for the Lord. [13]Greetings to Rufus, who is a special person in the Lord, and to his mother, who has been like a mother to me also. [14]Greetings to Asyncritus, Phlegon, Hermes, Patrobas, Hermas, and all the brothers and sisters who are with them. [15]Greetings to Philologus and Julia, Nereus and his sister, and Olympas, and to all God's people with them. [16]Greet each other with a holy kiss. All of Christ's churches send greetings to you.

[17]Brothers and sisters, I ask you to look out for those who cause people to be against each other and who upset other people's faith. They are against the true teaching you learned, so stay away from them. [18]Such people are not serving our Lord Christ but are only doing what pleases themselves. They use fancy talk and fine words to fool the minds of those who do not know about evil. [19]All the believers have heard that you obey, so I am very happy because of you. But I want you to be wise in what is good and innocent in what is evil.

[20]The God who brings peace will soon defeat Satan and give you power over him.

STEP 10

The grace of our Lord Jesus be with you.

[21]Timothy, a worker together with me, sends greetings, as well as Lucius, Jason, and Sosipater, my relatives.

[22]I am Tertius, and I am writing this letter from Paul. I send greetings to you in the Lord.

[23]Gaius is letting me and the whole church here use his home. He also sends greetings to you, as do Erastus, the city treasurer, and our brother Quartus. [[24]The grace of our Lord Jesus Christ be with all of you. Amen.]

[25]Glory to God who can make you strong in faith by the Good News that I tell people and by the message about Jesus Christ. The message about Christ is the secret that was hidden for long ages past but is now made known. [26]It has been made clear through the writings of the prophets. And by the command of the eternal God it is made known to all nations that they might believe and obey.

[27]To the only wise God be glory forever through Jesus Christ! Amen.

I CORINTHIANS

Help for a Church with Problems

1 From Paul. God called me to be an apostle of Christ Jesus because that is what God wanted. Also from Sosthenes, our brother in Christ.

²To the church of God in Corinth, to you who have been made holy in Christ Jesus. You were called to be God's holy people with all people everywhere who pray in the name of the Lord Jesus Christ—their Lord and ours:

³Grace and peace to you from God our Father and the Lord Jesus Christ.

⁴I always thank my God for you because of the grace God has given you in Christ Jesus. ⁵I thank God because in Christ you have been made rich in every way, in all your speaking and in all your knowledge. ⁶Just as our witness about Christ has been guaranteed to you, ⁷so you have every gift from God while you wait for our Lord Jesus Christ to come again. ⁸Jesus will keep you strong until the end so that there will be no wrong in you on the day our Lord Jesus Christ comes again. ⁹God, who has called you into fellowship with his Son, Jesus Christ our Lord, is faithful.

¹⁰I beg you, brothers and sisters, by the name of our Lord Jesus Christ that all of you agree with each other and not be split into groups. I beg that you be completely joined together by having the same kind of thinking and the same purpose. ¹¹My brothers and sisters, some people from Chloe's family have told me quite plainly that there are quarrels among you. ¹²This is what I mean: One of you says, "I follow Paul"; another says, "I follow Apollos"; another says, "I follow Peter"; and another says, "I follow Christ." ¹³Christ has been divided up into different groups! Did Paul die on the cross for you? No! Were you baptized in the name of Paul? No! ¹⁴I thank God I did not baptize any of you except Crispus and Gaius ¹⁵so that now no one can say you were baptized in my name. ¹⁶(I also baptized the family of Stephanas, but I do not remember that I baptized anyone else.) ¹⁷Christ did not send me to baptize people but to preach the Good News. And he sent me to preach the Good News without using words of human wisdom so that the cross of Christ would not lose its power.

¹⁸The teaching about the cross is foolishness to those who are being lost, but to us who are being saved it is the power of God. ¹⁹It is written in the Scriptures:

"I will cause the wise to lose their wisdom;
I will make the wise unable to understand." *Isaiah 29:14*

²⁰Where is the wise person? Where is the educated person? Where is the skilled talker of this world? God has made the wisdom of the world foolish. ²¹In the wisdom of God the world did not know God through its own wisdom. So God chose to use the message that sounds foolish to save those who believe. ²²The Jews ask for miracles, and the Greeks want wisdom. ²³But we preach a crucified Christ. This causes the Jews to stumble and is foolishness to non-Jews. ²⁴But Christ is the power of God and the wisdom of God to those people God has called—Jews and Greeks. ²⁵Even the foolishness of God is wiser than human wisdom, and the weakness of God is stronger than human strength.

²⁶Brothers and sisters, look at what

STEP 2

you were when God called you. Not many of you were wise in the way the world judges wisdom. Not many of you had great influence. Not many of you came from important families. ²⁷But God chose the foolish things of the world to shame the wise, and he chose the weak things of the world to shame the strong. ²⁸He chose what the world thinks is unimportant and what the world looks down on and thinks is nothing in order to destroy what the world thinks is important. ²⁹God did this so that no one can brag in his presence. ³⁰Because of God you are in Christ Jesus, who has become for us wisdom from God. In Christ we are put right with God, and have been made holy, and have been set free from sin. ³¹So, as the Scripture says, "If people want to brag, they should brag only about the Lord."

2 Dear brothers and sisters, when I came to you, I did not come preaching God's secret with fancy words or a show of human wisdom. ²I decided that while I was with you I would forget about everything except Jesus Christ and his death on the cross. ³So when I came to you, I was weak and fearful and trembling. ⁴My teaching and preaching were not with words of human wisdom that persuade people but with proof of the power that the Spirit gives. ⁵This was so that your faith would be in God's power and not in human wisdom.

⁶However, I speak a wisdom to those who are mature. But this wisdom is not from this world or from the rulers of this world, who are losing their power. ⁷I speak God's secret wisdom, which he has kept hidden. Before the world began, God planned this wisdom for our glory. ⁸None of the rulers of this world understood it. If they had, they would not have crucified the Lord of glory. ⁹But as it is written in the Scriptures:

"No one has ever seen this,
    and no one has ever heard about
        it.
No one has ever imagined
    what God has prepared for those
        who love him."   Isaiah 64:4

¹⁰But God has shown us these things through the Spirit.

The Spirit searches out all things, even the deep secrets of God. ¹¹Who knows the thoughts that another person has? Only a person's spirit that lives within him knows his thoughts. It is the same with God. No one knows the thoughts of God except the Spirit of God. ¹²Now we did not receive the spirit of the world, but we received the Spirit that is from God so that we can know all that God has given us. ¹³And we speak about these things, not with words taught us by human wisdom but with words taught us by the Spirit. And so we explain spiritual truths to spiritual people. ¹⁴A person who does not have the Spirit does not accept the truths that come from the Spirit of God. That person thinks they are foolish and cannot understand them, because they can only be judged to be true by the Spirit. ¹⁵The spiritual person is able to judge all things, but no one can judge him. The Scripture says:

¹⁶"Who has known the mind of the
        Lord?
    Who has been able to teach him?"
                            Isaiah 40:13

But we have the mind of Christ.

3 Brothers and sisters, in the past I could not talk to you as I talk to spiritual people. I had to talk to you as I would to people without the Spirit—babies in Christ. ²The teaching I gave you was like milk, not solid food, because you were not able to take solid food. And even now you are not ready. ³You are still not spiritual, because there is jealousy and quarreling

STEP 4

among you, and this shows that you are not spiritual. You are acting like people of the world. ⁴One of you says, "I belong to Paul," and another says, "I belong to Apollos." When you say things like this, you are acting like people of the world.

⁵Is Apollos important? No! Is Paul important? No! We are only servants of God who helped you believe. Each one of us did the work God gave us to do. ⁶I planted the seed, and Apollos watered it. But God is the One who made it grow. ⁷So the one who plants is not important, and the one who waters is not important. Only God, who makes things grow, is important. ⁸The one who plants and the one who waters have the same purpose, and each will be rewarded for his own work. ⁹We are God's workers, working together; you are like God's farm, God's house.

¹⁰Using the gift God gave me, I laid the foundation of that house like an expert builder. Others are building on that foundation, but all people should be careful how they build on it. ¹¹The foundation that has already been laid is Jesus Christ, and no one can lay down any other foundation. ¹²But if people build on that foundation, using gold, silver, jewels, wood, grass, or straw, ¹³their work will be clearly seen, because the Day of Judgment will make it visible. That Day will appear with fire, and the fire will test everyone's work to show what sort of work it was. ¹⁴If the building that has been put on the foundation still stands, the builder will get a reward. ¹⁵But if the building is burned up, the builder will suffer loss. The builder will be saved, but it will be as one who escaped from a fire.

¹⁶Don't you know that you are God's temple and that God's Spirit lives in you? ¹⁷If anyone destroys God's temple, God will destroy that person, because God's temple is holy and you are that temple.

¹⁸Do not fool yourselves. If you think you are wise in this world, you should become a fool so that you can become truly wise, ¹⁹because the wisdom of this world is foolishness with God. It is written in the Scriptures, "He catches those who are wise in their own clever traps." ²⁰It is also written in the Scriptures, "The Lord knows what wise people think. He knows their thoughts are just a puff of wind." ²¹So you should not brag about human leaders. All things belong to you: ²²Paul, Apollos, and Peter; the world, life, death, the present, and the future—all these belong to you. ²³And you belong to Christ, and Christ belongs to God.

4 People should think of us as servants of Christ, the ones God has trusted with his secrets. ²Now in this way those who are trusted with something valuable must show they are worthy of that trust. ³As for myself, I do not care if I am judged by you or by any human court. I do not even judge myself. ⁴I know of no wrong I have done, but this does not make me right before the Lord. The Lord is the One who judges me. ⁵So do not judge before the right time; wait until the Lord comes. He will bring to light things that are now hidden in darkness, and will make known the secret purposes of people's hearts. Then God will praise each one of them.

⁶Brothers and sisters, I have used Apollos and myself as examples so you could learn through us the meaning of the saying, "Follow only what is written in the Scriptures." Then you will not be more proud of one person than another. ⁷Who says you are better than others? What do you have that was not given to you? And if it was given to you, why do you brag as if you did not receive it as a gift?

⁸You think you already have everything you need. You think you are rich.

STEP 10

STEP 8

You think you have become kings without us. I wish you really were kings so we could be kings together with you. ⁹But it seems to me that God has put us apostles in last place, like those sentenced to die. We are like a show for the whole world to see—angels and people. ¹⁰We are fools for Christ's sake, but you are very wise in Christ. We are weak, but you are strong. You receive honor, but we are shamed. ¹¹Even to this very hour we do not have enough to eat or drink or to wear. We are often beaten, and we have no homes in which to live. ¹²We work hard with our own hands for our food. When people curse us, we bless them. When they hurt us, we put up with it. ¹³When they tell evil lies about us, we speak nice words about them. Even today, we are treated as though we were the garbage of the world—the filth of the earth.

¹⁴I am not trying to make you feel ashamed. I am writing this to give you a warning as my own dear children. ¹⁵For though you may have ten thousand teachers in Christ, you do not have many fathers. Through the Good News I became your father in Christ Jesus, ¹⁶so I beg you, please follow my example. ¹⁷That is why I am sending to you Timothy, my son in the Lord. I love Timothy, and he is faithful. He will help you remember my way of life in Christ Jesus, just as I teach it in all the churches everywhere.

¹⁸Some of you have become proud, thinking that I will not come to you again. ¹⁹But I will come to you very soon if the Lord wishes. Then I will know what the proud ones do, not what they say, ²⁰because the kingdom of God is present not in talk but in power. ²¹Which do you want: that I come to you with punishment or with love and gentleness?

5 It is actually being said that there is sexual sin among you. And it is a kind

that does not happen even among people who do not know God. A man there has his father's wife. ²And you are proud! You should have been filled with sadness so that the man who did this should be put out of your group. ³I am not there with you in person, but I am with you in spirit. And I have already judged the man who did that sin as if I were really there. ⁴When you meet together in the name of our Lord Jesus, and I meet with you in spirit with the power of our Lord Jesus, ⁵then hand this man over to Satan. So his sinful self will be destroyed, and his spirit will be saved on the day of the Lord.

⁶Your bragging is not good. You know the saying, "Just a little yeast makes the whole batch of dough rise." ⁷Take out all the old yeast so that you will be a new batch of dough without yeast, which you really are. For Christ, our Passover lamb, has been sacrificed. ⁸So let us celebrate this feast, but not with the bread that has the old yeast—the yeast of sin and wickedness. Let us celebrate this feast with the bread that has no yeast—the bread of goodness and truth.

⁹I wrote you in my earlier letter not to associate with those who sin sexually. ¹⁰But I did not mean you should not associate with those of this world who sin sexually, or with the greedy, or robbers, or those who worship idols. To get away from them you would have to leave this world. ¹¹I am writing to tell you that you must not associate with those who call themselves believers in Christ but who sin sexually, or are greedy, or worship idols, or abuse others with words, or get drunk, or cheat people. Do not even eat with people like that.

¹²⁻¹³It is not my business to judge those who are not part of the church. God will judge them. But you must judge the people who are part of the church. The

STEP 4

Made a searching and fearless moral
inventory of ourselves.

1 Corinthians 4:19–20

Nothing gets in the way of an honest Step 4 inventory like denial. You can know in your heart that your life is full of pain you need to admit and grieve over and still talk big as though things aren't so bad. You can pretend you haven't hurt anyone too much and no one's really gotten to you either. But it isn't true. It's just the empty words of big talk—big talk that comes from phony pride and wishful thinking.

Why would anyone do that? Why resort to smoke and mirrors when brutal honesty is what's needed? You hear it all the time, though. Jared claims it didn't bother him that his dad worked all the time, never came to one of his games, and missed his high school graduation. Melissa talks like she really believes her doctor "ordered" her to take sleeping pills the way she does. Tina says she sleeps with lots of guys because she believes in love. Pierce says he looks at Internet pornography because it's a natural, healthy way to handle his sexuality.

For nearly seventy years, A.A. literature has stated the cold, hard truth that anyone can recover from addiction except those "who are constitutionally incapable of being honest with themselves" (*Alcoholics Anonymous*, p. 58). The kingdom of God belongs to those who learn how to confess the garbage in their lives.

FOR YOUR NEXT **STEP 4** MEDITATION, TURN TO **PAGE 266.** ▶▶

Scripture says, "You must get rid of the evil person among you."

6 When you have something against another Christian, how can you bring yourself to go before judges who are not right with God? Why do you not let God's people decide who is right? ²Surely you know that God's people will judge the world. So if you are to judge the world, are you not able to judge small cases as well? ³You know that in the future we will judge angels, so surely we can judge the ordinary things of this life. ⁴If you have ordinary cases that must be judged, are you going to appoint people as judges who mean nothing to the church? ⁵I say this to shame you. Surely there is someone among you wise enough to judge a complaint between believers. ⁶But now one believer goes to court against another believer—and you do this in front of unbelievers!

⁷The fact that you have lawsuits against each other shows that you are already defeated. Why not let yourselves be wronged? Why not let yourselves be cheated? ⁸But you yourselves do wrong and cheat, and you do this to other believers!

⁹⁻¹⁰Surely you know that the people who do wrong will not inherit God's kingdom. Do not be fooled. Those who sin sexually, worship idols, take part in adultery, those who are male prostitutes, or men who have sexual relations with other men, those who steal, are greedy, get drunk, lie about others, or rob—these people will not inherit God's kingdom. ¹¹In the past, some of you were like that, but you were washed clean. You were made holy, and you were made right with God in the name of the Lord Jesus Christ and in the Spirit of our God.

STEP 10 ¹²"I am allowed to do all things," but not all things are good for me to do. "I am allowed to do all things," but I will not let anything make me its slave. ¹³"Food is for the stomach, and the stomach for food," but God will destroy them both. The body is not for sexual sin but for the Lord, and the Lord is for the body. ¹⁴By his power God has raised the Lord from the dead and will also raise us from the dead. ¹⁵Surely you know that your bodies are parts of Christ himself. So I must never take the parts of Christ and join them to a prostitute! ¹⁶It is written in the Scriptures, "The two will become one body." So you should know that anyone who joins with a prostitute becomes one body with the prostitute. ¹⁷But the one who joins with the Lord is one spirit with the Lord.

¹⁸So run away from sexual sin. Every other sin people do is outside their bodies, but those who sin sexually sin against their own bodies. ¹⁹You should know that your body is a temple for the Holy Spirit who is in you. You have received the Holy Spirit from God. So you do not belong to yourselves, ²⁰because you were bought by God for a price. So honor God with your bodies.

7 Now I will discuss the things you wrote me about. It is good for a man not to have sexual relations with a woman. ²But because sexual sin is a danger, each man should have his own wife, and each woman should have her own husband. ³The husband should give his wife all that he owes her as his wife. And the wife should give her husband all that she owes him as her husband. ⁴The wife does not have full rights over her own body; her husband shares them. And the husband does not have full rights over his own body; his wife shares them. ⁵Do not refuse to give your bodies to each other, unless you both agree to stay away from sexual relations for a time so you can give STEP 4

your time to prayer. Then come together again so Satan cannot tempt you because of a lack of self-control. [6]I say this to give you permission to stay away from sexual relations for a time. It is not a command to do so. [7]I wish that everyone were like me, but each person has his own gift from God. One has one gift, another has another gift.

[8]Now for those who are not married and for the widows I say this: It is good for them to stay unmarried as I am. [9]But if they cannot control themselves, they should marry. It is better to marry than to burn with sexual desire.

[10]Now I give this command for the married people. (The command is not from me; it is from the Lord.) A wife should not leave her husband. [11]But if she does leave, she must not marry again, or she should make up with her husband. Also the husband should not divorce his wife.

[12]For all the others I say this (I am saying this, not the Lord): If a Christian man has a wife who is not a believer, and she is happy to live with him, he must not divorce her. [13]And if a Christian woman has a husband who is not a believer, and he is happy to live with her, she must not divorce him. [14]The husband who is not a believer is made holy through his believing wife. And the wife who is not a believer is made holy through her believing husband. If this were not true, your children would not be clean, but now your children are holy.

[15]But if those who are not believers decide to leave, let them leave. When this happens, the Christian man or woman is free. But God called us to live in peace. [16]Wife, you don't know; maybe you will save your husband. And husband, you don't know; maybe you will save your wife.

[17]But in any case each one of you should continue to live the way God has given you to live—the way you were when God called you. This is a rule I make in all the churches. [18]If a man was already circumcised when he was called, he should not undo his circumcision. If a man was without circumcision when he was called, he should not be circumcised. [19]It is not important if a man is circumcised or not. The important thing is obeying God's commands. [20]Each one of you should stay the way you were when God called you. [21]If you were a slave when God called you, do not let that bother you. But if you can be free, then make good use of your freedom. [22]Those who were slaves when the Lord called them are free persons who belong to the Lord. In the same way, those who were free when they were called are now Christ's slaves. [23]You all were bought at a great price, so do not become slaves of people. [24]Brothers and sisters, each of you should stay as you were when you were called, and stay there with God.

[25]Now I write about people who are not married. I have no command from the Lord about this; I give my opinion. But I can be trusted, because the Lord has shown me mercy. [26]The present time is a time of trouble, so I think it is good for you to stay the way you are. [27]If you have a wife, do not try to become free from her. If you are not married, do not try to find a wife. [28]But if you decide to marry, you have not sinned. And if a girl who has never married decides to marry, she has not sinned. But those who marry will have trouble in this life, and I want you to be free from trouble.

[29]Brothers and sisters, this is what I mean: We do not have much time left. So starting now, those who have wives should live as if they had no wives. [30]Those

who are crying should live as if they were not crying. Those who are happy should live as if they were not happy. Those who buy things should live as if they own nothing. ³¹Those who use the things of the world should live as if they were not using them, because this world in its present form will soon be gone.

³²I want you to be free from worry. A man who is not married is busy with the Lord's work, trying to please the Lord. ³³But a man who is married is busy with things of the world, trying to please his wife. ³⁴He must think about two things—pleasing his wife and pleasing the Lord. A woman who is not married or a girl who has never married is busy with the Lord's work. She wants to be holy in body and spirit. But a married woman is busy with things of the world, as to how she can please her husband. ³⁵I am saying this to help you, not to limit you. But I want you to live in the right way, to give yourselves fully to the Lord without concern for other things.

³⁶If a man thinks he is not doing the right thing with the girl he is engaged to, if she is almost past the best age to marry and he feels he should marry her, he should do what he wants. They should get married. It is no sin. ³⁷But if a man is sure in his mind that there is no need for marriage, and has his own desires under control, and has decided not to marry the one to whom he is engaged, he is doing the right thing. ³⁸So the man who marries his girl does right, but the man who does not marry will do better.

³⁹A woman must stay with her husband as long as he lives. But if her husband dies, she is free to marry any man she wants, but she must marry another believer. ⁴⁰The woman is happier if she does not marry again. This is my opinion, but I believe I also have God's Spirit.

8 Now I will write about meat that is sacrificed to idols. We know that "we all have knowledge." Knowledge puffs you up with pride, but love builds up. ²If you think you know something, you do not yet know anything as you should. ³But if any person loves God, that person is known by God.

STEP
9

⁴So this is what I say about eating meat sacrificed to idols: We know that an idol is really nothing in the world, and we know there is only one God. ⁵Even though there are things called gods, in heaven or on earth (and there are many "gods" and "lords"), ⁶for us there is only one God—our Father. All things came from him, and we live for him. And there is only one Lord—Jesus Christ. All things were made through him, and we also were made through him.

⁷But not all people know this. Some people are still so used to idols that when they eat meat, they still think of it as being sacrificed to an idol. Because their conscience is weak, when they eat it, they feel guilty. ⁸But food will not bring us closer to God. Refusing to eat does not make us less pleasing to God, and eating does not make us better in God's sight.

⁹But be careful that your freedom does not cause those who are weak in faith to fall into sin. ¹⁰Suppose one of you who has knowledge eats in an idol's temple. Someone who is weak in faith might see you eating there and be encouraged to eat meat sacrificed to idols while thinking it is wrong to do so. ¹¹This weak believer for whom Christ died is ruined because of your "knowledge." ¹²When you sin against your brothers and sisters in Christ like this and cause them to do what they feel is wrong, you are also sinning against Christ. ¹³So if the food I eat causes them to fall into sin, I will

never eat meat again so that I will not cause any of them to sin.

9 I am a free man. I am an apostle. I have seen Jesus our Lord. You people are all an example of my work in the Lord. ²If others do not accept me as an apostle, surely you do, because you are proof that I am an apostle in the Lord.

³This is the answer I give people who want to judge me: ⁴Do we not have the right to eat and drink? ⁵Do we not have the right to bring a believing wife with us when we travel as do the other apostles and the Lord's brothers and Peter? ⁶Are Barnabas and I the only ones who must work to earn our living? ⁷No soldier ever serves in the army and pays his own salary. No one ever plants a vineyard without eating some of the grapes. No person takes care of a flock without drinking some of the milk.

⁸I do not say this by human authority; God's law also says the same thing. ⁹It is written in the law of Moses: "When an ox is working in the grain, do not cover its mouth to keep it from eating." When God said this, was he thinking only about oxen? No. ¹⁰He was really talking about us. Yes, that Scripture was written for us, because it goes on to say: "The one who plows and the one who works in the grain should hope to get some of the grain for their work." ¹¹Since we planted spiritual seed among you, is it too much if we should harvest material things? ¹²If others have the right to get something from you, surely we have this right, too. But we do not use it. No, we put up with everything ourselves so that we will not keep anyone from believing the Good News of Christ. ¹³Surely you know that those who work at the Temple get their food from the Temple, and those who serve at the altar get part of what is offered at the altar. ¹⁴In the same way, the Lord has commanded that those who tell the Good News should get their living from this work.

¹⁵But I have not used any of these rights. And I am not writing this now to get anything from you. I would rather die than to have my reason for bragging taken away. ¹⁶Telling the Good News does not give me any reason for bragging. Telling the Good News is my duty— something I must do. And how terrible it will be for me if I do not tell the Good News. ¹⁷If I preach because it is my own choice, I have a reward. But if I preach and it is not my choice to do so, I am only doing the duty that was given to me. ¹⁸So what reward do I get? This is my reward: that when I tell the Good News I can offer it freely. I do not use my full rights in my work of preaching the Good News.

¹⁹I am free and belong to no one. But I make myself a slave to all people to win as many as I can. ²⁰To the Jews I became like a Jew to win the Jews. I myself am not ruled by the law. But to those who are ruled by the law I became like a person who is ruled by the law. I did this to win those who are ruled by the law. ²¹To those who are without the law I became like a person who is without the law. I did this to win those people who are without the law. (But really, I am not without God's law—I am ruled by Christ's law.) ²²To those who are weak, I became weak so I could win the weak. I have become all things to all people so I could save some of them in any way possible. ²³I do all this because of the Good News and so I can share in its blessings.

²⁴You know that in a race all the runners run, but only one gets the prize. So run to win! ²⁵All those who compete in the games use self-control so they can win a crown. That crown is an earthly thing that lasts only a short time, but our crown

STEP 12

will never be destroyed. ²⁶So I do not run without a goal. I fight like a boxer who is hitting something—not just the air. ²⁷I treat my body hard and make it my slave so that I myself will not be disqualified after I have preached to others.

10 Brothers and sisters, I want you to know what happened to our ancestors who followed Moses. They were all under the cloud and all went through the sea. ²They were all baptized as followers of Moses in the cloud and in the sea. ³They all ate the same spiritual food, ⁴and all drank the same spiritual drink. They drank from that spiritual rock that followed them, and that rock was Christ. ⁵But God was not pleased with most of them, so they died in the desert.

STEP 10

⁶And these things happened as examples for us, to stop us from wanting evil things as those people did. ⁷Do not worship idols, as some of them did. Just as it is written in the Scriptures: "They sat down to eat and drink, and then they got up and sinned sexually." ⁸We must not take part in sexual sins, as some of them did. In one day twenty-three thousand of them died because of their sins. ⁹We must not test Christ as some of them did; they were killed by snakes. ¹⁰Do not complain as some of them did; they were killed by the angel that destroys.

¹¹The things that happened to those people are examples. They were written down to teach us, because we live in a time when all these things of the past have reached their goal. ¹²If you think you are strong, you should be careful not to fall. ¹³The only temptation that has come to you is that which everyone has. But you can trust God, who will not permit you to be tempted more than you can stand. But when you are tempted, he will also give you a way to escape so that you will be able to stand it.

¹⁴So, my dear friends, run away from the worship of idols. ¹⁵I am speaking to you as to reasonable people; judge for yourselves what I say. ¹⁶We give thanks for the cup of blessing, which is a sharing in the blood of Christ. And the bread that we break is a sharing in the body of Christ. ¹⁷Because there is one loaf of bread, we who are many are one body, because we all share that one loaf.

¹⁸Think about the Israelites: Do not those who eat the sacrifices share in the altar? ¹⁹I do not mean that the food sacrificed to an idol is important. I do not mean that an idol is anything at all. ²⁰But I say that what is sacrificed to idols is offered to demons, not to God. And I do not want you to share anything with demons. ²¹You cannot drink the cup of the Lord and the cup of demons also. You cannot share in the Lord's table and the table of demons. ²²Are we trying to make the Lord jealous? We are not stronger than he is, are we?

STEP 10

²³"We are allowed to do all things," but not all things are good for us to do. "We are allowed to do all things," but not all things help others grow stronger. ²⁴Do not look out only for yourselves. Look out for the good of others also.

²⁵Eat any meat that is sold in the meat market. Do not ask questions about it. ²⁶You may eat it, "because the earth belongs to the Lord, and everything in it."

²⁷Those who are not believers may invite you to eat with them. If you want to go, eat anything that is put before you. Do not ask questions about it. ²⁸But if anyone says to you, "That food was offered to idols," do not eat it. Do not eat it because of that person who told you and because eating it might be thought to be wrong. ²⁹I don't mean you think it is wrong, but the other person might. But why, you ask, should my freedom be

STEP 12

Having had a spiritual awakening as the result of these steps, we tried to carry this message to others, and to practice these principles in all our affairs.

1 Corinthians 9:22-27

It may seem funny to you, but Christians are both free people and servants. God sets you free from sin and selfishness. That freedom lets you become the servants of Christ. Once you belong to God, you are free from other people's control. They have no power over your life. You can freely choose to share the Good News of God's love and salvation with people who need to hear about it. Keep working hard on your recovery and spiritual growth. At the same time, keep your eyes open for times when you can share your experiences with others struggling with addictions.

The last part of this passage can be summed up in one word— "vigilance." You never stop needing spiritual self-discipline. This is why Step 12 urges us to "practice these principles in all our affairs." You won't slip up as often, and you'll stay close to God where you can feel his presence and peace.

FOR YOUR NEXT **STEP 12** MEDITATION, TURN TO **PAGE 244.** ▶▶

judged by someone else's conscience? ³⁰If I eat the meal with thankfulness, why am I criticized because of something for which I thank God?

STEP 11

³¹The answer is, if you eat or drink, or if you do anything, do it all for the glory of God. ³²Never do anything that might hurt others—Jews, Greeks, or God's church— ³³just as I, also, try to please everybody in every way. I am not trying to do what is good for me but what is good for most people so they can be saved.

11 Follow my example, as I follow the example of Christ.

²I praise you because you remember me in everything, and you follow closely the teachings just as I gave them to you. ³But I want you to understand this: The head of every man is Christ, the head of a woman is the man, and the head of Christ is God. ⁴Every man who prays or prophesies with his head covered brings shame to his head. ⁵But every woman who prays or prophesies with her head uncovered brings shame to her head. She is the same as a woman who has her head shaved. ⁶If a woman does not cover her head, she should have her hair cut off. But since it is shameful for a woman to cut off her hair or to shave her head, she should cover her head. ⁷But a man should not cover his head, because he is the likeness and glory of God. But woman is man's glory. ⁸Man did not come from woman, but woman came from man. ⁹And man was not made for woman, but woman was made for man. ¹⁰So that is why a woman should have a symbol of authority on her head, because of the angels.

¹¹But in the Lord women are not independent of men, and men are not independent of women. ¹²This is true because woman came from man, but also man is born from woman. But everything comes from God. ¹³Decide this for your-

selves: Is it right for a woman to pray to God with her head uncovered? ¹⁴Even nature itself teaches you that wearing long hair is shameful for a man. ¹⁵But long hair is a woman's glory. Long hair is given to her as a covering. ¹⁶Some people may still want to argue about this, but I would add that neither we nor the churches of God have any other practice.

¹⁷In the things I tell you now I do not praise you, because when you come together you do more harm than good. ¹⁸First, I hear that when you meet together as a church you are divided, and I believe some of this. ¹⁹(It is necessary to have differences among you so that it may be clear which of you really have God's approval.) ²⁰When you come together, you are not really eating the Lord's Supper. ²¹This is because when you eat, each person eats without waiting for the others. Some people do not get enough to eat, while others have too much to drink. ²²You can eat and drink in your own homes! You seem to think God's church is not important, and you embarrass those who are poor. What should I tell you? Should I praise you? I do not praise you for doing this.

²³The teaching I gave you is the same teaching I received from the Lord: On the night when the Lord Jesus was handed over to be killed, he took bread ²⁴and gave thanks for it. Then he broke the bread and said, "This is my body; it is for you. Do this to remember me." ²⁵In the same way, after they ate, Jesus took the cup. He said, "This cup is the new agreement that is sealed with the blood of my death. When you drink this, do it to remember me." ²⁶Every time you eat this bread and drink this cup you are telling others about the Lord's death until he comes.

²⁷So a person who eats the bread or drinks the cup of the Lord in a way that is

STEP 5

not worthy of it will be guilty of sinning against the body and the blood of the Lord. [28]Look into your own hearts before you eat the bread and drink the cup, [29]because all who eat the bread and drink the cup without recognizing the body eat and drink judgment against themselves. [30]That is why many in your group are sick and weak, and some of you have died. [31]But if we judged ourselves in the right way, God would not judge us. [32]But when the Lord judges us, he disciplines us so that we will not be destroyed along with the world.

[33]So my brothers and sisters, when you come together to eat, wait for each other. [34]Anyone who is too hungry should eat at home so that in meeting together you will not bring God's judgment on yourselves. I will tell you what to do about the other things when I come.

12Now, brothers and sisters, I want you to understand about spiritual gifts. [2]You know the way you lived before you were believers. You let yourselves be influenced and led away to worship idols—things that could not speak. [3]So I want you to understand that no one who is speaking with the help of God's Spirit says, "Jesus be cursed." And no one can say, "Jesus is Lord," without the help of the Holy Spirit.

[4]There are different kinds of gifts, but they are all from the same Spirit. [5]There are different ways to serve but the same Lord to serve. [6]And there are different ways that God works through people but the same God. God works in all of us in everything we do. [7]Something from the Spirit can be seen in each person, for the common good. [8]The Spirit gives one person the ability to speak with wisdom, and the same Spirit gives another the ability to speak with knowledge. [9]The same Spirit gives faith to one person. And, to

another, that one Spirit gives gifts of healing. [10]The Spirit gives to another person the power to do miracles, to another the ability to prophesy. And he gives to another the ability to know the difference between good and evil spirits. The Spirit gives one person the ability to speak in different kinds of languages and to another the ability to interpret those languages. [11]One Spirit, the same Spirit, does all these things, and the Spirit decides what to give each person.

[12]A person's body is one thing, but it has many parts. Though there are many parts to a body, all those parts make only one body. Christ is like that also. [13]Some of us are Jews, and some are Greeks. Some of us are slaves, and some are free. But we were all baptized into one body through one Spirit. And we were all made to share in the one Spirit.

[14]The human body has many parts. [15]The foot might say, "Because I am not a hand, I am not part of the body." But saying this would not stop the foot from being a part of the body. [16]The ear might say, "Because I am not an eye, I am not part of the body." But saying this would not stop the ear from being a part of the body. [17]If the whole body were an eye, it would not be able to hear. If the whole body were an ear, it would not be able to smell. [18-19]If each part of the body were the same part, there would be no body. But truly God put all the parts, each one of them, in the body as he wanted them. [20]So then there are many parts, but only one body.

[21]The eye cannot say to the hand, "I don't need you!" And the head cannot say to the foot, "I don't need you!" [22]No! Those parts of the body that seem to be the weaker are really necessary. [23]And the parts of the body we think are less deserving are the parts to which we give the most honor. We give special respect to

the parts we want to hide. 24The more respectable parts of our body need no special care. But God put the body together and gave more honor to the parts that need it 25so our body would not be divided. God wanted the different parts to care the same for each other. 26If one part of the body suffers, all the other parts suffer with it. Or if one part of our body is honored, all the other parts share its honor.

27Together you are the body of Christ, and each one of you is a part of that body. 28In the church God has given a place first to apostles, second to prophets, and third to teachers. Then God has given a place to those who do miracles, those who have gifts of healing, those who can help others, those who are able to govern, and those who can speak in different languages. 29Not all are apostles. Not all are prophets. Not all are teachers. Not all do miracles. 30Not all have gifts of healing. Not all speak in different languages. Not all interpret those languages. 31But you should truly want to have the greater gifts.

And now I will show you the best way of all.

STEP 8

13I may speak in different languages of people or even angels. But if I do not have love, I am only a noisy bell or a crashing cymbal. 2I may have the gift of prophecy. I may understand all the secret things of God and have all knowledge, and I may have faith so great I can move mountains. But even with all these things, if I do not have love, then I am nothing. 3I may give away everything I have, and I may even give my body as an offering to be burned. But I gain nothing if I do not have love.

4Love is patient and kind. Love is not jealous, it does not brag, and it is not proud. 5Love is not rude, is not selfish, and does not get upset with others. Love does not count up wrongs that have been done. 6Love takes no pleasure in evil but rejoices over the truth. 7Love patiently accepts all things. It always trusts, always hopes, and always endures.

8Love never ends. There are gifts of prophecy, but they will be ended. There are gifts of speaking in different languages, but those gifts will stop. There is the gift of knowledge, but it will come to an end. 9The reason is that our knowledge and our ability to prophesy are not perfect. 10But when perfection comes, the things that are not perfect will end. 11When I was a child, I talked like a child, I thought like a child, I reasoned like a child. When I became a man, I stopped those childish ways. 12It is the same with us. Now we see a dim reflection, as if we were looking into a mirror, but then we shall see clearly. Now I know only a part, but then I will know fully, as God has known me. 13So these three things continue forever: faith, hope, and love. And the greatest of these is love.

14You should seek after love, and you should truly want to have the spiritual gifts, especially the gift of prophecy. 2I will explain why. Those who have the gift of speaking in different languages are not speaking to people; they are speaking to God. No one understands them; they are speaking secret things through the Spirit. 3But those who prophesy are speaking to people to give them strength, encouragement, and comfort. 4The ones who speak in different languages are helping only themselves, but those who prophesy are helping the whole church. 5I wish all of you had the gift of speaking in different kinds of languages, but more, I wish you would prophesy. Those who prophesy are greater than those who can only speak in

STEP 8

Made a list of all persons we had harmed,
and became willing to make amends to them all.

1 Corinthians 13

The Corinthians must have thought they were really something. So the apostle Paul told them that it didn't matter how smart they were, how talented they were, or how religious they were. What mattered was how loving they were. If they didn't have God's kind of love, they were nothing. That's as true today as it was then.

In 1 Corinthians 13:3, Paul described the codependent personality type long before twentieth-century psychiatrists gave it a name. He said some people will sacrifice themselves in the hope that their sacrifice will earn them approval and happiness.

Step 8 can help you replace old codependent feelings with feelings of genuine love and compassion. You don't have to hate yourself and involve yourself in destructive relationships. Each verse in this chapter can point you to the kind of love God wants you to have.

FOR YOUR NEXT **STEP 8** MEDITATION, TURN TO **PAGE 302.** ▶▶

different languages—unless someone is there who can explain what is said so that the whole church can be helped.

⁶Brothers and sisters, will it help you if I come to you speaking in different languages? No! It will help you only if I bring you a new truth or some new knowledge, or prophecy, or teaching. ⁷It is the same as with lifeless things that make sounds—like a flute or a harp. If they do not make clear musical notes, you will not know what is being played. ⁸And in a war, if the trumpet does not give a clear sound, who will prepare for battle? ⁹It is the same with you. Unless you speak clearly with your tongue, no one can understand what you are saying. You will be talking into the air! ¹⁰It may be true that there are all kinds of sounds in the world, and none is without meaning. ¹¹But unless I understand the meaning of what someone says to me, we will be like foreigners to each other. ¹²It is the same with you. Since you want spiritual gifts very much, seek most of all to have the gifts that help the church grow stronger.

¹³The one who has the gift of speaking in a different language should pray for the gift to interpret what is spoken. ¹⁴If I pray in a different language, my spirit is praying, but my mind does nothing. ¹⁵So what should I do? I will pray with my spirit, but I will also pray with my mind. I will sing with my spirit, but I will also sing with my mind. ¹⁶If you praise God with your spirit, those persons there without understanding cannot say amen to your prayer of thanks, because they do not know what you are saying. ¹⁷You may be thanking God in a good way, but the other person is not helped.

¹⁸I thank God that I speak in different kinds of languages more than all of you. ¹⁹But in the church meetings I would rather speak five words I understand in order to teach others than thousands of words in a different language.

²⁰Brothers and sisters, do not think like children. In evil things be like babies, but in your thinking you should be like adults. ²¹It is written in the Scriptures:

> "With people who use strange words
> and foreign languages
> I will speak to these people.
> But even then they will not listen to
> me,"   Isaiah 28:11–12

says the Lord.

²²So the gift of speaking in different kinds of languages is a sign for those who do not believe, not for those who do believe. And prophecy is for people who do believe, not for those who do not believe. ²³Suppose the whole church meets together and everyone speaks in different languages. If some people come in who do not understand or do not believe, they will say you are crazy. ²⁴But suppose everyone is prophesying and some people come in who do not believe or do not understand. If everyone is prophesying, their sin will be shown to them, and they will be judged by all that they hear. ²⁵The secret things in their hearts will be made known. So they will bow down and worship God saying, "Truly, God is with you."

²⁶So, brothers and sisters, what should you do? When you meet together, one person has a song, and another has a teaching. Another has a new truth from God. Another speaks in a different language, and another person interprets that language. The purpose of all these things should be to help the church grow strong. ²⁷When you meet together, if anyone speaks in a different language, it should be only two, or not more than three, who speak. They should speak one after the other, and someone should interpret. ²⁸But if there is no interpreter, then those who speak in a different lan-

STEP
11

guage should be quiet in the church meeting. They should speak only to themselves and to God.

²⁹Only two or three prophets should speak, and the others should judge what they say. ³⁰If a message from God comes to another person who is sitting, the first speaker should stop. ³¹You can all prophesy one after the other. In this way all the people can be taught and encouraged. ³²The spirits of prophets are under the control of the prophets themselves. ³³God is not a God of confusion but a God of peace.

As is true in all the churches of God's people, ³⁴women should keep quiet in the church meetings. They are not allowed to speak, but they must yield to this rule as the law says. ³⁵If they want to learn something, they should ask their own husbands at home. It is shameful for a woman to speak in the church meeting. ³⁶Did God's teaching come from you? Or are you the only ones to whom it has come?

³⁷Those who think they are prophets or spiritual persons should understand that what I am writing to you is the Lord's command. ³⁸Those who ignore this will be ignored by God.

³⁹So my brothers and sisters, you should truly want to prophesy. But do not stop people from using the gift of speaking in different kinds of languages. ⁴⁰But let everything be done in a right and orderly way.

15 Now, brothers and sisters, I want you to remember the Good News I brought to you. You received this Good News and continue strong in it. ²And you are being saved by it if you continue believing what I told you. If you do not, then you believed for nothing.

³I passed on to you what I received, of which this was most important: that Christ died for our sins, as the Scriptures say; ⁴that he was buried and was raised to life on the third day as the Scriptures say; ⁵and that he was seen by Peter and then by the twelve apostles. ⁶After that, Jesus was seen by more than five hundred of the believers at the same time. Most of them are still living today, but some have died. ⁷Then he was seen by James and later by all the apostles. ⁸Last of all he was seen by me—as by a person not born at the normal time. ⁹All the other apostles are greater than I am. I am not even good enough to be called an apostle, because I persecuted the church of God. ¹⁰But God's grace has made me what I am, and his grace to me was not wasted. I worked harder than all the other apostles. (But it was not I really; it was God's grace that was with me.) ¹¹So if I preached to you or the other apostles preached to you, we all preach the same thing, and this is what you believed.

¹²Now since we preached that Christ was raised from the dead, why do some of you say that people will not be raised from the dead? ¹³If no one is ever raised from the dead, then Christ has not been raised. ¹⁴And if Christ has not been raised, then our preaching is worth nothing, and your faith is worth nothing. ¹⁵And also, we are guilty of lying about God, because we testified of him that he raised Christ from the dead. But if people are not raised from the dead, then God never raised Christ. ¹⁶If the dead are not raised, Christ has not been raised either. ¹⁷And if Christ has not been raised, then your faith has nothing to it; you are still guilty of your sins. ¹⁸And those in Christ who have already died are lost. ¹⁹If our hope in Christ is for this life only, we should be pitied more than anyone else in the world.

²⁰But Christ has truly been raised from the dead—the first one and proof that those who sleep in death will also be

STEP 12

STEP 2

243

STEP 12

Having had a spiritual awakening as the result of these steps, we tried to carry this message to others, and to practice these principles in all our affairs.

1 Corinthians 15:10

A great recovery slogan is "But for the grace of God." This slogan can mean several things to you. But for the grace of God, you might not have broken out of denial and recognized how bad your dependency was. But for the grace of God, you might not have found a support group, a Twelve Step recovery organization, or the church community to help you break your addiction. But for the grace of God, you might not have "hit bottom" and finally recognized that you had to get help. But for the grace of God, you might not have found God and had a new spiritual birth.

When you take Step 12, you take a grace-filled step. God has given you a spiritual awakening. Now you need to reflect God's grace to those around you. As you work hard to practice these principles in all of your affairs, you tell everybody watching that God's grace was "not wasted" and that "God's grace has made me what I am."

FOR YOUR NEXT **STEP 12** MEDITATION, TURN TO **PAGE 296.** ▶▶

raised. ²¹Death has come because of what one man did, but the rising from death also comes because of one man. ²²In Adam all of us die. In the same way, in Christ all of us will be made alive again. ²³But everyone will be raised to life in the right order. Christ was first to be raised. When Christ comes again, those who belong to him will be raised to life, ²⁴and then the end will come. At that time Christ will destroy all rulers, authorities, and powers, and he will hand over the kingdom to God the Father. ²⁵Christ must rule until he puts all enemies under his control. ²⁶The last enemy to be destroyed will be death. ²⁷The Scripture says that God put all things under his control. When it says "all things" are under him, it is clear this does not include God himself. God is the One who put everything under his control. ²⁸After everything has been put under the Son, then he will put himself under God, who had put all things under him. Then God will be the complete ruler over everything.

²⁹If the dead are never raised, what will people do who are being baptized for the dead? If the dead are not raised at all, why are people being baptized for them? ³⁰And what about us? Why do we put ourselves in danger every hour? ³¹I die every day. That is true, brothers and sisters, just as it is true that I brag about you in Christ Jesus our Lord. ³²If I fought wild animals in Ephesus only with human hopes, I have gained nothing. If the dead are not raised, "Let us eat and drink, because tomorrow we will die."

³³Do not be fooled: "Bad friends will ruin good habits." ³⁴Come back to your right way of thinking and stop sinning. Some of you do not know God—I say this to shame you.

³⁵But someone may ask, "How are the dead raised? What kind of body will they have?" ³⁶Foolish person! When you sow a seed, it must die in the ground before it can live and grow. ³⁷And when you sow it, it does not have the same "body" it will have later. What you sow is only a bare seed, maybe wheat or something else. ³⁸But God gives it a body that he has planned for it, and God gives each kind of seed its own body. ³⁹All things made of flesh are not the same: People have one kind of flesh, animals have another, birds have another, and fish have another. ⁴⁰Also there are heavenly bodies and earthly bodies. But the beauty of the heavenly bodies is one kind, and the beauty of the earthly bodies is another. ⁴¹The sun has one kind of beauty, the moon has another beauty, and the stars have another. And each star is different in its beauty.

⁴²It is the same with the dead who are raised to life. The body that is "planted" will ruin and decay, but it is raised to a life that cannot be destroyed. ⁴³When the body is "planted," it is without honor, but it is raised in glory. When the body is "planted," it is weak, but when it is raised, it is powerful. ⁴⁴The body that is "planted" is a physical body. When it is raised, it is a spiritual body.

There is a physical body, and there is also a spiritual body. ⁴⁵It is written in the Scriptures: "The first man, Adam, became a living person." But the last Adam became a spirit that gives life. ⁴⁶The spiritual did not come first, but the physical and then the spiritual. ⁴⁷The first man came from the dust of the earth. The second man came from heaven. ⁴⁸People who belong to the earth are like the first man of earth. But those people who belong to heaven are like the man of heaven. ⁴⁹Just as we were made like the man of earth, so we will also be made like the man of heaven.

STEP 4

⁵⁰I tell you this, brothers and sisters: Flesh and blood cannot have a part in the kingdom of God. Something that will ruin cannot have a part in something that never ruins. ⁵¹But look! I tell you this secret: We will not all sleep in death, but we will all be changed. ⁵²It will take only a second—as quickly as an eye blinks—when the last trumpet sounds. The trumpet will sound, and those who have died will be raised to live forever, and we will all be changed. ⁵³This body that can be destroyed must clothe itself with something that can never be destroyed. And this body that dies must clothe itself with something that can never die. ⁵⁴So this body that can be destroyed will clothe itself with that which can never be destroyed, and this body that dies will clothe itself with that which can never die. When this happens, this Scripture will be made true:

"Death is destroyed forever in
        victory."   *Isaiah 25:8*
⁵⁵"Death, where is your victory?
    Death, where is your pain?"
                        Hosea 13:14

⁵⁶Death's power to hurt is sin, and the power of sin is the law. ⁵⁷But we thank God! He gives us the victory through our Lord Jesus Christ.

⁵⁸So my dear brothers and sisters, stand strong. Do not let anything move you. Always give yourselves fully to the work of the Lord, because you know that your work in the Lord is never wasted.

16 Now I will write about the collection of money for God's people. Do the same thing I told the Galatian churches to do: ²On the first day of every week, each one of you should put aside money as you have been blessed. Save it up so you will not have to collect money after I come. ³When I arrive, I will send whomever you approve to take your gift to Jerusalem. I will send them with letters of introduction, ⁴and if it seems good for me to go also, they will go along with me.

⁵I plan to go through Macedonia, so I will come to you after I go through there. ⁶Perhaps I will stay with you for a time or even all winter. Then you can help me on my trip, wherever I go. ⁷I do not want to see you now just in passing. I hope to stay a longer time with you if the Lord allows it. ⁸But I will stay at Ephesus until Pentecost, ⁹because a good opportunity for a great and growing work has been given to me now. And there are many people working against me.

¹⁰If Timothy comes to you, see to it that he has nothing to fear with you, because he is working for the Lord just as I am. ¹¹So none of you should treat Timothy as unimportant, but help him on his trip in peace so that he can come back to me. I am expecting him to come with the brothers.

¹²Now about our brother Apollos: I strongly encouraged him to visit you with the other brothers. He did not at all want to come now; he will come when he has the opportunity.

¹³Be alert. Continue strong in the faith. Have courage, and be strong. ¹⁴Do everything in love.

¹⁵You know that the family of Stephanas were the first believers in Southern Greece and that they have given themselves to the service of God's people. I ask you, brothers and sisters, ¹⁶to follow the leading of people like these and anyone else who works and serves with them.

¹⁷I am happy that Stephanas, Fortunatus, and Achaicus have come. You are not here, but they have filled your place. ¹⁸They have refreshed my spirit and yours. You should recognize the value of people like these.

[19]The churches in Asia send greetings to you. Aquila and Priscilla greet you in the Lord, as does the church that meets in their house. [20]All the brothers and sisters here send greetings. Give each other a holy kiss when you meet.

[21]I, Paul, am writing this greeting with my own hand.

[22]If anyone does not love the Lord, let him be separated from God—lost forever!

Come, O Lord!

[23]The grace of the Lord Jesus be with you.

[24]My love be with all of you in Christ Jesus.

2 CORINTHIANS

Paul Answers Those Who Accuse Him

---

1 From Paul, an apostle of Christ Jesus. I am an apostle because that is what God wanted. Also from Timothy our brother in Christ.

To the church of God in Corinth, and to all of God's people everywhere in Southern Greece:

²Grace and peace to you from God our Father and the Lord Jesus Christ.

STEP 3

³Praise be to the God and Father of our Lord Jesus Christ. God is the Father who is full of mercy and all comfort. ⁴He comforts us every time we have trouble, so when others have trouble, we can comfort them with the same comfort God gives us. ⁵We share in the many sufferings of Christ. In the same way, much comfort comes to us through Christ. ⁶If we have troubles, it is for your comfort and salvation, and if we have comfort, you also have comfort. This helps you to accept patiently the same sufferings we have. ⁷Our hope for you is strong, knowing that you share in our sufferings and also in the comfort we receive.

STEP 2

⁸Brothers and sisters, we want you to know about the trouble we suffered in Asia. We had great burdens there that were beyond our own strength. We even gave up hope of living. ⁹Truly, in our own hearts we believed we would die. But this happened so we would not trust in ourselves but in God, who raises people from the dead. ¹⁰God saved us from these great dangers of death, and he will continue to save us. We have put our hope in him, and he will save us again. ¹¹And you can help us with your prayers. Then many people will give thanks for us—that God blessed us because of their many prayers.

¹²This is what we are proud of, and I can say it with a clear conscience: In everything we have done in the world, and especially with you, we have had an honest and sincere heart from God. We did this by God's grace, not by the kind of wisdom the world has. ¹³⁻¹⁴We write to you only what you can read and understand. And I hope that as you have understood some things about us, you may come to know everything about us. Then you can be proud of us, as we will be proud of you on the day our Lord Jesus Christ comes again.

¹⁵I was so sure of all this that I made plans to visit you first so you could be blessed twice. ¹⁶I planned to visit you on my way to Macedonia and again on my way back. I wanted to get help from you for my trip to Judea. ¹⁷Do you think that I made these plans without really meaning it? Or maybe you think I make plans as the world does, so that I say yes, yes and at the same time no, no.

¹⁸But since you can believe God, you can believe that what we tell you is never both yes and no. ¹⁹The Son of God, Jesus Christ, that Silas and Timothy and I preached to you, was not yes and no. In Christ it has always been yes. ²⁰The yes to all of God's promises is in Christ, and through Christ we say yes to the glory of God. ²¹Remember, God is the One who makes you and us strong in Christ. God made us his chosen people. ²²He put his mark on us to show that we are his, and he put his Spirit in our hearts to be a guarantee for all he has promised.

²³I tell you this, and I ask God to be my witness that this is true: The reason I did not come back to Corinth was to keep

you from being punished or hurt. [24]We are not trying to control your faith. You are strong in faith. But we are workers with you for your own joy.

2 So I decided that my next visit to you would not be another one to make you sad. [2]If I make you sad, who will make me glad? Only you can make me glad—particularly the person whom I made sad. [3]I wrote you a letter for this reason: that when I came to you I would not be made sad by the people who should make me happy. I felt sure of all of you, that you would share my joy. [4]When I wrote to you before, I was very troubled and unhappy in my heart, and I wrote with many tears. I did not write to make you sad, but to let you know how much I love you.

[5]Someone there among you has caused sadness, not to me, but to all of you. I mean he caused sadness to all in some way. (I do not want to make it sound worse than it really is.) [6]The punishment that most of you gave him is enough for him. [7]But now you should forgive him and comfort him to keep him from having too much sadness and giving up completely. [8]So I beg you to show that you love him. [9]I wrote you to test you and to see if you obey in everything. [10]If you forgive someone, I also forgive him. And what I have forgiven—if I had anything to forgive—I forgave it for you, as if Christ were with me. [11]I did this so that Satan would not win anything from us, because we know very well what Satan's plans are.

[12]When I came to Troas to preach the Good News of Christ, the Lord gave me a good opportunity there. [13]But I had no peace, because I did not find my brother Titus. So I said good-bye to them at Troas and went to Macedonia.

STEP 12

[14]But thanks be to God, who always leads us as captives in Christ's victory parade. God uses us to spread his knowledge everywhere like a sweet-smelling perfume. [15]Our offering to God is this: We are the sweet smell of Christ among those who are being saved and among those who are being lost. [16]To those who are lost, we are the smell of death that brings death, but to those who are being saved, we are the smell of life that brings life. So who is able to do this work? [17]We do not sell the word of God for a profit as many other people do. But in Christ we speak the truth before God, as messengers of God.

3 Are we starting to brag about ourselves again? Do we need letters of introduction to you or from you, like some other people? [2]You yourselves are our letter, written on our hearts, known and read by everyone. [3]You show that you are a letter from Christ sent through us. This letter is not written with ink but with the Spirit of the living God. It is not written on stone tablets but on human hearts.

[4]We can say this, because through Christ we feel certain before God. [5]We are not saying that we can do this work ourselves. It is God who makes us able to do all that we do. [6]He made us able to be servants of a new agreement from himself to his people. This new agreement is not a written law, but it is of the Spirit. The written law brings death, but the Spirit gives life.

[7]The law that brought death was written in words on stone. It came with God's glory, which made Moses' face so bright that the Israelites could not continue to look at it. But that glory later disappeared. [8]So surely the new way that brings the Spirit has even more glory. [9]If the law that judged people guilty of sin had glory, surely the new way that makes people right with God has much greater glory. [10]That old law had glory, but it really loses its glory when it is compared to the

much greater glory of this new way. ¹¹If that law which disappeared came with glory, then this new way which continues forever has much greater glory.

¹²We have this hope, so we are very bold. ¹³We are not like Moses, who put a covering over his face so the Israelites would not see it. The glory was disappearing, and Moses did not want them to see it end. ¹⁴But their minds were closed, and even today that same covering hides the meaning when they read the old agreement. That covering is taken away only through Christ. ¹⁵Even today, when they read the law of Moses, there is a covering over their minds. ¹⁶But when a person changes and follows the Lord, that covering is taken away. ¹⁷The Lord is the Spirit, and where the Spirit of the Lord is, there is freedom. ¹⁸Our faces, then, are not covered. We all show the Lord's glory, and we are being changed to be like him. This change in us brings ever greater glory, which comes from the Lord, who is the Spirit.

4 God, with his mercy, gave us this work to do, so we don't give up. ²But we have turned away from secret and shameful ways. We use no trickery, and we do not change the teaching of God. We teach the truth plainly, showing everyone who we are. Then they can know in their hearts what kind of people we are in God's sight. ³If the Good News that we preach is hidden, it is hidden only to those who are lost. ⁴The devil who rules this world has blinded the minds of those who do not believe. They cannot see the light of the Good News—the Good News about the glory of Christ, who is exactly like God. ⁵We do not preach about ourselves, but we preach that Jesus Christ is Lord and that we are your servants for Jesus. ⁶God once said, "Let the light shine out of the darkness!"

This is the same God who made his light shine in our hearts by letting us know the glory of God that is in the face of Christ.

⁷We have this treasure from God, but we are like clay jars that hold the treasure. This shows that the great power is from God, not from us. ⁸We have troubles all around us, but we are not defeated. We do not know what to do, but we do not give up the hope of living. ⁹We are persecuted, but God does not leave us. We are hurt sometimes, but we are not destroyed. ¹⁰We carry the death of Jesus in our own bodies so that the life of Jesus can also be seen in our bodies. ¹¹We are alive, but for Jesus we are always in danger of death so that the life of Jesus can be seen in our bodies that die. ¹²So death is working in us, but life is working in you.

¹³It is written in the Scriptures, "I believed, so I spoke." Our faith is like this, too. We believe, and so we speak. ¹⁴God raised the Lord Jesus from the dead, and we know that God will also raise us with Jesus. God will bring us together with you, and we will stand before him. ¹⁵All these things are for you. And so the grace of God that is being given to more and more people will bring increasing thanks to God for his glory.

¹⁶So we do not give up. Our physical body is becoming older and weaker, but our spirit inside us is made new every day. ¹⁷We have small troubles for a while now, but they are helping us gain an eternal glory that is much greater than the troubles. ¹⁸We set our eyes not on what we see but on what we cannot see. What we see will last only a short time, but what we cannot see will last forever.

5 We know that our body—the tent we live in here on earth—will be destroyed. But when that happens, God will have a house for us. It will not be a house made by human hands; instead, it will be

a home in heaven that will last forever. [2]But now we groan in this tent. We want God to give us our heavenly home, [3]because it will clothe us so we will not be naked. [4]While we live in this body, we have burdens, and we groan. We do not want to be naked, but we want to be clothed with our heavenly home. Then this body that dies will be fully covered with life. [5]This is what God made us for, and he has given us the Spirit to be a guarantee for this new life.

STEP 11

[6]So we always have courage. We know that while we live in this body, we are away from the Lord. [7]We live by what we believe, not by what we can see. [8]So I say that we have courage. We really want to be away from this body and be at home with the Lord. [9]Our only goal is to please God whether we live here or there, [10]because we must all stand before Christ to be judged. Each of us will receive what we should get—good or bad—for the things we did in the earthly body.

STEP 12

[11]Since we know what it means to fear the Lord, we try to help people accept the truth about us. God knows what we really are, and I hope that in your hearts you know, too. [12]We are not trying to prove ourselves to you again, but we are telling you about ourselves so you will be proud of us. Then you will have an answer for those who are proud about things that can be seen rather than what is in the heart. [13]If we are out of our minds, it is for God. If we have our right minds, it is for you. [14]The love of Christ controls us, because we know that One died for all, so all have died. [15]Christ died for all so that those who live would not continue to live for themselves. He died for them and was raised from the dead so that they would live for him.

STEP 11

[16]From this time on we do not think of anyone as the world does. In the past we thought of Christ as the world thinks, but we no longer think of him in that way. [17]If anyone belongs to Christ, there is a new creation. The old things have gone; everything is made new! [18]All this is from God. Through Christ, God made peace between us and himself, and God gave us the work of telling everyone about the peace we can have with him. [19]God was in Christ, making peace between the world and himself. In Christ, God did not hold the world guilty of its sins. And he gave us this message of peace. [20]So we have been sent to speak for Christ. It is as if God is calling to you through us. We speak for Christ when we beg you to be at peace with God. [21]Christ had no sin, but God made him become sin so that in Christ we could become right with God.

STEP 6

STEP 12

STEP 2

6 We are workers together with God, so we beg you: Do not let the grace that you received from God be for nothing. [2]God says,

> "At the right time I heard your
> prayers.
> On the day of salvation I helped
> you."   *Isaiah 49:8*

I tell you that the "right time" is now, and the "day of salvation" is now.

[3]We do not want anyone to find fault with our work, so nothing we do will be a problem for anyone. [4]But in every way we show we are servants of God: in accepting many hard things, in troubles, in difficulties, and in great problems. [5]We are beaten and thrown into prison. We meet those who become upset with us and start riots. We work hard, and sometimes we get no sleep or food. [6]We show we are servants of God by our pure lives, our understanding, patience, and kindness, by the Holy Spirit, by true love, [7]by speaking the truth, and by God's power. We use our right living to defend ourselves against everything. [8]Some people honor us, but

others blame us. Some people say evil things about us, but others say good things. Some people say we are liars, but we speak the truth. ⁹We are not known, but we are well known. We seem to be dying, but we continue to live. We are punished, but we are not killed. ¹⁰We have much sadness, but we are always rejoicing. We are poor, but we are making many people rich in faith. We have nothing, but really we have everything.

¹¹We have spoken freely to you in Corinth and have opened our hearts to you. ¹²Our feelings of love for you have not stopped, but you have stopped your feelings of love for us. ¹³I speak to you as if you were my children. Do to us as we have done—open your hearts to us.

STEP 4

¹⁴You are not the same as those who do not believe. So do not join yourselves to them. Good and bad do not belong together. Light and darkness cannot share together. ¹⁵How can Christ and Belial, the devil, have any agreement? What can a believer have together with a non-believer? ¹⁶The temple of God cannot have any agreement with idols, and we are the temple of the living God. As God said: "I will live with them and walk with them. And I will be their God, and they will be my people."

¹⁷"Leave those people,
    and be separate, says the Lord.
  Touch nothing that is unclean,
    and I will accept you."
                    Isaiah 52:11; Ezekiel 20:34, 41

¹⁸"I will be your father,
    and you will be my sons and
        daughters,
    says the Lord Almighty."
                    2 Samuel 7:14

7 Dear friends, we have these promises from God, so we should make ourselves pure—free from anything that makes body or soul unclean. We should try to become holy in the way we live, because we respect God.

²Open your hearts to us. We have not done wrong to anyone, we have not ruined the faith of anyone, and we have not cheated anyone. ³I do not say this to blame you. I told you before that we love you so much we would live or die with you. ⁴I feel very sure of you and am very proud of you. You give me much comfort, and in all of our troubles I have great joy.

⁵When we came into Macedonia, we had no rest. We found trouble all around us. We had fighting on the outside and fear on the inside. ⁶But God, who comforts those who are troubled, comforted us when Titus came. ⁷We were comforted, not only by his coming but also by the comfort you gave him. Titus told us about your wish to see me and that you are very sorry for what you did. He also told me about your great care for me, and when I heard this, I was much happier.

⁸Even if my letter made you sad, I am not sorry I wrote it. At first I was sorry, because it made you sad, but you were sad only for a short time. ⁹Now I am happy, not because you were made sad, but because your sorrow made you change your lives. You became sad in the way God wanted you to, so you were not hurt by us in any way. ¹⁰The kind of sorrow God wants makes people change their hearts and lives. This leads to salvation, and you cannot be sorry for that. But the kind of sorrow the world has brings death. ¹¹See what this sorrow—the sorrow God wanted you to have—has done to you: It has made you very serious. It made you want to restore yourselves. It made you angry and afraid. It made you want to see me. It made you care. It made you want to do the right thing. In every way you have regained

STEP 6

your innocence. [12]I wrote that letter, not because of the one who did the wrong or because of the person who was hurt. I wrote the letter so you could see, before God, the great care you have for us. [13]That is why we were comforted.

Not only were we very comforted, we were even happier to see that Titus was so happy. All of you made him feel much better. [14]I bragged to Titus about you, and you showed that I was right. Everything we said to you was true, and you have proved that what we bragged about to Titus is true. [15]And his love for you is stronger when he remembers that you were all ready to obey. You welcomed him with respect and fear. [16]I am very happy that I can trust you fully.

8 And now, brothers and sisters, we want you to know about the grace God gave the churches in Macedonia. [2]They have been tested by great troubles, and they are very poor. But they gave much because of their great joy. [3]I can tell you that they gave as much as they were able and even more than they could afford. No one told them to do it. [4]But they begged and pleaded with us to let them share in this service for God's people. [5]And they gave in a way we did not expect: They first gave themselves to the Lord and to us. This is what God wants. [6]So we asked Titus to help you finish this special work of grace since he is the one who started it. [7]You are rich in everything—in faith, in speaking, in knowledge, in truly wanting to help, and in the love you learned from us. In the same way, be strong also in the grace of giving.

[8]I am not commanding you to give. But I want to see if your love is true by comparing you with others that really want to help. [9]You know the grace of our Lord Jesus Christ. You know that Christ was rich, but for you he became poor so that by his becoming poor you might become rich.

[10]This is what I think you should do: Last year you were the first to want to give, and you were the first who gave. [11]So now finish the work you started. Then your "doing" will be equal to your "wanting to do." Give from what you have. [12]If you want to give, your gift will be accepted. It will be judged by what you have, not by what you do not have. [13]We do not want you to have troubles while other people are at ease, but we want everything to be equal. [14]At this time you have plenty. What you have can help others who are in need. Then later, when they have plenty, they can help you when you are in need, and all will be equal. [15]As it is written in the Scriptures, "The person who gathered more did not have too much, nor did the person who gathered less have too little."

[16]I thank God because he gave Titus the same love for you that I have. [17]Titus accepted what we asked him to do. He wanted very much to go to you, and this was his own idea. [18]We are sending with him the brother who is praised by all the churches because of his service in preaching the Good News. [19]Also, this brother was chosen by the churches to go with us when we deliver this gift of money. We are doing this service to bring glory to the Lord and to show that we really want to help.

[20]We are being careful so that no one will criticize us for the way we are handling this large gift. [21]We are trying hard to do what the Lord accepts as right and also what people think is right.

[22]Also, we are sending with them our brother, who is always ready to help. He has proved this to us in many ways, and he wants to help even more now, because he has much faith in you.

²³Now about Titus—he is my partner who is working with me to help you. And about the other brothers—they are sent from the churches, and they bring glory to Christ. ²⁴So show these men the proof of your love and the reason we are proud of you. Then all the churches can see it.

9 I really do not need to write you about this help for God's people. ²I know you want to help. I have been bragging about this to the people in Macedonia, telling them that you in Southern Greece have been ready to give since last year. And your desire to give has made most of them ready to give also. ³But I am sending the brothers to you so that our bragging about you in this will not be empty words. I want you to be ready, as I said you would be. ⁴If any of the people from Macedonia come with me and find that you are not ready, we will be ashamed that we were so sure of you. (And you will be ashamed, too!) ⁵So I thought I should ask these brothers to go to you before we do. They will finish getting in order the generous gift you promised so it will be ready when we come. And it will be a generous gift— not one that you did not want to give.

STEP 11

⁶Remember this: The person who plants a little will have a small harvest, but the person who plants a lot will have a big harvest. ⁷Each of you should give as you have decided in your heart to give. You should not be sad when you give, and you should not give because you feel forced to give. God loves the person who gives happily. ⁸And God can give you more blessings than you need. Then you will always have plenty of everything— enough to give to every good work. ⁹It is written in the Scriptures:

"He gives freely to the poor.
The things he does are right and
will continue forever."
Psalm 112:9

¹⁰God is the One who gives seed to the farmer and bread for food. He will give you all the seed you need and make it grow so there will be a great harvest from your goodness. ¹¹He will make you rich in every way so that you can always give freely. And your giving through us will cause many to give thanks to God. ¹²This service you do not only helps the needs of God's people, it also brings many more thanks to God. ¹³It is a proof of your faith. Many people will praise God because you obey the Good News of Christ—the gospel you say you believe—and because you freely share with them and with all others. ¹⁴And when they pray, they will wish they could be with you because of the great grace that God has given you. ¹⁵Thanks be to God for his gift that is too wonderful for words.

10 I, Paul, am begging you with the gentleness and the kindness of Christ. Some people say that I am easy on you when I am with you and bold when I am away. ²They think we live in a worldly way, and I plan to be very bold with them when I come. I beg you that when I come I will not need to use that same boldness with you. ³We do live in the world, but we do not fight in the same way the world fights. ⁴We fight with weapons that are different from those the world uses. Our weapons have power from God that can destroy the enemy's strong places. We destroy people's arguments ⁵and every proud thing that raises itself against the knowledge of God. We capture every thought and make it give up and obey Christ. ⁶We are ready to punish anyone there who does not obey, but first we want you to obey fully.

STEP 5

⁷You must look at the facts before you. If you feel sure that you belong to

STEP 5

Admitted to God, to ourselves, and to another
human being the exact nature of our wrongs.

2 Corinthians 10:3–5

A good recovery grabs you by the back of the neck and shakes you
hard. It wakes you up spiritually and makes everything in your life
new and fresh.

So a recovery requires new ways of thinking and looking at life. This
passage reminds us that "we do live in the world, but we do not fight
in the same way the world fights" (verse 3). In your Step 5 sharing,
you'll talk about a lot of worldly sins; but in the end, you find out that
you don't fight the true recovery battle on a physical level where all
those sins are. It is a spiritual struggle.

When you have that "Aha!" moment, you know from then on you
have to change completely from the inside out. Maybe at the start of
your recovery, you felt the faith and prayer parts would be temporary
until you got over the hump and could handle life on your own. By
now your perspective may have flip-flopped so you know that faith
and prayer last forever and it's the troubles of life that are temporary.
From this new perspective, children of God can say, "We fight with
weapons that are different from those the world uses. Our weapons
have power from God" (verse 4). When tempted to think the old
thoughts of addiction, God's children can say, "We capture every
thought and make it give up and obey Christ" (verse 5).

FOR YOUR NEXT **STEP 5** MEDITATION, TURN TO **PAGE 315**. ▶▶

Christ, you must remember that we belong to Christ just as you do. [8]It is true that we brag freely about the authority the Lord gave us. But this authority is to build you up, not to tear you down. So I will not be ashamed. [9]I do not want you to think I am trying to scare you with my letters. [10]Some people say, "Paul's letters are powerful and sound important, but when he is with us, he is weak. And his speaking is nothing." [11]They should know this: We are not there with you now, so we say these things in letters. But when we are there with you, we will show the same authority that we show in our letters.

STEP 4 [12]We do not dare to compare ourselves with those who think they are very important. They use themselves to measure themselves, and they judge themselves by what they themselves are. This shows that they know nothing. [13]But we will not brag about things outside the work that was given us to do. We will limit our bragging to the work that God gave us, and this includes our work with you. [14]We are not bragging too much, as we would be if we had not already come to you. But we have come to you with the Good News of Christ. [15]We limit our bragging to the work that is ours, not what others have done. We hope that as your faith continues to grow, you will help our work to grow much larger. [16]We want to tell the Good News in the areas beyond your city. We do not want to brag about work that has already been done in another person's area. [17]But, "If people want to brag, they should brag only about the Lord." [18]It is not those who say they are good who are accepted but those the Lord thinks are good.

STEP 10

11 [1]I wish you would be patient with me even when I am a little foolish, but you are already doing that. [2]I am jealous over you with a jealousy that comes from God. I promised to give you to Christ, as your only husband. I want to give you as his pure bride. [3]But I am afraid that your minds will be led away from your true and pure following of Christ just as Eve was tricked by the snake with his evil ways. [4]You are very patient with anyone who comes to you and preaches a different Jesus from the one we preached. You are very willing to accept a spirit or gospel that is different from the Spirit and Good News you received from us.

[5]I do not think that those "great apostles" are any better than I am. [6]I may not be a trained speaker, but I do have knowledge. We have shown this to you clearly in every way.

[7]I preached God's Good News to you without pay. I made myself unimportant to make you important. Do you think that was wrong? [8]I accepted pay from other churches, taking their money so I could serve you. [9]If I needed something when I was with you, I did not trouble any of you. The brothers who came from Macedonia gave me all that I needed. I did not allow myself to depend on you in any way, and I will never depend on you. [10]No one in Southern Greece will stop me from bragging about that. I say this with the truth of Christ in me. [11]And why do I not depend on you? Do you think it is because I do not love you? God knows that I love you.

[12]And I will continue doing what I am doing now, because I want to stop those people from having a reason to brag. They would like to say that the work they brag about is the same as ours. [13]Such men are not true apostles but are workers who lie. They change themselves to look like apostles of Christ.

¹⁴This does not surprise us. Even Satan changes himself to look like an angel of light. ¹⁵So it does not surprise us if Satan's servants also make themselves look like servants who work for what is right. But in the end they will be punished for what they do.

¹⁶I tell you again: No one should think I am a fool. But if you think so, accept me as you would accept a fool. Then I can brag a little, too. ¹⁷When I brag because I feel sure of myself, I am not talking as the Lord would talk but as a fool. ¹⁸Many people are bragging about their lives in the world. So I will brag too. ¹⁹You are wise, so you will gladly be patient with fools! ²⁰You are even patient with those who order you around, or use you, or trick you, or think they are better than you, or hit you in the face. ²¹It is shameful to me to say this, but we were too "weak" to do those things to you!

But if anyone else is brave enough to brag, then I also will be brave and brag. (I am talking as a fool.) ²²Are they Hebrews? So am I. Are they Israelites? So am I. Are they from Abraham's family? So am I. ²³Are they serving Christ? I am serving him more. (I am crazy to talk like this.) I have worked much harder than they. I have been in prison more often. I have been hurt more in beatings. I have been near death many times. ²⁴Five times the Jews have given me their punishment of thirty-nine lashes with a whip. ²⁵Three different times I was beaten with rods. One time I was almost stoned to death. Three times I was in ships that wrecked, and one of those times I spent a night and a day in the sea. ²⁶I have gone on many travels and have been in danger from rivers, thieves, my own people, the Jews, and those who are not Jews. I have been in danger in cities, in places where no one

lives, and on the sea. And I have been in danger with false Christians. ²⁷I have done hard and tiring work, and many times I did not sleep. I have been hungry and thirsty, and many times I have been without food. I have been cold and without clothes. ²⁸Besides all this, there is on me every day the load of my concern for all the churches. ²⁹I feel weak every time someone is weak, and I feel upset every time someone is led into sin.

³⁰If I must brag, I will brag about the things that show I am weak. ³¹God knows I am not lying. He is the God and Father of the Lord Jesus Christ, and he is to be praised forever. ³²When I was in Damascus, the governor under King Aretas wanted to arrest me, so he put guards around the city. ³³But my friends lowered me in a basket through a hole in the city wall. So I escaped from the governor.

12 I must continue to brag. It will do no good, but I will talk now about visions and revelations from the Lord. ²I know a man in Christ who was taken up to the third heaven fourteen years ago. I do not know whether the man was in his body or out of his body, but God knows. ³⁻⁴And I know that this man was taken up to paradise. I don't know if he was in his body or away from his body, but God knows. He heard things he is not able to explain, things that no human is allowed to tell. ⁵I will brag about a man like that, but I will not brag about myself, except about my weaknesses. ⁶But if I wanted to brag about myself, I would not be a fool, because I would be telling the truth. But I will not brag about myself. I do not want people to think more of me than what they see me do or hear me say.

⁷So that I would not become too proud of the wonderful things that were

shown to me, a painful physical problem was given to me. This problem was a messenger from Satan, sent to beat me and keep me from being too proud. ⁸I begged the Lord three times to take this problem away from me. ⁹But he said to me, "My grace is enough for you. When you are weak, my power is made perfect in you." So I am very happy to brag about my weaknesses. Then Christ's power can live in me. ¹⁰For this reason I am happy when I have weaknesses, insults, hard times, sufferings, and all kinds of troubles for Christ. Because when I am weak, then I am truly strong.

¹¹I have been talking like a fool, but you made me do it. You are the ones who should say good things about me. I am worth nothing, but those "great apostles" are not worth any more than I am!

¹²When I was with you, I patiently did the things that prove I am an apostle— signs, wonders, and miracles. ¹³So you received everything that the other churches have received. Only one thing was different: I was not a burden to you. Forgive me for this!

¹⁴I am now ready to visit you the third time, and I will not be a burden to you. I want nothing from you, except you. Children should not have to save up to give to their parents. Parents should save to give to their children. ¹⁵So I am happy to give everything I have for you, even myself. If I love you more, will you love me less?

¹⁶It is clear I was not a burden to you, but you think I was tricky and lied to catch you. ¹⁷Did I cheat you by using any of the messengers I sent to you? No, you know I did not. ¹⁸I asked Titus to go to you, and I sent our brother with him. Titus did not cheat you, did he? No, you

know that Titus and I did the same thing and with the same spirit.

¹⁹Do you think we have been defending ourselves to you all this time? We have been speaking in Christ and before God. You are our dear friends, and everything we do is to make you stronger. ²⁰I am afraid that when I come, you will not be what I want you to be, and I will not be what you want me to be. I am afraid that among you there may be arguing, jealousy, anger, selfish fighting, evil talk, gossip, pride, and confusion. ²¹I am afraid that when I come to you again, my God will make me ashamed before you. I may be saddened by many of those who have sinned because they have not changed their hearts or turned from their sexual sins and the shameful things they have done.

13¹I will come to you for the third time. "Every case must be proved by two or three witnesses." ²When I was with you the second time, I gave a warning to those who had sinned. Now I am away from you, and I give a warning to all the others. When I come to you again, I will not be easy with them. ³You want proof that Christ is speaking through me. My proof is that he is not weak among you, but he is powerful. ⁴It is true that he was weak when he was killed on the cross, but he lives now by God's power. It is true that we are weak in Christ, but for you we will be alive in Christ by God's power.

⁵Look closely at yourselves. Test yourselves to see if you are living in the faith. You know that Jesus Christ is in you—unless you fail the test. ⁶But I hope you will see that we ourselves have not failed the test. ⁷We pray to God that you will not do anything wrong. It is not important to see that we have passed the

STEP
4

test, but it is important that you do what is right, even if it seems we have failed. [8]We cannot do anything against the truth, but only for the truth. [9]We are happy to be weak, if you are strong, and we pray that you will become complete. [10]I am writing this while I am away from you so that when I come I will not have to be harsh in my use of authority. The Lord gave me this authority to build you up, not to tear you down.

[11]Now, brothers and sisters, I say good-bye. Live in harmony. Do what I have asked you to do. Agree with each other, and live in peace. Then the God of love and peace will be with you.

[12]Greet each other with a holy kiss. [13]All of God's holy people send greetings to you.

[14]The grace of the Lord Jesus Christ, the love of God, and the fellowship of the Holy Spirit be with you all.

GALATIANS

Christians Are Saved by Grace

1 From Paul, an apostle. I was not chosen to be an apostle by human beings, nor was I sent from human beings. I was made an apostle through Jesus Christ and God the Father who raised Jesus from the dead. ²This letter is also from all those of God's family who are with me.

To the churches in Galatia:

³Grace and peace to you from God our Father and the Lord Jesus Christ. ⁴Jesus gave himself for our sins to free us from this evil world we live in, as God the Father planned. ⁵The glory belongs to God forever and ever. Amen.

⁶God, by his grace through Christ, called you to become his people. So I am amazed that you are turning away so quickly and believing something different than the Good News. ⁷Really, there is no other Good News. But some people are confusing you; they want to change the Good News of Christ. ⁸We preached to you the Good News. So if we ourselves, or even an angel from heaven, should preach to you something different, we should be judged guilty! ⁹I said this before, and now I say it again: You have already accepted the Good News. If anyone is preaching something different to you, let that person be judged guilty!

¹⁰Do you think I am trying to make people accept me? No, God is the One I am trying to please. Am I trying to please people? If I still wanted to please people, I would not be a servant of Christ.

¹¹Brothers and sisters, I want you to know that the Good News I preached to you was not made up by human beings. ¹²I did not get it from humans, nor did anyone teach it to me, but Jesus Christ showed it to me.

¹³You have heard about my past life in the Jewish religion. I attacked the church of God and tried to destroy it. ¹⁴I was becoming a leader in the Jewish religion, doing better than most other Jews of my age. I tried harder than anyone else to follow the teachings handed down by our ancestors.

¹⁵But God had special plans for me and set me apart for his work even before I was born. He called me through his grace ¹⁶and showed his son to me so that I might tell the Good News about him to those who are not Jewish. When God called me, I did not get advice or help from any person. ¹⁷I did not go to Jerusalem to see those who were apostles before I was. But, without waiting, I went away to Arabia and later went back to Damascus.

¹⁸After three years I went to Jerusalem to meet Peter and stayed with him for fifteen days. ¹⁹I met no other apostles, except James, the brother of the Lord. ²⁰God knows that these things I write are not lies. ²¹Later, I went to the areas of Syria and Cilicia.

²²In Judea the churches in Christ had never met me. ²³They had only heard it said, "This man who was attacking us is now preaching the same faith that he once tried to destroy." ²⁴And these believers praised God because of me.

2 After fourteen years I went to Jerusalem again, this time with Barnabas. I also took Titus with me. ²I went because God showed me I should go. I met with the believers there, and in private I told their leaders the Good News that I preach to the non-Jewish people. I did not want my past work and the work I am

now doing to be wasted. [3]Titus was with me, but he was not forced to be circumcised, even though he was a Greek. [4]We talked about this problem because some false believers had come into our group secretly. They came in like spies to overturn the freedom we have in Christ Jesus. They wanted to make us slaves. [5]But we did not give in to those false believers for a minute. We wanted the truth of the Good News to continue for you.

[6]Those leaders who seemed to be important did not change the Good News that I preach. (It doesn't matter to me if they were "important" or not. To God everyone is the same.) [7]But these leaders saw that I had been given the work of telling the Good News to those who are not Jewish, just as Peter had the work of telling the Jews. [8]God gave Peter the power to work as an apostle for the Jewish people. But he also gave me the power to work as an apostle for those who are not Jews. [9]James, Peter, and John, who seemed to be the leaders, understood that God had given me this special grace, so they accepted Barnabas and me. They agreed that they would go to the Jewish people and that we should go to those who are not Jewish. [10]The only thing they asked us was to remember to help the poor—something I really wanted to do.

[11]When Peter came to Antioch, I challenged him to his face, because he was wrong. [12]Peter ate with the non-Jewish people until some Jewish people sent from James came to Antioch. When they arrived, Peter stopped eating with those who weren't Jewish, and he separated himself from them. He was afraid of the Jews. [13]So Peter was a hypocrite, as were the other Jewish believers who joined with him. Even Barnabas was influenced by what these Jewish believers did.

[14]When I saw they were not following the truth of the Good News, I spoke to Peter in front of them all. I said, "Peter, you are a Jew, but you are not living like a Jew. You are living like those who are not Jewish. So why do you now try to force those who are not Jewish to live like Jews?"

[15]We were not born as non-Jewish "sinners," but as Jews. [16]Yet we know that a person is made right with God not by following the law, but by trusting in Jesus Christ. So we, too, have put our faith in Christ Jesus, that we might be made right with God because we trusted in Christ. It is not because we followed the law, because no one can be made right with God by following the law.

[17]We Jews came to Christ, trying to be made right with God, and it became clear that we are sinners, too. Does this mean that Christ encourages sin? No! [18]But I would really be wrong to begin teaching again those things that I gave up. [19]It was the law that put me to death, and I died to the law so that I can now live for God. [20]I was put to death on the cross with Christ, and I do not live anymore—it is Christ who lives in me. I still live in my body, but I live by faith in the Son of God who loved me and gave himself to save me. [21]By saying these things I am not going against God's grace. Just the opposite, if the law could make us right with God, then Christ's death would be useless.

3 You people in Galatia were told very clearly about the death of Jesus Christ on the cross. But you were foolish; you let someone trick you. [2]Tell me this one thing: How did you receive the Holy Spirit? Did you receive the Spirit by following the law? No, you received the Spirit because you heard the Good News and believed it. [3]You began your life in Christ by the Spirit. Now are you trying to make it complete by your own power?

STEP 11

STEP 11

Sought through prayer and meditation to improve
our conscious contact with God **as we understood
Him,** praying only for knowledge of His will
for us and the power to carry that out.

G a l a t i a n s   2 : 2 0

There's an old saying that captures what happens when you hit
bottom. It goes like this: "Let go, and let God." When you lived in
your addiction, your compulsive cravings filled the center of your
universe. When you hit bottom you had to stop being your own
higher power, trying to handle the mess your life was in. You had to
be "put to death on the cross with Christ." You had to die to
codependent reliance on people and things.

When you come to Christ in faith, you experience a spiritual rebirth.
God takes his rightful place at the center of your life. Now you need
to look for spiritual solutions to the old dependent hungers of your
body. When we do, "we will intuitively know how to handle
situations which used to baffle us. We will suddenly realize that
God is doing for us what we could not do for ourselves" (*Alcoholics
Anonymous*, p. 84).

FOR YOUR NEXT **STEP 11** MEDITATION, TURN TO **PAGE 280.** ▶▶

That is foolish. [4]Were all your experiences wasted? I hope not! [5]Does God give you the Spirit and work miracles among you because you follow the law? No, he does these things because you heard the Good News and believed it.

[6]The Scriptures say the same thing about Abraham: "Abraham believed God, and God accepted Abraham's faith, and that faith made him right with God." [7]So you should know that the true children of Abraham are those who have faith. [8]The Scriptures, telling what would happen in the future, said that God would make the non-Jewish people right through their faith. This Good News was told to Abraham beforehand, as the Scripture says: "All nations will be blessed through you." [9]So all who believe as Abraham believed are blessed just as Abraham was. [10]But those who depend on following the law to make them right are under a curse, because the Scriptures say, "Anyone will be cursed who does not always obey what is written in the Book of the Law." [11]Now it is clear that no one can be made right with God by the law, because the Scriptures say, "Those who are right with God will live by faith." [12]The law is not based on faith. It says, "A person who obeys these things will live because of them." [13]Christ took away the curse the law put on us. He changed places with us and put himself under that curse. It is written in the Scriptures, "Anyone whose body is displayed on a tree is cursed." [14]Christ did this so that God's blessing promised to Abraham might come through Jesus Christ to those who are not Jews. Jesus died so that by our believing we could receive the Spirit that God promised.

[15]Brothers and sisters, let us think in human terms: Even an agreement made between two persons is firm. After that agreement is accepted by both people, no one can stop it or add anything to it. [16]God made promises both to Abraham and to his descendant. God did not say, "and to your descendants." That would mean many people. But God said, "and to your descendant." That means only one person; that person is Christ. [17]This is what I mean: God had an agreement with Abraham and promised to keep it. The law, which came four hundred thirty years later, cannot change that agreement and so destroy God's promise to Abraham. [18]If the law could give us Abraham's blessing, then the promise would not be necessary. But that is not possible, because God freely gave his blessings to Abraham through the promise he had made.

[19]So what was the law for? It was given to show that the wrong things people do are against God's will. And it continued until the special descendant, who had been promised, came. The law was given through angels who used Moses for a mediator to give the law to people. [20]But a mediator is not needed when there is only one side, and God is only one.

[21]Does this mean that the law is against God's promises? Never! That would be true only if the law could make us right with God. But God did not give a law that can bring life. [22]Instead, the Scriptures showed that the whole world is bound by sin. This was so the promise would be given through faith to people who believe in Jesus Christ.

[23]Before this faith came, we were all held prisoners by the law. We had no freedom until God showed us the way of faith that was coming. [24]In other words, the law was our guardian leading us to Christ so that we could be made right with God through faith. [25]Now the way of

faith has come, and we no longer live under a guardian.

²⁶⁻²⁷You were all baptized into Christ, and so you were all clothed with Christ. This means that you are all children of God through faith in Christ Jesus. ²⁸In Christ, there is no difference between Jew and Greek, slave and free person, male and female. You are all the same in Christ Jesus. ²⁹You belong to Christ, so you are Abraham's descendants. You will inherit all of God's blessings because of the promise God made to Abraham.

4 I want to tell you this: While those who will inherit their fathers' property are still children, they are no different from slaves. It does not matter that the children own everything. ²While they are children, they must obey those who are chosen to care for them. But when the children reach the age set by their fathers, they are free. ³It is the same for us. We were once like children, slaves to the useless rules of this world. ⁴But when the right time came, God sent his Son who was born of a woman and lived under the law. ⁵God did this so he could buy freedom for those who were under the law and so we could become his children.

⁶Since you are God's children, God sent the Spirit of his Son into your hearts, and the Spirit cries out, "Father." ⁷So now you are not a slave; you are God's child, and God will give you the blessing he promised, because you are his child.

⁸In the past you did not know God. You were slaves to gods that were not real.

STEP 10 ⁹But now you know the true God. Really, it is God who knows you. So why do you turn back to those weak and useless rules you followed before? Do you want to be slaves to those things again? ¹⁰You still follow teachings about special days, months, seasons, and years. ¹¹I am afraid

for you, that my work for you has been wasted.

¹²Brothers and sisters, I became like you, so I beg you to become like me. You were very good to me before. ¹³You remember that it was because of an illness that I came to you the first time, preaching the Good News. ¹⁴Though my sickness was a trouble for you, you did not hate me or make me leave. But you welcomed me as an angel from God, as if I were Jesus Christ himself! ¹⁵You were very happy then, but where is that joy now? I am ready to testify that you would have taken out your eyes and given them to me if that were possible. ¹⁶Now am I your enemy because I tell you the truth?

¹⁷Those people are working hard to persuade you, but this is not good for you. They want to persuade you to turn against us and follow only them. ¹⁸It is good for people to show interest in you, but only if their purpose is good. This is always true, not just when I am with you. ¹⁹My little children, again I feel the pain of childbirth for you until you truly become like Christ. ²⁰I wish I could be with you now and could change the way I am talking to you, because I do not know what to think about you.

²¹Some of you still want to be under the law. Tell me, do you know what the law says? ²²The Scriptures say that Abraham had two sons. The mother of one son was a slave woman, and the mother of the other son was a free woman. ²³Abraham's son from the slave woman was born in the normal human way. But the son from the free woman was born because of the promise God made to Abraham.

²⁴This story teaches something else: The two women are like the two agreements between God and his people. One agreement is the law that God made

on Mount Sinai, and the people who are under this agreement are like slaves. The mother named Hagar is like that agreement. ²⁵She is like Mount Sinai in Arabia and is a picture of the earthly city of Jerusalem. This city and its people are slaves to the law. ²⁶But the heavenly Jerusalem, which is above, is like the free woman. She is our mother. ²⁷It is written in the Scriptures:

"Be happy, Jerusalem.
> You are like a woman who never gave birth to children.
Start singing and shout for joy.
> You never felt the pain of giving birth,
but you will have more children
> than the woman who has a husband." *Isaiah 54:1*

²⁸My brothers and sisters, you are God's children because of his promise, as Isaac was then. ²⁹The son who was born in the normal way treated the other son badly. It is the same today. ³⁰But what does the Scripture say? "Throw out the slave woman and her son. The son of the slave woman should not inherit anything. The son of the free woman should receive it all." ³¹So, my brothers and sisters, we are not children of the slave woman, but of the free woman.

5 We have freedom now, because Christ made us free. So stand strong. Do not change and go back into the slavery of the law. ²Listen, I Paul tell you that if you go back to the law by being circumcised, Christ does you no good. ³Again, I warn every man: If you allow yourselves to be circumcised, you must follow all the law. ⁴If you try to be made right with God through the law, your life with Christ is over—you have left God's grace. ⁵But we have the true hope that comes from being made right with God, and by the Spirit we wait eagerly for this hope. ⁶When we

are in Christ Jesus, it is not important if we are circumcised or not. The important thing is faith—the kind of faith that works through love.

⁷You were running a good race. Who stopped you from following the true way? ⁸This change did not come from the One who chose you. ⁹Be careful! "Just a little yeast makes the whole batch of dough rise." ¹⁰But I trust in the Lord that you will not believe those different ideas. Whoever is confusing you with such ideas will be punished.

¹¹My brothers and sisters, I do not teach that a man must be circumcised. If I teach circumcision, why am I still being attacked? If I still taught circumcision, my preaching about the cross would not be a problem. ¹²I wish the people who are bothering you would castrate themselves!

¹³My brothers and sisters, God called you to be free, but do not use your freedom as an excuse to do what pleases your sinful self. Serve each other with love. ¹⁴The whole law is made complete in this one command: "Love your neighbor as you love yourself." ¹⁵If you go on hurting each other and tearing each other apart, be careful, or you will completely destroy each other.

¹⁶So I tell you: Live by following the Spirit. Then you will not do what your sinful selves want. ¹⁷Our sinful selves want what is against the Spirit, and the Spirit wants what is against our sinful selves. The two are against each other, so you cannot do just what you please. ¹⁸But if the Spirit is leading you, you are not under the law.

¹⁹The wrong things the sinful self does are clear: being sexually unfaithful, not being pure, taking part in sexual sins, ²⁰worshiping gods, doing witchcraft, hating, making trouble, being jealous, being angry, being selfish, making people angry

STEP 4

Made a searching and fearless moral
inventory of ourselves.

Galatians 6:3-5

It may surprise you to know that most people with really low self-esteem spend much of their time thinking about themselves and imagining they are successful and important. Most addicts have self-esteem issues and need to gain a more realistic and balanced perspective on themselves. Maybe you do, too. Your Step 4 personal inventory can help you do just that.

What is this balance you're looking for? On the one hand, the Bible tells you not to try to be something you're not. It asks that you deflate your ego. On the other hand, the Bible encourages you to be happy about and take credit for what you accomplish.

Getting a balanced perspective through your Step 4 inventory is important for two reasons. First, you get away from daydreams of glory and bouts of beating up on yourself. Second, you don't need other people to tell you you're okay. You can examine yourself and know what you've done well and what you need to work on. A person is well on the way to recovery who can "be responsible for himself" or herself (verse 5).

FOR YOUR NEXT **STEP 4** MEDITATION, TURN TO **PAGE 504.** ▶▶

with each other, causing divisions among people, ²¹feeling envy, being drunk, having wild and wasteful parties, and doing other things like these. I warn you now as I warned you before: Those who do these things will not inherit God's kingdom. ²²But the Spirit produces the fruit of love, joy, peace, patience, kindness, goodness, faithfulness, ²³gentleness, self-control. There is no law that says these things are wrong. ²⁴Those who belong to Christ Jesus have crucified their own sinful selves. They have given up their old selfish feelings and the evil things they wanted to do. ²⁵We get our new life from the Spirit, so we should follow the Spirit. ²⁶We must not be proud or make trouble with each other or be jealous of each other.

6 Brothers and sisters, if someone in your group does something wrong, you who are spiritual should go to that person and gently help make him right again. But be careful, because you might be tempted to sin, too. ²By helping each other with your troubles, you truly obey the law of Christ. ³If anyone thinks he is important when he really is not, he is only fooling himself. ⁴Each person should judge his own actions and not compare himself with others. Then he can be proud for what he himself has done. ⁵Each person must be responsible for himself.

⁶Anyone who is learning the teaching of God should share all the good things he has with his teacher.

⁷Do not be fooled: You cannot cheat God. People harvest only what they plant.

⁸If they plant to satisfy their sinful selves, their sinful selves will bring them ruin. But if they plant to please the Spirit, they will receive eternal life from the Spirit. ⁹We must not become tired of doing good. We will receive our harvest of eternal life at the right time if we do not give up. ¹⁰When we have the opportunity to help anyone, we should do it. But we should give special attention to those who are in the family of believers.

¹¹See what large letters I use to write this myself. ¹²Some people are trying to force you to be circumcised so the Jews will accept them. They are afraid they will be attacked if they follow only the cross of Christ. ¹³Those who are circumcised do not obey the law themselves, but they want you to be circumcised so they can brag about what they forced you to do. ¹⁴I hope I will never brag about things like that. The cross of our Lord Jesus Christ is my only reason for bragging. Through the cross of Jesus my world was crucified, and I died to the world. ¹⁵It is not important if a man is circumcised or uncircumcised. The important thing is being the new people God has made. ¹⁶Peace and mercy to those who follow this rule—and to all of God's people.

¹⁷So do not give me any more trouble. I have scars on my body that show I belong to Christ Jesus.

¹⁸My brothers and sisters, the grace of our Lord Jesus Christ be with your spirit. Amen.

EPHESIANS

God Unites His People

1 From Paul, an apostle of Christ Jesus. I am an apostle because that is what God wanted.

To God's holy people living in Ephesus, believers in Christ Jesus:

[2]Grace and peace to you from God our Father and the Lord Jesus Christ.

STEP 3

[3]Praise be to the God and Father of our Lord Jesus Christ. In Christ, God has given us every spiritual blessing in the heavenly world. [4]That is, in Christ, he chose us before the world was made so that we would be his holy people—people without blame before him. [5]Because of his love, God had already decided to make us his own children through Jesus Christ. That was what he wanted and what pleased him, [6]and it brings praise to God because of his wonderful grace. God gave that grace to us freely, in Christ, the One he loves. [7]In Christ we are set free by the blood of his death, and so we have forgiveness of sins. How rich is God's grace, [8]which he has given to us so fully and freely. God, with full wisdom and understanding, [9]let us know his secret purpose. This was what God wanted, and he planned to do it through Christ. [10]His goal was to carry out his plan, when the right time came, that all things in heaven and on earth would be joined together in Christ as the head.

[11]In Christ we were chosen to be God's people, because from the very beginning God had decided this in keeping with his plan. And he is the One who makes everything agree with what he decides and wants. [12]We are the first people who hoped in Christ, and we were chosen so that we would bring praise to God's glory. [13]So it is with you. When you heard the true teaching—the Good News about your salvation—you believed in Christ. And in Christ, God put his special mark of ownership on you by giving you the Holy Spirit that he had promised. [14]That Holy Spirit is the guarantee that we will receive what God promised for his people until God gives full freedom to those who are his—to bring praise to God's glory.

[15]That is why since I heard about your faith in the Lord Jesus and your love for all God's people, [16]I have not stopped giving thanks to God for you. I always remember you in my prayers, [17]asking the God of our Lord Jesus Christ, the glorious Father, to give you a spirit of wisdom and revelation so that you will know him better. [18]I pray also that you will have greater understanding in your heart so you will know the hope to which he has called us and that you will know how rich and glorious are the blessings God has promised his holy people. [19]And you will know that God's power is very great for us who believe. That power is the same as the great strength [20]God used to raise Christ from the dead and put him at his right side in the heavenly world. [21]God has put Christ over all rulers, authorities, powers, and kings, not only in this world but also in the next. [22]God put everything under his power and made him the head over everything for the church, [23]which is Christ's body. The church is filled with Christ, and Christ fills everything in every way.

STEP 11

2 In the past you were spiritually dead because of your sins and the things you did against God. [2]Yes, in the past you lived the way the world lives, following the ruler of the evil powers that are above

STEP 1

the earth. That same spirit is now working in those who refuse to obey God. ³In the past all of us lived like them, trying to please our sinful selves and doing all the things our bodies and minds wanted. We should have suffered God's anger because we were sinful by nature. We were the same as all other people.

STEP 2
⁴But God's mercy is great, and he loved us very much. ⁵Though we were spiritually dead because of the things we did against God, he gave us new life with Christ. You have been saved by God's grace. ⁶And he raised us up with Christ and gave us a seat with him in the heavens. He did this for those in Christ Jesus ⁷so that for all future time he could show the very great riches of his grace by being kind to us in Christ Jesus. **STEP 3** ⁸I mean that you have been saved by grace through believing. You did not save yourselves; it was a gift from God. ⁹It was not the result of your own efforts, so you cannot brag about it. **STEP 12** ¹⁰God has made us what we are. In Christ Jesus, God made us to do good works, which God planned in advance for us to live our lives doing.

¹¹You were not born Jewish. You are the people the Jews call "uncircumcised." Those who call you "uncircumcised" call themselves "circumcised." (Their circumcision is only something they themselves do on their bodies.) ¹²Remember that in the past you were without Christ. You were not citizens of Israel, and you had no part in the agreements with the promise that God made to his people. You had no hope, and you did not know God. ¹³But now in Christ Jesus, you who were far away from God are brought near through the blood of Christ's death. ¹⁴Christ himself is our peace. He made both Jewish people and those who are not Jews one people. They were separated as if there were a wall between them, but Christ broke down that wall of hate by giving his own body. ¹⁵The Jewish law had many commands and rules, but Christ ended that law. His purpose was to make the two groups of people become one new people in him and in this way make peace. ¹⁶It was also Christ's purpose to end the hatred between the two groups, to make them into one body, and to bring them back to God. Christ did all this with his death on the cross. ¹⁷Christ came and preached peace to you who were far away from God, and to those who were near to God. ¹⁸Yes, it is through Christ we all have the right to come to the Father in one Spirit.

¹⁹Now you who are not Jewish are not foreigners or strangers any longer, but are citizens together with God's holy people. You belong to God's family. ²⁰You are like a building that was built on the foundation of the apostles and prophets. Christ Jesus himself is the most important stone in that building, ²¹and that whole building is joined together in Christ. He makes it grow and become a holy temple in the Lord. ²²And in Christ you, too, are being built together with the Jews into a place where God lives through the Spirit.

3 So I, Paul, am a prisoner of Christ Jesus for you who are not Jews. ²Surely you have heard that God gave me this work to tell you about his grace. ³He let me know his secret by showing it to me. I have already written a little about this. ⁴If you read what I wrote then, you can see that I truly understand the secret about the Christ. ⁵People who lived in other times were not told that secret. But now, through the Spirit, God has shown that secret to his holy apostles and prophets. ⁶This is that secret: that through the Good News those who are not Jews will share with the Jews in God's blessing.

STEP 3

Made a decision to turn our will and our lives
over to the care of God **as we understood Him.**

Ephesians 2:8–9

There's a recovery slogan that may confuse newcomers to the Twelve
Steps. It's the incomplete thought "But for the grace of God. . . ." What
does that mean? Why leave the sentence dangling? It dangles
because everybody finishes the sentence differently. At some point,
everybody in recovery realizes that God has bailed them out of some
tough spots. If he hadn't . . . well, they wouldn't be working on their
recoveries. They'd be sinking deeper into their addictions.

"But for the grace of God" also means that the miracle of your
recovery isn't due to your own efforts. God isn't keeping a ledger
where he balances the good you do against the bad to see if you earn
salvation. Maybe you've been a perfectionist who thought you had to
get a handle on everything and do it just to be happy. That's not the
good news of the gospel, which says salvation is God's gift. It's not
something you can boast about deserving based on what you've done.

Be glad that your recovery doesn't hinge on being perfect. Wrap your
arms around the merciful grace of God and hang on. If you feel the
need to be perfect, those feelings aren't from God. That's a trick to
pull you back toward your addiction. God is the Creator; you're his
creation. "In Christ Jesus, God made us to do good works" (verse 10).
Trust God's grace to do this for you.

FOR YOUR NEXT **STEP 3** MEDITATION, TURN TO **PAGE 383.** ▶▶

They belong to the same body, and they share together in the promise that God made in Christ Jesus.

⁷By God's special gift of grace given to me through his power, I became a servant to tell that Good News. ⁸I am the least important of all God's people, but God gave me this gift—to tell those who are not Jews the Good News about the riches of Christ, which are too great to understand fully. ⁹And God gave me the work of telling all people about the plan for his secret, which has been hidden in him since the beginning of time. He is the One who created everything. ¹⁰His purpose was that through the church all the rulers and powers in the heavenly world will now know God's wisdom, which has so many forms. ¹¹This agrees with the purpose God had since the beginning of time, and he carried out his plan through Christ Jesus our Lord. ¹²In Christ we can come before God with freedom and without fear. We can do this through faith in Christ. ¹³So I ask you not to become discouraged because of the sufferings I am having for you. My sufferings are for your glory.

STEP
11

¹⁴So I bow in prayer before the Father ¹⁵from whom every family in heaven and on earth gets its true name. ¹⁶I ask the Father in his great glory to give you the power to be strong inwardly through his Spirit. ¹⁷I pray that Christ will live in your hearts by faith and that your life will be strong in love and be built on love. ¹⁸And I pray that you and all God's holy people will have the power to understand the greatness of Christ's love—how wide and how long and how high and how deep that love is. ¹⁹Christ's love is greater than anyone can ever know, but I pray that you will be able to know that love. Then you can be filled with the fullness of God.

²⁰With God's power working in us, God can do much, much more than anything we can ask or imagine. ²¹To him be glory in the church and in Christ Jesus for all time, forever and ever. Amen.

4 I am in prison because I belong to the Lord. Therefore I urge you who have been chosen by God to live up to the life to which God called you. ²Always be humble, gentle, and patient, accepting each other in love. ³You are joined together with peace through the Spirit, so make every effort to continue together in this way. ⁴There is one body and one Spirit, and God called you to have one hope. ⁵There is one Lord, one faith, and one baptism. ⁶There is one God and Father of everything. He rules everything and is everywhere and is in everything.

⁷Christ gave each one of us the special gift of grace, showing how generous he is. ⁸That is why it says in the Scriptures,

"When he went up to the heights,
    he led a parade of captives,
    and he gave gifts to people."
                              Psalm 68:18

⁹When it says, "He went up," what does it mean? It means that he first came down to the earth. ¹⁰So Jesus came down, and he is the same One who went up above all the heaven. Christ did that to fill everything with his presence. ¹¹And Christ gave gifts to people—he made some to be apostles, some to be prophets, some to go and tell the Good News, and some to have the work of caring for and teaching God's people. ¹²Christ gave those gifts to prepare God's holy people for the work of serving, to make the body of Christ stronger. ¹³This work must continue until we are all joined together in the same faith and in the same knowledge of the Son of God. We must become like a mature person, growing until we become like Christ and have his perfection.

STEP 5
[14]Then we will no longer be babies. We will not be tossed about like a ship that the waves carry one way and then another. We will not be influenced by every new teaching we hear from people who are trying to fool us. They make plans and try any kind of trick to fool people into following the wrong path. [15]No! Speaking the truth with love, we will grow up in every way into Christ, who is the head. [16]The whole body depends on Christ, and all the parts of the body are joined and held together. Each part does its own work to make the whole body grow and be strong with love.

STEP 6
[17]In the Lord's name, I tell you this. Do not continue living like those who do not believe. Their thoughts are worth nothing. [18]They do not understand, and they know nothing, because they refuse to listen. So they cannot have the life that God gives. [19]They have lost all feeling of shame, and they use their lives for doing evil. They continually want to do all kinds of evil. [20]But what you learned in Christ was not like this. [21]I know that you heard about him, and you are in him, so you were taught the truth that is in Jesus. [22]You were taught to leave your old self—to stop living the evil way you lived before. That old self becomes worse, because people are fooled by the evil things they want to do. [23]But you were taught to be made new in your hearts, [24]to become a new person. That new person is made to be like God—made to be truly good and holy.

STEP 5
[25]So you must stop telling lies. Tell each other the truth, because we all belong to each other in the same body. [26]When you are angry, do not sin, and be sure to stop being angry before the end of the day. [27]Do not give the devil a way to defeat you. [28]Those who are stealing must stop stealing and start working. They should earn an honest living for themselves. Then they will have something to share with those who are poor.

[29]When you talk, do not say harmful things, but say what people need—words that will help others become stronger. Then what you say will do good to those who listen to you. [30]And do not make the Holy Spirit sad. The Spirit is God's proof that you belong to him. God gave you the Spirit to show that God will make you free when the final day comes. [31]Do not be bitter or angry or mad. Never shout angrily or say things to hurt others. Never do anything evil. [32]Be kind and loving to each other, and forgive each other just as God forgave you in Christ.

5 You are God's children whom he loves, so try to be like him. [2]Live a life of love just as Christ loved us and gave himself for us as a sweet-smelling offering and sacrifice to God.

STEP 4
[3]But there must be no sexual sin among you, or any kind of evil or greed. Those things are not right for God's holy people. [4]Also, there must be no evil talk among you, and you must not speak foolishly or tell evil jokes. These things are not right for you. Instead, you should be giving thanks to God. [5]You can be sure of this: No one will have a place in the kingdom of Christ and of God who sins sexually, or does evil things, or is greedy. Anyone who is greedy is serving a false god.

[6]Do not let anyone fool you by telling you things that are not true, because these things will bring God's anger on those who do not obey him. [7]So have nothing to do with them. **STEP 6** [8]In the past you were full of darkness, but now you are full of light in the Lord. So live like children who belong to the light. [9]Light brings every kind of goodness, right living, and truth. [10]Try to learn what pleases the Lord. [11]Have nothing to do with the things done in darkness, which are not worth

STEP 6

Were entirely ready to have God
remove all these defects of character.

Ephesians 4:17–23

It's easier to talk about breaking addictions than to do it. Obviously!
You have to get to the point where breaking with the past is the
most important thing there is, no matter how much it hurts in the
process.

There's a situation that pops up repeatedly in the old *Peanuts*
comic strip. Linus decides it's time to give up his blanket. It
shouldn't be hard. The old thing is tattered and dirty. He's
embarrassed to hang onto it when Lucy laughs at him. So he
throws it away and resolves to face life without it. Well, you know
what happens. Linus's willpower crumbles, and it's back to the
blanket and his thumb for a security fix.

In Ephesians 4, the apostle Paul encouraged Christians at Ephesus
to depend on God's help to get rid of their dirty, worn-out
"blankets" of character defects once and for all in order to be
completely "made new in [their] hearts" (verse 23). You, too, can
have a complete heart makeover when you become totally willing
and ready for God to work radically in your life.

FOR YOUR NEXT **STEP 6** MEDITATION, TURN TO **PAGE 285.** ▶▶

anything. But show that they are wrong. [12]It is shameful even to talk about what those people do in secret. [13]But the light makes all things easy to see, [14]and everything that is made easy to see can become light. This is why it is said:

"Wake up, sleeper!
    Rise from death,
and Christ will shine on you."

STEP 10

[15]So be very careful how you live. Do not live like those who are not wise, but live wisely. [16]Use every chance you have for doing good, because these are evil times. [17]So do not be foolish but learn what the Lord wants you to do.

STEP 4

[18]Do not be drunk with wine, which will ruin you, but be filled with the Spirit.

STEP 11

[19]Speak to each other with psalms, hymns, and spiritual songs, singing and making music in your hearts to the Lord. [20]Always give thanks to God the Father for everything, in the name of our Lord Jesus Christ.

[21]Yield to obey each other as you would to Christ.

STEP 4

[22]Wives, yield to your husbands, as you do to the Lord, [23]because the husband is the head of the wife, as Christ is the head of the church. And he is the Savior of the body, which is the church. [24]As the church yields to Christ, so you wives should yield to your husbands in everything.

[25]Husbands, love your wives as Christ loved the church and gave himself for it [26]to make it belong to God. Christ used the word to make the church clean by washing it with water. [27]He died so that he could give the church to himself like a bride in all her beauty. He died so that the church could be pure and without fault, with no evil or sin or any other wrong thing in it. [28]In the same way, husbands should love their wives as they love their own bodies. The man who loves his wife loves himself. [29]No one ever hates his own body, but feeds and takes care of it. And

that is what Christ does for the church, [30]because we are parts of his body. [31]The Scripture says, "So a man will leave his father and mother and be united with his wife, and the two will become one body." [32]That secret is very important—I am talking about Christ and the church. [33]But each one of you must love his wife as he loves himself, and a wife must respect her husband.

6 Children, obey your parents as the Lord wants, because this is the right thing to do.

STEP 4

[2]The command says, "Honor your father and mother." This is the first command that has a promise with it— [3]"Then everything will be well with you, and you will have a long life on the earth."

[4]Fathers, do not make your children angry, but raise them with the training and teaching of the Lord.

[5]Slaves, obey your masters here on earth with fear and respect and from a sincere heart, just as you obey Christ. [6]You must do this not only while they are watching you, to please them. With all your heart you must do what God wants as people who are obeying Christ. [7]Do your work with enthusiasm. Work as if you were serving the Lord, not as if you were serving only men and women. [8]Remember that the Lord will give a reward to everyone, slave or free, for doing good.

[9]Masters, in the same way, be good to your slaves. Do not threaten them. Remember that the One who is your Master and their Master is in heaven, and he treats everyone alike.

STEP 11

[10]Finally, be strong in the Lord and in his great power. [11]Put on the full armor of God so that you can fight against the devil's evil tricks. [12]Our fight is not against people on earth but against the rulers and authorities and the powers of this world's darkness, against the spiritual

powers of evil in the heavenly world. [13]That is why you need to put on God's full armor. Then on the day of evil you will be able to stand strong. And when you have finished the whole fight, you will still be standing. [14]So stand strong, with the belt of truth tied around your waist and the protection of right living on your chest. [15]On your feet wear the Good News of peace to help you stand strong. [16]And also use the shield of faith with which you can stop all the burning arrows of the Evil One. [17]Accept God's salvation as your helmet, and take the sword of the Spirit, which is the word of God. [18]Pray in the Spirit at all times with all kinds of prayers, asking for everything you need. To do this you must always be ready and never give up. Always pray for all God's people.

[19]Also pray for me that when I speak, God will give me words so that I can tell the secret of the Good News without fear. [20]I have been sent to preach this Good News, and I am doing that now, here in prison. Pray that when I preach the Good News I will speak without fear, as I should.

[21]I am sending to you Tychicus, our brother whom we love and a faithful servant of the Lord's work. He will tell you everything that is happening with me. Then you will know how I am and what I am doing. [22]I am sending him to you for this reason—so that you will know how we are, and he can encourage you.

[23]Peace and love with faith to you brothers and sisters from God the Father and the Lord Jesus Christ. [24]Grace to all of you who love our Lord Jesus Christ with love that never ends.

PHILIPPIANS

Serve Others with Joy

1 From Paul and Timothy, servants of Christ Jesus.

To all of God's holy people in Christ Jesus who live in Philippi, including your overseers and deacons:

[2]Grace and peace to you from God our Father and the Lord Jesus Christ.

[3]I thank my God every time I remember you, [4]always praying with joy for all of you. [5]I thank God for the help you gave me while I preached the Good News—help you gave from the first day you believed until now. [6]God began doing a good work in you, and I am sure he will continue it until it is finished when Jesus Christ comes again.

STEP 12

[7]And I know that I am right to think like this about all of you, because I have you in my heart. All of you share in God's grace with me while I am in prison and while I am defending and proving the truth of the Good News. [8]God knows that I want to see you very much, because I love all of you with the love of Christ Jesus.

STEP 9

[9]This is my prayer for you: that your love will grow more and more; that you will have knowledge and understanding with your love; [10]that you will see the difference between good and bad and will choose the good; that you will be pure and without wrong for the coming of Christ; [11]that you will be filled with the good things produced in your life by Christ to bring glory and praise to God.

[12]I want you brothers and sisters to know that what has happened to me has helped to spread the Good News. [13]All the palace guards and everyone else knows that I am in prison because I am a believer in Christ. [14]Because I am in prison, most of the believers have become more bold in Christ and are not afraid to speak the word of God.

[15]It is true that some preach about Christ because they are jealous and ambitious, but others preach about Christ because they want to help. [16]They preach because they have love, and they know that God gave me the work of defending the Good News. [17]But the others preach about Christ for selfish and wrong reasons, wanting to make trouble for me in prison.

[18]But it doesn't matter. The important thing is that in every way, whether for right or wrong reasons, they are preaching about Christ. So I am happy, and I will continue to be happy. [19]Because you are praying for me and the Spirit of Jesus Christ is helping me, I know this trouble will bring my freedom. [20]I expect and hope that I will not fail Christ in anything but that I will have the courage now, as always, to show the greatness of Christ in my life here on earth, whether I live or die.

STEP 11

[21]To me the only important thing about living is Christ, and dying would be profit for me. [22]If I continue living in my body, I will be able to work for the Lord. I do not know what to choose—living or dying. [23]It is hard to choose between the two. I want to leave this life and be with Christ, which is much better, [24]but you need me here in my body. [25]Since I am sure of this, I know I will stay with you to help you grow and have joy in your faith. [26]You will be very happy in Christ Jesus when I am with you again.

[27]Only one thing concerns me: Be sure that you live in a way that brings honor to the Good News of Christ. Then whether I

STEP 11

STEP 9

Made direct amends to such people
wherever possible, except when to
do so would injure them or others.

Philippians 1:9–11

When you work Step 9, you make yourself transparent and vulnerable to people you've hurt in the past. That's risky business, but it's the only way to heal damaged relationships. Time does not heal these wounds; only courageous confession does. However, you probably feel overwhelmed as you try to decide what to say, who to say it to, and how to say it honestly and tactfully.

This gets beyond mere human capability. Fortunately, you can ask God's Spirit to guide you in your preparation and to accompany you when you go talk to people. Let this passage from Philippians remind you that as you spend time talking to God and listening to his Word, you will "grow more and more; that you will have knowledge and understanding" (verse 9). When you meet with someone to speak your words of amends, you aren't just speaking in your own power. As you do it, trust God to speak through you to your friends. Trust him, even if you don't feel his presence at the moment. He's promised to empower you to "see the difference between good and bad and . . . choose the good" and to "be pure and without wrong" (verse 10).

FOR YOUR NEXT **STEP 9** MEDITATION, TURN TO **PAGE 285.** ▶▶

come and visit you or am away from you, I will hear that you are standing strong with one purpose, that you work together as one for the faith of the Good News, [28]and that you are not afraid of those who are against you. All of this is proof that your enemies will be destroyed but that you will be saved by God. [29]God gave you the honor not only of believing in Christ but also of suffering for him, both of which bring glory to Christ. [30]When I was with you, you saw the struggles I had, and you hear about the struggles I am having now. You yourselves are having the same kind of struggles.

2 Does your life in Christ give you strength? Does his love comfort you? Do we share together in the spirit? Do you have mercy and kindness? [2]If so, make me very happy by having the same thoughts, sharing the same love, and having one mind and purpose. [3]When you do things, do not let selfishness or pride be your guide. Instead, be humble and give more honor to others than to yourselves. [4]Do not be interested only in your own life, but be interested in the lives of others.

[5]In your lives you must think and act like Christ Jesus.

[6]Christ himself was like God in
       everything.
   But he did not think that being
       equal with God was
       something to be used for his
       own benefit.
[7]But he gave up his place with God
       and made himself nothing.
   He was born as a man
   and became like a servant.
[8]And when he was living as a man,
   he humbled himself and was fully
       obedient to God,
   even when that caused his
       death—death on a cross.

[9]So God raised him to the highest
       place.
   God made his name greater than
       every other name
[10]so that every knee will bow to the
       name of Jesus—
   everyone in heaven, on earth, and
       under the earth.
[11]And everyone will confess that Jesus
       Christ is Lord
   and bring glory to God the Father.

[12]My dear friends, you have always obeyed God when I was with you. It is even more important that you obey now while I am away from you. Keep on working to complete your salvation with fear and trembling, [13]because God is working in you to help you want to do and be able to do what pleases him.

[14]Do everything without complaining or arguing. [15]Then you will be innocent and without any wrong. You will be God's children without fault. But you are living with crooked and mean people all around you, among whom you shine like stars in the dark world. [16]You offer the teaching that gives life. So when Christ comes again, I can be happy because my work was not wasted. I ran the race and won.

[17]Your faith makes you offer your lives as a sacrifice in serving God. If I have to offer my own blood with your sacrifice, I will be happy and full of joy with all of you. [18]You also should be happy and full of joy with me.

[19]I hope in the Lord Jesus to send Timothy to you soon. I will be happy to learn how you are. [20]I have no one else like Timothy, who truly cares for you. [21]Other people are interested only in their own lives, not in the work of Jesus Christ. [22]You know the kind of person Timothy is. You know he has served with me in telling the Good News, as a son serves his father. [23]I plan to send him to you quickly when I

STEP 8

STEP 2

STEP 10

know what will happen to me. [24]I am sure that the Lord will help me to come to you soon.

[25]Epaphroditus, my brother in Christ, works and serves with me in the army of Christ. When I needed help, you sent him to me. I think now that I must send him back to you, [26]because he wants very much to see all of you. He is worried because you heard that he was sick. [27]Yes, he was sick, and nearly died, but God had mercy on him and me too so that I would not have more sadness. [28]I want very much to send him to you so that when you see him you can be happy, and I can stop worrying about you. [29]Welcome him in the Lord with much joy. Give honor to people like him, [30]because he almost died for the work of Christ. He risked his life to give me the help you could not give in your service to me.

3 My brothers and sisters, be full of joy in the Lord. It is no trouble for me to write the same things to you again, and it will help you to be more ready. [2]Watch out for those who do evil, who are like dogs, who demand to cut the body. [3]We are the ones who are truly circumcised. We worship God through his Spirit, and our pride is in Christ Jesus. We do not put trust in ourselves or anything we can do, [4]although I might be able to put trust in myself. If anyone thinks he has a reason to trust in himself, he should know that I have greater reason for trusting in myself. [5]I was circumcised eight days after my birth. I am from the people of Israel and the tribe of Benjamin. I am a Hebrew, and my parents were Hebrews. I had a strict view of the law, which is why I became a Pharisee. [6]I was so enthusiastic I tried to hurt the church. No one could find fault with the way I obeyed the law of Moses.

STEP 11

[7]Those things were important to me, but now I think they are worth nothing because of Christ. [8]Not only those things, but I think that all things are worth nothing compared with the greatness of knowing Christ Jesus my Lord. Because of him, I have lost all those things, and now I know they are worthless trash. This allows me to have Christ [9]and to belong to him. Now I am right with God, not because I followed the law, but because I believed in Christ. God uses my faith to make me right with him. [10]I want to know Christ and the power that raised him from the dead. I want to share in his sufferings and become like him in his death. [11]Then I have hope that I myself will be raised from the dead.

[12]I do not mean that I am already as God wants me to be. I have not yet reached that goal, but I continue trying to reach it and to make it mine. Christ wants me to do that, which is the reason he made me his. [13]Brothers and sisters, I know that I have not yet reached that goal, but there is one thing I always do. Forgetting the past and straining toward what is ahead, [14]I keep trying to reach the goal and get the prize for which God called me through Christ to the life above.

[15]All of us who are spiritually mature should think this way, too. And if there are things you do not agree with, God will make them clear to you. [16]But we should continue following the truth we already have.

[17]Brothers and sisters, all of you should try to follow my example and to copy those who live the way we showed you. [18]Many people live like enemies of the cross of Christ. I have often told you about them, and it makes me cry to tell you about them now. [19]In the end, they will be destroyed. They do whatever bodies want, they are proud of their shameful acts, and they think only about

STEP 11

Sought through prayer and meditation to improve
our conscious contact with God **as we understood
Him,** praying only for knowledge of His will
for us and the power to carry that out.

Philippians 4:6–9

Step 11 urges you to grow closer and closer to God by means of
prayer and meditation. How can you build these important spiritual
disciplines into your life?

In these verses from Philippians, the apostle Paul suggests five
ways to strengthen your intimacy with God: First, quiet your
anxieties. They interfere with sensing God's promptings. You have
to be still inside to sense the greatness and power of God (Psalm
46:10). Second, thank God for all the good things in your life. Third,
openly and honestly lay before him all your sincere needs. Share
your fears along with the facts. Fourth, use your meditation time to
open your heart to receive the peace of God, a peace that goes
beyond human understanding. And fifth, meditate on things of
highest value: "the things that are good and worthy of praise, . . .
the things that are true and honorable and right and pure and
beautiful and respected" (verse 8).

FOR YOUR NEXT **STEP 11** MEDITATION, TURN TO **PAGE 307.** ▶▶

earthly things. [20]But our homeland is in heaven, and we are waiting for our Savior, the Lord Jesus Christ, to come from heaven. [21]By his power to rule all things, he will change our humble bodies and make them like his own glorious body.

4 My dear brothers and sisters, I love you and want to see you. You bring me joy and make me proud of you, so stand strong in the Lord as I have told you.

STEP 9

[2]I ask Euodia and Syntyche to agree in the Lord. [3]And I ask you, my faithful friend, to help these women. They served with me in telling the Good News, together with Clement and others who worked with me, whose names are written in the book of life.

[4]Be full of joy in the Lord always. I will say again, be full of joy.

STEP 8

[5]Let everyone see that you are gentle and kind. The Lord is coming soon.

STEP 11

[6]Do not worry about anything, but pray and ask God for everything you need, always giving thanks. [7]And God's peace, which is so great we cannot understand it, will keep your hearts and minds in Christ Jesus.

[8]Brothers and sisters, think about the things that are good and worthy of praise. Think about the things that are true and honorable and right and pure and beautiful and respected. [9]Do what you learned and received from me, what I told you, and what you saw me do. And the God who gives peace will be with you.

[10]I am very happy in the Lord that you have shown your care for me again. You continued to care about me, but there was no way for you to show it. [11]I am not telling you this because I need anything. I have learned to be satisfied with the things I have and with everything that happens. [12]I know how to live when I am poor, and I know how to live when I have plenty. I have learned the secret of being happy at any time in everything that happens, when I have enough to eat and when I go hungry, when I have more than I need and when I do not have enough. [13]I can do all things through Christ, because he gives me strength.

STEP 6

[14]But it was good that you helped me when I needed it. [15]You Philippians remember when I first preached the Good News there. When I left Macedonia, you were the only church that gave me help. [16]Several times you sent me things I needed when I was in Thessalonica. [17]Really, it is not that I want to receive gifts from you, but I want you to have the good that comes from giving. [18]And now I have everything, and more. I have all I need, because Epaphroditus brought your gift to me. It is like a sweet-smelling sacrifice offered to God, who accepts that sacrifice and is pleased with it. [19]My God will use his wonderful riches in Christ Jesus to give you everything you need.

STEP 7

[20]Glory to our God and Father forever and ever! Amen.

[21]Greet each of God's people in Christ Jesus. Those who are with me send greetings to you. [22]All of God's people greet you, particularly those from the palace of Caesar.

[23]The grace of the Lord Jesus Christ be with you all.

COLOSSIANS

Only Christ Can Save People

1 From Paul, an apostle of Christ Jesus. I am an apostle because that is what God wanted. Also from Timothy, our brother.

²To the holy and faithful brothers and sisters in Christ that live in Colossae:

Grace and peace to you from God our Father.

³In our prayers for you we always thank God, the Father of our Lord Jesus Christ, ⁴because we have heard about the faith you have in Christ Jesus and the love you have for all of God's people. ⁵You have this faith and love because of your hope, and what you hope for is kept safe for you in heaven. You learned about this hope when you heard the message about the truth, the Good News ⁶that was told to you. Everywhere in the world that Good News is bringing blessings and is growing. This has happened with you, too, since you heard the Good News and understood the truth about the grace of God. ⁷You learned about God's grace from Epaphras, whom we love. He works together with us and is a faithful servant of Christ for us. ⁸He also told us about the love you have from the Holy Spirit.

STEP 12 ⁹Because of this, since the day we heard about you, we have continued praying for you, asking God that you will know fully what he wants. We pray that you will also have great wisdom and understanding in spiritual things ¹⁰so that you will live the kind of life that honors and pleases the Lord in every way. You will produce fruit in every good work and grow in the knowledge of God. ¹¹God will strengthen you with his own great power so that you will not give up when troubles come, but you will be patient. ¹²And you will joyfully give thanks to the Father who has made you able to have a share in all that he has prepared for his people in the kingdom of light. ¹³God has freed us from the power of darkness, and he brought us into the kingdom of his dear Son. ¹⁴The Son paid for our sins, and in him we have forgiveness.

¹⁵No one can see God, but Jesus Christ is exactly like him. He ranks higher than everything that has been made. ¹⁶Through his power all things were made—things in heaven and on earth, things seen and unseen, all powers, authorities, lords, and rulers. All things were made through Christ and for Christ. ¹⁷He was there before anything was made, and all things continue because of him. ¹⁸He is the head of the body, which is the church. Everything comes from him. He is the first one who was raised from the dead. So in all things Jesus has first place. ¹⁹God was pleased for all of himself to live in Christ. ²⁰And through Christ, God has brought all things back to himself again—things on earth and things in heaven. God made peace through the blood of Christ's death on the cross.

²¹At one time you were separated from God. You were his enemies in your minds, and the evil things you did were against God. ²²But now God has made you his friends again. He did this through Christ's death in the body so that he might bring you into God's presence as people who are holy, with no wrong, and with nothing of which God can judge you guilty. ²³This will happen if you continue strong and sure in your faith. You must not be moved away from the hope brought to you by

the Good News that you heard. That same Good News has been told to everyone in the world, and I, Paul, help in preaching that Good News.

²⁴I am happy in my sufferings for you. There are things that Christ must still suffer through his body, the church. I am accepting, in my body, my part of these things that must be suffered. ²⁵I became a servant of the church because God gave me a special work to do that helps you, and that work is to tell fully the message of God. ²⁶This message is the secret that was hidden from everyone since the beginning of time, but now it is made known to God's holy people. ²⁷God decided to let his people know this rich and glorious secret which he has for all people. This secret is Christ himself, who is in you. He is our only hope for glory. ²⁸So we continue to preach Christ to each person, using all wisdom to warn and to teach everyone, in order to bring each one into God's presence as a mature person in Christ. ²⁹To do this, I work and struggle, using Christ's great strength that works so powerfully in me.

2 I want you to know how hard I work for you, those in Laodicea, and others who have never seen me. ²I want them to be strengthened and joined together with love so that they may be rich in their understanding. This leads to their knowing fully God's secret, that is, Christ himself. ³In him all the treasures of wisdom and knowledge are safely kept.

⁴I say this so that no one can fool you by arguments that seem good, but are false. ⁵Though I am absent from you in my body, my heart is with you, and I am happy to see your good lives and your strong faith in Christ.

⁶As you received Christ Jesus the Lord, so continue to live in him. ⁷Keep your roots deep in him and have your lives built on him. Be strong in the faith, just as you were taught, and always be thankful.

⁸Be sure that no one leads you away with false and empty teaching that is only human, which comes from the ruling spirits of this world, and not from Christ. ⁹All of God lives fully in Christ (even when Christ was on earth), ¹⁰and you have a full and true life in Christ, who is ruler over all rulers and powers.

¹¹Also in Christ you had a different kind of circumcision, a circumcision not done by hands. It was through Christ's circumcision, that is, his death, that you were made free from the power of your sinful self. ¹²When you were baptized, you were buried with Christ, and you were raised up with him through your faith in God's power that was shown when he raised Christ from the dead. ¹³When you were spiritually dead because of your sins and because you were not free from the power of your sinful self, God made you alive with Christ, and he forgave all our sins. ¹⁴He canceled the debt, which listed all the rules we failed to follow. He took away that record with its rules and nailed it to the cross. ¹⁵God stripped the spiritual rulers and powers of their authority. With the cross, he won the victory and showed the world that they were powerless.

¹⁶So do not let anyone make rules for you about eating and drinking or about a religious feast, a New Moon Festival, or a Sabbath day. ¹⁷These things were like a shadow of what was to come. But what is true and real has come and is found in Christ. ¹⁸Do not let anyone disqualify you by making you humiliate yourself and worship angels. Such people enter into visions, which fill them with foolish pride because of their human way of thinking. ¹⁹They do not hold tightly to Christ, the head. It is from him that all the parts of the body are cared for and held together.

So it grows in the way God wants it to grow.

²⁰Since you died with Christ and were made free from the ruling spirits of the world, why do you act as if you still belong to this world by following rules like these: ²¹"Don't handle this," "Don't taste that," "Don't even touch that thing"? ²²These rules refer to earthly things that are gone as soon as they are used. They are only human commands and teachings. ²³They seem to be wise, but they are only part of a human religion. They make people pretend not to be proud and make them punish their bodies, but they do not really control the evil desires of the sinful self.

STEP 10

3 Since you were raised from the dead with Christ, aim at what is in heaven, where Christ is sitting at the right hand of God. ²Think only about the things in heaven, not the things on earth. ³Your old sinful self has died, and your new life is kept with Christ in God. ⁴Christ is your life, and when he comes again, you will share in his glory.

STEP 6

⁵So put all evil things out of your life: sexual sinning, doing evil, letting evil thoughts control you, wanting things that are evil, and greed. This is really serving a false god. ⁶These things make God angry. ⁷In your past, evil life you also did these things.

⁸But now also put these things out of your life: anger, bad temper, doing or saying things to hurt others, and using evil words when you talk. ⁹Do not lie to each other. You have left your old sinful life and the things you did before. ¹⁰You have begun to live the new life, in which you are being made new and are becoming like the One who made you. This new life brings you the true knowledge of God. ¹¹In the new life there is no difference between Greeks and Jews, those who are

STEP 5

circumcised and those who are not circumcised, or people who are foreigners, or Scythians. There is no difference between slaves and free people. But Christ is in all believers, and Christ is all that is important.

¹²God has chosen you and made you his holy people. He loves you. So you should always clothe yourselves with mercy, kindness, humility, gentleness, and patience. ¹³Bear with each other, and forgive each other. If someone does wrong to you, forgive that person because the Lord forgave you. ¹⁴Even more than all this, clothe yourself in love. Love is what holds you all together in perfect unity. ¹⁵Let the peace that Christ gives control your thinking, because you were all called together in one body to have peace. Always be thankful. ¹⁶Let the teaching of Christ live in you richly. Use all wisdom to teach and instruct each other by singing psalms, hymns, and spiritual songs with thankfulness in your hearts to God. ¹⁷Everything you do or say should be done to obey Jesus your Lord. And in all you do, give thanks to God the Father through Jesus.

STEP 9
STEP 11

¹⁸Wives, yield to the authority of your husbands, because this is the right thing to do in the Lord.

STEP 9

¹⁹Husbands, love your wives and be gentle with them.

²⁰Children, obey your parents in all things, because this pleases the Lord. ²¹Fathers, do not nag your children. If you are too hard to please, they may want to stop trying.

²²Slaves, obey your masters in all things. Do not obey just when they are watching you, to gain their favor, but serve them honestly, because you respect the Lord. ²³In all the work you are doing, work the best you can. Work as if you were doing it for the Lord, not for

STEP 11

STEP 6

Were entirely ready to have God
remove all these defects of character.

Colossians 3:5–8

Once you've been an addict given to compulsive behavior, it's really hard to get some parts of life back in proper balance. One thing that's especially hard to balance is your God-given need for love, security, and acceptance. Addictive personalities swing from one extreme to another in this area.

Here are the extremes to avoid: 1) denying that God wants you to feel loved and accepted and 2) obsessing about needing more and more love and acceptance.

When you go to either of these extremes, you'll end up frustrated. You need to receive your foundational love and acceptance from God. Looking for it from people or things doesn't work. You looked for security in your addiction. You wanted your habit to satisfy some deep needs of your heart. You treated sexuality, drugs, food, money, power, or something else almost like a god. The Bible warns you to put these false gods "out of your life." In Step 6, you ask God to remove all these defects of character so you can find genuine, lasting love and acceptance in him.

FOR YOUR NEXT **STEP 6** MEDITATION, TURN TO **PAGE 335.** ▶▶

STEP 9

Made direct amends to such people
wherever possible, except when to
do so would injure them or others.

Colossians 4:5-6

Steps 8 and 9 are steps about repairing broken relationships. Who should you be thinking about reconciling with?

First, you want to be reconciled with your own conscience. Here you work on any lingering guilt and remorse for your addictive behavior. You don't want to dislike yourself as you pursue recovery.

Second, you want to reconcile with the important people in your life. Step 9 gives you a handy tool for reaching back through years of broken relationships and making amends for the hurts you've caused.

Third, and perhaps most importantly, once you start reconciling with yourself and others, you can reconcile with God. Step 9 lets you reach out to God free from feelings of regret and guilt. Don't get confused here. Theologically, God reconciles you to himself when you trust Jesus to deliver you from your sins. That's when you receive eternal salvation. Relationally, you reconcile to God—get closer and closer to him—as you tell him all the things you discover about yourself in your Step 4 personal inventory.

When you make amends, don't hint that the other person is to blame, too. Talk calmly and humbly about your role in causing pain. Make no excuses. Ask the person you're talking to for forgiveness. As you attempt to reunite with those who still aren't believers, give Jesus credit for the harmony and peace you are discovering.

FOR YOUR NEXT **STEP 9** MEDITATION, TURN TO **PAGE 310.** ▶▶

people. ²⁴Remember that you will receive your reward from the Lord, which he promised to his people. You are serving the Lord Christ. ²⁵But remember that anyone who does wrong will be punished for that wrong, and the Lord treats everyone the same.

4 Masters, give what is good and fair to your slaves. Remember that you have a Master in heaven.

²Continue praying, keeping alert, and always thanking God. ³Also pray for us that God will give us an opportunity to tell people his message. Pray that we can preach the secret that God has made known about Christ. This is why I am in prison. ⁴Pray that I can speak in a way that will make it clear, as I should.

⁵Be wise in the way you act with people who are not believers, making the most of every opportunity. ⁶When you talk, you should always be kind and pleasant so you will be able to answer everyone in the way you should.

⁷Tychicus is my dear brother in Christ and a faithful minister and servant with me in the Lord. He will tell you all the things that are happening to me. ⁸This is why I am sending him: so you may know how we are and he may encourage you. ⁹I send him with Onesimus, a faithful and dear brother in Christ, and one of your group. They will tell you all that has happened here.

¹⁰Aristarchus, a prisoner with me, and Mark, the cousin of Barnabas, greet you. (I have already told you what to do about Mark. If he comes, welcome him.) ¹¹Jesus, who is called Justus, also greets you. These are the only Jewish believers who work with me for the kingdom of God, and they have been a comfort to me.

¹²Epaphras, a servant of Jesus Christ, from your group, also greets you. He always prays for you that you will grow to be spiritually mature and have everything God wants for you. ¹³I know he has worked hard for you and the people in Laodicea and in Hierapolis. ¹⁴Demas and our dear friend Luke, the doctor, greet you.

¹⁵Greet the brothers and sisters in Laodicea. And greet Nympha and the church that meets in her house. ¹⁶After this letter is read to you, be sure it is also read to the church in Laodicea. And you read the letter that I wrote to Laodicea. ¹⁷Tell Archippus, "Be sure to finish the work the Lord gave you."

¹⁸I, Paul, greet you and write this with my own hand. Remember me in prison. Grace be with you.

1 THESSALONIANS

Paul Encourages New Christians

1 From Paul, Silas, and Timothy.
To the church in Thessalonica, the church in God the Father and the Lord Jesus Christ:

Grace and peace to you.

STEP
12

²We always thank God for all of you and mention you when we pray. ³We continually recall before God our Father the things you have done because of your faith and the work you have done because of your love. And we thank him that you continue to be strong because of your hope in our Lord Jesus Christ.

⁴Brothers and sisters, God loves you, and we know he has chosen you, ⁵because the Good News we brought to you came not only with words, but with power, with the Holy Spirit, and with sure knowledge that it is true. Also you know how we lived when we were with you in order to help you. ⁶And you became like us and like the Lord. You suffered much, but still you accepted the teaching with the joy that comes from the Holy Spirit. ⁷So you became an example to all the believers in Macedonia and Southern Greece. ⁸And the Lord's teaching spread from you not only into Macedonia and Southern Greece, but now your faith in God has become known everywhere. So we do not need to say anything about it. ⁹People everywhere are telling about the way you accepted us when we were there with you. They tell how you stopped worshiping idols and began serving the living and true God. ¹⁰And you wait for God's Son, whom God raised from the dead, to come from heaven. He is Jesus, who saves us from God's angry judgment that is sure to come.

2 Brothers and sisters, you know our visit to you was not a failure. ²Before we came to you, we suffered in Philippi. People there insulted us, as you know, and many people were against us. But our God helped us to be brave and to tell you his Good News. ³Our appeal does not come from lies or wrong reasons, nor were we trying to trick you. ⁴But we speak the Good News because God tested us and trusted us to do it. When we speak, we are not trying to please people, but God, who tests our hearts. ⁵You know that we never tried to influence you by saying nice things about you. We were not trying to get your money; we had no selfishness to hide from you. God knows that this is true. ⁶We were not looking for human praise, from you or anyone else, ⁷even though as apostles of Christ we could have used our authority over you.

STEP
12

But we were very gentle with you, like a mother caring for her little children. ⁸Because we loved you, we were happy to share not only God's Good News with you, but even our own lives. You had become so dear to us! ⁹Brothers and sisters, I know you remember our hard work and difficulties. We worked night and day so we would not burden any of you while we preached God's Good News to you.

STEP
12

¹⁰When we were with you, we lived in a holy and honest way, without fault. You know this is true, and so does God. ¹¹You know that we treated each of you as a father treats his own children. ¹²We encouraged you, we urged you, and we insisted that you live good lives for God, who calls you to his glorious kingdom.

¹³Also, we always thank God because when you heard his message from us,

you accepted it as the word of God, not the words of humans. And it really is God's message which works in you who believe. ¹⁴Brothers and sisters, your experiences have been like those of God's churches in Christ that are in Judea. You suffered from the people of your own country, as they suffered from the Jews ¹⁵who killed both the Lord Jesus and the prophets and forced us to leave that country. They do not please God and are against all people. ¹⁶They try to stop us from teaching those who are not Jews so they may be saved. By doing this, they are increasing their sins to the limit. The anger of God has come to them at last.

¹⁷Brothers and sisters, though we were separated from you for a short time, our thoughts were still with you. We wanted very much to see you and tried hard to do so. ¹⁸We wanted to come to you. I, Paul, tried to come more than once, but Satan stopped us. ¹⁹You are our hope, our joy, and the crown we will take pride in when our Lord Jesus Christ comes. ²⁰Truly you are our glory and our joy.

3 When we could not wait any longer, we decided it was best to stay in Athens alone ²and send Timothy to you. Timothy, our brother, works with us for God and helps us tell people the Good News about Christ. We sent him to strengthen and encourage you in your faith ³so none of you would be upset by these troubles. You yourselves know that we must face these troubles. ⁴Even when we were with you, we told you we all would have to suffer, and you know it has happened. ⁵Because of this, when I could wait no longer, I sent Timothy to you so I could learn about your faith. I was afraid the devil had tempted you, and perhaps our hard work would have been wasted.

⁶But Timothy now has come back to us from you and has brought us good news

about your faith and love. He told us that you always remember us in a good way and that you want to see us just as much as we want to see you. ⁷So, brothers and sisters, while we have much trouble and suffering, we are encouraged about you because of your faith. ⁸Our life is really full if you stand strong in the Lord. ⁹We have so much joy before our God because of you. We cannot thank him enough for all the joy we feel. ¹⁰Night and day we continue praying with all our heart that we can see you again and give you all the things you need to make your faith strong.

¹¹Now may our God and Father himself and our Lord Jesus prepare the way for us to come to you. ¹²May the Lord make your love grow more and multiply for each other and for all people so that you will love others as we love you. ¹³May your hearts be made strong so that you will be holy and without fault before our God and Father when our Lord Jesus comes with all his holy ones.

4 Brothers and sisters, we taught you how to live in a way that will please God, and you are living that way. Now we ask and encourage you in the Lord Jesus to live that way even more. ²You know what we told you to do by the authority of the Lord Jesus. ³God wants you to be holy and to stay away from sexual sins. ⁴He wants each of you to learn to control your own body in a way that is holy and honorable. ⁵Don't use your body for sexual sin like the people who do not know God. ⁶Also, do not wrong or cheat another Christian in this way. The Lord will punish people who do those things as we have already told you and warned you. ⁷God called us to be holy and does not want us to live in sin. ⁸So the person who refuses to obey this teaching is disobeying God, not simply a human

STEP 8

STEP 6

teaching. And God is the One who gives us his Holy Spirit.

STEP
11

⁹We do not need to write you about having love for your Christian family, because God has already taught you to love each other. ¹⁰And truly you do love the Christians in all of Macedonia. Brothers and sisters, now we encourage you to love them even more.

¹¹Do all you can to live a peaceful life. Take care of your own business, and do your own work as we have already told you. ¹²If you do, then people who are not believers will respect you, and you will not have to depend on others for what you need.

¹³Brothers and sisters, we want you to know about those Christians who have died so you will not be sad, as others who have no hope. ¹⁴We believe that Jesus died and that he rose again. So, because of him, God will raise with Jesus those who have died. ¹⁵What we tell you now is the Lord's own message. We who are living when the Lord comes again will not go before those who have already died. ¹⁶The Lord himself will come down from heaven with a loud command, with the voice of the archangel, and with the trumpet call of God. And those who have died believing in Christ will rise first. ¹⁷After that, we who are still alive will be gathered up with them in the clouds to meet the Lord in the air. And we will be with the Lord forever. ¹⁸So encourage each other with these words.

5 Now, brothers and sisters, we do not need to write you about times and dates. ²You know very well that the day the Lord comes again will be a surprise, like a thief that comes in the night. ³While people are saying, "We have peace and we are safe," they will be destroyed quickly. It is like pains that come quickly

to a woman having a baby. Those people will not escape. ⁴But you, brothers and sisters, are not living in darkness, and so that day will not surprise you like a thief. ⁵You are all people who belong to the light and to the day. We do not belong to the night or to darkness. ⁶So we should not be like other people who are sleeping, but we should be alert and have self-control. ⁷Those who sleep, sleep at night. Those who get drunk, get drunk at night. ⁸But we belong to the day, so we should control ourselves. We should wear faith and love to protect us, and the hope of salvation should be our helmet. ⁹God did not choose us to suffer his anger but to have salvation through our Lord Jesus Christ. ¹⁰Jesus died for us so that we can live together with him, whether we are alive or dead when he comes. ¹¹So encourage each other and give each other strength, just as you are doing now.

¹²Now, brothers and sisters, we ask you to appreciate those who work hard among you, who lead you in the Lord and teach you. ¹³Respect them with a very special love because of the work they do. Live in peace with each other. ¹⁴We ask you, brothers and sisters, to warn those who do not work. Encourage the people who are afraid. Help those who are weak. Be patient with everyone. ¹⁵Be sure that no one pays back wrong for wrong, but always try to do what is good for each other and for all people.

STEP
12

STEP
9

¹⁶Always be joyful. ¹⁷Pray continually, ¹⁸and give thanks whatever happens. That is what God wants for you in Christ Jesus.

STEP
10

¹⁹Do not hold back the work of the Holy Spirit. ²⁰Do not treat prophecy as if it were unimportant. ²¹But test everything. Keep what is good, ²²and stay away from everything that is evil.

²³Now may God himself, the God of

STEP 10

Continued to take personal inventory
and when we were wrong promptly admitted it.

1 Thessalonians 5:17–22

Steps 10, 11, and 12 are called the maintenance steps of recovery. Recovery literature describes the first nine steps as conditions for new life. Step 10 actually starts the adventure of putting the new life into day-to-day practice.

The obvious question about Step 10 is how do you conduct a daily personal inventory? What goes into one? This passage from 1 Thessalonians suggests five components of a daily inventory:

1) Pray continually.

2) Thank God regularly. In Twelve Step groups, you often hear references to keeping a daily "gratitude list."

3) Invite God's Spirit into your heart each day.

4) Search for God's direction and will for all of your future activities.

5) Regularly assess your strengths and weaknesses. We are indeed called to "keep what is good, and stay away from everything that is evil."

FOR YOUR NEXT **STEP 10** MEDITATION, TURN TO **PAGE 312.** ▶▶

peace, make you pure, belonging only to him. May your whole self—spirit, soul, and body—be kept safe and without fault when our Lord Jesus Christ comes. [24]You can trust the One who calls you to do that for you.

[25]Brothers and sisters, pray for us.

[26]Give each other a holy kiss when you meet. [27]I tell you by the authority of the Lord to read this letter to all the believers.

[28]The grace of our Lord Jesus Christ be with you.

2 THESSALONIANS

The Problems of New Christians

1 From Paul, Silas, and Timothy.
To the church in Thessalonica in God our Father and the Lord Jesus Christ:

²Grace and peace to you from God the Father and the Lord Jesus Christ.

³We must always thank God for you, brothers and sisters. This is only right, because your faith is growing more and more, and the love that every one of you has for each other is increasing. ⁴So we brag about you to the other churches of God. We tell them about the way you continue to be strong and have faith even though you are being treated badly and are suffering many troubles.

⁵This is proof that God is right in his judgment. He wants you to be counted worthy of his kingdom for which you are suffering. ⁶God will do what is right. He will give trouble to those who trouble you. ⁷And he will give rest to you who are troubled and to us also when the Lord Jesus appears with burning fire from heaven with his powerful angels. ⁸Then he will punish those who do not know God and who do not obey the Good News about our Lord Jesus Christ. ⁹Those people will be punished with a destruction that continues forever. They will be kept away from the Lord and from his great power. ¹⁰This will happen on the day when the Lord Jesus comes to receive glory because of his holy people. And all the people who have believed will be amazed at Jesus. You will be in that group, because you believed what we told you.

¹¹That is why we always pray for you, asking our God to help you live the kind of life he called you to live. We pray that with his power God will help you do the good things you want and perform the works that come from your faith. ¹²We pray all this so that the name of our Lord Jesus Christ will have glory in you, and you will have glory in him. That glory comes from the grace of our God and the Lord Jesus Christ.

2 Brothers and sisters, we have something to say about the coming of our Lord Jesus Christ and the time when we will meet together with him. ²Do not become easily upset in your thinking or afraid if you hear that the day of the Lord has already come. Someone may have said this in a prophecy or in a message or in a letter as if it came from us. ³Do not let anyone fool you in any way. That day of the Lord will not come until the turning away from God happens and the Man of Evil, who is on his way to hell, appears. ⁴He will be against and put himself above any so-called god or anything that people worship. And that Man of Evil will even go into God's Temple and sit there and say that he is God.

⁵I told you when I was with you that all this would happen. Do you not remember? ⁶And now you know what is stopping that Man of Evil so he will appear at the right time. ⁷The secret power of evil is already working in the world, but there is one who is stopping that power. And he will continue to stop it until he is taken out of the way. ⁸Then that Man of Evil will appear, and the Lord Jesus will kill him with the breath that comes from his mouth and will destroy him with the glory of his coming. ⁹The Man of Evil will come by the power of Satan. He will have great power, and he will do many different false miracles, signs, and wonders. ¹⁰He will use every kind of evil to trick those who are

lost. They will die, because they refused to love the truth. (If they loved the truth, they would be saved.) [11]For this reason God sends them something powerful that leads them away from the truth so they will believe a lie. [12]So all those will be judged guilty who did not believe the truth, but enjoyed doing evil.

[13]Brothers and sisters, whom the Lord loves, God chose you from the beginning to be saved. So we must always thank God for you. You are saved by the Spirit that makes you holy and by your faith in the truth. [14]God used the Good News that we preached to call you to be saved so you can share in the glory of our Lord Jesus Christ. [15]So, brothers and sisters, stand strong and continue to believe the teachings we gave you in our speaking and in our letter.

STEP 11 [16-17]May our Lord Jesus Christ himself and God our Father encourage you and strengthen you in every good thing you do and say. God loved us, and through his grace he gave us a good hope and encouragement that continues forever.

3 And now, brothers and sisters, pray for us that the Lord's teaching will continue to spread quickly and that people will give honor to that teaching, just as happened with you. [2]And pray that we will be protected from stubborn and evil people, because not all people believe.

STEP 10 [3]But the Lord is faithful and will give you strength and will protect you from the Evil One. [4]The Lord makes us feel sure that you are doing and will continue to do the things we told you. [5]May the Lord lead your hearts into God's love and Christ's patience.

[6]Brothers and sisters, by the authority of our Lord Jesus Christ we command you to stay away from any believer who refuses to work and does not follow the teaching we gave you. [7]You yourselves know that you should live as we live. We were not lazy when we were with you. [8]And when we ate another person's food, we always paid for it. We worked very hard night and day so we would not be an expense to any of you. [9]We had the right to ask you to help us, but we worked to take care of ourselves so we would be an example for you to follow. [10]When we were with you, we gave you this rule: "Anyone who refuses to work should not eat."

[11]We hear that some people in your group refuse to work. They do nothing but busy themselves in other people's lives. [12]We command those people and beg them in the Lord Jesus Christ to work quietly and earn their own food. [13]But you, brothers and sisters, never become tired of doing good.

[14]If some people do not obey what we tell you in this letter, then take note of them. Have nothing to do with them so they will feel ashamed. [15]But do not treat them as enemies. Warn them as fellow believers.

[16]Now may the Lord of peace give you peace at all times and in every way. The Lord be with all of you.

[17]I, Paul, end this letter now in my own handwriting. All my letters have this to show they are from me. This is the way I write. [18]The grace of our Lord Jesus Christ be with you all.

I TIMOTHY

Advice to a Young Preacher

---

1 From Paul, an apostle of Christ Jesus, by the command of God our Savior and Christ Jesus our hope.

²To Timothy, a true child to me because you believe:

Grace, mercy, and peace from God the Father and Christ Jesus our Lord.

³I asked you to stay longer in Ephesus when I went into Macedonia so you could command some people there to stop teaching false things. ⁴Tell them not to spend their time on stories that are not true and on long lists of names in family histories. These things only bring arguments; they do not help God's work, which is done in faith. ⁵The purpose of this command is for people to have love, a love that comes from a pure heart and a good conscience and a true faith. ⁶Some people have missed these things and turned to useless talk. ⁷They want to be teachers of the law, but they do not understand either what they are talking about or what they are sure about.

⁸But we know that the law is good if someone uses it lawfully. ⁹We also know that the law is not made for good people but for those who are against the law and for those who refuse to follow it. It is for people who are against God and are sinful, who are unholy and ungodly, who kill their fathers and mothers, who murder, ¹⁰who take part in sexual sins, who have sexual relations with people of the same sex, who sell slaves, who tell lies, who speak falsely, and who do anything against the true teaching of God. ¹¹That teaching is part of the Good News of the blessed God that he gave me to tell.

¹²I thank Christ Jesus our Lord, who gave me strength, because he trusted me and gave me this work of serving him. ¹³In the past I spoke against Christ and persecuted him and did all kinds of things to hurt him. But God showed me mercy, because I did not know what I was doing. I did not believe. ¹⁴But the grace of our Lord was fully given to me, and with that grace came the faith and love that are in Christ Jesus.

¹⁵What I say is true, and you should fully accept it: Christ Jesus came into the world to save sinners, of whom I am the worst. ¹⁶But I was given mercy so that in me, the worst of all sinners, Christ Jesus could show that he has patience without limit. His patience with me made me an example for those who would believe in him and have life forever. ¹⁷To the King that rules forever, who will never die, who cannot be seen, the only God, be honor and glory forever and ever. Amen.

¹⁸Timothy, my child, I am giving you a command that agrees with the prophecies that were given about you in the past. I tell you this so you can follow them and fight the good fight. ¹⁹Continue to have faith and do what you know is right. Some people have rejected this, and their faith has been shipwrecked. ²⁰Hymenaeus and Alexander have done that, and I have given them to Satan so they will learn not to speak against God.

2 First, I tell you to pray for all people, asking God for what they need and being thankful to him. ²Pray for rulers and for all who have authority so that we can have quiet and peaceful lives full of worship and respect for God. ³This is good, and it pleases God our Savior, ⁴who wants all people to be saved and to know the truth. ⁵There is one God and one

STEP 12

Having had a spiritual awakening as the
result of these steps, we tried to carry
this message to others, and to practice
these principles in all our affairs.

1 Timothy 1:12–16

The apostle Paul was surprisingly transparent about his pre-Christian past. He admitted that he "spoke against Christ and persecuted him and did all kinds of things to hurt him." In this way, Paul showed how merciful and patient God is.

Step 12 encourages you to be just as candid about your past. Let God use your recovery from past hurts, habits, and hang-ups to glorify himself. Be sensitive to the inner urgings of his Spirit, and you'll discover important opportunities to share how your life has changed.

A lot of people limp through life thinking they're not good enough for God to love or save. Your story could be the turning point for someone like that. You might help a friend break free from the same kind of addiction you've struggled with.

Keep practicing the Twelve Steps, and your life story can be "an example for those who would believe in him."

FOR YOUR NEXT **STEP 12** MEDITATION, TURN TO **PAGE 456.** ▶▶

mediator so that human beings can reach God. That way is through Christ Jesus, who is himself human. [6]He gave himself as a payment to free all people. He is proof that came at the right time. [7]That is why I was chosen to tell the Good News and to be an apostle. (I am telling the truth; I am not lying.) I was chosen to teach those who are not Jews to believe and to know the truth.

[8]So, I want the men everywhere to pray, lifting up their hands in a holy manner, without anger and arguments.

[9]Also, women should wear proper clothes that show respect and self-control, not using braided hair or gold or pearls or expensive clothes. [10]Instead, they should do good deeds, which is right for women who say they worship God.

[11]Let a woman learn by listening quietly and being ready to cooperate in everything. [12]But I do not allow a woman to teach or to have authority over a man, but to listen quietly, [13]because Adam was formed first and then Eve. [14]And Adam was not tricked, but the woman was tricked and became a sinner. [15]But she will be saved through having children if she continues in faith, love, and holiness, with self-control.

3 What I say is true: Anyone wanting to become an overseer desires a good work. [2]An overseer must not give people a reason to criticize him, and he must have only one wife. He must be self-controlled, wise, respected by others, ready to welcome guests, and able to teach. [3]He must not drink too much wine or like to fight, but rather be gentle and peaceable, not loving money. [4]He must be a good family leader, having children who cooperate with full respect. [5](If someone does not know how to lead the family, how can that person take care of God's church?) [6]But an elder must not be a new believer,

or he might be too proud of himself and be judged guilty just as the devil was. [7]An elder must also have the respect of people who are not in the church so he will not be criticized by others and caught in the devil's trap.

[8]In the same way, deacons must be respected by others, not saying things they do not mean. They must not drink too much wine or try to get rich by cheating others. [9]With a clear conscience they must follow the secret of the faith that God made known to us. [10]Test them first. Then let them serve as deacons if you find nothing wrong in them. [11]In the same way, women must be respected by others. They must not speak evil of others. They must be self-controlled and trustworthy in everything. [12]Deacons must have only one wife and be good leaders of their children and their own families. [13]Those who serve well as deacons are making an honorable place for themselves, and they will be very bold in their faith in Christ Jesus.

[14]Although I hope I can come to you soon, I am writing these things to you now. [15]Then, even if I am delayed, you will know how to live in the family of God. That family is the church of the living God, the support and foundation of the truth. [16]Without doubt, the secret of our life of worship is great:

He was shown to us in a human
        body,
    proved right in spirit,
and seen by angels.
    He was proclaimed to the nations,
    believed in by the world,
        and taken up in glory.

4 Now the Holy Spirit clearly says that in the later times some people will stop believing the faith. They will follow spirits that lie and teachings of demons. [2]Such teachings come from the false words of liars whose consciences are destroyed as if by a hot iron. ³They forbid people to marry and tell them not to eat certain foods which God created to be eaten with thanks by people who believe and know the truth. ⁴Everything God made is good, and nothing should be refused if it is accepted with thanks, ⁵because it is made holy by what God has said and by prayer.

⁶By telling these things to the brothers and sisters, you will be a good servant of Christ Jesus. You will be made strong by the words of the faith and the good teaching which you have been following. ⁷But do not follow foolish stories that disagree with God's truth, but train yourself to serve God. ⁸Training your body helps you in some ways, but serving God helps you in every way by bringing you blessings in this life and in the future life, too. ⁹What I say is true, and you should fully accept it. ¹⁰This is why we work and struggle: We hope in the living God who is the Savior of all people, especially of those who believe.

¹¹Command and teach these things. ¹²Do not let anyone treat you as if you are unimportant because you are young. Instead, be an example to the believers with your words, your actions, your love, your faith, and your pure life. ¹³Until I come, continue to read the Scriptures to the people, strengthen them, and teach them. ¹⁴Use the gift you have, which was given to you through prophecy when the group of elders laid their hands on you. ¹⁵Continue to do those things; give your life to doing them so your progress may be seen by everyone. ¹⁶Be careful in your life and in your teaching. If you continue to live and teach rightly, you will save both yourself and those who listen to you.

5 Do not speak angrily to an older man, but plead with him as if he were your father. Treat younger men like brothers, ²older women like mothers, and younger women like sisters. Always treat them in a pure way.

³Take care of widows who are truly widows. ⁴But if a widow has children or grandchildren, let them first learn to do their duty to their own family and to repay their parents or grandparents. That pleases God. ⁵The true widow, who is all alone, puts her hope in God and continues to pray night and day for God's help. ⁶But the widow who uses her life to please herself is really dead while she is alive. ⁷Tell the believers to do these things so that no one can criticize them. ⁸Whoever does not care for his own relatives, especially his own family members, has turned against the faith and is worse than someone who does not believe in God.

⁹To be on the list of widows, a woman must be at least sixty years old. She must have been faithful to her husband. ¹⁰She must be known for her good works—works such as raising her children, welcoming strangers, washing the feet of God's people, helping those in trouble, and giving her life to do all kinds of good deeds.

¹¹But do not put younger widows on that list. After they give themselves to Christ, they are pulled away from him by their physical desires, and then they want to marry again. ¹²They will be judged for not doing what they first promised to do. ¹³Besides that, they learn to waste their time, going from house to house. And they not only waste their time but also begin to gossip and busy themselves with other people's lives, saying things they should not say. ¹⁴So I want the younger widows to marry, have children, and manage their homes. Then no enemy will have any reason to criticize them.

STEP 4

[15]But some have already turned away to follow Satan.

[16]If any woman who is a believer has widows in her family, she should care for them herself. The church should not have to care for them. Then it will be able to take care of those who are truly widows.

[17]The elders who lead the church well should receive double honor, especially those who work hard by speaking and teaching, [18]because the Scripture says: "When an ox is working in the grain, do not cover its mouth to keep it from eating," and "A worker should be given his pay."

[19]Do not listen to someone who accuses an elder, without two or three witnesses. [20]Tell those who continue sinning that they are wrong. Do this in front of the whole church so that the others will have a warning.

[21]Before God and Christ Jesus and the chosen angels, I command you to do these things without showing favor of any kind to anyone.

[22]Think carefully before you lay your hands on anyone, and don't share in the sins of others. Keep yourself pure.

[23]Stop drinking only water, but drink a little wine to help your stomach and your frequent sicknesses.

[24]The sins of some people are easy to see even before they are judged, but the sins of others are seen only later. [25]So also good deeds are easy to see, but even those that are not easily seen cannot stay hidden.

6 All who are slaves under a yoke should show full respect to their masters so no one will speak against God's name and our teaching. [2]The slaves whose masters are believers should not show their masters any less respect because they are believers. They should serve their mas-

ters even better, because they are helping believers they love.

You must teach and preach these things.

[3]Anyone who has a different teaching does not agree with the true teaching of our Lord Jesus Christ and the teaching that shows the true way to serve God. [4]This person is full of pride and understands nothing, but is sick with a love for arguing and fighting about words. This brings jealousy, fighting, speaking against others, evil mistrust, [5]and constant quarrels from those who have evil minds and have lost the truth. They think that serving God is a way to get rich.

[6]Serving God does make us very rich, if we are satisfied with what we have. [7]We brought nothing into the world, so we can take nothing out. [8]But, if we have food and clothes, we will be satisfied with that. [9]Those who want to become rich bring temptation to themselves and are caught in a trap. They want many foolish and harmful things that ruin and destroy people. [10]The love of money causes all kinds of evil. Some people have left the faith, because they wanted to get more money, but they have caused themselves much sorrow.

[11]But you, man of God, run away from all those things. Instead, live in the right way, serve God, have faith, love, patience, and gentleness. [12]Fight the good fight of faith, grabbing hold of the life that continues forever. You were called to have that life when you confessed the good confession before many witnesses. [13]In the sight of God, who gives life to everything, and of Christ Jesus, I give you a command. Christ Jesus made the good confession when he stood before Pontius Pilate. [14]Do what you were commanded to do without wrong or blame until our Lord Jesus Christ comes again. [15]God will make

that happen at the right time. He is the blessed and only Ruler, the King of all kings and the Lord of all lords. [16]He is the only One who never dies. He lives in light so bright no one can go near it. No one has ever seen God, or can see him. May honor and power belong to God forever. Amen.

[17]Command those who are rich with things of this world not to be proud. Tell them to hope in God, not in their uncertain riches. God richly gives us everything to enjoy. [18]Tell the rich people to do good, to be rich in doing good deeds, to be generous and ready to share. [19]By doing that, they will be saving a treasure for themselves as a strong foundation for the future. Then they will be able to have the life that is true life.

[20]Timothy, guard what God has trusted to you. Stay away from foolish, useless talk and from the arguments of what is falsely called "knowledge." [21]By saying they have that "knowledge," some have missed the true faith.

Grace be with you.

2 TIMOTHY

Paul Encourages Timothy

1 From Paul, an apostle of Christ Jesus by the will of God. God sent me to tell about the promise of life that is in Christ Jesus.

² To Timothy, a dear child to me:

Grace, mercy, and peace to you from God the Father and Christ Jesus our Lord.

³ I thank God as I always mention you in my prayers, day and night. I serve him, doing what I know is right as my ancestors did. ⁴ Remembering that you cried for me, I want very much to see you so I can be filled with joy. ⁵ I remember your true faith. That faith first lived in your grandmother Lois and in your mother Eunice, and I know you now have that same faith. ⁶ This is why I remind you to keep using the gift God gave you when I laid my hands on you. Now let it grow, as a small flame grows into a fire. ⁷ God did not give us a spirit that makes us afraid but a spirit of power and love and self-control.

STEP 8

⁸ So do not be ashamed to tell people about our Lord Jesus, and do not be ashamed of me, in prison for the Lord. But suffer with me for the Good News. God, who gives us the strength to do that, ⁹ saved us and made us his holy people. That was not because of anything we did ourselves but because of God's purpose and grace. That grace was given to us through Christ Jesus before time began, ¹⁰ but it is now shown to us by the coming of our Savior Christ Jesus. He destroyed death, and through the Good News he showed us the way to have life that cannot be destroyed. ¹¹ I was chosen to tell that Good News and to be an apostle and a teacher. ¹² I am suffering now because I tell the Good News, but I am not

STEP 11

ashamed, because I know Jesus, the One in whom I have believed. And I am sure he is able to protect what he has trusted me with until that day. ¹³ Follow the pattern of true teachings that you heard from me in faith and love, which are in Christ Jesus. ¹⁴ Protect the truth that you were given; protect it with the help of the Holy Spirit who lives in us.

¹⁵ You know that everyone in Asia has left me, even Phygelus and Hermogenes. ¹⁶ May the Lord show mercy to the family of Onesiphorus, who has often helped me and was not ashamed that I was in prison. ¹⁷ When he came to Rome, he looked eagerly for me until he found me. ¹⁸ May the Lord allow him to find mercy from the Lord on that day. You know how many ways he helped me in Ephesus.

2 You then, Timothy, my child, be strong in the grace we have in Christ Jesus. ² You should teach people whom you can trust the things you and many others have heard me say. Then they will be able to teach others. ³ Share in the troubles we have like a good soldier of Christ Jesus. ⁴ A soldier wants to please the enlisting officer, so no one serving in the army wastes time with everyday matters. ⁵ Also an athlete who takes part in a contest must obey all the rules in order to win. ⁶ The farmer who works hard should be the first person to get some of the food that was grown. ⁷ Think about what I am saying, because the Lord will give you the ability to understand everything.

STEP 10

⁸ Remember Jesus Christ, who was raised from the dead, who is from the family of David. This is the Good News I preach, ⁹ and I am suffering because of it to the point of being bound with chains

STEP 8

Made a list of all persons we had harmed,
and became willing to make amends to them all.

2 Timothy 1:7

Most people dread the thought of facing somebody else and talking honestly about past hurts, regrets, bitterness, or hard feelings. Almost nothing could be harder to do, but this is what Steps 8 and 9 are all about

In the Bible, Timothy was a young pastor that the apostle Paul mentored. He may have had this fear of facing people he needed to talk to. So Paul had a heart-to-heart with Timothy and gave him the encouragement found in 2 Timothy 1:7. Paul told his friend that God had given him three gifts to replace the natural fear he felt about confronting problems. God replaces your fearful spirit with "a spirit of power and love and self-control."

As you work through Step 8, think often about this verse. Let it encourage and comfort you. God's Holy Spirit gives you a lot of resources for life. Among these is the **power** to forgive and ask to be forgiven. Let God's **love** enable you to make amends. Remember. You have God's love motivating you to care for those you talk with, and you have the God-given **self-control** to work through this challenging recovery step.

FOR YOUR NEXT **STEP 8** MEDITATION, TURN TO **PAGE 331.** ▶▶

like a criminal. But God's teaching is not in chains. [10]So I patiently accept all these troubles so that those whom God has chosen can have the salvation that is in Christ Jesus. With that salvation comes glory that never ends.

[11]This teaching is true:
If we died with him, we will also live
with him.
[12]If we accept suffering, we will also
rule with him.
If we say we don't know him, he will
say he doesn't know us.
[13]If we are not faithful, he will still be
faithful,
because he must be true to who
he is.

[14]Continue teaching these things, warning people in God's presence not to argue about words. It does not help anyone, and it ruins those who listen. [15]Make every effort to give yourself to God as the kind of person he will approve. Be a worker who is not ashamed and who uses the true teaching in the right way. [16]Stay away from foolish, useless talk, because that will lead people further away from God. [17]Their evil teaching will spread like a sickness inside the body. Hymenaeus and Philetus are like that. [18]They have left the true teaching, saying that the rising from the dead has already taken place, and so they are destroying the faith of some people. [19]But God's strong foundation continues to stand. These words are written on the seal: "The Lord knows those who belong to him," and "Everyone who wants to belong to the Lord must stop doing wrong."

[20]In a large house there are not only things made of gold and silver, but also things made of wood and clay. Some things are used for special purposes, and others are made for ordinary jobs. [21]All who make themselves clean from evil will be used for special purposes. They will be made holy, useful to the Master, ready to do any good work.

[22]But run away from the evil desires of youth. Try hard to live right and to have faith, love, and peace, together with those who trust in the Lord from pure hearts. [23]Stay away from foolish and stupid arguments, because you know they grow into quarrels. [24]And a servant of the Lord must not quarrel but must be kind to everyone, a good teacher, and patient. [25]The Lord's servant must gently teach those who disagree. Then maybe God will let them change their minds so they can accept the truth. [26]And they may wake up and escape from the trap of the devil, who catches them to do what he wants.

3 Remember this! In the last days there will be many troubles, [2]because people will love themselves, love money, brag, and be proud. They will say evil things against others and will not obey their parents or be thankful or be the kind of people God wants. [3]They will not love others, will refuse to forgive, will gossip, and will not control themselves. They will be cruel, will hate what is good, [4]will turn against their friends, and will do foolish things without thinking. They will be conceited, will love pleasure instead of God, [5]and will act as if they serve God but will not have his power. Stay away from those people. [6]Some of them go into homes and get control of silly women who are full of sin and are led by many evil desires. [7]These women are always learning new teachings, but they are never able to understand the truth fully. [8]Just as Jannes and Jambres were against Moses, these people are against the truth. Their thinking has been ruined, and they have failed in trying to follow the faith. [9]But they will not be successful in what they do,

because as with Jannes and Jambres, everyone will see that they are foolish.

¹⁰But you have followed what I teach, the way I live, my goal, faith, patience, and love. You know I never give up. ¹¹You know how I have been hurt and have suffered, as in Antioch, Iconium, and Lystra. I have suffered, but the Lord saved me from all those troubles. ¹²Everyone who wants to live as God desires, in Christ Jesus, will be persecuted. ¹³But people who are evil and cheat others will go from bad to worse. They will fool others, but they will also be fooling themselves.

STEP 11

¹⁴But you should continue following the teachings you learned. You know they are true, because you trust those who taught you. ¹⁵Since you were a child you have known the Holy Scriptures which are able to make you wise. And that wisdom leads to salvation through faith in Christ Jesus. ¹⁶All Scripture is inspired by God and is useful for teaching, for showing people what is wrong in their lives, for correcting faults, and for teaching how to live right. ¹⁷Using the Scriptures, the person who serves God will be capable, having all that is needed to do every good work.

4 I give you a command in the presence of God and Christ Jesus, the One who will judge the living and the dead, and by his coming and his kingdom: ²Preach the Good News. Be ready at all times, and tell people what they need to do. Tell them when they are wrong. Encourage them with great patience and careful teaching, ³because the time will come when people will not listen to the true teaching but will find many more teachers who please them by saying the things they want to hear. ⁴They will stop listening to the truth and will begin to follow false stories. ⁵But you should control yourself at all times, accept troubles, do the work of telling

the Good News, and complete all the duties of a servant of God.

⁶My life is being given as an offering to God, and the time has come for me to leave this life. ⁷I have fought the good fight, I have finished the race, I have kept the faith. ⁸Now, a crown is being held for me—a crown for being right with God. The Lord, the judge who judges rightly, will give the crown to me on that day—not only to me but to all those who have waited with love for him to come again.

⁹Do your best to come to me as soon as you can, ¹⁰because Demas, who loved this world, left me and went to Thessalonica. Crescens went to Galatia, and Titus went to Dalmatia. ¹¹Luke is the only one still with me. Get Mark and bring him with you when you come, because he can help me in my work here. ¹²I sent Tychicus to Ephesus. ¹³When I was in Troas, I left my coat there with Carpus. So when you come, bring it to me, along with my books, particularly the ones written on parchment.

¹⁴Alexander the metalworker did many harmful things against me. The Lord will punish him for what he did. ¹⁵You also should be careful that he does not hurt you, because he fought strongly against our teaching.

¹⁶The first time I defended myself, no one helped me; everyone left me. May they be forgiven. ¹⁷But the Lord stayed with me and gave me strength so I could fully tell the Good News to all those who are not Jews. So I was saved from the lion's mouth. ¹⁸The Lord will save me when anyone tries to hurt me, and he will bring me safely to his heavenly kingdom. Glory forever and ever be the Lord's. Amen.

¹⁹Greet Priscilla and Aquila and the family of Onesiphorus. ²⁰Erastus stayed in

Corinth, and I left Trophimus sick in Miletus. ²¹Try as hard as you can to come to me before winter.

Eubulus sends greetings to you. Also Pudens, Linus, Claudia, and all the brothers and sisters in Christ greet you.

²²The Lord be with your spirit. Grace be with you.

TITUS

Paul Instructs Titus

1 From Paul, a servant of God and an apostle of Jesus Christ. I was sent to help the faith of God's chosen people and to help them know the truth that shows people how to serve God. ²That faith and that knowledge come from the hope for life forever, which God promised to us before time began. And God cannot lie. ³At the right time God let the world know about that life through preaching. He trusted me with that work, and I preached by the command of God our Savior.

⁴To Titus, my true child in the faith we share:

Grace and peace from God the Father and Christ Jesus our Savior.

⁵I left you in Crete so you could finish doing the things that still needed to be done and so you could appoint elders in every town, as I directed you. ⁶An elder must not be guilty of doing wrong, must have only one wife, and must have believing children. They must not be known as children who are wild and do not cooperate. ⁷As God's managers, overseers must not be guilty of doing wrong, being selfish, or becoming angry quickly. They must not drink too much wine, like to fight, or try to get rich by cheating others. ⁸Overseers must be ready to welcome guests, love what is good, be wise, live right, and be holy and self-controlled. ⁹By holding on to the trustworthy word just as we teach it, overseers can help people by using true teaching, and they can show those who are against the true teaching that they are wrong.

¹⁰There are many people who refuse to cooperate, who talk about worthless things and lead others into the wrong way—mainly those who insist on circumcision to be saved. ¹¹These people must be stopped, because they are upsetting whole families by teaching things they should not teach, which they do to get rich by cheating people. ¹²Even one of their own prophets said, "Cretans are always liars, evil animals, and lazy people who do nothing but eat." ¹³The words that prophet said are true. So firmly tell those people they are wrong so they may become strong in the faith, ¹⁴not accepting Jewish false stories and the commands of people who reject the truth. ¹⁵To those who are pure, all things are pure, but to those who are full of sin and do not believe, nothing is pure. Both their minds and their consciences have been ruined. ¹⁶They say they know God, but their actions show they do not accept him. They are hateful people, they refuse to obey, and they are useless for doing anything good.

2 But you must tell everyone what to do to follow the true teaching. ²Teach older men to be self-controlled, serious, wise, strong in faith, in love, and in patience.

³In the same way, teach older women to be holy in their behavior, not speaking against others or enslaved to too much wine, but teaching what is good. ⁴Then they can teach the young women to love their husbands, to love their children, ⁵to be wise and pure, to be good workers at home, to be kind, and to yield to their husbands. Then no one will be able to criticize the teaching God gave us.

⁶In the same way, encourage young men to be wise. ⁷In every way be an example of doing good deeds. When you teach, do it with honesty and seriousness.

STEP 11

Sought through prayer and meditation to improve our conscious contact with God **as we understood Him,** praying only for knowledge of His will for us and the power to carry that out.

Titus 3:1–7

Maybe your addictive personality plays tricks on you and makes you feel you have to somehow work your way to heaven. Start thinking like that and you'll end up feeling like a failure who has to try harder and harder to jump through all the hoops set up for you by your own perfectionism.

You know you need deliverance from your faults. Before recovery we all were "foolish. We did not obey, we were wrong, and we were slaves to many things our bodies wanted" (verse 3). You were no different from any other sinner.

Isn't it good news that you don't have to try to be your own redeemer? You don't have to try to win, buy, or bargain for your salvation "because of good deeds we did" (verse 5). Redemption comes as a gift from God, "through the washing that made us new people through the Holy Spirit. God poured out richly upon us that Holy Spirit through Jesus Christ our Savior" (verses 5–6).

FOR YOUR NEXT **STEP 11** MEDITATION, TURN TO **PAGE 446.** ▶▶

⁸Speak the truth so that you cannot be criticized. Then those who are against you will be ashamed because there is nothing bad to say about us.

⁹Slaves should yield to their own masters at all times, trying to please them and not arguing with them. ¹⁰They should not steal from them but should show their masters they can be fully trusted so that in everything they do they will make the teaching of God our Savior attractive.

STEP
6

¹¹That is the way we should live, because God's grace that can save everyone has come. ¹²It teaches us not to live against God nor to do the evil things the world wants to do. Instead, that grace teaches us to live in the present age in a wise and right way and in a way that shows we serve God. ¹³We should live like that while we wait for our great hope and the coming of the glory of our great God and Savior Jesus Christ. ¹⁴He gave himself for us so he might pay the price to free us from all evil and to make us pure people who belong only to him—people who are always wanting to do good deeds.

¹⁵Say these things and encourage the people and tell them what is wrong in their lives, with all authority. Do not let anyone treat you as if you were unimportant.

STEP
11

3 Remind the believers to yield to the authority of rulers and government leaders, to obey them, to be ready to do good, ²to speak no evil about anyone, to live in peace, and to be gentle and polite to all people.

³In the past we also were foolish. We did not obey, we were wrong, and we were slaves to many things our bodies wanted and enjoyed. We spent our lives doing evil and being jealous. People hated us, and we hated each other. ⁴But when the kindness and love of God our Savior was shown, ⁵he saved us because of his mercy. It was not because of good deeds we did to be right with him. He saved us through the washing that made us new people through the Holy Spirit. ⁶God poured out richly upon us that Holy Spirit through Jesus Christ our Savior. ⁷Being made right with God by his grace, we could have the hope of receiving the life that never ends.

⁸This teaching is true, and I want you to be sure the people understand these things. Then those who believe in God will be careful to use their lives for doing good. These things are good and will help everyone.

⁹But stay away from those who have foolish arguments and talk about useless family histories and argue and quarrel about the law. Those things are worth nothing and will not help anyone. ¹⁰After a first and second warning, avoid someone who causes arguments. ¹¹You can know that such people are evil and sinful; their own sins prove them wrong.

¹²When I send Artemas or Tychicus to you, make every effort to come to me at Nicopolis, because I have decided to stay there this winter. ¹³Do all you can to help Zenas the lawyer and Apollos on their journey so that they have everything they need. ¹⁴Our people must learn to use their lives for doing good deeds to provide what is necessary so that their lives will not be useless.

STEP
11

¹⁵All who are with me greet you. Greet those who love us in the faith.

Grace be with you all.

PHILEMON

A Slave Becomes a Christian

---

[1]From Paul, a prisoner of Christ Jesus, and from Timothy, our brother.

To Philemon, our dear friend and worker with us; [2]to Apphia, our sister; to Archippus, a worker with us; and to the church that meets in your home:

[3]Grace and peace to you from God our Father and the Lord Jesus Christ.

[4]I always thank my God when I mention you in my prayers, [5]because I hear about the love you have for all God's holy people and the faith you have in the Lord Jesus. [6]I pray that the faith you share may make you understand every blessing we have in Christ. [7]I have great joy and comfort, my brother, because the love you have shown to God's people has refreshed them.

STEP 9

[8]So, in Christ, I could be bold and order you to do what is right. [9]But because I love you, I am pleading with you instead. I, Paul, an old man now and also a prisoner for Christ Jesus, [10]am pleading with you for my child Onesimus, who became my child while I was in prison. [11]In the past he was useless to you, but now he has become useful for both you and me.

[12]I am sending him back to you, and with him I am sending my own heart. [13]I wanted to keep him with me so that in your place he might help me while I am in prison for the Good News. [14]But I did not want to do anything without asking you first so that any good you do for me will be because you want to do it, not because I forced you. [15]Maybe Onesimus was separated from you for a short time so you could have him back forever— [16]no longer as a slave, but better than a slave, as a loved brother. I love him very much, but you will love him even more, both as a person and as a believer in the Lord.

[17]So if you consider me your partner, welcome Onesimus as you would welcome me. [18]If he has done anything wrong to you or if he owes you anything, charge that to me. [19]I, Paul, am writing this with my own hand. I will pay it back, and I will say nothing about what you owe me for your own life. [20]So, my brother, I ask that you do this for me in the Lord: Refresh my heart in Christ. [21]I write this letter, knowing that you will do what I ask you and even more.

[22]One more thing—prepare a room for me in which to stay, because I hope God will answer your prayers and I will be able to come to you.

[23]Epaphras, a prisoner with me for Christ Jesus, sends greetings to you. [24]And also Mark, Aristarchus, Demas, and Luke, workers together with me, send greetings.

[25]The grace of our Lord Jesus Christ be with your spirit.

STEP 9

Made direct amends to such people
wherever possible, except when to
do so would injure them or others.

Philemon 8–17

One of the sneakiest things an addiction does to you is weaken
your sense of responsibility. In fact, one of the best ways to gauge
how well your recovery is going is to look at how well you accept
responsibility for what you do.

The apostle Paul wrote an extraordinary little letter to a man named
Philemon asking him to take on a big responsibility. Paul asked
Philemon to forgive an act of betrayal and welcome home
Onesimus, the man who had betrayed him. In fact, Paul asked
Philemon to treat Onesimus "as a loved brother" (verse 16).

You need that same maturity and responsibility to do the work of
Step 9. In Step 9, you offer to reconcile with those who have
wronged you and those you have wronged. You do it even if some
of these people aren't ready or willing to respond to you the way
you'd like them to. When you accept this responsibility, you become
God's representative as a peacemaker, just as Paul was doing
between Philemon and Onesimus.

FOR YOUR NEXT **STEP 9** MEDITATION, TURN TO **PAGE 422.** ▶▶

HEBREWS

A Better Life Through Christ

1 In the past God spoke to our ancestors through the prophets many times and in many different ways. ²But now in these last days God has spoken to us through his Son. God has chosen his Son to own all things, and through him he made the world. ³The Son reflects the glory of God and shows exactly what God is like. He holds everything together with his powerful word. When the Son made people clean from their sins, he sat down at the right side of God, the Great One in heaven. ⁴The Son became much greater than the angels, and God gave him a name that is much greater than theirs.

⁵This is because God never said to any of the angels,

"You are my Son.
    Today I have become your Father."
                                    Psalm 2:7

Nor did God say of any angel,

"I will be his Father,
    and he will be my Son." *2 Samuel 7:14*

⁶And when God brings his firstborn Son into the world, he says,

"Let all God's angels worship him."
                                    Psalm 97:7

⁷This is what God said about the angels:

"God makes his angels become like
    winds.
He makes his servants become
    like flames of fire."
                                    Psalm 104:4

⁸But God said this about his Son:

"God, your throne will last forever and
    ever.
You will rule your kingdom with
    fairness.
⁹You love right and hate evil,
    so God has chosen you from
        among your friends;

he has set you apart with much
    joy."   *Psalm 45:6–7*

¹⁰God also says,

"Lord, in the beginning you made the
    earth,
and your hands made the skies.
¹¹They will be destroyed, but you will
    remain.
They will all wear out like clothes.
¹²You will fold them like a coat.
    And, like clothes, you will change
        them.
But you never change,
    and your life will never end."
                                    Psalm 102:25–27

¹³And God never said this to an angel:

"Sit by me at my right side
    until I put your enemies under your
        control."   *Psalm 110:1*

¹⁴All the angels are spirits who serve God and are sent to help those who will receive salvation.

2 So we must be more careful to follow what we were taught. Then we will not stray away from the truth. ²The teaching God spoke through angels was shown to be true, and anyone who did not follow it or obey it received the punishment that was earned. ³So surely we also will be punished if we ignore this great salvation. The Lord himself first told about this salvation, and those who heard him testified it was true. ⁴God also testified to the truth of the message by using wonders, great signs, many kinds of miracles, and by giving people gifts through the Holy Spirit, just as he wanted.

⁵God did not choose angels to be the rulers of the new world that was coming, which is what we have been talking about. ⁶It is written in the Scriptures,

STEP 10

STEP 10

Continued to take personal inventory
and when we were wrong promptly admitted it.

Hebrews 2:1–3

Three brothers—young boys—took the family rowboat out on the lake to enjoy a sunny summer day. The one rule they had to obey was to stay away from the power plant where they could get sucked into the huge intake pipe. They rowed to the side of the lake away from the plant and began to play. They swam and wrestled one another in the water. They took a breather in the bottom of the boat and felt the wind on their faces as they watched the clouds in the sky.

Suddenly the fun ended. The oldest brother cried out because they had drifted clear across the lake into the pull of the intake pipe. Fear froze their hearts. Were they glad to get a lecture from the patrolman who spotted them and towed them to safety! They learned an important lesson: "Give the more earnest heed . . . lest [you] drift away" (verse 3 NKJV).

Sometimes something similar happens when you enjoy the sweet success of a solid recovery from addiction. It feels so good. It would be nice to relax and drift a while in the good feelings. The danger comes when relaxing means neglecting Steps 10, 11, and 12, your maintenance steps. You can drift into disaster that way. Let Step 10 warns you, "Take inventory; take heed." Don't drift toward the sinister power plant of your old character defects.

FOR YOUR NEXT **STEP 10** MEDITATION, TURN TO **PAGE 337.** ►►

"Why are people even important to
you?
Why do you take care of human
beings?
[7]You made them a little lower than the
angels
and crowned them with glory and
honor.
[8]You put all things under their control."

Psalm 8:4–6

When God put everything under their
control, there was nothing left that they
did not rule. Still, we do not yet see them
ruling over everything. [9]But we see Jesus,
who for a short time was made lower than
the angels. And now he is wearing a
crown of glory and honor because he suffered and died. And by God's grace, he
died for everyone.

[10]God is the One who made all things,
and all things are for his glory. He wanted
to have many children share his glory, so
he made the One who leads people to
salvation perfect through suffering.

[11]Jesus, who makes people holy, and
those who are made holy are from the
same family. So he is not ashamed to call
them his brothers and sisters. [12]He says,
"Then, I will tell my brothers and
sisters about you;
I will praise you in the public
meeting."   *Psalm 22:22*
[13]He also says,
"I will trust in God."   *Isaiah 8:17*
And he also says,
"I am here, and with me are the
children God has given me."
Isaiah 8:18

STEP
2 [14]Since these children are people with
physical bodies, Jesus himself became
like them. He did this so that, by dying, he
could destroy the one who has the power
of death—the devil— [15]and free those
who were like slaves all their lives because of their fear of death. [16]Clearly, it is

not angels that Jesus helps, but the people who are from Abraham. [17]For this
reason Jesus had to be made like his
brothers and sisters in every way so he
could be their merciful and faithful high
priest in service to God. Then Jesus could
die in their place to take away their sins.
[18]And now he can help those who are
tempted, because he himself suffered
and was tempted.

3 So all of you holy brothers and sisters,
who were called by God, think about
Jesus, who was sent to us and is the high
priest of our faith. [2]Jesus was faithful to
God as Moses was in God's family. [3]Jesus
has more honor than Moses, just as the
builder of a house has more honor than
the house itself. [4]Every house is built by
someone, but the builder of everything is
God himself. [5]Moses was faithful in God's
family as a servant, and he told what God
would say in the future. [6]But Christ is
faithful as a Son over God's house. And
we are God's house if we confidently
maintain our hope.

[7]So it is as the Holy Spirit says: STEP
10
"Today listen to what he says.
[8]Do not be stubborn as in the past
when you turned against God,
when you tested God in the desert.
[9]There your ancestors tried me and
tested me
and saw the things I did for forty
years.
[10]I was angry with them.
I said, 'They are not loyal to me
and have not understood my
ways.'
[11]I was angry and made a promise,
'They will never enter my rest.' "
Psalm 95:7–11

[12]So brothers and sisters, be careful
that none of you has an evil, unbelieving
heart that will turn you away from the living God. [13]But encourage each other

every day while it is "today." Help each other so none of you will become hardened because sin has tricked you. ¹⁴We all share in Christ if we keep till the end the sure faith we had in the beginning. ¹⁵This is what the Scripture says:

"Today listen to what he says.
    Do not be stubborn as in the past
        when you turned against God."

Psalm 95:7–8

¹⁶Who heard God's voice and was against him? It was all those people Moses led out of Egypt. ¹⁷And with whom was God angry for forty years? He was angry with those who sinned, who died in the desert. ¹⁸And to whom was God talking when he promised that they would never enter his rest? He was talking to those who did not obey him. ¹⁹So we see they were not allowed to enter and have God's rest, because they did not believe.

STEP 3

4 Now, since God has left us the promise that we may enter his rest, let us be very careful so none of you will fail to enter. ²The Good News was preached to us just as it was to them. But the teaching they heard did not help them, because they heard it but did not accept it with faith. ³We who have believed are able to enter and have God's rest. As God has said,

"I was angry and made a promise,
    'They will never enter my rest.'"

Psalm 95:11

But God's work was finished from the time he made the world. ⁴In the Scriptures he talked about the seventh day of the week: "And on the seventh day God rested from all his works." ⁵And again in the Scripture God said, "They will never enter my rest."

⁶It is still true that some people will enter God's rest, but those who first heard the way to be saved did not enter, because they did not obey. ⁷So God planned

another day, called "today." He spoke about that day through David a long time later in the same Scripture used before:

"Today listen to what he says.
    Do not be stubborn."   *Psalm 95:7–8*

⁸We know that Joshua did not lead the people into that rest, because God spoke later about another day. ⁹This shows that the rest for God's people is still coming. ¹⁰Anyone who enters God's rest will rest from his work as God did. ¹¹Let us try as hard as we can to enter God's rest so that no one will fail by following the example of those who refused to obey.

STEP 5

¹²God's word is alive and working and is sharper than a double-edged sword. It cuts all the way into us, where the soul and the spirit are joined, to the center of our joints and bones. And it judges the thoughts and feelings in our hearts. ¹³Nothing in all the world can be hidden from God. Everything is clear and lies open before him, and to him we must explain the way we have lived.

¹⁴Since we have a great high priest, Jesus the Son of God, who has gone into heaven, let us hold on to the faith we have. ¹⁵For our high priest is able to understand our weaknesses. He was tempted in every way that we are, but he did not sin. ¹⁶Let us, then, feel very sure that we can come before God's throne where there is grace. There we can receive mercy and grace to help us when we need it.

5 Every high priest is chosen from among other people. He is given the work of going before God for them to offer gifts and sacrifices for sins. ²Since he himself is weak, he is able to be gentle with those who do not understand and who are doing wrong things. ³Because he is weak, the high priest must offer sacrifices for his own sins and also for the sins of the people.

STEP 5

Admitted to God, to ourselves, and to another human being the exact nature of our wrongs.

Hebrews 4:12–16

You have to be very careful in choosing who you make your Step 5 confession to. When you tell someone secrets, you're letting them into parts of your personality and feelings where, perhaps, no one else has been. You may reveal some things you've done that you're deeply ashamed of.

It's easy to understand why you might hesitate to admit "the exact nature of [your] wrongs." Maybe you expect to be judged or criticized by the person you tell. Maybe, since Step 5 involves confessing "to God, to ourselves, and to another human being," you expect God to get mad at you. Or maybe it's the critical voice in your head you don't want to hear. What you need to do is trust God's mercy and forgiveness, cut yourself some slack, and choose a mature, compassionate person to hear your confession.

At the very least you can trust God to accept your confession gladly. Jesus, his Son, fully understands from experience what you go through when you are tempted to sin. The Father and the Son never tire of reaching out to you with amazing grace!

FOR YOUR NEXT **STEP 5** MEDITATION, TURN TO **PAGE 332.** ▶▶

[4]To be a high priest is an honor, but no one chooses himself for this work. He must be called by God as Aaron was. [5]So also Christ did not choose himself to have the honor of being a high priest, but God chose him. God said to him,

"You are my Son.

Today I have become your Father."

Psalm 2:7

[6]And in another Scripture God says,

"You are a priest forever,

a priest like Melchizedek."

Psalm 110:4

[7]While Jesus lived on earth, he prayed to God and asked God for help. He prayed with loud cries and tears to the One who could save him from death, and his prayer was heard because he trusted God. [8]Even though Jesus was the Son of God, he learned obedience by what he suffered. [9]And because his obedience was perfect, he was able to give eternal salvation to all who obey him. [10]In this way God made Jesus a high priest, a priest like Melchizedek.

[11]We have much to say about this, but it is hard to explain because you are so slow to understand. [12]By now you should be teachers, but you need someone to teach you again the first lessons of God's message. You still need the teaching that is like milk. You are not ready for solid food. [13]Anyone who lives on milk is still a baby and knows nothing about right teaching. [14]But solid food is for those who are grown up. They are mature enough to know the difference between good and evil.

6 So let us go on to grown-up teaching. Let us not go back over the beginning lessons we learned about Christ. We should not again start teaching about faith in God and about turning away from those acts that lead to death. [2]We should not return to the teaching about bap-

tisms, about laying on of hands, about the raising of the dead and eternal judgment. [3]And we will go on to grown-up teaching if God allows.

[4]Some people cannot be brought back again to a changed life. They were once in God's light, and enjoyed heaven's gift, and shared in the Holy Spirit. [5]They found out how good God's word is, and they received the powers of his new world. [6]But they fell away from Christ. It is impossible to bring them back to a changed life again, because they are nailing the Son of God to a cross again and are shaming him in front of others.

[7]Some people are like land that gets plenty of rain. The land produces a good crop for those who work it, and it receives God's blessings. [8]Other people are like land that grows thorns and weeds and is worthless. It is about to be cursed by God and will be destroyed by fire.

[9]Dear friends, we are saying this to you, but we really expect better things from you that will lead to your salvation. [10]God is fair; he will not forget the work you did and the love you showed for him by helping his people. And he will remember that you are still helping them. [11]We want each of you to go on with the same hard work all your lives so you will surely get what you hope for. [12]We do not want you to become lazy. Be like those who through faith and patience will receive what God has promised.

[13]God made a promise to Abraham. And as there is no one greater than God, he used himself when he swore to Abraham, [14]saying, "I will surely bless you and give you many descendants." [15]Abraham waited patiently for this to happen, and he received what God promised.

[16]People always use the name of someone greater than themselves when they swear. The oath proves that what

STEP 5

they say is true, and this ends all arguing. [17]God wanted to prove that his promise was true to those who would get what he promised. And he wanted them to understand clearly that his purposes never change, so he made an oath. [18]These two things cannot change: God cannot lie when he makes a promise, and he cannot lie when he makes an oath. These things encourage us who came to God for safety. They give us strength to hold on to the hope we have been given. [19]We have this hope as an anchor for the soul, sure and strong. It enters behind the curtain in the Most Holy Place in heaven, [20]where Jesus has gone ahead of us and for us. He has become the high priest forever, a priest like Melchizedek.

7 Melchizedek was the king of Salem and a priest for God Most High. He met Abraham when Abraham was coming back after defeating the kings. When they met, Melchizedek blessed Abraham, [2]and Abraham gave him a tenth of everything he had brought back from the battle. First, Melchizedek's name means "king of goodness," and he is king of Salem, which means "king of peace." [3]No one knows who Melchizedek's father or mother was, where he came from, when he was born, or when he died. Melchizedek is like the Son of God; he continues being a priest forever.

[4]You can see how great Melchizedek was. Abraham, the great father, gave him a tenth of everything that he won in battle. [5]Now the law says that those in the tribe of Levi who become priests must collect a tenth from the people—their own people—even though the priests and the people are from the family of Abraham. [6]Melchizedek was not from the tribe of Levi, but he collected a tenth from Abraham. And he blessed Abraham, the man who had God's promises. [7]Now

everyone knows that the more important person blesses the less important person. [8]Priests receive a tenth, even though they are only men who live and then die. But Melchizedek, who received a tenth from Abraham, continues living, as the Scripture says. [9]We might even say that Levi, who receives a tenth, also paid it when Abraham paid Melchizedek a tenth. [10]Levi was not yet born, but he was in the body of his ancestor when Melchizedek met Abraham.

[11]The people were given the law concerning the system of priests from the tribe of Levi, but they could not be made perfect through that system. So there was a need for another priest to come, a priest like Melchizedek, not Aaron. [12]And when a different kind of priest comes, the law must be changed, too. [13]We are saying these things about Christ, who belonged to a different tribe. No one from that tribe ever served as a priest at the altar. [14]It is clear that our Lord came from the tribe of Judah, and Moses said nothing about priests belonging to that tribe.

[15]And this becomes even more clear when we see that another priest comes who is like Melchizedek. [16]He was not made a priest by human rules and laws but through the power of his life, which continues forever. [17]It is said about him,

"You are a priest forever,
    a priest like Melchizedek."

Psalm 110:4

[18]The old rule is now set aside, because it was weak and useless. [19]The law of Moses could not make anything perfect. But now a better hope has been given to us, and with this hope we can come near to God. [20]It is important that God did this with an oath. Others became priests without an oath, [21]but Christ became a priest with God's oath. God said:

"The Lord has made a promise
and will not change his mind.
'You are a priest forever.'"

Psalm 110:4

²²This means that Jesus is the guarantee of a better agreement from God to his people.

²³When one of the other priests died, he could not continue being a priest. So there were many priests. ²⁴But because Jesus lives forever, he will never stop serving as priest. ²⁵So he is able always to save those who come to God through him because he always lives, asking God to help them.

²⁶Jesus is the kind of high priest we need. He is holy, sinless, pure, not influenced by sinners, and he is raised above the heavens. ²⁷He is not like the other priests who had to offer sacrifices every day, first for their own sins, and then for the sins of the people. Christ offered his sacrifice only once and for all time when he offered himself. ²⁸The law chooses high priests who are people with weaknesses, but the word of God's oath came later than the law. It made God's Son to be the high priest, and that Son has been made perfect forever.

8 Here is the point of what we are saying: We have a high priest who sits on the right side of God's throne in heaven. ²Our high priest serves in the Most Holy Place, the true place of worship that was made by God, not by humans.

³Every high priest has the work of offering gifts and sacrifices to God. So our high priest must also offer something to God. ⁴If our high priest were now living on earth, he would not be a priest, because there are already priests here who follow the law by offering gifts to God. ⁵The work they do as priests is only a copy and a shadow of what is in heaven. This is why God warned Moses when he was ready to build the Holy Tent: "Be very careful to make everything by the plan I showed you on the mountain." ⁶But the priestly work that has been given to Jesus is much greater than the work that was given to the other priests. In the same way, the new agreement that Jesus brought from God to his people is much greater than the old one. And the new agreement is based on promises of better things.

⁷If there had been nothing wrong with the first agreement, there would have been no need for a second agreement. ⁸But God found something wrong with his people. He says:
"Look, the time is coming, says the
Lord,
when I will make a new agreement
with the people of Israel
and the people of Judah.
⁹It will not be like the agreement
I made with their ancestors
when I took them by the hand
to bring them out of Egypt.
But they broke that agreement,
and I turned away from them, says
the Lord.
¹⁰This is the agreement I will make
with the people of Israel at that
time, says the Lord.
I will put my teachings in their minds
and write them on their hearts.
I will be their God,
and they will be my people.
¹¹People will no longer have to teach
their neighbors and relatives
to know the Lord,
because all people will know me,
from the least to the most
important.
¹²I will forgive them for the wicked
things they did,
and I will not remember their sins
anymore." *Jeremiah 31:31–34*
¹³God called this a new agreement, so

he has made the first agreement old. And anything that is old and worn out is ready to disappear.

9 The first agreement had rules for worship and a place on earth for worship. [2]The Holy Tent was set up for this. The first area in the Tent was called the Holy Place. In it were the lamp and the table with the bread that was made holy for God. [3]Behind the second curtain was a room called the Most Holy Place. [4]In it was a golden altar for burning incense and the Ark covered with gold that held the old agreement. Inside this Ark was a golden jar of manna, Aaron's rod that once grew leaves, and the stone tablets of the old agreement. [5]Above the Ark were the creatures that showed God's glory, whose wings reached over the lid. But we cannot tell everything about these things now.

[6]When everything in the Tent was made ready in this way, the priests went into the first room every day to worship. [7]But only the high priest could go into the second room, and he did that only once a year. He could never enter the inner room without taking blood with him, which he offered to God for himself and for sins the people did without knowing they did them. [8]The Holy Spirit uses this to show that the way into the Most Holy Place was not open while the system of the old Holy Tent was still being used. [9]This is an example for the present time. It shows that the gifts and sacrifices offered cannot make the conscience of the worshiper perfect. [10]These gifts and sacrifices were only about food and drink and special washings. They were rules for the body, to be followed until the time of God's new way.

[11]But when Christ came as the high priest of the good things we now have, he entered the greater and more perfect tent. It is not made by humans and does not belong to this world. [12]Christ entered the Most Holy Place only once—and for all time. He did not take with him the blood of goats and calves. His sacrifice was his own blood, and by it he set us free from sin forever. [13]The blood of goats and bulls and the ashes of a cow are sprinkled on the people who are unclean, and this makes their bodies clean again. [14]How much more is done by the blood of Christ. He offered himself through the eternal Spirit as a perfect sacrifice to God. His blood will make our consciences pure from useless acts so we may serve the living God.

[15]For this reason Christ brings a new agreement from God to his people. Those who are called by God can now receive the blessings he has promised, blessings that will last forever. They can have those things because Christ died so that the people who lived under the first agreement could be set free from sin.

[16]When there is a will, it must be proven that the one who wrote that will is dead. [17]A will means nothing while the person is alive; it can be used only after the person dies. [18]This is why even the first agreement could not begin without blood to show death. [19]First, Moses told all the people every command in the law. Next he took the blood of calves and mixed it with water. Then he used red wool and a branch of the hyssop plant to sprinkle it on the book of the law and on all the people. [20]He said, "This is the blood that begins the Agreement that God commanded you to obey." [21]In the same way, Moses sprinkled the blood on the Holy Tent and over all the things used in worship. [22]The law says that almost everything must be made clean by blood, and sins cannot be forgiven without blood to show death.

²³So the copies of the real things in heaven had to be made clean by animal sacrifices. But the real things in heaven need much better sacrifices. ²⁴Christ did not go into the Most Holy Place made by humans, which is only a copy of the real one. He went into heaven itself and is there now before God to help us. ²⁵The high priest enters the Most Holy Place once every year with blood that is not his own. But Christ did not offer himself many times. ²⁶Then he would have had to suffer many times since the world was made. But Christ came only once and for all time at just the right time to take away all sin by sacrificing himself. ²⁷Just as everyone must die once and then be judged, ²⁸so Christ was offered as a sacrifice one time to take away the sins of many people. And he will come a second time, not to offer himself for sin, but to bring salvation to those who are waiting for him.

10 The law is only an unclear picture of the good things coming in the future; it is not the real thing. The people under the law offer the same sacrifices every year, but these sacrifices can never make perfect those who come near to worship God. ²If the law could make them perfect, the sacrifices would have already stopped. The worshipers would be made clean, and they would no longer have a sense of sin. ³But these sacrifices remind them of their sins every year, ⁴because it is impossible for the blood of bulls and goats to take away sins.

⁵So when Christ came into the world, he said:

"You do not want sacrifices and offerings,
but you have prepared a body for me.
⁶You do not ask for burnt offerings and offerings to take away sins.
⁷Then I said, 'Look, I have come.
It is written about me in the book.
God, I have come to do what you want.'" *Psalm 40:6–8*

⁸In this Scripture he first said, "You do not want sacrifices and offerings. You do not ask for burnt offerings and offerings to take away sins." (These are all sacrifices that the law commands.) ⁹Then he said, "Look, I have come to do what you want." God ends the first system of sacrifices so he can set up the new system. ¹⁰And because of this, we are made holy through the sacrifice Christ made in his body once and for all time.

¹¹Every day the priests stand and do their religious service, often offering the same sacrifices. Those sacrifices can never take away sins. ¹²But after Christ offered one sacrifice for sins, forever, he sat down at the right side of God. ¹³And now Christ waits there for his enemies to be put under his power. ¹⁴With one sacrifice he made perfect forever those who are being made holy.

¹⁵The Holy Spirit also tells us about this. First he says:

¹⁶"This is the agreement I will make with them at that time, says the Lord.
I will put my teachings in their hearts and write them on their minds." *Jeremiah 31:33*

¹⁷Then he says:

"Their sins and the evil things they do—
I will not remember anymore." *Jeremiah 31:34*

¹⁸Now when these have been forgiven, there is no more need for a sacrifice for sins.

¹⁹So, brothers and sisters, we are completely free to enter the Most Holy Place without fear because of the blood of Jesus' death. ²⁰We can enter through a new

and living way that Jesus opened for us. It leads through the curtain—Christ's body. [21]And since we have a great priest over God's house, [22]let us come near to God with a sincere heart and a sure faith, because we have been made free from a guilty conscience, and our bodies have been washed with pure water. [23]Let us hold firmly to the hope that we have confessed, because we can trust God to do what he promised.

STEP 12

[24]Let us think about each other and help each other to show love and do good deeds. [25]You should not stay away from the church meetings, as some are doing, but you should meet together and encourage each other. Do this even more as you see the day coming.

[26]If we decide to go on sinning after we have learned the truth, there is no longer any sacrifice for sins. [27]There is nothing but fear in waiting for the judgment and the terrible fire that will destroy all those who live against God. [28]Anyone who refused to obey the law of Moses was found guilty from the proof given by two or three witnesses. He was put to death without mercy. [29]So what do you think should be done to those who do not respect the Son of God, who look at the blood of the agreement that made them holy as no different from others' blood, who insult the Spirit of God's grace? Surely they should have a much worse punishment. [30]We know that God said, "I will punish those who do wrong; I will repay them." And he also said, "The Lord will judge his people." [31]It is a terrible thing to fall into the hands of the living God.

[32]Remember those days in the past when you first learned the truth. You had a hard struggle with many sufferings, but you continued strong. [33]Sometimes you were hurt and attacked before crowds of people, and sometimes you shared with those who were being treated that way. [34]You helped the prisoners. You even had joy when all that you owned was taken from you, because you knew you had something better and more lasting.

[35]So do not lose the courage you had in the past, which has a great reward. [36]You must hold on, so you can do what God wants and receive what he has promised. [37]For in a very short time,

"The One who is coming will come
    and will not be delayed.
[38]Those who are right with me
    will live by faith.
But if they turn back with fear,
    I will not be pleased with them."

Habakkuk 2:3–4

STEP 10

[39]But we are not those who turn back and are lost. We are people who have faith and are saved.

11 Faith means being sure of the things we hope for and knowing that something is real even if we do not see it. [2]Faith is the reason we remember great people who lived in the past.

[3]It is by faith we understand that the whole world was made by God's command so what we see was made by something that cannot be seen.

[4]It was by faith that Abel offered God a better sacrifice than Cain did. God said he was pleased with the gifts Abel offered and called Abel a good man because of his faith. Abel died, but through his faith he is still speaking.

[5]It was by faith that Enoch was taken to heaven so he would not die. He could not be found, because God had taken him away. Before he was taken, the Scripture says that he was a man who truly pleased God. [6]Without faith no one can please God. Anyone who comes to God must believe that he is real and that he rewards those who truly want to find him.

⁷It was by faith that Noah heard God's warnings about things he could not yet see. He obeyed God and built a large boat to save his family. By his faith, Noah showed that the world was wrong, and he became one of those who are made right with God through faith.

⁸It was by faith Abraham obeyed God's call to go to another place God promised to give him. He left his own country, not knowing where he was to go. ⁹It was by faith that he lived like a foreigner in the country God promised to give him. He lived in tents with Isaac and Jacob, who had received that same promise from God. ¹⁰Abraham was waiting for the city that has real foundations—the city planned and built by God.

¹¹He was too old to have children, and Sarah could not have children. It was by faith that Abraham was made able to become a father, because he trusted God to do what he had promised. ¹²This man was so old he was almost dead, but from him came as many descendants as there are stars in the sky. Like the sand on the seashore, they could not be counted.

¹³All these great people died in faith. They did not get the things that God promised his people, but they saw them coming far in the future and were glad. They said they were like visitors and strangers on earth. ¹⁴When people say such things, they show they are looking for a country that will be their own. ¹⁵If they had been thinking about the country they had left, they could have gone back. ¹⁶But they were waiting for a better country—a heavenly country. So God is not ashamed to be called their God, because he has prepared a city for them.

¹⁷It was by faith that Abraham, when God tested him, offered his son Isaac as a sacrifice. God made the promises to Abraham, but Abraham was ready to offer his own son as a sacrifice. ¹⁸God had said, "The descendants I promised you will be from Isaac." ¹⁹Abraham believed that God could raise the dead, and really, it was as if Abraham got Isaac back from death.

²⁰It was by faith that Isaac blessed the future of Jacob and Esau. ²¹It was by faith that Jacob, as he was dying, blessed each one of Joseph's sons. Then he worshiped as he leaned on the top of his walking stick.

²²It was by faith that Joseph, while he was dying, spoke about the Israelites leaving Egypt and gave instructions about what to do with his body.

²³It was by faith that Moses' parents hid him for three months after he was born. They saw that Moses was a beautiful baby, and they were not afraid to disobey the king's order.

²⁴It was by faith that Moses, when he grew up, refused to be called the son of the king of Egypt's daughter. ²⁵He chose to suffer with God's people instead of enjoying sin for a short time. ²⁶He thought it was better to suffer for the Christ than to have all the treasures of Egypt, because he was looking for God's reward. ²⁷It was by faith that Moses left Egypt and was not afraid of the king's anger. Moses continued strong as if he could see the God that no one can see. ²⁸It was by faith that Moses prepared the Passover and spread the blood on the doors so the one who brings death would not kill the firstborn sons of Israel.

²⁹It was by faith that the people crossed the Red Sea as if it were dry land. But when the Egyptians tried it, they were drowned.

³⁰It was by faith that the walls of Jericho fell after the people had marched around them for seven days.

³¹It was by faith that Rahab, the prostitute, welcomed the spies and was not killed with those who refused to obey God.

³²Do I need to give more examples? I do not have time to tell you about Gideon, Barak, Samson, Jephthah, David, Samuel, and the prophets. ³³Through their faith they defeated kingdoms. They did what was right, received God's promises, and shut the mouths of lions. ³⁴They stopped great fires and were saved from being killed with swords. They were weak, and yet were made strong. They were powerful in battle and defeated other armies. ³⁵Women received their dead relatives raised back to life. Others were tortured and refused to accept their freedom so they could be raised from the dead to a better life. ³⁶Some were laughed at and beaten. Others were put in chains and thrown into prison. ³⁷They were stoned to death, they were cut in half, and they were killed with swords. Some wore the skins of sheep and goats. They were poor, abused, and treated badly. ³⁸The world was not good enough for them! They wandered in deserts and mountains, living in caves and holes in the earth.

³⁹All these people are known for their faith, but none of them received what God had promised. ⁴⁰God planned to give us something better so that they would be made perfect, but only together with us.

STEP 6

12 We are surrounded by a great cloud of people whose lives tell us what faith means. So let us run the race that is before us and never give up. We should remove from our lives anything that would get in the way and the sin that so easily holds us back. ²Let us look only to Jesus, the One who began our faith and who makes it perfect. He suffered death on the cross. But he accepted the shame as if it were nothing because of the joy that God put before him. And now he is sitting at the right side of God's throne. ³Think about Jesus' example. He held on while wicked people were doing evil things to him. So do not get tired and stop trying.

⁴You are struggling against sin, but your struggles have not yet caused you to be killed. ⁵You have forgotten the encouraging words that call you his children:

STEP 7

> "My child, don't think the Lord's
>   discipline is worth nothing,
> and don't stop trying when he
>   corrects you.
> ⁶The Lord disciplines those he loves,
>   and he punishes everyone he
>   accepts as his child."
>
> *Proverbs 3:11–12*

⁷So hold on through your sufferings, because they are like a father's discipline. God is treating you as children. All children are disciplined by their fathers. ⁸If you are never disciplined (and every child must be disciplined), you are not true children. ⁹We have all had fathers here on earth who disciplined us, and we respected them. So it is even more important that we accept discipline from the Father of our spirits so we will have life. ¹⁰Our fathers on earth disciplined us for a short time in the way they thought was best. But God disciplines us to help us, so we can become holy as he is. ¹¹We do not enjoy being disciplined. It is painful at the time, but later, after we have learned from it, we have peace, because we start living in the right way.

¹²You have become weak, so make yourselves strong again. ¹³Keep on the right path, so the weak will not stumble but rather be strengthened.

¹⁴Try to live in peace with all people, and try to live free from sin. Anyone

STEP 9

STEP 7

Humbly asked Him to remove our shortcomings.

Hebrews 12:5–11

The key word in Hebrews 12:5–11 is "discipline." It repeats throughout this long paragraph that challenges you to humility and submission to God. These are key Step 7 qualities.

It would seem the Hebrew Christians didn't want to cooperate with the work God had set out to do in their lives. So the author reminded them that God disciplines them spiritually as an earthly father disciplines his son physically. The comparison reasons from lesser to greater. What's true in our relation to our earthly fathers should be more true in relation to our heavenly Father. Therefore, we should respond to God's discipline with more respect than we gave our human fathers, because—unlike everyday dads—God is infinitely wise and loving.

Step 7 calls on you to do what the Hebrew Christians needed to do. Humbly ask God to discipline out of your life those things that are damaging to you, to your relationships with others, and to your relationship with him.

Verse 11 admits that this discipline may be "painful" in the short term. However, as you keep humbly submitting to God's discipline and direction, you can look forward to experiencing "peace, because we start living in the right way."

FOR YOUR NEXT **STEP 7** MEDITATION, TURN TO **PAGE 340**. ▶▶

whose life is not holy will never see the Lord. ¹⁵Be careful that no one fails to receive God's grace and begins to cause trouble among you. A person like that can ruin many of you. ¹⁶Be careful that no one takes part in sexual sin or is like Esau and never thinks about God. As the oldest son, Esau would have received everything from his father, but he sold all that for a single meal. ¹⁷You remember that after Esau did this, he wanted to get his father's blessing, but his father refused. Esau could find no way to change what he had done, even though he wanted the blessing so much that he cried.

¹⁸You have not come to a mountain that can be touched and that is burning with fire. You have not come to darkness, sadness, and storms. ¹⁹You have not come to the noise of a trumpet or to the sound of a voice like the one the people of Israel heard and begged not to hear another word. ²⁰They did not want to hear the command: "If anything, even an animal, touches the mountain, it must be put to death with stones." ²¹What they saw was so terrible that Moses said, "I am shaking with fear."

²²But you have come to Mount Zion, to the city of the living God, the heavenly Jerusalem. You have come to thousands of angels gathered together with joy. ²³You have come to the meeting of God's firstborn children whose names are written in heaven. You have come to God, the judge of all people, and to the spirits of good people who have been made perfect. ²⁴You have come to Jesus, the One who brought the new agreement from God to his people, and you have come to the sprinkled blood that has a better message than the blood of Abel.

STEP
10

²⁵So be careful and do not refuse to listen when God speaks. Others refused to listen to him when he warned them on earth, and they did not escape. So it will be worse for us if we refuse to listen to God who warns us from heaven. ²⁶When he spoke before, his voice shook the earth, but now he has promised, "Once again I will shake not only the earth but also the heavens." ²⁷The words "once again" clearly show us that everything that was made—things that can be shaken—will be destroyed. Only the things that cannot be shaken will remain.

²⁸So let us be thankful, because we have a kingdom that cannot be shaken. We should worship God in a way that pleases him with respect and fear, ²⁹because our God is like a fire that burns things up.

STEP
10

13 Keep on loving each other as brothers and sisters. ²Remember to welcome strangers, because some who have done this have welcomed angels without knowing it. ³Remember those who are in prison as if you were in prison with them. Remember those who are suffering as if you were suffering with them.

STEP
11

⁴Marriage should be honored by everyone, and husband and wife should keep their marriage pure. God will judge as guilty those who take part in sexual sins. ⁵Keep your lives free from the love of money, and be satisfied with what you have. God has said,

"I will never leave you;
    I will never abandon you."

Deuteronomy 31:6

⁶So we can be sure when we say,

"I will not be afraid, because the Lord
    is my helper.
People can't do anything to me."

Psalm 118:6

⁷Remember your leaders who taught God's message to you. Remember how they lived and died, and copy their faith. ⁸Jesus Christ is the same yesterday, today, and forever.

⁹Do not let all kinds of strange teachings lead you into the wrong way. Your hearts should be strengthened by God's grace, not by obeying rules about foods, which do not help those who obey them. ¹⁰We have a sacrifice, but the priests who serve in the Holy Tent cannot eat from it. ¹¹The high priest carries the blood of animals into the Most Holy Place where he offers this blood for sins. But the bodies of the animals are burned outside the camp. ¹²So Jesus also suffered outside the city to make his people holy with his own blood. ¹³So let us go to Jesus outside the camp, holding on as he did when we are abused.

¹⁴Here on earth we do not have a city that lasts forever, but we are looking for the city that we will have in the future. ¹⁵So through Jesus let us always offer to God our sacrifice of praise, coming from lips that speak his name. ¹⁶Do not forget to do good to others, and share with them, because such sacrifices please God.

¹⁷Obey your leaders and act under their authority. They are watching over you, because they are responsible for your souls. Obey them so that they will do this work with joy, not sadness. It will not help you to make their work hard.

¹⁸Pray for us. We are sure that we have a clear conscience, because we always want to do the right thing. ¹⁹I especially beg you to pray so that God will send me back to you soon.

²⁰⁻²¹I pray that the God of peace will give you every good thing you need so you can do what he wants. God raised from the dead our Lord Jesus, the Great Shepherd of the sheep, because of the blood of his death. His blood began the eternal agreement that God made with his people. I pray that God will do in us what pleases him, through Jesus Christ, and to him be glory forever and ever. Amen.

²²My brothers and sisters, I beg you to listen patiently to this message I have written to encourage you, because it is not very long. ²³I want you to know that our brother Timothy has been let out of prison. If he arrives soon, we will both come to see you.

²⁴Greet all your leaders and all of God's people. Those from Italy send greetings to you.

²⁵Grace be with you all.

JAMES

How to Live as a Christian

1 From James, a servant of God and of the Lord Jesus Christ.

To all of God's people who are scattered everywhere in the world:

Greetings.

[2]My brothers and sisters, when you have many kinds of troubles, you should be full of joy, [3]because you know that these troubles test your faith, and this will give you patience. [4]Let your patience show itself perfectly in what you do. Then you will be perfect and complete and will have everything you need. [5]But if any of you needs wisdom, you should ask God for it. He is generous to everyone and will give you wisdom without criticizing you. [6]But when you ask God, you must believe and not doubt. Anyone who doubts is like a wave in the sea, blown up and down by the wind. [7-8]Such doubters are thinking two different things at the same time, and they cannot decide about anything they do. They should not think they will receive anything from the Lord.

[9]Believers who are poor should take pride that God has made them spiritually rich. [10]Those who are rich should take pride that God has shown them that they are spiritually poor. The rich will die like a wild flower in the grass. [11]The sun rises with burning heat and dries up the plants. The flower falls off, and its beauty is gone. In the same way the rich will die while they are still taking care of business.

[12]When people are tempted and still continue strong, they should be happy. After they have proved their faith, God will reward them with life forever. God promised this to all those who love him.

STEP 6

STEP 10

[13]When people are tempted, they should not say, "God is tempting me." Evil cannot tempt God, and God himself does not tempt anyone. [14]But people are tempted when their own evil desire leads them away and traps them. [15]This desire leads to sin, and then the sin grows and brings death.

STEP 2

[16]My dear brothers and sisters, do not be fooled about this. [17]Every good action and every perfect gift is from God. These good gifts come down from the Creator of the sun, moon, and stars, who does not change like their shifting shadows. [18]God decided to give us life through the word of truth so we might be the most important of all the things he made.

STEP 10

STEP 6

[19]My dear brothers and sisters, always be willing to listen and slow to speak. Do not become angry easily, [20]because anger will not help you live the right kind of life God wants. [21]So put out of your life every evil thing and every kind of wrong. Then in gentleness accept God's teaching that is planted in your hearts, which can save you.

STEP 11

[22]Do what God's teaching says; when you only listen and do nothing, you are fooling yourselves. [23]Those who hear God's teaching and do nothing are like people who look at themselves in a mirror. [24]They see their faces and then go away and quickly forget what they looked like. [25]But the truly happy people are those who carefully study God's perfect law that makes people free, and they continue to study it. They do not forget what they heard, but they obey what God's teaching says. Those who do this will be made happy.

[26]People who think they are religious

but say things they should not say are just fooling themselves. Their "religion" is worth nothing. [27]Religion that God accepts as pure and without fault is this: caring for orphans or widows who need help, and keeping yourself free from the world's evil influence.

2 My dear brothers and sisters, as believers in our glorious Lord Jesus Christ, never think some people are more important than others. [2]Suppose someone comes into your church meeting wearing nice clothes and a gold ring. At the same time a poor person comes in wearing old, dirty clothes. [3]You show special attention to the one wearing nice clothes and say, "Please, sit here in this good seat." But you say to the poor person, "Stand over there," or, "Sit on the floor by my feet." [4]What are you doing? You are making some people more important than others, and with evil thoughts you are deciding that one person is better.

[5]Listen, my dear brothers and sisters! God chose the poor in the world to be rich with faith and to receive the kingdom God promised to those who love him. [6]But you show no respect to the poor. The rich are always trying to control your lives. They are the ones who take you to court. [7]And they are the ones who speak against Jesus, who owns you.

[8]This royal law is found in the Scriptures: "Love your neighbor as you love yourself." If you obey this law, you are doing right. [9]But if you treat one person as being more important than another, you are sinning. You are guilty of breaking God's law. [10]A person who follows all of God's law but fails to obey even one command is guilty of breaking all the commands in that law. [11]The same God who said, "You must not be guilty of adultery," also said, "You must not murder

anyone." So if you do not take part in adultery but you murder someone, you are guilty of breaking all of God's law. [12]In everything you say and do, remember that you will be judged by the law that makes people free. [13]So you must show mercy to others, or God will not show mercy to you when he judges you. But the person who shows mercy can stand without fear at the judgment.

[14]My brothers and sisters, if people say they have faith, but do nothing, their faith is worth nothing. Can faith like that save them? [15]A brother or sister in Christ might need clothes or food. [16]If you say to that person, "God be with you! I hope you stay warm and get plenty to eat," but you do not give what that person needs, your words are worth nothing. [17]In the same way, faith by itself—that does nothing— is dead.

[18]Someone might say, "You have faith, but I have deeds." Show me your faith without doing anything, and I will show you my faith by what I do. [19]You believe there is one God. Good! But the demons believe that, too, and they tremble with fear.

[20]You foolish person! Must you be shown that faith that does nothing is worth nothing? [21]Abraham, our ancestor, was made right with God by what he did when he offered his son Isaac on the altar. [22]So you see that Abraham's faith and the things he did worked together. His faith was made perfect by what he did. [23]This shows the full meaning of the Scripture that says: "Abraham believed God, and God accepted Abraham's faith, and that faith made him right with God." And Abraham was called God's friend. [24]So you see that people are made right with God by what they do, not by faith only.

[25]Another example is Rahab, a prosti-

tute, who was made right with God by something she did. She welcomed the spies into her home and helped them escape by a different road.

²⁶Just as a person's body that does not have a spirit is dead, so faith that does nothing is dead!

3 My brothers and sisters, not many of you should become teachers, because you know that we who teach will be judged more strictly. ²We all make many mistakes. If people never said anything wrong, they would be perfect and able to control their entire selves, too. ³When we put bits into the mouths of horses to make them obey us, we can control their whole bodies. ⁴Also a ship is very big, and it is pushed by strong winds. But a very small rudder controls that big ship, making it go wherever the pilot wants. ⁵It is the same with the tongue. It is a small part of the body, but it brags about great things.

A big forest fire can be started with only a little flame. ⁶And the tongue is like a fire. It is a whole world of evil among the parts of our bodies. The tongue spreads its evil through the whole body. The tongue is set on fire by hell, and it starts a fire that influences all of life. ⁷People can tame every kind of wild animal, bird, reptile, and fish, and they have tamed them, ⁸but no one can tame the tongue. It is wild and evil and full of deadly poison. ⁹We use our tongues to praise our Lord and Father, but then we curse people, whom God made like himself. ¹⁰Praises and curses come from the same mouth! My brothers and sisters, this should not happen. ¹¹Do good and bad water flow from the same spring? ¹²My brothers and sisters, can a fig tree make olives, or can a grapevine make figs? No! And a well full of salty water cannot give good water.

¹³Are there those among you who are truly wise and understanding? Then they should show it by living right and doing good things with a gentleness that comes from wisdom. ¹⁴But if you are selfish and have bitter jealousy in your hearts, do not brag. Your bragging is a lie that hides the truth. ¹⁵That kind of "wisdom" does not come from God but from the world. It is not spiritual; it is from the devil. ¹⁶Where jealousy and selfishness are, there will be confusion and every kind of evil. ¹⁷But the wisdom that comes from God is first of all pure, then peaceful, gentle, and easy to please. This wisdom is always ready to help those who are troubled and to do good for others. It is always fair and honest. ¹⁸People who work for peace in a peaceful way plant a good crop of right-living.

4 Do you know where your fights and arguments come from? They come from the selfish desires that war within you. ²You want things, but you do not have them. So you are ready to kill and are jealous of other people, but you still cannot get what you want. So you argue and fight. You do not get what you want, because you do not ask God. ³Or when you ask, you do not receive because the reason you ask is wrong. You want things so you can use them for your own pleasures.

⁴So, you are not loyal to God! You should know that loving the world is the same as hating God. Anyone who wants to be a friend of the world becomes God's enemy. ⁵Do you think the Scripture means nothing that says, "The Spirit that God made to live in us wants us for himself alone"? ⁶But God gives us even more grace, as the Scripture says,

"God is against the proud,
   but he gives grace to the humble."
Proverbs 3:34

STEP 9

STEP 7

STEP 5

⁷So give yourselves completely to God. Stand against the devil, and the devil will run from you. ⁸Come near to God, and God will come near to you. You sinners, clean sin out of your lives. You who are trying to follow God and the world at the same time, make your thinking pure. ⁹Be sad, cry, and weep! Change your laughter into crying and your joy into sadness. ¹⁰Humble yourself in the Lord's presence, and he will honor you.

STEP 8

¹¹Brothers and sisters, do not tell evil lies about each other. If you speak against your fellow believers or judge them, you are judging and speaking against the law they follow. And when you are judging the law, you are no longer a follower of the law. You have become a judge. ¹²God is the only Lawmaker and Judge. He is the only One who can save and destroy. So it is not right for you to judge your neighbor.

¹³Some of you say, "Today or tomorrow we will go to some city. We will stay there a year, do business, and make money." ¹⁴But you do not know what will happen tomorrow! Your life is like a mist. You can see it for a short time, but then it goes away. ¹⁵So you should say, "If the Lord wants, we will live and do this or that." ¹⁶But now you are proud and you brag. All of this bragging is wrong. ¹⁷Anyone who knows the right thing to do, but does not do it, is sinning.

5 You rich people, listen! Cry and be very sad because of the troubles that are coming to you. ²Your riches have rotted, and your clothes have been eaten by moths. ³Your gold and silver have rusted, and that rust will be a proof that you were wrong. It will eat your bodies like fire. You saved your treasure for the last days. ⁴The pay you did not give the workers who mowed your fields cries out against you, and the cries of the workers have been heard by the Lord All-Powerful. ⁵Your life on earth was full of rich living and pleasing yourselves with everything you wanted. You made yourselves fat, like an animal ready to be killed. ⁶You have judged guilty and then murdered innocent people, who were not against you.

⁷Brothers and sisters, be patient until the Lord comes again. A farmer patiently waits for his valuable crop to grow from the earth and for it to receive the autumn and spring rains. ⁸You, too, must be patient. Do not give up hope, because the Lord is coming soon. ⁹Brothers and sisters, do not complain against each other or you will be judged guilty. And the Judge is ready to come! ¹⁰Brothers and sisters, follow the example of the prophets who spoke for the Lord. They suffered many hard things, but they were patient. ¹¹We say they are happy because they did not give up. You have heard about Job's patience, and you know the Lord's purpose for him in the end. You know the Lord is full of mercy and is kind.

STEP 12

STEP 8

¹²My brothers and sisters, above all, do not use an oath when you make a promise. Don't use the name of heaven, earth, or anything else to prove what you say. When you mean yes, say only yes, and when you mean no, say only no so you will not be judged guilty.

¹³Anyone who is having troubles should pray. Anyone who is happy should sing praises. ¹⁴Anyone who is sick should call the church's elders. They should pray for and pour oil on the person in the name of the Lord. ¹⁵And the prayer that is said with faith will make the sick person well; the Lord will heal that person. And if the person has sinned, the sins will be forgiven. ¹⁶Confess your sins to each other and pray for each other so God can heal you. When a believing person prays,

STEP 5

STEP 8

Made a list of all persons we had harmed,
and became willing to make amends to them all.

James 4:11–12

Both Step 8 and James 4:11–12 ask you to do something very hard. They ask you to let go of anger and bitterness toward people who have hurt you. You may find yourself saying, "I'm willing to forgive anybody who apologizes for what they did to me." Step 8, however, challenges you to make amends to everyone you've hurt, whether or not they are sorry about their part in what happened.

How can you forgive and make amends to people you know have caused you a lot of pain? How can you forgive when the stings of their words and actions are still fresh and alive in your heart?

Sometimes you have to cycle through a series of God-given feelings before you can let go of the past and forgive. If you've been physically or emotionally abused by someone, you have to think about what happened and let yourself be shocked by it, work through any denial issues, let yourself feel legitimate anger, deal with any depression, and feel sadness for what you lost. Once you've worked through these emotions, you can really forgive. You can forgive with a healthy heart and without any resentment.

SEE **PAGE 56** OF THE INTRODUCTORY MATERIAL FOR **STEP 9.**

STEP 5

Admitted to God, to ourselves, and to another human being the exact nature of our wrongs.

James 5:16

Many people live isolated lives with few connections to others—even to their family members. On top of that, most of us don't want to be accountable to anybody else. We want to do what we want, when we want, and how we want. If you stop and think about it, living that way makes it easy to slip into addictions and selfish behaviors. Accountability may not be a popular idea today, but the Bible says a lot about it.

God says you are accountable to him, and you need to make yourself accountable to other Christians, too. The world around may think that's letting somebody stick their nose in your business, but God says this is a way you get rid of character defects.

You will find that when you have the courage to tell another believer about your wrongs, you will find new energy and motivation to change your life. In some way, confession actually strengthens your commitment to grow spiritually. You know you have a friend who's praying for you, who's cheering you on to success, and who's always willing to talk with you about how your struggle's going. You may have times of weakness when you fall back into your old ways, but you will also have the love and support of God and of your friends to pick you up and get you back onto the road to recovery.

FOR YOUR NEXT **STEP 5** MEDITATION, TURN TO **PAGE 346.** ▶▶

great things happen. ¹⁷Elijah was a human being just like us. He prayed that it would not rain, and it did not rain on the land for three and a half years! ¹⁸Then Elijah prayed again, and the rain came down from the sky, and the land produced crops again.

¹⁹My brothers and sisters, if one of you wanders away from the truth, and someone helps that person come back, ²⁰remember this: Anyone who brings a sinner back from the wrong way will save that sinner's soul from death and will cause many sins to be forgiven.

STEP
12

1 PETER

Encouragement for Suffering Christians

1 From Peter, an apostle of Jesus Christ. To God's chosen people who are away from their homes and are scattered all around Pontus, Galatia, Cappadocia, Asia, and Bithynia. ²God planned long ago to choose you by making you his holy people, which is the Spirit's work. God wanted you to obey him and to be made clean by the blood of the death of Jesus Christ.

Grace and peace be yours more and more.

STEP 3
³Praise be to the God and Father of our Lord Jesus Christ. In God's great mercy he has caused us to be born again into a living hope, because Jesus Christ rose from the dead. ⁴Now we hope for the blessings God has for his children. These blessings, which cannot be destroyed or be spoiled or lose their beauty, are kept in heaven for you. ⁵God's power protects you through your faith until salvation is shown to you at the end of time. ⁶This makes you very happy, even though now for a short time different kinds of troubles may make you sad. ⁷These troubles come to prove that your faith is pure. This purity of faith is worth more than gold, which can be proved to be pure by fire but will ruin. But the purity of your faith will bring you praise and glory and honor when Jesus Christ is shown to you. ⁸You have not seen Christ, but still you love him. You cannot see him now, but you believe in him. So you are filled with a joy that cannot be explained, a joy full of glory. ⁹And you are receiving the goal of your faith—the salvation of your souls.

¹⁰The prophets searched carefully and tried to learn about this salvation. They prophesied about the grace that was coming to you. ¹¹The Spirit of Christ was in the prophets, telling in advance about the sufferings of Christ and about the glory that would follow those sufferings. The prophets tried to learn about what the Spirit was showing them, when those things would happen, and what the world would be like at that time. ¹²It was shown them that their service was not for themselves but for you, when they told about the truths you have now heard. Those who preached the Good News to you told you those things with the help of the Holy Spirit who was sent from heaven—things into which angels desire to look.

STEP 5
¹³So prepare your minds for service and have self-control. All your hope should be for the gift of grace that will be yours when Jesus Christ is shown to you. ¹⁴Now that you are obedient children of God do not live as you did in the past. You did not understand, so you did the evil things you wanted. ¹⁵But be holy in all you do, just as God, the One who called you, is holy. ¹⁶It is written in the Scriptures: "You must be holy, because I am holy."

¹⁷You pray to God and call him Father, and he judges each person's work equally. So while you are here on earth, you should live with respect for God. ¹⁸You know that in the past you were living in a worthless way, a way passed down from the people who lived before you. But you were saved from that useless life. You were bought, not with something that ruins like gold or silver, ¹⁹but with the precious blood of Christ, who was like a pure and perfect lamb. ²⁰Christ was chosen before the world was made, but he was shown to the world in these last times for your sake. ²¹Through Christ you believe in God, who raised Christ from the dead

STEP 6

Were entirely ready to have God
remove all these defects of character.

1 Peter 1:13-16

The first five steps of recovery focus on digging up painful stuff in your past that contributed to your addiction. Step 6 is a turning point. From here on recovery involves positive action to build a new future. This passage in 1 Peter suggests three things you need to do in order to accomplish the work of Step 6 successfully. First, you need to "prepare your minds" (verse 13). You need to think more like God does, and the Bible teaches you how. Second, you need to "have self-control." The Holy Spirit gives you self-control as you let him fill your life (Galatians 5:16, 18, 22–23). Third, "all your hope" should be focused on the clean, recovered life God promises you. With these three spiritual disciplines in place, you can live the "holy" life commanded in 1 Peter 1:14–16.

Maybe you think holiness sounds pious, dull, and stuffy. Actually, being holy simply means living the way God made people to live in relationship with him. Holiness should be exciting, joyous, and harmonious living.

FOR YOUR NEXT **STEP 6** MEDITATION, TURN TO **PAGE 350.** ▶▶

and gave him glory. So your faith and your hope are in God.

STEP 9

²²Now that your obedience to the truth has purified your souls, you can have true love for your Christian brothers and sisters. So love each other deeply with all your heart. ²³You have been born again, and this new life did not come from something that dies, but from something that cannot die. You were born again through God's living message that continues forever. ²⁴The Scripture says,

"All people are like the grass,
and all their glory is like the
flowers of the field.
The grass dies and the flowers fall,
²⁵   but the word of the Lord will live
forever."   *Isaiah 40:6–8*

And this is the word that was preached to you.

STEP 6

2 So then, rid yourselves of all evil, all lying, hypocrisy, jealousy, and evil speech. ²As newborn babies want milk, you should want the pure and simple teaching. By it you can mature in your salvation, ³because you have already examined and seen how good the Lord is.

⁴Come to the Lord Jesus, the "stone" that lives. The people of the world did not want this stone, but he was the stone God chose, and he was precious. ⁵You also are like living stones, so let yourselves be used to build a spiritual temple—to be holy priests who offer spiritual sacrifices to God. He will accept those sacrifices through Jesus Christ. ⁶The Scripture says:

"I will put a stone in the ground in
Jerusalem.
Everything will be built on this
important and precious
rock.
Anyone who trusts in him
will never be disappointed."
Isaiah 28:16

⁷This stone is worth much to you who believe. But to the people who do not believe,

"the stone that the builders rejected
has become the cornerstone."
Psalm 118:22

⁸Also, he is

"a stone that causes people to
stumble,
a rock that makes them fall."
Isaiah 8:14

They stumble because they do not obey what God says, which is what God planned to happen to them.

STEP 12

⁹But you are a chosen people, royal priests, a holy nation, a people for God's own possession. You were chosen to tell about the wonderful acts of God, who called you out of darkness into his wonderful light. ¹⁰At one time you were not a people, but now you are God's people. In the past you had never received mercy, but now you have received God's mercy.

STEP 10

¹¹Dear friends, you are like foreigners and strangers in this world. I beg you to avoid the evil things your bodies want to do that fight against your soul. ¹²People who do not believe are living all around you and might say that you are doing wrong. Live such good lives that they will see the good things you do and will give glory to God on the day when Christ comes again.

¹³For the Lord's sake, yield to the people who have authority in this world: the king, who is the highest authority, ¹⁴and the leaders who are sent by him to punish those who do wrong and to praise those who do right. ¹⁵It is God's desire that by doing good you should stop foolish people from saying stupid things about you. ¹⁶Live as free people, but do not use your freedom as an excuse to do evil. Live as servants of God. ¹⁷Show respect for all people: Love the brothers

STEP 10

Continued to take personal inventory
and when we were wrong promptly admitted it.

1 Peter 2:11

At times, it will surprise you how your old addiction can tempt you with the same power as when you were practicing it. You know that if you slide back into your habit, you'll find nothing but pain and shame. Still, you can hear it calling to you, making the same empty promises that food, sexuality, money, relationships, power, drugs, and so on, will make you happy and will satisfy the spiritual emptiness in your heart.

What can you do? How do you handle the sudden, compelling urges to slip into the "evil things your bodies want to do that fight against your soul"? At the heart of Twelve Step recovery teaching is the truth that addictive hungers can never be satisfied by anything of this world. You have to train yourself to look to God and his Word so you can "grow in the grace and knowledge of our Lord and Savior Jesus Christ" (2 Peter 3:18). Only peace in your heart can quiet the voices in your mind that lie to you and claim your addiction will set you free.

FOR YOUR NEXT **STEP 10** MEDITATION, TURN TO **PAGE 449.** ▶▶

and sisters of God's family, respect God, honor the king.

¹⁸Slaves, yield to the authority of your masters with all respect, not only those who are good and kind, but also those who are dishonest. ¹⁹A person might have to suffer even when it is unfair, but if he thinks of God and can stand the pain, God is pleased. ²⁰If you are beaten for doing wrong, there is no reason to praise you for being patient in your punishment. But if you suffer for doing good, and you are patient, then God is pleased. ²¹This is what you were called to do, because Christ suffered for you and gave you an example to follow. So you should do as he did.

²²"He had never sinned,
    and he had never lied."   *Isaiah 53:9*
²³People insulted Christ, but he did not insult them in return. Christ suffered, but he did not threaten. He let God, the One who judges rightly, take care of him. ²⁴Christ carried our sins in his body on the cross so we would stop living for sin and start living for what is right. And you are healed because of his wounds. ²⁵You were like sheep that wandered away, but now you have come back to the Shepherd and Overseer of your souls.

3 In the same way, you wives should yield to your husbands. Then, if some husbands do not obey God's teaching, they will be persuaded to believe without anyone's saying a word to them. They will be persuaded by the way their wives live. ²Your husbands will see the pure lives you live with your respect for God. ³It is not fancy hair, gold jewelry, or fine clothes that should make you beautiful. ⁴No, your beauty should come from within you— the beauty of a gentle and quiet spirit that will never be destroyed and is very precious to God. ⁵In this same way, the holy women who lived long ago and fol-

lowed God made themselves beautiful, yielding to their own husbands. ⁶Sarah obeyed Abraham, her husband, and called him her master. And you women are true children of Sarah if you always do what is right and are not afraid.

⁷In the same way, you husbands should live with your wives in an understanding way, since they are weaker than you. But show them respect, because God gives them the same blessing he gives you—the grace that gives true life. Do this so that nothing will stop your prayers.

⁸Finally, all of you should be in agreement, understanding each other, loving each other as family, being kind and humble. ⁹Do not do wrong to repay a wrong, and do not insult to repay an insult. But repay with a blessing, because you yourselves were called to do this so that you might receive a blessing. ¹⁰The Scripture says,

"A person must do these things
    to enjoy life and have many happy days.
He must not say evil things,
    and he must not tell lies.
¹¹He must stop doing evil and do good.
    He must look for peace and work for it.
¹²The Lord sees the good people
    and listens to their prayers.
But the Lord is against
    those who do evil."   *Psalm 34:12–16*
¹³If you are trying hard to do good, no one can really hurt you. ¹⁴But even if you suffer for doing right, you are blessed.
"Don't be afraid of what they fear;
    do not dread those things."
                              Isaiah 8:12–13
¹⁵But respect Christ as the holy Lord in your hearts. Always be ready to answer everyone who asks you to explain about the hope you have, ¹⁶but answer in a gen-

tle way and with respect. Keep a clear conscience so that those who speak evil of your good life in Christ will be made ashamed. [17]It is better to suffer for doing good than for doing wrong if that is what God wants. [18]Christ himself suffered for sins once. He was not guilty, but he suffered for those who are guilty to bring you to God. His body was killed, but he was made alive in the spirit. [19]And in the spirit he went and preached to the spirits in prison [20]who refused to obey God long ago in the time of Noah. God was waiting patiently for them while Noah was building the boat. Only a few people—eight in all—were saved by water. [21]And that water is like baptism that now saves you—not the washing of dirt from the body, but the promise made to God from a good conscience. And this is because Jesus Christ was raised from the dead. [22]Now Jesus has gone into heaven and is at God's right side ruling over angels, authorities, and powers.

4 Since Christ suffered while he was in his body, strengthen yourselves with the same way of thinking Christ had. The person who has suffered in the body is finished with sin. [2]Strengthen yourselves so that you will live here on earth doing what God wants, not the evil things people want. [3]In the past you wasted too much time doing what nonbelievers enjoy. You were guilty of sexual sins, evil desires, drunkenness, wild and drunken parties, and hateful idol worship. [4]Nonbelievers think it is strange that you do not do the many wild and wasteful things they do, so they insult you. [5]But they will have to explain this to God, who is ready to judge the living and the dead. [6]For this reason the Good News was preached to those who are now dead. Even though they were judged like all people, the Good News was preached to them so they could live in the spirit as God lives.

[7]The time is near when all things will end. So think clearly and control yourselves so you will be able to pray. [8]Most importantly, love each other deeply, because love will cause people to forgive each other for many sins. [9]Open your homes to each other, without complaining. [10]Each of you has received a gift to use to serve others. Be good servants of God's various gifts of grace. [11]Anyone who speaks should speak words from God. Anyone who serves should serve with the strength God gives so that in everything God will be praised through Jesus Christ. Power and glory belong to him forever and ever. Amen.

STEP 11

[12]My friends, do not be surprised at the terrible trouble which now comes to test you. Do not think that something strange is happening to you. [13]But be happy that you are sharing in Christ's sufferings so that you will be happy and full of joy when Christ comes again in glory. [14]When people insult you because you follow Christ, you are blessed, because the glorious Spirit, the Spirit of God, is with you. [15]Do not suffer for murder, theft, or any other crime, nor because you trouble other people. [16]But if you suffer because you are a Christian, do not be ashamed. Praise God because you wear that name. [17]It is time for judgment to begin with God's family. And if that judging begins with us, what will happen to those people who do not obey the Good News of God?

[18]"If it is very hard for a good person to
be saved,
the wicked person and the sinner
will surely be lost!"

[19]So those who suffer as God wants should trust their souls to the faithful Creator as they continue to do what is right.

STEP 7

Humbly asked Him to remove our shortcomings.

1 Peter 5:6–7

As you work on Step 7, you may have some confusion about the difference between humility, which God expects of you, and humiliation, which God doesn't want you to experience any longer. In fact, your addiction may have humiliated you many times, leaving you feeling worthless and hopeless. That humiliation may have caused you to hit bottom.

The humility God wants from you in Step 7 is based on a calm assessment of who you are and who God is. He wants you to have a realistic sense of your strengths and weaknesses, so you can submit your will to his. Step 7 involves the humble confession that God's way is the best way for you to go. When you humble yourself before God as his child in need, he lifts you up and satisfies your innermost hungers. Step 7 is the humble confession that you can't meet your needs by your own efforts. Instead, you cast your worries and cares into God's lap.

FOR YOUR NEXT **STEP 7** MEDITATION, TURN TO **PAGE 351.** ▶▶

5 Now I have something to say to the elders in your group. I also am an elder. I have seen Christ's sufferings, and I will share in the glory that will be shown to us. I beg you to ²shepherd God's flock, for whom you are responsible. Watch over them because you want to, not because you are forced. That is how God wants it. Do it because you are happy to serve, not because you want money. ³Do not be like a ruler over people you are responsible for, but be good examples to them. ⁴Then when Christ, the Chief Shepherd, comes, you will get a glorious crown that will never lose its beauty.

⁵In the same way, younger people should be willing to be under older people. And all of you should be very humble with each other.

   "God is against the proud,
      but he gives grace to the humble."

Proverbs 3:34

STEP 7

⁶Be humble under God's powerful hand so he will lift you up when the right time comes. ⁷Give all your worries to him, because he cares about you.

⁸Control yourselves and be careful! The devil, your enemy, goes around like a roaring lion looking for someone to eat. ⁹Refuse to give in to him, by standing strong in your faith. You know that your Christian family all over the world is having the same kinds of suffering.

STEP 11

¹⁰And after you suffer for a short time, God, who gives all grace, will make everything right. He will make you strong and support you and keep you from falling. He called you to share in his glory in Christ, a glory that will continue forever. ¹¹All power is his forever and ever. Amen.

¹²I wrote this short letter with the help of Silas, who I know is a faithful brother in Christ. I wrote to encourage you and to tell you that this is the true grace of God. Stand strong in that grace.

¹³The church in Babylon, who was chosen like you, sends you greetings. Mark, my son in Christ, also greets you. ¹⁴Give each other a kiss of Christian love when you meet.

Peace to all of you who are in Christ.

2 PETER

Correcting False Teachings

1 From Simon Peter, a servant and apostle of Jesus Christ.

To you who have received a faith as valuable as ours, because our God and Savior Jesus Christ does what is right.

STEP 11

²Grace and peace be given to you more and more, because you truly know God and Jesus our Lord.

³Jesus has the power of God, by which he has given us everything we need to live and to serve God. We have these things because we know him. Jesus called us by his glory and goodness. ⁴Through these he gave us the very great and precious promises. With these gifts you can share in God's nature, and the world will not ruin you with its evil desires.

⁵Because you have these blessings, do your best to add these things to your lives: to your faith, add goodness; and to your goodness, add knowledge; ⁶and to your knowledge, add self-control; and to your self-control, add patience; and to your patience, add service for God; ⁷and to your service for God, add kindness for your brothers and sisters in Christ; and to this kindness, add love. ⁸If all these things are in you and are growing, they will help you to be useful and productive in your knowledge of our Lord Jesus Christ. ⁹But anyone who does not have these things cannot see clearly. He is blind and has forgotten that he was made clean from his past sins.

¹⁰My brothers and sisters, try hard to be certain that you really are called and chosen by God. If you do all these things, you will never fall. ¹¹And you will be given a very great welcome into the eternal kingdom of our Lord and Savior Jesus Christ.

¹²You know these things, and you are very strong in the truth, but I will always help you remember them. ¹³I think it is right for me to help you remember as long as I am in this body. ¹⁴I know I must soon leave this body, as our Lord Jesus Christ has shown me. ¹⁵I will try my best so that you may be able to remember these things even after I am gone.

¹⁶When we told you about the powerful coming of our Lord Jesus Christ, we were not telling just clever stories that someone invented. But we saw the greatness of Jesus with our own eyes. ¹⁷Jesus heard the voice of God, the Greatest Glory, when he received honor and glory from God the Father. The voice said, "This is my Son, whom I love, and I am very pleased with him." ¹⁸We heard that voice from heaven while we were with Jesus on the holy mountain.

¹⁹This makes us more sure about the message the prophets gave. It is good for you to follow closely what they said as you would follow a light shining in a dark place, until the day begins and the morning star rises in your hearts. ²⁰Most of all, you must understand this: No prophecy in the Scriptures ever comes from the prophet's own interpretation. ²¹No prophecy ever came from what a person wanted to say, but people led by the Holy Spirit spoke words from God.

2 There used to be false prophets among God's people, just as you will have some false teachers in your group. They will secretly teach things that are wrong—teachings that will cause people to be lost. They will even refuse to accept the Master, Jesus, who bought their freedom. So they will bring quick ruin on

themselves. ²Many will follow their evil ways and say evil things about the way of truth. ³Those false teachers only want your money, so they will use you by telling you lies. Their judgment spoken against them long ago is still coming, and their ruin is certain.

⁴When angels sinned, God did not let them go free without punishment. He sent them to hell and put them in caves of darkness where they are being held for judgment. ⁵And God punished the world long ago when he brought a flood to the world that was full of people who were against him. But God saved Noah, who preached about being right with God, and seven other people with him. ⁶And God also destroyed the evil cities of Sodom and Gomorrah by burning them until they were ashes. He made those cities an example of what will happen to those who are against God. ⁷But he saved Lot from those cities. Lot, a good man, was troubled because of the filthy lives of evil people. ⁸(Lot was a good man, but because he lived with evil people every day, his good heart was hurt by the evil things he saw and heard.) ⁹So the Lord knows how to save those who serve him when troubles come. He will hold evil people and punish them, while waiting for the Judgment Day. ¹⁰That punishment is especially for those who live by doing the evil things their sinful selves want and who hate authority.

These false teachers are bold and do anything they want. They are not afraid to speak against the angels. ¹¹But even the angels, who are much stronger and more powerful than false teachers, do not accuse them with insults before the Lord. ¹²But these people speak against things they do not understand. They are like animals that act without thinking, animals born to be caught and killed. And, like an-imals, these false teachers will be destroyed. ¹³They have caused many people to suffer, so they themselves will suffer. That is their pay for what they have done. They take pleasure in openly doing evil, so they are like dirty spots and stains among you. They delight in deceiving you while eating meals with you. ¹⁴Every time they look at a woman they want her, and their desire for sin is never satisfied. They lead weak people into the trap of sin, and they have taught their hearts to be greedy. God will punish them! ¹⁵These false teachers left the right road and lost their way, following the way Balaam went. Balaam was the son of Beor, who loved being paid for doing wrong. ¹⁶But a donkey, which cannot talk, told Balaam he was sinning. It spoke with a man's voice and stopped the prophet's crazy thinking.

¹⁷Those false teachers are like springs without water and clouds blown by a storm. A place in the blackest darkness has been kept for them. ¹⁸They brag with words that mean nothing. By their evil desires they lead people into the trap of sin—people who are just beginning to escape from others who live in error. ¹⁹They promise them freedom, but they themselves are not free. They are slaves of things that will be destroyed. For people are slaves of anything that controls them. ²⁰They were made free from the evil in the world by knowing our Lord and Savior Jesus Christ. But if they return to evil things and those things control them, then it is worse for them than it was before. ²¹Yes, it would be better for them to have never known the right way than to know it and to turn away from the holy teaching that was given to them. ²²What they did is like this true saying: "A dog goes back to what it has thrown up," and, "After a pig is washed, it goes back and rolls in the mud."

STEP 1

3 My friends, this is the second letter I have written you to help your honest minds remember. ²I want you to think about the words the holy prophets spoke in the past, and remember the command our Lord and Savior gave us through your apostles. ³It is most important for you to understand what will happen in the last days. People will laugh at you. They will live doing the evil things they want to do. ⁴They will say, "Jesus promised to come again. Where is he? Our fathers have died, but the world continues the way it has been since it was made." ⁵But they do not want to remember what happened long ago. By the word of God heaven was made, and the earth was made from water and with water. ⁶Then the world was flooded and destroyed with water. ⁷And that same word of God is keeping heaven and earth that we now have in order to be destroyed by fire. They are being kept for the Judgment Day and the destruction of all who are against God.

⁸But do not forget this one thing, dear friends: To the Lord one day is as a thousand years, and a thousand years is as one day. ⁹The Lord is not slow in doing what he promised—the way some people understand slowness. But God is being patient with you. He does not want anyone to be lost, but he wants all people to change their hearts and lives.

¹⁰But the day of the Lord will come like a thief. The skies will disappear with a loud noise. Everything in them will be destroyed by fire, and the earth and everything in it will be exposed. ¹¹In that way everything will be destroyed. So what kind of people should you be? You should live holy lives and serve God, ¹²as you wait for and look forward to the coming of the day of God. When that day comes, the skies will be destroyed with fire, and everything in them will melt with heat. ¹³But God made a promise to us, and we are waiting for a new heaven and a new earth where goodness lives.

¹⁴Dear friends, since you are waiting for this to happen, do your best to be without sin and without fault. Try to be at peace with God. ¹⁵Remember that we are saved because our Lord is patient. Our dear brother Paul told you the same thing when he wrote to you with the wisdom that God gave him. ¹⁶He writes about this in all his letters. Some things in Paul's letters are hard to understand, and people who are ignorant and weak in faith explain these things falsely. They also falsely explain the other Scriptures, but they are destroying themselves by doing this.

¹⁷Dear friends, since you already know about this, be careful. Do not let those evil people lead you away by the wrong they do. Be careful so you will not fall from your strong faith. ¹⁸But grow in the grace and knowledge of our Lord and Savior Jesus Christ. Glory be to him now and forever! Amen.

STEP 10

I JOHN

Love One Another

1 We write you now about what has always existed, which we have heard, we have seen with our own eyes, we have looked at, and we have touched with our hands. We write to you about the Word that gives life. ²He who gives life was shown to us. We saw him and can give proof about it. And now we announce to you that he has life that continues forever. He was with God the Father and was shown to us. ³We announce to you what we have seen and heard, because we want you also to have fellowship with us. Our fellowship is with God the Father and with his Son, Jesus Christ. ⁴We write this to you so we may be full of joy.

⁵Here is the message we have heard from Christ and now announce to you: God is light, and in him there is no darkness at all. ⁶So if we say we have fellowship with God, but we continue living in darkness, we are liars and do not follow the truth.

STEP 11 ⁷But if we live in the light, as God is in the light, we can share fellowship with each other. Then the blood of Jesus, God's Son, cleanses us from every sin.

STEP 5 ⁸If we say we have no sin, we are fooling ourselves, and the truth is not in us. ⁹But if we confess our sins, he will forgive our sins, because we can trust God to do what is right. He will cleanse us from all the wrongs we have done. ¹⁰If we say we have not sinned, we make God a liar, and we do not accept God's teaching.

2 My dear children, I write this letter to you so you will not sin. But if anyone does sin, we have a helper in the presence of the Father—Jesus Christ, the One who does what is right. ²He died in our place to take away our sins, and not only our sins but the sins of all people.

STEP 10 ³We can be sure that we know God if we obey his commands. ⁴Anyone who says, "I know God," but does not obey God's commands is a liar, and the truth is not in that person. ⁵But if someone obeys God's teaching, then in that person God's love has truly reached its goal. This is how we can be sure we are living in God: ⁶Whoever says that he lives in God must live as Jesus lived.

⁷My dear friends, I am not writing a new command to you but an old command you have had from the beginning. It is the teaching you have already heard. ⁸But also I am writing a new command to you, and you can see its truth in Jesus and in you, because the darkness is passing away, and the true light is already shining.

STEP 8 ⁹Anyone who says, "I am in the light," but hates a brother or sister, is still in the darkness. ¹⁰Whoever loves a brother or sister lives in the light and will not cause anyone to stumble in his faith. ¹¹But whoever hates a brother or sister is in darkness, lives in darkness, and does not know where to go, because the darkness has made that person blind.

¹²I write to you, dear children,
    because your sins are forgiven
        through Christ.
¹³I write to you, fathers,
    because you know the One who
        existed from the beginning.
I write to you, young people,
    because you have defeated the
        Evil One.
¹⁴I write to you, children,
    because you know the Father.

STEP 5

Admitted to God, to ourselves, and to another
human being the exact nature of our wrongs.

1 John 1:8-9

Step 4 asked you to take a courageous look at what goes on inside
you that feeds your addictive urges. Maybe you faced some facts
about yourself for the first time. Step 5 takes you even farther
along the path of self-discovery and self-disclosure. Now you are
called on to confess openly to God, to yourself, and to somebody
else everything you've desperately tried for years to keep hidden.
The only way you can have the confidence to take this step is to
know that God loves you unconditionally. He already knows
everything about you; but he asks you to confess your wrongs to
him anyway, because once you admit those wrongs, you can start
moving toward a healthier life.

Confession opens your heart so you can soak in the love that God
already offers you. God's great love motivates him not only to
forgive you faithfully but to cleanse you faithfully. Once you are
clean you can ditch all those old "survival skills" that went with
your addiction. They weren't helping you survive, were they? They
were destroying you. Once rid of them, you can walk into the fresh
air of a stronger and more peaceful life.

FOR YOUR NEXT **STEP 5** MEDITATION, TURN TO **PAGE 535.** ▶▶

I write to you, fathers,
    because you know the One who
        existed from the beginning.
I write to you, young people,
    because you are strong;
    the teaching of God lives in you,
    and you have defeated the Evil
        One.

STEP 10

¹⁵Do not love the world or the things in the world. If you love the world, the love of the Father is not in you. ¹⁶These are the ways of the world: wanting to please our sinful selves, wanting the sinful things we see, and being too proud of what we have. None of these come from the Father, but all of them come from the world. ¹⁷The world and everything that people want in it are passing away, but the person who does what God wants lives forever.

¹⁸My dear children, these are the last days. You have heard that the enemy of Christ is coming, and now many enemies of Christ are already here. This is how we know that these are the last days. ¹⁹These enemies of Christ were in our fellowship, but they left us. They never really belonged to us; if they had been a part of us, they would have stayed with us. But they left, and this shows that none of them really belonged to us.

²⁰You have the gift that the Holy One gave you, so you all know the truth. ²¹I do not write to you because you do not know the truth but because you do know the truth. And you know that no lie comes from the truth. ²²Who is the liar? It is the person who does not accept Jesus as the Christ. This is the enemy of Christ: the person who does not accept the Father and his Son. ²³Whoever does not accept the Son does not have the Father. But whoever confesses the Son has the Father, too.

²⁴Be sure you continue to follow the teaching you heard from the beginning. If you continue to follow what you heard from the beginning, you will stay in the Son and in the Father. ²⁵And this is what the Son promised to us—life forever.

²⁶I am writing this letter about those people who are trying to lead you the wrong way. ²⁷Christ gave you a special gift that is still in you, so you do not need any other teacher. His gift teaches you about everything, and it is true, not false. So continue to live in Christ, as his gift taught you.

²⁸Yes, my dear children, live in him so that when Christ comes back, we can be without fear and not be ashamed in his presence. ²⁹Since you know that Christ is righteous, you know that all who do right are God's children.

STEP 6

3 The Father has loved us so much that we are called children of God. And we really are his children. The reason the people in the world do not know us is that they have not known him. ²Dear friends, now we are children of God, and we have not yet been shown what we will be in the future. But we know that when Christ comes again, we will be like him, because we will see him as he really is. ³Christ is pure, and all who have this hope in Christ keep themselves pure like Christ.

STEP 7

⁴The person who sins breaks God's law. Yes, sin is living against God's law. ⁵You know that Christ came to take away sins and that there is no sin in Christ. ⁶So anyone who lives in Christ does not go on sinning. Anyone who goes on sinning has never really understood Christ and has never known him.

⁷Dear children, do not let anyone lead you the wrong way. Christ is righteous. So to be like Christ a person must do what is right. ⁸The devil has been sinning

since the beginning, so anyone who continues to sin belongs to the devil. The Son of God came for this purpose: to destroy the devil's work.

⁹Those who are God's children do not continue sinning, because the new life from God remains in them. They are not able to go on sinning, because they have become children of God. ¹⁰So we can see who God's children are and who the devil's children are: Those who do not do what is right are not God's children, and those who do not love their brothers and sisters are not God's children.

¹¹This is the teaching you have heard from the beginning: We must love each other. ¹²Do not be like Cain who belonged to the Evil One and killed his brother. And why did he kill him? Because the things Cain did were evil, and the things his brother did were good.

¹³Brothers and sisters, do not be surprised when the people of the world hate you. ¹⁴We know we have left death and have come into life because we love each other. Whoever does not love is still dead. ¹⁵Everyone who hates a brother or sister is a murderer, and you know that no murderers have eternal life in them. ¹⁶This is how we know what real love is: Jesus gave his life for us. So we should give our lives for our brothers and sisters. ¹⁷Suppose someone has enough to live and sees a brother or sister in need, but does not help. Then God's love is not living in that person. ¹⁸My children, we should love people not only with words and talk, but by our actions and true caring.

¹⁹⁻²⁰This is the way we know that we belong to the way of truth. When our hearts make us feel guilty, we can still have peace before God. God is greater than our hearts, and he knows everything. ²¹My dear friends, if our hearts do not make us feel guilty, we can come without fear into God's presence. ²²And God gives us what we ask for because we obey God's commands and do what pleases him. ²³This is what God commands: that we believe in his Son, Jesus Christ, and that we love each other, just as he commanded. ²⁴The people who obey God's commands live in God, and God lives in them. We know that God lives in us because of the Spirit God gave us.

4 My dear friends, many false prophets have gone out into the world. So do not believe every spirit, but test the spirits to see if they are from God. ²This is how you can know God's Spirit: Every spirit who confesses that Jesus Christ came to earth as a human is from God. ³And every spirit who refuses to say this about Jesus is not from God. It is the spirit of the enemy of Christ, which you have heard is coming, and now he is already in the world.

⁴My dear children, you belong to God and have defeated them; because God's Spirit, who is in you, is greater than the devil, who is in the world. ⁵And they belong to the world, so what they say is from the world, and the world listens to them. ⁶But we belong to God, and those who know God listen to us. But those who are not from God do not listen to us. That is how we know the Spirit that is true and the spirit that is false.

⁷Dear friends, we should love each other, because love comes from God. Everyone who loves has become God's child and knows God. ⁸Whoever does not love does not know God, because God is love. ⁹This is how God showed his love to us: He sent his one and only Son into the world so that we could have life through him. ¹⁰This is what real love is: It is not our love for God; it is God's love for

us. He sent his Son to die in our place to take away our sins.

¹¹Dear friends, if God loved us that much we also should love each other. ¹²No one has ever seen God, but if we love each other, God lives in us, and his love is made perfect in us.

¹³We know that we live in God and he lives in us, because he gave us his Spirit. ¹⁴We have seen and can testify that the Father sent his Son to be the Savior of the world. ¹⁵Whoever confesses that Jesus is the Son of God has God living inside, and that person lives in God. ¹⁶And so we know the love that God has for us, and we trust that love.

God is love. Those who live in love live in God, and God lives in them. ¹⁷This is how love is made perfect in us: that we can be without fear on the day God judges us, because in this world we are like him. ¹⁸Where God's love is, there is no fear, because God's perfect love drives out fear. It is punishment that makes a person fear, so love is not made perfect in the person who fears.

¹⁹We love because God first loved us. ²⁰If people say, "I love God," but hate their brothers or sisters, they are liars. Those who do not love their brothers and sisters, whom they have seen, cannot love God, whom they have never seen. ²¹And God gave us this command: Those who love God must also love their brothers and sisters.

5 Everyone who believes that Jesus is the Christ is God's child, and whoever loves the Father also loves the Father's children. ²This is how we know we love God's children: when we love God and obey his commands. ³Loving God means obeying his commands. And God's commands are not too hard for us, ⁴because everyone who is a child of God conquers the world. And this is the victory that conquers the world—our faith. ⁵So the one who conquers the world is the person who believes that Jesus is the Son of God.

⁶Jesus Christ is the One who came by water and blood. He did not come by water only, but by water and blood. And the Spirit says that this is true, because the Spirit is the truth. ⁷So there are three witnesses: ⁸the Spirit, the water, and the blood; and these three witnesses agree. ⁹We believe people when they say something is true. But what God says is more important, and he has told us the truth about his own Son. ¹⁰Anyone who believes in the Son of God has the truth that God told us. Anyone who does not believe makes God a liar, because that person does not believe what God told us about his Son. ¹¹This is what God told us: God has given us eternal life, and this life is in his Son. ¹²Whoever has the Son has life, but whoever does not have the Son of God does not have life.

¹³I write this letter to you who believe in the Son of God so you will know you have eternal life. ¹⁴And this is the boldness we have in God's presence: that if we ask God for anything that agrees with what he wants, he hears us. ¹⁵If we know he hears us every time we ask him, we know we have what we ask from him.

¹⁶If anyone sees a brother or sister sinning (sin that does not lead to eternal death), that person should pray, and God will give the sinner life. I am talking about people whose sin does not lead to eternal death. There is sin that leads to death. I do not mean that a person should pray about that sin. ¹⁷Doing wrong is always sin, but there is sin that does not lead to eternal death.

STEP 6

STEP 8

STEP 11

STEP 7

STEP 6

Were entirely ready to have God
remove all these defects of character.

1 John 4:18

When you start working Step 6 of your recovery program, you may feel like an emotional cripple who needs "surgery" to be able to feel normal emotions again. You may feel as though you've been tied in tense emotional knots or drained of all feelings to the point of being numb. Even so, you may be leery of letting God act as the Great Physician and "operate" on your heart. It's frightening to move from the familiar—though destructive—ways of dealing with problems to the unknown—though life-giving—ways.

Let 1 John 4:18 remind you that God's love is greater than all your fears. You can trust him to replace your old crippled life with a robust new one. Get rid of your compulsive efforts to control everything and believe that the Lord loves you deeply. He wants you to know real joy, peace, and contentment. Trust him, and your fears will evaporate. At that point, you'll be more than ready for him get rid of every defect of character that has messed up your walk with him.

FOR YOUR NEXT **STEP 6** MEDITATION, TURN TO **PAGE 361.** ▶▶

STEP 7

Humbly asked Him to remove our shortcomings.

1 John 5:14–15

Step 7 says you should ask God to remove your shortcomings. Can you really expect God to do that? Why should he? First John 5:14 says there are prayers you can know will be answered. They're the ones when you "ask God for anything that agrees with what he wants." What prayer could make your heavenly Father happier than one asking him to make your life over in line with his Word and his Spirit?

If you read the Gospels, you learn right away that Jesus wants you to follow him and copy his way of living. When you pray a Step 7 prayer, you're starting to do that. You're lining yourself up with Jesus. In Psalm 37:4, David wrote, "Enjoy serving the Lord, and he will give you what you want." That's another promise that God will answer your prayers to be more like him.

In Step 7, you turn away from trying to do things your way to doing things God's way. That's where the power is for a new, better life. Ask humbly, but ask with confidence that God wants this for you, too.

FOR YOUR NEXT **STEP 7** MEDITATION, TURN TO **PAGE 405.** ▶▶

STEP
11

¹⁸We know that those who are God's children do not continue to sin. The Son of God keeps them safe, and the Evil One cannot touch them. ¹⁹We know that we belong to God, but the Evil One controls the whole world. ²⁰We also know that the Son of God has come and has given us understanding so that we can know the True One. And our lives are in the True One and in his Son, Jesus Christ. He is the true God and the eternal life.

²¹So, dear children, keep yourselves away from false gods.

2 JOHN

Do Not Help False Teachers

¹From the Elder.

To the chosen lady and her children:

I love all of you in the truth, and all those who know the truth love you. ²We love you because of the truth that lives in us and will be with us forever.

³Grace, mercy, and peace from God the Father and his Son, Jesus Christ, will be with us in truth and love.

⁴I was very happy to learn that some of your children are following the way of truth, as the Father commanded us. ⁵And now, dear lady, this is not a new command but is the same command we have had from the beginning. I ask you that we all love each other. ⁶And love means living the way God commanded us to live. As you have heard from the beginning, his command is this: Live a life of love.

⁷Many false teachers are in the world now who do not confess that Jesus Christ came to earth as a human. Anyone who does not confess this is a false teacher and an enemy of Christ. ⁸Be careful yourselves that you do not lose everything you have worked for, but that you receive your full reward.

⁹Anyone who goes beyond Christ's teaching and does not continue to follow only his teaching does not have God. But whoever continues to follow the teaching of Christ has both the Father and the Son. ¹⁰If someone comes to you and does not bring this teaching, do not welcome or accept that person into your house. ¹¹If you welcome such a person, you share in the evil work.

¹²I have many things to write to you, but I do not want to use paper and ink. Instead, I hope to come to you and talk face to face so we can be full of joy. ¹³The children of your chosen sister greet you.

3 JOHN

Help Christians Who Teach Truth

¹From the Elder.

To my dear friend Gaius, whom I love in the truth:

²My dear friend, I know your soul is doing fine, and I pray that you are doing well in every way and that your health is good. ³I was very happy when some brothers and sisters came and told me about the truth in your life and how you are following the way of truth. ⁴Nothing gives me greater joy than to hear that my children are following the way of truth.

⁵My dear friend, it is good that you help the brothers and sisters, even those you do not know. ⁶They told the church about your love. Please help them to continue their trip in a way worthy of God. ⁷They started out in service to Christ, and they have been accepting nothing from nonbelievers. ⁸So we should help such people; when we do, we share in their work for the truth.

⁹I wrote something to the church, but Diotrephes, who loves to be their leader, will not listen to us. ¹⁰So if I come, I will talk about what Diotrephes is doing, about how he lies and says evil things about us. But more than that, he refuses to accept the other brothers and sisters; he even stops those who do want to accept them and puts them out of the church.

¹¹My dear friend, do not follow what is bad; follow what is good. The one who does good belongs to God. But the one who does evil has never known God.

¹²Everyone says good things about Demetrius, and the truth agrees with what they say. We also speak well of him, and you know what we say is true.

¹³I have many things I want to write you, but I do not want to use pen and ink. ¹⁴I hope to see you soon and talk face to face. ¹⁵Peace to you. The friends here greet you. Please greet each friend there by name.

JUDE

Warnings About False Teachers

¹From Jude, a servant of Jesus Christ and a brother of James.

To all who have been called by God. God the Father loves you, and you have been kept safe in Jesus Christ:

²Mercy, peace, and love be yours richly.

³Dear friends, I wanted very much to write you about the salvation we all share. But I felt the need to write you about something else: I want to encourage you to fight hard for the faith that was given the holy people of God once and for all time. ⁴Some people have secretly entered your group. Long ago the prophets wrote about these people who will be judged guilty. They are against God and have changed the grace of our God into a reason for sexual sin. They also refuse to accept Jesus Christ, our only Master and Lord.

⁵I want to remind you of some things you already know: Remember that the Lord saved his people by bringing them out of the land of Egypt. But later he destroyed all those who did not believe. ⁶And remember the angels who did not keep their place of power but left their proper home. The Lord has kept these angels in darkness, bound with everlasting chains, to be judged on the great day. ⁷Also remember the cities of Sodom and Gomorrah and the other towns around them. In the same way they were full of sexual sin and people who desired sexual relations that God does not allow. They suffer the punishment of eternal fire, as an example for all to see.

⁸It is the same with these people who have entered your group. They are guided by dreams and make themselves filthy with sin. They reject God's authority and speak against the angels. ⁹Not even the archangel Michael, when he argued with the devil about who would have the body of Moses, dared to judge the devil guilty. Instead, he said, "The Lord punish you." ¹⁰But these people speak against things they do not understand. And what they do know, by feeling, as dumb animals know things, are the very things that destroy them. ¹¹It will be terrible for them. They have followed the way of Cain, and for money they have given themselves to doing the wrong that Balaam did. They have fought against God as Korah did, and like Korah, they surely will be destroyed. ¹²They are like dirty spots in your special Christian meals you share. They eat with you and have no fear, caring only for themselves. They are clouds without rain, which the wind blows around. They are autumn trees without fruit that are pulled out of the ground. So they are twice dead. ¹³They are like wild waves of the sea, tossing up their own shameful actions like foam. They are like stars that wander in the sky. A place in the blackest darkness has been kept for them forever.

¹⁴Enoch, the seventh descendant from Adam, said about these people: "Look, the Lord is coming with many thousands of his holy angels to ¹⁵judge every person. He is coming to punish all who are against God for all the evil they have done against him. And he will punish the sinners who are against God for all the evil they have said against him."

¹⁶These people complain and blame others, doing the evil things they want to

do. They brag about themselves, and they flatter others to get what they want.

¹⁷Dear friends, remember what the apostles of our Lord Jesus Christ said before. ¹⁸They said to you, "In the last times there will be people who laugh about God, following their own evil desires which are against God." ¹⁹These are the people who divide you, people whose thoughts are only of this world, who do not have the Spirit.

²⁰But dear friends, use your most holy faith to build yourselves up, praying in the Holy Spirit. ²¹Keep yourselves in God's love as you wait for the Lord Jesus Christ with his mercy to give you life forever.

²²Show mercy to some people who have doubts. ²³Take others out of the fire, and save them. Show mercy mixed with fear to others, hating even their clothes which are dirty from sin.

²⁴God is strong and can help you not to fall. He can bring you before his glory without any wrong in you and can give you great joy. ²⁵He is the only God, the One who saves us. To him be glory, greatness, power, and authority through Jesus Christ our Lord for all time past, now, and forever. Amen.

REVELATION

Christ Will Win over Evil

1 This is the revelation of Jesus Christ, which God gave to him, to show his servants what must soon happen. And Jesus sent his angel to show it to his servant John, [2] who has told everything he has seen. It is the word of God; it is the message from Jesus Christ. [3] Blessed is the one who reads the words of God's message, and blessed are the people who hear this message and do what is written in it. The time is near when all of this will happen.

[4] From John.

To the seven churches in Asia:

Grace and peace to you from the One who is and was and is coming, and from the seven spirits before his throne, [5] and from Jesus Christ. Jesus is the faithful witness, the first among those raised from the dead. He is the ruler of the kings of the earth.

He is the One who loves us, who made us free from our sins with the blood of his death. [6] He made us to be a kingdom of priests who serve God his Father. To Jesus Christ be glory and power forever and ever! Amen.

[7] Look, Jesus is coming with the clouds, and everyone will see him, even those who stabbed him. And all peoples of the earth will cry loudly because of him. Yes, this will happen! Amen.

[8] The Lord God says, "I am the Alpha and the Omega. I am the One who is and was and is coming. I am the Almighty."

[9] I, John, am your brother. All of us share with Christ in suffering, in the kingdom, and in patience to continue. I was on the island of Patmos, because I had preached the word of God and the message about Jesus. [10] On the Lord's day I was in the Spirit, and I heard a loud voice behind me that sounded like a trumpet. [11] The voice said, "Write what you see in a book and send it to the seven churches: to Ephesus, Smyrna, Pergamum, Thyatira, Sardis, Philadelphia, and Laodicea."

[12] I turned to see who was talking to me. When I turned, I saw seven golden lampstands [13] and someone among the lampstands who was "like a Son of Man." He was dressed in a long robe and had a gold band around his chest. [14] His head and hair were white like wool, as white as snow, and his eyes were like flames of fire. [15] His feet were like bronze that glows hot in a furnace, and his voice was like the noise of flooding water. [16] He held seven stars in his right hand, and a sharp double-edged sword came out of his mouth. He looked like the sun shining at its brightest time.

[17] When I saw him, I fell down at his feet like a dead man. He put his right hand on me and said, "Do not be afraid. I am the First and the Last. [18] I am the One who lives; I was dead, but look, I am alive forever and ever! And I hold the keys to death and to the place of the dead. [19] So write the things you see, what is now and what will happen later. [20] Here is the secret of the seven stars that you saw in my right hand and the seven golden lampstands: The seven lampstands are the seven churches, and the seven stars are the angels of the seven churches.

2 "Write this to the angel of the church in Ephesus:

"The One who holds the seven stars in his right hand and walks among the seven golden lampstands says this:

²I know what you do, how you work hard and never give up. I know you do not put up with the false teachings of evil people. You have tested those who say they are apostles but really are not, and you found they are liars. ³You have patience and have suffered troubles for my name and have not given up.

⁴"But I have this against you: You have left the love you had in the beginning. ⁵So remember where you were before you fell. Change your hearts and do what you did at first. If you do not change, I will come to you and will take away your lampstand from its place. ⁶But there is something you do that is right: You hate what the Nicolaitans do, as much as I.

⁷"Every person who has ears should listen to what the Spirit says to the churches. To those who win the victory I will give the right to eat the fruit from the tree of life, which is in the garden of God.

⁸"Write this to the angel of the church in Smyrna:

"The One who is the First and the Last, who died and came to life again, says this: ⁹I know your troubles and that you are poor, but really you are rich! I know the bad things some people say about you. They say they are Jews, but they are not true Jews. They are a synagogue that belongs to Satan. ¹⁰Do not be afraid of what you are about to suffer. I tell you, the devil will put some of you in prison to test you, and you will suffer for ten days. But be faithful, even if you have to die, and I will give you the crown of life.

¹¹"Everyone who has ears should listen to what the Spirit says to the churches. Those who win the victory will not be hurt by the second death.

¹²"Write this to the angel of the church in Pergamum:

"The One who has the sharp, double-edged sword says this: ¹³I know where you live. It is where Satan has his throne. But you are true to me. You did not refuse to tell about your faith in me even during the time of Antipas, my faithful witness who was killed in your city, where Satan lives.

¹⁴"But I have a few things against you: You have some there who follow the teaching of Balaam. He taught Balak how to cause the people of Israel to sin by eating food offered to idols and by taking part in sexual sins. ¹⁵You also have some who follow the teaching of the Nicolaitans. ¹⁶So change your hearts and lives. If you do not, I will come to you quickly and fight against them with the sword that comes out of my mouth.

¹⁷"Everyone who has ears should listen to what the Spirit says to the churches.

"I will give some of the hidden manna to everyone who wins the victory. I will also give to each one who wins the victory a white stone with a new name written on it. No one knows this new name except the one who receives it.

¹⁸"Write this to the angel of the church in Thyatira:

"The Son of God, who has eyes that blaze like fire and feet like shining bronze, says this: ¹⁹I know what you do. I know about your love, your faith, your service, and your patience. I know that you are doing more now than you did at first.

²⁰"But I have this against you: You let that woman Jezebel spread false teachings. She says she is a prophetess, but by her teaching she leads my people to take part in sexual sins and to eat food that is offered to idols. ²¹I have given her time to change her heart and turn away from her sin, but she does not want to change. ²²So I will throw her on a bed of suffering. And all those who take part in adultery with her will suffer greatly if they do not turn

away from the wrongs she does. [23]I will also kill her followers. Then all the churches will know I am the One who searches hearts and minds, and I will repay each of you for what you have done.

[24]"But others of you in Thyatira have not followed her teaching and have not learned what some call Satan's deep secrets. I say to you that I will not put any other load on you. [25]Only continue in your loyalty until I come.

[26]"I will give power over the nations to everyone who wins the victory and continues to be obedient to me until the end.

[27]'You will rule over them with an iron rod,

as when pottery is broken into pieces.'   *Psalm 2:9*

[28]This is the same power I received from my Father. I will also give him the morning star. [29]Everyone who has ears should listen to what the Spirit says to the churches.

3 "Write this to the angel of the church in Sardis:

"The One who has the seven spirits and the seven stars says this: I know what you do. People say that you are alive, but really you are dead. [2]Wake up! Strengthen what you have left before it dies completely. I have found that what you are doing is less than what my God wants. [3]So do not forget what you have received and heard. Obey it, and change your hearts and lives. So you must wake up, or I will come like a thief, and you will not know when I will come to you. [4]But you have a few there in Sardis who have kept their clothes unstained, so they will walk with me and will wear white clothes, because they are worthy. [5]Those who win the victory will be dressed in white clothes like them. And I will not erase their names from the book of life, but I will say they belong to me before my Father and be-

fore his angels. [6]Everyone who has ears should listen to what the Spirit says to the churches.

[7]"Write this to the angel of the church in Philadelphia:

"This is what the One who is holy and true, who holds the key of David, says. When he opens a door, no one can close it. And when he closes it, no one can open it. [8]I know what you do. I have put an open door before you, which no one can close. I know you have little strength, but you have obeyed my teaching and were not afraid to speak my name. [9]Those in the synagogue that belongs to Satan say they are Jews, but they are not true Jews; they are liars. I will make them come before you and bow at your feet, and they will know that I have loved you. [10]You have obeyed my teaching about not giving up your faith. So I will keep you from the time of trouble that will come to the whole world to test those who live on earth.

[11]"I am coming soon. Continue strong in your faith so no one will take away your crown. [12]I will make those who win the victory pillars in the temple of my God, and they will never have to leave it. I will write on them the name of my God and the name of the city of my God, the new Jerusalem, that comes down out of heaven from my God. I will also write on them my new name. [13]Everyone who has ears should listen to what the Spirit says to the churches.

[14]"Write this to the angel of the church in Laodicea:

"The Amen, the faithful and true witness, the ruler of all God has made, says this: [15]I know what you do, that you are not hot or cold. I wish that you were hot or cold! [16]But because you are lukewarm—neither hot, nor cold—I am ready to spit you out of my mouth. [17]You say, 'I am rich, and I have become wealthy and do not need anything.' But you do not know that you are really miserable, pitiful, poor, blind, and naked. [18]I advise you to buy from me gold made pure in fire so you can be truly rich. Buy from me white clothes so you can be clothed and so you can cover your shameful nakedness. Buy from me medicine to put on your eyes so you can truly see.

STEP 6 [19]"I correct and punish those whom I love. So be eager to do right, and change your hearts and lives. [20]Here I am! I stand at the door and knock. If you hear my voice and open the door, I will come in and eat with you, and you will eat with me.

[21]"Those who win the victory will sit with me on my throne in the same way that I won the victory and sat down with my Father on his throne. [22]Everyone who has ears should listen to what the Spirit says to the churches."

4 After the vision of these things I looked, and there before me was an open door in heaven. And the same voice that spoke to me before, that sounded like a trumpet, said, "Come up here, and I will show you what must happen after this." [2]Immediately I was in the Spirit, and before me was a throne in heaven, and someone was sitting on it. [3]The One who sat on the throne looked like precious stones, like jasper and carnelian. All around the throne was a rainbow the color of an emerald. [4]Around the throne there were twenty-four other thrones with twenty-four elders sitting on them. They were dressed in white and had golden crowns on their heads. [5]Lightning flashes and noises and thunder came from the throne. Before the throne seven lamps were burning, which are the seven spirits of God. [6]Also before the throne there was something that looked like a sea of glass, clear like crystal.

In the center and around the throne were four living creatures with eyes all over them, in front and in back. [7]The first living creature was like a lion. The second was like a calf. The third had a face like a man. The fourth was like a flying eagle. [8]Each of these four living creatures had six wings and was covered all over with eyes, inside and out. Day and night they never stop saying:

"Holy, holy, holy is the Lord God
        Almighty.
    He was, he is, and he is coming."

[9]These living creatures give glory, honor, and thanks to the One who sits on the throne, who lives forever and ever. [10]Then the twenty-four elders bow down before the One who sits on the throne, and they worship him who lives forever and ever. They put their crowns down before the throne and say:

[11]"You are worthy, our Lord and God,
        to receive glory and honor and
            power,
    because you made all things.
        Everything existed and was made,
        because you wanted it."

5 Then I saw a scroll in the right hand of the One sitting on the throne. The scroll had writing on both sides and was kept closed with seven seals. [2]And I saw a powerful angel calling in a loud voice, "Who is worthy to break the seals and open the scroll?" [3]But there was no one in heaven or on earth or under the earth who could open the scroll or look inside it. [4]I cried bitterly because there was no one who was worthy to open the scroll or look inside. [5]But one of the elders said to me, "Do not cry! The Lion from the tribe of Judah, David's descendant, has won the victory so that he is able to open the scroll and its seven seals."

[6]Then I saw a Lamb standing in the center of the throne and in the middle of the four living creatures and the elders.

STEP 6

Were entirely ready to have God
remove all these defects of character.

Revelation 3:19–20

You may be surprised at times to find yourself feeling sad at the prospect of losing your character defects. After all, they've been "old friends" for a long time. They haven't helped you. In fact, they've hurt you deeply. But they can feel like family.

This Bible passage points out that you need to look at getting rid of your defects of character as more than a good-bye. It is a life-changing hello. You're saying "Hello" to God who's been standing patiently at the door of your heart waiting for you to let him in. Don't look at getting rid of your character defects as losing old friends. Look at it as welcoming in the best friend you'll ever have.

What can you expect to happen when God makes himself at home in your life? Your anger may give way and reveal a calm, reasonable person. Your worry may be replaced with feelings of peace and security. Maybe you've been a possessive person—a "taker" in your relationships with others. God can make you a "giver," one who can share life with others. All of these changes—and more—wait on your opening the door and asking God to remove your defects of character.

FOR YOUR NEXT **STEP 6** MEDITATION, TURN TO **PAGE 478.** ▶▶

The Lamb looked as if he had been killed. He had seven horns and seven eyes, which are the seven spirits of God that were sent into all the world. [7]The Lamb came and took the scroll from the right hand of the One sitting on the throne. [8]When he took the scroll, the four living creatures and the twenty-four elders bowed down before the Lamb. Each one of them had a harp and golden bowls full of incense, which are the prayers of God's holy people. [9]And they all sang a new song to the Lamb:

"You are worthy to take the scroll
    and to open its seals,
because you were killed,
    and with the blood of your death
        you bought people for God
    from every tribe, language, people,
        and nation.
[10]You made them to be a kingdom of
        priests for our God,
    and they will rule on the earth."

[11]Then I looked, and I heard the voices of many angels around the throne, and the four living creatures, and the elders. There were thousands and thousands of angels, [12]saying in a loud voice:

"The Lamb who was killed is worthy
    to receive power, wealth, wisdom,
        and strength,
    honor, glory, and praise!"

[13]Then I heard all creatures in heaven and on earth and under the earth and in the sea saying:

"To the One who sits on the throne
    and to the Lamb
be praise and honor and glory and
        power
    forever and ever."

[14]The four living creatures said, "Amen," and the elders bowed down and worshiped.

6 Then I watched while the Lamb opened the first of the seven seals. I heard one of the four living creatures say with a voice like thunder, "Come!" [2]I looked, and there before me was a white horse. The rider on the horse held a bow, and he was given a crown, and he rode out, determined to win the victory.

[3]When the Lamb opened the second seal, I heard the second living creature say, "Come!" [4]Then another horse came out, a red one. Its rider was given power to take away peace from the earth and to make people kill each other, and he was given a big sword.

[5]When the Lamb opened the third seal, I heard the third living creature say, "Come!" I looked, and there before me was a black horse, and its rider held a pair of scales in his hand. [6]Then I heard something that sounded like a voice coming from the middle of the four living creatures. The voice said, "A quart of wheat for a day's pay, and three quarts of barley for a day's pay, and do not damage the olive oil and wine!"

[7]When the Lamb opened the fourth seal, I heard the voice of the fourth living creature say, "Come!" [8]I looked, and there before me was a pale horse. Its rider was named death, and Hades was following close behind him. They were given power over a fourth of the earth to kill people by war, by starvation, by disease, and by the wild animals of the earth.

[9]When the Lamb opened the fifth seal, I saw under the altar the souls of those who had been killed because they were faithful to the word of God and to the message they had received. [10]These souls shouted in a loud voice, "Holy and true Lord, how long until you judge the people of the earth and punish them for killing us?" [11]Then each one of them was given a white robe and was told to wait a short time longer. There were still some of their fellow servants and brothers and sisters

in the service of Christ who must be killed as they were. They had to wait until all of this was finished.

[12]Then I watched while the Lamb opened the sixth seal, and there was a great earthquake. The sun became black like rough black cloth, and the whole moon became red like blood. [13]And the stars in the sky fell to the earth like figs falling from a fig tree when the wind blows. [14]The sky disappeared as a scroll when it is rolled up, and every mountain and island was moved from its place.

[15]Then the kings of the earth, the rulers, the generals, the rich people, the powerful people, the slaves, and the free people hid themselves in caves and in the rocks on the mountains. [16]They called to the mountains and the rocks, "Fall on us. Hide us from the face of the One who sits on the throne and from the anger of the Lamb! [17]The great day for their anger has come, and who can stand against it?"

7 After the vision of these things I saw four angels standing at the four corners of the earth. The angels were holding the four winds of the earth to keep them from blowing on the land or on the sea or on any tree. [2]Then I saw another angel coming up from the east who had the seal of the living God. And he called out in a loud voice to the four angels to whom God had given power to harm the earth and the sea. [3]He said to them, "Do not harm the land or the sea or the trees until we mark with a sign the foreheads of the people who serve our God." [4]Then I heard how many people were marked with the sign. There were one hundred forty-four thousand from every tribe of the people of Israel.

[5]From the tribe of Judah twelve thousand were marked with the sign,

from the tribe of Reuben twelve thousand,
from the tribe of Gad twelve thousand,
[6]from the tribe of Asher twelve thousand,
from the tribe of Naphtali twelve thousand,
from the tribe of Manasseh twelve thousand,
[7]from the tribe of Simeon twelve thousand,
from the tribe of Levi twelve thousand,
from the tribe of Issachar twelve thousand,
[8]from the tribe of Zebulun twelve thousand,
from the tribe of Joseph twelve thousand,
and from the tribe of Benjamin twelve thousand were marked with the sign.

[9]After the vision of these things I looked, and there was a great number of people, so many that no one could count them. They were from every nation, tribe, people, and language of the earth. They were all standing before the throne and before the Lamb, wearing white robes and holding palm branches in their hands. [10]They were shouting in a loud voice, "Salvation belongs to our God, who sits on the throne, and to the Lamb." [11]All the angels were standing around the throne and the elders and the four living creatures. They all bowed down on their faces before the throne and worshiped God, [12]saying, "Amen! Praise, glory, wisdom, thanks, honor, power, and strength belong to our God forever and ever. Amen!"

[13]Then one of the elders asked me, "Who are these people dressed in white robes? Where did they come from?"

¹⁴I answered, "You know, sir."

And the elder said to me, "These are the people who have come out of the great distress. They have washed their robes and made them white in the blood of the Lamb. ¹⁵Because of this, they are before the throne of God. They worship him day and night in his temple. And the One who sits on the throne will be present with them. ¹⁶Those people will never be hungry again, and they will never be thirsty again. The sun will not hurt them, and no heat will burn them, ¹⁷because the Lamb at the center of the throne will be their shepherd. He will lead them to springs of water that give life. And God will wipe away every tear from their eyes."

8 When the Lamb opened the seventh seal, there was silence in heaven for about half an hour. ²And I saw the seven angels who stand before God and to whom were given seven trumpets.

³Another angel came and stood at the altar, holding a golden pan for incense. He was given much incense to offer with the prayers of all God's holy people. The angel put this offering on the golden altar before the throne. ⁴The smoke from the incense went up from the angel's hand to God with the prayers of God's people. ⁵Then the angel filled the incense pan with fire from the altar and threw it on the earth, and there were flashes of lightning, thunder and loud noises, and an earthquake.

⁶Then the seven angels who had the seven trumpets prepared to blow them.

⁷The first angel blew his trumpet, and hail and fire mixed with blood were poured down on the earth. And a third of the earth, and all the green grass, and a third of the trees were burned up.

⁸Then the second angel blew his trumpet, and something that looked like a big mountain, burning with fire, was thrown into the sea. And a third of the sea became blood, ⁹a third of the living things in the sea died, and a third of the ships were destroyed.

¹⁰Then the third angel blew his trumpet, and a large star, burning like a torch, fell from the sky. It fell on a third of the rivers and on the springs of water. ¹¹The name of the star is Wormwood. And a third of all the water became bitter, and many people died from drinking the water that was bitter.

¹²Then the fourth angel blew his trumpet, and a third of the sun, and a third of the moon, and a third of the stars were struck. So a third of them became dark, and a third of the day was without light, and also the night.

¹³While I watched, I heard an eagle that was flying high in the air cry out in a loud voice, "Trouble! Trouble! Trouble for those who live on the earth because of the remaining sounds of the trumpets that the other three angels are about to blow!"

9 Then the fifth angel blew his trumpet, and I saw a star fall from the sky to the earth. The star was given the key to the deep hole that leads to the bottomless pit. ²Then it opened up the hole that leads to the bottomless pit, and smoke came up from the hole like smoke from a big furnace. Then the sun and sky became dark because of the smoke from the hole. ³Then locusts came down to the earth out of the smoke, and they were given the power to sting like scorpions. ⁴They were told not to harm the grass on the earth or any plant or tree. They could harm only the people who did not have the sign of God on their foreheads. ⁵These locusts were not given the power to kill anyone, but to cause pain to the people for five months. And the pain they felt was like the pain a scorpion

gives when it stings someone. ⁶During those days people will look for a way to die, but they will not find it. They will want to die, but death will run away from them.

⁷The locusts looked like horses prepared for battle. On their heads they wore what looked like crowns of gold, and their faces looked like human faces. ⁸Their hair was like women's hair, and their teeth were like lions' teeth. ⁹Their chests looked like iron breastplates, and the sound of their wings was like the noise of many horses and chariots hurrying into battle. ¹⁰The locusts had tails with stingers like scorpions, and in their tails was their power to hurt people for five months. ¹¹The locusts had a king who was the angel of the bottomless pit. His name in the Hebrew language is Abaddon and in the Greek language is Apollyon.

¹²The first trouble is past; there are still two other troubles that will come.

¹³Then the sixth angel blew his trumpet, and I heard a voice coming from the horns on the golden altar that is before God. ¹⁴The voice said to the sixth angel who had the trumpet, "Free the four angels who are tied at the great river Euphrates." ¹⁵And they let loose the four angels who had been kept ready for this hour and day and month and year so they could kill a third of all people on the earth. ¹⁶I heard how many troops on horses were in their army—two hundred million.

¹⁷The horses and their riders I saw in the vision looked like this: They had breastplates that were fiery red, dark blue, and yellow like sulfur. The heads of the horses looked like heads of lions, with fire, smoke, and sulfur coming out of their mouths. ¹⁸A third of all the people on earth were killed by these three terrible disasters coming out of the horses'

mouths: the fire, the smoke, and the sulfur. ¹⁹The horses' power was in their mouths and in their tails; their tails were like snakes with heads, and with them they hurt people.

²⁰The other people who were not killed by these terrible disasters still did not change their hearts and turn away from what they had made with their own hands. They did not stop worshiping demons and idols made of gold, silver, bronze, stone, and wood—things that cannot see or hear or walk. ²¹These people did not change their hearts and turn away from murder or evil magic, from their sexual sins or stealing.

10 Then I saw another powerful angel coming down from heaven dressed in a cloud with a rainbow over his head. His face was like the sun, and his legs were like pillars of fire. ²The angel was holding a small scroll open in his hand. He put his right foot on the sea and his left foot on the land. ³Then he shouted loudly like the roaring of a lion. And when he shouted, the voices of seven thunders spoke. ⁴When the seven thunders spoke, I started to write. But I heard a voice from heaven say, "Keep hidden what the seven thunders said, and do not write them down."

⁵Then the angel I saw standing on the sea and on the land raised his right hand to heaven, ⁶and he made a promise by the power of the One who lives forever and ever. He is the One who made the skies and all that is in them, the earth and all that is in it, and the sea and all that is in it. The angel promised, "There will be no more waiting! ⁷In the days when the seventh angel is ready to blow his trumpet, God's secret will be finished. This secret is the Good News God told to his servants, the prophets."

⁸Then I heard the same voice from

heaven again, saying to me: "Go and take the open scroll that is in the hand of the angel that is standing on the sea and on the land."

⁹So I went to the angel and told him to give me the small scroll. And he said to me, "Take the scroll and eat it. It will be sour in your stomach, but in your mouth it will be sweet as honey." ¹⁰So I took the small scroll from the angel's hand and ate it. In my mouth it tasted sweet as honey, but after I ate it, it was sour in my stomach. ¹¹Then I was told, "You must prophesy again about many peoples, nations, languages, and kings."

11 I was given a measuring stick like a rod, and I was told, "Go and measure the temple of God and the altar, and count the people worshiping there. ²But do not measure the yard outside the temple. Leave it alone, because it has been given to those who are not God's people. And they will trample on the holy city for forty-two months. ³And I will give power to my two witnesses to prophesy for one thousand two hundred sixty days, and they will be dressed in rough cloth to show their sadness."

⁴These two witnesses are the two olive trees and the two lampstands that stand before the Lord of the earth. ⁵And if anyone tries to hurt them, fire comes from their mouths and kills their enemies. And if anyone tries to hurt them in whatever way, in that same way that person will die. ⁶These witnesses have the power to stop the sky from raining during the time they are prophesying. And they have power to make the waters become blood, and they have power to send every kind of trouble to the earth as many times as they want.

⁷When the two witnesses have finished telling their message, the beast that comes up from the bottomless pit will fight a war against them. He will defeat them and kill them. ⁸The bodies of the two witnesses will lie in the street of the great city where the Lord was killed. This city is named Sodom and Egypt, which has a spiritual meaning. ⁹Those from every race of people, tribe, language, and nation will look at the bodies of the two witnesses for three and one-half days, and they will refuse to bury them. ¹⁰People who live on the earth will rejoice and be happy because these two are dead. They will send each other gifts, because these two prophets brought much suffering to those who live on the earth.

¹¹But after three and one-half days, God put the breath of life into the two prophets again. They stood on their feet, and everyone who saw them became very afraid. ¹²Then the two prophets heard a loud voice from heaven saying, "Come up here!" And they went up into heaven in a cloud as their enemies watched.

¹³In the same hour there was a great earthquake, and a tenth of the city was destroyed. Seven thousand people were killed in the earthquake, and those who did not die were very afraid and gave glory to the God of heaven.

¹⁴The second trouble is finished. Pay attention: The third trouble is coming soon.

¹⁵Then the seventh angel blew his trumpet. And there were loud voices in heaven, saying:

"The power to rule the world now
            belongs to our Lord and his
            Christ,
      and he will rule forever and ever."

¹⁶Then the twenty-four elders, who sit on their thrones before God, bowed down on their faces and worshiped God. ¹⁷They said:

"We give thanks to you, Lord God
Almighty,
who is and who was,
because you have used your great
power
and have begun to rule!
¹⁸The people of the world were angry,
but your anger has come.
The time has come to judge the dead,
and to reward your servants the
prophets
and your holy people,
all who respect you, great and
small.
The time has come to destroy those
who destroy the earth!"

¹⁹Then God's temple in heaven was opened. The Ark that holds the agreement God gave to his people could be seen in his temple. Then there were flashes of lightning, noises, thunder, an earthquake, and a great hailstorm.

12 And then a great wonder appeared in heaven: A woman was clothed with the sun, and the moon was under her feet, and a crown of twelve stars was on her head. ²She was pregnant and cried out with pain, because she was about to give birth. ³Then another wonder appeared in heaven: There was a giant red dragon with seven heads and seven crowns on each head. He also had ten horns. ⁴His tail swept a third of the stars out of the sky and threw them down to the earth. He stood in front of the woman who was ready to give birth so he could eat her baby as soon as it was born. ⁵Then the woman gave birth to a son who will rule all the nations with an iron rod. And her child was taken up to God and to his throne. ⁶The woman ran away into the desert to a place God prepared for her where she would be taken care of for one thousand two hundred sixty days.

⁷Then there was a war in heaven. Michael and his angels fought against the dragon, and the dragon and his angels fought back. ⁸But the dragon was not strong enough, and he and his angels lost their place in heaven. ⁹The giant dragon was thrown down out of heaven. (He is that old snake called the devil or Satan, who tricks the whole world.) The dragon with his angels was thrown down to the earth.

¹⁰Then I heard a loud voice in heaven saying:
"The salvation and the power and the
kingdom of our God
and the authority of his Christ
have now come.
The accuser of our brothers and
sisters,
who accused them day and night
before our God,
has been thrown down.
¹¹And our brothers and sisters defeated
him
by the blood of the Lamb's death
and by the message they
preached.
They did not love their lives so much
that they were afraid of death.
¹²So rejoice, you heavens
and all who live there!
But it will be terrible for the earth and
the sea,
because the devil has come down
to you!
He is filled with anger,
because he knows he does not
have much time."

¹³When the dragon saw he had been thrown down to the earth, he hunted for the woman who had given birth to the son. ¹⁴But the woman was given the two wings of a great eagle so she could fly to the place prepared for her in the desert. There she would be taken care of for

three and one-half years, away from the snake. [15]Then the snake poured water out of its mouth like a river toward the woman so the flood would carry her away. [16]But the earth helped the woman by opening its mouth and swallowing the river that came from the mouth of the dragon. [17]Then the dragon was very angry at the woman, and he went off to make war against all her other children—those who obey God's commands and who have the message Jesus taught.

[18]And the dragon stood on the seashore.

13 Then I saw a beast coming up out of the sea. It had ten horns and seven heads, and there was a crown on each horn. A name against God was written on each head. [2]This beast looked like a leopard, with feet like a bear's feet and a mouth like a lion's mouth. And the dragon gave the beast all of his power and his throne and great authority. [3]One of the heads of the beast looked as if it had been killed by a wound, but this death wound was healed. Then the whole world was amazed and followed the beast. [4]People worshiped the dragon because he had given his power to the beast. And they also worshiped the beast, asking, "Who is like the beast? Who can make war against it?"

[5]The beast was allowed to say proud words and words against God, and it was allowed to use its power for forty-two months. [6]It used its mouth to speak against God, against God's name, against the place where God lives, and against all those who live in heaven. [7]It was given power to make war against God's holy people and to defeat them. It was given power over every tribe, people, language, and nation. [8]And all who live on earth will worship the beast—all the people since the beginning of the world whose names are not written in the Lamb's book of life. The Lamb is the One who was killed.

[9]Anyone who has ears should listen:

[10]If you are to be a prisoner,
then you will be a prisoner.
If you are to be killed with the sword,
then you will be killed with the
sword.

This means that God's holy people must have patience and faith.

[11]Then I saw another beast coming up out of the earth. It had two horns like a lamb, but it spoke like a dragon. [12]This beast stands before the first beast and uses the same power the first beast has. By this power it makes everyone living on earth worship the first beast, who had the death wound that was healed. [13]And the second beast does great miracles so that it even makes fire come down from heaven to earth while people are watching. [14]It fools those who live on earth by the miracles it has been given the power to do. It does these miracles to serve the first beast. The second beast orders people to make an idol to honor the first beast, the one that was wounded by the deadly sword but sprang to life again. [15]The second beast was given power to give life to the idol of the first one so that the idol could speak. And the second beast was given power to command all who will not worship the image of the beast to be killed. [16]The second beast also forced all people, small and great, rich and poor, free and slave, to have a mark on their right hand or on their forehead. [17]No one could buy or sell without this mark, which is the name of the beast or the number of its name. [18]This takes wisdom. Let the one who has understanding find the meaning of the number, which is the number of a person. Its number is 666.

14 Then I looked, and there before me was the Lamb standing on Mount Zion. With him were one hundred forty-four thousand people who had his name and his Father's name written on their foreheads. ²And I heard a sound from heaven like the noise of flooding water and like the sound of loud thunder. The sound I heard was like people playing harps. ³And they sang a new song before the throne and before the four living creatures and the elders. No one could learn the new song except the one hundred forty-four thousand who had been bought from the earth. ⁴These are the ones who did not do sinful things with women, because they kept themselves pure. They follow the Lamb every place he goes. These one hundred forty-four thousand were bought from among the people of the earth as people to be offered to God and the Lamb. ⁵They were not guilty of telling lies; they are without fault.

⁶Then I saw another angel flying high in the air. He had the eternal Good News to preach to those who live on earth—to every nation, tribe, language, and people. ⁷He preached in a loud voice, "Fear God and give him praise, because the time has come for God to judge all people. So worship God who made the heavens and the earth, and the sea, and the springs of water."

⁸Then the second angel followed the first angel and said, "Ruined, ruined is the great city of Babylon! She made all the nations drink the wine of the anger of her adultery."

⁹Then a third angel followed the first two angels, saying in a loud voice: "If anyone worships the beast and his idol and gets the beast's mark on the forehead or on the hand, ¹⁰that one also will drink the wine of God's anger, which is prepared with all its strength in the cup of his anger. And that person will be put in pain with burning sulfur before the holy angels and the Lamb. ¹¹And the smoke from their burning pain will rise forever and ever. There will be no rest, day or night, for those who worship the beast and his idol or who get the mark of his name." ¹²This means God's holy people must be patient. They must obey God's commands and keep their faith in Jesus.

¹³Then I heard a voice from heaven saying, "Write this: Blessed are the dead who die from now on in the Lord."

The Spirit says, "Yes, they will rest from their hard work, and the reward of all they have done stays with them."

¹⁴Then I looked, and there before me was a white cloud, and sitting on the white cloud was One who looked like a Son of Man. He had a gold crown on his head and a sharp sickle in his hand. ¹⁵Then another angel came out of the temple and called out in a loud voice to the One who was sitting on the cloud, "Take your sickle and harvest from the earth, because the time to harvest has come, and the fruit of the earth is ripe." ¹⁶So the One who was sitting on the cloud swung his sickle over the earth, and the earth was harvested.

¹⁷Then another angel came out of the temple in heaven, and he also had a sharp sickle. ¹⁸And then another angel, who has power over the fire, came from the altar. This angel called to the angel with the sharp sickle, saying, "Take your sharp sickle and gather the bunches of grapes from the earth's vine, because its grapes are ripe." ¹⁹Then the angel swung his sickle over the earth. He gathered the earth's grapes and threw them into the great winepress of God's anger. ²⁰They were trampled in the winepress outside the city, and blood flowed out of the

winepress as high as horses' bridles for a distance of about one hundred eighty miles.

15Then I saw another wonder in heaven that was great and amazing. There were seven angels bringing seven disasters. These are the last disasters, because after them, God's anger is finished.

²I saw what looked like a sea of glass mixed with fire. All of those who had won the victory over the beast and his idol and over the number of his name were standing by the sea of glass. They had harps that God had given them. ³They sang the song of Moses, the servant of God, and the song of the Lamb:

"You do great and wonderful things,
Psalm 111:2

Lord God Almighty.   *Amos 3:13*
Everything the Lord does is right and
    true,   *Psalm 145:17*
King of the nations.
⁴Everyone will respect you, Lord,
Jeremiah 10:7
    and will honor you.
Only you are holy.
All the nations will come
    and worship you,   *Psalm 86:9–10*
because the right things you have
    done
    are now made known."
Deuteronomy 32:4

⁵After this I saw that the temple (the Tent of the Agreement) in heaven was opened. ⁶And the seven angels bringing the seven disasters came out of the temple. They were dressed in clean, shining linen and wore golden bands tied around their chests. ⁷Then one of the four living creatures gave to the seven angels seven golden bowls filled with the anger of God, who lives forever and ever. ⁸The temple was filled with smoke from the glory and the power of God, and no one could enter the temple until the seven disasters of the seven angels were finished.

16Then I heard a loud voice from the temple saying to the seven angels, "Go and pour out the seven bowls of God's anger on the earth."

²The first angel left and poured out his bowl on the land. Then ugly and painful sores came upon all those who had the mark of the beast and who worshiped his idol.

³The second angel poured out his bowl on the sea, and it became blood like that of a dead man, and every living thing in the sea died.

⁴The third angel poured out his bowl on the rivers and the springs of water, and they became blood. ⁵Then I heard the angel of the waters saying:

"Holy One, you are the One who is
    and who was.
You are right to decide to punish
    these evil people.
⁶They have poured out the blood of
    your holy people and your
    prophets.
So now you have given them
    blood to drink as they
    deserve."

⁷And I heard a voice coming from the altar saying:

"Yes, Lord God Almighty,
    the way you punish evil people is
    right and fair."

⁸The fourth angel poured out his bowl on the sun, and he was given power to burn the people with fire. ⁹They were burned by the great heat, and they cursed the name of God, who had control over these disasters. But the people refused to change their hearts and lives and give glory to God.

¹⁰The fifth angel poured out his bowl on the throne of the beast, and darkness covered its kingdom. People gnawed

their tongues because of the pain. ¹¹They also cursed the God of heaven because of their pain and the sores they had, but they refused to change their hearts and turn away from the evil things they did.

¹²The sixth angel poured out his bowl on the great river Euphrates so that the water in the river was dried up to prepare the way for the kings from the east to come. ¹³Then I saw three evil spirits that looked like frogs coming out of the mouth of the dragon, out of the mouth of the beast, and out of the mouth of the false prophet. ¹⁴These evil spirits are the spirits of demons, which have power to do miracles. They go out to the kings of the whole world to gather them together for the battle on the great day of God Almighty.

¹⁵"Listen! I will come as a thief comes! Blessed are those who stay awake and keep their clothes on so that they will not walk around naked and have people see their shame."

¹⁶Then the evil spirits gathered the kings together to the place that is called Armageddon in the Hebrew language.

¹⁷The seventh angel poured out his bowl into the air. Then a loud voice came out of the temple from the throne, saying, "It is finished!" ¹⁸Then there were flashes of lightning, noises, thunder, and a big earthquake—the worst earthquake that has ever happened since people have been on earth. ¹⁹The great city split into three parts, and the cities of the nations were destroyed. And God remembered the sins of Babylon the Great, so he gave that city the cup filled with the wine of his terrible anger. ²⁰Then every island ran away, and mountains disappeared. ²¹Giant hailstones, each weighing about a hundred pounds, fell from the sky upon people. People cursed God for the disaster of the hail, because this disaster was so terrible.

17 Then one of the seven angels who had the seven bowls came and spoke to me. He said, "Come, and I will show you the punishment that will be given to the great prostitute, the one sitting over many waters. ²The kings of the earth sinned sexually with her, and the people of the earth became drunk from the wine of her sexual sin."

³Then the angel carried me away by the Spirit to the desert. There I saw a woman sitting on a red beast. It was covered with names against God written on it, and it had seven heads and ten horns. ⁴The woman was dressed in purple and red and was shining with the gold, precious jewels, and pearls she was wearing. She had a golden cup in her hand, a cup filled with evil things and the uncleanness of her sexual sin. ⁵On her forehead a title was written that was secret. This is what was written:

THE GREAT BABYLON

MOTHER OF PROSTITUTES

AND OF THE EVIL THINGS OF THE EARTH

⁶Then I saw that the woman was drunk with the blood of God's holy people and with the blood of those who were killed because of their faith in Jesus.

When I saw the woman, I was very amazed. ⁷Then the angel said to me, "Why are you amazed? I will tell you the secret of this woman and the beast she rides—the one with seven heads and ten horns. ⁸The beast you saw was once alive but is not alive now. But soon it will come up out of the bottomless pit and go away to be destroyed. There are people who live on earth whose names have not been written in the book of life since the beginning of the world. They will be amazed when they see the beast, because he was once alive, is not alive now, but will come again.

⁹"You need a wise mind to understand

this. The seven heads on the beast are seven mountains where the woman sits. [10]And they are seven kings. Five of the kings have already been destroyed, one of the kings lives now, and another has not yet come. When he comes, he must stay a short time. [11]The beast that was once alive, but is not alive now, is also an eighth king. He belongs to the first seven kings, and he will go away to be destroyed.

[12]"The ten horns you saw are ten kings who have not yet begun to rule, but they will receive power to rule with the beast for one hour. [13]All ten of these kings have the same purpose, and they will give their power and authority to the beast. [14]They will make war against the Lamb, but the Lamb will defeat them, because he is Lord of lords and King of kings. He will defeat them with his called, chosen, and faithful followers."

[15]Then the angel said to me, "The waters that you saw, where the prostitute sits, are peoples, races, nations, and languages. [16]The ten horns and the beast you saw will hate the prostitute. They will take everything she has and leave her naked. They will eat her body and burn her with fire. [17]God made the ten horns want to carry out his purpose by agreeing to give the beast their power to rule, until what God has said comes about. [18]The woman you saw is the great city that rules over the kings of the earth."

18 After the vision of these things, I saw another angel coming down from heaven. This angel had great power, and his glory made the earth bright. [2]He shouted in a powerful voice:

"Ruined, ruined is the great city of Babylon!
    She has become a home for demons
and a prison for every evil spirit,

and a prison for every unclean bird and unclean beast.
[3]She has been ruined, because all the peoples of the earth
    have drunk the wine of the desire of her sexual sin.
She has been ruined also because the kings of the earth
    have sinned sexually with her,
and the merchants of the earth
    have grown rich from the great wealth of her luxury."

[4]Then I heard another voice from heaven saying:
"Come out of that city, my people,
    so that you will not share in her sins,
    so that you will not receive the disasters that will come to her.
[5]Her sins have piled up as high as the sky,
    and God has not forgotten the wrongs she has done.
[6]Give that city the same as she gave to others.
    Pay her back twice as much as she did.
Prepare wine for her that is twice as strong
    as the wine she prepared for others.
[7]She gave herself much glory and rich living.
    Give her that much suffering and sadness.
She says to herself, 'I am a queen sitting on my throne.
    I am not a widow; I will never be sad.'
[8]So these disasters will come to her in one day:
    death, and crying, and great hunger,
and she will be destroyed by fire,

because the Lord God who judges her is powerful."

⁹The kings of the earth who sinned sexually with her and shared her wealth will see the smoke from her burning. Then they will cry and be sad because of her death. ¹⁰They will be afraid of her suffering and stand far away and say:

"Terrible! How terrible for you, great city,
    powerful city of Babylon,
because your punishment has come in one hour!"

¹¹And the merchants of the earth will cry and be sad about her, because now there is no one to buy their cargoes— ¹²cargoes of gold, silver, jewels, pearls, fine linen, purple cloth, silk, red cloth; all kinds of citron wood and all kinds of things made from ivory, expensive wood, bronze, iron, and marble; ¹³cinnamon, spice, incense, myrrh, frankincense, wine, olive oil, fine flour, wheat, cattle, sheep, horses, carriages, slaves, and human lives.

¹⁴The merchants will say,
"Babylon, the good things you wanted are gone from you.
All your rich and fancy things have disappeared.
    You will never have them again."

¹⁵The merchants who became rich from selling to her will be afraid of her suffering and will stand far away. They will cry and be sad ¹⁶and say:

"Terrible! How terrible for the great city!
She was dressed in fine linen, purple and red cloth,
and she was shining with gold, precious jewels, and pearls!
¹⁷All these riches have been destroyed in one hour!"

Every sea captain, every passenger, the sailors, and all those who earn their living from the sea stood far away from Babylon. ¹⁸As they saw the smoke from her burning, they cried out loudly, "There was never a city like this great city!" ¹⁹And they threw dust on their heads and cried out, weeping and being sad. They said:

"Terrible! How terrible for the great city!
All the people who had ships on the sea
    became rich because of her wealth!
But she has been destroyed in one hour!
²⁰Be happy because of this, heaven!
Be happy, God's holy people and apostles and prophets!
God has punished her because of what she did to you."

²¹Then a powerful angel picked up a large stone, like one used for grinding grain, and threw it into the sea. He said:

"In the same way, the great city of Babylon will be thrown down,
    and it will never be found again.
²²The music of people playing harps and other instruments,
    flutes, and trumpets,
    will never be heard in you again.
No workman doing any job
    will ever be found in you again.
The sound of grinding grain
    will never be heard in you again.
²³The light of a lamp
    will never shine in you again,
and the voices of a bridegroom and bride
    will never be heard in you again.
Your merchants were the world's great people,
    and all the nations were tricked by your magic.
²⁴You are guilty of the death of the prophets and God's holy people

and all who have been killed on earth."

19 After this vision and announcement I heard what sounded like a great many people in heaven saying:

"Hallelujah!
Salvation, glory, and power belong to
our God,
² because his judgments are true
and right.
He has punished the prostitute
who made the earth evil with her
sexual sin.
He has paid her back for the death of
his servants."

³Again they said:

"Hallelujah!
She is burning, and her smoke will
rise forever and ever."

⁴Then the twenty-four elders and the four living creatures bowed down and worshiped God, who sits on the throne. They said:

"Amen, Hallelujah!"

⁵Then a voice came from the throne, saying:

"Praise our God, all you who serve him
and all you who honor him, both
small and great!"

⁶Then I heard what sounded like a great many people, like the noise of flooding water, and like the noise of loud thunder. The people were saying:

"Hallelujah!
Our Lord God, the Almighty, rules.
⁷Let us rejoice and be happy
and give God glory,
because the wedding of the Lamb
has come,
and the Lamb's bride has made
herself ready.
⁸Fine linen, bright and clean, was
given to her to wear."

(The fine linen means the good things done by God's holy people.)

⁹And the angel said to me, "Write this: Blessed are those who have been invited to the wedding meal of the Lamb!" And the angel said, "These are the true words of God."

¹⁰Then I bowed down at the angel's feet to worship him, but he said to me, "Do not worship me! I am a servant like you and your brothers and sisters who have the message of Jesus. Worship God, because the message about Jesus is the spirit that gives all prophecy."

¹¹Then I saw heaven opened, and there before me was a white horse. The rider on the horse is called Faithful and True, and he is right when he judges and makes war. ¹²His eyes are like burning fire, and on his head are many crowns. He has a name written on him, which no one but himself knows. ¹³He is dressed in a robe dipped in blood, and his name is the Word of God. ¹⁴The armies of heaven, dressed in fine linen, white and clean, were following him on white horses. ¹⁵Out of the rider's mouth comes a sharp sword that he will use to defeat the nations, and he will rule them with a rod of iron. He will crush out the wine in the winepress of the terrible anger of God the Almighty. ¹⁶On his robe and on his upper leg was written this name: KING OF KINGS AND LORD OF LORDS.

¹⁷Then I saw an angel standing in the sun, and he called with a loud voice to all the birds flying in the sky: "Come and gather together for the great feast of God ¹⁸so that you can eat the bodies of kings, generals, mighty people, horses and their riders, and the bodies of all people—free, slave, small, and great."

¹⁹Then I saw the beast and the kings of the earth. Their armies were gathered together to make war against the rider on the horse and his army. ²⁰But the beast was captured and with him the false

prophet who did the miracles for the beast. The false prophet had used these miracles to trick those who had the mark of the beast and worshiped his idol. The false prophet and the beast were thrown alive into the lake of fire that burns with sulfur. ²¹And their armies were killed with the sword that came out of the mouth of the rider on the horse, and all the birds ate the bodies until they were full.

20 I saw an angel coming down from heaven. He had the key to the bottomless pit and a large chain in his hand. ²The angel grabbed the dragon, that old snake who is the devil and Satan, and tied him up for a thousand years. ³Then he threw him into the bottomless pit, closed it, and locked it over him. The angel did this so he could not trick the people of the earth anymore until the thousand years were ended. After a thousand years he must be set free for a short time.

⁴Then I saw some thrones and people sitting on them who had been given the power to judge. And I saw the souls of those who had been killed because they were faithful to the message of Jesus and the message from God. They had not worshiped the beast or his idol, and they had not received the mark of the beast on their foreheads or on their hands. They came back to life and ruled with Christ for a thousand years. ⁵(The others that were dead did not live again until the thousand years were ended.) This is the first raising of the dead. ⁶Blessed and holy are those who share in this first raising of the dead. The second death has no power over them. They will be priests for God and for Christ and will rule with him for a thousand years.

⁷When the thousand years are over, Satan will be set free from his prison. ⁸Then he will go out to trick the nations in all the earth—Gog and Magog—to gather them for battle. There are so many people they will be like sand on the seashore. ⁹And Satan's army marched across the earth and gathered around the camp of God's people and the city God loves. But fire came down from heaven and burned them up. ¹⁰And Satan, who tricked them, was thrown into the lake of burning sulfur with the beast and the false prophet. There they will be punished day and night forever and ever.

¹¹Then I saw a great white throne and the One who was sitting on it. Earth and sky ran away from him and disappeared. ¹²And I saw the dead, great and small, standing before the throne. Then books were opened, and the book of life was opened. The dead were judged by what they had done, which was written in the books. ¹³The sea gave up the dead who were in it, and Death and Hades gave up the dead who were in them. Each person was judged by what he had done. ¹⁴And Death and Hades were thrown into the lake of fire. The lake of fire is the second death. ¹⁵And anyone whose name was not found written in the book of life was thrown into the lake of fire.

21 Then I saw a new heaven and a new earth. The first heaven and the first earth had disappeared, and there was no sea anymore. ²And I saw the holy city, the new Jerusalem, coming down out of heaven from God. It was prepared like a bride dressed for her husband. ³And I heard a loud voice from the throne, saying, "Now God's presence is with people, and he will live with them, and they will be his people. God himself will be with them and will be their God. ⁴He will wipe away every tear from their eyes, and there will be no more death, sadness, crying, or pain, because all the old ways are gone."

⁵The One who was sitting on the

throne said, "Look! I am making everything new!" Then he said, "Write this, because these words are true and can be trusted."

⁶The One on the throne said to me, "It is finished. I am the Alpha and the Omega, the Beginning and the End. I will give free water from the spring of the water of life to anyone who is thirsty. ⁷Those who win the victory will receive this, and I will be their God, and they will be my children. ⁸But cowards, those who refuse to believe, who do evil things, who kill, who sin sexually, who do evil magic, who worship idols, and who tell lies—all these will have a place in the lake of burning sulfur. This is the second death."

⁹Then one of the seven angels who had the seven bowls full of the seven last troubles came to me, saying, "Come with me, and I will show you the bride, the wife of the Lamb." ¹⁰And the angel carried me away by the Spirit to a very large and high mountain. He showed me the holy city, Jerusalem, coming down out of heaven from God. ¹¹It was shining with the glory of God and was bright like a very expensive jewel, like a jasper, clear as crystal. ¹²The city had a great high wall with twelve gates with twelve angels at the gates, and on each gate was written the name of one of the twelve tribes of Israel. ¹³There were three gates on the east, three on the north, three on the south, and three on the west. ¹⁴The walls of the city were built on twelve foundation stones, and on the stones were written the names of the twelve apostles of the Lamb.

¹⁵The angel who talked with me had a measuring rod made of gold to measure the city, its gates, and its wall. ¹⁶The city was built in a square, and its length was equal to its width. The angel measured the city with the rod. The city was 1,500 miles long, 1,500 miles wide, and 1,500 miles high. ¹⁷The angel also measured the wall. It was 216 feet high, by human measurements, which the angel was using. ¹⁸The wall was made of jasper, and the city was made of pure gold, as pure as glass. ¹⁹The foundation stones of the city walls were decorated with every kind of jewel. The first foundation was jasper, the second was sapphire, the third was chalcedony, the fourth was emerald, ²⁰the fifth was onyx, the sixth was carnelian, the seventh was chrysolite, the eighth was beryl, the ninth was topaz, the tenth was chrysoprase, the eleventh was jacinth, and the twelfth was amethyst. ²¹The twelve gates were twelve pearls, each gate having been made from a single pearl. And the street of the city was made of pure gold as clear as glass.

²²I did not see a temple in the city, because the Lord God Almighty and the Lamb are the city's temple. ²³The city does not need the sun or the moon to shine on it, because the glory of God is its light, and the Lamb is the city's lamp. ²⁴By its light the people of the world will walk, and the kings of the earth will bring their glory into it. ²⁵The city's gates will never be shut on any day, because there is no night there. ²⁶The glory and the honor of the nations will be brought into it. ²⁷Nothing unclean and no one who does shameful things or tells lies will ever go into it. Only those whose names are written in the Lamb's book of life will enter the city.

22 Then the angel showed me the river of the water of life. It was shining like crystal and was flowing from the throne of God and of the Lamb ²down the middle of the street of the city. The tree of life was on each side of the river. It produces fruit twelve times a year, once each month. The leaves of the tree are for the healing of all the nations. ³Nothing that God judges guilty will be in that city. The throne of God and of the Lamb will be there, and God's servants will worship him. ⁴They will see his face, and his name will be written on their foreheads. ⁵There will never be night again. They will not need the light of a lamp or the light of the sun, because the Lord God will give them light. And they will rule as kings forever and ever.

⁶The angel said to me, "These words can be trusted and are true." The Lord, the God of the spirits of the prophets, sent his angel to show his servants the things that must happen soon.

⁷"Listen! I am coming soon! Blessed is the one who obeys the words of prophecy in this book."

⁸I, John, am the one who heard and saw these things. When I heard and saw them, I bowed down to worship at the feet of the angel who showed these things to me. ⁹But the angel said to me, "Do not worship me! I am a servant like you, your brothers the prophets, and all those who obey the words in this book. Worship God!"

¹⁰Then the angel told me, "Do not keep secret the words of prophecy in this book, because the time is near for all this to happen. ¹¹Let whoever is doing evil continue to do evil. Let whoever is unclean continue to be unclean. Let whoever is doing right continue to do right. Let whoever is holy continue to be holy."

¹²"Listen! I am coming soon! I will bring my reward with me, and I will repay each one of you for what you have done. ¹³I am the Alpha and the Omega, the First and the Last, the Beginning and the End.

¹⁴"Blessed are those who wash their robes so that they will receive the right to eat the fruit from the tree of life and may go through the gates into the city. ¹⁵Outside the city are the evil people, those who do evil magic, who sin sexually, who murder, who worship idols, and who love lies and tell lies.

¹⁶"I, Jesus, have sent my angel to tell you these things for the churches. I am the descendant from the family of David, and I am the bright morning star."

¹⁷The Spirit and the bride say, "Come!" Let the one who hears this say, "Come!" Let whoever is thirsty come; whoever wishes may have the water of life as a free gift.

¹⁸I warn everyone who hears the words of the prophecy of this book: If anyone adds anything to these words, God will add to that person the disasters written about in this book. ¹⁹And if anyone takes away from the words of this book of prophecy, God will take away that one's share of the tree of life and of the holy city, which are written about in this book.

²⁰Jesus, the One who says these things are true, says, "Yes, I am coming soon."

Amen. Come, Lord Jesus!

²¹The grace of the Lord Jesus be with all. Amen.

THE BOOKS

OF

PSALMS

AND

PROVERBS

PSALMS

The Songbook of Israel

Book 1

PSALM 1

¹Happy are those who don't listen to
the wicked,
who don't go where sinners go,
who don't do what evil people do.
²They love the LORD's teachings,
and they think about those
teachings day and night.
³They are strong, like a tree planted by
a river.
The tree produces fruit in season,
and its leaves don't die.
Everything they do will succeed.

⁴But wicked people are not like that.
They are like chaff that the wind
blows away.
⁵So the wicked will not escape God's
punishment.
Sinners will not worship with
God's people.
⁶This is because the LORD takes care
of his people,
but the wicked will be destroyed.

PSALM 2

¹Why are the nations so angry?
Why are the people making
useless plans?
²The kings of the earth prepare to
fight,
and their leaders make plans
together
against the LORD
and his appointed one.
³They say, "Let's break the chains that
hold us back
and throw off the ropes that tie us
down."

⁴But the one who sits in heaven laughs;
the Lord makes fun of them.
⁵Then the LORD warns them
and frightens them with his anger.
⁶He says, "I have appointed my own
king
to rule in Jerusalem on my holy
mountain, Zion."

⁷Now I will tell you what the LORD has
declared:
He said to me, "You are my son.
Today I have become your father.
⁸If you ask me, I will give you the
nations;
all the people on earth will be
yours.
⁹You will rule over them with an iron
rod.
You will break them into pieces
like pottery."

¹⁰So, kings, be wise;
rulers, learn this lesson.
¹¹Obey the LORD with great fear.
Be happy, but tremble.
¹²Show that you are loyal to his son,
or you will be destroyed by his
anger,
because he can quickly become
angry.
But happy are those who trust him
for protection.

PSALM 3

David sang this when he ran away
from his son Absalom.

¹LORD, I have many enemies!
Many people have turned
against me.
²Many are saying about me,
"God won't rescue him."   *Selah*

381

³But, LORD, you are my shield,
　　my wonderful God who gives me
　　　　courage.
⁴I will pray to the LORD,
　　and he will answer me from his
　　　　holy mountain.　　　*Selah*

STEP 3

⁵I can lie down and go to sleep,
　　and I will wake up again,
　　because the LORD gives me
　　　　strength.
⁶Thousands of troops may
　　　　surround me,
　　but I am not afraid.

⁷LORD, rise up!
　　My God, come save me!
　　You have struck my enemies on the
　　　　cheek;
　　　　you have broken the teeth of the
　　　　　　wicked.
⁸The LORD can save his people.
　　LORD, bless your people.　　*Selah*

PSALM 4

For the director of music. With stringed instruments.
A psalm of David.

¹Answer me when I pray to you,
　　my God who does what is right.
　　Make things easier for me when I am
　　　　in trouble.
　　　　Have mercy on me and hear my
　　　　　　prayer.

²People, how long will you turn my
　　　　honor into shame?
　　How long will you love what is
　　　　false and look for new lies?
　　　　　　　　　　　　　　Selah
³You know that the LORD has chosen
　　for himself those who are
　　　　loyal to him.
　　The LORD listens when I pray to
　　　　him.

STEP 6

⁴When you are angry, do not sin.
　　Think about these things quietly
　　　　as you go to bed.　　*Selah*

⁵Do what is right as a sacrifice to the
　　　　LORD
　　and trust the LORD.

⁶Many people ask,
　　"Who will give us anything good?"
　　LORD, be kind to us.
⁷But you have made me very happy,
　　happier than they are,
　　even with all their grain and new
　　　　wine.

⁸I go to bed and sleep in peace,
　　because, LORD, only you keep me
　　　　safe.

STEP 3

PSALM 5

For the director of music. For flutes.
A psalm of David.

¹LORD, listen to my words.
　　Understand my sadness.

STEP 1

²Listen to my cry for help, my King and
　　my God,
　　because I pray to you.
³LORD, every morning you hear my
　　voice.
　　Every morning, I tell you what I
　　　　need,
　　and I wait for your answer.

⁴You are not a God who is pleased with
　　　　the wicked;
　　you do not live with those who do
　　　　evil.
⁵Those people who make fun of you
　　　　cannot stand before you.
　　You hate all those who do evil.
⁶You destroy liars;
　　the LORD hates those who kill and
　　　　trick others.

⁷Because of your great love,
　　I can come into your Temple.
　　Because I fear and respect you,
　　I can worship in your holy Temple.
⁸LORD, since I have many enemies,
　　show me the right thing to do.

STEP 3

Made a decision to turn our will and our lives
over to the care of God **as we understood Him.**

Psalm 3:5-6

As he started Psalm 3, David quoted the taunt of his enemies: "God won't rescue him" (verse 2).

We don't need enemies to say things like that about us. We say them ourselves. Have you ever felt a gnawing doubt about whether God will take care of you? If you're normal, you've wondered, *Is there a God, and does he know the tough things I'm facing? Does he care how lonely, sick, and hurting I am?* Now that you realize you can't go on living with your addiction, you need to settle these questions about whether God is interested in you.

David wasn't worried because his enemies thought God had deserted him. David knew better. He could go to bed and sleep like a baby. He trusted God's care more than he trusted an army of bodyguards. God's always there. He cares, and he will watch over you. Throw open your hungry heart, and let him satisfy your deepest needs. Turn your will and your life over to him. He's up to the job.

FOR YOUR NEXT **STEP 3** MEDITATION, TURN TO **PAGE 397.** ▶▶

Show me clearly how you want me
to live.

⁹My enemies' mouths do not tell the
truth;
in their hearts they want to
destroy others.
Their throats are like open graves;
they use their tongues for telling
lies.
¹⁰God, declare them guilty!
Let them fall into their own
traps.
Send them away because their sins
are many;
they have turned against you.

¹¹But let everyone who trusts you be
happy;
let them sing glad songs forever.
Protect those who love you
and who are happy because of
you.
¹²LORD, you bless those who do what is
right;
you protect them like a soldier's
shield.

PSALM 6

For the director of music. With stringed instruments.
Upon the sheminith. A psalm of David.

¹LORD, don't correct me when you are
angry;
don't punish me when you are
very angry.

STEP
I

²LORD, have mercy on me because I
am weak.
Heal me, LORD, because my bones
ache.
³I am very upset.
LORD, how long will it be?

⁴LORD, return and save me;
save me because of your kindness.
⁵Dead people don't remember you;
those in the grave don't praise
you.

STEP
I

⁶I am tired of crying to you.
Every night my bed is wet with
tears;
my bed is soaked from my crying.
⁷My eyes are weak from so much
crying;
they are weak from crying about
my enemies.

⁸Get away from me, all you who do
evil,
because the LORD has heard my
crying.
⁹The LORD has heard my cry for help;
the LORD will answer my prayer.
¹⁰All my enemies will be ashamed and
troubled.
They will turn and suddenly leave
in shame.

PSALM 7

A shiggaion of David which he sang to the LORD
about Cush, from the tribe of Benjamin.

¹LORD my God, I trust in you for
protection.
Save me and rescue me
from those who are chasing me.
²Otherwise, like a lion they will tear me
apart.
They will rip me to pieces, and no
one can save me.

³LORD my God, what have I done?
Have my hands done something
wrong?
⁴Have I done wrong to my friend
or stolen without reason from my
enemy?
⁵If I have, let my enemy chase me and
capture me.
Let him trample me into the dust
and bury me in the ground.   *Selah*

⁶LORD, rise up in your anger;
stand up against my enemies'
anger.
Get up and demand fairness.

STEP 1

We admitted we were powerless
over our dependencies—that our lives
had become unmanageable.

Psalm 6:2–4

Most people want to be in control of how they live and of what happens to them. Some people think they have to be. Happy are the truly grown-up adults who realize they aren't in control of everything and don't even want to be. Do you know how you get to that point? You get there by coming to the end of yourself and your strength and discovering that only God has enough resources to face the really big challenges of life.

That's the point David had reached when he penned Psalm 6. Physically and emotionally he was a wreck. "My bones ache," David complained. That was a Hebrew way of saying "I'm shot through with pain." David, the famous warrior, admitted his weakness and his emotional collapse. But he wasn't defeated by his admission. David had placed himself in the strongest position possible. He didn't have to pretend he was strong when he wasn't. He could turn to God for strength and help—and do it publicly. Everyone else could be encouraged to trust God in tough times. That's an honest, helpful way to live.

FOR YOUR NEXT **STEP 1** MEDITATION, TURN TO **PAGE 403.** ▶▶

⁷Gather the nations around you
   and rule them from above.
⁸LORD, judge the people.
      LORD, defend me because I am
         right,
      because I have done no wrong,
         God Most High.
⁹God, you do what is right.
      You know our thoughts and
         feelings.
   Stop those wicked actions done by
      evil people,
      and help those who do what is
         right.

¹⁰God protects me like a shield;
      he saves those whose hearts are
         right.
¹¹God judges by what is right,
      and God is always ready to punish
         the wicked.
¹²If they do not change their lives,
      God will sharpen his sword;
      he will string his bow and take
         aim.
¹³He has prepared his deadly weapons;
      he has made his flaming arrows.

¹⁴There are people who think up evil
      and plan trouble and tell lies.
¹⁵They dig a hole to trap others,
      but they will fall into it themselves.
¹⁶They will get themselves into trouble;
      the violence they cause will hurt
         only themselves.

¹⁷I praise the LORD because he does
      what is right.
      I sing praises to the LORD Most
         High.

PSALM 8

For the director of music. On the gittith.
A psalm of David.

¹LORD our Lord,
      your name is the most wonderful
         name in all the earth!

It brings you praise in heaven
   above.
²You have taught children and babies
      to sing praises to you
      because of your enemies.
   And so you silence your enemies
      and destroy those who try to get
         even.

³I look at your heavens,
      which you made with your fingers.
   I see the moon and stars,
      which you created.
⁴But why are people even important to
      you?
      Why do you take care of human
         beings?
⁵You made them a little lower than the
      angels
      and crowned them with glory and
         honor.
⁶You put them in charge of everything
      you made.
      You put all things under their
         control:
⁷all the sheep, the cattle,
      and the wild animals,
⁸the birds in the sky,
      the fish in the sea,
      and everything that lives under
         water.

⁹LORD our Lord,
      your name is the most wonderful
         name in all the earth!

PSALM 9

For the director of music. To the tune of "The Death
of the Son." A psalm of David.

¹I will praise you, LORD, with all my
      heart.
      I will tell all the miracles you have
         done.
²I will be happy because of you;
      God Most High, I will sing praises
         to your name.

³My enemies turn back;
they are overwhelmed and die
because of you.
⁴You have heard my complaint;
you sat on your throne and judged
by what was right.
⁵You spoke strongly against the
foreign nations and
destroyed the wicked;
you wiped out their names forever
and ever.
⁶The enemy is gone forever.
You destroyed their cities;
no one even remembers them.

⁷But the LORD rules forever.
He sits on his throne to judge,
⁸and he will judge the world in
fairness;
he will decide what is fair for the
nations.

⁹The LORD defends those who suffer;
he defends them in times of
trouble.
¹⁰Those who know the LORD trust him,
because he will not leave those
who come to him.

¹¹Sing praises to the LORD who is king
on Mount Zion.
Tell the nations what he has done.
¹²He remembers who the murderers are;
he will not forget the cries of
those who suffer.
¹³LORD, have mercy on me.
See how my enemies hurt me.
Do not let me go through the
gates of death.
¹⁴Then, at the gates of Jerusalem, I will
praise you;
I will rejoice because you saved me.

¹⁵The nations have fallen into the pit
they dug.
Their feet are caught in the nets
they laid.

¹⁶The LORD has made himself known by
his fair decisions;
the wicked get trapped by what
they do.   *Higgaion. Selah*

¹⁷Wicked people will go to the grave,
and so will all those who forget
God.
¹⁸But those who have troubles will not
be forgotten.
The hopes of the poor will never
die.

¹⁹LORD, rise up and judge the nations.
Don't let people think they are
strong.
²⁰Teach them to fear you, LORD.
The nations must learn that they
are only human.   *Selah*

PSALM 10

¹LORD, why are you so far away?
Why do you hide when there is
trouble?
²Proudly the wicked chase down those
who suffer.
Let them be caught in their own
traps.
³They brag about the things they
want.
They bless the greedy but hate
the LORD.
⁴The wicked people are too proud.
They do not look for God;
there is no room for God in their
thoughts.
⁵They always succeed.
They are far from keeping your
laws;
they make fun of their enemies.
⁶They say to themselves, "Nothing
bad will ever happen
to me;
I will never be ruined."
⁷Their mouths are full of curses, lies,
and threats;

they use their tongues for sin and evil.

⁸They hide near the villages.
　　They look for innocent people to kill;
　　they watch in secret for the helpless.
⁹They wait in hiding like a lion.
　　They wait to catch poor people;
　　they catch the poor in nets.
¹⁰The poor are thrown down and crushed;
　　they are defeated because the others are stronger.
¹¹The wicked think, "God has forgotten us.
　　He doesn't see what is happening."

¹²LORD, rise up and punish the wicked.
　　Don't forget those who need help.
¹³Why do wicked people hate God?
　　They say to themselves, "God won't punish us."

STEP 1
¹⁴LORD, surely you see these cruel and evil things;
　　look at them and do something.
People in trouble look to you for help.
You are the one who helps the orphans.

¹⁵Break the power of wicked people.
　　Punish them for the evil they have done.

¹⁶The LORD is King forever and ever.
　　Destroy from your land those nations that do not worship you.

STEP 7
¹⁷LORD, you have heard what the poor people want.
　　Do what they ask, and listen to them.

¹⁸Protect the orphans and put an end to suffering
　　so they will no longer be afraid of evil people.

PSALM 11
For the director of music. Of David.

¹I trust in the LORD for protection.
　　So why do you say to me,
　　"Fly like a bird to your mountain.
²Like hunters, the wicked string their bows;
　　they set their arrows on the bowstrings.
They shoot from dark places
　　at those who are honest.
³When the foundations for good collapse,
　　what can good people do?"

⁴The LORD is in his holy temple;
　　the LORD sits on his throne in heaven.
He sees what people do;
　　he keeps his eye on them.
⁵The LORD tests those who do right,
　　but he hates the wicked and those who love to hurt others.
⁶He will send hot coals and burning sulfur on the wicked.
　　A whirlwind is what they will get.
⁷The LORD does what is right, and he loves justice,
　　so honest people will see his face.

PSALM 12
For the director of music. Upon the sheminith.
A psalm of David.

¹Save me, LORD, because the good people are all gone;
　　no true believers are left on earth.
²Everyone lies to his neighbors;
　　they say one thing and mean another.

³The LORD will stop those flattering lips
　　and cut off those bragging tongues.
⁴They say, "Our tongues will help us win.
　　We can say what we wish; no one is our master."

388

STEP 1

⁵But the LORD says,
"I will now rise up,
    because the poor are being hurt.
Because of the moans of the helpless,
    I will give them the help they
        want."
⁶The LORD's words are pure,
    like silver purified by fire,
    like silver purified seven times
        over.

⁷LORD, you will keep us safe;
    you will always protect us from
        such people.
⁸But the wicked are all around us;
    everyone loves what is wrong.

PSALM 13

For the director of music. A psalm of David.

STEP 1

¹How long will you forget me, LORD?
        Forever?
    How long will you hide from me?
²How long must I worry
    and feel sad in my heart all day?
    How long will my enemy win over
        me?

³LORD, look at me.
    Answer me, my God;
    tell me, or I will die.
⁴Otherwise my enemy will say, "I have
        won!"
    Those against me will rejoice that
        I've been defeated.

⁵I trust in your love.
    My heart is happy because you
        saved me.
⁶I sing to the LORD
    because he has taken care of me.

PSALM 14

For the director of music. Of David.

¹Fools say to themselves,
    "There is no God."
Fools are evil and do terrible things;
    there is no one who does anything
        good.

²The LORD looked down from heaven
        on all people
    to see if anyone understood,
    if anyone was looking to God for
        help.
³But all have turned away.
    Together, everyone has become
        evil.
There is no one who does anything
        good,
    not even one.

⁴Don't the wicked understand?
    They destroy my people as if they
        were eating bread.
    They do not ask the LORD for help.
⁵But the wicked are filled with terror,
    because God is with those who do
        what is right.
⁶The wicked upset the plans of the
        poor,
    but the LORD will protect them.

⁷I pray that victory will come to Israel
        from Mount Zion!
    May the LORD bring them back.
Then the people of Jacob will rejoice,
    and the people of Israel will be
        glad.

PSALM 15

A psalm of David.

¹LORD, who may enter your Holy Tent?
    Who may live on your holy
        mountain?

²Only those who are innocent
    and who do what is right.
Such people speak the truth from
        their hearts
³   and do not tell lies about others.
    They do no wrong to their neighbors
    and do not gossip.
⁴They do not respect hateful people

but honor those who honor the
LORD.
They keep their promises to their
neighbors,
even when it hurts.
⁵They do not charge interest on
money they lend
and do not take money to hurt
innocent people.

Whoever does all these things will
never be destroyed.

PSALM 16
A miktam of David.

¹Protect me, God,
because I trust in you.
²I said to the LORD, "You are my Lord.
Every good thing I have comes
from you."
³As for the godly people in the world,
they are the wonderful ones I
enjoy.

STEP
1

⁴But those who turn to idols
will have much pain.
I will not offer blood to those idols
or even speak their names.

⁵No, the LORD is all I need.
He takes care of me.
⁶My share in life has been pleasant;
my part has been beautiful.

STEP
6

⁷I praise the LORD because he
advises me.
Even at night, I feel his leading.
⁸I keep the LORD before me always.
Because he is close by my side,
I will not be hurt.
⁹So I rejoice and am glad.
Even my body has hope,
¹⁰because you will not leave me in the
grave.
You will not let your holy one rot.
¹¹You will teach me how to live a holy
life.

Being with you will fill me with joy;
at your right hand I will find
pleasure forever.

PSALM 17
A prayer of David.

¹LORD, hear me begging for fairness;
listen to my cry for help.
Pay attention to my prayer,
because I speak the truth.
²You will judge that I am right;
your eyes can see what is true.
³You have examined my heart;
you have tested me all night.
You questioned me without finding
anything wrong;
I have not sinned with my mouth.
⁴I have obeyed your commands,
so I have not done what evil
people do.
⁵I have done what you told me;
I have not failed.

⁶I call to you, God,
and you answer me.
Listen to me now,
and hear what I say.
⁷Your love is wonderful.
By your power you save those who
trust you
from their enemies.
⁸Protect me as you would protect your
own eye.
Hide me under the shadow of your
wings.
⁹Keep me from the wicked who attack
me,
from my enemies who
surround me.
¹⁰They are selfish
and brag about themselves.
¹¹They have chased me until they have
surrounded me.
They plan to throw me to the
ground.

STEP
3

¹²They are like lions ready to kill;
  like lions, they sit in hiding.

¹³Lord, rise up, face the enemy, and
    throw them down.
  Save me from the wicked with
    your sword.
¹⁴Lord, save me by your power
    from those whose reward is in this
    life.
They have plenty of food.
  They have many sons
    and leave much money to their
    children.

¹⁵Because I have lived right, I will see
    your face.
  When I wake up, I will see your
    likeness and be satisfied.

PSALM 18

For the director of music. By the Lord's servant, David.
David sang this song to the Lord when the Lord had
saved him from Saul and all his other enemies.

STEP 2

¹I love you, Lord. You are my strength.

²The Lord is my rock, my protection,
    my Savior.
  My God is my rock.
  I can run to him for safety.
  He is my shield and my saving
    strength, my defender.
³I will call to the Lord, who is worthy of
    praise,
  and I will be saved from my
    enemies.

⁴The ropes of death came around me;
    the deadly rivers
      overwhelmed me.
⁵The ropes of death wrapped
    around me.
  The traps of death were
    before me.
STEP 1
⁶In my trouble I called to the Lord.
  I cried out to my God for help.
  From his temple he heard my voice;
    my call for help reached his ears.

⁷The earth trembled and shook.
  The foundations of the mountains
    began to shake.
  They trembled because the Lord
    was angry.
⁸Smoke came out of his nose,
    and burning fire came out of his
    mouth.
  Burning coals went before him.
⁹He tore open the sky and came down
    with dark clouds under his feet.
¹⁰He rode a creature with wings and
    flew.
  He raced on the wings of the
    wind.
¹¹He made darkness his covering, his
    shelter around him,
    surrounded by fog and clouds.
¹²Out of the brightness of his presence
    came clouds
    with hail and lightning.
¹³The Lord thundered from heaven;
    the Most High raised his voice,
    and there was hail and lightning.
¹⁴He shot his arrows and scattered his
    enemies.
  His many bolts of lightning
    confused them with fear.
¹⁵Lord, you spoke strongly.
  The wind blew from your nose.
  Then the valleys of the sea appeared,
    and the foundations of the earth
    were seen.

¹⁶The Lord reached down from above
    and took me;
  he pulled me from the deep water.
¹⁷He saved me from my powerful
    enemies,
    from those who hated me,
      because they were too
      strong for me.
¹⁸They attacked me at my time of
    trouble,
  but the Lord supported me.

STEP 2

STEP 2

Came to believe that a Power greater than
ourselves could restore us to sanity.

Psalm 18:1-3

Steps 1 and 2 set out intentionally to deflate your ego big time. Like
everyone else in recovery, you have to realize just how badly your
efforts at self-control and willpower have worked against your "Big
Three" enemies: compulsiveness, drivenness, and neediness.

When you start a recovery program, you're at a crossroads. Your
addiction keeps on luring you with promises of escape, pleasure,
and freedom from pain. But you've begun to realize these promises
are lies—lies of the worst kind. The addiction doesn't really deliver
what it promises. You have a sneaking suspicion that your life is
headed for a shipwreck of epic proportions.

That's a bleak prospect. It takes the wind out of your sails and
leaves you dead in the water. At a time like that in his experience,
David celebrated a God he called "my rock, my protection, my
Savior" (verse 2). Let your addiction deflate your ego. Admit your
powerlessness. Celebrate it! Powerlessness introduces you to God,
who has unlimited strength to deliver you from addiction and
shame.

FOR YOUR NEXT **STEP 2** MEDITATION, TURN TO **PAGE 493**. ▶▶

¹⁹He took me to a safe place.
Because he delights in me, he
saved me.

²⁰The LORD spared me because I did
what was right.
Because I have not done evil, he
has rewarded me.
²¹I have followed the ways of the LORD;
I have not done evil by turning
away from my God.
²²I remember all his laws
and have not broken his rules.
²³I am innocent before him;
I have kept myself from doing evil.
²⁴The LORD rewarded me because I did
what was right,
because I did what the LORD said
was right.

²⁵LORD, you are loyal to those who are
loyal,
and you are good to those who are
good.
²⁶You are pure to those who are pure,
but you are against those who are
bad.

²⁷You save the humble,
but you bring down those who are
proud.
²⁸LORD, you give light to my lamp.
My God brightens the darkness
around me.
²⁹With your help I can attack an army.
With God's help I can jump over a
wall.

³⁰The ways of God are without fault.
The LORD's words are pure.
He is a shield to those who trust him.
³¹Who is God? Only the LORD.
Who is the Rock? Only our God.
³²God is my protection.
He makes my way free from fault.
³³He makes me like a deer that does
not stumble;

he helps me stand on the steep
mountains.
³⁴He trains my hands for battle
so my arms can bend a bronze
bow.
³⁵You protect me with your saving
shield.
You support me with your right
hand.
You have stooped to make me
great.
³⁶You give me a better way to live,
so I live as you want me to.
³⁷I chased my enemies and caught
them.
I did not quit until they were
destroyed.
³⁸I crushed them so they couldn't rise
up again.
They fell beneath my feet.
³⁹You gave me strength in battle.
You made my enemies bow
before me.
⁴⁰You made my enemies turn back,
and I destroyed those who
hated me.
⁴¹They called for help,
but no one came to save them.
They called to the LORD,
but he did not answer them.
⁴²I beat my enemies into pieces, like
dust in the wind.
I poured them out like mud in the
streets.

⁴³You saved me when the people
attacked me.
You made me the leader of
nations.
People I never knew serve me.
⁴⁴As soon as they hear me, they
obey me.
Foreigners obey me.
⁴⁵They all become afraid
and tremble in their hiding places.

STEP
I

⁴⁶The LORD lives!
> May my Rock be praised.
> Praise the God who saves me!

⁴⁷God gives me victory over my
> enemies
> and brings people under my rule.

⁴⁸He saves me from my enemies.

You set me over those who hate me.
> You saved me from violent people.

⁴⁹So I will praise you, LORD, among the
> nations.
> I will sing praises to your name.

⁵⁰The LORD gives great victories to his
> king.
> He is loyal to his appointed king,
> to David and his descendants
> forever.

PSALM 19

For the director of music. A psalm of David.

¹The heavens declare the glory of
> God,
> and the skies announce what his
> hands have made.

²Day after day they tell the story;
> night after night they tell it again.

³They have no speech or words;
> they have no voice to be heard.

⁴But their message goes out through
> all the world;
> their words go everywhere on
> earth.

The sky is like a home for the sun.

⁵   The sun comes out like a
> bridegroom from his
> bedroom.
> It rejoices like an athlete eager to
> run a race.

⁶The sun rises at one end of the sky
> and follows its path to the other
> end.
> Nothing hides from its heat.

⁷The teachings of the LORD are perfect;
> they give new strength.

The rules of the LORD can be trusted;
> they make plain people wise.

⁸The orders of the LORD are right;
> they make people happy.

The commands of the LORD are pure;
> they light up the way.

⁹Respect for the LORD is good;
> it will last forever.

The judgments of the LORD are true;
> they are completely right.

¹⁰They are worth more than gold,
> even the purest gold.

They are sweeter than honey,
> even the finest honey.

¹¹By them your servant is warned.
> Keeping them brings great
> reward.

¹²People cannot see their own mistakes. | STEP 6
> Forgive me for my secret sins.

¹³Keep me from the sins of pride;
> don't let them rule me.

Then I can be pure
> and innocent of the greatest of
> sins.

¹⁴I hope my words and thoughts please
> you.
> LORD, you are my Rock, the one
> who saves me.

PSALM 20

For the director of music. A psalm of David.

¹May the LORD answer you in times of
> trouble.
> May the God of Jacob protect you.

²May he send you help from his Temple
> and support you from Mount Zion.

³May he remember all your offerings
> and accept all your sacrifices. *Selah*

⁴May he give you what you want
> and make all your plans succeed,

⁵and we will shout for joy when you
> succeed,
> and we will raise a flag in the
> name of our God.

May the LORD give you all that you ask for.

6Now I know the LORD helps his
appointed king.
He answers him from his holy
heaven
and saves him with his strong
right hand.

STEP 2
7Some trust in chariots, others in
horses,
but we trust the LORD our God.
8They are overwhelmed and defeated,
but we march forward and win.
9LORD, save the king!
Answer us when we call for help.

PSALM 21

For the director of music. A psalm of David.

1LORD, the king rejoices because of
your strength;
he is so happy when you save him!
2You gave the king what he wanted
and did not refuse what he asked
for. *Selah*
3You put good things before him
and placed a gold crown on his
head.
4He asked you for life,
and you gave it to him,
so his years go on and on.
5He has great glory because you gave
him victories;
you gave him honor and praise.
6You always gave him blessings;
you made him glad because you
were with him.
7The king truly trusts the LORD.
Because God Most High always
loves him,
he will not be overwhelmed.
8Your hand is against all your enemies;
those who hate you will feel your
power.
9When you appear,
you will burn them as in a furnace.

In your anger you will swallow them
up,
and fire will burn them up.
10You will destroy their families from
the earth;
their children will not live.
11They made evil plans against you,
but their traps won't work.
12You will make them turn their backs
when you aim your arrows at
them.
13Be supreme, LORD, in your power.
We sing and praise your greatness.

PSALM 22

For the director of music. To the tune of "The Doe
of Dawn." A psalm of David.

STEP 1
1My God, my God, why have you
abandoned me?
You seem far from saving me,
far away from my groans.
2My God, I call to you during the day,
but you do not answer.
I call at night;
I am not silent.

3You sit as the Holy One.
The praises of Israel are your
throne.
4Our ancestors trusted you;
they trusted, and you saved them.
5They called to you for help
and were rescued.
They trusted you
and were not disappointed.

6But I am like a worm instead of a man.
People make fun of me and
hate me.
7Those who look at me laugh.
They stick out their tongues and
shake their heads.
8They say, "Turn to the LORD for help.
Maybe he will save you.
If he likes you,
maybe he will rescue you."

9You had my mother give birth to me.
   You made me trust you
   while I was just a baby.
10I have leaned on you since the day I
      was born;
   you have been my God since my
      mother gave me birth.

STEP 1
11So don't be far away from me.
   Now trouble is near,
   and there is no one to help.
12People have surrounded me like
      angry bulls.
   Like the strong bulls of Bashan,
   they are on every side.
13Like hungry, roaring lions
   they open their mouths at me.

14My strength is gone,
   like water poured out onto the
      ground,
   and my bones are out of joint.
My heart is like wax;
   it has melted inside me.
15My strength has dried up like a clay
      pot,
   and my tongue sticks to the top of
      my mouth.
   You laid me in the dust of death.
16Evil people have surrounded me;
   like dogs they have trapped me.
   They have bitten my arms and
      legs.
17I can count all my bones;
   people look and stare at me.
18They divided my clothes among
      them,
   and they threw lots for my
      clothing.

19But, LORD, don't be far away.
   You are my strength; hurry to
      help me.
20Save me from the sword;
   save my life from the dogs.
21Rescue me from the lion's mouth;
   save me from the horns of the
      bulls.

STEP 12
22Then I will tell my brothers and sisters
      about you;
   I will praise you in the public
      meeting.
23Praise the LORD, all you who respect
      him.
   All you descendants of Jacob,
      honor him;
   fear him, all you Israelites.
24He does not ignore those in trouble.
   He doesn't hide from them
   but listens when they call out to
      him.
25LORD, I praise you in the great
      meeting of your people;
   these worshipers will see me do
      what I promised.
26Poor people will eat until they are full;
   those who look to the LORD will
      praise him.
   May your hearts live forever!
27People everywhere will remember
   and will turn to the LORD.
All the families of the nations
   will worship him
28because the LORD is King,
   and he rules the nations.

29All the powerful people on earth will
      eat and worship.
   Everyone will bow down to him,
   all who will one day die.
30The people in the future will serve him;
   they will always be told about the
      Lord.
31They will tell that he does what is
      right.
   People who are not yet born
   will hear what God has done.

PSALM 23

A psalm of David.

STEP 3
1The LORD is my shepherd;
   I have everything I need.
2He lets me rest in green pastures.
   He leads me to calm water.

STEP 3

Made a decision to turn our will and our lives over to the care of God **as we understood Him.**

Psalm 23

Several places in the Bible compare people to sheep and God to a shepherd. In John 10:14, Jesus called himself "the good shepherd" who gives his life for his sheep. A thousand years before Jesus, David knew what it felt like to be a "sheep" taken care of by the Good Shepherd; and he described his experience in what has become the most familiar of all the psalms. You, too, can know what it's like to be watched over, nurtured, and guided by the Good Shepherd. The Good Shepherd gave his life for you. On your part, you need to turn your life over to him and become his sheep. When you give up your determination to run your own life, your ambitions that drive you toward selfish goals, and your destructive addiction, you can experience some "green pastures" and "calm water."

Nothing else on earth comes close to the sense of security you will find when you become one of the Good Shepherd's sheep. Your Shepherd is good, in the sense that he's kind to you and concerned about your well-being and success. Your Shepherd is also all-powerful. His rod and his shepherd's staff can beat off every enemy. No wonder David wasn't afraid to walk through the darkest valley. You may feel like the path out of your addiction looks like a death march through a minefield. The Good Shepherd can get you through that "dark valley." Let him comfort and protect you.

FOR YOUR NEXT **STEP 3** MEDITATION, TURN TO **PAGE 454.** ▶▶

³He gives me new strength.
　He leads me on paths that are right
　　for the good of his name.
⁴Even if I walk through a very dark
　　valley,
　I will not be afraid,
because you are with me.
　　Your rod and your shepherd's staff
　　comfort me.

⁵You prepare a meal for me
　in front of my enemies.
You pour oil of blessing on my head;
　you fill my cup to overflowing.
⁶Surely your goodness and love will be
　　with me
　all my life,
and I will live in the house of the LORD
　　forever.

PSALM 24

A psalm of David.

¹The earth belongs to the LORD, and
　　everything in it—
　the world and all its people.
²He built it on the waters
　and set it on the rivers.

³Who may go up on the mountain of
　　the LORD?
　Who may stand in his holy Temple?
⁴Only those with clean hands and pure
　　hearts,
　who have not worshiped idols,
　who have not made promises in
　　the name of a false god.
⁵They will receive a blessing from the
　　LORD;
　the God who saves them will
　　declare them right.
⁶They try to follow God;
　they look to the God of Jacob for
　　help.　　　　　　　　　　　Selah

⁷Open up, you gates.
　Open wide, you aged doors
　and the glorious King will come in.

⁸Who is this glorious King?
　The LORD, strong and mighty.
　The LORD, the powerful warrior.
⁹Open up, you gates.
　Open wide, you aged doors
　and the glorious King will come in.
¹⁰Who is this glorious King?
　The LORD All-Powerful—
　he is the glorious King.　　Selah

PSALM 25

Of David.

¹LORD, I give myself to you;
²　　my God, I trust you.
　Do not let me be disgraced;
　　do not let my enemies laugh
　　　at me.
³No one who trusts you will be
　　disgraced,
　but those who sin without excuse
　　will be disgraced.

⁴LORD, tell me your ways.
　Show me how to live.
⁵Guide me in your truth,
　and teach me, my God, my Savior.
　I trust you all day long.
⁶LORD, remember your mercy and love
　　that you have shown since long
　　　ago.
⁷Do not remember the sins
　and wrong things I did when I was
　　young.
But remember to love me always
　because you are good, LORD.

⁸The LORD is good and right;
　he points sinners to the right way.
⁹He shows those who are humble how
　　to do right,
　and he teaches them his ways.
¹⁰All the LORD's ways are loving and true
　for those who follow the demands
　　of his agreement.
¹¹For the sake of your name, LORD,
　forgive my many sins.

¹²Are there those who respect the
LORD?
   He will point them to the best way.
¹³They will enjoy a good life,
   and their children will inherit the
   land.
¹⁴The LORD tells his secrets to those
   who respect him;
   he tells them about his
   agreement.
¹⁵My eyes are always looking to the
   LORD for help.
   He will keep me from any traps.

STEP
I
¹⁶Turn to me and have mercy on me,
   because I am lonely and hurting.
¹⁷My troubles have grown larger;
   free me from my problems.
¹⁸Look at my suffering and troubles,
   and take away all my sins.
¹⁹Look at how many enemies I have!
   See how much they hate me!
²⁰Protect me and save me.
   I trust you, so do not let me be
   disgraced.
²¹My hope is in you,
   so may goodness and honesty
   guard me.
²²God, save Israel from all their troubles!

PSALM 26
Of David.

¹LORD, defend me because I have lived
   an innocent life.
   I have trusted the LORD and never
   doubted.
²LORD, try me and test me;
   look closely into my heart and
   mind.
³I see your love,
   and I live by your truth.
⁴I do not spend time with liars,
   nor do I make friends with those
   who hide their sin.
⁵I hate the company of evil people,
   and I won't sit with the wicked.

⁶I wash my hands to show I am
   innocent,
   and I come to your altar, LORD.
⁷I raise my voice in praise
   and tell of all the miracles you
   have done.
⁸LORD, I love the Temple where you
   live,
   where your glory is.
⁹Do not kill me with those sinners
   or take my life with those
   murderers.
¹⁰Evil is in their hands,
   and they do wrong for money.
¹¹But I have lived an innocent life,
   so save me and have mercy on me.
¹²I stand in a safe place.
   LORD, I praise you in the great
   meeting.

PSALM 27
Of David.

¹The LORD is my light and the one who
   saves me.
   So why should I fear anyone?
   The LORD protects my life.
   So why should I be afraid?
²Evil people may try to destroy my
   body.
   My enemies and those who hate
   me attack me,
   but they are overwhelmed and
   defeated.
³If an army surrounds me,
   I will not be afraid.
   If war breaks out,
   I will trust the LORD.

⁴I ask only one thing from the LORD.
   This is what I want:
   Let me live in the LORD's house
   all my life.
   Let me see the LORD's beauty
   and look with my own eyes at his
   Temple.

⁵During danger he will keep me safe in
    his shelter.
He will hide me in his Holy Tent,
    or he will keep me safe on a high
      mountain.
⁶My head is higher than my enemies
    around me.
I will offer joyful sacrifices in his Holy
    Tent.
I will sing and praise the LORD.

⁷LORD, hear me when I call;
    have mercy and answer me.
⁸My heart said of you, "Go, worship
    him."
So I come to worship you, LORD.
⁹Do not turn away from me.
    Do not turn your servant away in
      anger;
    you have helped me.
Do not push me away or leave me
    alone,
    God, my Savior.
¹⁰If my father and mother leave me,
    the LORD will take me in.
¹¹LORD, teach me your ways,
    and guide me to do what is right
    because I have enemies.
¹²Do not hand me over to my enemies,
    because they tell lies about me
    and say they will hurt me.

STEP 2

¹³I truly believe
    I will live to see the LORD's
      goodness.
¹⁴Wait for the LORD's help.
    Be strong and brave,
    and wait for the LORD's help.

PSALM 28
Of David.

STEP 1

¹LORD, my Rock, I call out to you for
    help.
    Do not be deaf to me.
If you are silent,
    I will be like those in the grave.

²Hear the sound of my prayer,
    when I cry out to you for help.
I raise my hands
    toward your Most Holy Place.
³Don't drag me away with the wicked,
    with those who do evil.
They say "Peace" to their neighbors,
    but evil is in their hearts.
⁴Pay them back for what they have
    done,
    for their evil deeds.
Pay them back for what they have
    done;
    give them their reward.
⁵They don't understand what the LORD
    has done
    or what he has made.
So he will knock them down
    and not lift them up.

⁶Praise the LORD,
    because he heard my prayer for
      help.
⁷The LORD is my strength and shield.
    I trust him, and he helps me.
I am very happy,
    and I praise him with my song.
⁸The LORD is powerful;
    he gives victory to his chosen one.
⁹Save your people
    and bless those who are your own.
    Be their shepherd and carry them
      forever.

STEP 3

PSALM 29
A psalm of David.

¹Praise the LORD, you angels;
    praise the LORD's glory and power.
²Praise the LORD for the glory of his
    name;
    worship the LORD because he is
      holy.

³The LORD's voice is heard over the sea.
    The glorious God thunders;
    the LORD thunders over the ocean.

⁴The LORD's voice is powerful;
     the LORD's voice is majestic.
⁵The LORD's voice breaks the trees;
     the LORD breaks the cedars of
          Lebanon.
⁶He makes the land of Lebanon dance
          like a calf
     and Mount Hermon jump like a
          baby bull.
⁷The LORD's voice makes the lightning
          flash.
⁸The LORD's voice shakes the desert;
     the LORD shakes the Desert of
          Kadesh.
⁹The LORD's voice shakes the oaks
     and strips the leaves off the trees.
In his Temple everyone says, "Glory
     to God!"

¹⁰The LORD controls the flood.
     The LORD will be King forever.
¹¹The LORD gives strength to his people;
     the LORD blesses his people with
          peace.

PSALM 30

A psalm of David. A song for giving the Temple
to the LORD.

¹I will praise you, LORD,
     because you rescued me.
     You did not let my enemies laugh
          at me.
²LORD, my God, I prayed to you,
     and you healed me.
³You lifted me out of the grave;
     you spared me from going down
          to the place of the dead.

⁴Sing praises to the LORD, you who
          belong to him;
     praise his holy name.
⁵His anger lasts only a moment,
     but his kindness lasts for a
          lifetime.
Crying may last for a night,
     but joy comes in the morning.

⁶When I felt safe, I said,
     "I will never fear."
⁷LORD, in your kindness you made my
          mountain safe.
     But when you turned away, I was
          frightened.

⁸I called to you, LORD,
     and asked you to have mercy
          on me.
⁹I said, "What good will it do if I die
     or if I go down to the grave?
Dust cannot praise you;
     it cannot speak about your truth.
¹⁰LORD, hear me and have mercy on me.
     LORD, help me."

STEP
I

¹¹You changed my sorrow into dancing.
     You took away my clothes of
          sadness,
     and clothed me in happiness.
¹²I will sing to you and not be silent.
     LORD, my God, I will praise you
          forever.

PSALM 31

For the director of music. A psalm of David.

¹LORD, I trust in you;
     let me never be disgraced.
     Save me because you do what is
          right.
²Listen to me
     and save me quickly.
Be my rock of protection,
     a strong city to save me.
³You are my rock and my protection.
     For the good of your name, lead
          me and guide me.
⁴Set me free from the trap they set for
          me,
     because you are my protection.
⁵I give you my life.
     Save me, LORD, God of truth.

⁶I hate those who worship false gods.
     I trust only in the LORD.

⁷I will be glad and rejoice in your love,
 because you saw my suffering;
 you knew my troubles.
⁸You have not handed me over to my
   enemies
 but have set me in a safe place.

STEP 1

⁹LORD, have mercy, because I am in
   misery.
 My eyes are weak from so much
   crying,
 and my whole being is tired from
   grief.
¹⁰My life is ending in sadness,
 and my years are spent in crying.
 My troubles are using up my strength,
 and my bones are getting weaker.
¹¹Because of all my troubles, my
   enemies hate me,
 and even my neighbors look down
   on me.
When my friends see me,
 they are afraid and run.
¹²I am like a piece of a broken pot.
 I am forgotten as if I were dead.
¹³I have heard many insults.
 Terror is all around me.
They make plans against me
 and want to kill me.

¹⁴LORD, I trust you.
 I have said, "You are my God."
¹⁵My life is in your hands.
 Save me from my enemies
 and from those who are
   chasing me.
¹⁶Show your kindness to me, your
   servant.
 Save me because of your love.
¹⁷LORD, I called to you,
 so do not let me be disgraced.
Let the wicked be disgraced
 and lie silent in the grave.
¹⁸With pride and hatred
 they speak against those who do
   right.
So silence their lying lips.

¹⁹How great is your goodness
 that you have stored up for those
   who fear you,
that you have given to those who
   trust you.
 You do this for all to see.
²⁰You protect them by your presence
 from what people plan against
   them.
 You shelter them from evil words.
²¹Praise the LORD.
 His love to me was wonderful
 when my city was attacked.
²²In my distress, I said,
 "God cannot see me!"
But you heard my prayer
 when I cried out to you for help.
²³Love the LORD, all you who belong to
   him.
 The LORD protects those who truly
   believe,
 but he punishes the proud as
   much as they have sinned.
²⁴All you who put your hope in the LORD
 be strong and brave.

STEP 3

STEP 1

PSALM 32

A maskil of David.

¹Happy is the person
 whose sins are forgiven,
 whose wrongs are pardoned.
²Happy is the person
 whom the LORD does not consider
   guilty
 and in whom there is nothing
   false.

STEP 7

³When I kept things to myself,
 I felt weak deep inside me.
 I moaned all day long.
⁴Day and night you punished me.
 My strength was gone as in the
   summer heat. *Selah*
⁵Then I confessed my sins to you
 and didn't hide my guilt.

STEP 5

STEP 1

We admitted we were powerless
over our dependencies—that our lives
had become unmanageable.

Psalm 31:9–10

David cried out, "My life is ending in sadness." Anyone battling a tenacious addiction has to go through a similar desperate moment when it seems like you're almost going to die. Only then can you surrender your broken life to God and really mean it.

You make a serious, though common, mistake if you equate brokenness with defeat. Brokenness is the first step toward final victory over your addiction. This is another of those recovery paradoxes—things that work the opposite way from what you expect. You have to give up in order to win!

Most people aren't the least bit interested in admitting they're powerless until it dawns on them that their addiction is wrecking their lives and their relationships with everyone around them. You may need to make a list of the losses you've suffered because of your addiction. What's it cost you at school or at work? What's it done to your health? To your family relationships? To your friendships? How far has your addiction taken you from God?

Make your list. Take a good look at it. Feel the losses at the depth of your being. Let yourself grieve like David did. That can help you achieve the kind of surrender Step 1 requires. That grief can be healthy. It helps clean the "dirt" out of your emotional wounds so they can heal fully.

FOR YOUR NEXT **STEP 1** MEDITATION, TURN TO **PAGE 412.** ▶▶

I said, "I will confess my sins to the
LORD,"
and you forgave my guilt.   *Selah*

⁶For this reason, all who obey you
should pray to you while they still
can.
When troubles rise like a flood,
they will not reach them.
⁷You are my hiding place.
You protect me from my troubles
and fill me with songs of salvation.
Selah

⁸The LORD says, "I will make you wise
and show you where to go.
I will guide you and watch over you.
⁹So don't be like a horse or donkey,
that doesn't understand.
They must be led with bits and reins,
or they will not come near you."

¹⁰Wicked people have many troubles,
but the LORD's love surrounds
those who trust him.
¹¹Good people, rejoice and be happy in
the LORD.
Sing all you whose hearts are
right.

PSALM 33

¹Sing to the LORD, you who do what is
right;
honest people should praise him.
²Praise the LORD on the harp;
make music for him on a
ten-stringed lyre.
³Sing a new song to him;
play well and joyfully.

⁴God's word is true,
and everything he does is right.
⁵He loves what is right and fair;
the LORD's love fills the earth.

⁶The sky was made at the LORD's
command.

By the breath from his mouth, he
made all the stars.
⁷He gathered the water of the sea into
a heap.
He made the great ocean stay in
its place.
⁸All the earth should worship the LORD;
the whole world should fear him.
⁹He spoke, and it happened.
He commanded, and it appeared.
¹⁰The LORD upsets the plans of nations;
he ruins all their plans.
¹¹But the LORD's plans will stand
forever;
his ideas will last from now on.
¹²Happy is the nation whose God is the
LORD,
the people he chose for his very
own.
¹³The LORD looks down from heaven
and sees every person.
¹⁴From his throne he watches
all who live on earth.
¹⁵He made their hearts
and understands everything
they do.
¹⁶No king is saved by his great army.
No warrior escapes by his great
strength.
¹⁷Horses can't bring victory;
they can't save by their strength.
¹⁸But the LORD looks after those who
fear him,
those who put their hope in his
love.
¹⁹He saves them from death
and spares their lives in times of
hunger.
²⁰So our hope is in the LORD.
He is our help, our shield to
protect us.
²¹We rejoice in him,
because we trust his holy name.
²²LORD, show your love to us
as we put our hope in you.

STEP 7

Humbly asked Him to remove our shortcomings.

Psalm 32:6–8

When you read David's psalms, you know he had total confidence in God. In this psalm, he called God his "hiding place." David trusted God so much that his heart was filled with "songs of salvation." In the same way God delivered David from his enemies, he will deliver you from your shortcomings and old behavior patterns. God will respond to your humility and faith by changing your life, repairing the damage your addiction has caused, and making you healthy and whole.

God promises: "I will make you wise and show you where to go. I will guide you and watch over you" (verse 8). He takes special, personal interest in each person who belongs to him. Get excited about his love and care for you! You will never be just a number or a computer file to God. He highly values the relationship you are developing with him. And because he does, you can dare to humble yourself before him. You can trust him to make your life over into a living example of his peace and his love.

FOR YOUR NEXT **STEP 7** MEDITATION, TURN TO **PAGE 410.** ▶▶

PSALM 34

David's song from the time he acted crazy so
Abimelech would send him away, and David did leave.

[1] I will praise the LORD at all times;
his praise is always on my lips.
[2] My whole being praises the LORD.
The poor will hear and be glad.
[3] Glorify the LORD with me,
and let us praise his name
together.

STEP 7

[4] I asked the LORD for help, and he
answered me.
He saved me from all that I feared.
[5] Those who go to him for help are
happy,
and they are never disgraced.
[6] This poor man called, and the LORD
heard him
and saved him from all his
troubles.
[7] The angel of the LORD camps around
those who fear God,
and he saves them.

[8] Examine and see how good the LORD is.
Happy is the person who trusts
him.
[9] You who belong to the LORD, fear him!
Those who fear him will have
everything they need.
[10] Even lions may get weak and hungry,
but those who look to the LORD
will have every good thing.
[11] Children, come and listen to me.
I will teach you to worship the LORD.
[12] You must do these things
to enjoy life and have many happy
days.
[13] You must not say evil things,
and you must not tell lies.
[14] Stop doing evil and do good.
Look for peace and work for it.

STEP 7

[15] The LORD sees the good people
and listens to their prayers.

[16] But the LORD is against those who do
evil;
he makes the world forget them.
[17] The LORD hears good people when
they cry out to him,
and he saves them from all their
troubles.
[18] The LORD is close to the
brokenhearted,
and he saves those whose spirits
have been crushed.

STEP I

[19] People who do what is right may have
many problems,
but the LORD will solve them all.
[20] He will protect their very bones;
not one of them will be broken.
[21] Evil will kill the wicked;
those who hate good people will
be judged guilty.
[22] But the LORD saves his servants'
lives;
no one who trusts him will be
judged guilty.

PSALM 35

Of David.

[1] LORD, battle with those who battle
with me.
Fight against those who fight
against me.
[2] Pick up the shield and armor.
Rise up and help me.
[3] Lift up your spears, both large and
small,
against those who chase me.
Tell me, "I will save you."

[4] Make those who want to kill me
be ashamed and disgraced.
Make those who plan to harm me
turn back and run away.
[5] Make them like chaff blown by the
wind
as the angel of the LORD forces
them away.

⁶Let their road be dark and slippery
  as the angel of the LORD chases
    them.
⁷For no reason they spread out their
    net to trap me;
  for no reason they dug a pit for me.
⁸So let ruin strike them suddenly.
  Let them be caught in their own
    nets;
  let them fall into the pit and die.
⁹Then I will rejoice in the LORD;
  I will be happy when he saves me.
¹⁰Even my bones will say,
  "LORD, who is like you?
You save the weak from the strong,
  the weak and poor from robbers."

¹¹Men without mercy stand up to testify.
  They ask me things I do not know.
¹²They repay me with evil for the good I
    have done,
  and they make me very sad.
¹³Yet when they were sick, I put on
    clothes of sadness
  and showed my sorrow by fasting.
But my prayers were not answered.
¹⁴ I acted as if they were my friends
    or brothers.
I bowed in sadness as if I were crying
    for my mother.
¹⁵But when I was in trouble, they
    gathered and laughed;
  they gathered to attack before I
    knew it.
  They insulted me without
    stopping.
¹⁶They made fun of me and were cruel
    to me
  and ground their teeth at me in
    anger.

¹⁷Lord, how long will you watch this
    happen?
  Save my life from their attacks;
  save me from these people who
    are like lions.

¹⁸I will praise you in the great meeting.
  I will praise you among crowds of
    people.
¹⁹Do not let my enemies laugh at me;
  they hate me for no reason.
Do not let them make fun of me;
  they have no cause to hate me.
²⁰Their words are not friendly
  but are lies about peace-loving
    people.
²¹They speak against me
  and say, "Aha! We saw what you
    did!"

²²LORD, you have been watching. Do not
    keep quiet.
  Lord, do not leave me alone.
²³Wake up! Come and defend me!
  My God and Lord, fight for me!
²⁴LORD my God, defend me with your
    justice.
  Don't let them laugh at me.
²⁵Don't let them think, "Aha! We got
    what we wanted!"
  Don't let them say, "We destroyed
    him."
²⁶Let them be ashamed and
    embarrassed,
  because they were happy when I
    hurt.
Cover them with shame and disgrace,
  because they thought they were
    better than I was.
²⁷May my friends sing and shout for joy.
  May they always say, "Praise the
    greatness of the LORD,
  who loves to see his servants do
    well."
²⁸I will tell of your goodness
  and will praise you every day.

PSALM 36

For the director of music. Of David, the servant
of the LORD.

¹Sin speaks to the wicked in their
    hearts.
  They have no fear of God.

²They think too much of themselves
    so they don't see their sin and
        hate it.
³Their words are wicked lies;
    they are no longer wise or good.
⁴At night they make evil plans;
    what they do leads to nothing
        good.
    They don't refuse things that are
        evil.

⁵LORD, your love reaches to the heavens,
    your loyalty to the skies.
⁶Your goodness is as high as the
        mountains.
    Your justice is as deep as the great
        ocean.
LORD, you protect both people and
    animals.
⁷God, your love is so precious!
    You protect people in the shadow
        of your wings.
⁸They eat the rich food in your house,
    and you let them drink from your
        river of pleasure.
⁹You are the giver of life.
    Your light lets us enjoy life.

¹⁰Continue to love those who know you
    and to do good to those who are
        good.
¹¹Don't let proud people attack me
    and the wicked force me away.
¹²Those who do evil have been
        defeated.
    They are overwhelmed;
    they cannot do evil any longer.

PSALM 37
Of David.

¹Don't be upset because of evil
    people.
    Don't be jealous of those who do
        wrong,
²because like the grass, they will soon
    dry up.

Like green plants, they will soon
    die away.
³Trust the LORD and do good.
    Live in the land and feed on truth.
⁴Enjoy serving the LORD,
    and he will give you what you
        want.
⁵Depend on the LORD;
    trust him, and he will take care of
        you.
⁶Then your goodness will shine like the
        sun,
    and your fairness like the noonday
        sun.

STEP 7

⁷Wait and trust the LORD.
    Don't be upset when others get
        rich
    or when someone else's plans
        succeed.
⁸Don't get angry.
    Don't be upset; it only leads to
        trouble.
⁹Evil people will be sent away,
    but those who trust the LORD will
        inherit the land.
¹⁰In a little while the wicked will be no
        more.
    You may look for them, but they
        will be gone.
¹¹People who are not proud will inherit
    the land
    and will enjoy complete peace.

¹²The wicked make evil plans against
    good people.
    They grind their teeth at them in
        anger.
¹³But the Lord laughs at the wicked,
    because he sees that their day is
        coming.
¹⁴The wicked draw their swords
    and bend their bows
    to kill the poor and helpless,
        to kill those who are honest.

¹⁵But their swords will stab their own
hearts,
and their bows will break.

¹⁶It is better to have little and be right
than to have much and be wrong.
¹⁷The power of the wicked will be
broken,
but the Lord supports those who
do right.
¹⁸The Lord watches over the lives of
the innocent,
and their reward will last forever.
¹⁹They will not be ashamed when
trouble comes.
They will be full in times of hunger.
²⁰But the wicked will die.
The Lord's enemies will be like
the flowers of the fields;
they will disappear like smoke.
²¹The wicked borrow and don't pay
back,
but those who do right give freely
to others.
²²Those whom the Lord blesses will
inherit the land,
but those he curses will be sent
away.

STEP
7
²³When people's steps follow the Lord,
God is pleased with their ways.
²⁴If they stumble, they will not fall,
because the Lord holds their
hand.

²⁵I was young, and now I am old,
but I have never seen good people
left helpless
or their children begging for food.
²⁶Good people always lend freely to
others,
and their children are a blessing.

²⁷Stop doing evil and do good,
so you will live forever.
²⁸The Lord loves justice
and will not leave those who
worship him.

He will always protect them,
but the children of the wicked will
die.
²⁹Good people will inherit the land
and will live in it forever.

³⁰Good people speak with wisdom,
and they say what is fair.
³¹The teachings of their God are in their
heart,
so they do not fail to keep them.
³²The wicked watch for good people
so that they may kill them.
³³But the Lord will not take away his
protection
or let good people be judged
guilty.

³⁴Wait for the Lord's help
and follow him.
He will honor you and give you the
land,
and you will see the wicked sent
away.

³⁵I saw a wicked and cruel man
who looked strong like a healthy
tree in good soil.
³⁶But he died and was gone;
I looked for him, but he couldn't
be found.

³⁷Think of the innocent person,
and watch the honest one.
The man who has peace
will have children to live
after him.
³⁸But sinners will be destroyed;
in the end the wicked will die.

³⁹The Lord saves good people;
he is their strength in times of
trouble.
⁴⁰The Lord helps them and saves them;
he saves them from the wicked,
because they trust in him for
protection.

STEP 7

Humbly asked Him to remove our shortcomings.

Psalm 37:23-24

David said, "When people's steps follow the LORD, God is pleased with their ways" (verse 23). We say something similar when we pray the recovery prayer "Let go, and let God." How orderly and successful our steps turn out depends on how willing we are to surrender humbly to God's guidance.

You may find the most serious challenge you face in day-to-day recovery will be putting aside your long-established patterns of relying on relationships and addictive behavior to function as gods in your life. These are destructive patterns, but they're familiar to you. Each day you have to choose who will be your Lord. You must choose whether your old addiction will direct your life or whether God will direct you.

Seek God's guidance with a humble heart. Then you will find him weeding out your most damaging shortcomings. At the same time you'll find him guiding you. "If [you] stumble, [you] will not fall, because the LORD holds [your] hand" (verse 24).

SEE **PAGE 52** OF THE INTRODUCTORY MATERIAL FOR **STEP 8.**

PSALM 38

A psalm of David to remember.

STEP 1

¹LORD, don't correct me when you are angry.
Don't punish me when you are furious.
²Your arrows have wounded me,
and your hand has come down on me.
³My body is sick from your punishment.
Even my bones are not healthy because of my sin.
⁴My guilt has overwhelmed me;
like a load it weighs me down.

⁵My sores stink and become infected because I was foolish.
⁶I am bent over and bowed down;
I am sad all day long.
⁷I am burning with fever,
and my whole body is sore.
⁸I am weak and faint.
I moan from the pain I feel.

⁹Lord, you know everything I want;
my cries are not hidden from you.
¹⁰My heart pounds, and my strength is gone.
I am losing my sight.
¹¹Because of my wounds, my friends and neighbors avoid me,
and my relatives stay far away.
¹²Some people set traps to kill me.
Those who want to hurt me plan trouble;
all day long they think up lies.

¹³I am like the deaf; I cannot hear.
Like the mute, I cannot speak.
¹⁴I am like those who do not hear,
who have no answer to give.
¹⁵I trust you, LORD.
You will answer, my Lord and God.
¹⁶I said, "Don't let them laugh at me
or brag when I am defeated."

¹⁷I am about to die,
and I cannot forget my pain.

STEP 5

¹⁸I confess my guilt;
I am troubled by my sin.
¹⁹My enemies are strong and healthy,
and many hate me for no reason.
²⁰They repay me with evil for the good I did.
They lie about me because I try to do good.

²¹LORD, don't leave me;
my God, don't go away.
²²Quickly come and help me,
my Lord and Savior.

PSALM 39

For the director of music. For Jeduthun.
A psalm of David.

¹I said, "I will be careful how I act
and will not sin by what I say.
I will be careful what I say
around wicked people."
²So I kept very quiet.
I didn't even say anything good,
but I became even more upset.
³I became very angry inside,
and as I thought about it, my anger burned.
So I spoke:

⁴"LORD, tell me when the end will come
and how long I will live.
Let me know how long I have.

STEP 1

⁵You have given me only a short life;
my lifetime is like nothing to you.
Everyone's life is only a breath.

Selah

⁶People are like shadows moving about.
All their work is for nothing;
they collect things but don't know who will get them.

⁷"So, Lord, what hope do I have?
You are my hope.

STEP 7

STEP 1

We admitted we were powerless
over our dependencies—that our lives
had become unmanageable.

Psalm 38:1-9

The Bible calls David "the kind of man [the LORD] wants" (see 1 Samuel 13:14; Acts 13:22). You might think a guy with that reputation would live a life of peace and contentment. The fact is that David's life was characterized by conflict and tough times. In Psalm 38, David shared about a time in his life when he had to go back to Square One. He mourned about how unmanageable everything had become. He had stopped letting God control his life. As a result, he admitted, he had become "foolish" (verse 5) and "weigh[ed] down" by his bad choices (verse 4). Finally, David admitted that his behavior was causing him a bunch of physical and emotional pain. In verse 8, he complained, "I am weak and faint." In spite of all that, surrender to God did not come easily. He still moaned from the pain he felt (verse 8).

It's sad but true that letting go of the things that cause us misery is one of the hardest parts of beating an addiction. But with David we can say to God, "My cries are not hidden from you" (verse 9). God knows our struggles and will give us the power to look to him for help.

FOR YOUR NEXT **STEP 1** MEDITATION, TURN TO **PAGE 417.** ▶▶

⁸Save me from all my sins.
    Don't let wicked fools make fun
        of me.
⁹I am quiet; I do not open my mouth,
    because you are the one who has
        done this.
¹⁰Quit punishing me;
    your beating is about to kill me.
¹¹You correct and punish people for
        their sins;
    like a moth, you destroy what they
        love.
    Everyone's life is only a breath.

Selah

¹²"LORD, hear my prayer,
    and listen to my cry.
    Do not ignore my tears.
I am like a visitor with you.
    Like my ancestors, I'm only here a
        short time.
¹³Leave me alone so I can be happy
    before I leave and am no more."

PSALM 40

For the director of music. A psalm of David.

STEP 12

¹I waited patiently for the LORD.
    He turned to me and heard my
        cry.
²He lifted me out of the pit of
        destruction,
    out of the sticky mud.
    He stood me on a rock
        and made my feet steady.
³He put a new song in my mouth,
    a song of praise to our God.
Many people will see this and worship
        him.
    Then they will trust the LORD.

⁴Happy is the person
    who trusts the LORD,
who doesn't turn to those who are
        proud
    or to those who worship false
        gods.

⁵LORD my God, you have done many
        miracles.
    Your plans for us are many.
If I tried to tell them all,
    there would be too many to count.

⁶You do not want sacrifices and
        offerings.
    But you have made a hole in my
        ear
    to show that my body and life are
        yours.
You do not ask for burnt offerings
    and sacrifices to take away sins.
⁷Then I said, "Look, I have come.
    It is written about me in the book.
⁸My God, I want to do what you want.
    Your teachings are in my heart."

⁹I will tell about your goodness in the
        great meeting of your
        people.
    LORD, you know my lips are not
        silent.
¹⁰I do not hide your goodness in my
        heart;
    I speak about your loyalty and
        salvation.
I do not hide your love and truth
    from the people in the great
        meeting.

¹¹LORD, do not hold back your mercy
        from me;
    let your love and truth always
        protect me.
¹²Troubles have surrounded me;
    there are too many to count.
My sins have caught me
    so that I cannot see a way to
        escape.
I have more sins than hairs on my
        head,
    and I have lost my courage.
¹³Please, LORD, save me.
    Hurry, LORD, to help me.

STEP 5

413

¹⁴People are trying to kill me.
>Shame them and disgrace them.

People want to hurt me.
>Let them run away in disgrace.

¹⁵People are making fun of me.
>Let them be shamed into silence.

¹⁶But let those who follow you
>be happy and glad.

They love you for saving them.
>May they always say, "Praise the
>LORD!"

STEP 1

¹⁷Lord, because I am poor and helpless,
>please remember me.

You are my helper and savior.
>My God, do not wait.

PSALM 41

For the director of music. A psalm of David.

¹Happy are those who think about the
>poor.

>When trouble comes, the LORD will
>save them.

²The LORD will protect them and spare
>their life

>and will bless them in the land.

>He will not let their enemies take
>them.

³The LORD will give them strength
>when they are sick,

>and he will make them well again.

STEP 5

⁴I said, "LORD, have mercy on me.
>Heal me, because I have sinned
>against you."

⁵My enemies are saying evil things
>about me.

>They say, "When will he die and be
>forgotten?"

⁶Some people come to see me,
>but they lie.

They just come to get bad news.
>Then they go and gossip.

⁷All my enemies whisper about me
>and think the worst about me.

⁸They say, "He has a terrible disease.

He will never get out of bed
>again."

⁹My best and truest friend, who ate at
>my table,

>has even turned against me.

¹⁰LORD, have mercy on me.
>Give me strength so I can pay
>them back.

¹¹Because my enemies do not defeat
>me,

>I know you are pleased with me.

¹²Because I am innocent, you
>support me

>and will let me be with you
>forever.

¹³Praise the LORD, the God of Israel.
>He has always been,

>and he will always be.
>Amen and amen.

Book 2

PSALM 42

For the director of music. A maskil of the sons
of Korah.

¹As a deer thirsts for streams of
>water,

>so I thirst for you, God.

²I thirst for the living God.
>When can I go to meet with him?

³Day and night, my tears have been
>my food.

People are always saying,
>"Where is your God?"

⁴When I remember these things,
>I speak with a broken heart.

I used to walk with the crowd
>and lead them to God's Temple
>with songs of praise.

⁵Why am I so sad?
>Why am I so upset?

I should put my hope in God
>and keep praising him,

STEP 1

my Savior and ⁶my God.

I am very sad.
So I remember you where the
Jordan River begins,
near the peaks of Hermon and Mount
Mizar.
⁷Troubles have come again and again,
sounding like waterfalls.
Your waves are crashing all
around me.
⁸The LORD shows his true love every
day.
At night I have a song,
and I pray to my living God.

⁹I say to God, my Rock,
"Why have you forgotten me?
Why am I sad
and troubled by my enemies?"
¹⁰My enemies' insults make me feel
as if my bones were broken.
They are always saying,
"Where is your God?"

¹¹Why am I so sad?
Why am I so upset?
I should put my hope in God
and keep praising him,
my Savior and my God.

PSALM 43

¹God, defend me.
Argue my case against those who
don't follow you.
Save me from liars and those who
do evil.
²God, you are my strength.
Why have you rejected me?
Why am I sad
and troubled by my enemies?
³Send me your light and truth
to guide me.
Let them lead me to your holy
mountain,
to where you live.
⁴Then I will go to the altar of God,
to God who is my joy and
happiness.

I will praise you with a harp,
God, my God.

⁵Why am I so sad?
Why am I so upset?
I should put my hope in God
and keep praising him,
my Savior and my God.

PSALM 44

For the director of music. A maskil of the sons
of Korah.

¹God, we have heard about you.
Our ancestors told us
what you did in their days,
in days long ago.
²With your power you forced the
nations out of the land
and placed our ancestors here.
You destroyed those other nations,
but you made our ancestors grow
strong.
³It wasn't their swords that took the
land.
It wasn't their power that gave
them victory.
But it was your great power and
strength.
You were with them because you
loved them.

⁴My God, you are my King.
Your commands led Jacob's people
to victory.
⁵With your help we pushed back our
enemies.
In your name we trampled those
who came against us.
⁶I don't trust my bow to help me,
and my sword can't save me.
⁷You saved us from our foes,
and you made our enemies
ashamed.
⁸We will praise God every day;
we will praise your name forever.
Selah

⁹But you have rejected us and
            shamed us.
      You don't march with our armies
            anymore.
¹⁰You let our enemies push us back,
      and those who hate us have taken
            our wealth.
¹¹You gave us away like sheep to be
            eaten
      and have scattered us among the
            nations.
¹²You sold your people for nothing
      and made no profit on the sale.

¹³You made us a joke to our neighbors;
      those around us laugh and make
            fun of us.
¹⁴You made us a joke to the other
            nations;
      people shake their heads.

STEP
1

¹⁵I am always in disgrace,
      and I am covered with shame.
¹⁶My enemy is getting even
      with insults and curses.

¹⁷All these things have happened to us,
      but we have not forgotten you
      or failed to keep our agreement
            with you.
¹⁸Our hearts haven't turned away from
            you,
      and we haven't stopped following
            you.
¹⁹But you crushed us in this place
            where wild dogs live,
      and you covered us with deep
            darkness.

²⁰If we had forgotten our God
      or lifted our hands in prayer to
            foreign gods,
²¹God would have known,
      because he knows what is in our
            hearts.
²²But for you we are in danger of death
      all the time.

People think we are worth no
      more than sheep to be
      killed.

²³Wake up, Lord! Why are you sleeping?
      Get up! Don't reject us forever.
²⁴Why do you hide from us?
      Have you forgotten our pain and
            troubles?

²⁵We have been pushed down into the
            dirt;
      we are flat on the ground.
²⁶Get up and help us.
      Because of your love, save us.

PSALM 45

For the director of music. To the tune of "Lilies."
A maskil. A love song of the sons of Korah.

¹Beautiful words fill my mind.
      I am speaking of royal things.
      My tongue is like the pen of a
            skilled writer.

²You are more handsome than anyone,
      and you are an excellent speaker,
      so God has blessed you forever.
³Put on your sword, powerful warrior.
      Show your glory and majesty.
⁴In your majesty win the victory
      for what is true and right.
      Your power will do amazing things.
⁵Your sharp arrows will enter
      the hearts of the king's enemies.
      Nations will be defeated before
            you.
⁶God, your throne will last forever and
            ever.
      You will rule your kingdom with
            fairness.
⁷You love right and hate evil,
      so God has chosen you from
            among your friends;
      he has set you apart with much
            joy.
⁸Your clothes smell like myrrh, aloes,
      and cassia.

STEP 1

We admitted we were powerless
over our dependencies—that our lives
had become unmanageable.

Psalm 44:15–16

Shame is one of the most crippling emotions you can feel. Modern medical research into addiction reports that people are driven to try to escape from a profound sense of shame and inadequacy. Thousands of years ago, a psalmist said much the same thing when he lamented that he was "covered with shame" (verse 15).

How is it that shame can cling to you like a dense fog and absolutely paralyze your efforts to be happy? Maybe you feel shame because you're a long way from God. Maybe your shame results from your inability to pull in the reins on your addiction. You might be ashamed of how much pain you've caused people around you because of the way you've been living. You might even be lugging around a load of false shame because you think it's your fault that someone abused you.

Step 1 says it's time to turn a corner. If you don't, your guilt and shame will force you back into addictive behavior. You need to give the whole out-of-control mess to God and count on his grace to fix things. The choice is yours.

FOR YOUR NEXT **STEP 1** MEDITATION, TURN TO **PAGE 436.** ▶▶

From palaces of ivory
music comes to make you happy.
⁹Kings' daughters are among your
honored women.
Your bride stands at your right side
wearing gold from Ophir.

¹⁰Listen to me, daughter; look and pay
attention.
Forget your people and your
father's family.
¹¹The king loves your beauty.
Because he is your master, you
should obey him.
¹²People from the city of Tyre have
brought a gift.
Wealthy people will want to meet
you.

¹³The princess is very beautiful.
Her gown is woven with gold.
¹⁴In her beautiful clothes she is brought
to the king.
Her bridesmaids follow behind her,
and they are also brought to him.
¹⁵They come with happiness and joy;
they enter the king's palace.

¹⁶You will have sons to replace your
fathers.
You will make them rulers through
all the land.
¹⁷I will make your name famous from
now on,
so people will praise you forever
and ever.

PSALM 46

For the director of music. By alamoth. A psalm
of the sons of Korah.

STEP 2

¹God is our protection and our
strength.
He always helps in times of
trouble.
²So we will not be afraid even if the
earth shakes,
or the mountains fall into the sea,

³even if the oceans roar and foam,
or the mountains shake at the
raging sea.   *Selah*

⁴There is a river that brings joy to the
city of God,
the holy place where God Most
High lives.
⁵God is in that city, and so it will not be
shaken.
God will help her at dawn.
⁶Nations tremble and kingdoms shake.
God shouts and the earth
crumbles.

⁷The Lord All-Powerful is with us;
the God of Jacob is our defender.
Selah

⁸Come and see what the Lord has done,
the amazing things he has done
on the earth.
⁹He stops wars everywhere on the
earth.
He breaks all bows and spears
and burns up the chariots with
fire.
¹⁰God says, "Be still and know that I am
God.
I will be praised in all the nations;
I will be praised throughout the
earth."

¹¹The Lord All-Powerful is with us;
the God of Jacob is our defender.
Selah

PSALM 47

For the director of music. A psalm
of the sons of Korah.

¹Clap your hands, all you people.
Shout to God with joy.
²The Lord Most High is wonderful.
He is the great King over all the
earth!
³He defeated nations for us
and put them under our control.

⁴He chose the land we would inherit.
    We are the children of Jacob,
        whom he loved.   *Selah*

⁵God has risen with a shout of joy;
    the LORD has risen as the trumpets
        sounded.
⁶Sing praises to God. Sing praises.
    Sing praises to our King. Sing
        praises.
⁷God is King of all the earth,
    so sing a song of praise to him.
⁸God is King over the nations.
    God sits on his holy throne.
⁹The leaders of the nations meet
    with the people of the God of
        Abraham,
because the leaders of the earth
        belong to God.
    He is supreme.

PSALM 48
A psalm of the sons of Korah.

¹The LORD is great; he should be praised
    in the city of our God, on his holy
        mountain.
²It is high and beautiful
    and brings joy to the whole world.
Mount Zion is like the high mountains
        of the north;
    it is the city of the Great King.
³God is within its palaces;
    he is known as its defender.
⁴Kings joined together
    and came to attack the city.
⁵But when they saw it, they were
        amazed.
    They ran away in fear.
⁶Fear took hold of them;
    they hurt like a woman having a
        baby.
⁷You destroyed the large trading ships
    with an east wind.

⁸First we heard
    and now we have seen

that God will always keep his city
        safe.
    It is the city of the LORD
        All-Powerful,
    the city of our God.   *Selah*

⁹God, we come into your Temple
    to think about your love.
¹⁰God, your name is known everywhere;
    all over the earth people praise you.
    Your right hand is full of goodness.
¹¹Mount Zion is happy
    and all the towns of Judah rejoice,
because your decisions are fair.

¹²Walk around Jerusalem
    and count its towers.
¹³Notice how strong they are.
    Look at the palaces.
    Then you can tell your children
        about them.
¹⁴This God is our God forever and ever.
    He will guide us from now on.

PSALM 49
For the director of music. A psalm
of the sons of Korah.

¹Listen to this, all you nations;
    listen, all you who live on earth.
²Listen, both great and small,
    rich and poor together.
³What I say is wise,
    and my heart speaks with
        understanding.
⁴I will pay attention to a wise saying;
    I will explain my riddle on the
        harp.

⁵Why should I be afraid of bad days?
    Why should I fear when evil people
        surround me?
⁶They trust in their money
    and brag about their riches.
⁷No one can buy back the life of
        another.
    No one can pay God for his own
        life,

⁸because the price of a life is high.
No payment is ever enough.
⁹Do people live forever?
Don't they all face death?

¹⁰See, even wise people die.
Fools and stupid people also die
and leave their wealth to others.
¹¹Their graves will always be their
homes.
They will live there from now on,
even though they named places
after themselves.
¹²Even rich people do not live forever;
like the animals, people die.

¹³This is what will happen to those who
trust in themselves
and to their followers who believe
them.   *Selah*
¹⁴Like sheep, they must die,
and death will be their shepherd.
Honest people will rule over them in
the morning,
and their bodies will rot in a grave
far from home.
¹⁵But God will save my life
and will take me from the grave.
Selah

¹⁶Don't be afraid of rich people
because their houses are more
beautiful.
¹⁷They don't take anything to the
grave;
their wealth won't go down with
them.
¹⁸Even though they were praised when
they were alive—
and people may praise you when
you succeed—
¹⁹they will go to where their ancestors
are.
They will never see light again.
²⁰Rich people with no understanding
are just like animals that die.

PSALM 50

A psalm of Asaph.

¹The God of gods, the LORD, speaks.
He calls the earth from the rising
to the setting sun.
²God shines from Jerusalem,
whose beauty is perfect.
³Our God comes, and he will not be
silent.
A fire burns in front of him,
and a powerful storm surrounds
him.
⁴He calls to the sky above and to the
earth
that he might judge his people.
⁵He says, "Gather around, you who
worship me,
who have made an agreement
with me, using a sacrifice."
⁶God is the judge,
and even the skies say he is right.
Selah

⁷God says, "My people, listen to me;
Israel, I will testify against you.
I am God, your God.
⁸I do not scold you for your sacrifices.
You always bring me your burnt
offerings.
⁹But I do not need bulls from your stalls
or goats from your pens,
¹⁰because every animal of the forest is
already mine.
The cattle on a thousand hills are
mine.
¹¹I know every bird on the mountains,
and every living thing in the fields
is mine.
¹²If I were hungry, I would not tell you,
because the earth and everything
in it are mine.
¹³I don't eat the meat of bulls
or drink the blood of goats.
¹⁴Give an offering to show thanks to
God.

STEP
11

420

Give God Most High what you
have promised.
¹⁵Call to me in times of trouble.
I will save you, and you will
honor me."

¹⁶But God says to the wicked,
"Why do you talk about my laws?
Why do you mention my
agreement?
¹⁷You hate my teachings
and turn your back on what I say.
¹⁸When you see a thief, you join him.
You take part in adultery.
¹⁹You don't stop your mouth from
speaking evil,
and your tongue makes up lies.
²⁰You speak against your brother
and lie about your mother's son.
²¹I have kept quiet while you did these
things,
so you thought I was just like you.
But I will scold you
and accuse you to your face.

²²"Think about this, you who forget
God.
Otherwise, I will tear you apart,
and no one will save you.
²³Those people honor me
who bring me offerings to show
thanks.
And I, God, will save those who do
that."

PSALM 51

For the director of music. A psalm of David
when the prophet Nathan came to David
after David's sin with Bathsheba.

STEP 7

¹God, be merciful to me
because you are loving.
Because you are always ready to be
merciful,
wipe out all my wrongs.
²Wash away all my guilt
and make me clean again.

STEP 5

³I know about my wrongs,
and I can't forget my sin.
⁴You are the only one I have sinned
against;
I have done what you say is wrong.
You are right when you speak
and fair when you judge.
⁵I was brought into this world in sin.
In sin my mother gave birth to me.

⁶You want me to be completely
truthful,
so teach me wisdom.
⁷Take away my sin, and I will be clean.
Wash me, and I will be whiter than
snow.
⁸Make me hear sounds of joy and
gladness;
let the bones you crushed be
happy again.
⁹Turn your face from my sins
and wipe out all my guilt.

STEP 7

¹⁰Create in me a pure heart, God,
and make my spirit right again.
¹¹Do not send me away from you
or take your Holy Spirit away
from me.
¹²Give me back the joy of your
salvation.
Keep me strong by giving me a
willing spirit.
¹³Then I will teach your ways to those
who do wrong,
and sinners will turn back to you.

STEP 9

¹⁴God, save me from the guilt of
murder,
God of my salvation,
and I will sing about your
goodness.
¹⁵Lord, let me speak
so I may praise you.
¹⁶You are not pleased by sacrifices, or I
would give them.
You don't want burnt offerings.

STEP 9

Made direct amends to such people
wherever possible, except when to
do so would injure them or others.

Psalm 51:14–17

David grew up as both a simple shepherd and a skilled musician.
But God had bigger plans for him and made him king of Israel.
There were several things about David that God liked. One of them
was his willingness to humble himself before God and others and
to admit when he was wrong. That kind of humility is an attitude
God will keep building in you all the way through your recovery
program. It certainly is a key component for the successful
completion of Step 9.

David said he was "broken and sorry for sin" (verse 17). That's the
attitude you need as you work through this step. When his sorrow
for sin was complete, David asked God, "Let me speak" (verse 15).
God will bring you to the point where there is a new power and a
new graciousness about your life that will let you correct past
wrongs and learn healthy new ways of relating to the people
around you.

Turn to God and let him make you willing to make amends. He will
release you from the power of old resentments that keep you a
prisoner of your past.

FOR YOUR NEXT **STEP 9** MEDITATION, TURN TO **PAGE 520.** ▶▶

¹⁷The sacrifice God wants is a broken
spirit.
God, you will not reject a heart
that is broken and sorry for
sin.

¹⁸Do whatever good you wish for
Jerusalem.
Rebuild the walls of Jerusalem.
¹⁹Then you will be pleased with right
sacrifices and whole burnt
offerings,
and bulls will be offered on your
altar.

PSALM 52

For the director of music. A maskil of David. When
Doeg the Edomite came to Saul and said to him,
"David is in Ahimelech's house."

¹Mighty warrior, why do you brag
about the evil you do?
God's love will continue forever.
²You think up evil plans.
Your tongue is like a sharp razor,
making up lies.
³You love wrong more than right
and lies more than truth.   *Selah*
⁴You love words that bite
and tongues that lie.

⁵But God will ruin you forever.
He will grab you and throw you
out of your tent;
he will tear you away from the
land of the living.   *Selah*
⁶Those who do right will see this and
fear God.
They will laugh at you and say,
⁷"Look what happened to the man
who did not depend on God
but depended on his money.
He grew strong by his evil plans."

⁸But I am like an olive tree
growing in God's Temple.
I trust God's love
forever and ever.

⁹God, I will thank you forever for what
you have done.
With those who worship you, I will
trust you because you are
good.

PSALM 53

For the director of music. By mahalath.
A maskil of David.

¹Fools say to themselves,
"There is no God."
Fools are evil and do terrible
things;
none of them does anything
good.

²God looked down from heaven on all
people
to see if anyone was wise,
if anyone was looking to God for
help.
³But all have turned away.
Together, everyone has become
evil;
none of them does anything
good.
Not a single person.

⁴Don't the wicked understand?
They destroy my people as if they
were eating bread.
They do not ask God for help.
⁵The wicked are filled with terror
where there had been nothing to
fear.
God will scatter the bones of your
enemies.
You will defeat them,
because God has rejected them.

⁶I pray that victory will come to Israel
from Mount Zion!
May God bring them back.
Then the people of Jacob will
rejoice,
and the people of Israel will be
glad.

PSALM 54

For the director of music. With stringed instruments.
A maskil of David when the Ziphites went to Saul and
said, "We think David is hiding among our people."

¹God, save me because of who you
are.
By your strength show that I am
innocent.
²Hear my prayer, God;
listen to what I say.
³Strangers turn against me,
and cruel people want to kill me.
They do not care about God. *Selah*

⁴See, God will help me;
the Lord will support me.
⁵Let my enemies be punished with
their own evil.
Destroy them because you are
loyal to me.

⁶I will offer a sacrifice as a special gift
to you.
I will thank you, LORD, because you
are good.
⁷You have saved me from all my
troubles,
and I have seen my enemies
defeated.

PSALM 55

For the director of music. With stringed instruments.
A maskil of David.

¹God, listen to my prayer
and do not ignore my cry for help.
²Pay attention to me and answer me.
I am troubled and upset
³by what the enemy says
and how the wicked look at me.
They bring troubles down on me,
and in anger they attack me.

STEP 1

⁴I am frightened inside;
the terror of death has
attacked me.
⁵I am scared and shaking,
and terror grips me.

⁶I said, "I wish I had wings like a dove.
Then I would fly away and rest.
⁷I would wander far away
and stay in the desert.   *Selah*
⁸I would hurry to my place of escape,
far away from the wind and
storm."

⁹Lord, destroy and confuse their
words,
because I see violence and
fighting in the city.
¹⁰Day and night they are all around its
walls,
and evil and trouble are
everywhere inside.
¹¹Destruction is everywhere in the city;
trouble and lying never leave its
streets.

¹²It was not an enemy insulting me.
I could stand that.
It was not someone who hated me.
I could hide from him.
¹³But it is you, a person like me,
my companion and good friend.
¹⁴We had a good friendship
and walked together to God's
Temple.

¹⁵Let death take away my enemies.
Let them die while they are still
young
because evil lives with them.
¹⁶But I will call to God for help,
and the LORD will save me.
¹⁷Morning, noon, and night I am
troubled and upset,
but he will listen to me.
¹⁸Many are against me,
but he keeps me safe in battle.
¹⁹God who lives forever
will hear me and punish them.
Selah

But they will not change;
they do not fear God.

²⁰The one who was my friend attacks
his friends
and breaks his promises.
²¹His words are slippery like butter,
but war is in his heart.
His words are smoother than oil,
but they cut like knives.

STEP 11

²²Give your worries to the LORD,
and he will take care of you.
He will never let good people
down.
²³But, God, you will bring down
the wicked to the grave.
Murderers and liars will live
only half a lifetime.
But I will trust in you.

PSALM 56

For the director of music. To the tune of "The Dove
in the Distant Oak." A miktam of David when the
Philistines captured him in Gath.

¹God, be merciful to me because
people are chasing me;
the battle has pressed me all day
long.
²My enemies have chased me all day;
there are many proud people
fighting me.

STEP 3

³When I am afraid,
I will trust you.
⁴I praise God for his word.
I trust God, so I am not afraid.
What can human beings do to me?

⁵All day long they twist my words;
all their evil plans are against me.
⁶They wait. They hide.
They watch my steps,
hoping to kill me.
⁷God, do not let them escape;
punish the foreign nations in your
anger.
⁸You have recorded my troubles.
You have kept a list of my tears.
Aren't they in your records?

⁹On the day I call for help, my enemies
will be defeated.
I know that God is on my side.
¹⁰I praise God for his word to me;
I praise the LORD for his word.
¹¹I trust in God. I will not be afraid.
What can people do to me?

¹²God, I must keep my promises to you.
I will give you my offerings to
thank you,
¹³because you have saved me from
death.
You have kept me from being
defeated.
So I will walk with God
in light among the living.

PSALM 57

For the director of music. To the tune of "Do Not
Destroy." A miktam of David when he escaped
from Saul in the cave.

¹Be merciful to me, God; be merciful to
me
because I come to you for
protection.
Let me hide under the shadow of
your wings
until the trouble has passed.

²I cry out to God Most High,
to the God who does everything
for me.
³He sends help from heaven and
saves me.
He punishes those who chase me.
                                                    Selah
God sends me his love and truth.

⁴Enemies, like lions, are all around me;
I must lie down among them.
Their teeth are like spears and
arrows,
their tongues as sharp as swords.

⁵God is supreme over the skies;
his majesty covers the earth.

⁶They set a trap for me.
  I am very worried.
 They dug a pit in my path,
  but they fell into it themselves.
                                          Selah

⁷My heart is steady, God; my heart is
    steady.
  I will sing and praise you.
⁸Wake up, my soul.
  Wake up, harp and lyre!
  I will wake up the dawn.
⁹Lord, I will praise you among the
    nations;
  I will sing songs of praise about
    you to all the nations.
¹⁰Your great love reaches to the skies,
  your truth to the clouds.
¹¹God, you are supreme above the
    skies.
  Let your glory be over all the
    earth.

⁷Let them disappear like water that
    flows away.
  Let them be cut short like a
    broken arrow.
⁸Let them be like snails that melt as
    they move.
  Let them be like a child born
    dead who never saw
    the sun.
⁹His anger will blow them away alive
    faster than burning thorns can
    heat a pot.
¹⁰Good people will be glad when they
    see him get even.
  They will wash their feet in the
    blood of the wicked.
¹¹Then people will say,
  "There really are rewards for
    doing what is right.
  There really is a God who judges
    the world."

PSALM 58

For the director of music. To the tune of "Do Not
Destroy." A miktam of David.

¹Do you rulers really say what is right?
  Do you judge people fairly?
²No, in your heart you plan evil;
  you think up violent crimes in the
    land.
³From birth, evil people turn away
    from God;
  they wander off and tell lies as
    soon as they are born.
⁴They are like poisonous snakes,
  like deaf cobras that stop up their
    ears
⁵so they cannot hear the music of the
    snake charmer
  no matter how well he plays.

⁶God, break the teeth in their
    mouths!
  Tear out the fangs of those lions,
    Lord!

PSALM 59

For the director of music. To the tune of "Do Not
Destroy." A miktam of David when Saul sent men
to watch David's house to kill him.

¹God, save me from my enemies.
  Protect me from those who come
    against me.
²Save me from those who do evil
  and from murderers.

³Look, they are waiting to
    ambush me.
  Cruel people attack me,
  but I have not sinned or done
    wrong, Lord.
⁴I have done nothing wrong, but they
    are ready to attack me.
  Wake up to help me, and look.
⁵You are the Lord God All-Powerful,
    the God of Israel.
  Arise and punish those people.
  Do not give those traitors any
    mercy.   *Selah*

⁶They come back at night.
  Like dogs they growl and roam
    around the city.
⁷Notice what comes from their mouths.
  Insults come from their lips,
  because they say, "Who's
    listening?"
⁸But, LORD, you laugh at them;
  you make fun of all of them.

⁹God, my strength, I am looking to you,
  because God is my defender.
¹⁰My God loves me, and he goes in
    front of me.
  He will help me defeat my
    enemies.
¹¹Lord, our protector, do not kill them,
  or my people will forget.
  With your power scatter them and
    defeat them.
¹²They sin by what they say;
  they sin with their words.
  They curse and tell lies,
    so let their pride trap them.
¹³Destroy them in your anger;
  destroy them completely!
  Then they will know
    that God rules over Israel
    and to the ends of the earth. *Selah*

¹⁴They come back at night.
  Like dogs they growl
  and roam around the city.
¹⁵They wander about looking for food,
  and they howl if they do not find
    enough.
¹⁶But I will sing about your strength.
  In the morning I will sing about
    your love.
  You are my defender,
    my place of safety in times of
      trouble.
¹⁷God, my strength, I will sing praises to
    you.
  God, my defender, you are the
    God who loves me.

PSALM 60

For the director of music. To the tune of "Lily of the
Agreement." A miktam of David. For teaching.
When David fought the Arameans of Northwest
Mesopotamia and Zobah, and when Joab returned
and defeated twelve thousand Edomites
at the Valley of Salt.

¹God, you have rejected us and
    scattered us.
  You have been angry, but please
    come back to us.
²You made the earth shake and crack.
  Heal its breaks because it is
    shaking.
³You have given your people trouble.
  You made us unable to walk
    straight, like people drunk
    with wine.
⁴You have raised a banner to gather
    those who fear you.
  Now they can stand up against the
    enemy.   *Selah*

⁵Answer us and save us by your power
  so the people you love will be
    rescued.

⁶God has said from his Temple,
  "When I win, I will divide Shechem
  and measure off the Valley of
    Succoth.
⁷Gilead and Manasseh are mine.
  Ephraim is like my helmet.
  Judah holds my royal scepter.
⁸Moab is like my washbowl.
  I throw my sandals at Edom.
  I shout at Philistia."

⁹Who will bring me to the strong,
    walled city?
  Who will lead me to Edom?
¹⁰God, surely you have rejected us;
  you do not go out with our armies.
¹¹Help us fight the enemy.
  Human help is useless,
¹²but we can win with God's help.
  He will defeat our enemies.

PSALM 61

For the director of music. With stringed instruments.
Of David.

¹God, hear my cry;
    listen to my prayer.
²I call to you from the ends of the
        earth
    when I am afraid.
    Carry me away to a high mountain.
³You have been my protection,
    like a strong tower against my
        enemies.

⁴Let me live in your Holy Tent forever.
    Let me find safety in the shelter of
        your wings.   *Selah*

⁵God, you have heard my promises.
    You have given me what belongs
        to those who fear you.

⁶Give the king a long life;
    let him live many years.
⁷Let him rule in the presence of God
        forever.
    Protect him with your love and
        truth.
⁸Then I will praise your name forever,
    and every day I will keep my
        promises.

PSALM 62

For the director of music. For Jeduthun.
A psalm of David.

¹I find rest in God;
    only he can save me.
²He is my rock and my salvation.
    He is my defender;
    I will not be defeated.

³How long will you attack someone?
    Will all of you kill that person?
    Who is like a leaning wall, like a
        fence ready to fall?
⁴They are planning to make that
        person fall.
    They enjoy telling lies.

With their mouths they bless,
    but in their hearts they curse. *Selah*

⁵I find rest in God;
    only he gives me hope.
⁶He is my rock and my salvation.
    He is my defender;
    I will not be defeated.
⁷My honor and salvation come from
        God.
    He is my mighty rock and my
        protection.

⁸People, trust God all the time.
    Tell him all your problems,
    because God is our protection.
                                        Selah

⁹The least of people are only a breath,
    and even the greatest are just
        a lie.
On the scales, they weigh nothing;
    together they are only a breath.
¹⁰Do not trust in force.
    Stealing is of no use.
Even if you gain more riches,
    don't put your trust in them.

¹¹God has said this,
    and I have heard it over and over:
        God is strong.
¹²The Lord is loving.
    You reward people for what they
        have done.

PSALM 63

A psalm of David when he was in the desert of Judah.

¹God, you are my God.
    I search for you.
I thirst for you
    like someone in a dry, empty land
        where there is no water.
²I have seen you in the Temple
    and have seen your strength and
        glory.
³Because your love is better than life,
    I will praise you.

⁴I will praise you as long as I live.
    I will lift up my hands in prayer to
        your name.
⁵I will be content as if I had eaten the
        best foods.
    My lips will sing, and my mouth
        will praise you.

⁶I remember you while I'm lying in bed;
    I think about you through the
        night.
⁷You are my help.
    Because of your protection, I sing.
⁸I stay close to you;
    you support me with your right
        hand.

⁹Some people are trying to kill me,
    but they will go down to the grave.
¹⁰They will be killed with swords
    and eaten by wild dogs.
¹¹But the king will rejoice in his God.
    All who make promises in his
        name will praise him,
    but the mouths of liars will be
        shut.

PSALM 64

For the director of music. A psalm of David.

¹God, listen to my complaint.
    I am afraid of my enemies;
        protect my life from them.
²Hide me from those who plan wicked
        things,
    from that gang who does evil.
³They sharpen their tongues like
        swords
    and shoot bitter words like arrows.
⁴From their hiding places they shoot at
        innocent people;
    they shoot suddenly and are not
        afraid.
⁵They encourage each other to do
        wrong.
    They talk about setting traps,
        thinking no one will see them.

⁶They plan wicked things and say,
    "We have a perfect plan."
    The mind of human beings is hard
        to understand.

⁷But God will shoot them with arrows;
    they will suddenly be struck down.
⁸Their own words will be used against
        them.
    All who see them will shake their
        heads.
⁹Then everyone will fear God.
    They will tell what God has done,
    and they will learn from what he
        has done.
¹⁰Good people will be happy in the Lord
    and will find protection in him.
    Let everyone who is honest praise
        the Lord.

PSALM 65

For the director of music. A psalm of David. A song.

¹God, you will be praised in Jerusalem.
    We will keep our promises to you.
²You hear our prayers.
    All people will come to you.
³Our guilt overwhelms us,
    but you forgive our sins.
⁴Happy are the people you choose
    and invite to stay in your court.
    We are filled with good things in your
        house,
    your holy Temple.

⁵You answer us in amazing ways,
    God our Savior.
    People everywhere on the earth
        and beyond the sea trust you.
⁶You made the mountains by your
        strength;
    you are dressed in power.
⁷You stopped the roaring seas,
    the roaring waves,
    and the uproar of the nations.
⁸Even those people at the ends of the
        earth fear your miracles.

You are praised from where the
   sun rises to where it sets.

9You take care of the land and water it;
   you make it very fertile.
The rivers of God are full of water.
   Grain grows because you make it
      grow.
10You send rain to the plowed fields;
   you fill the rows with water.
You soften the ground with rain,
   and then you bless it with crops.
11You give the year a good harvest,
   and you load the wagons with
      many crops.
12The desert is covered with grass
   and the hills with happiness.
13The pastures are full of flocks,
   and the valleys are covered with
      grain.
   Everything shouts and sings for joy.

PSALM 66

For the director of music. A song. A psalm.

1Everything on earth, shout with joy to
      God!
2Sing about his glory!
   Make his praise glorious!
3Say to God, "Your works are amazing!
   Because your power is great,
   your enemies fall before you.
4All the earth worships you
   and sings praises to you.
   They sing praises to your name."
                                    Selah

5Come and see what God has done,
   the amazing things he has done
      for people.
6He turned the sea into dry land.
   The people crossed the river on
      foot.
   So let us rejoice because of what
      he did.
7He rules forever with his power.
   He keeps his eye on the nations,

so people should not turn against
   him.   Selah

8You people, praise our God;
   loudly sing his praise.
9He protects our lives
   and does not let us be defeated.
10God, you have tested us;
   you have purified us like silver.
11You let us be trapped
   and put a heavy load on us.
12You let our enemies walk on our
      heads.
   We went through fire and flood,
   but you brought us to a place with
      good things.

13I will come to your Temple with burnt
      offerings.
   I will give you what I promised,
14   things I promised when I was in
      trouble.
15I will bring you offerings of fat
      animals,
   and I will offer sheep, bulls, and
      goats.   Selah

16All of you who fear God, come and
      listen,
   and I will tell you what he has
      done for me.
17I cried out to him with my mouth
   and praised him with my tongue.
18If I had known of any sin in my heart,
   the Lord would not have listened
      to me.   **STEP 4**
19But God has listened;
   he has heard my prayer.
20Praise God,
   who did not ignore my prayer
   or hold back his love from me.

PSALM 67

For the director of music. With stringed instruments.
A psalm. A song.

1God, have mercy on us and bless us
   and show us your kindness   Selah

²so the world will learn your ways,
and all nations will learn that you
can save.

³God, the people should praise you;
all people should praise you.
⁴The nations should be glad and sing
because you judge people fairly.
You guide all the nations on earth.
Selah

⁵God, the people should praise you;
all people should praise you.

⁶The land has given its crops.
God, our God, blesses us.
⁷God blesses us
so people all over the earth will
fear him.

PSALM 68

For the director of music. A psalm of David. A song.

¹Let God rise up and scatter his
enemies;
let those who hate him run away
from him.
²Blow them away as smoke
is driven away by the wind.
As wax melts before a fire,
let the wicked be destroyed
before God.
³But those who do right should be glad
and should rejoice before God;
they should be happy and glad.

⁴Sing to God; sing praises to his name.
Prepare the way for him
who rides through the desert,
whose name is the LORD.
Rejoice before him.

STEP 10

⁵God is in his holy Temple.
He is a father to orphans,
and he defends the widows.
⁶God gives the lonely a home.
He leads prisoners out with joy,
but those who turn against God
will live in a dry land.

⁷God, you led your people out
when you marched through the
desert. *Selah*

⁸The ground shook
and the sky poured down rain
before God, the God of Mount Sinai,
before God, the God of Israel.
⁹God, you sent much rain;
you refreshed your tired land.
¹⁰Your people settled there.
God, in your goodness
you took care of the poor.

¹¹The Lord gave the command,
and a great army told the news:
¹²"Kings and their armies run away.
In camp they divide the wealth
taken in war.
¹³Those who stayed by the campfires
will share the riches taken in
battle."
¹⁴The Almighty scattered kings
like snow on Mount Zalmon.

¹⁵The mountains of Bashan are high;
the mountains of Bashan have
many peaks.
¹⁶Why do you mountains with many
peaks look with envy
on the mountain that God chose
for his home?
The LORD will live there forever.
¹⁷God comes with millions of chariots;
the Lord comes from Mount Sinai
to his holy place.
¹⁸When you went up to the heights,
you led a parade of captives.
You received gifts from the people,
even from those who turned against
you.
And the LORD God will live there.

STEP 3

¹⁹Praise the Lord, God our Savior,
who helps us every day. *Selah*
²⁰Our God is a God who saves us;
the LORD God saves us from death.

431

²¹God will crush his enemies' heads,
the hairy skulls of those who
continue to sin.
²²The Lord said, "I will bring the enemy
back from Bashan;
I will bring them back from the
depths of the sea.
²³Then you can stick your feet in their
blood,
and your dogs can lick their share."

²⁴God, people have seen your victory
march;
God my King marched into the
holy place.
²⁵The singers are in front and the
instruments are behind.
In the middle are the girls with the
tambourines.
²⁶Praise God in the meeting place;
praise the LORD in the gathering of
Israel.
²⁷There is the smallest tribe, Benjamin,
leading them.
And there are the leaders of Judah
with their group.
There also are the leaders of
Zebulun and of Naphtali.

²⁸God, order up your power;
show the mighty power you have
used for us before.
²⁹Kings will bring their wealth to you,
to your Temple in Jerusalem.
³⁰Punish Egypt, the beast in the tall
grass along the river.
Punish the leaders of nations,
those bulls among the cows.
Defeated, they will bring you their
silver.
Scatter those nations that love war.
³¹Messengers will come from Egypt;
the people of Cush will pray to God.

³²Kingdoms of the earth, sing to God;
sing praises to the Lord.   *Selah*

³³Sing to the one who rides through the
skies, which are from long
ago.
He speaks with a thundering
voice.
³⁴Announce that God is powerful.
He rules over Israel,
and his power is in the skies.
³⁵God, you are wonderful in your
Temple.
The God of Israel gives his people
strength and power.

Praise God!

PSALM 69

For the director of music. To the tune of "Lilies."
A psalm of David.

¹God, save me,
because the water has risen to my
neck.
²I'm sinking down into the mud,
and there is nothing to stand on.
I am in deep water,
and the flood covers me.
³I am tired from calling for help;
my throat is sore.
My eyes are tired from waiting
for God to help me.

STEP
1

⁴There are more people who hate me
for no reason than hairs on
my head;
powerful enemies want to destroy
me for no reason.
They make me pay back
what I did not steal.

⁵God, you know what I have done
wrong;
I cannot hide my guilt from you.

STEP
5

⁶Lord GOD All-Powerful,
do not let those who hope in you
be ashamed because of me.
God of Israel,
do not let your worshipers be
disgraced because of me.

⁷For you, I carry this shame,
and my face is covered with
disgrace.
⁸I am like a stranger to my closest
relatives
and a foreigner to my mother's
children.
⁹My strong love for your Temple
completely controls me.
When people insult you, it
hurts me.
¹⁰When I cry and fast,
they make fun of me.
¹¹When I wear clothes of sadness,
they joke about me.
¹²They make fun of me in public places,
and the drunkards make up songs
about me.

¹³But I pray to you, LORD, for favor.
God, because of your great love,
answer me.
You are truly able to save.
¹⁴Pull me from the mud,
and do not let me sink.
Save me from those who hate me
and from the deep water.
¹⁵Do not let the flood drown me
or the deep water swallow me
or the grave close its mouth
over me.
¹⁶LORD, answer me because your love is
so good.
Because of your great kindness,
turn to me.
¹⁷Do not hide from me, your servant.
I am in trouble. Hurry to
help me!
¹⁸Come near and save me;
rescue me from my enemies.

¹⁹You see my shame and disgrace.
You know all my enemies and
what they have said.
²⁰Insults have broken my heart
and left me weak.

I looked for sympathy, but there was
none;
I found no one to comfort me.
²¹They put poison in my food
and gave me vinegar to drink.

²²Let their own feasts cause their ruin;
let their feasts trap them and pay
them back.
²³Let their eyes be closed so they
cannot see
and their backs be forever weak
from troubles.
²⁴Pour your anger out on them;
let your anger catch up with them.
²⁵May their place be empty;
leave no one to live in their tents.
²⁶They chase after those you have hurt,
and they talk about the pain of
those you have wounded.
²⁷Charge them with crime after crime,
and do not let them have anything
good.
²⁸Wipe their names from the book of
life,
and do not list them with those
who do what is right.

²⁹I am sad and hurting.
God, save me and protect me.
³⁰I will praise God in a song
and will honor him by giving
thanks.
³¹That will please the LORD more than
offering him cattle,
more than sacrificing a bull with
horns and hoofs.
³²Poor people will see this and be glad.
Be encouraged, you who worship
God.
³³The LORD listens to those in need
and does not look down on
captives.

³⁴Heaven and earth should praise him,
the seas and everything in them.

STEP
I

STEP
I

³⁵God will save Jerusalem
and rebuild the cities of Judah.
Then people will live there and own
the land.
³⁶ The descendants of his servants
will inherit that land,
and those who love him will live
there.

PSALM 70

For the director of music. A psalm of David.
To help people remember.

¹God, come quickly and save me.
LORD, hurry to help me.
²Let those who are trying to kill me
be ashamed and disgraced.
Let those who want to hurt me
run away in disgrace.
³Let those who make fun of me
stop because of their shame.
⁴But let all those who worship you
rejoice and be glad.
Let those who love your salvation
always say, "Praise the greatness
of God."
⁵I am poor and helpless;
God, hurry to me.
You help me and save me.
LORD, do not wait.

PSALM 71

STEP
2

¹In you, LORD, is my protection.
Never let me be ashamed.
²Because you do what is right, save
and rescue me;
listen to me and save me.
³Be my place of safety
where I can always come.
Give the command to save me,
because you are my rock and my
strong, walled city.
⁴My God, save me from the power of
the wicked
and from the hold of evil and cruel
people.

⁵LORD, you are my hope.
LORD, I have trusted you since I
was young.
⁶I have depended on you since I was
born;
you helped me even on the day of
my birth.
I will always praise you.

⁷I am an example to many people,
because you are my strong
protection.
⁸I am always praising you;
all day long I honor you.
⁹Do not reject me when I am old;
do not leave me when my strength
is gone.
¹⁰My enemies make plans against me,
and they meet together to kill me.
¹¹They say, "God has left him.
Go after him and take him,
because no one will save him."

¹²God, don't be far off.
My God, hurry to help me.
¹³Let those who accuse me
be ashamed and destroyed.
Let those who are trying to hurt me
be covered with shame and
disgrace.
¹⁴But I will always have hope
and will praise you more and
more.
¹⁵I will tell how you do what is right.
I will tell about your salvation all
day long,
even though it is more than I can
tell.
¹⁶I will come and tell about your
powerful works, Lord GOD.
I will remind people that only you
do what is right.

¹⁷God, you have taught me since I was
young.
To this day I tell about the
miracles you do.

¹⁸Even though I am old and gray,
    do not leave me, God.
I will tell the children about your
      power;
    I will tell those who live after me
      about your might.

¹⁹God, your justice reaches to the skies.
    You have done great things;
    God, there is no one like you.
²⁰You have given me many troubles and
      bad times,
    but you will give me life again.
When I am almost dead,
    you will keep me alive.
²¹You will make me greater than ever,
    and you will comfort me again.

²²I will praise you with the harp.
    I trust you, my God.
I will sing to you with the lyre,
    Holy One of Israel.
²³I will shout for joy when I sing praises
      to you.
    You have saved me.
²⁴I will tell about your justice all day long.
    And those who want to hurt me
    will be ashamed and disgraced.

PSALM 72
Of Solomon.

¹God, give the king your good
      judgment
    and the king's son your goodness.
²Help him judge your people fairly
    and decide what is right for the
      poor.
³Let there be peace on the mountains
    and goodness on the hills for the
      people.
⁴Help him be fair to the poor
    and save the needy
    and punish those who hurt them.

⁵May they respect you as long as the
      sun shines
    and as long as the moon glows.

⁶Let him be like rain on the grass,
    like showers that water the earth.
⁷Let goodness be plentiful while he
      lives.
    Let peace continue as long as
      there is a moon.

⁸Let his kingdom go from sea to sea,
    and from the Euphrates River to
      the ends of the earth.
⁹Let the people of the desert bow
      down to him,
    and make his enemies lick the
      dust.
¹⁰Let the kings of Tarshish and the
      faraway lands
    bring him gifts.
Let the kings of Sheba and Seba
    bring their presents to him.
¹¹Let all kings bow down to him
    and all nations serve him.

¹²He will help the poor when they cry
      out
    and will save the needy when no
      one else will help.
¹³He will be kind to the weak and poor,
    and he will save their lives.

STEP 1

¹⁴He will save them from cruel people
      who try to hurt them,
    because their lives are precious to
      him.

¹⁵Long live the king!
    Let him receive gold from Sheba.
Let people always pray for him
    and bless him all day long.
¹⁶Let the fields grow plenty of grain
    and the hills be covered with
      crops.
Let the land be as fertile as Lebanon,
    and let the cities grow like the
      grass in a field.
¹⁷Let the king be famous forever;
    let him be remembered as long as
      the sun shines.

STEP 1

We admitted we were powerless
over our dependencies—that our lives
had become unmanageable.

Psalm 72:12-13

If you pretend to be strong enough and capable enough to run your own life, you won't be able to take the first step toward physical, emotional, and spiritual healing. King Solomon wrote many of the proverbs, but he also wrote this psalm. He was the most powerful man in his part of the world, but the point he chose to make is that God saves those who humble themselves and cry out to him for help. Deliverance comes to those who admit their lives are unmanageable. If you're too proud to admit your failures, you won't see God work in your life.

Getting handles on this unmanageability issue is hard to do. Even when you say the right words about relying on God alone, you may still find yourself looking to friends and relatives to rescue you. You have to come to grips with the fact that God alone can heal you of your addictions. When you get your arms around that idea, you're ready to be set free.

SEE **PAGE 24** OF THE INTRODUCTORY MATERIAL FOR **STEP 2**.

Let the nations be blessed because
        of him,
    and may they all bless him.

¹⁸Praise the LORD God, the God of Israel,
    who alone does such miracles.
¹⁹Praise his glorious name forever.
    Let his glory fill the whole world.
        Amen and amen.

²⁰This ends the prayers of David son of
        Jesse.

Book 3

PSALM 73

A psalm of Asaph.

¹God is truly good to Israel,
    to those who have pure hearts.
²But I had almost stopped believing;
    I had almost lost my faith
³because I was jealous of proud
        people.
    I saw wicked people doing well.

⁴They are not suffering;
    they are healthy and strong.
⁵They don't have troubles like the rest
        of us;
    they don't have problems like
        other people.
⁶They wear pride like a necklace
    and put on violence as their
        clothing.
⁷They are looking for profits
    and do not control their selfish
        desires.
⁸They make fun of others and speak
        evil;
    proudly they speak of hurting
        others.
⁹They brag to the sky.
    They say that they own the earth.
¹⁰So their people turn to them
    and give them whatever they
        want.

¹¹They say, "How can God know?
    What does God Most High know?"
¹²These people are wicked,
    always at ease, and getting richer.
¹³So why have I kept my heart pure?
    Why have I kept my hands from
        doing wrong?
¹⁴I have suffered all day long;
    I have been punished every
        morning.

¹⁵God, if I had decided to talk like this,
    I would have let your people down.
¹⁶I tried to understand all this,
    but it was too hard for me to see
¹⁷until I went to the Temple of God.
    Then I understood what will
        happen to them.
¹⁸You have put them in danger;
    you cause them to be destroyed.
¹⁹They are destroyed in a moment;
    they are swept away by terrors.
²⁰It will be like waking from a dream.
    Lord, when you rise up, they will
        disappear.

²¹When my heart was sad
        and I was angry,   STEP 4
²²I was senseless and stupid.
    I acted like an animal toward you.
²³But I am always with you;
    you have held my hand.
²⁴You guide me with your advice,
    and later you will receive me in
        honor.
²⁵I have no one in heaven but you;
    I want nothing on earth besides
        you.
²⁶My body and my mind may become
        weak,
    but God is my strength.
        He is mine forever.

²⁷Those who are far from God will die;
    you destroy those who are
        unfaithful.

²⁸But I am close to God, and that is
good.
The Lord GOD is my protection.
I will tell all that you have done.

PSALM 74

A maskil of Asaph.

¹God, why have you rejected us for so
long?
Why are you angry with us, the
sheep of your pasture?
²Remember the people you bought
long ago.
You saved us, and we are your very
own.
After all, you live on Mount Zion.
³Make your way through these old
ruins;
the enemy wrecked everything in
the Temple.

⁴Those who were against you shouted
in your meeting place
and raised their flags there.
⁵They came with axes raised
as if to cut down a forest of
trees.
⁶They smashed the carved panels
with their axes and hatchets.
⁷They burned your Temple to the
ground;
they have made the place where
you live unclean.
⁸They thought, "We will completely
crush them!"
They burned every place where
God was worshiped in the
land.
⁹We do not see any signs.
There are no more prophets,
and no one knows how long this
will last.
¹⁰God, how much longer will the enemy
make fun of you?
Will they insult you forever?

¹¹Why do you hold back your power?
Bring your power out in the open
and destroy them!

¹²God, you have been our king for a long
time.
You bring salvation to the earth.
¹³You split open the sea by your power
and broke the heads of the sea
monster.
¹⁴You smashed the heads of the
monster Leviathan
and gave it to the desert creatures
as food.
¹⁵You opened up the springs and
streams
and made the flowing rivers run
dry.
¹⁶Both the day and the night are yours;
you made the sun and the moon.
¹⁷You set all the limits on the earth;
you created summer and winter.

¹⁸LORD, remember how the enemy
insulted you.
Remember how those foolish
people made fun of you.
¹⁹Do not give us, your doves, to those
wild animals.
Never forget your poor people.
²⁰Remember the agreement you made
with us,
because violence fills every dark
corner of this land.
²¹Do not let your suffering people be
disgraced.
Let the poor and helpless praise
you.

²²God, arise and defend yourself.
Remember the insults that come
from those foolish people all
day long.
²³Don't forget what your enemies said;
don't forget their roar as they rise
against you always.

PSALM 75

For the director of music. To the tune of "Do Not Destroy." A psalm of Asaph. A song.

¹God, we thank you;
    we thank you because you are near.
    We tell about the miracles you do.

²You say, "I set the time for trial,
    and I will judge fairly.
³The earth with all its people may
      shake,
    but I am the one who holds it
      steady.   *Selah*
⁴I say to those who are proud, 'Don't
      brag,'
    and to the wicked, 'Don't show
      your power.
⁵Don't try to use your power against
      heaven.
    Don't be stubborn.' "

⁶No one from the east or the west
    or the desert can judge you.
⁷God is the judge;
    he judges one person as guilty and
      another as innocent.
⁸The Lord holds a cup of anger in his
      hand;
    it is full of wine mixed with spices.
He pours it out even to the last drop,
    and the wicked drink it all.

⁹I will tell about this forever;
    I will sing praise to the God of
      Jacob.
¹⁰He will take all power away from the
      wicked,
    but the power of good people will
      grow.

PSALM 76

For the director of music. With stringed instruments. A psalm of Asaph. A song.

¹People in Judah know God;
    his fame is great in Israel.
²His Tent is in Jerusalem;
    his home is on Mount Zion.

³There God broke the flaming arrows,
    the shields, the swords, and the
      weapons of war.   *Selah*

⁴God, how wonderful you are!
    You are more splendid than the
      hills full of animals.
⁵The brave soldiers were stripped
    as they lay asleep in death.
 Not one warrior
    had the strength to stop it.
⁶God of Jacob, when you spoke
      strongly,
    horses and riders fell dead.
⁷You are feared;
    no one can stand against you
      when you are angry.
⁸From heaven you gave the decision,
    and the earth was afraid and
      silent.
⁹God, you stood up to judge
    and to save the needy people of
      the earth.   *Selah*
¹⁰People praise you for your anger
      against evil.
    Those who live through your anger
      are stopped from doing
      more evil.

¹¹Make and keep your promises to the
      Lord your God.
    From all around, gifts should come
      to the God we worship.
¹²God breaks the spirits of great leaders;
    the kings on earth fear him.

PSALM 77

For the director of music. For Jeduthun. A psalm of Asaph.

¹I cry out to God;
    I call to God, and he will hear me.
²I look for the Lord on the day of
      trouble.
    All night long I reach out my
      hands,
    but I cannot be comforted.

³When I remember God, I become
        upset;
    when I think, I become afraid. *Selah*

⁴You keep my eyes from closing.
    I am too upset to say anything.
⁵I keep thinking about the old days,
    the years of long ago.
⁶At night I remember my songs.
    I think and I ask myself:
⁷"Will the Lord reject us forever?
    Will he never be kind to us again?
⁸Is his love gone forever?
    Has he stopped speaking for all
        time?
⁹Has God forgotten mercy?
    Is he too angry to pity us?"   *Selah*
¹⁰Then I say, "This is what makes me
        sad:
    For years the power of God Most
        High was with us."

¹¹I remember what the LORD did;
    I remember the miracles you did
        long ago.
¹²I think about all the things you did
    and consider your deeds.

¹³God, your ways are holy.
    No god is as great as our God.
¹⁴You are the God who does miracles;
    you have shown people your
        power.
¹⁵By your power you have saved your
        people,
    the descendants of Jacob and
        Joseph.   *Selah*

¹⁶God, the waters saw you;
    they saw you and became afraid;
    the deep waters shook with fear.
¹⁷The clouds poured down their rain.
    The sky thundered.
    Your lightning flashed back and
        forth like arrows.
¹⁸Your thunder sounded in the
        whirlwind.

Lightning lit up the world.
    The earth trembled and shook.
¹⁹You made a way through the sea
    and paths through the deep
        waters,
    but your footprints were not seen.
²⁰You led your people like a flock
    by using Moses and Aaron.

PSALM 78

A maskil of Asaph.

¹My people, listen to my teaching;
    listen to what I say.
²I will speak using stories;
    I will tell secret things from long
        ago.
³We have heard them and known
        them
    by what our ancestors have
        told us.
⁴We will not keep them from our
        children;   STEP
    we will tell those who come later   12
        about the praises of the LORD.
We will tell about his power
    and the miracles he has done.

⁵The LORD made an agreement with
        Jacob
    and gave the teachings to Israel,
    which he commanded our ancestors
        to teach to their children.
⁶Then their children would know
        them,
    even their children not yet born.
    And they would tell their children.
⁷So they would all trust God
    and would not forget what he had
        done
    but would obey his commands.
⁸They would not be like their ancestors
    who were stubborn and
        disobedient.
    Their hearts were not loyal to God,
    and they were not true to him.

⁹The men of Ephraim had bows for
weapons,
but they ran away on the day of
battle.
¹⁰They didn't keep their agreement
with God
and refused to live by his
teachings.
¹¹They forgot what he had done
and the miracles he had shown
them.
¹²He did miracles while their ancestors
watched,
in the fields of Zoan in Egypt.
¹³He divided the Red Sea and led them
through.
He made the water stand up like a
wall.
¹⁴He led them with a cloud by day
and by the light of a fire by night.
¹⁵He split the rocks in the desert
and gave them more than enough
water, as if from the deep
ocean.
¹⁶He brought streams out of the rock
and caused water to flow down
like rivers.

¹⁷But the people continued to sin
against him;
in the desert they turned against
God Most High.
¹⁸They decided to test God
by asking for the food they wanted.
¹⁹Then they spoke against God,
saying, "Can God prepare food in
the desert?
²⁰When he hit the rock, water poured
out
and rivers flowed down.
But can he give us bread also?
Will he provide his people with
meat?"
²¹When the LORD heard them, he was
very angry.

His anger was like fire to the
people of Jacob;
his anger grew against the people
of Israel.
²²They had not believed God
and had not trusted him to save
them.
²³But he gave a command to the clouds
above
and opened the doors of heaven.
²⁴He rained manna down on them to
eat;
he gave them grain from heaven.
²⁵So they ate the bread of angels.
He sent them all the food they
could eat.
²⁶He sent the east wind from heaven
and led the south wind by his
power.
²⁷He rained meat on them like dust.
The birds were as many as the
sand of the sea.
²⁸He made the birds fall inside the camp,
all around the tents.
²⁹So the people ate and became very
full.
God had given them what they
wanted.
³⁰While they were still eating,
and while the food was still in
their mouths,
³¹God became angry with them.
He killed some of the healthiest of
them;
he struck down the best young
men of Israel.

³²But they kept on sinning;
they did not believe even with the
miracles.
³³So he ended their days without
meaning
and their years in terror.
³⁴Anytime he killed them, they would
look to him for help;

they would come back to God and
follow him.
³⁵They would remember that God was
their Rock,
that God Most High had saved
them.
³⁶But their words were false,
and their tongues lied to him.
³⁷Their hearts were not really loyal to
God;
they did not keep his agreement.
³⁸Still God was merciful.
He forgave their sins
and did not destroy them.
Many times he held back his anger
and did not stir up all his anger.
³⁹He remembered that they were only
human,
like a wind that blows and does
not come back.

⁴⁰They turned against God so often in
the desert
and grieved him there.
⁴¹Again and again they tested God
and brought pain to the Holy One
of Israel.
⁴²They did not remember his power
or the time he saved them from
the enemy.
⁴³They forgot the signs he did in Egypt
and his wonders in the fields of
Zoan.
⁴⁴He turned their rivers to blood
so no one could drink the water.
⁴⁵He sent flies that bit the people.
He sent frogs that destroyed them.
⁴⁶He gave their crops to grasshoppers
and what they worked for to
locusts.
⁴⁷He destroyed their vines with hail
and their sycamore trees with
sleet.
⁴⁸He killed their animals with hail
and their cattle with lightning.

⁴⁹He showed them his hot anger.
He sent his strong anger against
them,
his destroying angels.
⁵⁰He found a way to show his anger.
He did not keep them from dying
but let them die by a terrible
disease.
⁵¹God killed all the firstborn sons in
Egypt,
the oldest son of each family of
Ham.
⁵²But God led his people out like
sheep
and he guided them like a flock
through the desert.
⁵³He led them to safety so they had
nothing to fear,
but their enemies drowned in the
sea.
⁵⁴So God brought them to his holy land,
to the mountain country he took
with his own power.
⁵⁵He forced out the other nations,
and he had his people inherit the
land.
He let the tribes of Israel settle
there in tents.

⁵⁶But they tested God
and turned against God Most
High;
they did not keep his rules.
⁵⁷They turned away and were disloyal
just like their ancestors.
They were like a crooked bow that
does not shoot straight.
⁵⁸They made God angry by building
places to worship gods;
they made him jealous with their
idols.
⁵⁹When God heard them, he became
very angry
and rejected the people of Israel
completely.

⁶⁰He left his dwelling at Shiloh,
the Tent where he lived among
the people.
⁶¹He let the Ark, his power, be
captured;
he let the Ark, his glory, be taken
by enemies.
⁶²He let his people be killed;
he was very angry with his
children.
⁶³The young men died by fire,
and the young women had no one
to marry.
⁶⁴Their priests fell by the sword,
but their widows were not allowed
to cry.

⁶⁵Then the Lord got up as if he had
been asleep;
he awoke like a man who had
been drunk with wine.
⁶⁶He struck down his enemies
and disgraced them forever.
⁶⁷But God rejected the family of Joseph;
he did not choose the tribe of
Ephraim.
⁶⁸Instead, he chose the tribe of Judah
and Mount Zion, which he loves.
⁶⁹And he built his Temple high like the
mountains.
Like the earth, he built it to last
forever.
⁷⁰He chose David to be his servant
and took him from the sheep
pens.
⁷¹He brought him from tending the
sheep
so he could lead the flock, the
people of Jacob,
his own people, the people of
Israel.
⁷²And David led them with an innocent
heart
and guided them with skillful
hands.

PSALM 79

A psalm of Asaph.

¹God, nations have come against your
chosen people.
They have ruined your holy Temple.
They have turned Jerusalem into
ruins.
²They have given the bodies of your
servants as food to the wild
birds.
They have given the bodies of those
who worship you to the wild
animals.
³They have spilled blood like water all
around Jerusalem.
No one was left to bury the dead.
⁴We are a joke to the other nations;
they laugh and make fun of us.

⁵LORD, how long will this last?
Will you be angry forever?
How long will your jealousy burn
like a fire?
⁶Be angry with the nations that do not
know you
and with the kingdoms that do not
honor you.
⁷They have gobbled up the people of
Jacob
and destroyed their land.
⁸Don't punish us for our past sins.
Show your mercy to us soon,
because we are helpless!
⁹God our Savior, help us
so people will praise you.
Save us and forgive our sins
so people will honor you.
¹⁰Why should the nations say,
"Where is their God?"
Tell the other nations in our presence
that you punish those who kill
your servants.
¹¹Hear the moans of the prisoners.
Use your great power
to save those sentenced to die.

STEP
7

¹²Repay those around us seven times
over
for their insults to you, Lord.
¹³We are your people, the sheep of your
flock.
We will thank you always;
forever and ever we will praise you.

PSALM 80

For the director of music. To the tune of "Lilies
of the Agreement." A psalm of Asaph.

¹Shepherd of Israel, listen to us.
You lead the people of Joseph like
a flock.
You sit on your throne between the
gold creatures with wings.
Show your greatness ²to the
people of Ephraim,
Benjamin, and Manasseh.
Use your strength,
and come to save us.

³God, take us back.
Show us your kindness so we can
be saved.

⁴Lord God All-Powerful,
how long will you be angry
at the prayers of your people?
⁵You have fed your people with tears;
you have made them drink many
tears.
⁶You made those around us fight over
us,
and our enemies make fun of us.

⁷God All-Powerful, take us back.
Show us your kindness so we can
be saved.

⁸You brought us out of Egypt as if we
were a vine.
You forced out other nations and
planted us in the land.
⁹You cleared the ground for us.
Like a vine, we took root and filled
the land.

¹⁰We covered the mountains with our
shade.
We had limbs like the mighty
cedar tree.
¹¹Our branches reached the
Mediterranean Sea,
and our shoots went to the
Euphrates River.

¹²So why did you pull down our walls?
Now everyone who passes by
steals from us.
¹³Like wild pigs they walk over us;
like wild animals they feed on us.

¹⁴God All-Powerful, come back.
Look down from heaven and see.
Take care of us, your vine.
¹⁵   You planted this shoot with your
own hands
and strengthened this child.
¹⁶Now it is cut down and burned with
fire;
you destroyed us by your angry
looks.
¹⁷With your hand,
strengthen the one you have
chosen for yourself.
¹⁸Then we will not turn away from you.
Give us life again, and we will call
to you for help.

¹⁹Lord God All-Powerful, take us back.
Show us your kindness so we can
be saved.

PSALM 81

For the director of music. By the gittith.
A psalm of Asaph.

¹Sing for joy to God, our strength;
shout out loud to the God of Jacob.
²Begin the music. Play the
tambourines.
Play pleasant music on the harps
and lyres.
³Blow the trumpet at the time of the
New Moon,

when the moon is full, when our
feast begins.
⁴This is the law for Israel;
it is the command of the God of
Jacob.
⁵He gave this rule to the people of
Joseph
when they went out of the land of
Egypt.

I heard a language I did not know,
saying:
⁶"I took the load off their shoulders;
I let them put down their baskets.
⁷When you were in trouble, you called,
and I saved you.
I answered you with thunder.
I tested you at the waters of
Meribah.   Selah
⁸My people, listen. I am warning you.
Israel, please listen to me!
⁹You must not have foreign gods;
you must not worship any false
god.
¹⁰I, the LORD, am your God,
who brought you out of Egypt.
Open your mouth and I will feed
you.

¹¹"But my people did not listen to me;
Israel did not want me.
¹²So I let them go their stubborn way
and follow their own advice.
¹³I wish my people would listen to me;
I wish Israel would live my way.
¹⁴Then I would quickly defeat their
enemies
and turn my hand against their
foes.
¹⁵Those who hate the LORD would bow
before him.
Their punishment would continue
forever.
¹⁶But I would give you the finest wheat
and fill you with honey from the
rocks."

PSALM 82

A psalm of Asaph.

¹God is in charge of the great meeting;
he judges among the "gods."
²He says, "How long will you defend
evil people?
How long will you show greater
kindness to the wicked?
                              Selah
³Defend the weak and the orphans;
defend the rights of the poor and
suffering.
⁴Save the weak and helpless;
free them from the power of the
wicked.

⁵"You know nothing. You don't
understand.
You walk in the dark,
while the world is falling apart.
⁶I said, 'You are "gods."
You are all sons of God Most
High.'
⁷But you will die like any other person;
you will fall like all the leaders."

⁸God, come and judge the earth,
because you own all the nations.

PSALM 83

A song. A psalm of Asaph.

¹God, do not keep quiet;
God, do not be silent or still.
²Your enemies are making noises;
those who hate you are getting
ready to attack.
³They are making secret plans against
your people;
they plot against those you love.
⁴They say, "Come, let's destroy them
as a nation.
Then no one will ever remember
the name 'Israel.' "
⁵They are united in their plan.
These have made an agreement
against you:

⁶the families of Edom and the
Ishmaelites,
Moab and the Hagrites,
⁷the people of Byblos, Ammon,
Amalek,
Philistia, and Tyre.
⁸Even Assyria has joined them
to help Ammon and Moab, the
descendants of Lot.   *Selah*

⁹God, do to them what you did to
Midian,
what you did to Sisera and Jabin at
the Kishon River.
¹⁰They died at Endor,
and their bodies rotted on the
ground.
¹¹Do to their important leaders what
you did to Oreb and Zeeb.
Do to their princes what you did to
Zebah and Zalmunna.
¹²They said, "Let's take for ourselves
the pasturelands that belong to
God."
¹³My God, make them like tumbleweed,
like chaff blown away by the wind.
¹⁴Be like a fire that burns a forest
or like flames that blaze through
the hills.
¹⁵Chase them with your storm,
and frighten them with your wind.
¹⁶Cover them with shame.
Then people will look for you, LORD.
¹⁷Make them afraid and ashamed
forever.
Disgrace them and destroy them.
¹⁸Then they will know that you are the
LORD,
that only you are God Most High
over all the earth.

PSALM 84

For the director of music. On the gittith.
A psalm of the sons of Korah.

¹LORD All-Powerful,
how lovely is your Temple!

²I want more than anything
to be in the courtyards of the
LORD's Temple.
My whole being wants
to be with the living God.
³The sparrows have found a home,
and the swallows have nests.
They raise their young near your
altars,
LORD All-Powerful, my King and my
God.
⁴Happy are the people who live at your
Temple;
they are always praising you.   *Selah*

⁵Happy are those whose strength
comes from you,
who want to travel to Jerusalem.
⁶As they pass through the Valley of
Baca,
they make it like a spring.
The autumn rains fill it with pools
of water.
⁷The people get stronger as they go,
and everyone meets with God in
Jerusalem.

⁸LORD God All-Powerful, hear my
prayer;
God of Jacob, listen to me.   *Selah*
⁹God, look at our shield;
be kind to your appointed king.

¹⁰One day in the courtyards of your
Temple is better
than a thousand days anywhere
else.
I would rather be a doorkeeper in the
Temple of my God
than live in the homes of the
wicked.
¹¹The LORD God is like a sun and shield;
the LORD gives us kindness and
honor.
He does not hold back anything good
from those whose lives are
innocent.

STEP
11

STEP 11

Sought through prayer and meditation to improve
our conscious contact with God **as we understood
Him,** praying only for knowledge of His will
for us and the power to carry that out.

Psalm 84:5–12

In Old Testament times, devout Jews made one or more annual
pilgrimages to the Temple in Jerusalem to offer sacrifices, pray, and
worship. Psalm 84 captures a sense of the commitment it took to
overcome the obstacles inherent in making a long trip on foot and
a sense of how such concentrated effort strengthened the faith of
the pilgrims.

You may not set out to keep an appointment with God in a Temple,
but you are on a quest to get to know him personally. And it's
possible to think of recovery from an addiction as a difficult journey.
Temptations to go back to your addiction try to get you to leave
Freedom Road and go down dead-end alleys. You may think some
stretches of Freedom Road wind through endless deserts where you
feel alone, hopeless, and discouraged. Keep trusting and obeying
God, and he will give you strength to make it all the way.

Verse 10 says it's better to be an usher in God's Temple than the
owner of a glitzy mansion built with the profits of sin. Why?
Because it's better to enjoy his guidance and protection forever
than to have some temporary pleasures that disappoint you in the
end. Since God "does not hold back anything good from those
whose lives are innocent" (verse 11), you can tell him, "Happy are
the people who trust you!" (verse 12).

FOR YOUR NEXT **STEP 11** MEDITATION, TURN TO **PAGE 485.** ▶▶

¹²Lᴏʀᴅ All-Powerful,
   happy are the people who trust
      you!

PSALM 85

For the director of music. A psalm of the sons of Korah.

¹Lᴏʀᴅ, you have been kind to your
      land;
   you brought back the people of
      Jacob.
²You forgave the guilt of the people
   and covered all their sins.   *Selah*
³You stopped all your anger;
   you turned back from your strong
      anger.

⁴God our Savior, bring us back again.
   Stop being angry with us.
⁵Will you be angry with us forever?
   Will you stay angry from now on?
⁶Won't you give us life again?
   Your people would rejoice
      in you.
⁷Lᴏʀᴅ, show us your love,
   and save us.

STEP 10

⁸I will listen to God the Lᴏʀᴅ.
   He has ordered peace for those
      who worship him.
   Don't let them go back to
      foolishness.
⁹God will soon save those who respect
      him,
   and his glory will be seen in our
      land.

¹⁰Love and truth belong to God's
      people;
   goodness and peace will be theirs.
¹¹On earth people will be loyal to God,
   and God's goodness will shine
      down from heaven.
¹²The Lᴏʀᴅ will give his goodness,
   and the land will give its crops.
¹³Goodness will go before God
   and prepare the way for him.

PSALM 86

A prayer of David.

¹Lᴏʀᴅ, listen to me and answer me.
   I am poor and helpless.
²Protect me, because I worship you.
   My God, save me, your servant
      who trusts in you.
³Lord, have mercy on me,
   because I have called to you all
      day.
⁴Give happiness to me, your servant,
   because I give my life to you, Lord.
⁵Lord, you are kind and forgiving
   and have great love for those who
      call to you.
⁶Lᴏʀᴅ, hear my prayer,
   and listen when I ask for mercy.
⁷I call to you in times of trouble,
   because you will answer me.

⁸Lord, there is no god like you
   and no works like yours.
⁹Lord, all the nations you have made
   will come and worship you.
   They will honor you.
¹⁰You are great and you do miracles.
   Only you are God.

STEP 3

¹¹Lᴏʀᴅ, teach me what you want me to
      do,
   and I will live by your truth.
   Teach me to respect you completely.
¹²Lord, my God, I will praise you with all
      my heart,
   and I will honor your name forever.
¹³You have great love for me.
   You have saved me from death.

¹⁴God, proud people are attacking me;
   a gang of cruel people is trying to
      kill me.
   They do not respect you.
¹⁵But, Lord, you are a God who shows
      mercy and is kind.
   You don't become angry quickly.
   You have great love and
      faithfulness.

STEP 10

Continued to take personal inventory
and when we were wrong promptly admitted it.

Psalm 85:8–9

The first nine steps of recovery start you on a life-changing journey. The maintenance steps—Steps 10, 11, and 12—keep you on track so you don't lose your way and "go back to foolishness" (verse 8). Your ongoing life inventory is the tool you use to keep your bearings.

If you don't keep doing self-evaluation, you run the risk of slipping back into some form of denial. You might tend to deny that your addiction or dependency was all that bad. You might deny that your willpower isn't enough to beat your habits. You might deny that you used to use and abuse people. You might even begin to deny God cares about you or has power to help you. It's surprising how easily a person can slip back into old, negative patterns of thinking and feeling. Envy, fear, resentment, and self-pity are just waiting for you to stop taking your personal inventory.

The antidote to self-delusion is rigorous honesty in your personal inventory. That way you can "listen to God the LORD" instead of to the deadly voices of denial.

FOR YOUR NEXT **STEP 10** MEDITATION, TURN TO **PAGE 463.** ▶▶

¹⁶Turn to me and have mercy.
Give me, your servant, strength.
Save me, the son of your female
servant.
¹⁷Show me a sign of your goodness.
When my enemies look, they will
be ashamed.
You, LORD, have helped me and
comforted me.

PSALM 87

A song. A psalm of the sons of Korah.

¹The LORD built Jerusalem on the holy
mountain.
² He loves its gates more than any
other place in Israel.
³City of God,
wonderful things are said about
you. *Selah*
⁴God says, "I will put Egypt and
Babylonia
on the list of nations that
know me.
People from Philistia, Tyre, and Cush
will be born there."

⁵They will say about Jerusalem,
"This one and that one were born
there.
God Most High will strengthen
her."
⁶The LORD will keep a list of the
nations.
He will note, "This person was
born there." *Selah*

⁷They will dance and sing,
"All good things come from
Jerusalem."

PSALM 88

A song. A psalm of the sons of Korah. For the
director of music. By the mahalath leannoth.
A maskil of Heman the Ezrahite.

STEP
1
¹LORD, you are the God who saves me.
I cry out to you day and night.

²Receive my prayer,
and listen to my cry.

³My life is full of troubles,
and I am nearly dead.
⁴They think I am on the way to my
grave.
I am like a man with no strength.
⁵I have been left as dead,
like a body lying in a grave
whom you don't remember
anymore,
cut off from your care.
⁶You have brought me close to death;
I am almost in the dark place of
the dead.
⁷You have been very angry with me;
all your waves crush me. *Selah*
⁸You have taken my friends away
from me
and have made them hate me.
I am trapped and cannot escape.
⁹ My eyes are weak from crying.
LORD, I have prayed to you every day;
I have lifted my hands in prayer to
you.

¹⁰Do you show your miracles for the
dead?
Do their spirits rise up and praise
you? *Selah*

¹¹Will your love be told in the grave?
Will your loyalty be told in the
place of death?
¹²Will your miracles be known in the
dark grave?
Will your goodness be known in
the land of forgetfulness?

¹³But, LORD, I have called out to you for
help;
every morning I pray to you.
¹⁴LORD, why do you reject me?
Why do you hide from me?
¹⁵I have been weak and dying since I
was young.

I suffer from your terrors, and I am helpless.
¹⁶You have been angry with me,
and your terrors have destroyed me.
¹⁷They surround me daily like a flood;
they are all around me.
¹⁸You have taken away my loved ones and friends.
Darkness is my only friend.

PSALM 89

A maskil of Ethan the Ezrahite.

¹I will always sing about the LORD's love;
I will tell of his loyalty from now on.
²I will say, "Your love continues forever;
your loyalty goes on and on like the sky."
³You said, "I made an agreement with the man of my choice;
I made a promise to my servant David.
⁴I told him, 'I will make your family continue forever.
Your kingdom will go on and on.' "
Selah

⁵LORD, the heavens praise you for your miracles
and for your loyalty in the meeting of your holy ones.
⁶Who in heaven is equal to the LORD?
None of the angels is like the LORD.
⁷When the holy ones meet, it is God they fear.
He is more frightening than all who surround him.
⁸LORD God All-Powerful, who is like you?
LORD, you are powerful and completely trustworthy.
⁹You rule the mighty sea
and calm the stormy waves.

¹⁰You crushed the sea monster Rahab;
by your power you scattered your enemies.

¹¹The skies and the earth belong to you.
You made the world and everything in it.
¹²You created the north and the south.
Mount Tabor and Mount Hermon sing for joy at your name.
¹³Your arm has great power.
Your hand is strong; your right hand is lifted up.
¹⁴Your kingdom is built on what is right and fair.
Love and truth are in all you do.

¹⁵Happy are the people who know how to praise you.
LORD, let them live in the light of your presence.
¹⁶In your name they rejoice
and continually praise your goodness.
¹⁷You are their glorious strength,
and in your kindness you honor our king.
¹⁸Our king, our shield, belongs to the LORD,
to the Holy One of Israel.

¹⁹Once, in a vision, you spoke
to those who worship you.
You said, "I have given strength to a warrior;
I have raised up a young man from my people.
²⁰I have found my servant David;
I appointed him by pouring holy oil on him.
²¹I will steady him with my hand
and strengthen him with my arm.
²²No enemy will make him give forced payments,
and wicked people will not defeat him.

²³I will crush his enemies in front of
     him;
   I will defeat those who hate him.
²⁴My loyalty and love will be with him.
   Through me he will be strong.
²⁵I will give him power over the sea
   and control over the rivers.
²⁶He will say to me, 'You are my father,
   my God, the Rock, my Savior.'
²⁷I will make him my firstborn son,
   the greatest king on earth.
²⁸My love will watch over him forever,
   and my agreement with him will
     never end.
²⁹I will make his family continue,
   and his kingdom will last as long
     as the skies.

³⁰"If his descendants reject my
     teachings
   and do not follow my laws,
³¹if they ignore my demands
   and disobey my commands,
³²then I will punish their sins with a rod
   and their wrongs with a whip.
³³But I will not hold back my love from
     David,
   nor will I stop being loyal.
³⁴I will not break my agreement
   nor change what I have said.
³⁵I have promised by my holiness,
   I will not lie to David.
³⁶His family will go on forever.
   His kingdom will last before me
     like the sun.
³⁷It will continue forever, like the
     moon,
   like a dependable witness in the
     sky."   Selah

³⁸But now you have refused and
     rejected your appointed
     king.
   You have been angry with him.
³⁹You have abandoned the agreement
   with your servant

and thrown his crown to the
     ground.
⁴⁰You have torn down all his city walls;
   you have turned his strong cities
     into ruins.
⁴¹Everyone who passes by steals from
     him.
   His neighbors insult him.
⁴²You have given strength to his
     enemies
   and have made them all happy.
⁴³You have made his sword useless;
   you did not help him stand in
     battle.
⁴⁴You have kept him from winning
   and have thrown his throne to the
     ground.
⁴⁵You have cut his life short
   and covered him with shame. Selah

⁴⁶Lord, how long will this go on?
   Will you ignore us forever?
   How long will your anger burn like
     a fire?
⁴⁷Remember how short my life is.
   Why did you create us? For
     nothing?
⁴⁸What person alive will not die?
   Who can escape the grave?   Selah

⁴⁹Lord, where is your love from times
     past,
   which in your loyalty you promised
     to David?
⁵⁰Lord, remember how they insulted
     your servant;
   remember how I have suffered the
     insults of the nations.
⁵¹Lord, remember how your enemies
     insulted you
   and how they insulted your
     appointed king wherever he
     went.

⁵²Praise the Lord forever!
   Amen and amen.

Book 4

PSALM 90

A prayer of Moses, the man of God.

¹Lord, you have been our home
since the beginning.
²Before the mountains were born
and before you created the earth
and the world,
you are God.
You have always been, and you
will always be.

³You turn people back into dust.
You say, "Go back into dust,
human beings."
⁴To you, a thousand years
is like the passing of a day,
or like a few hours in the night.
⁵While people sleep, you take their
lives.
They are like grass that grows up
in the morning.
⁶In the morning they are fresh and
new,
but by evening they dry up and
die.

⁷We are destroyed by your anger;
we are terrified by your hot anger.

STEP 4

⁸You have put the evil we have done
right in front of you;
you clearly see our secret sins.
⁹All our days pass while you are angry.
Our years end with a moan.
¹⁰Our lifetime is seventy years
or, if we are strong, eighty years.
But the years are full of hard work
and pain.
They pass quickly, and then we are
gone.

¹¹Who knows the full power of your
anger?
Your anger is as great as our fear of
you should be.

¹²Teach us how short our lives really are
so that we may be wise.

¹³LORD, how long before you return
and show kindness to your
servants?
¹⁴Fill us with your love every morning.
Then we will sing and rejoice all
our lives.
¹⁵We have seen years of trouble.
Now give us as much joy as you
gave us sorrow.
¹⁶Show your servants the wonderful
things you do;
show your greatness to their
children.

STEP 9

¹⁷Lord our God, treat us well.
Give us success in what we do;
yes, give us success in what we do.

PSALM 91

STEP 3

¹Those who go to God Most High for
safety
will be protected by the Almighty.
²I will say to the LORD, "You are my place
of safety and protection.
You are my God and I trust you."

³God will save you from hidden traps
and from deadly diseases.
⁴He will cover you with his feathers,
and under his wings you can hide.
His truth will be your shield and
protection.
⁵You will not fear any danger by night
or an arrow during the day.
⁶You will not be afraid of diseases that
come in the dark
or sickness that strikes at noon.
⁷At your side one thousand people
may die,
or even ten thousand right beside
you,
but you will not be hurt.
⁸You will only watch
and see the wicked punished.

STEP 3

Made a decision to turn our will and our lives
over to the care of God **as we understood Him.**

Psalm 91:1–4

When you choose to trust God as your Savior and turn your will and
your life over to him, he shelters you in a "place of safety." There
God wraps his love and protection around you like a warm quilt on
a cold night, or like the wings of a mother bird. You can get into
trouble, however, if you think of your "place of safety" as more like
a temporary safe house than as your permanent home. The Bible
uses the expressions "cover you" and "you can hide" (verse 4) to
suggest permanence. A primary feature of this permanent
arrangement is constant two-way communication. You listen to
God through his Word. You talk to him in prayer. As long as you
keep the dialogue going, you'll steer clear of your old negative
thinking and your addiction.

It's amazing how the truth of God's Word shields your mind from
fear and doubt. Keeping those negative emotions away from your
heart lets your faith grow. Faith will give you confidence about
today and hope for tomorrow.

FOR YOUR NEXT **STEP 3** MEDITATION, TURN TO **PAGE 501.** ▶▶

⁹The Lᴏʀᴅ is your protection;
  you have made God Most High
      your place of safety.
¹⁰Nothing bad will happen to you;
  no disaster will come to your home.
¹¹He has put his angels in charge of you
  to watch over you wherever
      you go.
¹²They will catch you in their hands
  so that you will not hit your foot on
      a rock.
¹³You will walk on lions and cobras;
  you will step on strong lions and
      snakes.

STEP 7

¹⁴The Lᴏʀᴅ says, "Whoever loves me, I
      will save.
  I will protect those who know me.
¹⁵They will call to me, and I will answer
      them.
  I will be with them in trouble;
  I will rescue them and honor them.
¹⁶I will give them a long, full life,
  and they will see how I can save."

PSALM 92

A psalm. A song for the Sabbath day.

STEP 12

¹It is good to praise you, Lᴏʀᴅ,
  to sing praises to God Most High.
²It is good to tell of your love in the
      morning
  and of your loyalty at night.
³It is good to praise you with the ten-
      stringed lyre
  and with the soft-sounding harp.

⁴Lᴏʀᴅ, you have made me happy by
      what you have done;
  I will sing for joy about what your
      hands have done.
⁵Lᴏʀᴅ, you have done such great
      things!
  How deep are your thoughts!
⁶Stupid people don't know these
      things,
  and fools don't understand.

⁷Wicked people grow like the grass.
  Evil people seem to do well,
  but they will be destroyed forever.
⁸But, Lᴏʀᴅ, you will be honored
      forever.

⁹Lᴏʀᴅ, surely your enemies,
  surely your enemies will be
      destroyed,
  and all who do evil will be
      scattered.
¹⁰But you have made me as strong as
      an ox.
  You have poured fine oils on me.
¹¹When I looked, I saw my enemies;
  I heard the cries of those who are
      against me.

¹²But good people will grow like palm
      trees;
  they will be tall like the cedars of
      Lebanon.
¹³Like trees planted in the Temple of
      the Lᴏʀᴅ,
  they will grow strong in the
      courtyards of our God.
¹⁴When they are old, they will still
      produce fruit;
  they will be healthy and fresh.
¹⁵They will say that the Lᴏʀᴅ is good.
  He is my Rock, and there is no
      wrong in him.

PSALM 93

¹The Lᴏʀᴅ is king. He is clothed in
      majesty.
  The Lᴏʀᴅ is clothed in majesty
  and armed with strength.
  The world is set,
  and it cannot be moved.
²Lᴏʀᴅ, your kingdom was set up long
      ago;
  you are everlasting.

³Lᴏʀᴅ, the seas raise,
  the seas raise their voice.

STEP 12

Having had a spiritual awakening as the
result of these steps, we tried to carry
this message to others, and to practice
these principles in all our affairs.

Psalm 92:1–4

Step 12 points ahead to the payoff of your whole recovery process.
All of your sacrifices made during the first eleven steps have gained
for you something you probably weren't expecting when you
started work on Step 1—a spiritual awakening that connects you
with God. You started out to break with your past and have ended
up with a personal relationship with God himself. Now you can join
the psalmist in saying, "It is good to praise you, LORD, to sing
praises to God Most High" (verse 1).

Step 12 goes on to remind you that your "spiritual awakening" isn't
a one-time, historical event that you look back on. It's an ongoing,
unfolding adventure that you experience every day. Step 12
encourages you to "carry this message to others." When you do,
you join the psalmist to "tell of [God's] love in the morning and of
[his] loyalty at night" (verse 2).

FOR YOUR NEXT **STEP 12** MEDITATION, TURN TO **PAGE 459.** ▶▶

The seas raise up their pounding
waves.
⁴The sound of the water is loud;
the ocean waves are powerful,
but the LORD above is much
greater.

⁵LORD, your laws will stand forever.
Your Temple will be holy
forevermore.

PSALM 94

¹The LORD is a God who punishes.
God, show your greatness and
punish!
²Rise up, Judge of the earth,
and give the proud what they
deserve.
³How long will the wicked be happy?
How long, LORD?

⁴They are full of proud words;
those who do evil brag about what
they have done.
⁵LORD, they crush your people
and make your children suffer.
⁶They kill widows and foreigners
and murder orphans.
⁷They say, "The LORD doesn't see;
the God of Jacob doesn't notice."

⁸You stupid ones among the people,
pay attention.
You fools, when will you
understand?
⁹Can't the creator of ears hear?
Can't the maker of eyes see?
¹⁰Won't the one who corrects nations
punish you?
Doesn't the teacher of people
know everything?
¹¹The LORD knows what people think.
He knows their thoughts are just a
puff of wind.

STEP
6
¹²LORD, those you correct are happy;
you teach them from your law.

¹³You give them rest from times of
trouble
until a pit is dug for the wicked.
¹⁴The LORD won't leave his people
nor give up his children.
¹⁵Judgment will again be fair,
and all who are honest will
follow it.

¹⁶Who will help me fight against the
wicked?
Who will stand with me against
those who do evil?

STEP
3
¹⁷If the LORD had not helped me,
I would have died in a minute.
¹⁸I said, "I am about to fall,"
but, LORD, your love kept me safe.
¹⁹I was very worried,
but you comforted me and made
me happy.

²⁰Crooked leaders cannot be your
friends.
They use the law to cause
suffering.
²¹They join forces against people who
do right
and sentence to death the
innocent.
²²But the LORD is my defender;
my God is the rock of my
protection.
²³God will pay them back for their sins
and will destroy them for their evil.
The LORD our God will destroy
them.

PSALM 95

¹Come, let's sing for joy to the LORD.
Let's shout praises to the Rock
who saves us.
²Let's come to him with thanksgiving.
Let's sing songs to him,
³because the LORD is the great God,
the great King over all gods.
⁴The deepest places on earth are his,

and the highest mountains belong
　　to him.
⁵The sea is his because he made it,
　　and he created the land with his
　　　own hands.

⁶Come, let's worship him and bow
　　down.
　　Let's kneel before the LORD who
　　　made us,
⁷because he is our God
　　and we are the people he takes
　　　care of,
　　the sheep that he tends.

Today listen to what he says:
⁸　　"Do not be stubborn, as your
　　　ancestors were at Meribah,
　　as they were that day at Massah in
　　　the desert.
⁹There your ancestors tested me
　　and tried me even though they
　　　saw what I did.
¹⁰I was angry with those people for
　　forty years.
　　I said, 'They are not loyal to me
　　　and have not understood my
　　　ways.'
¹¹I was angry and made a promise,
　　'They will never enter my rest.' "

PSALM 96

STEP 12

¹Sing to the LORD a new song;
　　sing to the LORD, all the earth.
²Sing to the LORD and praise his name;
　　every day tell how he saves us.
³Tell the nations of his glory;
　　tell all peoples the miracles he
　　　does,

⁴because the LORD is great; he should
　　be praised at all times.
　　He should be honored more than
　　　all the gods,
⁵because all the gods of the nations
　　are only idols,
　　but the LORD made the heavens.

⁶The LORD has glory and majesty;
　　he has power and beauty in his
　　　Temple.

⁷Praise the LORD, all nations on earth;
　　praise the LORD's glory and power.
⁸Praise the glory of the LORD's name.
　　Bring an offering and come into
　　　his Temple courtyards.
⁹Worship the LORD because he is holy.
　　Tremble before him, everyone on
　　　earth.
¹⁰Tell the nations, "The LORD is king."
　　The earth is set, and it cannot be
　　　moved.
　　He will judge the people fairly.
¹¹Let the skies rejoice and the earth be
　　glad;
　　let the sea and everything in it
　　　shout.
¹²　　Let the fields and everything in
　　　them rejoice.
　　Then all the trees of the forest will
　　　sing for joy
¹³　　before the LORD, because he is
　　　coming.
　　He is coming to judge the world;
he will judge the world with fairness
　　and the peoples with truth.

PSALM 97

¹The LORD is king. Let the earth
　　rejoice;
　　faraway lands should be glad.
²Thick, dark clouds surround him.
　　His kingdom is built on what is
　　　right and fair.
³A fire goes before him
　　and burns up his enemies all
　　　around.
⁴His lightning lights up the world;
　　when the people see it, they
　　　tremble.
⁵The mountains melt like wax before
　　the LORD,
　　before the Lord of all the earth.

STEP 12

Having had a spiritual awakening as the result of these steps, we tried to carry this message to others, and to practice these principles in all our affairs.

Psalm 96:1-2

As your recovery brings healing and strength to your life, the Lord will start using you as an instrument of his healing for people around you. Can you imagine that God wants you to "every day tell how he saves us" (verse 2)?

You tell about God's deliverance in two ways. First, you "tell" by the way you live. As people see the strength and love God has built into your life, they will know something miraculous has happened to you. And second, you "tell" with words. You share the story of your recovery with people who need to hear it. God will use your story to bring glory to his name and help other addicts. You will be a little unsure the first time you feel the Holy Spirit encouraging you to tell what he's done for you. But when you tell your story, you will not only help others see their need, but you will be encouraged in your own spiritual growth.

FOR YOUR NEXT **STEP 12** MEDITATION, TURN TO **PAGE 539.** ▶▶

⁶The heavens tell about his goodness,
and all the people see his glory.

⁷Those who worship idols should be
ashamed;
they brag about their gods.
All the gods should worship the
LORD.
⁸When Jerusalem hears this, she is glad,
and the towns of Judah rejoice.
They are happy because of your
judgments, LORD.
⁹You are the LORD Most High over all
the earth;
you are supreme over all gods.

¹⁰People who love the LORD hate evil.
The LORD watches over those who
follow him
and frees them from the power of
the wicked.
¹¹Light shines on those who do right;
joy belongs to those who are
honest.
¹²Rejoice in the LORD, you who do right.
Praise his holy name.

PSALM 98
A psalm.

¹Sing to the LORD a new song,
because he has done miracles.
By his right hand and holy arm
he has won the victory.
²The LORD has made known his power
to save;
he has shown the other nations his
victory for his people.
³He has remembered his love
and his loyalty to the people of
Israel.
All the ends of the earth have seen
God's power to save.

⁴Shout with joy to the LORD, all the
earth;
burst into songs and make music.

⁵Make music to the LORD with harps,
with harps and the sound of
singing.
⁶Blow the trumpets and the sheep's
horns;
shout for joy to the LORD the King.

⁷Let the sea and everything in it shout;
let the world and everyone in it
sing.
⁸Let the rivers clap their hands;
let the mountains sing together for
joy.
⁹Let them sing before the LORD,
because he is coming to judge the
world.
He will judge the world fairly;
he will judge the peoples with
fairness.

PSALM 99

¹The LORD is king.
Let the peoples shake with fear.
He sits between the gold creatures
with wings.
Let the earth shake.
²The LORD in Jerusalem is great;
he is supreme over all the peoples.
³Let them praise your name;
it is great, holy and to be feared.

⁴The King is powerful and loves justice.
LORD, you made things fair;
you have done what is fair and right
for the people of Jacob.
⁵Praise the LORD our God,
and worship at the Temple, his
footstool.
He is holy.

⁶Moses and Aaron were among his
priests,
and Samuel was among his
worshipers.
They called to the LORD,
and he answered them.

⁷He spoke to them from the pillar of
cloud.
They kept the rules and laws he
gave them.

⁸LORD our God, you answered them.
You showed them that you are a
forgiving God,
but you punished them for their
wrongs.
⁹Praise the LORD our God,
and worship at his holy mountain,
because the LORD our God is holy.

PSALM 100

A psalm of thanks.

¹Shout to the LORD, all the earth.
²   Serve the LORD with joy;
come before him with singing.
³Know that the LORD is God.
He made us, and we belong to
him;
we are his people, the sheep he
tends.

⁴Come into his city with songs of
thanksgiving
and into his courtyards with songs
of praise.
Thank him and praise his name.
⁵The LORD is good. His love is forever,
and his loyalty goes on and on.

PSALM 101

A psalm of David.

¹I will sing of your love and fairness;
LORD, I will sing praises to you.

²I will be careful to live an innocent life.
When will you come to me?

I will live an innocent life in my house.
³   I will not look at anything wicked.
I hate those who turn against you;
they will not be found near me.
⁴Let those who want to do wrong stay
away from me;
I will have nothing to do with evil.

⁵If anyone secretly says things against
his neighbor,
I will stop him.
I will not allow people
to be proud and look down on
others.

⁶I will look for trustworthy people
so I can live with them in the land.
Only those who live innocent lives
will be my servants.
⁷No one who is dishonest will live in
my house;
no liars will stay around me.
⁸Every morning I will destroy the
wicked in the land.
I will rid the LORD's city of people
who do evil.

PSALM 102

A prayer of a person who is suffering when he is
discouraged and tells the LORD his complaints.

¹LORD, listen to my prayer;
let my cry for help come to you.
²Do not hide from me
in my time of trouble.
Pay attention to me.
When I cry for help, answer me
quickly.

³My life is passing away like smoke,
and my bones are burned up with
fire.
⁴My heart is like grass
that has been cut and dried.
I forget to eat.
⁵Because of my grief,
my skin hangs on my bones.
⁶I am like a desert owl,
like an owl living among the ruins.
⁷I lie awake.
I am like a lonely bird on a
housetop.
⁸All day long enemies insult me;
those who make fun of me use my
name as a curse.

STEP
I

STEP
10

⁹I eat ashes for food,
    and my tears fall into my drinks.
¹⁰Because of your great anger,
    you have picked me up and
        thrown me away.
¹¹My days are like a passing shadow;
    I am like dried grass.

¹²But, LORD, you rule forever,
    and your fame goes on and on.
¹³You will come and have mercy on
        Jerusalem,
    because the time has now come to
        be kind to her;
    the right time has come.
¹⁴Your servants love even her stones;
    they even care about her dust.
¹⁵Nations will fear the name of the
        LORD,
    and all the kings on earth will
        honor you.
¹⁶The LORD will rebuild Jerusalem;
    there his glory will be seen.
¹⁷He will answer the prayers of the
        needy;
    he will not reject their prayers.

¹⁸Write these things for the future
    so that people who are not yet
        born will praise the LORD.
¹⁹The LORD looked down from his holy
        place above;
    from heaven he looked down at
        the earth.
²⁰He heard the moans of the prisoners,
    and he freed those sentenced to
        die.
²¹The name of the LORD will be heard in
        Jerusalem;
    his praise will be heard there.
²²People will come together,
    and kingdoms will serve the LORD.

²³God has made me tired of living;
    he has cut short my life.
²⁴So I said, "My God, do not take me in
        the middle of my life.

Your years go on and on.
²⁵In the beginning you made the earth,
    and your hands made the skies.
²⁶They will be destroyed, but you will
        remain.
    They will all wear out like clothes.
    And, like clothes, you will change
        them
    and throw them away.
²⁷But you never change,
    and your life will never end.
²⁸Our children will live in your presence,
    and their children will remain with
        you."

PSALM 103
Of David.

¹All that I am, praise the LORD;
    everything in me, praise his holy
        name.
²My whole being, praise the LORD
    and do not forget all his
        kindnesses. | STEP 7 |
³He forgives all my sins
    and heals all my diseases.
⁴He saves my life from the grave
    and loads me with love and mercy.
⁵He satisfies me with good things
    and makes me young again, like
        the eagle.

⁶The LORD does what is right and fair
    for all who are wronged by others.
⁷He showed his ways to Moses
    and his deeds to the people of
        Israel.
⁸The LORD shows mercy and is kind.
    He does not become angry
        quickly, and he has great
        love. | STEP 10 |
⁹He will not always accuse us,
    and he will not be angry forever.
¹⁰He has not punished us as our sins
        should be punished;
    he has not repaid us for the evil we
        have done.

STEP 10

Continued to take personal inventory
and when we were wrong promptly admitted it.

Psalm 103:8–18

Step 10 asks you to reassess your life continually. You have to ask, "Am I being careful to honor, obey, and serve God with humility? Am I at any point slipping back into my old, addictive behavior patterns?" Each day you need to honestly, humbly inventory yourself, admit your shortcomings to God, and ask him for strength to overcome them. If you carefully maintain this honest, humble frame of mind, God will respond to you with mercy. "He has not punished us as our sins should be punished" (verse 10). Instead, he remembers that we are fragile and weak, and he has pity on us as a father pities his children.

God is merciful and gracious to you, so you shouldn't be too hard on yourself either. Each day is a chance for new growth. If you mess up, Jesus is there to pick you up, forgive you, and set you on the right track again. "The LORD's love for those who respect him continues forever and ever" (verse 17).

SEE **PAGE 65** OF THE INTRODUCTORY MATERIAL FOR **STEP 11.**

¹¹As high as the sky is above the earth,
    so great is his love for those who
        respect him.
¹²He has taken our sins away from us
    as far as the east is from west.
¹³The LORD has mercy on those who
        respect him,
    as a father has mercy on his
        children.
¹⁴He knows how we were made;
    he remembers that we are dust.

¹⁵Human life is like grass;
    we grow like a flower in the field.
¹⁶After the wind blows, the flower is
        gone,
    and there is no sign of where it
        was.
¹⁷But the LORD's love for those who
        respect him
    continues forever and ever,
    and his goodness continues to
        their grandchildren
¹⁸and to those who keep his agreement
    and who remember to obey his
        orders.

¹⁹The LORD has set his throne in heaven,
    and his kingdom rules over
        everything.
²⁰You who are his angels, praise the
        LORD.
    You are the mighty warriors who
        do what he says
    and who obey his voice.
²¹You, his armies, praise the LORD;
    you are his servants who do what
        he wants.
²²Everything the LORD has made
    should praise him in all the places
        he rules.
    My whole being, praise the LORD.

PSALM 104

¹My whole being, praise the LORD.
    LORD my God, you are very great.

You are clothed with glory and
        majesty;
²   you wear light like a robe.
You stretch out the skies like a tent.
³   You build your room above the
        clouds.
You make the clouds your chariot,
    and you ride on the wings of the
        wind.
⁴You make the winds your messengers,
    and flames of fire are your
        servants.

⁵You built the earth on its foundations
    so it can never be moved.
⁶You covered the earth with oceans;
    the water was above the
        mountains.
⁷But at your command, the water
        rushed away.
    When you thundered your orders,
        it hurried away.
⁸The mountains rose; the valleys sank.
    The water went to the places you
        made for it.
⁹You set borders for the seas that they
        cannot cross,
    so water will never cover the earth
        again.

¹⁰You make springs pour into the
        ravines;
    they flow between the mountains.
¹¹They water all the wild animals;
    the wild donkeys come there to
        drink.
¹²Wild birds make nests by the water;
    they sing among the tree
        branches.
¹³You water the mountains from above.
    The earth is full of the things you
        made.
¹⁴You make the grass for cattle
    and vegetables for the people.
    You make food grow from the
        earth.

¹⁵You give us wine that makes happy
    hearts
        and olive oil that makes our faces
            shine.
        You give us bread that gives us
            strength.
¹⁶The LORD's trees have plenty of water;
    they are the cedars of Lebanon,
        which he planted.
¹⁷The birds make their nests there;
    the stork's home is in the fir trees.
¹⁸The high mountains belong to the
    wild goats.
        The rocks are hiding places for the
            badgers.

¹⁹You made the moon to mark the
    seasons,
        and the sun always knows when to
            set.
²⁰You make it dark, and it becomes
    night.
        Then all the wild animals creep
            around.
²¹The lions roar as they attack.
    They look to God for food.
²²When the sun rises, they leave
    and go back to their dens to lie
        down.
²³Then people go to work
    and work until evening.

²⁴LORD, you have made many things;
    with your wisdom you made them
        all.
        The earth is full of your riches.
²⁵Look at the sea, so big and wide,
    with creatures large and small that
        cannot be counted.
²⁶Ships travel over the ocean,
    and there is the sea monster
        Leviathan,
        which you made to play there.

²⁷All these things depend on you
    to give them their food at the right
        time.

²⁸When you give it to them,
    they gather it up.
    When you open your hand,
        they are filled with good food.
²⁹When you turn away from them,
    they become frightened.
    When you take away their breath,
        they die and turn to dust.
³⁰When you breathe on them,
    they are created,
        and you make the land new again.

³¹May the glory of the LORD be forever.
    May the LORD enjoy what he has
        made.
³²He just looks at the earth, and it
    shakes.
        He touches the mountains, and
            they smoke.

³³I will sing to the LORD all my life;
    I will sing praises to my God as
        long as I live.
³⁴May my thoughts please him;
    I am happy in the LORD.
³⁵Let sinners be destroyed from the
    earth,
        and let the wicked live no longer.

My whole being, praise the LORD.
    Praise the LORD.

PSALM 105

¹Give thanks to the LORD and pray to
    him.
        Tell the nations what he has done.
²Sing to him; sing praises to him.
    Tell about all his miracles.
³Be glad that you are his;
    let those who seek the LORD be
        happy.
⁴Depend on the LORD and his strength;
    always go to him for help.
⁵Remember the miracles he has done;
    remember his wonders and his
        decisions.

⁶You are descendants of his servant
　　Abraham,
　　　the children of Jacob, his chosen
　　　　people.
⁷He is the LORD our God.
　　　His laws are for all the world.

⁸He will keep his agreement forever;
　　　he will keep his promises always.
⁹He will keep the agreement he made
　　　with Abraham
　　　and the promise he made to Isaac.
¹⁰He made it a law for the people of
　　Jacob;
　　　he made it an agreement with
　　　　Israel to last forever.
¹¹The LORD said, "I will give you the land
　　of Canaan,
　　　and it will belong to you."

¹²Then God's people were few in
　　number.
　　　They were strangers in the land.
¹³They went from one nation to
　　another,
　　　from one kingdom to another.
¹⁴But the LORD did not let anyone hurt
　　them;
　　　he warned kings not to harm
　　　　them.
¹⁵He said, "Don't touch my chosen
　　people,
　　　and don't harm my prophets."

¹⁶God ordered a time of hunger in the
　　land,
　　　and he destroyed all the food.
¹⁷Then he sent a man ahead of them—
　　　Joseph, who was sold as a slave.
¹⁸They put chains around his feet
　　　and an iron ring around his neck.
¹⁹Then the time he had spoken of came,
　　　and the LORD's words proved that
　　　　Joseph was right.
²⁰The king of Egypt sent for Joseph and
　　freed him;
　　　the ruler of the people set him
　　　　free.
²¹He made him the master of his house;
　　　Joseph was in charge of his riches.
²²He could order the princes as he
　　wished.
　　　He taught the older men to be wise.
²³Then his father Israel came to Egypt;
　　　Jacob lived in Egypt.
²⁴The LORD made his people grow in
　　number,
　　　and he made them stronger than
　　　　their enemies.
²⁵He caused the Egyptians to hate his
　　people
　　　and to make plans against his
　　　　servants.
²⁶Then he sent his servant Moses,
　　　and Aaron, whom he had chosen.
²⁷They did many signs among the
　　Egyptians
　　　and worked wonders in Egypt.
²⁸The LORD sent darkness and made
　　the land dark,
　　　but the Egyptians turned against
　　　　what he said.
²⁹So he changed their water into blood
　　　and made their fish die.
³⁰Then their country was filled with
　　frogs,
　　　even in the bedrooms of their
　　　　rulers.
³¹The LORD spoke and flies came,
　　　and gnats were everywhere in the
　　　　country.
³²He made hail fall like rain
　　　and sent lightning through their
　　　　land.
³³He struck down their grapevines and
　　fig trees,
　　　and he destroyed every tree in the
　　　　country.
³⁴He spoke and grasshoppers came;
　　　the locusts were too many to
　　　　count.

³⁵They ate all the plants in the land
and everything the earth produced.
³⁶The Lord also killed all the firstborn
sons in the land,
the oldest son of each family.

³⁷Then he brought his people out,
and they carried with them silver
and gold.
Not one of his people stumbled.
³⁸The Egyptians were glad when they
left,
because the Egyptians were afraid
of them.
³⁹The Lord covered them with a cloud
and lit up the night with fire.
⁴⁰When they asked, he brought them
quail
and filled them with bread from
heaven.
⁴¹God split the rock, and water flowed
out;
it ran like a river through the
desert.
⁴²He remembered his holy promise
to his servant Abraham.

⁴³So God brought his people out with
joy,
his chosen ones with singing.
⁴⁴He gave them lands of other nations,
so they received what others had
worked for.
⁴⁵This was so they would keep his
orders
and obey his teachings.

Praise the Lord!

PSALM 106

¹Praise the Lord!

Thank the Lord because he is good.
His love continues forever.
²No one can tell all the mighty things
the Lord has done;
no one can speak all his praise.

³Happy are those who do right,
who do what is fair at all times.

⁴Lord, remember me when you are
kind to your people;
help me when you save them.
⁵Let me see the good things you do
for your chosen people.
Let me be happy along with your
happy nation;
let me join your own people in
praising you.

⁶We have sinned just as our ancestors
did.
We have done wrong; we have
done evil.
⁷Our ancestors in Egypt
did not learn from your miracles.
They did not remember all your
kindnesses,
so they turned against you at the
Red Sea.
⁸But the Lord saved them for his own
sake,
to show his great power.
⁹He commanded the Red Sea, and it
dried up.
He led them through the deep sea
as if it were a desert.
¹⁰He saved them from those who hated
them.
He saved them from their
enemies,
¹¹and the water covered their foes.
Not one of them escaped.
¹²Then the people believed what the
Lord said,
and they sang praises to him.

¹³But they quickly forgot what he had
done;
they did not wait for his advice.
¹⁴They became greedy for food in the
desert,
and they tested God there.

¹⁵So he gave them what they wanted,
   but he also sent a terrible disease
      among them.

¹⁶The people in the camp were jealous
      of Moses
   and of Aaron, the holy priest of the
      LORD.
¹⁷Then the ground opened up and
      swallowed Dathan
   and closed over Abiram's group.
¹⁸A fire burned among their followers,
   and flames burned up the wicked.

¹⁹The people made a gold calf at Mount
      Sinai
   and worshiped a metal statue.
²⁰They exchanged their glorious God
   for a statue of a bull that eats grass.
²¹They forgot the God who saved them,
   who had done great things in
      Egypt,
²²who had done miracles in Egypt
   and amazing things by the Red
      Sea.
²³So God said he would destroy them.
   But Moses, his chosen one, stood
      before him
   and stopped God's anger from
      destroying them.

²⁴Then they refused to go into the
      beautiful land of Canaan;
   they did not believe what God
      promised.
²⁵They grumbled in their tents
   and did not obey the LORD.
²⁶So he swore to them
   that they would die in the desert.
²⁷He said their children would be killed
      by other nations
   and that they would be scattered
      among other countries.

²⁸They joined in worshiping Baal at Peor
   and ate meat that had been
      sacrificed to lifeless statues.

²⁹They made the LORD angry by what
      they did,
   so many people became sick with
      a terrible disease.
³⁰But Phinehas prayed to the LORD,
   and the disease stopped.
³¹Phinehas did what was right,
   and it will be remembered from
      now on.

³²The people also made the LORD angry
      at Meribah,
   and Moses was in trouble because
      of them.
³³The people turned against the Spirit
      of God,
   so Moses spoke without stopping
      to think.

³⁴The people did not destroy the other
      nations
   as the LORD had told them to do.
³⁵Instead, they mixed with the other
      nations
   and learned their customs.
³⁶They worshiped other nations' idols
   and were trapped by them.
³⁷They even killed their sons and
      daughters
   as sacrifices to demons.
³⁸They killed innocent people,
   their own sons and daughters,
   as sacrifices to the idols of Canaan.
   So the land was made unholy by
      their blood.
³⁹The people became unholy by their
      sins;
   they were unfaithful to God in
      what they did.

⁴⁰So the LORD became angry with his
      people
   and hated his own children.
⁴¹He handed them over to other nations
   and let their enemies rule over
      them.

⁴²Their enemies were cruel to them
and kept them under their power.
⁴³The LORD saved his people many
times,
but they continued to turn against
him.
So they became even more
wicked.

⁴⁴But God saw their misery
when he heard their cry.
⁴⁵He remembered his agreement with
them,
and he felt sorry for them because
of his great love.
⁴⁶He caused them to be pitied
by those who held them captive.

⁴⁷LORD our God, save us
and bring us back from other
nations.
Then we will thank you
and will gladly praise you.

⁴⁸Praise the LORD, the God of Israel.
He always was and always will be.
Let all the people say, "Amen!"

Praise the LORD!

Book 5

PSALM 107

STEP 12

¹Thank the LORD because he is good.
His love continues forever.
²That is what those whom the LORD
has saved should say.
He has saved them from the
enemy
³and has gathered them from other
lands,
from east and west, north and
south.

⁴Some people had wandered in the
desert lands.
They found no city in which to live.

⁵They were hungry and thirsty,
and they were discouraged.
⁶In their misery they cried out to the
LORD,
and he saved them from their
troubles.
⁷He led them on a straight road
to a city where they could live.
⁸Let them give thanks to the LORD for
his love
and for the miracles he does for
people.
⁹He satisfies the thirsty
and fills up the hungry.

¹⁰Some sat in gloom and darkness;
they were prisoners suffering in
chains.
¹¹They had turned against the words of
God
and had refused the advice of God
Most High.
¹²So he broke their pride by hard
work.
They stumbled, and no one
helped.
¹³In their misery they cried out to the
LORD,
and he saved them from their
troubles.
¹⁴He brought them out of their gloom
and darkness
and broke their chains.
¹⁵Let them give thanks to the LORD for
his love
and for the miracles he does for
people.
¹⁶He breaks down bronze gates
and cuts apart iron bars.

¹⁷Some fools turned against God
and suffered for the evil they did.
¹⁸They refused to eat anything,
so they almost died.
¹⁹In their misery they cried out to the
LORD,

and he saved them from their
troubles.
²⁰God gave the command and healed
them,
so they were saved from dying.

STEP 12

²¹Let them give thanks to the LORD for
his love
and for the miracles he does for
people.
²²Let them offer sacrifices to thank him.
With joy they should tell what he
has done.

²³Others went out to sea in ships
and did business on the great
oceans.
²⁴They saw what the LORD could do,
the miracles he did in the deep
oceans.
²⁵He spoke, and a storm came up,
which blew up high waves.
²⁶The ships were tossed as high as the
sky and fell low to the
depths.
The storm was so bad that they
lost their courage.

STEP 2

²⁷They stumbled and fell like people
who were drunk.
They did not know what to do.
²⁸In their misery they cried out to the
LORD,
and he saved them from their
troubles.
²⁹He stilled the storm
and calmed the waves.
³⁰They were happy that it was quiet,
and God guided them to the port
they wanted.
³¹Let them give thanks to the LORD for
his love
and for the miracles he does for
people.
³²Let them praise his greatness in the
meeting of the people;
let them praise him in the meeting
of the elders.

³³He changed rivers into a desert
and springs of water into dry
ground.
³⁴He made fertile land salty,
because the people there did evil.
³⁵He changed the desert into pools of
water
and dry ground into springs of
water.
³⁶He had the hungry settle there
so they could build a city in which
to live.
³⁷They planted seeds in the fields and
vineyards,
and they had a good harvest.
³⁸God blessed them, and they grew in
number.
Their cattle did not become fewer.

³⁹Because of disaster, troubles, and
sadness,
their families grew smaller and
weaker.
⁴⁰He showed he was displeased with
their leaders
and made them wander in a
pathless desert.

STEP 2

⁴¹But he lifted the poor out of their
suffering
and made their families grow like
flocks of sheep.
⁴²Good people see this and are happy,
but the wicked say nothing.

⁴³Whoever is wise will remember these
things
and will think about the love of
the LORD.

PSALM 108

A song. A psalm of David.

¹God, my heart is steady.
I will sing and praise you with all
my being.
²Wake up, harp and lyre!
I will wake up the dawn.

³LORD, I will praise you among the
nations;
I will sing songs of praise about
you to all the nations.
⁴Your great love reaches to the skies,
your truth to the heavens.
⁵God, you are supreme above the
skies.
Let your glory be over all the
earth.

⁶Answer us and save us by your power
so the people you love will be
rescued.
⁷God has said from his Temple,
"When I win, I will divide
Shechem
and measure off the Valley of
Succoth.
⁸Gilead and Manasseh are mine.
Ephraim is like my helmet.
Judah holds my royal scepter.
⁹Moab is like my washbowl.
I throw my sandals at Edom.
I shout at Philistia."

¹⁰Who will bring me to the strong,
walled city?
Who will lead me to Edom?
¹¹God, surely you have rejected us;
you do not go out with our armies.
¹²Help us fight the enemy.
Human help is useless,
¹³but we can win with God's help.
He will defeat our enemies.

PSALM 109

For the director of music. A psalm of David.

¹God, I praise you.
Do not be silent.
²Wicked people and liars have spoken
against me;
they have told lies about me.
³They have said hateful things
about me
and attack me for no reason.

⁴They attacked me, even though I
loved them
and prayed for them.
⁵I was good to them, but they repay
me with evil.
I loved them, but they hate me in
return.

⁶They say about me, "Have an evil
person work against him,
and let an accuser stand against
him.
⁷When he is judged, let him be found
guilty,
and let even his prayers show his
guilt.
⁸Let his life be cut short,
and let another man replace him
as leader.
⁹Let his children become orphans
and his wife a widow.
¹⁰Make his children wander around,
begging for food.
Let them be forced out of the
ruins in which they live.
¹¹Let the people to whom he owes
money take everything he
owns,
and let strangers steal everything
he has worked for.
¹²Let no one show him love
or have mercy on his orphaned
children.
¹³Let all his descendants die
and be forgotten by those who live
after him.
¹⁴LORD, remember how wicked his
ancestors were,
and don't let the sins of his
mother be wiped out.
¹⁵LORD, always remember their sins.
Then make people forget about
them completely.

¹⁶"He did not remember to be
loving.

He hurt the poor, the needy, and
those who were sad
until they were nearly dead.
¹⁷He loved to put curses on others,
so let those same curses fall on
him.
He did not like to bless others,
so do not let good things happen
to him.
¹⁸He cursed others as often as he wore
clothes.
Cursing others filled his body and
his life,
like drinking water and using olive
oil.
¹⁹So let curses cover him like clothes
and wrap around him like a
belt."
²⁰May the Lord do these things to
those who accuse me,
to those who speak evil
against me.

STEP 2

²¹But you, Lord GOD,
be kind to me so others will know
you are good.
Because your love is good,
save me.
²²I am poor and helpless
and very sad.
²³I am dying like an evening shadow;
I am shaken off like a locust.
²⁴My knees are weak from fasting,
and I have grown thin.
²⁵My enemies insult me;
they look at me and shake their
heads.

²⁶LORD my God, help me;
because you are loving, save me.
²⁷Then they will know that your power
has done this;
they will know that you have done
it, LORD.
²⁸They may curse me, but you
bless me.

They may attack me, but they will
be disgraced.
Then I, your servant, will be glad.
²⁹Let those who accuse me be
disgraced
and covered with shame like a
coat.

³⁰I will thank the LORD very much;
I will praise him in front of many
people.
³¹He defends the helpless
and saves them from those who
accuse them.

PSALM 110

A psalm of David.

¹The LORD said to my Lord,
"Sit by me at my right side
until I put your enemies under your
control."
²The LORD will enlarge your kingdom
beyond Jerusalem,
and you will rule over your
enemies.
³Your people will join you on your day
of battle.
You have been dressed in holiness
from birth;
you have the freshness of a child.

⁴The LORD has made a promise
and will not change his mind.
He said, "You are a priest forever,
a priest like Melchizedek."

⁵The Lord is beside you to help you.
When he becomes angry, he will
crush kings.
⁶He will judge those nations, filling
them with dead bodies;
he will defeat rulers all over the
world.
⁷The king will drink from the brook on
the way.
Then he will be strengthened.

PSALM 111

STEP 12

¹Praise the Lord!

I will thank the Lord with all my heart
in the meeting of his good people.
²The Lord does great things;
those who enjoy them seek them.
³What he does is glorious and
splendid,
and his goodness continues
forever.
⁴His miracles are unforgettable.
The Lord is kind and merciful.
⁵He gives food to those who fear him.
He remembers his agreement
forever.
⁶He has shown his people his power
when he gave them the lands of
other nations.

⁷Everything he does is good and fair;
all his orders can be trusted.
⁸They will continue forever.
They were made true and right.
⁹He sets his people free.
He made his agreement
everlasting.
He is holy and wonderful.

¹⁰Wisdom begins with respect for the
Lord;
those who obey his orders have
good understanding.
He should be praised forever.

PSALM 112

¹Praise the Lord!

Happy are those who respect the
Lord,
who want what he commands.
²Their descendants will be powerful in
the land;
the children of honest people will
be blessed.
³Their houses will be full of wealth and
riches,

and their goodness will continue
forever.
⁴A light shines in the dark for honest
people,
for those who are merciful and
kind and good.
⁵It is good to be merciful and
generous.
Those who are fair in their
business
⁶will never be defeated.
Good people will always be
remembered.
⁷They won't be afraid of bad news;
their hearts are steady because
they trust the Lord.
⁸They are confident and will not be
afraid;
they will look down on their
enemies.
⁹They give freely to the poor.
The things they do are right and
will continue forever.
They will be given great honor.

¹⁰The wicked will see this and become
angry;
they will grind their teeth in anger
and then disappear.
The wishes of the wicked will
come to nothing.

PSALM 113

¹Praise the Lord!

Praise him, you servants of the
Lord;
praise the name of the Lord.
²The Lord's name should be praised
now and forever.
³The Lord's name should be praised
from where the sun rises to where
it sets.
⁴The Lord is supreme over all the
nations;
his glory reaches to the skies.

⁵No one is like the LORD our God,
    who rules from heaven,
⁶who bends down to look
    at the skies and the earth.
⁷The LORD lifts the poor from the dirt
    and takes the helpless from the
    ashes.
⁸He seats them with princes,
    the princes of his people.
⁹He gives children to the woman who
    has none
    and makes her a happy mother.

Praise the LORD!

PSALM 114

¹When the Israelites went out of
    Egypt,
    the people of Jacob left that
    foreign country.
²Then Judah became God's holy place;
    Israel became the land he ruled.

³The Red Sea looked and ran away;
    the Jordan River turned back.
⁴The mountains danced like sheep
    and the hills like little lambs.
⁵Sea, why did you run away?
    Jordan, why did you turn back?
⁶Mountains, why did you dance like
    sheep?
    Hills, why did you dance like little
    lambs?

⁷Earth, shake with fear before the
    Lord,
    before the God of Jacob.
⁸He turned a rock into a pool of water,
    a hard rock into a spring of water.

PSALM 115

¹It does not belong to us, LORD.
    The glory belongs to you
    because of your love and loyalty.

²Why do the nations ask,
    "Where is their God?"

³Our God is in heaven.
    He does what he pleases.
⁴Their idols are made of silver and
    gold,
    the work of human hands.
⁵They have mouths, but they cannot
    speak.
    They have eyes, but they cannot
    see.
⁶They have ears, but they cannot hear.
    They have noses, but they cannot
    smell.
⁷They have hands, but they cannot
    feel.
    They have feet, but they cannot
    walk.
    No sounds come from their
    throats.
⁸People who make idols will be like
    them,
    and so will those who trust them.

⁹Family of Israel, trust the LORD;
    he is your helper and your
    protection.
¹⁰Family of Aaron, trust the LORD;
    he is your helper and your
    protection.
¹¹You who respect the LORD should
    trust him;
    he is your helper and your
    protection.

¹²The LORD remembers us and will
    bless us.
    He will bless the family of Israel;
    he will bless the family of Aaron.
¹³The LORD will bless those who respect
    him,
    from the smallest to the greatest.

¹⁴May the LORD give you success,
    and may he give you and your
    children success.
¹⁵May you be blessed by the LORD,
    who made heaven and earth.

¹⁶Heaven belongs to the LORD,
　　but he gave the earth to people.
¹⁷Dead people do not praise the LORD;
　　those in the grave are silent.
¹⁸But we will praise the LORD
　　now and forever.

Praise the LORD!

PSALM 116

STEP 3

¹I love the LORD,
　　because he listens to my prayers
　　　for help.
²He paid attention to me,
　　so I will call to him for help as long
　　　as I live.
³The ropes of death bound me,
　　and the fear of the grave took hold
　　　of me.
　　I was troubled and sad.
⁴Then I called out the name of the
　　LORD.
　　I said, "Please, LORD, save me!"

⁵The LORD is kind and does what is
　　right;
　　our God is merciful.
⁶The LORD watches over the foolish;
　　when I was helpless, he saved me.
⁷I said to myself, "Relax,
　　because the LORD takes care of
　　　you."
⁸LORD, you saved me from death.
　　You stopped my eyes from crying;
　　you kept me from being
　　　defeated.
⁹So I will walk with the LORD
　　in the land of the living.
¹⁰I believed, so I said,
　　"I am completely ruined."
¹¹In my distress I said,
　　"All people are liars."

¹²What can I give the LORD
　　for all the good things he has
　　　given to me?

¹³I will lift up the cup of salvation,
　　and I will pray to the LORD.
¹⁴I will give the LORD what I promised
　　in front of all his people.

¹⁵The death of one that belongs to the
　　LORD
　　is precious in his sight.
¹⁶LORD, I am your servant;
　　I am your servant and the son of
　　　your female servant.
　　You have freed me from my chains.
¹⁷I will give you an offering to show
　　　thanks to you,
　　and I will pray to the LORD.
¹⁸I will give the LORD what I promised
　　in front of all his people,
¹⁹in the Temple courtyards
　　in Jerusalem.

Praise the LORD!

PSALM 117

¹All you nations, praise the LORD.
　　All you people, praise him
²because the LORD loves us very much,
　　and his truth is everlasting.

Praise the LORD!

PSALM 118

¹Thank the LORD because he is good.
　　His love continues forever.
²Let the people of Israel say,
　　"His love continues forever."
³Let the family of Aaron say,
　　"His love continues forever."
⁴Let those who respect the LORD say,
　　"His love continues forever."

⁵I was in trouble, so I called to the
　　LORD.
　　The LORD answered me and set
　　　me free.
⁶I will not be afraid, because the LORD
　　is with me.
　　People can't do anything to me.

⁷The LORD is with me to help me,
    so I will see my enemies
        defeated.
⁸It is better to trust the LORD
    than to trust people.
⁹It is better to trust the LORD
    than to trust princes.

¹⁰All the nations surrounded me,
    but I defeated them in the name
        of the LORD.
¹¹They surrounded me on every side,
    but with the LORD's power I
        defeated them.
¹²They surrounded me like a swarm of
        bees,
    but they died as quickly as thorns
        burn.
    By the LORD's power, I defeated
        them.
¹³They chased me until I was almost
        defeated,
    but the LORD helped me.
¹⁴The LORD gives me strength and a
        song.
    He has saved me.

¹⁵Shouts of joy and victory
    come from the tents of those who
        do right:
    "The LORD has done powerful
        things."
¹⁶The power of the LORD has won the
        victory;
    with his power the LORD has done
        mighty things.

¹⁷I will not die, but live,
    and I will tell what the LORD has
        done.
¹⁸The LORD has taught me a hard
        lesson,
    but he did not let me die.

¹⁹Open for me the Temple gates.
    Then I will come in and thank the
        LORD.

²⁰This is the LORD's gate;
    only those who are good may
        enter through it.
²¹Lord, I thank you for answering me.
    You have saved me.

²²The stone that the builders rejected
    became the cornerstone.
²³The LORD did this,
    and it is wonderful to us.
²⁴This is the day that the LORD has
        made.
    Let us rejoice and be glad today!

²⁵Please, LORD, save us;
    please, LORD, give us success.
²⁶God bless the one who comes in the
        name of the LORD.
    We bless all of you from the
        Temple of the LORD.
²⁷The LORD is God,
    and he has shown kindness to us.
    With branches in your hands, join the
        feast.
    Come to the corners of the altar.

²⁸You are my God, and I will thank you;
    you are my God, and I will praise
        your greatness.

²⁹Thank the LORD because he is good.
    His love continues forever.

PSALM 119

¹Happy are those who live pure lives,
    who follow the LORD's teachings.
²Happy are those who keep his rules,
    who try to obey him with their
        whole heart.
³They don't do what is wrong;
    they follow his ways.
⁴LORD, you gave your orders
    to be obeyed completely.
⁵I wish I were more loyal
    in obeying your demands.
⁶Then I would not be ashamed
    when I study your commands.

⁷When I learned that your laws are fair,
    I praised you with an honest heart.
⁸I will obey your demands,
    so please don't ever leave me.

⁹How can a young person live a pure
    life?
    By obeying your word.

STEP 6

¹⁰With all my heart I try to obey you.
    Don't let me break your commands.
¹¹I have taken your words to heart
    so I would not sin against you.
¹²LORD, you should be praised.
    Teach me your demands.
¹³My lips will tell about
    all the laws you have spoken.
¹⁴I enjoy living by your rules
    as people enjoy great riches.
¹⁵I think about your orders
    and study your ways.
¹⁶I enjoy obeying your demands,
    and I will not forget your word.

¹⁷Do good to me, your servant, so I can
    live,
    so I can obey your word.
¹⁸Open my eyes to see
    the miracles in your teachings.
¹⁹I am a stranger on earth.
    Do not hide your commands
    from me.
²⁰I wear myself out with desire
    for your laws all the time.
²¹You scold proud people;
    those who ignore your commands
    are cursed.
²²Don't let me be insulted and hated
    because I keep your rules.
²³Even if princes speak against me,
    I, your servant, will think about
    your demands.
²⁴Your rules give me pleasure;
    they give me good advice.

²⁵I am about to die.
    Give me life, as you have promised.

²⁶I told you about my life, and you
    answered me.
    Teach me your demands.
²⁷Help me understand your orders.
    Then I will think about your
    miracles.

STEP 6

²⁸I am sad and tired.
    Make me strong again as you have
    promised.
²⁹Don't let me be dishonest;
    have mercy on me by helping me
    obey your teachings.
³⁰I have chosen the way of truth;
    I have obeyed your laws.
³¹I hold on to your rules.
    LORD, do not let me be disgraced.
³²I will quickly obey your commands,
    because you have made me happy.

³³LORD, teach me your demands,
    and I will keep them until the end.
³⁴Help me understand, so I can keep
    your teachings,
    obeying them with all my heart.
³⁵Lead me in the path of your
    commands,
    because that makes me happy.
³⁶Make me want to keep your rules
    instead of wishing for riches.
³⁷Keep me from looking at worthless
    things.
    Let me live by your word.
³⁸Keep your promise to me, your servant,
    so you will be respected.
³⁹Take away the shame I fear,
    because your laws are good.
⁴⁰How I want to follow your orders.
    Give me life because of your
    goodness.

⁴¹LORD, show me your love,
    and save me as you have
    promised.
⁴²I have an answer for people who
    insult me,
    because I trust what you say.

STEP 6

Were entirely ready to have God
remove all these defects of character.

Psalm 119:28–40

Psalm 119 is sometimes called "the wisdom psalm." Step 6 in your recovery plan depends on learning about God's wisdom. The truth is that if you plant seeds of wisdom in your life, you eventually reap a harvest of peace and joy.

As you read through this lengthy psalm, you may find the psalmist expressing feelings and longings much like your own. He grieves over his shortcomings and longs for God to change him. He expresses one of his deepest concerns when he prays, "Don't let me be dishonest" (verse 29). In the part of this psalm you just read, the poet essentially tells God to do whatever it takes to transform his life to conform to God's ways.

Because the writer places his life squarely in God's hands, he shifts his focus from how big his problems are to how big God's power to change them is. You also need to fix your attention on God and his will. God's power alone can change your life. This starts when you are totally ready to let him remove all your defects of character.

SEE **PAGE 48** OF THE INTRODUCTORY MATERIAL FOR **STEP 7**.

⁴³Never keep me from speaking your
truth,
because I depend on your fair laws.
⁴⁴I will obey your teachings
forever and ever.
⁴⁵So I will live in freedom,
because I want to follow your
orders.
⁴⁶I will discuss your rules with kings
and will not be ashamed.
⁴⁷I enjoy obeying your commands,
which I love.
⁴⁸I praise your commands, which I love,
and I think about your demands.

⁴⁹Remember your promise to me, your
servant;
it gives me hope.
⁵⁰When I suffer, this comforts me:
Your promise gives me life.
⁵¹Proud people always make fun of me,
but I do not reject your teachings.
⁵²I remember your laws from long ago,
and they comfort me, LORD.
⁵³I become angry with wicked people
who do not keep your teachings.
⁵⁴I sing about your demands
wherever I live.
⁵⁵LORD, I remember you at night,
and I will obey your teachings.
⁵⁶This is what I do:
I follow your orders.

⁵⁷LORD, you are my share in life;
I have promised to obey your
words.
⁵⁸I prayed to you with all my heart.
Have mercy on me as you have
promised.
⁵⁹I thought about my life,
and I decided to follow your rules.
⁶⁰I hurried and did not wait
to obey your commands.
⁶¹Wicked people have tied me up,
but I have not forgotten your
teachings.

⁶²In the middle of the night, I get up to
thank you
because your laws are right.
⁶³I am a friend to everyone who fears
you,
to anyone who obeys your orders.
⁶⁴LORD, your love fills the earth.
Teach me your demands.

⁶⁵You have done good things for your
servant,
as you have promised, LORD.
⁶⁶Teach me wisdom and knowledge
because I trust your commands.
⁶⁷Before I suffered, I did wrong,
but now I obey your word.
⁶⁸You are good, and you do what is
good.
Teach me your demands.
⁶⁹Proud people have made up lies about
me,
but I will follow your orders with all
my heart.
⁷⁰Those people have no feelings,
but I love your teachings.
⁷¹It was good for me to suffer
so I would learn your demands.
⁷²Your teachings are worth more to me
than thousands of pieces of gold
and silver.

⁷³You made me and formed me with
your hands.
Give me understanding so I can
learn your commands.
⁷⁴Let those who respect you rejoice
when they see me,
because I put my hope in your
word.
⁷⁵LORD, I know that your laws are right
and that it was right for you to
punish me.
⁷⁶Comfort me with your love,
as you promised me, your servant.
⁷⁷Have mercy on me so that I may live.
I love your teachings.

STEP
5

78Make proud people ashamed because
      they lied about me.
    But I will think about your orders.
79Let those who respect you return to
      me,
    those who know your rules.
80Let me obey your demands perfectly
    so I will not be ashamed.

81I am weak from waiting for you to
      save me,
    but I hope in your word.
82My eyes are tired from looking for your
      promise.
    When will you comfort me?
83Even though I am like a wine bag
      going up in smoke,
    I do not forget your demands.
84How long will I live?
    When will you judge those who are
      hurting me?
85Proud people have dug pits to trap me.
    They have nothing to do with your
      teachings.
86All of your commands can be trusted.
    Liars are hurting me. Help me!
87They have almost put me in the
      grave,
    but I have not rejected your orders.
88Give me life by your love
    so I can obey your rules.

89Lord, your word is everlasting;
    it continues forever in heaven.
90Your loyalty will go on and on;
    you made the earth, and it still
      stands.
91All things continue to this day because
      of your laws,
    because all things serve you.
92If I had not loved your teachings,
    I would have died from my
      sufferings.
93I will never forget your orders,
    because you have given me life by
      them.

94I am yours. Save me.
    I want to obey your orders.
95Wicked people are waiting to destroy
      me,
    but I will think about your rules.
96Everything I see has its limits,
    but your commands have none.

97How I love your teachings!
    I think about them all day long.
98Your commands make me wiser than
      my enemies,
    because they are mine forever.
99I am wiser than all my teachers,
    because I think about your rules.
100I have more understanding than the
      elders,
    because I follow your orders.
101I have avoided every evil way
    so I could obey your word.
102I haven't walked away from your laws,
    because you yourself are my
      teacher.
103Your promises are sweet to me,
    sweeter than honey in my mouth!
104Your orders give me understanding,
    so I hate lying ways.

105Your word is like a lamp for my feet
    and a light for my path.
106I will do what I have promised
    and obey your fair laws.
107I have suffered for a long time.
    Lord, give me life by your word.
108Lord, accept my willing praise
    and teach me your laws.
109My life is always in danger,
    but I haven't forgotten your
      teachings.
110Wicked people have set a trap for me,
    but I haven't strayed from your
      orders.
111I will follow your rules forever,
    because they make me happy.
112I will try to do what you demand
    forever, until the end.

¹¹³I hate disloyal people,
> but I love your teachings.

¹¹⁴You are my hiding place and my shield;
> I hope in your word.

¹¹⁵Get away from me, you who do evil,
> so I can keep my God's commands.

¹¹⁶Support me as you promised so I can
> live.
> Don't let me be embarrassed
> because of my hopes.

¹¹⁷Help me, and I will be saved.
> I will always respect your demands.

¹¹⁸You reject those who ignore your
> demands,
> because their lies mislead them.

¹¹⁹You throw away the wicked of the
> world like trash.
> So I will love your rules.

¹²⁰I shake in fear of you;
> I respect your laws.

¹²¹I have done what is fair and right.
> Don't leave me to those who
> wrong me.

¹²²Promise that you will help me, your
> servant.
> Don't let proud people wrong me.

[STEP 2] ¹²³My eyes are tired from looking for your
> salvation
> and for your good promise.

¹²⁴Show your love to me, your servant,
> and teach me your demands.

¹²⁵I am your servant. Give me wisdom
> so I can understand your rules.

¹²⁶LORD, it is time for you to do something,
> because people have disobeyed
> your teachings.

¹²⁷I love your commands
> more than the purest gold.

¹²⁸I respect all your orders,
> so I hate lying ways.

¹²⁹Your rules are wonderful.
> That is why I keep them.

¹³⁰Learning your words gives wisdom
> and understanding for the foolish.

¹³¹I am nearly out of breath.
> I really want to learn your
> commands.

¹³²Look at me and have mercy on me
> as you do for those who love you.

[STEP 7] ¹³³Guide my steps as you promised;
> don't let any sin control me.

¹³⁴Save me from harmful people
> so I can obey your orders.

¹³⁵Show your kindness to me, your
> servant.
> Teach me your demands.

¹³⁶Tears stream from my eyes,
> because people do not obey your
> teachings.

¹³⁷LORD, you do what is right,
> and your laws are fair.

¹³⁸The rules you commanded are right
> and completely trustworthy.

¹³⁹I am so upset I am worn out,
> because my enemies have
> forgotten your words.

¹⁴⁰Your promises are proven,
> so I, your servant, love them.

¹⁴¹I am unimportant and hated,
> but I have not forgotten your orders.

¹⁴²Your goodness continues forever,
> and your teachings are true.

¹⁴³I have had troubles and misery,
> but I love your commands.

¹⁴⁴Your rules are always good.
> Help me understand so I can live.

¹⁴⁵LORD, I call to you with all my heart.
> Answer me, and I will keep your
> demands.

¹⁴⁶I call to you.
> Save me so I can obey your rules.

¹⁴⁷I wake up early in the morning and cry
> out.
> I hope in your word.

¹⁴⁸I stay awake all night
> so I can think about your promises.

¹⁴⁹Listen to me because of your love;
> LORD, give me life by your laws.

¹⁵⁰Those who love evil are near,
    but they are far from your
        teachings.
¹⁵¹But, LORD, you are also near,
    and all your commands are true.
¹⁵²Long ago I learned from your rules
    that you made them to continue
        forever.

¹⁵³See my suffering and rescue me,
    because I have not forgotten your
        teachings.
¹⁵⁴Argue my case and save me.
    Let me live by your promises.
¹⁵⁵Wicked people are far from being
        saved,
    because they do not want your
        demands.
¹⁵⁶LORD, you are very kind;
    give me life by your laws.
¹⁵⁷Many enemies are after me,
    but I have not rejected your rules.
¹⁵⁸I see those traitors, and I hate them,
    because they do not obey what
        you say.
¹⁵⁹See how I love your orders.
    LORD, give me life by your love.
¹⁶⁰Your words are true from the start,
    and all your laws will be fair
        forever.

¹⁶¹Leaders attack me for no reason,
    but I fear your law in my heart.

STEP 2

¹⁶²I am as happy over your promises
    as if I had found a great treasure.
¹⁶³I hate and despise lies,
    but I love your teachings.
¹⁶⁴Seven times a day I praise you
    for your fair laws.
¹⁶⁵Those who love your teachings will
        find true peace,
    and nothing will defeat them.
¹⁶⁶I am waiting for you to save me, LORD.
    I will obey your commands.

¹⁶⁷I obey your rules,
    and I love them very much.

¹⁶⁸I obey your orders and rules,
    because you know everything I do.

¹⁶⁹Hear my cry to you, LORD.
    Let your word help me understand.
¹⁷⁰Listen to my prayer;
    save me as you promised.
¹⁷¹Let me speak your praise,
    because you have taught me your
        demands.
¹⁷²Let me sing about your promises,
    because all your commands are
        fair.
¹⁷³Give me your helping hand,
    because I have chosen your
        commands.
¹⁷⁴I want you to save me, LORD.
    I love your teachings.
¹⁷⁵Let me live so I can praise you,
    and let your laws help me.
¹⁷⁶I have wandered like a lost sheep.
    Look for your servant, because I
        have not forgotten your
        commands.

PSALM 120

A psalm for going up to worship.

¹When I was in trouble, I called to the
        LORD,
    and he answered me.
²LORD, save me from liars
    and from those who plan evil.

³You who plan evil, what will God do to
        you?
    How will he punish you?
⁴He will punish you with the sharp
        arrows of a warrior
    and with burning coals of wood.

⁵How terrible it is for me to live in the
        land of Meshech,
    to live among the people of Kedar.
⁶I have lived too long
    with people who hate peace.
⁷When I talk peace,
    they want war.

PSALM 121

A song for going up to worship.

STEP 2

¹I look up to the hills,
but where does my help come
from?
²My help comes from the LORD,
who made heaven and earth.

³He will not let you be defeated.
He who guards you never sleeps.
⁴He who guards Israel
never rests or sleeps.
⁵The LORD guards you.
The LORD is the shade that
protects you from the sun.
⁶The sun cannot hurt you during the
day,
and the moon cannot hurt you at
night.
⁷The LORD will protect you from all
dangers;
he will guard your life.
⁸The LORD will guard you as you come
and go,
both now and forever.

PSALM 122

A song for going up to worship. Of David.

¹I was happy when they said to me,
"Let's go to the Temple of the
LORD."
²Jerusalem, we are standing
at your gates.

³Jerusalem is built as a city
with the buildings close together.
⁴The tribes go up there,
the tribes who belong to the LORD.
It is the rule in Israel
to praise the LORD at Jerusalem.
⁵There the descendants of David
set their thrones to judge the
people.

⁶Pray for peace in Jerusalem:
"May those who love her be safe.

⁷May there be peace within her walls
and safety within her strong
towers."
⁸To help my relatives and friends,
I say, "Let Jerusalem have peace."
⁹For the sake of the Temple of the
LORD our God,
I wish good for her.

PSALM 123

A song for going up to worship.

¹LORD, I look upward to you,
you who live in heaven.
²Slaves depend on their masters,
and a female servant depends on
her mistress.
In the same way, we depend on the
LORD our God;
we wait for him to show us mercy.

³Have mercy on us, LORD. Have mercy
on us,
because we have been insulted.
⁴We have suffered many insults from
lazy people
and much cruelty from the proud.

PSALM 124

A song for going up to worship. Of David.

¹What if the LORD had not been on our
side?
(Let Israel repeat this.)
²What if the LORD had not been on our
side
when we were attacked?
³When they were angry with us,
they would have swallowed us
alive.
⁴They would have been like a flood
drowning us;
they would have poured over us
like a river.
⁵   They would have swept us away
like a mighty stream.

⁶Praise the LORD,
who did not let them chew us up.

⁷We escaped like a bird
    from the hunter's trap.
The trap broke,
    and we escaped.
⁸Our help comes from the LORD,
    who made heaven and earth.

PSALM 125

A song for going up to worship.

¹Those who trust the LORD are like
    Mount Zion,
    which sits unmoved forever.
²As the mountains surround Jerusalem,
    the LORD surrounds his people
    now and forever.

³The wicked will not rule
    over those who do right.
If they did, the people who do right
    might use their power to do evil.

⁴LORD, be good to those who are good,
    whose hearts are honest.
⁵But, LORD, when you remove those
    who do evil,
    also remove those who stop
    following you.

Let there be peace in Israel.

PSALM 126

A song for going up to worship.

¹When the LORD brought the prisoners
    back to Jerusalem,
    it seemed as if we were dreaming.
²Then we were filled with laughter,
    and we sang happy songs.
Then the other nations said,
    "The LORD has done great things
    for them."
³The LORD has done great things for us,
    and we are very glad.

⁴LORD, return our prisoners again,
    as you bring streams to the desert.

STEP 9
⁵Those who cry as they plant crops
    will sing at harvest time.

⁶Those who cry
    as they carry out the seeds
will return singing
    and carrying bundles of grain.

PSALM 127

A song for going up to worship. Of Solomon.

STEP 11
¹If the LORD doesn't build the house,
    the builders are working for
    nothing.
If the LORD doesn't guard the city,
    the guards are watching for
    nothing.
²It is no use for you to get up early
    and stay up late,
working for a living.
    The LORD gives sleep to those he
    loves.
³Children are a gift from the LORD;
    babies are a reward.
⁴Children who are born to a young
    man
    are like arrows in the hand of a
    warrior.
⁵Happy is the man
    who has his bag full of arrows.
They will not be defeated
    when they fight their enemies at
    the city gate.

PSALM 128

A song for going up to worship.

STEP 11
¹Happy are those who respect the
    LORD and obey him.
²You will enjoy what you work for,
    and you will be blessed with good
    things.
³Your wife will give you many
    children,
    like a vine that produces much
    fruit.
Your children will bring you much
    good,
    like olive branches that produce
    many olives.

STEP 11

Sought through prayer and meditation to improve our conscious contact with God **as we understood Him,** praying only for knowledge of His will for us and the power to carry that out.

Psalm 127:1–2

Maybe you grew up thinking you measure a person's worth by how hard he or she works. Maybe you thought that if you wanted something badly enough and worked hard enough, you were bound to get it.

By this point in your Twelve Step recovery, you know those aren't realistic rules to live by. There are jerks who work hard; and there are lots of dreams that never come true, no matter how hard you chase them. In fact, you can end up driving yourself into addictive or obsessive behavior trying to make unrealistic dreams come true.

The first two verses of Psalm 127 give you God's wise perspective on pursuing big plans. You start by admitting your utter dependence on God for success. Second, you find courage in knowing that God likes to give good gifts to his children. You also find peace in knowing that rest is one of his gifts to you.

Make it part of the routine of your life to let God direct your work and your dreams. Meditate on his Word and pray regularly as ways to find his guidance. Then obey him; and you will experience his blessing, protection, and restful peace.

SEE **PAGE 70** OF THE INTRODUCTORY MATERIAL FOR **STEP 12.**

⁴This is how the man who respects
the Lord
will be blessed.
⁵May the Lord bless you from Mount
Zion;
may you enjoy the good things of
Jerusalem all your life.
⁶May you see your grandchildren.

Let there be peace in Israel.

PSALM 129

A song for going up to worship.

¹They have treated me badly all my
life.
(Let Israel repeat this.)
²They have treated me badly all my life,
but they have not defeated me.
³Like farmers plowing, they plowed
over my back,
making long wounds.
⁴But the Lord does what is right;
he has set me free from those
wicked people.

⁵Let those who hate Jerusalem
be turned back in shame.
⁶Let them be like the grass on the roof
that dries up before it has grown.
⁷There is not enough of it to fill a hand
or to make into a bundle to fill
one's arms.
⁸Let those who pass by them not say,
"May the Lord bless you.
We bless you by the power of the
Lord."

PSALM 130

A song for going up to worship.

STEP 2

¹Lord, I am in great trouble,
so I call out to you.
²Lord, hear my voice;
listen to my prayer for help.
³Lord, if you punished people for all
their sins,
no one would be left, Lord.

⁴But you forgive us,
so you are respected.

⁵I wait for the Lord to help me,
and I trust his word.
⁶I wait for the Lord to help me
more than night watchmen wait
for the dawn,
more than night watchmen wait
for the dawn.

⁷People of Israel, put your hope in the
Lord
because he is loving
and able to save.
⁸He will save Israel
from all their sins.

PSALM 131

A song for going up to worship. Of David.

¹Lord, my heart is not proud;
I don't look down on others.
I don't do great things,
and I can't do miracles.
²But I am calm and quiet,
like a baby with its mother.
I am at peace, like a baby with its
mother.

³People of Israel, put your hope in the
Lord
now and forever.

PSALM 132

A song for going up to worship.

¹Lord, remember David
and all his suffering.
²He made an oath to the Lord,
a promise to the Mighty God of
Jacob.
³He said, "I will not go home to my
house,
or lie down on my bed,
⁴or close my eyes,
or let myself sleep,
⁵until I find a place for the Lord.

I want to provide a home for the
    Mighty God of Jacob."

[6]We heard about the Ark in
    Bethlehem.
    We found it at Kiriath Jearim.
[7]Let's go to the LORD's house.
    Let's worship at his footstool.
[8]Rise, LORD, and come to your resting
    place;
    come with the Ark that shows your
    strength.
[9]May your priests do what is right.
    May your people sing for joy.

[10]For the sake of your servant David,
    do not reject your appointed
    king.
[11]The LORD made a promise to David,
    a sure promise that he will not
    take back.
He promised, "I will make one of your
    descendants
    rule as king after you.
[12]If your sons keep my agreement
    and the rules that I teach them,
then their sons after them will rule
    on your throne forever and ever."

[13]The LORD has chosen Jerusalem;
    he wants it for his home.
[14]He says, "This is my resting place
    forever.
    Here is where I want to stay.
[15]I will bless her with plenty;
    I will fill her poor with food.
[16]I will cover her priests with salvation,
    and those who worship me will
    really sing for joy.

[17]"I will make a king come from the
    family of David.
    I will provide my appointed one
    descendants to rule after
    him.
[18]I will cover his enemies with shame,
    but his crown will shine."

PSALM 133

A song for going up to worship. Of David.

[1]It is good and pleasant
    when God's people live together in
    peace!
[2]It is like perfumed oil poured on the
    priest's head
    and running down his beard.
It ran down Aaron's beard
    and on to the collar of his robes.
[3]It is like the dew of Mount Hermon
    falling on the hills of Jerusalem.
There the LORD gives his blessing
    of life forever.

STEP
8

PSALM 134

A song for going up to worship.

[1]Praise the LORD, all you servants of
    the LORD,
    you who serve at night in the
    Temple of the LORD.
[2]Raise your hands in the Temple
    and praise the LORD.

[3]May the LORD bless you from Mount
    Zion,
    he who made heaven and earth.

PSALM 135

[1]Praise the LORD!

Praise the name of the LORD;
    praise him, you servants of the
    LORD,
[2]you who stand in the LORD's Temple
    and in the Temple courtyards.
[3]Praise the LORD, because he is good;
    sing praises to him, because it is
    pleasant.

[4]The LORD has chosen the people of
    Jacob for himself;
    he has chosen the people of Israel
    for his very own.
[5]I know that the LORD is great.
    Our Lord is greater than all the
    gods.

6The LORD does what he pleases,
   in heaven and on earth,
   in the seas and the deep oceans.
7He brings the clouds from the ends
      of the earth.
   He sends the lightning with the
      rain.
   He brings out the wind from his
      storehouses.

8He destroyed the firstborn sons in
      Egypt
   the firstborn of both people and
      animals.
9He did many signs and miracles in
      Egypt
   against the king and his servants.
10He defeated many nations
   and killed powerful kings:
11Sihon king of the Amorites,
   Og king of Bashan,
   and all the kings of Canaan.
12Then he gave their land as a gift,
   a gift to his people, the Israelites.

13LORD, your name is everlasting;
   LORD, you will be remembered
      forever.
14The LORD defends his people
   and has mercy on his servants.

15The idols of other nations are made of
      silver and gold,
   the work of human hands.
16They have mouths, but they cannot
      speak.
   They have eyes, but they cannot
      see.
17They have ears, but they cannot hear.
   They have no breath in their
      mouths.
18People who make idols will be like
      them,
   and so will those who trust them.

19Family of Israel, praise the LORD.
   Family of Aaron, praise the LORD.

20Family of Levi, praise the LORD.
   You who respect the LORD should
      praise him.
21You people of Jerusalem, praise the
      LORD on Mount Zion.
   Praise the LORD!

PSALM 136

1Give thanks to the LORD because he is
      good.
   His love continues forever.
2Give thanks to the God of gods.
   His love continues forever.
3Give thanks to the Lord of lords.
   His love continues forever.

4Only he can do great miracles.
   His love continues forever.
5With his wisdom he made the skies.
   His love continues forever.
6He spread out the earth on the seas.
   His love continues forever.
7He made the sun and the moon.
   His love continues forever.
8He made the sun to rule the day.
   His love continues forever.
9He made the moon and stars to rule
      the night.
   His love continues forever.

10He killed the firstborn sons of the
      Egyptians.
   His love continues forever.
11He brought the people of Israel out of
      Egypt.
   His love continues forever.
12He did it with his great power and
      strength.
   His love continues forever.
13He parted the water of the Red Sea.
   His love continues forever.
14He brought the Israelites through the
      middle of it.
   His love continues forever.
15But the king of Egypt and his army
      drowned in the Red Sea.
   His love continues forever.

¹⁶He led his people through the desert.
  His love continues forever.
¹⁷He defeated great kings.
  His love continues forever.
¹⁸He killed powerful kings.
  His love continues forever.
¹⁹He defeated Sihon king of the
    Amorites.
  His love continues forever.
²⁰He defeated Og king of Bashan.
  His love continues forever.
²¹He gave their land as a gift.
  His love continues forever.
²²It was a gift to his servants, the
    Israelites.
  His love continues forever.

²³He remembered us when we were in
    trouble.
  His love continues forever.
²⁴He freed us from our enemies.
  His love continues forever.
²⁵He gives food to every living creature.
  His love continues forever.

²⁶Give thanks to the God of heaven.
  His love continues forever.

PSALM 137

¹By the rivers in Babylon we sat and
    cried
  when we remembered Jerusalem.
²On the poplar trees nearby
  we hung our harps.
³Those who captured us asked us to
    sing;
  our enemies wanted happy songs.
  They said, "Sing us a song about
    Jerusalem!"

⁴But we cannot sing songs about the
    LORD
  while we are in this foreign
    country!
⁵Jerusalem, if I forget you,
  let my right hand lose its skill.

⁶Let my tongue stick to the roof of my
    mouth
  if I do not remember you,
 if I do not think about Jerusalem
  as my greatest joy.

⁷LORD, remember what the Edomites did
  on the day Jerusalem fell.
  They said, "Tear it down!
    Tear it down to its foundations!"

⁸People of Babylon, you will be
    destroyed.
    The people who pay you back for
      what you did to us will be
      happy.
⁹They will grab your babies
  and throw them against the rocks.

PSALM 138

A psalm of David.

¹LORD, I will thank you with all my
    heart;
  I will sing to you before the gods.
²I will bow down facing your holy
    Temple,
    and I will thank you for your love
      and loyalty.
  You have made your name and your
    word
    greater than anything.
³On the day I called to you, you
    answered me.
  You made me strong and brave.

⁴LORD, let all the kings of the earth
    praise you
  when they hear the words you
    speak.
⁵They will sing about what the LORD
    has done,
  because the LORD's glory is great.

⁶Though the LORD is supreme,
  he takes care of those who are
    humble,
  but he stays away from the proud.

⁷LORD, even when I have trouble all
around me,
    you will keep me alive.
When my enemies are angry,
    you will reach down and save me
    by your power.
⁸LORD, you do everything for me.
    LORD, your love continues forever.
    Do not leave us, whom you made.

PSALM 139

For the director of music. A psalm of David.

STEP 2

¹LORD, you have examined me
    and know all about me.
²You know when I sit down and when I
    get up.
    You know my thoughts before I
    think them.
³You know where I go and where I lie
    down.
    You know everything I do.
⁴LORD, even before I say a word,
    you already know it.
⁵You are all around me—in front and
    in back—
    and have put your hand on me.
⁶Your knowledge is amazing to me;
    it is more than I can understand.

⁷Where can I go to get away from your
    Spirit?
    Where can I run from you?
⁸If I go up to the heavens, you are
    there.
    If I lie down in the grave, you are
    there.
⁹If I rise with the sun in the east
    and settle in the west beyond the
    sea,
¹⁰even there you would guide me.
    With your right hand you would
    hold me.
¹¹I could say, "The darkness will
    hide me.
    Let the light around me turn into
    night."

¹²But even the darkness is not dark to
    you.
    The night is as light as the day;
    darkness and light are the same to
    you.

¹³You made my whole being;
    you formed me in my mother's
    body.
¹⁴I praise you because you made me in
    an amazing and wonderful
    way.
    What you have done is wonderful.
    I know this very well.
¹⁵You saw my bones being formed
    as I took shape in my mother's
    body.
When I was put together there,
¹⁶   you saw my body as it was
    formed.
All the days planned for me
    were written in your book
    before I was one day old.

¹⁷God, your thoughts are precious
    to me.
    They are so many!
¹⁸If I could count them,
    they would be more than all the
    grains of sand.
When I wake up,
    I am still with you.

¹⁹God, I wish you would kill the wicked!
    Get away from me, you murderers!
²⁰They say evil things about you.
    Your enemies use your name
    thoughtlessly.
²¹LORD, I hate those who hate you;
    I hate those who rise up against
    you.
²²I feel only hate for them;
    they are my enemies.

²³God, examine me and know my heart;
    test me and know my anxious
    thoughts.

STEP 6

²⁴See if there is any bad thing in me.
Lead me on the road to
everlasting life.

PSALM 140

For the director of music. A psalm of David.

¹Lᴏʀᴅ, rescue me from evil people;
protect me from cruel people
²who make evil plans,
who always start fights.
³They make their tongues sharp as a
snake's;
their words are like snake poison.
Selah

⁴Lᴏʀᴅ, guard me from the power of
wicked people;
protect me from cruel people
who plan to trip me up.
⁵The proud hid a trap for me.
They spread out a net beside the
road;
they set traps for me. *Selah*

⁶I said to the Lᴏʀᴅ, "You are my God."
Lᴏʀᴅ, listen to my prayer for help.
⁷Lᴏʀᴅ God, my mighty savior,
you protect me in battle.
⁸Lᴏʀᴅ, do not give the wicked what
they want.
Don't let their plans succeed,
or they will become proud. *Selah*

⁹Those around me have planned
trouble.
Now let it come to them.
¹⁰Let burning coals fall on them.
Throw them into the fire
or into pits from which they
cannot escape.
¹¹Don't let liars settle in the land.
Let evil quickly hunt down cruel
people.

¹²I know the Lᴏʀᴅ will get justice for the
poor
and will defend the needy in court.

¹³Good people will praise his name;
honest people will live in his
presence.

PSALM 141

A psalm of David.

¹Lᴏʀᴅ, I call to you. Come quickly.
Listen to me when I call to you.
²Let my prayer be like incense placed
before you,
and my praise like the evening
sacrifice.

³Lᴏʀᴅ, help me control my tongue;
help me be careful about what I
say.
⁴Take away my desire to do evil
or to join others in doing wrong.
Don't let me eat tasty food
with those who do evil.

STEP 6

⁵If a good person punished me, that
would be kind.
If he corrected me, that would be
like perfumed oil on my
head.
I shouldn't refuse it.
But I pray against those who do evil.
⁶ Let their leaders be thrown down
the cliffs.
Then people will know that I have
spoken correctly.
⁷"The ground is plowed and broken up.
In the same way, our bones have
been scattered at the
grave."

⁸Gᴏᴅ, I look to you for help.
I trust in you, Lᴏʀᴅ. Don't let me
die.
⁹Protect me from the traps they set
for me
and from the net that evil people
have spread.
¹⁰Let the wicked fall into their own nets,
but let me pass by safely.

PSALM 142

A maskil of David when he was in the cave. A prayer.

STEP 2

¹I cry out to the LORD;
    I pray to the LORD for mercy.
²I pour out my problems to him;
    I tell him my troubles.
³When I am afraid,
    you, LORD, know the way out.
In the path where I walk,
    a trap is hidden for me.
⁴Look around me and see.
    No one cares about me.
I have no place of safety;
    no one cares if I live.

⁵LORD, I cry out to you.
    I say, "You are my protection.
    You are all I want in this life."
⁶Listen to my cry,
    because I am helpless.
Save me from those who are
        chasing me,
    because they are too strong
        for me.
⁷Free me from my prison,
    and then I will praise your name.
Then good people will surround me,
    because you have taken care
        of me.

PSALM 143

A psalm of David.

¹LORD, hear my prayer;
    listen to my cry for mercy.
Answer me
    because you are loyal and good.
²Don't judge me, your servant,
    because no one alive is right
        before you.
³My enemies are chasing me;
    they crushed me to the ground.
They made me live in darkness
    like those long dead.
⁴I am afraid;
    my courage is gone.

⁵I remember what happened long ago;
    I consider everything you have
        done.
    I think about all you have made.
⁶I lift my hands to you in prayer.
    As a dry land needs rain, I thirst
        for you.   Selah

⁷LORD, answer me quickly,
    because I am getting weak.
Don't turn away from me,
    or I will be like those who are
        dead.
⁸Tell me in the morning about your love,
    because I trust you.
Show me what I should do,
    because my prayers go up to you.

STEP 3

⁹LORD, save me from my enemies;
    I hide in you.
¹⁰Teach me to do what you want,
    because you are my God.
Let your good Spirit
    lead me on level ground.

¹¹LORD, let me live
    so people will praise you.
In your goodness
    save me from my troubles.
¹²In your love defeat my enemies.
    Destroy all those who trouble me,
    because I am your servant.

PSALM 144

Of David.

¹Praise the LORD, my Rock,
    who trains me for war,
    who trains me for battle.
²He protects me like a strong, walled
        city, and he loves me.
He is my defender and my Savior,
    my shield and my protection.
    He helps me keep my people
        under control.

³LORD, why are people important to
        you?

STEP 2

Came to believe that a Power greater than
ourselves could restore us to sanity.

Psalm 142

Before David was king, he was an outlaw chased all over southern
Israel by the armies of King Saul. During one particularly desperate
time, David and his men hid in a cave. But David didn't trust the
cave to save him. His enemies were too strong and cunning. David
looked to the Lord for deliverance. He cried out to God, "Free me
from my prison" (verse 7).

When you wrestle with temptations to go back again to your
addition, your soul may feel like it's imprisoned and helpless.
Addictive behavior generates the kind of chaos and confusion in
your life that make you a prisoner of guilt, fear, frustration, and
pain. Those destructive emotions mess with your sanity and cripple
your decision making.

Look again at David's cure for such a situation. In verses 5–7, he
shifted his focus from his strong enemies to his stronger Lord. He
rejoiced that God was his true refuge. He declared confidently,
"You have taken care of me." Let David's example encourage you
to turn to God for strength, for comfort, and for restoration to
sanity.

SEE **PAGE 29** OF THE INTRODUCTORY MATERIAL FOR **STEP 3**.

Why do you even think about
human beings?
⁴People are like a breath;
their lives are like passing
shadows.

⁵LORD, tear open the sky and come
down.
Touch the mountains so they will
smoke.
⁶Send the lightning and scatter my
enemies.
Shoot your arrows and force them
away.
⁷Reach down from above.
Save me and rescue me out of this
sea of enemies,
from these foreigners.
⁸They are liars;
they are dishonest.

⁹God, I will sing a new song to you;
I will play to you on the ten-
stringed harp.
¹⁰You give victory to kings.
You save your servant David from
cruel swords.
¹¹Save me, rescue me from these
foreigners.
They are liars; they are
dishonest.

¹²Let our sons in their youth
grow like plants.
Let our daughters be
like the decorated stones in the
Temple.
¹³Let our barns be filled
with crops of all kinds.
Let our sheep in the fields have
thousands and tens of thousands
of lambs.
¹⁴   Let our cattle be strong.
Let no one break in.
Let there be no war,
no screams in our streets.

¹⁵Happy are those who are like this;
happy are the people whose God
is the LORD.

PSALM 145

A psalm of praise. Of David.

¹I praise your greatness, my God the
King;
I will praise you forever and ever.
²I will praise you every day;
I will praise you forever and ever.
³The LORD is great and worthy of our
praise;
no one can understand how great
he is.

⁴Parents will tell their children what
you have done.
They will retell your mighty acts,
⁵wonderful majesty, and glory.
And I will think about your
miracles.
⁶They will tell about the amazing
things you do,
and I will tell how great you are.
⁷They will remember your great
goodness
and will sing about your fairness.

⁸The LORD is kind and shows mercy.
He does not become angry quickly
but is full of love.
⁹The LORD is good to everyone;
he is merciful to all he has made.
¹⁰LORD, everything you have made will
praise you;
those who belong to you will bless
you.
¹¹They will tell about the glory of your
kingdom
and will speak about your
power.
¹²Then everyone will know the mighty
things you do
and the glory and majesty of your
kingdom.

STEP
12

¹³Your kingdom will go on and on,
and you will rule forever.

The Lord will keep all his
promises;
he is loyal to all he has made.
¹⁴The Lord helps those who have been
defeated
and takes care of those who are in
trouble.
¹⁵All living things look to you for food,
and you give it to them at the right
time.
¹⁶You open your hand,
and you satisfy all living things.

¹⁷Everything the Lord does is right.
He is loyal to all he has made.
¹⁸The Lord is close to everyone who
prays to him,
to all who truly pray to him.
¹⁹He gives those who respect him what
they want.
He listens when they cry, and he
saves them.
²⁰The Lord protects everyone who
loves him,
but he will destroy the wicked.

²¹I will praise the Lord.
Let everyone praise his holy name
forever.

PSALM 146

¹Praise the Lord!

My whole being, praise the Lord.
²I will praise the Lord all my life;
I will sing praises to my God as
long as I live.

³Do not put your trust in princes
or other people, who cannot save
you.
⁴When people die, they are buried.
Then all of their plans come to an
end.

⁵Happy are those who are helped by
the God of Jacob.
Their hope is in the Lord their
God.
⁶He made heaven and earth,
the sea and everything in it.
He remains loyal forever.
⁷He does what is fair for those who
have been wronged.
He gives food to the hungry.
The Lord sets the prisoners free.
⁸   The Lord gives sight to the blind.
The Lord lifts up people who are in
trouble.
The Lord loves those who do
right.
⁹The Lord protects the foreigners.
He defends the orphans and
widows,
but he blocks the way of the
wicked.

¹⁰The Lord will be King forever.
Jerusalem, your God is everlasting.

Praise the Lord!

PSALM 147

¹Praise the Lord!

It is good to sing praises to our God;
it is good and pleasant to praise
him.
²The Lord rebuilds Jerusalem;
he brings back the captured
Israelites.
³He heals the brokenhearted
and bandages their wounds.

⁴He counts the stars
and names each one.
⁵Our Lord is great and very powerful.
There is no limit to what he
knows.
⁶The Lord defends the humble,
but he throws the wicked to the
ground.

⁷Sing praises to the LORD;
  praise our God with harps.
⁸He fills the sky with clouds
  and sends rain to the earth
  and makes grass grow on the hills.
⁹He gives food to cattle
  and to the little birds that call.

¹⁰He is not impressed with the strength
    of a horse
  or with human might.

STEP 3

¹¹The LORD is pleased with those who
    respect him,
  with those who trust his love.

¹²Jerusalem, praise the LORD;
  Jerusalem, praise your God.
¹³He makes your city gates strong
  and blesses your children inside.
¹⁴He brings peace to your country
  and fills you with the finest grain.

¹⁵He gives a command to the earth,
  and it quickly obeys him.
¹⁶He spreads the snow like wool
  and scatters the frost like ashes.
¹⁷He throws down hail like rocks.
  No one can stand the cold he
    sends.
¹⁸Then he gives a command, and it
    melts.
  He sends the breezes, and the
    waters flow.

¹⁹He gave his word to Jacob,
  his laws and demands to Israel.
²⁰He didn't do this for any other
    nation.
  They don't know his laws.

Praise the LORD!

PSALM 148

¹Praise the LORD!

Praise the LORD from the skies.
  Praise him high above the earth.
²Praise him, all you angels.

Praise him, all you armies of
    heaven.
³Praise him, sun and moon.
  Praise him, all you shining stars.
⁴Praise him, highest heavens
  and you waters above the sky.
⁵Let them praise the LORD,
  because they were created by his
    command.
⁶He put them in place forever and
    ever;
  he made a law that will never
    change.

⁷Praise the LORD from the earth,
  you large sea animals and all the
    oceans,
⁸lightning and hail, snow and mist,
  and stormy winds that obey him,
⁹mountains and all hills,
  fruit trees and all cedars,
¹⁰wild animals and all cattle,
  crawling animals and birds,
¹¹kings of the earth and all nations,
  princes and all rulers of the earth,
¹²young men and women,
  old people and children.

¹³Praise the LORD,
  because he alone is great.
  He is more wonderful than heaven
    and earth.
¹⁴God has given his people a king.
  He should be praised by all who
    belong to him;
  he should be praised by the
    Israelites, the people closest
    to his heart.

Praise the LORD!

PSALM 149

¹Praise the LORD!

Sing a new song to the LORD;
  sing his praise in the meeting of
    his people.

²Let the Israelites be happy because of
God, their Maker.
Let the people of Jerusalem
rejoice because of their
King.
³They should praise him with
dancing.
They should sing praises to him
with tambourines and
harps.

STEP 2
⁴The LORD is pleased with his
people;
he saves the humble.

⁵Let those who worship him rejoice in
his glory.
Let them sing for joy even in bed!

⁶Let them shout his praise
with their two-edged swords in
their hands.
⁷They will punish the nations
and defeat the people.
⁸They will put those kings in chains
and those important men in iron
bands.

⁹They will punish them as God has
written.
God is honored by all who worship
him.

Praise the LORD!

PSALM 150

¹Praise the LORD!

Praise God in his Temple;
praise him in his mighty heaven.
²Praise him for his strength;
praise him for his greatness.
³Praise him with trumpet blasts;
praise him with harps and lyres.
⁴Praise him with tambourines and
dancing;
praise him with stringed
instruments and flutes.
⁵Praise him with loud cymbals;
praise him with crashing cymbals.
⁶Let everything that breathes praise
the LORD.

Praise the LORD!

PROVERBS

Wise Teachings for God's People

1 These are the wise words of Solomon son of David, king of Israel.
²They teach wisdom and self-control;
  they will help you understand wise words.
³They will teach you how to be wise
  and self-controlled
  and will teach you to do what is
  honest and fair and right.
⁴They make the uneducated wise
  and give knowledge and sense to
  the young.
⁵Wise people can also listen and learn;
  even they can find good advice in
  these words.
⁶Then anyone can understand wise
  words and stories,
  the words of the wise and their
  riddles.

⁷Knowledge begins with respect for the LORD,
  but fools hate wisdom and discipline.

⁸My child, listen to your father's teaching
  and do not forget your mother's advice.
⁹Their teaching will be like flowers in
  your hair
  or a necklace around your neck.

¹⁰My child, if sinners try to lead you into
  sin,
  do not follow them.
¹¹They will say, "Come with us.
  Let's ambush and kill someone;
  let's attack some innocent people
  just for fun.
¹²Let's swallow them alive, as death
  does;

let's swallow them whole, as the
  grave does.
¹³We will take all kinds of valuable
  things
  and fill our houses with stolen
  goods.
¹⁴Come join us,
  and we will share with you stolen
  goods."
¹⁵My child, do not go along with them;
  do not do what they do.
¹⁶They are eager to do evil
  and are quick to kill.
¹⁷It is useless to spread out a net
  right where the birds can see it.
¹⁸But sinners will fall into their own
  traps;
  they will only catch themselves!
¹⁹All greedy people end up this way;
  greed kills selfish people.

²⁰Wisdom is like a woman shouting in
  the street;
  she raises her voice in the city
  squares.
²¹She cries out in the noisy street
  and shouts at the city gates:
²²"You fools, how long will you be
  foolish?
  How long will you make fun of
  wisdom
  and hate knowledge?
²³If only you had listened when I
  corrected you,
  I would have told you what's in my
  heart;
  I would have told you what I am
  thinking.
²⁴I called, but you refused to listen;
  I held out my hand, but you paid
  no attention.

²⁵You did not follow my advice
  and did not listen when I corrected
    you.
²⁶So I will laugh when you are in trouble.
  I will make fun when disaster
    strikes you,
²⁷when disaster comes over you like a
    storm,
  when trouble strikes you like a
    whirlwind,
  when pain and trouble overwhelm
    you.

²⁸"Then you will call to me,
  but I will not answer.
  You will look for me,
    but you will not find me.
²⁹It is because you rejected knowledge
  and did not choose to respect the
    LORD.
³⁰You did not accept my advice,
  and you rejected my correction.
³¹So you will get what you deserve;
  you will get what you planned for
    others.
³²Fools will die because they refuse to
    listen;
  they will be destroyed because
    they do not care.
³³But those who listen to me will live in
    safety
  and be at peace, without fear of
    injury."

2 My child, listen to what I say
    and remember what I
    command you.

STEP
2
²Listen carefully to wisdom;
  set your mind on understanding.
³Cry out for wisdom,
  and beg for understanding.
⁴Search for it like silver,
  and hunt for it like hidden
    treasure.
⁵Then you will understand respect for
    the LORD,

and you will find that you know
    God.
⁶Only the LORD gives wisdom;
  he gives knowledge and
    understanding.
⁷He stores up wisdom for those who
    are honest.
  Like a shield he protects the
    innocent.
⁸He makes sure that justice is done,
  and he protects those who are
    loyal to him.

⁹Then you will understand what is
    honest and fair
  and what is the good and right
    thing to do.
¹⁰Wisdom will come into your mind,
  and knowledge will be pleasing to
    you.
¹¹Good sense will protect you;
  understanding will guard you.
¹²It will keep you from the wicked,
  from those whose words are bad,
¹³who don't do what is right
  but what is evil.
¹⁴They enjoy doing wrong
  and are happy to do what is
    crooked and evil.
¹⁵What they do is wrong,
  and their ways are dishonest.

¹⁶It will save you from the unfaithful
    wife
  who tries to lead you into adultery
    with pleasing words.
¹⁷She leaves the husband she married
    when she was young.
  She ignores the promise she made
    before God.
¹⁸Her house is on the way to death;
  those who took that path are now
    all dead.
¹⁹No one who goes to her comes back
  or walks the path of life again.

²⁰But wisdom will help you be good
and do what is right.
²¹Those who are honest will live in the
land,
and those who are innocent will
remain in it.
²²But the wicked will be removed from
the land,
and the unfaithful will be thrown
out of it.

3 My child, do not forget my teaching,
but keep my commands in mind.
²Then you will live a long time,
and your life will be successful.

³Don't ever forget kindness and truth.
Wear them like a necklace.
Write them on your heart as if on a
tablet.
⁴Then you will be respected
and will please both God and
people.

STEP 3

⁵Trust the LORD with all your heart,
and don't depend on your own
understanding.
⁶Remember the LORD in all you do,
and he will give you success.

⁷Don't depend on your own wisdom.
Respect the LORD and refuse to do
wrong.
⁸Then your body will be healthy,
and your bones will be strong.

⁹Honor the LORD with your wealth
and the firstfruits from all your
crops.
¹⁰Then your barns will be full,
and your wine barrels will overflow
with new wine.

STEP 5

¹¹My child, do not reject the LORD's
discipline,
and don't get angry when he
corrects you.
¹²The LORD corrects those he loves,

just as parents correct the child
they delight in.

¹³Happy is the person who finds
wisdom,
the one who gets understanding.
¹⁴Wisdom is worth more than silver;
it brings more profit than gold.
¹⁵Wisdom is more precious than
rubies;
nothing you could want is equal
to it.
¹⁶With her right hand wisdom offers you
a long life,
and with her left hand she gives
you riches and honor.
¹⁷Wisdom will make your life pleasant
and will bring you peace.
¹⁸As a tree produces fruit, wisdom gives
life to those who use it,
and everyone who uses it will be
happy.

¹⁹The LORD made the earth, using his
wisdom.
He set the sky in place, using his
understanding.
²⁰With his knowledge, he made springs
flow into rivers
and the clouds drop rain on the
earth.

²¹My child, hold on to wisdom and good
sense.
Don't let them out of your sight.
²²They will give you life
and beauty like a necklace around
your neck.
²³Then you will go your way in safety,
and you will not get hurt.
²⁴When you lie down, you won't be
afraid;
when you lie down, you will sleep
in peace.
²⁵You won't be afraid of sudden
trouble;

STEP 3

Made a decision to turn our will and our lives
over to the care of God **as we understood Him.**

Proverbs 3:5–6

Addicts can trick themselves by thinking in circles and failing to
break out of their mental ruts. A.A. makes this observation about
relying too much on what goes on in our heads: "We had been
faithful, abjectly faithful to the God of Reason" (*Alcoholics
Anonymous*, p. 54). It's as though King Solomon had addicts in mind
when he wrote, "Don't depend on your own understanding" (verse
5). Intelligence and reason are precious gifts from God, but the fact
of the matter is that friendships with other people and with God
are more matters of the heart than of the head. These
relationships are what got messed up by your addictive behavior.

When you lean on your own understanding, you run into countless
barriers to recovery. How many times have you tried to think your
way out of a temptation to your addictive behavior? How many
times have you tried to reason your way out of feelings of
emptiness and uselessness? All to no avail.

Decisions "to turn our will and our lives over to the care of God"
involve several kinds of surrender. One of them is the surrender of
an inflated sense of personal intellectual ability. In Step 3, you start
learning to lean, not on your own understanding, but on the God of
your understanding.

SEE **PAGE 33** OF THE INTRODUCTORY MATERIAL FOR **STEP 4.**

you won't fear the ruin that comes
to the wicked,
²⁶because the LORD will keep you safe.
He will keep you from being
trapped.

STEP
9 ²⁷Whenever you are able,
do good to people who need help.
²⁸If you have what your neighbor asks
for,
don't say, "Come back later.
I will give it to you tomorrow."
²⁹Don't make plans to hurt your
neighbor
who lives nearby and trusts you.
³⁰Don't accuse a person for no good
reason;
don't accuse someone who has
not harmed you.

³¹Don't be jealous of those who use
violence,
and don't choose to be like them.
³²The LORD hates those who do wrong,
but he is a friend to those who are
honest.
³³The LORD will curse the evil person's
house,
but he will bless the home of
those who do right.
³⁴The LORD laughs at those who laugh
at him,
but he gives grace to those who
are not proud.
³⁵Wise people will receive honor,
but fools will be disgraced.

4 My children, listen to your father's
teaching;
pay attention so you will
understand.
²What I am telling you is good,
so do not forget what I teach you.
³When I was a young boy in my
father's house
and like an only child to my
mother,

⁴my father taught me and said,
"Hold on to my words with all your
heart.
Keep my commands and you will
live.
⁵Get wisdom and understanding.
Don't forget or ignore my words.
⁶Hold on to wisdom, and it will take
care of you.
Love it, and it will keep you safe.
⁷Wisdom is the most important thing;
so get wisdom.
If it costs everything you have, get
understanding.
⁸Treasure wisdom, and it will make
you great;
hold on to it, and it will bring you
honor.
⁹It will be like flowers in your hair
and like a beautiful crown on your
head."

¹⁰My child, listen and accept what I say.
Then you will have a long life.
¹¹I am guiding you in the way of wisdom,
and I am leading you on the right
path.
¹²Nothing will hold you back;
you will not be overwhelmed.
¹³Always remember what you have
been taught,
and don't let go of it.
Keep all that you have learned;
it is the most important thing in
life.
¹⁴Don't follow the ways of the wicked;
don't do what evil people do.
¹⁵Avoid their ways, and don't follow
them.
Stay away from them and keep on
going,
¹⁶because they cannot sleep until they
do evil.
They cannot rest until they harm
someone.

¹⁷They feast on wickedness and cruelty
as if they were eating bread and
drinking wine.

¹⁸The way of the good person is like the
light of dawn,
growing brighter and brighter until
full daylight.
¹⁹But the wicked walk around in the
dark;
they can't even see what makes
them stumble.

²⁰My child, pay attention to my words;
listen closely to what I say.
²¹Don't ever forget my words;
keep them always in mind.
²²They are the key to life for those who
find them;
they bring health to the whole
body.
²³Be careful what you think,
because your thoughts run your
life.
²⁴Don't use your mouth to tell lies;
don't ever say things that are not
true.
²⁵Keep your eyes focused on what is
right,
and look straight ahead to what is
good.
²⁶Be careful what you do,
and always do what is right.
²⁷Don't turn off the road of goodness;
keep away from evil paths.

5 My son, pay attention to my wisdom;
listen to my words of
understanding.
²Be careful to use good sense,
and watch what you say.
³The words of another man's wife may
seem sweet as honey;
they may be as smooth as olive oil.
⁴But in the end she will bring you
sorrow,

causing you pain like a two-edged
sword.
⁵She is on the way to death;
her steps are headed straight to
the grave.
⁶She gives little thought to life.
She doesn't even know that her
ways are wrong.

⁷Now, my sons, listen to me,
and don't ignore what I say.
⁸Stay away from such a woman.
Don't even go near the door of her
house,
⁹or you will give your riches to others,
and the best years of your life will
be given to someone cruel.
¹⁰Strangers will enjoy your wealth,
and what you worked so hard for
will go to someone else.
¹¹You will groan at the end of your life
when your health is gone.
¹²Then you will say, "I hated being told
what to do!
I would not listen to correction!
¹³I would not listen to my teachers
or pay attention to my instructors.
¹⁴I came close to being completely
ruined
in front of a whole group of
people."

¹⁵Be faithful to your own wife,
just as you drink water from your
own well.
¹⁶Don't pour your water in the streets;
don't give your love to just any
woman.
¹⁷These things are yours alone
and shouldn't be shared with
strangers.
¹⁸Be happy with the wife you married
when you were young.
She gives you joy, as your fountain
gives you water.
¹⁹She is as lovely and graceful as a deer.

STEP
4

STEP 4

Made a searching and fearless moral
inventory of ourselves.

Proverbs 5:3–6

You may have read these verses and thought, *I don't run around with married people. I'm okay here.* Or maybe you thought, *Uh-oh. Been there. Done that. Is my goose cooked?* Neither ignore this scenario nor let it cause you to despair. These proverbs offer life, not judgment. You can learn from the woman warned against here.

This married woman who goes looking for other men to seduce thinks she's out for kicks. Actually, she's trying to fill an empty place in her heart. She's failed to make a satisfying marriage, so she settles for sex instead of love. She closes her eyes to the harsh reality that nobody cherishes her; everybody just uses her. She dares not think how this is all going to end. In time, her life goes downhill so fast, she can't even see the cruel fate rushing to meet her.

So the moral of this story is this: Regularly think about where your life is headed. That's what Step 4 is all about. Addicts have to deal with unstable ways of thinking and behaving. You can't deal with them fully until you understand them well. You can't understand them until you identify them and consider the negative impact they have on you. That's a big job, so you need God's help in understanding yourself. Ask him for wisdom and courage to see where your life is headed. Trust his love to take care of you through this journey of discovery.

FOR YOUR NEXT **STEP 4** MEDITATION, TURN TO **PAGE 518.** ▶▶

Let her love always make you
happy;
let her love always hold you
captive.
²⁰My son, don't be held captive by a
woman who takes part in
adultery.
Don't fondle a woman who is not
your wife.

²¹The LORD sees everything you do,
and he watches where you go.
²²An evil man will be caught in his
wicked ways;
the ropes of his sins will tie
him up.
²³He will die because he does not
control himself,
and he will be held captive by his
foolishness.

6 My child, be careful about giving a
guarantee for somebody else's
loan,
about promising to pay what
someone else owes.
²You might get trapped by what you
say;
you might be caught by your own
words.
³My child, if you have done this and
are under your neighbor's
control,
here is how to get free.
Don't be proud. Go to your neighbor
and beg to be free from your
promise.
⁴Don't go to sleep
or even rest your eyes,
⁵but free yourself like a deer running
from a hunter,
like a bird flying away from a
trapper.

⁶Go watch the ants, you lazy person.
Watch what they do and be wise.

⁷Ants have no commander,
no leader or ruler,
⁸but they store up food in the summer
and gather their supplies at
harvest.
⁹How long will you lie there, you lazy
person?
When will you get up from
sleeping?
¹⁰You sleep a little; you take a nap.
You fold your hands and lie down
to rest.
¹¹So you will be as poor as if you had
been robbed;
you will have as little as if you had
been held up.

¹²Some people are wicked and no good.
They go around telling lies,
¹³winking with their eyes, tapping with
their feet,
and making signs with their
fingers.
¹⁴They make evil plans in their hearts
and are always starting
arguments.
¹⁵So trouble will strike them in an
instant;
suddenly they will be so hurt no
one can help them.

¹⁶There are six things the LORD hates.
There are seven things he cannot
stand:
¹⁷ a proud look,
a lying tongue,
hands that kill innocent people,
¹⁸ a mind that thinks up evil plans,
feet that are quick to do evil,
¹⁹ a witness who lies,
and someone who starts
arguments among families.

²⁰My son, keep your father's commands,
and don't forget your mother's
teaching.

²¹Keep their words in mind forever
as though you had them tied
around your neck.
²²They will guide you when you walk.
They will guard you when you
sleep.
They will speak to you when you
are awake.
²³These commands are like a lamp;
this teaching is like a light.
And the correction that comes from
them
will help you have life.
²⁴They will keep you from sinful women
and from the pleasing words of
another man's unfaithful
wife.
²⁵Don't desire her because she is
beautiful.
Don't let her capture you by the
way she looks at you.
²⁶A prostitute will treat you like a loaf of
bread,
and a woman who takes part in
adultery may cost you your
life.
²⁷You cannot carry hot coals against
your chest
without burning your clothes,
²⁸and you cannot walk on hot coals
without burning your feet.
²⁹The same is true if you have sexual
relations with another man's
wife.
Anyone who does so will be
punished.

³⁰People don't hate a thief
when he steals because he is
hungry.
³¹But if he is caught, he must pay back
seven times what he
stole,
and it may cost him everything he
owns.

³²A man who takes part in adultery has
no sense;
he will destroy himself.
³³He will be beaten up and disgraced,
and his shame will never go away.
³⁴Jealousy makes a husband very angry,
and he will have no pity when he
gets revenge.
³⁵He will accept no payment for the
wrong;
he will take no amount of money.

7 My son, remember what I say, and
treasure my commands.
²Obey my commands, and you will live.
Guard my teachings as you would
your own eyes.
³Remind yourself of them;
write them on your heart as if on a
tablet.
⁴Treat wisdom as a sister,
and make understanding your
closest friend.
⁵Wisdom and understanding will keep
you away from adultery,
away from the unfaithful wife and
her pleasing words.

⁶Once while I was at the window of my
house
I looked out through the shutters
⁷and saw some foolish, young men.
I noticed one of them had no
wisdom.
⁸He was walking down the street near
the corner
on the road leading to her
house.
⁹It was the twilight of the evening;
the darkness of the night was just
beginning.
¹⁰Then the woman approached him,
dressed like a prostitute
and planning to trick him.
¹¹She was loud and stubborn
and never stayed at home.

¹²She was always out in the streets or in
the city squares,
waiting around on the corners of
the streets.
¹³She grabbed him and kissed him.
Without shame she said to him,
¹⁴"I made my fellowship offering and
took some of the meat
home.
Today I have kept my special
promises.
¹⁵So I have come out to meet you;
I have been looking for you and
have found you.
¹⁶I have covered my bed
with colored sheets from Egypt.
¹⁷I have made my bed smell sweet
with myrrh, aloes, and cinnamon.
¹⁸Come, let's make love until morning.
Let's enjoy each other's love.
¹⁹My husband is not home;
he has gone on a long trip.
²⁰He took a lot of money with him
and won't be home for weeks."
²¹By her clever words she made him
give in;
by her pleasing words she led him
into doing wrong.
²²All at once he followed her,
like an ox led to the butcher,
like a deer caught in a trap
²³   and shot through the liver with an
arrow.
Like a bird caught in a trap,
he didn't know what he did would
kill him.

²⁴Now, my sons, listen to me;
pay attention to what I say.
²⁵Don't let yourself be tricked by such a
woman;
don't go where she leads you.
²⁶She has ruined many good men,
and many have died because of
her.

²⁷Her house is on the road to death,
the road that leads down to the
grave.

8 Wisdom calls to you like someone
shouting;
understanding raises her voice.
²On the hilltops along the road
and at the crossroads, she stands
calling.
³Beside the city gates,
at the entrances into the city, she
calls out:
⁴"Listen, everyone, I'm calling out to
you;
I am shouting to all people.
⁵You who are uneducated, seek
wisdom.
You who are foolish, get
understanding.
⁶Listen, because I have important
things to say,
and what I tell you is right.
⁷What I say is true,
I refuse to speak evil.
⁸Everything I say is honest;
nothing I say is crooked or false.
⁹People with good sense know what I
say is true;
and those with knowledge know
my words are right.
¹⁰Choose my teachings instead of silver,
and knowledge rather than the
finest gold.
¹¹Wisdom is more precious than rubies.
Nothing you could want is equal
to it.

¹²"I am wisdom, and I have good
judgment.
I also have knowledge and good
sense.
¹³If you respect the LORD, you will also
hate evil.
I hate pride and bragging,
evil ways and lies.

¹⁴I have good sense and advice,
  and I have understanding and
    power.
¹⁵I help kings to govern
  and rulers to make fair laws.
¹⁶Princes use me to lead,
  and so do all important people
    who judge fairly.
¹⁷I love those who love me,
  and those who seek me find me.
¹⁸Riches and honor are mine to give.
  So are wealth and lasting success.
¹⁹What I give is better than the finest
    gold,
  better than the purest silver.
²⁰I do what is right
  and follow the path of justice.
²¹I give wealth to those who love me,
  filling their houses with treasures.

²²"I, wisdom, was with the LORD when
    he began his work,
  long before he made anything
    else.
²³I was created in the very beginning,
  even before the world began.
²⁴I was born before there were oceans,
  or springs overflowing with water,
²⁵before the hills were there,
  before the mountains were put in
    place.
²⁶God had not made the earth or fields,
  not even the first dust of the earth.
²⁷I was there when God put the skies in
    place,
  when he stretched the horizon
    over the oceans,
²⁸when he made the clouds above
  and put the deep underground
    springs in place.
²⁹I was there when he ordered the sea
  not to go beyond the borders he
    had set.
  I was there when he laid the earth's
    foundation.

³⁰ I was like a child by his side.
  I was delighted every day,
    enjoying his presence all the time,
³¹enjoying the whole world,
  and delighted with all its people.

³²"Now, my children, listen to me,
  because those who follow my
    ways are happy.
³³Listen to my teaching, and you will be
    wise;
  do not ignore it.
³⁴Happy are those who listen to me,
  watching at my door every day,
  waiting at my open doorway.
³⁵Those who find me find life,
  and the LORD will be pleased with
    them.
³⁶Those who do not find me hurt
    themselves.
  Those who hate me love death."

9 Wisdom has built her house;
  she has made its seven columns.
²She has prepared her food and wine;
  she has set her table.
³She has sent out her servant girls,
  and she calls out from the highest
    place in the city.
⁴She says to those who are
    uneducated,
  "Come in here, you foolish people!
⁵Come and eat my food
  and drink the wine I have prepared.
⁶Stop your foolish ways, and you will
    live;
  take the road of understanding.

⁷"If you correct someone who makes
    fun of wisdom, you will be
    insulted.
  If you correct an evil person, you
    will get hurt.
⁸Do not correct those who make fun
    of wisdom, or they will hate
    you.

But correct the wise, and they will
love you.
⁹Teach the wise, and they will become
even wiser;
teach good people, and they will
learn even more.

¹⁰"Wisdom begins with respect for the
LORD,
and understanding begins with
knowing the Holy One.
¹¹If you live wisely, you will live a long
time;
wisdom will add years to your life.
¹²The wise person is rewarded by
wisdom,
but whoever makes fun of wisdom
will suffer for it."

¹³Foolishness is like a loud woman;
she does not have wisdom or
knowledge.
¹⁴She sits at the door of her house
at the highest place in the city.
¹⁵She calls out to those who are passing
by,
who are going along, minding
their own business.
¹⁶She says to those who are
uneducated,
"Come in here, you foolish people!
¹⁷Stolen water is sweeter,
and food eaten in secret tastes
better."
¹⁸But these people don't know that
everyone who goes there
dies,
that her guests end up deep in the
grave.

10 These are the wise words of Solomon:
Wise children make their father
happy,
but foolish children make their
mother sad.

²Riches gotten by doing wrong have no
value,
but right living will save you from
death.

³The LORD does not let good people go
hungry,
but he keeps evil people from
getting what they want.

⁴A lazy person will end up poor,
but a hard worker will become
rich.

⁵Those who gather crops on time are
wise,
but those who sleep through the
harvest are a disgrace.

⁶Good people will have rich blessings,
but the wicked will be
overwhelmed by violence.

⁷Good people will be remembered as a
blessing,
but evil people will soon be
forgotten.

⁸The wise do what they are told,
but a talkative fool will be ruined.

⁹The honest person will live in safety,
but the dishonest will be caught.

¹⁰A wink may get you into trouble,
and foolish talk will lead to your
ruin.

¹¹The words of a good person give life,
like a fountain of water,
but the words of the wicked
contain nothing but
violence.

¹²Hatred stirs up trouble,
but love forgives all wrongs.   **STEP 8**

¹³Wise people speak with
understanding,
but people without wisdom should
be punished.

¹⁴The wise don't tell everything they know,
  but the foolish talk too much and are ruined.

¹⁵Having lots of money protects the rich,
  but having no money destroys the poor.

¹⁶Good people are rewarded with life,
  but evil people are paid with punishment.

STEP 4

¹⁷Whoever accepts correction is on the way to life,
  but whoever ignores correction will lead others away from life.

¹⁸Whoever hides hate is a liar.
  Whoever tells lies is a fool.

¹⁹If you talk a lot, you are sure to sin;
  if you are wise, you will keep quiet.

²⁰The words of a good person are like pure silver,
  but an evil person's thoughts are worth very little.

²¹Good people's words will help many others,
  but fools will die because they don't have wisdom.

²²The LORD's blessing brings wealth,
  and no sorrow comes with it.

²³A foolish person enjoys doing wrong,
  but a person with understanding enjoys doing what is wise.

²⁴Evil people will get what they fear most,
  but good people will get what they want most.

²⁵A storm will blow the evil person away,
  but a good person will always be safe.

²⁶A lazy person affects the one he works for
  like vinegar on the teeth or smoke in the eyes.

²⁷Whoever respects the LORD will have a long life,
  but the life of an evil person will be cut short.

²⁸A good person can look forward to happiness,
  but an evil person can expect nothing.

²⁹The LORD will protect good people
  but will ruin those who do evil.

³⁰Good people will always be safe,
  but evil people will not remain in the land.

³¹A good person says wise things,
  but a liar's tongue will be stopped.

³²Good people know the right thing to say,
  but evil people only tell lies.

11 The LORD hates dishonest scales,
  but he is pleased with honest weights.

²Pride leads only to shame;
  it is wise to be humble.

³Good people will be guided by honesty;
  dishonesty will destroy those who are not trustworthy.

⁴Riches will not help when it's time to die,
  but right living will save you from death.

⁵The goodness of the innocent makes life easier,
  but the wicked will be destroyed by their wickedness.

⁶Doing right brings freedom to honest
people,
but those who are not trustworthy
will be caught by their own
desires.

⁷When the wicked die, hope dies with
them;
their hope in riches will come to
nothing.

⁸The good person is saved from trouble;
it comes to the wicked instead.

⁹With words an evil person can destroy
a neighbor,
but a good person will escape by
being resourceful.

¹⁰When good people succeed, the city is
happy.
When evil people die, there are
shouts of joy.

¹¹Good people bless and build up their
city,
but the wicked can destroy it with
their words.

¹²People without good sense find fault
with their neighbors,
but those with understanding
keep quiet.

¹³Gossips can't keep secrets,
but a trustworthy person can.

¹⁴Without leadership a nation falls,
but lots of good advice will save it.

¹⁵Whoever guarantees to pay somebody
else's loan will suffer.
It is safer to avoid such promises.

¹⁶A kind woman gets respect,
but cruel men get only wealth.

¹⁷Kind people do themselves a favor,
but cruel people bring trouble on
themselves.

¹⁸An evil person really earns nothing,
but a good person will surely be
rewarded.

¹⁹Those who are truly good will live,
but those who chase after evil will
die.

²⁰The LORD hates those with evil
hearts
but is pleased with those who are
innocent.

²¹Evil people will certainly be punished,
but those who do right will be set
free.

²²A beautiful woman without good
sense
is like a gold ring in a pig's snout.

²³Those who do right only wish for
good,
but the wicked can expect to be
defeated by God's anger.

²⁴Some people give much but get back
even more.
Others don't give what they
should and end up poor.
²⁵Whoever gives to others will get
richer;
those who help others will
themselves be helped.

²⁶People curse those who keep all the
grain,
but they bless the one who is
willing to sell it.

²⁷Whoever looks for good will find
kindness,
but whoever looks for evil will find
trouble.

²⁸Those who trust in riches will be
ruined,
but a good person will be healthy
like a green leaf.

²⁹Whoever brings trouble to his family
will be left with nothing but the
wind.
A fool will be a servant to the wise.

³⁰A good person gives life to others;
the wise person teaches others
how to live.

³¹Good people will be rewarded on
earth,
and the wicked and the sinners
will be punished.

STEP 10

12 Anyone who loves learning
accepts correction,
but a person who hates being
corrected is stupid.

²The LORD is pleased with a good
person,
but he will punish anyone who
plans evil.

³Doing evil brings no safety at all,
but a good person has safety and
security.

⁴A good wife is like a crown for her
husband,
but a disgraceful wife is like a
disease in his bones.

⁵The plans that good people make are
fair,
but the advice of the wicked will
trick you.

⁶The wicked talk about killing people,
but the words of good people will
save them.

⁷Wicked people die and they are no
more,
but a good person's family
continues.

⁸The wisdom of the wise wins praise,
but there is no respect for the
stupid.

⁹A person who is not important but has
a servant is better off
than someone who acts important
but has no food.

¹⁰Good people take care of their animals,
but even the kindest acts of the
wicked are cruel.

¹¹Those who work their land will have
plenty of food,
but the one who chases empty
dreams is not wise.

¹²The wicked want what other evil
people have stolen,
but good people want to give what
they have to others.

¹³Evil people are trapped by their evil
talk,
but good people stay out of
trouble.

¹⁴People will be rewarded for what they
say,
and they will also be rewarded for
what they do.

¹⁵Fools think they are doing right,
but the wise listen to advice.

¹⁶Fools quickly show that they are upset,
but the wise ignore insults.

¹⁷An honest witness tells the truth,
but a dishonest witness tells lies.

¹⁸Careless words stab like a sword,
but wise words bring healing.

STEP 9

¹⁹Truth will continue forever,
but lies are only for a moment.

²⁰Those who plan evil are full of lies,
but those who plan peace are
happy.

²¹No harm comes to a good person,
but an evil person's life is full of
trouble.

²²The LORD hates those who tell lies
 but is pleased with those who
  keep their promises.

²³Wise people keep what they know to
   themselves,
 but fools can't keep from showing
  how foolish they are.

²⁴Hard workers will become leaders,
 but those who are lazy will be
  slaves.

²⁵Worry is a heavy load,
 but a kind word cheers you up.

²⁶Good people take advice from their
   friends,
 but an evil person is easily led to
  do wrong.

²⁷The lazy catch no food to cook,
 but a hard worker will have great
  wealth.

²⁸Doing what is right is the way to life,
 but there is another way that leads
  to death.

13 Wise children take their parents'
   advice,
 but whoever makes fun of wisdom
  won't listen to correction.

²People will be rewarded for what they
   say,
 but those who can't be trusted
  want only violence.

³Those who are careful about what
   they say protect their lives,
 but whoever speaks without
  thinking will be ruined.

⁴The lazy will not get what they want,
 but those who work hard will.

⁵Good people hate what is false,
 but the wicked do shameful and
  disgraceful things.

⁶Doing what is right protects the
   honest person,
 but doing evil ruins the sinner.

⁷Some people pretend to be rich but
   really have nothing.
 Others pretend to be poor but
  really are wealthy.

⁸The rich may have to pay a ransom
   for their lives,
 but the poor will face no such
  danger.

⁹Good people can look forward to a
   bright future,
 but the future of the wicked is like
  a flame going out.

¹⁰Pride only leads to arguments,
 but those who take advice are
  wise.

¹¹Money that comes easily disappears
   quickly,
 but money that is gathered little
  by little will grow.

¹²It is sad not to get what you hoped for.
 But wishes that come true are like
  eating fruit from the tree of
  life.

¹³Those who reject what they are
   taught will pay for it,
 but those who obey what they are
  told will be rewarded.

STEP
4

¹⁴The teaching of a wise person gives
   life.
 It is like a fountain that can save
  people from death.

¹⁵People with good understanding will
   be well liked,
 but the lives of those who are not
  trustworthy are hard.

¹⁶Every wise person acts with good
   sense,

but fools show how foolish they are.

¹⁷A wicked messenger brings nothing but trouble,
but a trustworthy one makes everything right.

STEP 6
¹⁸A person who refuses correction will end up poor and disgraced,
but the one who accepts correction will be honored.

¹⁹It is so good when wishes come true,
but fools hate to stop doing evil.

²⁰Spend time with the wise and you will become wise,
but the friends of fools will suffer.

²¹Trouble always comes to sinners,
but good people enjoy success.

²²Good people leave their wealth to their grandchildren,
but a sinner's wealth is stored up for good people.

²³A poor person's field might produce plenty of food,
but others often steal it away.

²⁴If you do not punish your children, you don't love them,
but if you love your children, you will correct them.

²⁵Good people have enough to eat,
but the wicked will go hungry.

STEP 8
14 A wise woman strengthens her family,
but a foolish woman destroys hers by what she does.

²People who live good lives respect the LORD,
but those who live evil lives don't.

³Fools will be punished for their proud words,

but the words of the wise will protect them.

⁴When there are no oxen, no food is in the barn.
But with a strong ox, much grain can be grown.

⁵A truthful witness does not lie,
but a false witness tells nothing but lies.

⁶Those who make fun of wisdom look for it and do not find it,
but knowledge comes easily to those with understanding.

⁷Stay away from fools,
because they can't teach you anything.

⁸A wise person will understand what to do,
but a foolish person is dishonest.

⁹Fools don't care if they sin,
but honest people work at being right.

¹⁰No one else can know your sadness,
and strangers cannot share your joy.

¹¹The wicked person's house will be destroyed,
but a good person's tent will still be standing.

¹²Some people think they are doing right,
but in the end it leads to death.
STEP 1

¹³Someone who is laughing may be sad inside,
and joy may end in sadness.

¹⁴Evil people will be paid back for their evil ways,
and good people will be rewarded for their good ones.
STEP 4

¹⁵Fools will believe anything,
  but the wise think about what
    they do.

¹⁶Wise people are careful and stay out
    of trouble,
  but fools are careless and quick to
    act.

¹⁷Someone with a quick temper does
    foolish things,
  but someone with understanding
    remains calm.

¹⁸Fools are rewarded with nothing but
    more foolishness,
  but the wise are rewarded with
    knowledge.

¹⁹Evil people will bow down to those
    who are good;
  the wicked will bow down at the
    door of those who do right.

²⁰The poor are rejected, even by their
    neighbors,
  but the rich have many friends.

²¹It is a sin to hate your neighbor,
  but being kind to the needy brings
    happiness.

²²Those who make evil plans will be
    ruined,
  but those who plan to do good will
    be loved and trusted.

²³Those who work hard make a profit,
  but those who only talk will be
    poor.

²⁴Wise people are rewarded with wealth,
  but fools only get more
    foolishness.

²⁵A truthful witness saves lives,
  but a false witness is a traitor.

STEP 3
²⁶Those who respect the LORD will have
    security,

and their children will be
    protected.

²⁷Respect for the LORD gives life.
  It is like a fountain that can save
    people from death.

²⁸A king is honored when he has many
    people to rule,
  but a prince is ruined if he has
    none.

²⁹Patient people have great
    understanding,
  but people with quick tempers
    show their foolishness.

³⁰Peace of mind means a healthy body,
  but jealousy will rot your bones. **STEP 8**

³¹Whoever mistreats the poor insults
    their Maker,
  but whoever is kind to the needy
    honors God.

³²The wicked are ruined by their own
    evil,
  but those who do right are
    protected even in death.

³³Wisdom lives in those with
    understanding,
  and even fools recognize it.

³⁴Doing what is right makes a nation
    great,
  but sin will bring disgrace to any
    people.

³⁵A king is pleased with a wise servant,
  but he will become angry with one
    who causes him shame.

15 ¹A gentle answer will calm a
    person's anger,
  but an unkind answer will cause
    more anger. **STEP 9**

²Wise people use knowledge when
    they speak,
  but fools pour out foolishness.

³The LORD's eyes see everything;
he watches both evil and good
people.

⁴As a tree gives fruit, healing words
give life,
but dishonest words crush the
spirit.

⁵Fools reject their parents' correction,
but anyone who accepts
correction is wise.

⁶Much wealth is in the houses of good
people,
but evil people get nothing but
trouble.

⁷Wise people use their words to spread
knowledge,
but there is no knowledge in the
thoughts of fools.

⁸The LORD hates the sacrifice that the
wicked offer,
but he likes the prayers of honest
people.

⁹The LORD hates what evil people do,
but he loves those who do what is
right.

¹⁰The person who quits doing what is
right will be punished,
and the one who hates to be
corrected will die.

STEP
4

¹¹The LORD knows what is happening in
the world of the dead,
so he surely knows the thoughts
of the living.

¹²Those who make fun of wisdom don't
like to be corrected;
they will not ask the wise for
advice.

¹³Happiness makes a person smile,
but sadness can break a person's
spirit.

¹⁴People with understanding want more
knowledge,
but fools just want more
foolishness.

¹⁵Every day is hard for those who suffer,
but a happy heart is like a
continual feast.

¹⁶It is better to be poor and respect the
LORD
than to be wealthy and have much
trouble.

STEP
2

¹⁷It is better to eat vegetables with
those who love you
than to eat meat with those who
hate you.

¹⁸People with quick tempers cause
trouble,
but those who control their
tempers stop a quarrel.

¹⁹A lazy person's life is like a patch of
thorns,
but an honest person's life is like a
smooth highway.

²⁰Wise children make their father happy,
but foolish children disrespect
their mother.

²¹A person without wisdom enjoys being
foolish,
but someone with understanding
does what is right.

²²Plans fail without good advice,
but they succeed with the advice
of many others.

²³People enjoy giving good advice.
Saying the right word at the right
time is so pleasing.

²⁴Wise people's lives get better and
better.
They avoid whatever would cause
their death.

²⁵The LORD will tear down the proud
person's house,
but he will protect the widow's
property.

²⁶The LORD hates evil thoughts
but is pleased with kind words.

²⁷Greedy people bring trouble to their
families,
but the person who can't be paid
to do wrong will live.

²⁸Good people think before they answer,
but the wicked simply pour out evil.

²⁹The LORD does not listen to the wicked,
but he hears the prayers of those
who do right.

³⁰Good news makes you feel better.
Your happiness will show in your
eyes.

STEP 4
³¹If you listen to correction to improve
your life,
you will live among the wise.

³²Those who refuse correction hate
themselves,
but those who accept correction
gain understanding.

³³Respect for the LORD will teach you
wisdom.
If you want to be honored, you
must be humble.

16 People may make plans in their
minds,
but only the LORD can make them
come true.

STEP 4
²You may believe you are doing right,
but the LORD will judge your
reasons.

³Depend on the LORD in whatever
you do,
and your plans will succeed.

⁴The LORD makes everything go as he
pleases.
He has even prepared a day of
disaster for evil people.

⁵The LORD hates those who are proud.
They will surely be punished.

⁶Love and truth bring forgiveness of sin.   **STEP 9**
By respecting the LORD you will
avoid evil.

⁷When people live so that they please
the LORD,
even their enemies will make
peace with them.

⁸It is better to be poor and right
than to be wealthy and dishonest.

⁹People may make plans in their minds,
but the LORD decides what they
will do.

¹⁰The words of a king are like a
message from God,
so his decisions should be fair.

¹¹The LORD wants honest balances and
scales;
all the weights are his work.

¹²Kings hate those who do wrong,
because governments only
continue if they are fair.

¹³Kings like honest people;
they value someone who speaks
the truth.

¹⁴An angry king can put someone to
death,
so a wise person will try to make
him happy.

¹⁵A smiling king can give people life;
his kindness is like a spring
shower.

¹⁶It is better to get wisdom than gold,
and to choose understanding
rather than silver!

STEP 4

Made a searching and fearless moral
inventory of ourselves.

Proverbs 16:2-3

The instrument panel of an airplane includes a gadget called an artificial horizon indicator. It lets a pilot know in the dark or inside a cloud how to fly level. A flier's sense of up and down gets totally confused when he or she can't see the horizon. The horizon indicator is never fooled. Pilots flying blind always should rely on the artificial horizon indicator, even when what it says goes against their natural instincts.

That's the same way it is when your natural instincts disagree with the wisdom of God. "You may believe you are doing right" (verse 2); but if God's Word says it's wrong, go with God's wisdom. It's always right. Trying to run your own life is like trying to fly an airplane through a cloud bank without a horizon indicator.

Open your life completely and honestly to God's inspection. Accept his direction for the course of your life. That's a major step toward flying straight and true and staying off a collision course with trouble.

SEE **PAGE 40** OF THE INTRODUCTORY MATERIAL FOR **STEP 5.**

¹⁷Good people stay away from evil.
By watching what they do, they
protect their lives.

STEP
5

¹⁸Pride leads to destruction;
a proud attitude brings ruin.

¹⁹It is better to be humble and be with
those who suffer
than to share stolen property with
the proud.

STEP
9

²⁰Whoever listens to what is taught will
succeed,
and whoever trusts the LORD will
be happy.

²¹The wise are known for their
understanding.
Their pleasant words make them
better teachers.

²²Understanding is like a fountain which
gives life to those who use it,
but foolishness brings punishment
to fools.

²³Wise people's minds tell them what to
say,
and that helps them be better
teachers.

²⁴Pleasant words are like a honeycomb,
making people happy and
healthy.

²⁵Some people think they are doing
right,
but in the end it leads to death.

²⁶The workers' hunger helps them,
because their desire to eat makes
them work.

²⁷Useless people make evil plans,
and their words are like a burning
fire.

²⁸A useless person causes trouble,
and a gossip ruins friendships.

²⁹Cruel people trick their neighbors
and lead them to do wrong.

³⁰Someone who winks is planning evil,
and the one who grins is planning
something wrong.

³¹Gray hair is like a crown of honor;
it is earned by living a good life.

³²Patience is better than strength.
Controlling your temper is better
than capturing a city.

³³People throw lots to make a decision,
but the answer comes from the
LORD.

17 It is better to eat a dry crust of
bread in peace
than to have a feast where there is
quarreling.

²A wise servant will rule over the
master's disgraceful child
and will even inherit a share of
what the master leaves his
children.

³A hot furnace tests silver and gold,
but the LORD tests hearts.

⁴Evil people listen to evil words.
Liars pay attention to cruel words.

⁵Whoever mistreats the poor insults
their Maker;
whoever enjoys someone's trouble
will be punished.

⁶Old people are proud of their
grandchildren,
and children are proud of their
parents.

⁷Fools should not be proud,
and rulers should not be liars.

⁸Some people think they can pay others
to do anything they ask.
They think it will work every time.

STEP 9

Made direct amends to such people
wherever possible, except when to
do so would injure them or others.

Proverbs 16:20-24

You may find this hard to believe, but every day as you work at
your recovery, you are becoming wiser. Can you imagine some of
the people you hung out with during the days of your addiction
calling you wise? The wisdom you're learning will show itself in
everything you say and do. The way you respond to problems, to
other people, and even to your own shortcomings will be healthier
and more positive.

When you work on Step 9, as Proverbs 16:20 says, you will learn to
"listen to what is taught" and to "succeed." When you make
amends to people you have hurt, trust God to give you his wisdom
and direction for exactly the right words at the right time. When
you do, you'll find the courage you need both to ask for and to
grant forgiveness. Verses 22-24 say that when you talk to people
God's way, you will be "happy and healthy." At the same time, your
good words offer the same happiness and health to those you are
reconciling with.

SEE **PAGE 61** OF THE INTRODUCTORY MATERIAL FOR **STEP 10**.

⁹Whoever forgives someone's sin
makes a friend,
but gossiping about the sin breaks
up friendships.

STEP 6

¹⁰A wise person will learn more from a
warning
than a fool will learn from a
hundred lashings.

¹¹Disobedient people look only for
trouble,
so a cruel messenger will be sent
against them.

¹²It is better to meet a bear robbed of
her cubs
than to meet a fool doing foolish
things.

¹³Whoever gives evil in return for good
will always have trouble at home.

¹⁴Starting a quarrel is like a leak in a
dam,
so stop it before a fight breaks
out.

¹⁵The LORD hates both of these things:
freeing the guilty and punishing
the innocent.

¹⁶It won't do a fool any good to try to
buy wisdom,
because he doesn't have the
ability to be wise.

¹⁷A friend loves you all the time,
and a brother helps in time of
trouble.

¹⁸It is not wise to promise
to pay what your neighbor owes.

¹⁹Whoever loves to argue loves to sin.
Whoever brags a lot is asking for
trouble.

²⁰A person with an evil heart will find no
success,
and the person whose words are
evil will get into trouble.

²¹It is sad to have a foolish child;
there is no joy in being the parent
of a fool.

²²A happy heart is like good medicine,
but a broken spirit drains your
strength.

²³When the wicked accept money to do
wrong
there can be no justice.

²⁴The person with understanding is
always looking for wisdom,
but the mind of a fool wanders
everywhere.

²⁵Foolish children make their father sad
and cause their mother great
sorrow.

²⁶It is not good to punish the innocent
or to beat leaders for being honest.

²⁷The wise say very little,
and those with understanding stay
calm.

²⁸Even fools seem to be wise if they
keep quiet;
if they don't speak, they appear to
understand.

18 Unfriendly people are selfish
and hate all good sense.

²Fools do not want to understand
anything.
They only want to tell others what
they think.

³Do something evil, and people won't
like you.
Do something shameful, and they
will make fun of you.

⁴Spoken words can be like deep water,
but wisdom is like a flowing
stream.

⁵It is not good to honor the wicked
  or to be unfair to the innocent.

⁶The words of fools start quarrels.
  They make people want to beat
  them.

⁷The words of fools will ruin them;
  their own words will trap them.

⁸The words of a gossip are like tasty
  bits of food.
  People like to gobble them up.

⁹A person who doesn't work hard
  is just like someone who destroys
  things.

¹⁰The Lord is like a strong tower;
  those who do right can run to him
  for safety.

¹¹Rich people trust their wealth to
  protect them.
  They think it is like the high walls
  of a city.

STEP 7
¹²Proud people will be ruined,
  but the humble will be honored.

¹³Anyone who answers without listening
  is foolish and confused.

STEP 1
¹⁴The will to live can get you through
  sickness,
  but no one can live with a broken
  spirit.

¹⁵The mind of a person with
  understanding gets
  knowledge;
  the wise person listens to learn
  more.

¹⁶Taking gifts to important people
  will help get you in to see them.

¹⁷The person who tells one side of a
  story seems right,
  until someone else comes and
  asks questions.

¹⁸Throwing lots can settle arguments
  and keep the two sides from
  fighting.

¹⁹A brother who has been insulted is
  harder to win back than a
  walled city,
  and arguments separate people
  like the barred gates of a
  palace.

²⁰People will be rewarded for what they
  say;
  they will be rewarded by how they
  speak.

²¹What you say can mean life or death.
  Those who speak with care will be
  rewarded.

²²When a man finds a wife, he finds
  something good.
  It shows that the Lord is pleased
  with him.

²³The poor beg for mercy,
  but the rich give rude answers.

²⁴Some friends may ruin you,
  but a real friend will be more loyal
  than a brother.

19 It is better to be poor and honest
  than to be foolish and tell lies.

²Enthusiasm without knowledge is not
  good.
  If you act too quickly, you might
  make a mistake.

³People's own foolishness ruins their
  lives,
  but in their minds they blame the
  Lord.

⁴Wealthy people are always finding
  more friends,
  but the poor lose all theirs.

⁵A witness who lies will not go free;
  liars will never escape.

⁶Many people want to please a leader,
    and everyone is friends with those
        who give gifts.

⁷Poor people's relatives avoid them;
    even their friends stay far away.
  They run after them, begging,
    but they are gone.

⁸Those who get wisdom do
        themselves a favor,
    and those who love learning will
        succeed.

⁹A witness who lies will not go free,
    liars will die.

¹⁰A fool should not live in luxury.
    A slave should not rule over princes.

¹¹The wise are patient;
    they will be honored if they ignore
        insults.

¹²An angry king is like a roaring lion,
    but his kindness is like the dew on
        the grass.

¹³A foolish child brings disaster to a
        father,
    and a quarreling wife is like
        dripping water.

¹⁴Houses and wealth are inherited from
        parents,
    but a wise wife is a gift from the
        LORD.

¹⁵Lazy people sleep a lot,
    and idle people will go hungry.

¹⁶Those who obey the commands
        protect themselves,
    but those who are careless will
        die.

¹⁷Being kind to the poor is like lending
        to the LORD;
    he will reward you for what you
        have done.

¹⁸Correct your children while there is
        still hope;
    do not let them destroy
        themselves.

¹⁹People with quick tempers will have to
        pay for it.
    If you help them out once, you will
        have to do it again.

STEP 4

²⁰Listen to advice and accept
        correction,
    and in the end you will be wise.

²¹People can make all kinds of plans,
    but only the LORD's plan will
        happen.

²²People want others to be loyal,
    so it is better to be poor than to be
        a liar.

²³Those who respect the LORD will live
    and be satisfied, unbothered by
        trouble.

²⁴Though the lazy person puts his hand
        in the dish,
    he won't lift the food to his mouth.

²⁵Whip those who make fun of wisdom,
    and perhaps foolish people
        will gain some wisdom.
  Correct those with understanding,
    and they will gain
        knowledge.

²⁶A child who robs his father and sends
        away his mother
    brings shame and disgrace on
        himself.

²⁷Don't stop listening to correction, my
        child,
    or you will forget what you have
        already learned.

²⁸An evil witness makes fun of fairness,
    and wicked people love what is
        evil.

²⁹People who make fun of wisdom will
be punished,
and the backs of foolish people
will be beaten.

STEP 4 **20** Wine and beer make people loud
and uncontrolled;
it is not wise to get drunk on them.

²An angry king is like a roaring lion.
Making him angry may cost you
your life.

³Foolish people are always fighting,
but avoiding quarrels will bring
you honor.

⁴Lazy farmers don't plow when they
should;
they expect a harvest, but there is
none.

⁵People's thoughts can be like a deep
well,
but someone with understanding
can find the wisdom there.

⁶Many people claim to be loyal,
but it is hard to find a trustworthy
person.

⁷The good people who live honest lives
will be a blessing to their children.

⁸When a king sits on his throne to
judge,
he knows evil when he sees it.

⁹No one can say, "I am innocent;
I have never done anything
wrong."

¹⁰The LORD hates both these things:
dishonest weights and dishonest
measures.

¹¹Even children are known by their
behavior;
their actions show if they are
innocent and good.

¹²The LORD has made both these things:
ears to hear and eyes to see.

¹³If you love to sleep, you will be poor.
If you stay awake, you will have
plenty of food.

¹⁴Buyers say, "This is bad. It's no good."
Then they go away and brag
about what they bought.

¹⁵There is gold and plenty of rubies,
but only a few people speak with
knowledge.

¹⁶Take the coat of someone who
promises to pay a stranger's
debts,
and keep it until he pays what the
stranger owes.

¹⁷Stolen food may taste sweet at first,
but later it will feel like a mouth
full of gravel.

¹⁸Get advice if you want your plans to
work.
If you go to war, get the advice of
others.

¹⁹Gossips can't keep secrets,
so avoid people who talk too
much. **STEP 4**

²⁰Those who curse their father or
mother
will be like a light going out in
darkness.

²¹Wealth inherited quickly in the
beginning
will do you no good in the end.

²²Don't say, "I'll pay you back for the
wrong you did."
Wait for the LORD, and he will
make things right.

²³The LORD hates dishonest weights,
and dishonest scales do not please
him.

²⁴The LORD decides what a person
will do;
no one understands what his life is
all about.

²⁵It's dangerous to promise something
to God too quickly.
After you've thought about it, it
may be too late.

²⁶A wise king sorts out the evil people,
and he punishes them as they
deserve.

²⁷The LORD looks deep inside people
and searches through their
thoughts.

²⁸Loyalty and truth keep a king in power;
he continues to rule if he is loyal.

²⁹The young glory in their strength,
and the old are honored for their
gray hair.

³⁰Hard punishment will get rid of evil,
and whippings can change an evil
heart.

21 The LORD can control a king's
mind as he controls a river;
he can direct it as he pleases.

STEP 5
²You may believe you are doing right,
but the LORD judges your reasons.

³Doing what is right and fair
is more important to the LORD
than sacrifices.

⁴Proud looks, proud thoughts,
and evil actions are sin.

⁵The plans of hard-working people
earn a profit,
but those who act too quickly
become poor.

⁶Wealth that comes from telling lies
vanishes like a mist and leads to
death.

⁷The violence of the wicked will
destroy them,
because they refuse to do what is
right.

⁸Guilty people live dishonest lives,
but honest people do right.

STEP 4
⁹It is better to live in a corner on the
roof
than inside the house with a
quarreling wife.

¹⁰Evil people only want to harm
others.
Their neighbors get no mercy
from them.

¹¹If you punish those who make fun of
wisdom, a foolish person
may gain some wisdom.
But if you teach the wise, they will
get knowledge.

¹²God, who is always right, watches the
house of the wicked
and brings ruin on every evil
person.

¹³Whoever ignores the poor when they
cry for help
will also cry for help and not be
answered.

¹⁴A secret gift will calm an angry
person;
a present given in secrecy will
quiet great anger.

¹⁵When justice is done, good people are
happy,
but evil people are ruined.

¹⁶Whoever does not use good sense
will end up among the dead.

¹⁷Whoever loves pleasure will become
poor;
whoever loves wine and perfume
will never be rich.

¹⁸Wicked people will suffer instead of
good people,
and those who cannot be trusted
will suffer instead of those
who do right.

¹⁹It is better to live alone in the desert
than with a quarreling and
complaining wife.

²⁰Wise people's houses are full of the
best foods and olive oil,
but fools waste everything they
have.

²¹Whoever tries to live right and be loyal
finds life, success, and honor.

²²A wise person can defeat a city full of
warriors
and tear down the defenses they
trust in.

²³Those who are careful about what
they say
keep themselves out of trouble.

²⁴People who act with stubborn pride
are called "proud," "bragger," and
"mocker."

²⁵Lazy people's desire for sleep will kill
them,
because they refuse to work.
²⁶All day long they wish for more,
but good people give without
holding back.

²⁷The LORD hates sacrifices brought by
evil people,
particularly when they offer them
for the wrong reasons.

²⁸A lying witness will be forgotten,
but a truthful witness will
speak on.

²⁹Wicked people are stubborn,
but good people think carefully
about what they do.

³⁰There is no wisdom, understanding,
or advice
that can succeed against the LORD.

³¹You can get the horses ready for battle,
but it is the LORD who gives the
victory.

22 Being respected is more important
than having great riches.
To be well thought of is better
than silver or gold.

²The rich and the poor are alike
in that the LORD made them all.

³The wise see danger ahead and
avoid it,
but fools keep going and get into
trouble.

⁴Respecting the LORD and not being
proud
will bring you wealth, honor, and
life.

STEP
7

⁵Evil people's lives are like paths
covered with thorns and
traps.
People who guard themselves
don't have such problems.

⁶Train children to live the right way,
and when they are old, they will
not stray from it.

⁷The rich rule over the poor,
and borrowers are servants to
lenders.

⁸Those who plan evil will receive
trouble.
Their cruel anger will come to an
end.

⁹Generous people will be blessed,
because they share their food with
the poor.

¹⁰Get rid of the one who makes fun of
wisdom.

Then fighting, quarrels, and insults
will stop.

[11]Whoever loves pure thoughts and kind words
will have even the king as a friend.

[12]The Lord guards knowledge,
but he destroys false words.

[13]The lazy person says, "There's a lion outside!
I might get killed out in the street!"

[14]The words of an unfaithful wife are like a deep trap.
Those who make the Lord angry will get caught by them.

[15]Every child is full of foolishness,
but punishment can get rid of it.

[16]Whoever gets rich by mistreating the poor,
and gives presents to the wealthy,
will become poor.

[17]Listen carefully to what wise people say;
pay attention to what I am teaching you.

[18]It will be good to keep these things in mind
so that you are ready to repeat them.

[19]I am teaching them to you now
so that you will put your trust in the Lord.

[20]I have written thirty sayings for you,
which give knowledge and good advice.

[21]I am teaching you true and reliable words
so that you can give true answers to anyone who asks.

[22]Do not abuse poor people because they are poor,

and do not take away the rights of the needy in court.

[23]The Lord will defend them in court
and will take the life of those who take away their rights.

[24]Don't make friends with
quick-tempered people
or spend time with those who have bad tempers.
[25]If you do, you will be like them.
Then you will be in real danger.

STEP 4

[26]Don't promise to pay what someone else owes,
and don't guarantee anyone's loan.

[27]If you cannot pay the loan,
your own bed may be taken right out from under you.

[28]Don't move an old stone that marks a border,
because those stones were set up by your ancestors.

[29]Do you see people skilled in their work?
They will work for kings, not for ordinary people.

23 If you sit down to eat with a ruler,
notice the food that is in front of you.
[2]Control yourself
if you have a big appetite.
[3]Don't be greedy for his fine foods,
because that food might be a trick.

[4]Don't wear yourself out trying to get rich;
be wise enough to control yourself.
[5]Wealth can vanish in the wink of an eye.
It can seem to grow wings
and fly away like an eagle.

⁶Don't eat the food of selfish people;
   don't be greedy for their fine
      foods.
⁷Selfish people are always worrying
      about how much the food costs.
   They tell you, "Eat and drink,"
      but they don't really mean it.
⁸You will throw up the little you have
      eaten,
   and you will have wasted your kind
      words.

⁹Don't speak to fools;
   they will only ignore your wise
      words.

¹⁰Don't move an old stone that marks a
      border,
   and don't take fields that belong
      to orphans.
¹¹God, their defender, is strong;
   he will take their side
      against you.

¹²Remember what you are taught,
   and listen carefully to words of
      knowledge.

¹³Don't fail to punish children.
   If you spank them, they won't die.
¹⁴If you spank them,
   you will save them from death.

¹⁵My child, if you are wise,
   then I will be happy.
¹⁶I will be so pleased
   if you speak what is right.

¹⁷Don't envy sinners,
   but always respect the LORD.
¹⁸Then you will have hope for the
      future,
   and your wishes will come true.

¹⁹Listen, my child, and be wise.
   Keep your mind on what is right.
²⁰Don't drink too much wine
   or eat too much food.

²¹Those who drink and eat too much
      become poor.
   They sleep too much and end up
      wearing rags.

²²Listen to your father, who gave you life,
   and do not forget your mother
      when she is old.
²³Learn the truth and never reject it.
   Get wisdom, self-control, and
      understanding.
²⁴The father of a good child is very
      happy;
   parents who have wise children
      are glad because of them.
²⁵Make your father and mother happy;
   give your mother a reason to be
      glad.

²⁶My son, pay attention to me,
   and watch closely what I do.
²⁷A prostitute is as dangerous as a deep
      pit,
   and an unfaithful wife is like a
      narrow well. [STEP 4]
²⁸They ambush you like robbers
   and cause many men to be
      unfaithful to their wives.

²⁹Who has trouble? Who has pain? [STEP 4]
   Who fights? Who complains?
   Who has unnecessary bruises?
   Who has bloodshot eyes?
³⁰It is people who drink too much wine,
   who try out all different kinds of
      strong drinks.
³¹Don't stare at the wine when it is red,
   when it sparkles in the cup,
   when it goes down smoothly.
³²Later it bites like a snake
   with poison in its fangs.
³³Your eyes will see strange sights,
   and your mind will be confused.
³⁴You will feel dizzy as if you're in a
      storm on the ocean,
   as if you're on top of a ship's sails.

³⁵You will think, "They hit me, but I'm
not hurt.
They beat me up, but I don't
remember it.
I wish I could wake up.
Then I would get another drink."

24
Don't envy evil people or try to
be friends with them.
²Their minds are always planning
violence,
and they always talk about making
trouble.

³It takes wisdom to have a good family,
and it takes understanding to
make it strong.
⁴It takes knowledge to fill a home
with rare and beautiful treasures.

⁵Wise people have great power,
and those with knowledge have
great strength.
⁶So you need advice when you go to
war.
If you have lots of good advice,
you will win.

⁷Foolish people cannot understand
wisdom.
They have nothing to say in a
discussion.

⁸Whoever makes evil plans
will be known as a troublemaker.
⁹Making foolish plans is sinful,
and making fun of wisdom is
hateful.

¹⁰If you give up when trouble comes,
it shows that you are weak.

¹¹Save those who are being led to their
death;
rescue those who are about to be
killed.
¹²If you say, "We don't know anything
about this,"

God, who knows what's in your
mind, will notice.
He is watching you, and he will know.
He will reward each person for
what he has done.

¹³My child, eat honey because it is good.
Honey from the honeycomb tastes
sweet.
¹⁴In the same way, wisdom is pleasing
to you.
If you find it, you have hope for
the future,
and your wishes will come true.

¹⁵Don't be wicked and attack a good
family's house;
don't rob the place where they
live.
¹⁶Even though good people may be
bothered by trouble seven
times, they are never
defeated,
but the wicked are overwhelmed
by trouble.

¹⁷Don't be happy when your enemy is
defeated;
don't be glad when he is
overwhelmed.
¹⁸The LORD will notice and be
displeased.
He may not be angry with them
anymore.

¹⁹Don't envy evil people,
and don't be jealous of the
wicked.
²⁰An evil person has nothing to hope
for;
the wicked will die like a flame
that is put out.

²¹My child, respect the LORD and the
king.
Don't join those people who
refuse to obey them.

²²The Lord and the king will quickly
destroy such people.
Those two can cause great
disaster!

²³These are also sayings of the wise:
It is not good to take sides when you
are the judge.
²⁴Don't tell the wicked that they are
innocent;
people will curse you, and nations
will hate you.
²⁵But things will go well if you punish
the guilty,
and you will receive rich blessings.

²⁶An honest answer is as pleasing
as a kiss on the lips.

²⁷First, finish your outside work
and prepare your fields.
After that, you can build your house.

²⁸Don't testify against your neighbor for
no good reason.
Don't say things that are false.
²⁹Don't say, "I'll get even;
I'll do to him what he did to me."

³⁰I passed by a lazy person's field
and by the vineyard of someone
with no sense.
³¹Thorns had grown up everywhere.
The ground was covered with
weeds,
and the stone walls had fallen
down.
³²I thought about what I had seen;
I learned this lesson from what I
saw.
³³You sleep a little; you take a nap.
You fold your hands and lie down
to rest.
³⁴Soon you will be as poor as if you had
been robbed;
you will have as little as if you had
been held up.

25These are more wise sayings of
Solomon, copied by the men of
Hezekiah king of Judah.
²God is honored for what he keeps
secret.
Kings are honored for what they
can discover.

³No one can measure the height of the
skies or the depth of the
earth.
So also no one can understand the
mind of a king.

⁴Remove the scum from the silver,
so the silver can be used by the
silversmith.
⁵Remove wicked people from the
king's presence;
then his government will be
honest and last a long time.

⁶Don't brag to the king
and act as if you are great.
⁷It is better for him to give you a higher
position
than to bring you down in front of
the prince.

Because of something you have seen,
⁸ do not quickly take someone to
court.
What will you do later
when your neighbor proves you
wrong?

⁹If you have an argument with your
neighbor,
don't tell other people what was
said.
¹⁰Whoever hears it might shame you,
and you might not ever be
respected again.

¹¹The right word spoken at the right
time
is as beautiful as gold apples in a
silver bowl.

STEP
9

¹²A wise warning to someone who will
listen
is as valuable as gold earrings or
fine gold jewelry.

¹³Trustworthy messengers refresh
those who send them,
like the coolness of snow in the
summertime.

¹⁴People who brag about gifts they
never give
are like clouds and wind that give
no rain.

¹⁵With patience you can convince a ruler,
and a gentle word can get through
to the hard-headed.

¹⁶If you find honey, don't eat too much,
or it will make you throw up.
¹⁷Don't go to your neighbor's house too
often;
too much of you will make him
hate you.

¹⁸When you lie about your neighbors,
it hurts them as much as a club, a
sword, or a sharp arrow.

¹⁹Trusting unfaithful people when you
are in trouble
is like eating with a broken tooth
or walking with a crippled
foot.

²⁰Singing songs to someone who is sad
is like taking away his coat on a
cold day
or pouring vinegar on soda.

²¹If your enemy is hungry, feed him.
If he is thirsty, give him a drink.
²²Doing this will be like pouring burning
coals on his head,
and the LORD will reward you.

²³As the north wind brings rain,
telling gossip brings angry looks.

²⁴It is better to live in a corner on the roof
than inside the house with a
quarreling wife.

²⁵Good news from a faraway place
is like a cool drink when you are
tired.

²⁶A good person who gives in to evil
is like a muddy spring or a dirty
well.

²⁷It is not good to eat too much honey,
nor does it bring you honor to brag
about yourself.

²⁸Those who do not control themselves
are like a city whose walls are
broken down.

STEP 4

26 It shouldn't snow in summer or
rain at harvest.
Neither should a foolish person
ever be honored.

²Curses will not harm someone who is
innocent;
they are like sparrows or swallows
that fly around and never
land.

³Whips are for horses, and harnesses
are for donkeys,
so paddles are good for fools.

⁴Don't answer fools when they speak
foolishly,
or you will be just like them.

⁵Answer fools when they speak foolishly,
or they will think they are really
wise.

⁶Sending a message by a foolish person
is like cutting off your feet or
drinking poison.

⁷A wise saying spoken by a fool
is as useless as the legs of a
crippled person.

⁸Giving honor to a foolish person
  is like tying a stone in a slingshot.

⁹A wise saying spoken by a fool
  is like a thorn stuck in the hand of
    a drunk.

¹⁰Hiring a foolish person or anyone just
    passing by
  is like an archer shooting at just
    anything.

¹¹A fool who repeats his foolishness
  is like a dog that goes back to
    what it has thrown up.

STEP 1
¹²There is more hope for a foolish
    person
  than for those who think they are
    wise.

¹³The lazy person says, "There's a lion
    in the road!
  There's a lion in the streets!"

¹⁴Like a door turning back and forth on
    its hinges,
  the lazy person turns over and
    over in bed.

¹⁵Lazy people may put their hands in
    the dish,
  but they are too tired to lift the
    food to their mouths.

¹⁶The lazy person thinks he is wiser
  than seven people who give
    sensible answers.

¹⁷Interfering in someone else's quarrel
    as you pass by
  is like grabbing a dog by the ears.

¹⁸Like a madman shooting
    deadly, burning arrows
¹⁹is the one who tricks a neighbor
  and then says, "I was just joking."

STEP 4
²⁰Without wood, a fire will go out,
  and without gossip, quarreling will
    stop.

²¹Just as charcoal and wood keep a fire
    going,
  a quarrelsome person keeps an
    argument going.

²²The words of a gossip are like tasty
    bits of food;
  people like to gobble them up.

²³Kind words from a wicked mind
  are like a shiny coating on a clay
    pot.

²⁴Those who hate you may try to fool
    you with their words,
  but in their minds they are
    planning evil.

²⁵People's words may be kind, but don't
    believe them,
  because their minds are full of evil
    thoughts.

²⁶Lies can hide hate,
  but the evil will be plain to
    everyone.

²⁷Whoever digs a pit for others will fall
    into it.
  Whoever tries to roll a boulder
    down on others will be
    crushed by it.

²⁸Liars hate the people they hurt,
  and false praise can ruin others.

27 Don't brag about tomorrow;
    you don't know what may
      happen then.

²Don't praise yourself. Let someone
    else do it.
  Let the praise come from a
    stranger and not from your
      own mouth.

³Stone is heavy, and sand is weighty,
  but a complaining fool is worse
    than either.

⁴Anger is cruel and destroys like a
    flood,

but no one can put up with
jealousy!

⁵It is better to correct someone openly
than to have love and not show it.

⁶The slap of a friend can be trusted to
help you,
but the kisses of an enemy are
nothing but lies.

⁷When you are full, not even honey
tastes good,
but when you are hungry, even
something bitter tastes
sweet.

⁸A person who leaves his home
is like a bird that leaves its nest.

⁹The sweet smell of perfume and oils
is pleasant,
and so is good advice from a
friend.

¹⁰Don't forget your friend or your
parent's friend.
Don't always go to your family for
help when trouble comes.
A neighbor close by is better than
a family far away.

¹¹Be wise, my child, and make me
happy.
Then I can respond to any insult.

¹²The wise see danger ahead and avoid
it,
but fools keep going and get into
trouble.

¹³Take the coat of someone who
promises to pay a stranger's
loan,
and keep it until he pays what the
stranger owes.

¹⁴If you loudly greet your neighbor early
in the morning,
he will think of it as a curse.

¹⁵A quarreling wife is as bothersome
as a continual dripping on a rainy
day.

¹⁶Stopping her is like stopping the wind
or trying to grab oil in your hand.

¹⁷As iron sharpens iron,
so people can improve each
other.

STEP 5

¹⁸Whoever tends a fig tree gets to eat
its fruit,
and whoever takes care of his
master will receive honor.

¹⁹As water reflects your face,
so your mind shows what kind of
person you are.

²⁰People will never stop dying and being
destroyed,
and they will never stop wanting
more than they have.

²¹A hot furnace tests silver and gold,
and people are tested by the
praise they receive.

²²Even if you ground up a foolish person
like grain in a bowl,
you couldn't remove the
foolishness.

²³Be sure you know how your sheep are
doing,
and pay attention to the condition
of your cattle.

²⁴Riches will not go on forever,
nor do governments go on
forever.

²⁵Bring in the hay, and let the new grass
appear.
Gather the grass from the hills.

²⁶Make clothes from the lambs' wool,
and sell some goats to buy a field.

²⁷There will be plenty of goat's milk
to feed you and your family
and to make your servant girls
healthy.

28 Evil people run even though no one is chasing them,
but good people are as brave as a lion.

2 When a country is lawless, it has one ruler after another;
but when it is led by a leader with understanding and knowledge, it continues strong.

3 Rulers who mistreat the poor
are like a hard rain that destroys the crops.

4 Those who disobey what they have been taught praise the wicked,
but those who obey what they have been taught are against them.

5 Evil people do not understand justice,
but those who follow the LORD understand it completely.

6 It is better to be poor and innocent
than to be rich and wicked.

7 Children who obey what they have been taught are wise,
but friends of troublemakers disgrace their parents.

8 Some people get rich by overcharging others,
but their wealth will be given to those who are kind to the poor.

9 If you refuse to obey what you have been taught,
your prayers will not be heard.

10 Those who lead good people to do wrong
will be ruined by their own evil,
but the innocent will be rewarded with good things.

11 Rich people may think they are wise,
but the poor with understanding will prove them wrong.

12 When good people triumph, there is great happiness,
but when the wicked get control, everybody hides.

13 If you hide your sins, you will not succeed.
If you confess and reject them, you will receive mercy.

STEP 5

14 Those who are always respectful will be happy,
but those who are stubborn will get into trouble.

15 A wicked ruler is as dangerous to poor people
as a roaring lion or a charging bear.

16 A ruler without wisdom will be cruel,
but the one who refuses to take dishonest money will rule a long time.

17 Don't help those who are guilty of murder;
let them run until they die.

18 Innocent people will be kept safe,
but those who are dishonest will suddenly be ruined.

19 Those who work their land will have plenty of food,
but the ones who chase empty dreams instead will end up poor.

20 A truthful person will have many blessings,
but those eager to get rich will be punished.

21 It is not good for a judge to take sides,
but some will sin for only a piece of bread.

STEP 5

Admitted to God, to ourselves, and to another human being the exact nature of our wrongs.

Proverbs 28:13–14

Confession plays a central role in biblical faith, even if it isn't practiced in all of its aspects in some churches. Without confession, things like fear, anger, and resentment remain buried inside where they can do you the most harm.

Buried emotions can be as toxic as buried chemical waste dumps. Both eventually leak out and contaminate everything in the neighborhood. For instance, if you grew up resenting your father because he was way too strict, that resentment may fester until you're 30 or 40 when you find you're always furious with every authority figure around you. Or, if your mother smothered you and never let you make decisions for yourself, you may realize as a grown-up that you don't connect well with your spouse or your friends. You don't know how to commit to real intimacy. Such emotional poisons have to be dug up and removed from your life.

Confession is excavating equipment. You bring your damaged past to the surface, look at it, show it to God, and let those people you count on to help you stay on track see it, too. Honest confession invites God's healing mercy and your friends' support to do their work. Proverbs 28:13 says: "If you hide your sins, you will not succeed. If you confess and reject them, you will receive mercy." Step 5 is an active step. It breaks barriers surrounding your heart and exposes it to God's tender mercies.

SEE **PAGE 44** OF THE INTRODUCTORY MATERIAL FOR **STEP 6**.

22Selfish people are in a hurry to get rich
　　and do not realize they soon will
　　be poor.

23Those who correct others will later be
　　liked
　　more than those who give false
　　praise.

24Whoever robs father or mother
　　and says, "It's not wrong,"
　　is just like someone who destroys
　　things.

25A greedy person causes trouble,
　　but the one who trusts the LORD
　　will succeed.

STEP 1
26Those who trust in themselves are
　　foolish,
　　but those who live wisely will be
　　kept safe.

27Whoever gives to the poor will have
　　everything he needs,
　　but the one who ignores the poor
　　will receive many curses.

28When the wicked get control,
　　everybody hides,
　　but when they die, good people do
　　well.

STEP 4
29 Whoever is stubborn after being
　　corrected many times
　　will suddenly be hurt beyond cure.

2When good people do well, everyone
　　is happy,
　　but when evil people rule,
　　everyone groans.

3Those who love wisdom make their
　　parents happy,
　　but friends of prostitutes waste
　　their money.

4If a king is fair, he makes his country
　　strong,

　　but if he takes gifts dishonestly, he
　　tears his country down.

5Those who give false praise to their
　　neighbors
　　are setting a trap for them.

6Evil people are trapped by their own
　　sin,
　　but good people can sing and be
　　happy.

7Good people care about justice for the
　　poor,
　　but the wicked are not concerned.

8People who make fun of wisdom
　　cause trouble in a city,
　　but wise people calm anger down.

9When a wise person takes a foolish
　　person to court,
　　the fool only shouts or laughs, and
　　there is no peace.

10Murderers hate an honest person
　　and try to kill those who do right.

STEP 4
11Foolish people lose their tempers,
　　but wise people control theirs.

12If a ruler pays attention to lies,
　　all his officers will become wicked.

13The poor person and the cruel person
　　are alike
　　in that the LORD gave eyes to both
　　of them.

14If a king judges poor people fairly,
　　his government will continue
　　forever.

15Correction and punishment make
　　children wise,
　　but those left alone will disgrace
　　their mother.

16When there are many wicked people,
　　there is much sin,
　　but those who do right will see
　　them destroyed.

¹⁷Correct your children, and you will be
proud;
they will give you satisfaction.

¹⁸Where there is no word from God,
people are uncontrolled,
but those who obey what they
have been taught are happy.

¹⁹Words alone cannot correct a servant,
because even if they understand,
they won't respond.

STEP 4

²⁰Do you see people who speak too
quickly?
There is more hope for a foolish
person than for them.

²¹If you spoil your servants when they
are young,
they will bring you grief later on.

STEP 4

²²An angry person causes trouble;
a person with a quick temper sins
a lot.

²³Pride will ruin people,
but those who are humble will be
honored.

²⁴Partners of thieves are their own
worst enemies.
If they have to testify in court,
they are afraid to say
anything.

²⁵Being afraid of people can get you
into trouble,
but if you trust the LORD, you will
be safe.

²⁶Many people want to speak to a
ruler,
but justice comes only from the
LORD.

²⁷Good people hate those who are
dishonest,
and the wicked hate those who
are honest.

30 These are the words of Agur son of
Jakeh.
This is his message to Ithiel and Ucal:
²"I am the most stupid person there is,
and I have no understanding.
³I have not learned to be wise,
and I don't know much about God,
the Holy One.
⁴Who has gone up to heaven and
come back down?
Who can hold the wind in his
hand?
Who can gather up the waters in his
coat?
Who has set in place the ends of
the earth?
What is his name or his son's name?
Tell me, if you know!

⁵"Every word of God is true.
He guards those who come to him
for safety.
⁶Do not add to his words,
or he will correct you and prove
you are a liar.

⁷"I ask two things from you, LORD.
Don't refuse me before I die.
⁸Keep me from lying and being
dishonest.
And don't make me either rich or
poor;
just give me enough food for each
day.
⁹If I have too much, I might reject you
and say, 'I don't know the LORD.'
If I am poor, I might steal
and disgrace the name of my God.

¹⁰"Do not say bad things about
servants to their masters,
or they will curse you, and you will
suffer for it.

¹¹"Some people curse their fathers
and do not bless their mothers.
¹²Some people think they are pure,

STEP 4

but they are not really free from
evil.
¹³Some people have such a proud look!
They look down on others.
¹⁴Some people have teeth like swords;
their jaws seem full of knives.
They want to remove the poor from
the earth
and the needy from the land.

¹⁵"Greed has two daughters
named 'Give' and 'Give.'
There are three things that are never
satisfied,
really four that never say, 'I've had
enough!':
¹⁶the cemetery, the childless mother,
the land that never gets enough
rain,
and fire that never says, 'I've had
enough!'

¹⁷"If you make fun of your father
and refuse to obey your mother,
the birds of the valley will peck out
your eyes,
and the vultures will eat them.

¹⁸"There are three things that are too
hard for me,
really four I don't understand:
¹⁹the way an eagle flies in the sky,
the way a snake slides over a rock,
the way a ship sails on the sea,
and the way a man and a woman
fall in love.

²⁰"This is the way of a woman who
takes part in adultery:
She acts as if she had eaten and
washed her face;
she says, 'I haven't done anything
wrong.'

²¹"There are three things that make the
earth tremble,
really four it cannot stand:

²²a servant who becomes a king,
a foolish person who has plenty to
eat,
²³a hated woman who gets married,
and a maid who replaces her
mistress.

²⁴"There are four things on earth that
are small,
but they are very wise:
²⁵Ants are not very strong,
but they store up food in the
summer.
²⁶Rock badgers are not very powerful,
but they can live among the rocks.
²⁷Locusts have no king,
but they all go forward in
formation.
²⁸Lizards can be caught in the hand,
but they are found even in kings'
palaces.

²⁹"There are three things that strut
proudly,
really four that walk as if they
were important:
³⁰a lion, the proudest animal,
which is strong and runs from
nothing,
³¹a rooster, a male goat,
and a king when his army is
around him.

³²"If you have been foolish and proud,
or if you have planned evil, shut
your mouth.   STEP 5
³³Just as stirring milk makes butter,
and twisting noses makes them
bleed,
so stirring up anger causes
trouble."

31 These are the words of King
Lemuel, the message his mother
taught him:
²"My son, I gave birth to you.
You are the son I prayed for.

STEP 12

Having had a spiritual awakening as the
result of these steps, we tried to carry
this message to others, and to practice
these principles in all our affairs.

Proverbs 31:26–31

Proverbs 31:26–31 says a mother influences her children in three ways: by words, by actions, and by attitudes. What's true of mothers is true of fathers, too. And what's true of parental influence is also true of friends influencing friends.

When you fully surrender to God and his will for you, your words, actions, and attitudes begin to honor God in the eyes of everyone watching you. Your *words* reflect the wisdom and kindness described in verse 26. You get this wisdom and kindness from your daily meditation on God's Word and your prayers. Your *actions* show you care about others and want to be responsible (verses 27–28). Your *attitudes* show that you respect the Lord (verse 30). Your friends and acquaintances will notice that. They may not know what to make of it, but they will respect you for it. In fact, your attitudes becomes the message you carry to others by your words and your deeds.

Keep practicing Step 12 as a regular part of your life. As you do, you will, with God's help, have as much influence as the remarkable woman described in Proverbs 31.

THIS IS YOUR LAST **STEP 12** MEDITATION.

³Don't waste your strength on women
 or your time on those who ruin
  kings.

⁴"Kings should not drink wine, Lemuel,
 and rulers should not desire beer.
⁵If they drink, they might forget the
  law
 and keep the needy from getting
  their rights.
⁶Give beer to people who are dying
 and wine to those who are sad.
⁷Let them drink and forget their need
 and remember their misery no
  more.

⁸"Speak up for those who cannot
  speak for themselves;
 defend the rights of all those who
  have nothing.
⁹Speak up and judge fairly,
 and defend the rights of the poor
  and needy."

¹⁰It is hard to find a good wife,
 because she is worth more than
  rubies.
¹¹Her husband trusts her completely.
 With her, he has everything he
  needs.
¹²She does him good and not harm
 for as long as she lives.
¹³She looks for wool and flax
 and likes to work with her hands.
¹⁴She is like a trader's ship,
 bringing food from far away.
¹⁵She gets up while it is still dark
 and prepares food for her family
 and feeds her servant girls.
¹⁶She inspects a field and buys it.
 With money she earned, she
  plants a vineyard.
¹⁷She does her work with energy,
 and her arms are strong.

¹⁸She knows that what she makes is
  good.
 Her lamp burns late into the night.
¹⁹She makes thread with her hands
 and weaves her own cloth.
²⁰She welcomes the poor
 and helps the needy.
²¹She does not worry about her family
  when it snows,
 because they all have fine clothes
  to keep them warm.
²²She makes coverings for herself;
 her clothes are made of linen and
  other expensive material.
²³Her husband is known at the city
  meetings,
 where he makes decisions as one
  of the leaders of the land.
²⁴She makes linen clothes and sells
  them
 and provides belts to the
  merchants.
²⁵She is strong and is respected by the
  people.
 She looks forward to the future
  with joy.
²⁶She speaks wise words
 and teaches others to be kind.

STEP 12

²⁷She watches over her family
 and never wastes her time.
²⁸Her children speak well of her.
 Her husband also praises her,
²⁹saying, "There are many fine women,
 but you are better than all of
  them."
³⁰Charm can fool you, and beauty can
  trick you,
 but a woman who respects the
  LORD should be praised.
³¹Give her the reward she has earned;
 she should be praised in public for
  what she has done.

About the *New Century Version*®

God never intended the Bible to be too difficult for his people. To make sure God's message was clear, the authors of the Bible recorded God's word in familiar everyday language. These books brought a message that the original readers could understand. These first readers knew that God spoke through these books. Down through the centuries, many people wanted a Bible so badly that they copied different Bible books by hand!

Today, now that the Bible is readily available, many Christians do not regularly read it. Many feel that the Bible is too hard to understand or irrelevant to life.

The *New Century Version* captures the clear and simple message that the very first readers understood. This version presents the Bible as God intended it: clear and dynamic.

A team of scholars from the World Bible Translation Center worked together with twenty-one other experienced Bible scholars from all over the world to translate the text directly from the best available Greek and Hebrew texts. You can trust that this Bible accurately presents God's Word as it came to us in the original languages.

Translators kept sentences short and simple. They avoided difficult words and worked to make the text easier to read. They used modern terms for places and measurements. And they put figures of speech and idiomatic expressions ("he was gathered to his people") in language that even children understand ("he died").

Following the tradition of other English versions, the *New Century Version* indicates the divine name, *Yahweh*, by putting LORD, and sometimes GOD, in capital letters. This distinguishes it from *Adonai*, another Hebrew word that is translated "Lord."

We acknowledge the infallibility of God's Word and yet our own frailty. We pray that God will use this Bible to help you understand his rich truth for yourself. To God be the glory.